Handbook of Research on Innovative Approaches to Information Technology in Library and Information Science

Barbara Holland
Brooklyn Public Library, USA (Retired)

Keshav Sinha
University of Petroleum and Energy Studies, India

A volume in the Advances in Library and Information Science (ALIS) Book Series

IGI Global
PUBLISHER of TIMELY KNOWLEDGE

Published in the United States of America by
IGI Global
Information Science Reference (an imprint of IGI Global)
701 E. Chocolate Avenue
Hershey PA, USA 17033
Tel: 717-533-8845
Fax: 717-533-8661
E-mail: cust@igi-global.com
Web site: http://www.igi-global.com

Library of Congress Cataloging-in-Publication Data

CIP PENDING
ISBN: 9798369308073
eISBN: 9798369308080

This book is published in the IGI Global book series Advances in Library and Information Science (ALIS) (ISSN: 2326-4136; eISSN: 2326-4144)

British Cataloguing in Publication Data
A Cataloguing in Publication record for this book is available from the British Library.

For electronic access to this publication, please contact: eresources@igi-global.com.

Advances in Library and Information Science (ALIS) Book Series

Alfonso Ippolito
Sapienza University-Rome, Italy
Carlo Inglese
Sapienza University-Rome, Italy

ISSN:2326-4136
EISSN:2326-4144

MISSION

The **Advances in Library and Information Science (ALIS) Book Series** is comprised of high quality, research-oriented publications on the continuing developments and trends affecting the public, school, and academic fields, as well as specialized libraries and librarians globally. These discussions on professional and organizational considerations in library and information resource development and management assist in showcasing the latest methodologies and tools in the field.

The **ALIS Book Series** aims to expand the body of library science literature by covering a wide range of topics affecting the profession and field at large. The series also seeks to provide readers with an essential resource for uncovering the latest research in library and information science management, development, and technologies.

COVERAGE

- Continuing Education for Library Professionals
- Blogging in Libraries
- Children and Youth Services
- Web-Based Bibliographic Instruction
- Cataloging and Classification
- Virtual Reference Services
- Censorship
- Human Side of Information Services
- Cases on Library Management
- Institutional Repositories

IGI Global is currently accepting manuscripts for publication within this series. To submit a proposal for a volume in this series, please contact our Acquisition Editors at Acquisitions@igi-global.com or visit: http://www.igi-global.com/publish/.

The Advances in Library and Information Science (ALIS) Book Series (ISSN 2326-4136) is published by IGI Global, 701 E. Chocolate Avenue, Hershey, PA 17033-1240, USA, www.igi-global.com. This series is composed of titles available for purchase individually; each title is edited to be contextually exclusive from any other title within the series. For pricing and ordering information please visit http://www.igi-global.com/book-series/advances-library-information-science/73002. Postmaster: Send all address changes to above address.

Titles in this Series

For a list of additional titles in this series, please visit:
www.igi-global.com/book-series/advances-library-information-science/73002

Multidisciplinary Approach to Information Technology in Library and Information Science
Barbara Holland (Brooklyn Public Library, USA (Retired)) and Keshav Sinha (University of Petroleum and Energy Studies, India)
Information Science Reference • copyright 2024 • 350pp • H/C (ISBN: 9798369328415) • US $245.00 (our price)

Illuminating and Advancing the Path for Mathematical Writing Research
Madelyn W. Colonnese (Reading and Elementary Education Department, Cato College of Education, University of North Carolina at Charlotte, USA) Tutita M. Casa (Department of Curriculum and Instruction, Neag School of Education, University of Connecticut, USA) and Fabiana Cardetti (Department of Mathematics, College of Liberal Arts and Sciences, University of Connecticut, USA)
Information Science Reference • copyright 2024 • 389pp • H/C (ISBN: 9781668465387) • US $215.00 (our price)

Emerging Technology-Based Services and Systems in Libraries, Educational Institutions, and Non-Profit Organizations
Dickson K. W. Chiu (The University of Hong Kong, Hong Kong) and Kevin K. W. Ho (University of Tsukuba, Japan)
Information Science Reference • copyright 2023 • 353pp • H/C (ISBN: 9781668486719) • US $225.00 (our price)

Applying Positivist and Interpretivist Philosophies to Social Research Practices
C.C. Jayasundara (University of Kelaniya, Sri Lanka)
Information Science Reference • copyright 2023 • 300pp • H/C (ISBN: 9781668454312) • US $215.00 (our price)

Handbook of Research on Advancements of Contactless Technology and Service Innovation in Library and Information Science
Barbara Holland (Brooklyn Public Library, USA (Retired))
Information Science Reference • copyright 2023 • 388pp • H/C (ISBN: 9781668476932) • US $270.00 (our price)

Perspectives on Justice, Equity, Diversity, and Inclusion in Libraries
Nandita S. Mani (University of Massachusetts, Amherst, USA) Michelle A. Cawley (University of North Carolina at Chapel Hill, USA) and Emily P. Jones (University of North Carolina at Chapel Hill, USA)
Information Science Reference • copyright 2023 • 320pp • H/C (ISBN: 9781668472552) • US $215.00 (our price)

Handbook of Research on Technological Advances of Library and Information Science in Industry 5.0
Barbara Jane Holland (Independent Researcher, USA)
Information Science Reference • copyright 2023 • 549pp • H/C (ISBN: 9781668447550) • US $270.00 (our price)

IGI Global
PUBLISHER of TIMELY KNOWLEDGE

701 East Chocolate Avenue, Hershey, PA 17033, USA
Tel: 717-533-8845 x100 • Fax: 717-533-8661
E-Mail: cust@igi-global.com • www.igi-global.com

List of Contributors

Table of Contents

Detailed Table of Contents

One way to assess the IS and establish a foundation for improvement decisions is to evaluate its maturity using a maturity model (MM) tailored to the organization's type and the goals of these activities. The outcome is the determination of the assessed organization's maturity level, enabling the initiation of improvement activities and comparisons with similar organizations. Many such initiatives have been inspired by well-established maturity models, such as the capability maturity model (CMM). An organization with a higher level of maturity is considered more reliable and customer-friendly. This chapter delves into the issues of IS maturity, providing definitions of maturity, maturity models (with examples), models for implementing MM (change management), highlighting the distinctions and similarities between maturity, diffusion (acceptance), and innovation of information systems, as well as the relationships between methods for assessing IS maturity and the information/data literacy of its users.

Scheduling problems play a pivotal role in many of the fields today, such as manufacturing systems, industrial processes, production, etc. The job-shop scheduling problems are categorized as a non-deterministic NP hard problem. It is very complicated to find a better algorithm which can give an optimal solution under a given time constraint. A scheduling can be generally categorized as a set of jobs where each job can have greater than one operation to perform. The main aim of the scheduling would be to resolve the scheduling of the jobs that would minimize a measure of performance. A common measure of performance for dealing with the problems of the scheduling is the makespan of a schedule. Technique for calculating the shop scheduling problem ranges from simple FIFO and SPT to more sophisticated procedures, for instance branch and bound, tabu search, ant colony, genetic algorithm, and many others. The modified version of ABC is parallel ABC (PABC) for solving the JSSP. Projected method basically uses the concept of parallelism for the concept of scheduling.

The growing integration of information and communication technology (ICT) in today's world has led to the rise of crimes in the digital realm, specifically those linked to networks and computers. This surge in cybercrime presents substantial hurdles for forensic evaluation. A pivotal evidence source in cyber forensic probes, especially when pinpointing potential threats to confidential data, stems from the extensive data produced by network nodes. The primary goal of cyber forensics is to offer clear, well-documented evidence that can stand up in a courtroom. This chapter intends to deliver a thorough overview of the current scholarly material, emphasizing diverse aspects of cyber forensic endeavors. It encompasses foundational theories, prior data analysis blueprints, and initiatives to refine methods, thereby augmenting the reach, proficiency, and precision of the network forensic structure.

Recognizing that the sharing of information and knowledge is a preponderant factor for the generation of innovation and that innovative performance in a nation depends on the ability of innovation agents to share information and knowledge focusing on innovation, this chapter aims to highlight why and how information management (IG) and knowledge management (KM) processes constitute valuable subsidies for the generation of innovation. In addition, it presents and analyzes organizations whose purpose is the management of knowledge and information, such as archives, libraries, information/documentation centers, and museums seeking to show that these organizations have the potential to play an important role in the context of innovation systems.

The study explores the phenomenon of herding behavior among investors in the Indian financial market with a specific focus on the influence of social media. Herding bias impacts the cognitive functions of the investor by inducing them to take decisions based on the decisions of the crowd. Social media platforms have gained significant popularity, becoming a prominent source of financial information and market sentiment for investors. The study analyses the impact based on the social media messages, news, and discussions on popular platforms. A sample of 215 investors was collected through a questionnaire via Google Form. The respondents were selected through purposive sampling technique. The hypothesis is primarily tested using PLS-SEM. The results of this study indicate that influencer credibility for the investors shows a significant positive impact on herd behaviour. Financial literacy had a detrimental effect on herding but became significant when risk perception was used as a mediator. Lastly, risk perception in isolation also showed a significant impact on herding behaviour.

This chapter aims at understanding better the perceptions of academic libraries' top managers with regards to artificial intelligence (AI) and adoption decisions. Building on previous research, this study reports on the relationship between perceived familiarity with AI and the decision-makers' positive adoption attitude regarding AI in libraries. Results indicate that the main issues faced by senior-librarians when considering an AI implementation are the lack of maturity of the commercial solutions offered, security and privacy concerns, the library's core values, its funding capacity, and the need for technical expertise. The most popular AI applications currently implemented are natural language processing and virtual reference librarians (chatbots) while the least popular are robot guides and facial recognition.

Use of medicinal plants has a long history in traditional medicine around the world. It is critical to correctly identify medicinal plants in order to determine their therapeutic characteristics and prospective applications. However, due to the complexity of their appearance, it might be a challenging process. Variation in features of leaf restrict the use of existing plants identification methods. This research suggests a deep learning-based solution using VGG-19 model, which employs a convolutional neural network (CNN) that is capable of learning and encoding complex aspects of images, allowing it to recognize and classify medicinal plants with high accuracy. The experiment has been done with the help of Flavia dataset which complies 1000 images, and extracted features are classified using different classifiers. The research has the potential to provide a knowledge base for identifying herbal plants to healthcare providers and herbal medicine researchers.

This chapter delves into the evolution of library management systems (LMS) and the emergence of library services platforms (LSP) with a focus on FOLIO, an innovative open-source solution. Beginning with the historical context of open-source software in libraries, it dissects the architectural nuances between monolithic and micro-services systems in LMS development. The discussion shifts to a comprehensive understanding of FOLIO, exploring its installation, specialized apps, and pivotal features. Addressing challenges in FOLIO implementation, the chapter offers practical insights and best practices. It emphasizes enhancing user experience through accessibility and personalized options and elucidates FOLIO's robust security measures and data privacy in the open-source realm. Furthermore, it illuminates the thriving FOLIO community, encouraging active participation and collaboration. The chapter concludes by contemplating FOLIO's transformative impact on the future landscape of library management.

Digital technologies promoted innovation and proposed unprecedented opportunities to the sectors, one of which is cultural heritage. There are many benefits of digitization such as rapid access of data, cost-effectiveness according to benefit and loss assessment in a long term, and rapid identification of cultural heritage and risks. This study is the comprehensive bibliometric analysis that ensures statistical and all-embracing understanding in the digital technologies in cultural heritage literature, which was carried out in Web of Science between 1993 and 2022. The study is expected to spur scholars to perform more studies on digital technologies in cultural heritage. The analysis embodied 1826 publications written by 200 authors from 98 countries. Italy produced 24.20% of the world's publications on digital technologies in cultural heritage, which has the highest number of publications with 442 documents. The most used keywords in this literature are cultural heritage, virtual reality, and augmented reality.

Data security presents significant concerns for organizations and individuals in today's evolving digital landscape. Prominent challenges include sophisticated cyberattacks, remote work vulnerabilities, cloud security, phishing, insider threats, data privacy, encryption, and identity and access management. In addressing diverse challenges, a range of solutions can be implemented, such as using multi-factor authentication (MFA) to enhance user authentication. At the same time, zero trust networking (ZTN) ensures continuous authentication and authorization. Dynamic data masking (DDM) alters sensitive data during transit to thwart unauthorized access. Regular security training, cloud security tools, and insider

Systems for monitoring cybersecurity are now crucial instruments for safeguarding digital assets and fending off numerous attacks. This chapter covers the various uses, challenges, and new developments of using surveillance systems in order to enhance cybersecurity. Discussion themes include threat detection, incident response, insider threat identification, and vulnerability management. The primary challenges—including data overload, false positives, privacy concerns, skill gaps, regulatory compliance, adaptive threats, and cultural acceptance—are also exhaustively examined. The report also covers recent advancements, such as the use of zero trust architectures, the development of behavioral analytics, and the blending of AI and ML technologies. By addressing these problems and implementing these trends, organizations can strengthen their entire cybersecurity posture.

This chapter provides an overview of ocean data legislation in the context of EU maritime policy. Its analyses give an insight into the implementation of the regulations, directives, decisions, and recommendations that address the European Union's approach to the management of its ocean resources. Methods adopted by European legislators to foster collaboration and innovation and harness ocean data to inform policymakers and other stakeholders are discussed. It provides an overview of how the EU has adapted its legal framework to the changing landscape of data management in ocean research and resource management. This insight is given within the specific geographical context of the European Atlantic and Mediterranean regions, allowing readers to understand how these legal responses to the data revolution impact their seas. This chapter could be a valuable resource for those interested in the particular interplay between regulations, data, and the changing landscape of fisheries management in the European Union.

Preface

Information technology (IT) refers to the use of computers, software, networks, and other digital devices to create, store, process, transmit, and access data and information. This book covers the basic concepts, principles, and techniques of IT, in a variety of innovative uses depicting current trends, and future challenges.

IT has also transformed many aspects of library and information science (LIS), such as collection development, cataloging, reference, circulation, and user services. For example, IT allows libraries to acquire and provide access to a wide range of digital resources, such as e-books, databases, journals, and multimedia. IT also enables libraries to use online catalogs and discovery tools to organize and retrieve information. IT also enhances the interaction between libraries and users, such as through online reference services, chatbots, social media platforms, and mobile applications. Moreover, IT also enables new forms of information creation, dissemination, access, and use, such as e-books, digital libraries, and open-access repositories. IT also allows users to access and use information from anywhere and anytime. IT also allows users to create and share their information through blogs, wikis, podcasts, and other tools.

The quickly developing field of information technology (IT) has completely changed how libraries and information centers run and provide services to their patrons. Managing the growing volume and complexity of data, guaranteeing information security and privacy, improving user experience and satisfaction, and encouraging cooperation and innovation among library staff and stakeholders are just a few of the new opportunities and challenges that IT has brought to libraries, information centers, and the academia environment. The book's major ideas and subjects are introduced, featuring some of the most creative IT solutions found in libraries and information hubs worldwide.

Information technology (IT) is a rapidly evolving field that has transformed the way libraries and information centers operate and serve their users.

This book showcases successful examples and case studies of IT innovation in libraries and information centers from different regions and sectors.

Moreover, the book covers various aspects of IT applications, such as infrastructure, systems, standards, policies, strategies, best practices, trends, issues, and future directions. The book aims to provide practical guidance and inspiration for librarians, academia, information professionals, practitioners, and advanced students who want to enhance their skills and knowledge in using, implementing, and developing information technology solutions. The book covers a wide range of topics, including a study of Artificial Bee Colonies for solving productivity problems, Information System Maturity, Folio a Library Service Platform, Electronic Information and Health Libraries, and Artificial Intelligence in Libraries. The book also showcases examples of successful projects and best practices from different types of libraries, information centers around the world.

Moreover, this book consists of interdisciplinary methods, and applications of information in various domains, such as librarianship, business, education, health, culture, and society.

The book is intended for librarians, academia, researchers, practitioners, advanced students, and general readers who are interested in learning more about the role and impact of information in the modern world.

The book is intended to be both informative and engaging, as well as to stimulate further discussion and research on the role and impact of information technology in libraries and information centers.

Furthermore, this book aims to provide readers with a comprehensive and up-to-date overview of the current state and prospects of IT in libraries and information centers, as well as to inspire them to adopt, adapt, or develop their innovative approaches to IT in their settings.

This preface introduces chapters concerning the main topics and issues related to IT in libraries, information centers or hubs, and academia.

Chapter 1 explores IS maturity, offering definitions, maturity models (with examples), and models for MM (change management) implementation. It also highlights the differences and similarities between IS maturity, diffusion (acceptance), and innovation, and the connections between IS maturity assessment techniques and users' information/data literacy.

In Chapter 2, the Artificial Bee Colony (ABC) algorithm has proved to be useful in various fields of problems such as assignment problems, scheduling problems, transportation problems, etc.

Chapter 3 gives a thorough overview of the current scholarly material, emphasizing diverse aspects of cyber forensic endeavors is provided.

Chapter 4 illustrates the benefits that information management (IG) and knowledge management (KM) procedures provide as important catalysts for innovation.

Chapter 5 explores the phenomenon of herding behavior among investors in the Indian financial market, with a specific focus on the influence of social media. Herding bias impacts the cognitive functions of the investors by inducing them to make decisions based on the decisions of the crowd.

Chapter 6 reports on the relationship between perceived familiarity with AI and the decision-maker's positive adoption attitude regarding AI in libraries.

Chapter 7 proposes a deep learning-based method based on the VGG-19 model. The method makes use of a Convolutional Neural Network (CNN), which can learn and encode complicated features of images and identify and categorize medicinal plants with high accuracy.

Chapter 8 explores the development of Library Services Platforms (LSP) and Library Management Systems (LMS), emphasizing the novel open-source solution FOLIO. This chapter aims to inspire librarians to consider FOLIO as a promising solution to enhance their library services and meet the evolving needs of their patrons in the digital age.

Chapter 9, which was conducted in Web of Science between 1993 and 2022, is the only thorough bibliometric analysis that guarantees statistical and full comprehension of the digital technologies in cultural heritage literature.

In Chapter 10, data security is a major concern for both individuals and organizations in the rapidly changing digital ecosystem of today. Smart cyberattacks, vulnerabilities in remote work, cloud security, phishing, insider threats, data privacy, encryption, and identity and access management are some of the major issues.

In Chapter 11, an IoT adoption framework for enhancing library administration procedures in Ghana's public tertiary institution is presented. The library industry has been transformed by the Internet of Things (IoT).

Chapter 12 uses various rounds of household-level unit data from the National Sample Survey Office (NSSO) to estimate the occurrence, depth, and severity of poverty in India across the states. In this study, the authors individually calculated the various metrics of absolute and relative poverty for the rural and urban regions of India's 22 largest states, including the poverty rate, depth, and severity of poverty.

In Chapter 13, the first point of emphasis is the critical role that EHRs play in digitizing patient data, centralizing medical records, and facilitating efficient data sharing amongst healthcare providers. The use of machine learning algorithms to find patterns in patient data, pinpoint illness risks, and offer tailored therapy suggestions is thoroughly examined in this chapter.

In Chapter 14, different machine learning methods are being analyzed to showcase the application and importance of applying machine learning tools in the improvement of crop production.

Chapter 15 discusses the many applications, difficulties, and recent advancements of using surveillance systems to improve cybersecurity and the fusion of AI and ML technologies. Through the implementation of these trends and problem-solving techniques, organizations can enhance their overall cybersecurity posture.

In Chapter 16, an overview of ocean data regulation within the framework of EU maritime policy is given. Through its analysis, one can gain insight into how the rules, directives, decisions, and suggestions on the European Union's approach to ocean resource management are being implemented. For individuals who are specifically interested in the interactions between laws, data, and the evolving field of fisheries management in the European Union, this chapter is a great resource.

Barbara Holland
Brooklyn Public Library, USA (Retired)

Keshav Sinha
University of Petroleum and Energy Studies, India

Chapter 1
Information System Maturity

Marek Nahotko
https://orcid.org/0000-0002-4823-8080
Jagiellonian University, Krakow, Poland

ABSTRACT

One way to assess the IS and establish a foundation for improvement decisions is to evaluate its maturity using a maturity model (MM) tailored to the organization's type and the goals of these activities. The outcome is the determination of the assessed organization's maturity level, enabling the initiation of improvement activities and comparisons with similar organizations. Many such initiatives have been inspired by well-established maturity models, such as the capability maturity model (CMM). An organization with a higher level of maturity is considered more reliable and customer-friendly. This chapter delves into the issues of IS maturity, providing definitions of maturity, maturity models (with examples), models for implementing MM (change management), highlighting the distinctions and similarities between maturity, diffusion (acceptance), and innovation of information systems, as well as the relationships between methods for assessing IS maturity and the information/data literacy of its users.

INTRODUCTION

The creators and employees of libraries and other information systems (IS) have increasingly focused on assessing the success of their activities, particularly the services provided to clients/users. The need for special attention to monitoring IS work results from at least two factors. Firstly, rapid technological changes result in much easier and universal access to information through global networks. However, these changes also entail significant expenses for hardware, software, and employee training. Secondly, we observe changes in the information needs and behavior of users, which arise from their access to an increasingly competitive information market. In this market, traditional organizations such as libraries have to compete for users' attention with numerous commercial enterprises, including Internet search engines, as the most obvious example. The process of building a collection of digital resources, as well as organizing and sharing them, also presents challenges.

Many libraries have adopted tools such as balanced scorecards, value scorecards, performance indicator frameworks, benchmarking, and typologies to demonstrate their value and impact (Dash & Padhi,

DOI: 10.4018/979-8-3693-0807-3.ch001

2010). Libraries also cooperate in this area (Chadwell, 2011). The success of information activities can be understood through the six dimensions proposed by Petter, DeLone, and McLean (2008), which have been widely used by IS researchers to comprehend and measure these dimensions in functioning IS. Furthermore, each of the variables describing the success of the IS aligns with one or more of the six main dimensions of the model created by the cited authors (Petter, DeLone & McLean, 2008, p. 238). The following dimensions of success have been distinguished:

- System quality: desirable characteristics of the information system. They can be: ease of use, system flexibility, reliability, ease of learning, as well as features of intuitiveness, sophistication, flexibility and responsiveness;
- Information quality: desirable features of system outputs, e.g. reports, data displayed. Indicators such as relevance, understandability, timeliness, and usability can be distinguished;
- Service quality: the quality of the support that users can receive from the IS and its staff. E.g. responsiveness, accuracy, reliability, technical competence, as well as employee empathy. In this area, tools such as SERVQUAL, created in the area of marketing, and LibQUAL, adapted to the measurement of library services, are used. This tool is used to assess IS user satisfaction by measuring the differences (gaps) between three levels of maturity: minimal, actual and optimal (desired) of information services (Kamath et al., 2022);
- System use: the degree and manner in which employees and users/customers use IS capabilities. The measures here may be: level of use, frequency of use, manner of use, suitability of use, extent of use, purpose of use;
- User satisfaction: the level of user satisfaction with IS services, determining its acceptability;
- Net benefits: the degree of IS participation in the success of individuals, groups, organizations, industries and nations. E.g.: improving decision-making, improving productivity, increasing library loans, reducing costs, increasing income, market efficiency, customer/user satisfaction, economic development.

Researchers have developed numerous models to explain why some ISs succeed while others fail. One of the simpler models is the Technology Acceptance Model (TAM) by Davis (1989), which incorporates the Theory of Reasoned Action (TRA) and the Theory of Planned Behavior (TPB) (Fishbein & Ajzen, 1975). Using this model, attempts have been made to explain why some ISs (broadly understood) are more readily accepted by their users than others. Acceptance is not synonymous with success, but it is a necessary prerequisite for success. Therefore, the most important factor for the successful implementation of an IS is the presence of a community of users willing to use it (Shareef et al., 2011). Phenomena such as acceptance, diffusion (spread), and maturity of IS depend on the decisions of users to utilize these systems. While technological development and the diffusion of networked information systems of all kinds appear undeniable, the willingness of potential users to adopt them can sometimes be a subject of debate.

The role of users and their needs in evaluating IS has been emphasized in the ACRL (1998) standards. According to these standards, the assessment of information systems is based on three elements: inputs (the raw materials of information activities), outputs (the values used to quantify the work done), and outcomes, identifying how information users change as a result of their exposure to information resources and services. The assessment of the first two elements can be conducted in various ways by analyzing objective quantitative indicators. However, the third element, which is the most crucial, relies heavily on the user's perspective. The analysis of inputs and outputs provides an overview of the library's functioning, while the assessment of outcomes primarily aims to determine user satisfaction. It encompasses several dimensions, such as services, instructions, resources and access to them, staff, facilities, communication and collaboration, administration, and budget. This article primarily focuses on this area.

Success, understood in this manner, can be achieved by mature organizations and information systems. Both types of IS are relatively new solutions in information activities, although digital libraries have a longer tradition of use in information activities. These two examples demonstrate differences in the development of maturity models for different applications, particularly concerning the distinguished assessment dimensions and maturity levels. However, before delving into specific examples, general issues of maturity and its modeling will be presented. Additionally, it is important to establish the relationships between IS maturity and other IS assessment indicators, such as diffusion (acceptance) and excellence in the innovation process, which are integral to IS, as well as user information/data literacy (I/DL), which should be included in each IS maturity model.

The purpose of this chapter is to address the issue of information system maturity and the models operating in this area. This issue will be exemplified through the maturity of two types of these systems: digital libraries (DL) and research data services (RDS).

IS MATURITY DEFINITION

The term "maturity" is used to describe a concept of analytical, explanatory, or normative nature, which finds applications in various disciplines. Dictionary definitions indicate that maturity refers to the state of achieving full development or readiness for something, as well as the highest quality during the development of something. However, the term "quality" is ambiguous, and its meaning can be grouped into five separate but interrelated ways of thinking about quality: it can be treated as an indicator of something special (above a high standard), as excellence (or consistency), as a tool to achieve a goal, as financial value, or as transformation (qualitative changes) (Harvey & Green, 1993). Thus, achieving maturity is a process of evolutionary progress in quality (in its various meanings), involving specific opportunities or the achievement of a goal, from the initial stage of lower quality to the desired or most frequently occurring stage of higher quality (Mettler, 2009). Maturity assessment is thus a part of process management. This process constitutes a transformation characterized by the following features: 1. Has predictable and definable inputs that initiate the process; 2. Follows a linear, logical sequence or flow; 3. Involves a set of clearly definable and interrelated activities; 4. Results in predictable and desired outputs, which are the result of the process (Zairi, 1997). Later, additional features were added: 5. Is horizontal (sequential) and cross-functional; 6. Is performed by resources; 7. Is repeatable, and 8. Adds value for customers, stakeholders, or other interested parties (Palmberg, 2009).

In the literature, maturity has been defined in various ways, depending on the context in which the definitions were formulated. Moreover, there is no single prescribed path to achieve maturity. The differences between organizations with more or less mature IS result not only from the achieved values of the indicators used but also from the fact that more mature organizations use different indicators compared to those at a lower level of maturity.

However, comparisons in this area are hindered by the differentiated understanding of the maturity concept depending on the context. Maturity is defined as, among other things:

- A detailed process to clearly define, manage, measure and control the evolutionary growth of the individual unit being assessed (Paulk et al., 1993);
- A state in which the organization is perfectly capable of achieving the goals it has set for itself (Anderson & Jessen, 2003);
- Evaluation criterion or state of being complete, perfect and finished (Fitterer & Rohner, 2010);
- A concept, an idea that is developed from an initial state to a final (more advanced) state, i.e. to higher levels of maturity (Sen, Ramammurthy & Sinha, 2012);
- Evolutionary progress in the manifestation of specific capabilities or the pursuit of a designated goal (Mettler, 2009);
- Stages of evolution toward the full operationalization of technological processes (Goksen, Cevik & Avunduk, 2015);
- The ability to respond properly to environmental stimuli through management practices (Bititci et al., 2015, p. 3065);
- With regard to library services, Cox et al. (2017) believe that maturity in this context refers to a state where the knowledge and services of a specific area have reached a full and finite level of development.

There is no one universal way to achieve maturity (Mettler, 2009). Furthermore, in the real world, there are no fully mature organizations. Therefore, it makes sense to discuss a certain degree of maturity and make an effort to measure its actual level. The differences between organizations with more or less mature IS result not only from the achieved values of the indicators used but also from the fact that more mature organizations use different indicators than those at a lower level of maturity (Cooke-Davies & Arzymanow, 2003). It seems logical to assert that regardless of whether we apply the concept of maturity to the processes or organization of IS or whether we consider the perspective that takes into account the growing skills of participants in information processes (or a combination of both approaches), it is appropriate to believe that the longer an IS operates in today's competitive information market, the more likely it is that its processes and stakeholders will reach a higher level of maturity.

It is also necessary to distinguish between the concept of maturity, which applies to one or more features identified jointly as relevant, and the concept of system capability, which is used separately for each of these features and is defined as the power or ability in general, whether physical or mental, to fulfill specific tasks and goals (Wendler, 2012). These differences arise from the fact that maturity levels are applied to the entire IS, serving its improvement across all processes, while capabilities refer to individual processes and serve their individual improvement. In other words, maturity means that everything happening in the IS is properly documented, and everyone knows what is expected of them and adjusts their actions accordingly. Capability concerns ensuring the appropriate quality of a product, service, or process in the IS. As the IS evolves towards more mature stages of development, it simultaneously redefines its process capabilities (Gomes & Romão, 2018). Generally speaking, process capability refers to: 1.Controlling the variation in actual results; 2. Predicting process costs and performance; 3. Effectively achieving the targeted results; 4. Elevating the targeted results. This is achieved by establishing policies, standards, and organizational structures that support routine-based practices (Looy, Backer & Poels, 2011).

Successive levels of maturity should lead to the state of organizational excellence, including its information system. It can therefore be said that maturity signifies organizational capabilities that must develop over time to enable the efficient operation of the IS (thus achieving success), while excellence means attaining and maintaining the highest level of information services, deemed satisfactory by both IS creators and its users (IAM, 2021). Excellence should represent outstanding performance or reaching the upper limits of what is possible. Maturity is used to describe the entire spectrum and progression through various stages. Therefore, maturity relates to the IS organization, while excellence pertains to the results generated by that organization. Maturity models are used to enhance the organizational capacity of the IS to meet the information needs of its users. Achieving excellence involves producing complex results by improving organizational efficiency.

Despite its frequent use in many disciplines, understanding the term "maturity" can be problematic. Its use may suggest the existence of a single developmental path leading to a fixed (predictable) final state of maturity, ensuring the achievement of the appropriate effectiveness and/or usefulness of the IS. However, this is rarely the case in reality. Another issue is that terms such as "immature" or "undeveloped," sometimes found in maturity models, can be perceived as pejorative. Despite these challenges, the concept of IS maturity is valuable for conducting analyses of areas that are still in development (i.e., immature), where the quality of services and infrastructure should be continuously monitored. Maturity models (MM) are employed for this purpose.

IS MATURITY MODELS

The level of maturity achieved by IS can be assessed using maturity models (MM), which contain lists of features that determine the level of maturity. Their purpose is to illustrate the conditions that must be met for specific objects to attain the best (perfect) state of achieving their intended goals. Naturally, these models must be adapted to the type of organization and the systems it uses (specific objects), hence the existence of multiple such models. The concept of using maturity assessment models for information systems typically applies in two situations: they are used as a means of continuous improvement or ongoing assessment of the IS's functioning, conducted either independently or by an external organization (referred to as a "third party"). The popularity of such tools and similar methodologies (e.g., Six Sigma or the EFQM model of excellence) has significantly increased with the advent of general-purpose models of excellence like the Capability Maturity Model (CMM) and its successors (Mettler, 2011).

MM Nature, Structure, and Purposes

Maturity models are based on the assumption that individuals, organizations, functional areas, processes, and so on, progress in their development towards increasingly advanced maturity levels, which can be represented as moving to higher levels or reaching successive phases of development (Goksen, Cevik & Avunduk, 2015). The level in the model is a state in which it is possible to plan and implement the evolution of the system to a higher level of maturity (Santos et al., 2011). Maturity levels in the model are usually limited (typically less than 10). They conceptually represent stages of growth of a capability at a quantitative or qualitative level, in order to evaluate their progress relative to the defined maturity levels. Typically, the levels in MM are:

- Sequential and cumulative by nature;
- Indicating a hierarchical progression which is not easily reversible;
- Involve a broad array of structures as well human and organizational activities.

These features of MM are important because they allow for the combination of real, ideal, and potential situations related to the functioning of the IS at a given level of maturity, considering its resources and capabilities. Consequently, a MM is defined as a conceptual, multi-level framework that describes typical patterns of an organization's potential capability development (Harmon, 2004).

As Carneiro (2013) states, MM can be defined from three perspectives: operational, processual, and decisional, and are associated with corrective or enhancement actions. MM describes the development of an entity over time and possesses several properties. Firstly, an entity's development is simplified and described with a limited number of maturity levels. Secondly, these maturity levels are ordered sequentially and characterized by specific requirements that the entity must achieve. Thirdly, progress from one level to the next must occur without skipping any level. The MM identifies various organizational issues in IS implementation and development, highlighting the priorities requiring managerial attention at different stages of growth. In essence, the MM is a set of successive levels that together form the expected or desired logical transition path from the initial state to the final state, considered as maturity (Pöppelbuß & Röglinger, 2011). These maturity levels are assigned dimensions, depending on the domain for which the MM is designed. The maturity levels and dimensions form a matrix, the content of which describes activity features and determines the maturity achievement path for each dimension. The primary elements of an MM are thus:

- A certain number of maturity levels, usually from three to six, describing the development of the examined IS in a simplified way;
- Description (name) of each level;
- A general description of the features of each level;
- A certain number of dimensions, referring to capabilities of measured objects;
- A certain number of items or activities for each dimension;
- A description of each element or activity that can be used at each maturity level.

The achievement paths mentioned are constructed based on the maturity level indicators adopted in the model. These tools are used to assess the state of maturity of IS elements and to select actions aimed at elevating these elements to a higher level of maturity (Kohlegger et al., 2009). Conceptually, they represent the stages of potential development at the quantitative and qualitative levels of an IS element to assess the degree of its development relative to defined maturity levels. In the definitions of MM, concepts such as benchmarking, continuous improvement, and identifying the strengths and weaknesses of the organization (SWOT) are often used (Proença & Borbinha, 2016).

A model constructed in this manner can serve multiple purposes. Firstly, it acts as a signpost, indicating the position of the IS on the path to excellence and the directions of development necessary for success on this path. Secondly, it provides a framework that enables IS managers to choose priorities and methods for their implementation, thereby avoiding unnecessary expenses. Thirdly, MM can serve as a tool for IS assessment, encompassing its inputs, outputs, and outcomes. Fourth, MM can offer a common language and conceptual framework for the IS community, including librarians, library providers, and users (Wilson, 2015).

MM purposes can also be categorized into three groups: descriptive (evaluating current capabilities based on established criteria – MM serves as a diagnostic tool); prescriptive (indicating how to attain desirable maturity levels and providing improvement measures); and comparative (a tool for internal or

external benchmarking). These purposes mean that MMs are treated both as descriptions of the existing state and as the foundation for implementing improvement activities (Pöppelbuß & Röglinger, 2011).

MMs Origin and Development

Maturity Models (MM) have their origins in the field of quality assessment. The first papers on distinguishing stages of process development were written by Nolan (1973), who introduced the theory of stages of development and proposed a phased model of growth. In this model, he predicted the subsequent stages of development of information technologies (IT) and data processing within organizations. The initial four-phase model was later expanded to six phases, which are as follows: 1. Initiation (the organization focuses on operational efficiency and aims to derive limited value from the IS); 2. Contagion (the organization shifts toward online systems and accommodates more users); 3. Control (management exercises control and conducts cost-benefit assessments); 4. Integration (the organization transitions from ad-hoc, isolated solutions based on IS to service-based IS. This results in changes in the organization's behavior towards IS and initiates a new appreciation for data and information); 6. Data administration (the organization begins to recognize the value of information and works to centralize data management); 7. Maturity (the organization creates synergies between its corporate objectives and IS planning, enabling both to work in a synchronized manner).

Specific IT and IS that utilize it are assigned to the appropriate development phase based on an analysis of their properties in relation to model properties (determinants) characterizing successive levels of development, such as the IT budget and introduced technological changes (Hollyhead & Robson, 2012, p. 47). Several years later, Crosby (1979) proposed the Quality Management Process Maturity Grid, which categorized best practices across five maturity levels and six stages of growth that must be achieved to reach maturity.

Later studies in the field of maturity are rooted in quality management, where the Quality Management Maturity Grid (QMMG) has been utilized since the 1980s. It consisted of five levels of maturity: uncertainty, awakening, enlightenment, wisdom, and certainty (Gkinni, 2014). The popularity of MMs increased significantly following the introduction of the Capability Maturity Model (CMM) in the late 1980s and early 1990s. This model had many imitators, such as the ISO/IEC 15504 model (currently ISO/IEC 33004), also known as SPICE (Software Process Improvement and Capability Determination), and BOOTSTRAP, its European version, which considered the solutions of the ISO 9000 series of standards.

CMM was developed at the Software Engineering Institute (SEI) at Carnegie Mellon University in Pittsburgh, USA. This model is widely used as the primary method for evaluating software development processes. CMM defines five levels of maturity for the software development process: 1. Initial (processes are disorganized, ad hoc, and even chaotic, success depends on individual efforts, with no process definitions); 2. Repeatable (requisite processes are established, defined, and documented, enabling the repetition of success in key process areas); 3. Defined (the organization develops its own standard software development process); 4. Managed (the organization monitors and controls its own process through data collection and analysis); 5. Optimizing (processes are continually improved through monitoring feedback from the used processes and the introduction of innovative processes and functionality).

Based on the MMs mentioned, dozens of other MMs have been developed, especially in the areas of business, software engineering, and information systems. This indicates a significant interest in this issue, which is also reflected in the extensive literature (Kohlegger, Maier & Thalmann, 2009). Mutafelija and Stromberg (2003) calculated that the concept of maturity has been applied to more than 150 areas within the IS discipline. These models are quite commonly used in domains such as assisting organizations with digital government, IT management, knowledge management, or business process management (Pöppelbuß & Röglinger, 2011). Quite a few MMs can also be found in diverse, non-technical disciplines like biology, sociology, and psychology (Greenberg & Sørensen, 1974, p. 331).

In addition to the differences in their detailed characteristics, many similarities are also easily discernible because new MMs often emerge from pre-existing ones (CMM is particularly frequently mentioned in this regard). On one hand, this allows for some standardization, but on the other hand, solutions are sometimes adopted without proper theoretical consideration.

MATURITY MODEL IMPLEMENTATION

To support the implementation of maturity models, SEI developed an organizational change implementation model called IDEAL (McFeeley, 1996). This framework can be used as a tool to facilitate the implementation of maturity models. IDEAL is a standard that offers practical recommendations for change management and process improvement based on maturity models. The model defines a cycle of improvement activities consisting of five phases:

- **I** – initiating: preliminary definition of infrastructure enabling the effective implementation of the improvement process. Determining the goals and expected results of changes and necessary expenditures. Goals can be defined in general terms and are made more specific in the establishing phase. Management plays an important role in this phase.
- **D** – diagnosing: determining the current state of the organization and relating it to the desired state. Assessments are made based on measurements, the results of which are compared with reference standards. A description of the current state of the organization and the desired future state is created.
- **E** – establishing: planning and determining ways to achieve goals. A detailed MM implementation plan is created, along with recommendations. The general goals from the initiating phase are made more detailed.
- **A** – acting: implementation of the plan based on recommendations from previous stages. The most labor-intensive stage.
- **L** – leverage: acquiring knowledge based on experience gained and improving the ability to implement changes. An assessment of the achievement of goals and proposal of future actions are made.

It's evident that the IDEAL model, like other existing models of this type, is rooted in the PDCA (Plan-Do-Check-Act) cycle defined by Deming. The Deming cycle starts with the development of a plan that outlines improvement goals and the strategies for achieving them (Plan). Subsequently, these improvements are put into action (Do). In the following stage, the attainment of the planned benefits is assessed (Check). Based on this assessment, further actions are taken as necessary (Act).

SELECTED MATURITY MODELS: DIGITAL LIBRARIES (DL) AND RESEARCH DATA SERVICES (RDS)

For a better understanding of the MM concept, it's helpful to employ a method that models the reality of IS and assesses their maturity using selected examples from the field of Library and Information Science (LIS). To illustrate this, we will briefly introduce maturity models for two types of IS: digital libraries (DL) and research data services (RDS).

Digital Library Maturity Models

Despite the existence of numerous maturity models for information systems and information technology, there are few models specifically tailored to digital libraries. Existing models often share similarities, especially in terms of maturity levels, as they typically derive from variations of the CMM. Given that MMs guide the path to excellence in IS by presenting the structure of successive developmental stages, and digital libraries are complex systems requiring well-planned activities for their creation and enhancement, the application of a maturity model to a digital library as an information system can systematically improve it and enhance end-users' interest in the system. The development of a digital library can be visualized as a process of progressing through the successive stages of the maturity model. This approach allows the organization to manage the library and plan its activities while concurrently reducing the overall cost of its operations.

An example of a MM for digital libraries can be found in the work of Sheikhshoaei and his team (2018; 2021). They created such a model based on existing literature, utilizing the qualitative meta-synthesis method, and supplemented the obtained results with expert opinions through the Delphi technique. This model posits the existence of five maturity levels (initial, repeatable, defined, managed, optimizing), encompassing three categories (organizational governance, organizational-human factors, technical content) and seven core concepts (strategic management, continuous control, digital library manpower, support and organizational infrastructure, structures and processes, digital library content, IT infrastructure), which constitute the dimensions of the model. These dimensions form the rows and columns of a matrix filled with determinants of digital library maturity levels. These determinants enable the description of the conditions that must be met for a digital library to achieve a specific level within a particular dimension. Using this MM, one can assess the level of digital library maturity, taking into account its characteristics across three dimensions: organizational management, human factors, and IT applied. The assessed digital library may vary in maturity within each of these three dimensions, allowing for the identification of better and less developed elements. This, in turn, facilitates the planning of further actions aimed at achieving sustainable development for the digital library.

Another example is the work of Yang et al. (2016), who based their MM for knowledge management in digital libraries on the CMM. This effort resulted in the creation of a knowledge management capability maturity model for digital libraries, comprising five maturity levels: original (no conscious control of the knowledge process, no knowledge management), repeatable (acknowledgment of the vital role of knowledge management), general (externalization of tacit knowledge), management (standardized management integrated into a learning organization), and innovation (the digital library as a foundation for innovation). Except for the original level, which lacks any process areas, each maturity level is composed of 3 to 5 key process areas, totaling 18 areas. These process areas include knowledge processing, knowledge organization, knowledge marketing, knowledge innovation, and more.

RDS Maturity Models

In the realm of information management, more maturity models have been proposed for research data management (RDM) and its associated services (RDS) than for DL. A significant aspect of this work pertains to the involvement of libraries in these processes. Notable models include the Stewardship Maturity Model (Peng et al., 2015) and the CMM for RDM (Qin et al., 2017; Crowston & Qin, 2011). These models are employed to assess the maturity of projects or components of projects, aiming to enhance research data management and promote data reuse. One of the models that emerged from empirical research, particularly relevant to library RDS, is the one introduced by Cox & Pinfield (2014). Initially, it distinguished three levels of activities: basic, well-developed, and extensive. Subsequently, this model underwent further development (Cox et al., 2017; Cox et al., 2019), expanding to encompass four levels of maturity (see Table 1). Other authors have also contributed to discussions on the role of libraries in implementing mature RDM by preparing appropriate MMs (Kim, 2021; Kouper et al., 2017).

Table 1. Cox et al. (2019) model of evolving maturity of the RDM

Levels	Skills	Activities
0 none	Existing skills	Audit, survey
1 compliance	Translation of existing skills	RDM training, data literacy, DMP, publication, citation, storage, rights, policy
2 stewardship	Reskilling of existing staff	Data repository, selection, catalogue, curation, preservation, metadata
3 transformation	New skills acquisition	Data analysis, visualization, integrity

Source: Cox et al. (2019, p. 1453).

These studies demonstrate the positive impact of library participation in RDM; the greater the involvement of libraries in institutional RDM, the more mature RDS become. In the initial stages of RDS implementation in libraries, changes may appear to be of minor significance as activities are adapted to fit within the existing library structure and processes. However, as RDS matures, these changes can lead to a fundamental shift in the perception of the academic library's role (Cox et al., 2019). The increasing maturity of RDS may result in several transformative changes within the library, including: greater emphasis on supporting the university research process and direct involvement in its implementation; a shift from acquiring and organizing external (acquired from outside) collections towards a focus on managing resources created within the parent institution, such as research data; restructuring of professional relationships, fostering new forms of cooperation, and offering services tailored to the needs of researchers; the impact of RDS on the development of new competencies, influencing the librarian profession. It's important to note that more mature RDS are not necessarily those offering the longest list of services or employing the largest staff, but rather those whose activities are deeply integrated into the mission and functions of both the library and its parent institution (Kouper et al., 2017, p. 164).

RELATIONS BETWEEN MATURITY, DIFFUSION (ACCEPTANCE), AND EXCELLENCE OF INNOVATIVE IS

The constant growth of human capabilities, the creation of the potential for change, and the gradual maturation of applied solutions are the primary assumptions of innovation theory. Consequently, intriguing connections can be drawn between innovation theory and the development of maturity in organizations and their information systems. A crucial role is played by the diffusion of innovation and its associated theory, supported by Everett Rogers (2003). This theory offers a dynamic model that allows for the determination of the degree of innovation evolution within different user groups, taking into account variability over time. Diffusion is the process by which innovation is communicated through specific information channels over time among members of a social system. During diffusion, innovation matures, becoming increasingly appealing to subsequent user groups. Rogers categorized users into the following groups: innovators (2.5% of the market), early adopters (13.5%), early majority (34%), late majority (34%), and laggards (16%). When innovation reaches the critical mass point (16% of the market), the technology meets the basic needs of users, becoming mature enough for their requirements. From this juncture, the technology itself diminishes in significance, and the functionality of the solutions employed in its products, known as the perceived usefulness of the innovative technology, becomes paramount. Geoffrey Moore argued that there exists a boundary (critical mass point) between early acceptance and early majority that many technologies fail to reach. Critical mass occurs when the number of people accepting the innovation is so significant that further growth in innovation is sustained spontaneously (Moore, 1991, p. 16). After surpassing this point, technology becomes a secondary concern for most users, with their primary focus being on the suitability of functionality (convenience, reliability, low costs) offered by solutions. Surpassing the maturity level defined as critical mass leads to rapid technological advancement and widespread adoption of its products.

The theory of innovation underscores the critical importance of the level of acceptance of new technology, such as IT, by potential users in creating a market for products utilizing this technology. The success of a new product in the market depends on exceeding the critical mass of user acceptance. IS creators have explored the potential use of models from the field of psychology to describe intentions as a theoretical basis for researching user behavior with innovative systems. This effort led to the development of theories like the TRA, TPB, and TAM. These theories are rooted in cognitive psychology, which posits that a small number of variables can explain a significant portion of the variability in any behavior within a given population. Specifically, these models suggest that the intention to engage in a behavior is causally (though not necessarily rationally) linked to the specific beliefs individuals hold about that behavior, and this intention can serve as a basis for predicting behavior itself.

The TAM identifies two forms of motivation for using technological innovation: extrinsic and intrinsic. Extrinsic motivation pertains to the desire to achieve an outcome separate from the technology itself, such as using technology to enhance work efficiency. Intrinsic motivation involves using technology for its inherent value (Lin, 2007). Technology acceptance refers to a group of users' willingness to employ IT for the tasks it was designed to support (Dillon & Morris, 1998, p. 5). Acceptance of technology contributes to its maturity, and increased maturity, in turn, boosts its level of acceptance.

Advancing through successive levels of maturity should lead to a state referred to as excellence of the organization and its IS. In such a system, there exists an environment that ensures ongoing operational success, defined as functioning in the best interests of both the system and its users. Maturity, therefore, serves as one of the prerequisites for achieving excellence. Paradoxically, achieving excellence in the use of a particular IT carries the promise of obsolescence: it signifies the final stage of its use as it is eventually replaced by other innovative solutions. While these new IT innovations may not initially be as flawless, they introduce functionalities that were previously unavailable. This new wave of technological innovation matures through successive stages of development, continually striving for excellence.

This implies that the diffusion of innovation and the process of growing maturity are also related to disruptive innovations (Christensen, 1997) and the theories of creative destruction, which describe the fate of technologies replaced by innovation. Disruptive innovations often result in a product that is simpler (easier to use) and more affordable, but typically not as mature as the technology used before. The challenge lies in the fact that managers must compare the profitability of investing in a new business model with an immature product versus the profitability of an existing and mature product model. This can make the innovation business model seem less attractive to them. Meanwhile, new market entrants, who lack the choice of continuing with an established model, have to build their business from the ground up, maturing their products step by step. If they succeed in creating an accepted and innovative (sufficiently mature) product, it can disrupt the old technology market, sometimes dramatically. The effects of creative destruction are also felt by libraries, e.g. forced to withdraw resources stored on obsolete media, such as video tapes or CDs.

These issues are closely interconnected, leading to proposals for integrated models that simultaneously consider them (Drljevic, Aranda & Stantchev, 2022; Bach, Zoroja & Čeljo, 2017). Drljevic et al., while addressing the adoption of new IT, such as blockchain technology, recognized that there are two key aspects: novelty and complexity. To integrate these aspects, they proposed an adoption model that combines elements of the TAM and the CMM. Novelty relates to acceptance, while complexity pertains to maturity. Acceptance is a decision-making process influenced by users' attitudes, values, and intentions to use technology. Maturity, on the other hand, represents the successive stages of the evolution of a new technology, reflecting the various stages users go through in a complex environment. This model incorporates seven levels of maturity: awareness, knowledge, initiation, implementation, standardization, scale, and optimization. These levels are linked in a matrix with six dimensions: level of knowledge, perceived usefulness, perceived risk, perceived ease of use, intention to use, and active system use. Risk and success factors are then assigned to each element of the matrix, facilitating the operationalization, measurement, and management of technology usage in a sustainable manner. These factors include, but are not limited to, agility, architecture, cost, customer experience, and interoperability.

RELATIONS BETWEEN MATURITY MODELS AND INFORMATION/DATA LITERACY (I/DL) ASSESSMENT

In this section, we will compare Maturity Models (MMs) as tools for measuring Information Systems (IS) maturity and rubrics for Information/Data Literacy (I/DL) assessment. I/DL refers to the ability to consume knowledge, produce coherent information, and think critically about information and data (Kayser-Bril, 2012, p. 126). Rubrics are one of the tools used to assess I/DL. They are descriptive scoring schemes that enable consistent evaluation of users' progress in skills, as well as the analysis of their work and activities. Rubrics primarily serve to facilitate the assessment of the quality of various objects and activities (Moskal, 2000). When creating rubrics, it's important to define criteria for evaluating activities, methods for achieving success, levels of activity quality, and reasonable, reliable, and fair methods for determining scores, along with rules for describing and distinguishing successive quality levels. Thus, rubrics are utilized to assess the quality of task performance across a wide range of subjects.

Rubrics are typically presented in the form of a matrix, where rows contain evaluation criteria, and columns represent levels (successive steps) of I/DL, ranging from the lowest to the highest. Criteria are essential tasks or indicators that demonstrate the proper functioning of data services. Another crucial component of rubrics is performance descriptors, which indicate what is necessary for each assessment criterion to receive an appropriate rating (Popham, 2003). In libraries, rubrics can be applied to research and evaluate various library products and services (Oakleaf, 2007). They can provide valuable insights into information-seeking behavior, user services, marketing and improvement activities, the utility of collections, and the effectiveness of information services.

The information provided about I/DL rubrics and MMs suggests that these two tools share significant similarities. In fact, one could argue that rubrics are a type of MM that focuses on a specific entity: the user of information, often in need of I/DL training. Typically, the evaluation of the user training system, methods, processes used, and, most importantly, the training outcomes are assessed. The primary resemblance between these two tools pertains to their structure. Both are organized as matrices, with rows describing maturity levels or levels of understanding, and columns containing dimensions or objective indicators. The matrix encompasses a set of benchmarks that define I/DL or the maturity of the subject of the MM. Rubrics represent a component of the MM that outlines the organization at each maturity level for a specific assessment area (Qin, Crowston & Kirkland, 2017). Therefore, rubrics for I/DL can be regarded as an integral part of every IS MM.

I/DL rubrics are based on grading schemes, which include grading scales and attributes (skill levels) for each point on the grading scale. They are employed for specific purposes, such as assessing the impact of training users in the field of DL and indirectly evaluating training methods and the competence of trainers. By utilizing rubrics in the assessment process, it is possible to determine the maturity level of both students and their training system. On the other hand, MMs can be applied to every aspect of human activity, from the broadest to the most detailed scale of phenomena.

As Sternkopf and Mueller (2018) pointed out, frameworks that aim to describe I/DL must comprehend, appreciate, and represent its diversity. One approach to achieving this is through the application of a maturity model. A Data Literacy Maturity Model (DLMM) can help define data handling and data conversion capabilities, identify strengths and weaknesses, and provide guidance for future data practices. In their cited publication, the authors proposed the DLMM framework, which aims to focus on evaluating individual competences while also highlighting the key areas of capability, including governance, culture, technology, and people. The model consists of four levels of maturity: uncertainty, enlightenment, certainty, and data fluency. The authors address 11 data literacy dimensions (competencies), distinguished at both the organizational level (1-2) and the individual level (3-11). These dimensions are as follows: 1. Data culture, 2. Data ethics and security, 3. Asking questions and defining, 4. Finding, 5. Obtaining, 6. Verifying, 7. Cleaning, 8. Analyzing, 9. Visualizing, 10. Communicating, and 11. Assessing and interpreting (Sternkopf & Mueller, 2018, p. 5049). The primary objective of this work was to develop a maturity grid and translate it into an easy-to-use self-evaluation tool that can help assess current data-handling and data-conversion skills.

Siahaan and Gunawan (2021) proposed using a maturity model to measure information and communication technology (ICT) literacy. They employed the People Capability Maturity Model (P-CMM) to determine the level of ICT literacy. P-CMM defines five levels: initial, repeatable, defined, predictable, and optimized. To categorize ICT literacy, the Digital Competency framework was utilized (https://

ec.europa.eu/jrc/en/digcomp/digital-competence-framework), comprising five categories for measuring competencies: internet activity, communication and collaboration, digital content, security, and problem-solving.

RECOMMENDATIONS AND FUTURE RESEARCH

Proper recognition and integrated management of information processes are essential for the functioning of IS. This integration can be achieved through the use of appropriate IT. All processes within IS are organized to enhance their ability to disseminate relevant and useful information to users who require it. This ability can be assessed by using the MMs described in this article. The utilization of these models is akin to an expert evaluation method, particularly heuristic evaluation (Nielsen, 1993). This method involves comparing selected and significant IS features with an established set of criteria (i.e., some form of MM) that describes the desired state. However, it's worth noting that IS MMs do not solely focus on user experience (UX) issues, as is often the case in expert assessments. MMs describe and specify the steps necessary to achieve excellence or completeness (i.e., maturity) in specific capabilities. The concept of maturity can apply to any field, including the assessment of IS processes, where it is already well-established.

CONCLUSION

Progress towards maturity can be understood either as a defined evolutionary path (a life cycle perspective) or as potential or necessary improvements (a potential functioning perspective). MMs simplify the description of the successive stages of completeness of the analyzed objects using established and comprehensive criteria (Wendler, 2012). MMs are a valuable tool that allows for the assessment of information systems for both diagnostic purposes (defining the current state) and prognostic purposes (assessing IS development possibilities and user acceptance). Despite the assessment being based on subjectively selected criteria from the maturity model, it's possible to estimate the features of the system and its value for IS users. Thanks to this, MMs enable the presentation of the successive stages of development of the evaluated system. They also facilitate the comparison of different systems based on established criteria (benchmarking). Using MMs allows for the relatively easy determination of subsequent actions that will enhance IS maturity in the future, creating an action plan for the short or long term and setting further goals to be achieved. MMs, in this regard, provide measures for improvement. Most such models incorporate Deming's PDCA cycle (plan, do, check, act) in some form, which is also used in the ISO 9000 series standard.

IS maturity is a construct that assesses IS success more comprehensively than other measures such as effectiveness, usability, and acceptance. It offers a holistic view of any type of information system from various perspectives, including those of the system designer, information specialist, and end-users. Moreover, these perspectives consider the type of information system assessed, its goals, and tasks.

While MMs are not a universal solution for all IS problems, their relatively widespread use, expected to increase (Scott, 2007), results from several apparent benefits. MMs raise awareness of the analyzed aspects, including their status, importance, potential, requirements, complexity, and more. They can serve as a reference framework for improvement, ensure a certain level of quality, prevent errors, and assess one's own capabilities on a comparable basis (Wendler, 2012).

The literature (Cookie-Davies & Arzymow, 2003; Becker, Knackstedt & Pöppelbuß 2009; Pöppelbuß & Röglinger, 2011) also highlights the disadvantages of using MMs, primarily stemming from their simplicity (which is often mentioned as an advantage). The problems include:

- Oversimplifying the picture of the reality;
- Lack of strong theoretical foundation;
- Pointing to one path to achieving maturity and excellence, ignoring other, potentially beneficial paths;
- Their use may be limited by internal factors (availability of technology, property rights, relationships with suppliers) or external factors (e.g. market condition);
- The existence of many, very similar or even identical MMs prepared for different applications;
- Frequent lack of information about the method of MM creating (design process);
- Frequent adopting CMM solutions without sufficient reflection.

These shortcomings can be mitigated by ensuring continuous and repeatable evaluation and by comparing the results obtained by using different MMs to assess the same IS (Helgesson, Höst & Weyns, 2012).

REFERENCES

ACRL. (1998). *Task force on academic library outcomes assessment report.* https://www.ala.org/acrl/publications/whitepapers/taskforceacademic

Anderson, E., & Jessen, S. (2003). Project maturity in organizations. *International Journal of Project Management, 21*(6), 457–461. doi:10.1016/S0263-7863(02)00088-1

Bach, M., Zoroja, J., & Čeljo, A. (2017). An extension of the technology acceptance model for business intelligence system: Project management maturity perspective. *International Journal of Information Systems and Project Management, 5*(2), 5–21. doi:10.12821/ijispm050201

Becker, J., Knackstedt, R., & Pöppelbuß, J. (2009). Developing maturity models for IT management: A procedure model and its application. *Business & Information Systems Engineering, 1*(3), 213–222. doi:10.100712599-009-0044-5

Bititci, U., Garengo, P., Ates, A., & Nudurupati, S. (2015). Value of maturity models in performance measurement. *International Journal of Production Research, 53*(10), 3062–3085. doi:10.1080/00207543.2014.970709

Carneiro, A. (2013). Maturity and metrics in health organizations information systems. In M. Cruz-Cunha, I. Miranda, & P. Gonçalves (Eds.), *Handbook of research on ICTs and management systems for improving efficiency in Healthcare and social care* (pp. 937–952). IGI Global. doi:10.4018/978-1-4666-3990-4.ch049

Chadwell, F. (2011). Assessing the value of academic library consortia. *Journal of Library Administration, 51*(7/8), 645–661. doi:10.1080/01930826.2011.601268

Cooke-Davies, T., & Arzymanow, A. (2003). The maturity of project management in different industries: An investigation into variations between project management models. *International Journal of Project Management, 21*(6), 471–478. doi:10.1016/S0263-7863(02)00084-4

Cox, A., Kennan, M., Lyon, L., & Pinfield, S. (2017). Developments in research data management in academic libraries: Towards an understanding of research data service maturity. *Journal of the Association for Information Science and Technology, 68*(9), 2182–2200. doi:10.1002/asi.23781

Cox, A., Kennan, M., Lyon, L., Pinfield, S., & Sbaffi, L. (2019). Maturing research data services and the transformation of academic libraries. *The Journal of Documentation, 75*(6), 1432–1462. doi:10.1108/JD-12-2018-0211

Cox, A., & Pinfield, S. (2014). Research data management and libraries: Current activities and future priorities. *Journal of Librarianship and Information Science, 46*(4), 299–316. doi:10.1177/0961000613492542

Crosby, P. (1979). *Quality is free: the art of making quality certain.* McGraw-Hill.

Crowston, K., & Qin, J. (2011). A capability maturity model for scientific data management: Evidence from literature. *Proceedings of the American Society for Information Science and Technology, 48*(1), 1–9. doi:10.1002/meet.2011.14504801036

Davis, F. D. (1989). Perceived usefulness, perceived ease of use, and user acceptance of information technology. *Management Information Systems Quarterly, 13*(3), 318–346. doi:10.2307/249008

Deash, N., & Padhi, P. (2010). Quality assessment of libraries. *DESIDOC Journal of Library and Information Technology, 30*(6), 12–23. doi:10.14429/djlit.30.672

Dillon, A., & Morris, M. (1998). From "can they?" to "will they?" Extending usability evaluation to address acceptance. In E. Hoadley, I. Benbasat (Eds.) *Proceedings Americas Conference on Information Systems (AMCIS).* Univ. of Baltimore.

Drljevic, N., Aranda, D., & Stantchev, V. (2022). An integrated adoption model to manage blockchain-driven business innovation in a sustainable way. *Sustainability (Basel), 14*(4), 2873. doi:10.3390u14052873

Fishbein, M., & Ajzen, I. (1975). *Belief, attitude, intention, and behavior: an introduction to theory and research.* Addison-Wesley.

Fitterer, R., & Rohner, P. (2010). Towards assessing the networkability of health care provides: A maturity model approach. *Information Systems and e-Business Management, 8*(3), 309–333. doi:10.100710257-009-0121-9

Gkinni, Z. (2014). A preservation policy maturity model: A practical tool for Greek libraries and archives. *Journal of Insect Conservation, 37*(1), 1–10.

Goksen, Y., Cevik, E., & Avunduk, H. (2015). A case analysis on the focus on the maturity models and information technologies. *Procedia Economics and Finance, 19*, 208–216. doi:10.1016/S2212-5671(15)00022-2

Gomes, J., & Romão, M. (2018). Information system maturity models in healthcare. *Journal of Medical Systems, 42*(11), 235. doi:10.100710916-018-1097-0 PMID:30327955

Greenberg, E., & Sørensen, A. (1974). Towards a concept of psychological maturity. *Journal of Youth and Adolescence*, *3*(4), 329–358. doi:10.1007/BF02214746 PMID:24414373

Harmon, P. (2004). Evaluating an organization's business process maturity. *Business Process Trends*, *2*(3), 1–11.

Harvey, L., & Green, D. (1993). Defining quality. *Assessment & Evaluation in Higher Education*, *18*(1), 9–35. doi:10.1080/0260293930180102

Helgesson, Y., Höst, M., & Weyns, K. (2012). A review of methods for evaluation of maturity models for process improvement. *Journal of Software Maintenance and Evolution: Research and Practice*, *24*(4), 436–454.

Hollyhead, A., & Robson, A. (2012). A little bit of history repeating itself – Nolan's stages theory and modern IS auditor. *ISACA Journal*, *5*, 46–49.

IAM. (2021). *Pathway to excellence – maturity scale and guidance*. Institute of Asset Management.

Kamath, G., Mallya, J., Kamath, V., & Payini, V. (2022). LibQUAL+® based importance-performance matrix analysis for assessing library service quality: A case study. *Annals of Library and Information Studies*, *69*(4), 269–276.

Kayser-Bril, N. (2012). Become data literate in 3 simple steps. In J. Grey, L. Bounegru, & L. Chambers (Eds.), *The data journalism handbook*. O'Reilly Media.

Kim, J. (2021). Determining research data services maturity: The role of library leadership and stakeholder involvement. *Library & Information Science Research*, *43*(2), 101092. doi:10.1016/j.lisr.2021.101092

Kohlegger, M., Maier, R., & Thalmann, S. (2009). Understanding maturity models. Results of a structured content analysis. In K. Tochtermann, A. Paschke (Eds.), *Proceedings of I-KNOW'09 and I-SEMANTICS'09* (pp. 51-61). Verl. Technische Universitat Graz.

Kouper, I., Fear, K., Ishida, M., Kollen, Ch., & Williams, S. (2017). Research data services maturity in academic libraries. In L. Johnston (Ed.), Curating research data. Vol. 1: Practical strategies for your digital repository (pp. 153-170). ACRL.

Lin, H. (2007). Effects of extrinsic and intrinsic motivation on employee knowledge sharing intentions. *Journal of Information Science*, *33*(2), 135–149. doi:10.1177/0165551506068174

Looy, A., Backer, M., & Poels, G. (2011). Defining business process maturity. A journey towards excellence. *Total Quality Management & Business Excellence*, *22*(11), 1119–1137. doi:10.1080/14783363.2011.624779

McFeeley, B. (1996). *IDEAL^{SM}: a user's guide for software process improvement*. Carnegie Mellon University. doi:10.21236/ADA305472

Mettler, T. (2009). *A design science research perspective on maturity models in information systems*. Report no. BE IWI/HNE/03. Universität St. Galen. https://www.alexandria.unisg.ch/publications/214531

Mettler, T. (2011). Maturity assessment models: A design science research approach. *International Journal of Society Systems Science*, *3*(1/2), 81–98. doi:10.1504/IJSSS.2011.038934

Moore, G. (1991). *Crossing the chasm: marketing and selling high-tech products to mainstream customers*. Harper Business.

Moskal, B. (2000). Scoring rubrics: What, when and how? *Practical Assessment, Research & Evaluation*, *7*(3), 3.

Mutafelija, B., & Stromberg, H. (2003). *Systematic process improvement using ISO 9001:2000 and CMMI*. Artech House.

Nielsen, J. (1993). *Usability engineering*. Morgan Kaufmann Publ. doi:10.1016/B978-0-08-052029-2.50007-3

Nolan, R. (1973). Managing the computer resource: A stage hypothesis. *Communications of the ACM*, *16*(7), 399–405. doi:10.1145/362280.362284

Oakleaf, M. (2007). Using rubrics to collect evidence for decision-making: What do librarians need to learn? *Evidence Based Library and Information Practice*, *2*(3), 27–42. doi:10.18438/B8WS3W

Palmberg, K. (2009). Exploring process management: Are there any widespread models and definitions? *The TQM Journal*, *21*(2), 203–215. doi:10.1108/17542730910938182

Paulk, M., Curtis, B., Chrissis, M., & Weber, Ch. (1993). Capability maturity model, version 1.1. *IEEE Software*, *10*(4), 18–27. doi:10.1109/52.219617

Peng, G., Privette, J., Kearns, E., Ritchey, N., & Ansari, S. (2015). A unified framework for measuring stewardship practices applied to digital environmental datasets. *Data Science Journal*, *13*(0), 231–253. doi:10.2481/dsj.14-049

Petter, S., DeLone, W., & McLean, E. (2008). Measuring information systems success: Models, dimensions, measures, and interrelationships. *European Journal of Information Systems*, *17*(3), 236–263. doi:10.1057/ejis.2008.15

Popham, J. (2003). *Test better, teach better: the instructional role of assessment*. Assoc. for Supervision and Curriculum Development.

Pöppelbuß, J., & Röglinger, M. (2011). What makes a useful maturity model? A framework for general design principles for maturity models and its demonstration in business process management. In V. Tuunainen (Ed.), *Proceedings of the 19th European Conference on Information Systems*. https://fim-rc.de/Paperbibliothek/Verorffentlicht/327/wi-327.pdf

Proença, D., & Borbinha, J. (2016). Maturity models for information systems – a state of the art. *Procedia Computer Science*, *100*, 1042–1049. doi:10.1016/j.procs.2016.09.279

Qin, J., Crowston, K., & Kirkland, A. (2017). Pursuing best performance in research data management by using the capability maturity model and rubrics. *Journal of Escience Librarianship*, *6*(2), e1113. doi:10.7191/jeslib.2017.1113

Rogers, E. (2003). *Diffusion of innovations* (5th ed.). Free Press.

Santos, R., Borges, M., Canós, J., & Gomes, J. (2011). The assessment of information technology maturity in emergency response organization. *Group Decision and Negotiation*, *20*(5), 593–613. doi:10.100710726-011-9232-z

Scott, J. (2007). Mobility, business process management, software sourcing, and maturity model trends: Propositions for the IS organization of the future. *Information Systems Management*, *24*(2), 139–145. doi:10.1080/10580530701221031

Sen, A., Ramammurthy, K., & Sinha, A. (2012). A model of data warehousing process maturity. *IEEE Transactions on Software Engineering*, *38*(2), 336–353. doi:10.1109/TSE.2011.2

Shareef, M., Kumar, V., Kumar, U., & Dwivedi, Y. (2011). E-Government adoption model (GAM): Differing service maturity levels. *Government Information Quarterly*, *28*(1), 17–35. doi:10.1016/j.giq.2010.05.006

Sheikhshoaei, F., Naghshineh, N., Alidousti, S., & Nakhoda, M. (2018). Design of a digital library maturity model (DLMM). *The Electronic Library*, *36*(4), 607–619. doi:10.1108/EL-05-2017-0114

Sheikhshoaei, F., Naghshineh, N., Alidousti, S., Nakhoda, M., & Dehdarirad, H. (2021). Development and validation of a measuring instrument for digital library maturity. *Library & Information Science Research*, *43*(3), 101101. doi:10.1016/j.lisr.2021.101101

Siahaan, Y., & Gunawan, F. (2021). Measuring level of information and communication technology literacy of university students in Indonesia. *Advances in Economics. Business and Management Research*, *168*, 242–245.

Sternkopf, H., & Mueller, R. (2018). Doing good with data: development of a maturity model for data literacy in non-governmental organizations. In T. Bui (Ed.), *Proceedings of the 51st Hawaii Intern. Conference on System Sciences (HICSS-51)*, (pp. 5045-5054). Univ. of Hawaii at Manoa. 10.24251/HICSS.2018.630

Wendler, R. (2012). The maturity of maturity model research: A systematic mapping study. *Information and Software Technology*, *54*(12), 1317–1339. doi:10.1016/j.infsof.2012.07.007

Wilson, F. (2015). The Quality Maturity Model: Your roadmap to a culture of quality. *Library Management*, *36*(3), 258–267. doi:10.1108/LM-09-2014-0102

Yang, Z., Zhu, R., & Zhang, L. (2016). Research on the Capability Maturity Model of Digital Library Knowledge Management. In B. Xu (Ed.), *Proceedings of the 2nd Information Technology and Mechatronics Engineering Conference* (pp. 333-337). Atlantis Press. 10.2991/itoec-16.2016.63

Zairi, M. (1997). Business process management: A boundaryless approach to modern competitiveness. *Business Process Management Journal*, *3*(1), 64–80. doi:10.1108/14637159710161585

ADDITIONAL READING

Crawford, J. (2014). *Project management maturity model*. O'Reilly.

Galli, B. (2019). Continuous improvement maturity models: How to view them effectively. *International Journal of Service Science, Management, Engineering, and Technology, 10*(4), 26–38. doi:10.4018/IJSSMET.2019100102

Kaluu, S. (2019). *Diverse applications and transferability of maturity models*. IGI Global.

Marnewick, C., & Langerman, J. (2018). Agile maturity: the first step to information technology project success. In G. Silvius & G. Karayaz (Eds.), *Developing organizational maturity for effective project management* (pp. 233–252). IGI Global. doi:10.4018/978-1-5225-3197-5.ch012

KEY TERMS AND DEFINITIONS

Benchmarking: The process of measuring products, services, and processes against those of organizations known to be leaders in one or more aspects of their operations.

Information Literacy: A set of integrated abilities encompassing the reflective discovery of information, the understanding of how information is produced and valued, and the use of information in creating new knowledge and participating ethically in communities of learning to achieve personal, social, occupational, and educational goals.

Information System: An integrated set of components for collecting, storing, and processing data and for providing information that contributes to knowledge and information products, whether analog or digital, that facilitate decision making.

Innovation Diffusion: The way (pattern, speed etc.) new technologies and other advancements (ideas, goods, products, services, or behaviors) spread throughout societies and cultures, from their introduction to widespread adoption.

IT Acceptance: The perception of an IS after use, leading to a positive decision to use an innovation.

Maturity: A state where the knowledge about and services in a specific area has reached a fully or complete level of development.

Maturity Model: A framework (simplified representation) for measuring an organization's mature state: its ability to continuously improve in a specific discipline and its success in evolving from a particular criterion.

Research Data Management (RDM): A set of practices covering the entire lifecycle of data, including planning, storage, access, and preservation of data produced from a given investigation.

Research Data Service (RDS): Services aiming at providing information on how to organize, describe, preserve, and share research data (elements of RDM), intended to support researchers in working with data.

SWOT Analysis: A framework used to evaluate an organization's competitive position and to develop strategic planning, facilitating a realistic, fact-based, data-driven examination of the strengths, weaknesses, opportunities, and threads of an organization, its initiatives, or within its industry, leading to fact-based analysis, fresh perspectives, and new ideas.

Chapter 2
Parallel Artificial Bee Colony Algorithm for Solving Advance Industrial Productivity Problems

Annu Priya
https://orcid.org/0000-0001-6772-6509
Chitkara University Institute of Engineering and Technology, Chitkara University, Punjab, India

Shrabanti Mandal
https://orcid.org/0000-0003-3989-9503
Guru Ghasidas University, Bilaspur, India

Yogesh
https://orcid.org/0000-0002-0746-0558
Chitkara University Institute of Engineering and Technology, Chitkara University, Punjab, India

ABSTRACT

Scheduling problems play a pivotal role in many of the fields today, such as manufacturing systems, industrial processes, production, etc. The job-shop scheduling problems are categorized as a non-deterministic NP hard problem. It is very complicated to find a better algorithm which can give an optimal solution under a given time constraint. A scheduling can be generally categorized as a set of jobs where each job can have greater than one operation to perform. The main aim of the scheduling would be to resolve the scheduling of the jobs that would minimize a measure of performance. A common measure of performance for dealing with the problems of the scheduling is the makespan of a schedule. Technique for calculating the shop scheduling problem ranges from simple FIFO and SPT to more sophisticated procedures, for instance branch and bound, tabu search, ant colony, genetic algorithm, and many others. The modified version of ABC is parallel ABC (PABC) for solving the JSSP. Projected method basically uses the concept of parallelism for the concept of scheduling.

DOI: 10.4018/979-8-3693-0807-3.ch002

INTRODUCTION

In many industries today, including manufacturing systems, industrial processes, production, etc., scheduling issues are crucial. 'Productivity' is the most frequently used phrase in the industrial sphere, which is related to the conversion system where some value addition needs to be performed on the given input resources and quantitative measure of performance (Priya et al., 2023). Productivity identifies performance aspects of quality, efficiency, and effectiveness. So, productivity advancement is more important to do the right things better. It identifies the major concern of productivity improvement that depends on how successful the use of the major factor of the production system is. Job-shop scheduling problems are non-deterministic NP-hard problems, making it challenging to discover optimal algorithms under time restrictions, especially for large-scale scheduling difficulties. A scheduling approach can be seen as an allocation of jobs, each associated with more than one action to do (Sinha, 2023). A specific order of the given task is followed on the specific equipment to achieve the goal of the scheduling that would minimize a performance metric. The makespan of a schedule is a standard performance metric for dealing with our scheduling challenges. The techniques used to solve the shop scheduling problem range from simple FIFO and SPT to more complex procedures such as Branch and bound, tabu search, ant colony, genetic algorithm, etc. Parallel ABC (PABC) is a modified form of ABC used to solve the JSSP. The projected method uses the concept of parallelism for the concept of scheduling. The job shop scheduling approaches responsible for optimizing the mapping include constraints such as timing, energy consumption, and so on for a particular platform, even if only one optimization criterion is addressed, e.g., Throughput. It is an NP-complete problem. Researchers on this problem usually focus on specific application domain solutions and optimization aims (Jaiswal & Sinha, 2023). There are more heuristic approaches than exact ones. This chapter concludes with a case study for scheduling jobs on available machines. The processing time is measured for available machines, and jobs are scheduled on the machine based on the priorities. It also provides a comprehensive review of job-shop scheduling techniques in the industry environment and an overview of artificial bee colony techniques to solve the problem. The third phase of this chapter discusses the parallel artificial bee colony to solve the Jobshop scheduling problem. Finally, this paper highlights futuristic approaches in the Jobshop scheduling research and its application.

BACKGROUND

The scheduling not so new concept it was introduced in the past 3000- year ago. The science behind scheduling is to identify the tasks and resources that need to perform. In the 1980s, scheduling was used for very costly affairs which required extensive manual scheduling calculations (Jaiswal et al., 2023). In the current scenario, scheduling helps to develop a computer and information technology. The application of scheduling becomes very essential in every field such as computer science, business sector, cooperation, etc. to organize the data correctly, creating plains and structure complex processes efficiently and reliably (Gupta et al., 2023). It improves the effectiveness of the system by dividing the given problem into the process and assign them to the processors. The scheduling of the process is very tedious task in field of computer science. So, these tasks need a specific algorithm to reduce the time frame of the process in the waiting queue of the process onto the processor. Scheduling technique is a hot research topic these days, Today's many of the scheduling techniques in use have been adapted from management science and operations research studies. Multi-programed operation systems required scheduling to make the computer more productive. There is various stochastic scheduling techniques study as available to schedule the processor and process vice versa. It helps to find out that which process will get the computer resource to execute the process while another process is keeps on hold condition.

MOTIVATION

Dervis Karaboga introduced the Artificial Bee Colony (ABC) technique in 2005 that is built on population based the intelligent foraging behavior of the honey bees. This technique is easy to use as Particle Swarm Optimization (PSO) and Differential Evolution (DE) techniques. It just considers standard control variables like colony size and the maximum number of cycles. As an optimization tool, this technique offers a population-based search method where individuals, referred to as foods, are modified over time by artificial bees, with the bees' goal being to locate food sources with raised nectar amounts before arriving at the one with the most nectar (Kumar et al., 2023). The ABC system uses artificial bees that fly around in a multidimensional seeking region. Some of the bees selected food sources based on their own and their nest mates' prior experiences, and they also changed locations as needed. They memorize the new spot and forget the old one if the nectar yield of a new source is greater than that of the prior one in their memory. So, the ABC system basically combines the local search with global search approaches that carried out by employed as well as onlooker bees to balance examination and utilization process.

BACKGROUND OF THE WORK

Scheduling is not a new concept. It was introduced 3000 years ago. The science behind scheduling is identifying the tasks and resources that need to be performed. In the 1980s, scheduling was used for costly affairs requiring extensive manual scheduling calculations. In the current scenario, scheduling helps to develop computer and information technology. Scheduling has become essential in every field, such as computer science, business sector, cooperation, etc., to organize the data correctly, create plans, and structure complex processes efficiently and reliably. It improves the system's effectiveness by dividing the given problem into the process and assigning them to the processors. The scheduling of the process is a very tedious task in computer science. So, these tasks need a specific algorithm to reduce the process's time frame in the process's waiting queue onto the processor. Scheduling technique is a hot research topic these days (Karmakar et al., 2022). Today, many scheduling techniques have been adapted from management science and operations research studies. Multi-programmed operation systems required scheduling to make the computer more productive. Various stochastic scheduling techniques are available to schedule the processor and process vice versa. It helps to determine which process will get the computer resource to execute the process while another process is kept on hold condition.

Artificial Bee Colony (ABC Algorithm)

A new subset of swarm intelligence techniques, i.e., Artificial bee colony (ABC), has been developed. This technique used the concept of insect behavior to solve the problems. Karaboga first proposed ABC as an evolutionary algorithm in 2005. It attempts to mimic the natural foraging behavior of honeybees. The algorithm comprises three types of bees: employed bees, spectator bees, and scout bees. The colony is divided into two sections, with the primary section of hired bees and the secondary section of onlookers. There will be one employed bee for every available food source. As a result, the total number of bees equals the entire number of food sources present. The employed bees control accessing the nectar source first and then relaying this knowledge to the observer bees. The observer bees then select another viable food source. The spectator bees decide based on the waggle dance done by the employed bees. The hired bees use the waggle dance to communicate information about the food source, such as direction and distance. The ABC algorithm can be described in terms of "cycles of hunts," with each cycle consisting of three steps: Directing worker bees to sources of food and determining the amount of nectar content in the area; Choosing food sources while receiving guidance from working bees and determining the food source's nectar content; and deploying bee scouts to potential food sources. The bees randomly select food source locations and calculate their nectar levels in the first stage, the Initialization stage. After that, bees arrive at the hive, and communication has been established to source food, and bees are awaiting outside the hive's dance area. After the information is sent, Each worker bee visits the source region they were in during the previous cycle because that bee recalls the food source and uses visual cues to select a different food source nearby using that recollection as a guide. The third phase involves the nectar data provided by the employed bees in the dance area. An observer chooses a food supply region. Once the total nectar in the food source increases, the likelihood that an onlooker will select that food source increases. Thus, the dance of employed bees delivering advanced nectar attracts observers to food supply sites with advanced nectar amounts. Following hive-ward bound at the targeted region, the bee selects a new visual input and identifies a nearby food source to the one in memory. Visual information is provided by comparing where food sources are located. A scout bee discovers a new food source and replaces the one abandoned when the bees release the nectar of a food source. In the ABC technique, each food source position denotes a potential answer to the optimization issue.

In an optimization problem, each solution is associated with a fitness value, which decides which solution is superior based on the fitness value. Thus, in the ABC technique, the fitness function value of the associated result is inversely correlated with the nectar quantity of a food source. The number of worker or observer bees is the same as the population of offered solutions. The ABC technique creates a starting population or random solution of size SP, where SP represents the population size or overall number of food sources. Each solution is indicated as 'x', a D-dimensional vector solution, and 'i' stands for a particular solution (i=1, 2,....., SP), 'j' represents a certain dimension of a specific solution (j=1,2,...., D). The bees start looking after initializing the used random solution. Active bees explore for food close to the preceding food source, and if a new result is developed and is superior to the old one, the new solution takes the place of the old one. A food source's fitness value or nectar amount is used to compare food sources or solutions. After all hired bees have finished the search process, they communicate their position to observation bees and nectar information from food sources (solutions). According to the possibility value 'ρi, related to each food source, the spectator bee selects one. For each dietary source, the probability is determined using Eq (1).

$$\rho_i = \frac{f_i}{\sum_{n=1}^{SP} f_n} \quad (1)$$

Where, employed bees and SP, computed the nectar total value of food source or the fitness value of the obtain solution 'I'. So, after the active bees evaluate the food source, the likelihood value for each food source is established, which is used by observer bees. The candidate key solution is generated from the preceding key solution artificial bee procedures the following Eq (2).

$$V1_{ij} = X1_{ij} + \Phi1_{ij}\left(X1_{ij} + X2_{kj}\right) \tag{2}$$

Where,

j = Dimension index (j=1, 2... D).
k = Define Index that represents a specific individual or key solution from the population ('k'=1, 2, 3....., SP)
i = Define an index that represents an exact key solution ('i'=1, 2... SP).
ij = lies in between [-1, 1]

The adjacent food positions surrounding is represent X1_ij. The value of X_1ij become less as the gap between the parameter x1_ij and x2_kj gets closer. The length of each step gets shorter as the search gets closer to an optimized solution in their search space. The determined fitness value of the created candidate solution v1_ij and x1_ij's fitness are compared. The old candidate solution is replaced in memory if the new candidate solution has a nectar or fitness value that is at least as good as the old one. The old value of fitness function is taken if the solution is not developed further. A depleted food source is replenished by a fresh food source produced by scout bees.

Job Shop Scheduling Problem

In general, JSP problem is defined based on two basic constraint i.e. Precedence constraints and conflict constraints where set of 'n' jobs processed on m different machines. These assigned tasks performed some sequential operations to on a predefined machines with knowledge of deterministic processing time. Every machine process tasks independently from each other. The time required to set up the machine and transfer between processes is negligible. Furthermore, in this case, machine malfunction is not taken into account, and pre-emption is not permitted. Each operation of a given task is handled in the correct order by using precedence constraints whereas conflicts constraints give the assurance that each machine must processed only one operation at a time. The objective sequences are optimized based on the actions on the machine that has been take place also finding the starting and finishing times of each activity. Here, the main goal is to reduce the make span as short as possible. The JSP model used some of variable is given as Eq (3).

$P1_{i,k}$ =Define the proves time on machine k for Job 'j'
$S1_{i,k}$ = Define the staring time on machine k for Job 'j'
M1 = Represents Positive number
$r1_i$ = Represent ready tie for Job j
$y1_{j,j',k}$ = = the binary variable defined as:

$$y1_{j,j',k} = \begin{cases} 1 \; if \; job \; j' \; is \; before \; job \; j' on \; machine \; k \\ 0, otherwise \end{cases} \tag{3}$$

To reduce the makespan, the issue might be conceptualized as a mathematical model as shown Eq (4).

$$f1 : minimize \; \max \left\{ s1_{j,k} + p1_{jk} \right\} \tag{4}$$

$$S1_{j,k} + P1_{j,k} \le s1_{k} \; \forall \; \text{j,k,k'} \tag{5}$$

$$S1_{j,k} + P1_{j,k} \le s_{1k} + \text{M1 (1- } y_{j,j'k}\text{')} \; \forall \; \text{j, j', k'} \tag{6}$$

$$S1_{j',k} + P1_{j',k} \le s_{1k} + \text{M1 (} y_{j,j'k}\text{)} \; \forall \; \text{j, j', k} \tag{7}$$

$$S1_{j,k} r1_{j} \ge 0 \; \forall \; \text{j, k,} \tag{8}$$

Where, j,j" and k, k" is defined in between {1,2,….n} and {1,2,….m}.The objective function represented by Eq (4). The precedence constraint is defined by using Eq (5). The conflict constraints are defined by Eq (6) and Eq. (7). Eq (8) guarantees that no job will start until it is prepared.

There are numerous alternatives to Job Shop Scheduling. Initially very study has been done by Bruker and Schlie to handle the JSP with two jobs where, each task has assigned with same processing time on the distinct computers. So, basically to address realistic situations there are two types of technique developed (i). Hierarchical technique and (ii). Integrated technique. The hierarchical technique provides the way to handle routing and scheduling independently, whereas the integrated technique provide the way to handle both sub-problems concurrently. The routing and scheduling subproblems of the FJSP may be divided suitably, hierarchical techniques are natural for the FJSP established on the principle of breaking the original problem into sub-problems. Brandimarte suggested a hierarchical method to solve the FJSP problem that is based on decomposition. Where, the routing subproblem was dealt with via active dispatching rules, and the sequencing subproblem by tabu search (TS). Paulli proposed a hierarchical strategy similar to this for the flexible production system. Because of the high complexity problem of the FJSP's, meta-heuristics and evolutionary strategies have been applied to solve it. Researchers from a range of sectors have expressed interest in the localization strategy created to solve problems by using the ABC technique. The ABC technique was developed first to optimize multivariable and multi-modal continuous functions. Several comparison studies demonstrated that the performance of the ABC technique was economical from other population-based algorithms, with the benefit of using fewer control parameters in the continuous space. So, the applicability of ABC to combinatorial optimization problems is significantly fewer than that of its uses to continuous optimization problems. Baykasoglu et al. showed a comparison study of ABC and generated a fantastic artificial bee colony method to deal the given assignment problem. To solve the lot-streaming flow shop scheduling problem offered a discrete artificial bee colony technique that is established on a self-adaptive strategy. A novel bee colony optimization with local search introduced by to solve the travelling salesman problem.

Job Shop Scheduling (JSP) Using Bee Colony

Job Shop Scheduling has a extensive range of opportunities. Bruker and Schlie introduced a first study that deal with a polynomial approach to solve the JSP with two jobs, where every procedure has the same processing time on different computers technologies. Two different types of techniques—hierarchical methods and integrated approaches—have been developed to address scenarios that are realistic and involve more than two occupations. The hierarchical approaches deal with routing and scheduling separately, whereas the integrated approaches deal with both sub-problems concurrently. Hierarchical techniques are logical for the FJSP since the routing and scheduling subproblems of the FJSP may be divided suitably, based on the principle of dissecting the original problem into sub-problems. Brandimarte developed a hierarchical method based on decomposition that was able to solve the FJSP. The idea behind the method tabu search (TS) was to dealt with routing subproblem that using active dispatching rules, and the sequencing subproblem Paulli proposed a hierarchical strategy similar to this for the flexible production system. Meta-heuristics and evolutionary techniques have been commonly used to the FJSP because of its high complexity. The assignment problem was solved using a localization strategy, and the FJSP was proposed to use an evolutionary strategy controlled by the assignment model. The multi-objective problem has been solved by using particle swarm optimisation (PSO) technique to assign operations to machines and simulated annealing (SA) to schedule operations on each machine. Xia, Wu, and FJSP suggested a hierarchical approach. In order to learn and evolve solutions for the FJSP, a system known as learnable genetic architecture (LEGA) was created. To find a way to solve the FJSP with sequence-dependent setups, Saidi-mehrabad and Fattahi suggested a TS algorithm with two heuristics. In addition, SA and TS methods for solving the FJSP were also presented. To solve the multi-objective FJSP, the genetic algorithm (GA) was combined with uneven neighbourhood search. For the purpose of solving the FJSP with parallel machines and re-entrant processes, it was suggested to hybridise the machine assortment module and the operation scheduling module. The FJSP with make span criterion was introduced in a variable neighbourhood genetic algorithm. From the perspective of dynamic programming, a multistage operation-based GA was intended to handle the challenge. Yazdani et al. introduced a parallel variable neighbourhood search (PVNS) technique that was based on six neighbourhood structures. A knowledge-based ant colony optimisation algorithm (KBACO) was proposed to solve the FJSP. Moradi et al. carried out an effective architecture for scheduling the FJSP with machine accessibility restrictions. A parallel GA for the FJSP with sequence-dependent setups was presented by Defersha and Chen. To reduce make span time, Zhang et al. developed a successful GA for solving the FJSP. For the FJSP, Li et al. created a hybrid TS with a productive neighbourhood structure. Integrated techniques are more challenging to solve than hierarchical ones, but they typically produce superior outcomes. Based on the integrated method, Dauzere-Peres and Paulli developed a TS algorithm and created a new neighbourhood structure for the problem, where there was no difference between reassigning and resequencing an operation. The TS algorithm was enhanced by Mastrolilli and Gambardella, who created two neighbourhood functions and outperformed all other active meta-heuristics in terms of calculation time and solution quality. A method based on linguistics, SA, and a dispatching rule was put forth by Baykasoglu, in which the FJSP was referred to as an alternative process plan. Chan et al. solved the FJSP under resource restrictions using an integrated technique based on GA. In order to solve the FJSP, Pezzella et al. created a GA that integrated many methods for creating the initial population, choosing people for reproduction, and producing new individuals. To solve the multi-objective FJSP and minimise makes pan, mean tardiness, and mean flow times, Tay and Ho proposed an integrated strategy based on genetic programming. Most recently, for the multi-objective FJSP, Moslehi and Mahnam developed a Pareto technique employing PSO and limited investigation, and the computational outcomes demonstrated the effectiveness of the algorithm. Swarm intelligence's newest component, the artificial bee colony (ABC) approach, is based on collective behaviour. of self-organized systems. Researchers from many different domains have so far expressed interest in the ABC algorithm. The initial goal of the ABC method was to maximise continuous multivariable and multimodal functions. Numerous investigations in comparison revealed that the ABC algorithm's performance was comparable to that of other population-based algorithms, with the benefit of using fewer control parameters in the continuous space. The use of ABC in solving combinatorial optimisation issues is much more constrained than it is in solving continuous optimisation issues. Baykasoglu et al. has done comparative analysis of ABC technique and advanced effective artificial bee colony technique to deal with the generalised assignment problem. The author Pan et al. offered a discrete artificial bee colony technique that is mainly based on a self-adaptive policy to deal with the lot-streaming flow shop scheduling problem including the criterion of total weighted earliness and tardiness penalties. Wong et al. offered an innovative bee colony optimisation technique by using efficient local search that is able to solve the travelling salesman problem.

PARALLEL ARTIFICIAL BEE COLONY ALGORITHM

The TSP & JSSP problems are known as NP-hard problems. Their solution is identified in reasonable period of time by using heuristic intelligent exploring method called ABCA. However, when they are used to solve more challenging problems and the number of jobs increases noticeably, it takes much longer to locate the answer. In an effort to cut down on processing time, the artificial bee colony method has hidden parallelism that accelerates the algorithm's speed and allows it to find a better solution in a shorter period of time. In parallel artificial bee colony technique the entire colony of bees has been divide into sub-colonies. Here the number of sub-colonies is directly proportional to the number of processor resource that has been taken. The individual resource has been given a sub-colony and is free to independently identify the best solutions worldwide. The communication system between each sub colony helps to enables them which discard the worst answer, and at the end of the iteration, the best solution so far can be found. The master node oversees displaying results, establishing parameter setting, and allocating other computational resources in our master-slave paradigm. Additionally, the remaining nodes oversee performing the calculation. In addition to the various tasks mentioned above, the master node is also in charge of calculations. The parameter relation between the entire colony and sub-colony represented by the given equation below.

$$\text{sub\_SN1} = \frac{SN}{num} \tag{9}$$

$$\text{sub\_iteration1} = \frac{total\_iteration}{communi\_num} \tag{10}$$

$$\text{sub\_LIMIT1} = \text{LIMIT} \tag{11}$$

The population relation of entire colony and sub colony is represented by Equation 5. Here, the total number of the population is referred by 'Num'. The colony size of each sub colony is denoted by sub_SN1 and total size of the colony is SN. The equation 6 is defined as iteration in each sub-colony that is represented by sub_iteration1. The total_iteration is denoted by whole colony whereas communi_num is represents communication between each sub-colony. The limited value of whole colony is defined by LIMIT that is equal to the limited value of each sub colony.

MECHANISM FOR COMMUNICATION AND THE TOPOLOGICAL STRUCTURES

Since we are extracting the parallel property found in the sequential bee colony algorithm, hence it is very important that the communication mechanism and the required topology among each subcolony is of vital importance for the parallel ABC. Ring topology can be used to implement the communication for the data among each processor node. Each of the sub-colony will be pre-assigned with a serial number. So, during the communication each processor will know which object needs to be communicated with that serial number. As this is a ring topology, so each processor will communicate with the serial number which is next to it. So, each time a communication is done between two processors, they can share the information about the current best solution to the later processor. After which the node receiving the data can determine which will be the global best solution and pass that information to the next node. While receiving the best solution from their former nodes, the present node can update the current worst solution in it with the best solution received.

JOB SHOP SCHEDULING (JSSP)

To a specific target function fulfilment, the job shop scheduling problem (JSSP) look for to identify the best sequential allocation of competing resources. The goal of the JSSP in this paper is to reduce the make span. It consists of a collection of jobs on a set of machines. Only one machine can handle a job in the JSSP at once. We assume that one task consists of "m" actions that must be completed on a certain date. A job cannot be split up in the middle of processing after it has begun on a specific computer. The basic goal of job scheduling is to develop a timetable that will reduce the overall time needed to complete the jobs. A good timetable will be one that keeps the machines from being idle for long periods of time. A n-m job-shop scheduling issue can be formulated as follows. Let 'J' = 1, 2,..., n represent the set of operations to be scheduled, 'M' = 1, 2,..., m stand in for the set of machines, and 'O' = 0, 1,..., n, n+1 represent an operation. Dummy operations are 0 and n×m+1, which stand for the first and last operations, respectively. Two different types of restrictions connect the operations together. Priority constraints are used to guarantee that each operation j will be scheduled after all previous operations P have been completed. Additionally, scheduling operations j is only possible when the machine needed for them is not in use. Let dj and F stand for the operation's fixed duration time and finish time, respectively. Let A(t) be the set of operations being carried out at time t, and let ζj =1if processing machine m is necessary for action j, and ζ jm =0 otherwise. The model is as follows, in light of the conclusions drawn from the facts already stated: Minimize $F_{n\times m+1}$.

$F_K \le F_j - d_j; j = 1,\ldots..,n \times m+1; k \in P_j$ (12)

$$\sum_{j\in A(t)} \P_{\mathrm{jm}}\ 1,\ \mathrm{m} \in \mathrm{M},\ \mathrm{t} \geq 0 \tag{13}$$

$F_j \geq 0$ J= 1,2,……, n× m +1 (14)

Makespan is the name of the objective function (8), which seeks to minimize the time taken to complete the most recent operation. Equation (9) can be used to enforce the precedence constraint, while equation (10) makes sure that only one machine can execute one operation at a time. The final phrase guarantees the makespan's non-negative. Job shop scheduling is frequently shown visually as a disjunctive graph. Each operation in the graph has its own node, and there are source operations with order 0 and sink operations with order O = nxm+1. Each positive-weighted operation has a processing time that corresponds to its positive weight. The beginning and ending times of our job schedule will be determined by the beginning and ending times of the source and washbasin, respectively. Each positive-weighted operation has a processing time that corresponds to its positive weight. The beginning and ending times of our job schedule will be determined by the beginning and ending times of the source and washbasin, respectively. Figure 1 illustrates a 3X3 disjunctive as an example. Conjunctive arcs are represented by solid lines, while disjunctive arcs are represented by dotted lines. Oij stands for the jth operation of the task Ji, and M_1=O_11,O_22,O_32, M_2=O_12,O_23,O_33, and M_3=O_13,O_21,O_31, respectively, give the set of operations for each machine.

Figure 1. Flowchart of ABC algorithm

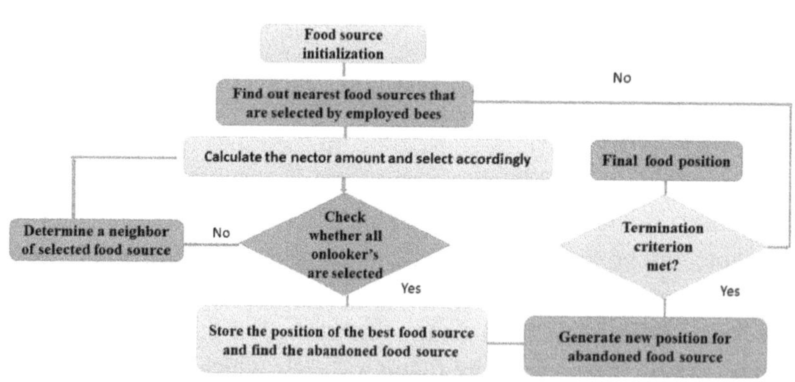

The scheduling problem is identified as a challenging JSSP problem. That can be able to resolve by finding a combination of the machines that makes the bidirectional arcs unidirectional. The makespan of the given problem is based on finding the length of the longest directed graph, which is calculated by summing the execution durations of all the operations on that path. The makespan of the problem can be determine by finding the length of the longest directed graph, which is calculated by summing the execution durations of all the operations on that path. A feasible method is shown in Figure 2 that illustrate a workable solution.

Figure 2. An example of a 3 by 3 instances in disjunctive form

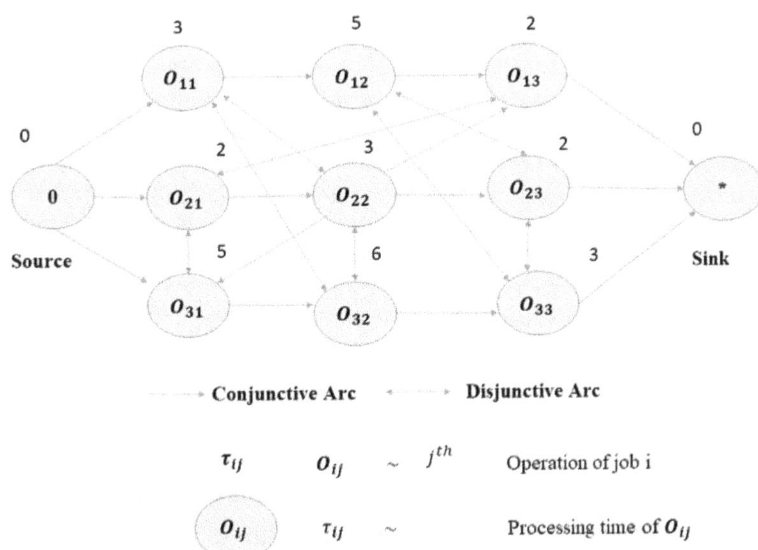

A visualization of the feasible solution can be given through the GANNT chart in Figure 3. The makespan is obtained from the operations $\{O_{23}, O_{31}, O_{32}\}$ which is 16

Figure 3. A possible solution

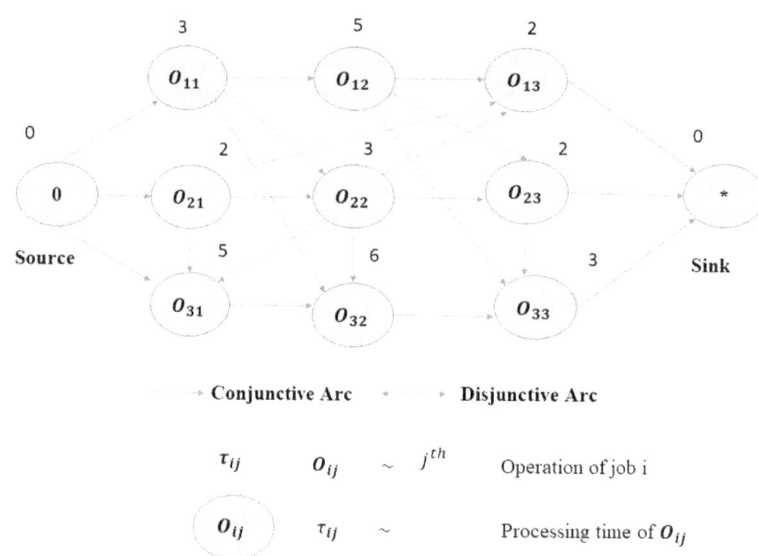

IMPLEMENTATION DETAILS

Parallel artificial bee colony algorithm in developed using C/C++ compiler on Window 7 platform. A solution's duration on the list is determined by the number of iterations for which it has been certified. The foragers are identified by the list of privileged number solutions. Here, the length of waggle dance is proportional to that number. Each data structure for these solutions contains the makespan of the forager's path based on the maximum number of allowable iterations as well as the total number of iterations when a key solution is added to the list. In the course of our implementation, the path is kept in a list. There are connections between the operations in the list. As a result, the edges for the solution in figure 3 are {O,O11}, {O11,O21}, {O21,O31}, {O31,O22}, {O22,O12}, {O12,O32}, {O32,O23}, {O23,O13}, {O13,O33}, and {O33,*}. Source and sink, respectively, are O and *. The present bee and the other bee in the same colony hunt for neighbors during the implementation procedure. Due to the division of the entire population across small sub-colonies, there will be fewer bees in the sub-colony. As a result, if we continue to use the standard ABC's local search method, the algorithm will inevitably find the closest best answer. So, in order to get out of this predicament, we came up with a novel method for conducting neighbor searches. To develop a fresh potential solution for the neighbor search, the algorithm randomly selects two parameters from the entire parameter space. By quantifying the amount of time, it takes for each sub-colony to finish as a unit of time, we were able to mimic the parallel process on a single computer. The initiation phase, employed bees' stage, and scout bee stage are the four phases of the ABC technique. The created algorithm is displayed below:

Initialization Stage

- Set the PABCA master node's initialization parameters. Bee population as a whole, iteration times, the value of the limitation, and communication times during computation are all included.

- Sub-colony parameter calculations. It provides the subcolony's population, sub-iteration times, and the locations where data communications were carried out.
- The data sent from the master node is received by each subcolony.
- In accordance with the parameters sent by the matrix node, each subcolony creates a number of random solutions and determines the fitness functions for those solutions. Once the minimum and maximum fitness function values in each sub-colony have been established, the best solution in each sub-colony should be substituted with the maximum fitness functions.

Employed Bee Stage

- Every subcolony follows the bees-in-work concept.
- Each subcolony decides the probability based on the fitness function.

Onlooker Bee Phase

- On the basis of the probability found during employed bee phase, onlookers make decisions. It then follows the employed bee of its choice in doing the neighbor search.
- Each sub colony updates with its best solution. When each subcolony has determined both the greatest and worst options currently available.

Scout Bee Stage

- The scouts model is implemented in every subcolony. Judge variables that track when each employed bee conducted a neighbor search. The employed bees of a variable return to zero if any variables exceed the limit then it has been established at the start of the method, and a new randomly generated solution takes its place.
- Every subcolony evaluates the iteration times; if the iteration times fall short of the maximum times, the employed bee phase is the next step. Move on to the next step if the iteration times exceed the maximum number.
- In accordance with the ring topological structure, each sub-colony communicates the best fitness function with the others. The variable that records the number of times each worker bee searched for neighbors returns to zero when the worst fitness function is get exchanged by the best fitness function achieved from other colonies.
- Each sub colony needs to calculate the communication times, if the estimated time doesn't reach the set limit time then go to worker bee phase. Once iteration time of the technique reaches the limit time go to next step.
- Exit from the methodology.

EXPERIMENTS AND RESULTS ANALYSIS

In this section we implemented some of the benchmark problems available, and then we compared our results with some of the benchmark problems that are genetic algorithm and ant algorithm.

Problem Instances

82 job shop problem instances (Ganesan et al., 2004) have been considered for checking the efficiency of our algorithm. Fisher & Thompson discussed ft06, ft10 and ft20 problems in 1963. In 1984 Lawrence referred the la01 – la10 10. swv11 – swv20 3 problems generated by Adams et al. (1988), referred as abz7 – abz9.

Format of Input File for the Standard Instances

The input file contain 82 JSP test instances. These instances submitted by Dirk C. Mattfeld and Rob J.M. Vaessens to the OR-Library. The input file is downloaded from the website "https://www.eii.uva.es/elena/JSSP/InstancesJSSP.htm". These instances provide details about the number of jobs and machines. These job with machine number associated with processing time in each stage of the work. Initially machine starting time is consider as 0. These issues can involve anywhere between 6 and 50 jobs and 5 and 20 machines. The effectiveness of the dispatching rules in relation to the store's size is unaffected. According to prior research, tests with relatively modest establishments could yield reliable results. For this reason, larger shop difficulties are not considered in the study. The generated programmes were ran in codeblock IDE on a computer with a specification of Intel Core i3 processor operating at 2.4 GHz with 4 GB of RAM, and Windows 7. 39 The ant colony algorithm, which belongs to swarm intelligence, was first put forth by Dorigo et al. in 1996. When ants find food, they start out randomly and then return to their colony while leaving pheromone trails. Other animals use this trail to follow that route instead than meandering aimlessly, and they also depart from the pheromone trail on their way back. The shortest path will automatically have more rather than a great distance because the pheromone will also evaporate with time. The genetic algorithm is a form of artificial intelligence that mimics the process of natural selection in search heuristics. A population of potential solutions to an optimization problem is evolved via a genetic algorithm towards a superior answer. Each potential solution has a unique set of properties that are malleable. Typically, the answers are shown as a binary string of 0's and 1's. A population of randomly created individuals is typically the starting point for evolution. Each individual's fitness function is assessed, and the more fit individuals are chosen, with each person's genome being changed to build a new generation of the string. When the maximum number of generations have been generated or a suitable fitness level has been attained, the algorithm ends. Table1. Shows comparison of experimental results of benchmark algorithms. Table size is defined as name of each test set problem. Here, BKS represent the best known solution. The last column is the output of each test instance according to the algorithm proposed in the paper.

Table 1. The GA, ant colony, and parallel ABC are compared

Problem Name	Size	BKS	GA	Ant Colony	Parallel ABC
1.Ft06	[6×6]	55.00	55.00	55.00	55.00
2. Ft10	[10×10]	930.00	930.00	980.00	980.00
3. Ft20	[20×5]	1165.00	1165.00	1194.00	1194.00
4. La01	[10×5]	666.00	666.00	666.00	666.00
5. La02	[10×5]	655.00	655.00	655.00	655.00
6. La03	[10×5]	597.00	597.00	597.00	597.00
7. La04	[10×5]	590.00	590.00	590.00	590.00
8. La05	[10×5]	593.00	593.00	593.00	593.00
9. La06	[15×5]	926.00	926.00	926.00	926.00
10. La07	[15×5]	890.00	890.00	890.00	890.00
11. La08	[15×5]	863.00	863.00	863.00	863.00
12. La09	[15×5]	951.00	951.00	951.00	951.00
13.La10	[15×5]	958.00	958.00	958.00	958.00
14. Swv11	[50×10]	3200.00	3200.00	-	3300.00
15. Swv12	[50×10]	3250.00	3250.00	-	3358.00
16. Swv13	[50×10]	3754.00	3754.00	-	3834.00
17.Swv14	[50×10]	3487.00	3487.00	-	3487.00
18. Swv15	[50×10]	4235.00	4235.00	-	4235.00
19. Swv16	[50×10]	3547.00	3547.00	-	3547.00
20. Swv17	[50×10]	3269.00	3269.00	-	3269.00
21. Swv18	[50×10]	3156.00	3156.00	-	3156.00
22. Swv19	[50×10]	3169.00	3169.00	-	3169.00
23. Swv20	[50×10]	3231.00	3231.00	-	3231.00
24. Abz7	[15×20]	656.00	655.00	775.00	656.00
25. Abz8	[15×20]	665.00	686.00	787.00	686.00
27. Abz9	[15×20]	661.00	697.00	-	697.00

The graphical representation of comparison for the GA, Ant colony and Parallel ABC is given below in Figure 4.

Figure 4. Comparison for the GA, ant colony, and parallel ABC

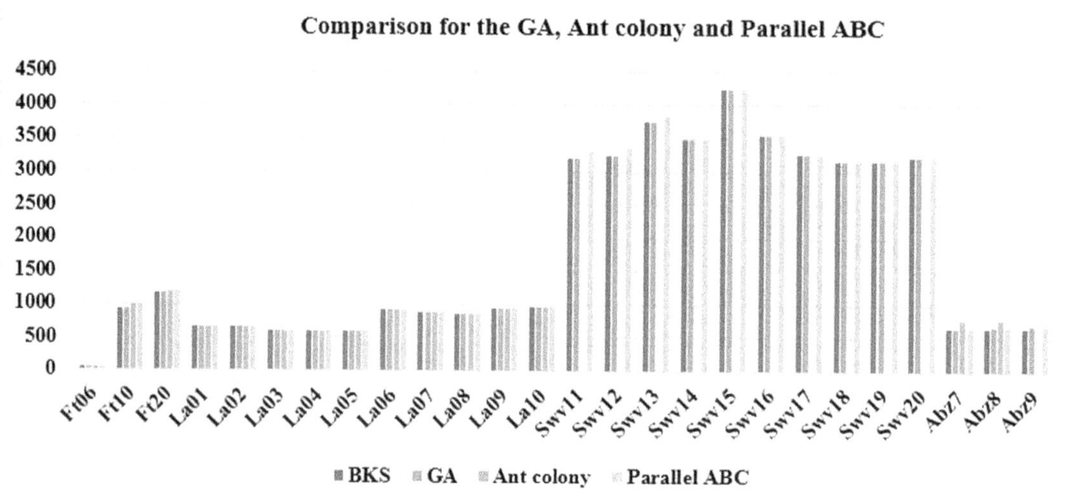

CASE STUDY 1: ARTIFICIAL BEE COLONY (ABC) ON TSP

In normal bee colony approximately 6,000 and 20,000 bees might be found in a hive. Active foragers, scout foragers, and inactive foragers are the three primary functions of foraging bees. The foraging bees are actively searching for food in the area, travelling to a food source to get food, and then returning to the hive. The Scout bees scour the vicinity of the hive, frequently a space of up to 50 square miles, in search of alluring new food sources. In a hive, about 10% of the foraging bees serve as scouts. The distances between cities wouldn't be calculated artificially in the majority of TSP scenarios. Instead, some type of lookup data structure would probably be used to store the distances. In some TSP versions it is consider that every single city is associated with other new city, whereas other problems assume that the connections between the cities are incomplete. Additionally, some TSP variations assume that the distance between any two cities Tc1 and Tc2 is equal to the distance between Tc2 and Tc1, while other problem variations do not make this assumption in both directions. At first the travelling salesman problem will find a random solution by using the bee algorithm, when the employee bee will go on. After the employee bee has generated a random solution, it will be stored in 'a' array best index. Once the problem has been initialized, then the fitness of each generated solution will be checked and then the scout will go on for the searching better solution. Once the optimal solution has been achieved, the algorithm will stop. The algorithm can also be terminated, if the entire food source has been exhausted, or code has run past its run time. Once a solution has been abandoned, the employee bee will become inactive and can go on for further searching of new solution.

CASE STUDY 2: ANT COLONY OPTIMIZATION (ACO) ON TSP

A collection of methods called ant colony optimisation are essentially used to identify the best paths through a graph. It does this by imitating an ant colony's foraging strategy. Ants utilise pheromones to communicate, as I previously stated, and the quantity of pheromone on each trail determines whether it is the best course of action. An ant will therefore be more inclined to follow a trail that has more pheromones on it. The term MAX_CITIES denotes the most cities we can fit onto the map. The maximum pair-wise distance between the cities is also set at 100. As a result, the worst-case scenario represented by 'MAX_TOUR'. That is the tour which requires the ant to pass through MAX_CITIES*MAX_DIST. In this case, we define the number of ants to be 30, or precisely the same as the number of cities on the map. Experimental research has shown that the optimal solution is produced faster with an equal number of ants to cities than with a higher number of ants. The x and y are members of a struct called cityType. These serve as a representation of the city's coordinates. Following this, we define the struct antType, which includes the members required for an ant to operate. The indices of the current city and the following city to be visited on the graph are represented by the integer values curCity and nextCity. The list of cities that an ant has already passed through is represented by the array tabu, while the path variable stores the path that the ant has taken. The distance the ant has covered as of the tour is represented by the value tourLength. Following the creation of the simulation's ants and the fundamental setup of the problem, now define the parameters through which the algorithm will converge to a solution. The significance of the trail is represented by one variable, and the relative significance of visibility is defined by another. The inverse of the distance between two nodes is used to model visibility in this case. RHO is a symbol for the factor that controls how quickly pheromones dissipate on the edges. For the purpose of defining the nodes in our graph, we declare a cityType struct array. The size of a city's worth of ants are also produced by our company. While the array 'phero' keeps track of the pheromone levels on each edge between the cities, the array 'dist' keeps track of the pairwise distances between the cities. The best tour is recorded using the variable best as a control variable once each iteration is complete. The complete graph will be initialized, as well as the Ants that will be used to navigate it. The cities are essentially given random coordinates, and then compute the distances between them on a pair-by-pair basis. Additionally, to start the ants, place an ant on each node of the graph.. Also set the path and the remaining characteristics of each Ant, including the tabu list. The ants are restarted by going back to their starting positions in the next step of the algorithm after each traverse. The global variables that we have constructed contain information about the optimum path as well as its value. In order to decide which edge to traverse next, a collection of functions is utilized. According to the equation given in the previous post, each ant in the environment chooses the following edge. Both the actual value of the pheromone itself and a straightforward reciprocal function of distance, which measures visibility, are used in this instance to represent pheromone. The extensive research that has been done in this field allows for the replacement of these functions by other suitable heuristic functions. The functions that we utilize show to be an adequate measure for the straightforward TSP that we will solve. The pheromone trails will then be updated using the function. When the number of iterations does not exceed MAX_TIME, we simply continue the simulation with the updated trails after running the simulations again. This makes sure that the simulation ends after a predetermined number of iterations, whether or not the ANT agents reach a solution.

SOLUTIONS AND RECOMMENDATIONS

In order to allocate competing resources in the best possible order, the job shop scheduling problem (JSSP) is used. that achieve a precise goal function. The goal of the JSSP in this study is to reduce the make span and consist of a collection of jobs on a set of machines. Only one machine at a time can handle a job in the JSSP. We assume that each job consists of "m" actions that must be completed on a particular day. A job cannot be divided up in the middle of processing after it has begun on a specific computer. Finding a timetable that will reduce the overall time it takes to complete the jobs is the major goal of job scheduling. A good schedule will be one that minimizes the idle time of the machines.

FUTURE RESEARCH DIRECTIONS

There is scope to address many aspects for improvement in the future. Some possible extensions of the work in terms of scheduling technique and model have also been suggested.

- The work is restricted to jo shop scheduling parallel artificial bee colony. The present work can be extended by considering hybrid flowshop scheduling in high-performance computing.
- The parallel artificial bee colony has considered in this chapter, but the work can be extended with hybridization of both the algorithms

CONCLUSION

We have implemented job-shop schedule problems using the parallel artificial bee colony. As can be concluded from the results obtained that parallel artificial bee colony is comparable to other heuristics algorithms, but still there are gaps between them. Since this is our first implementation, we intend to use the Message Passing Interfaces and more than one process, instead of simulating on a single processor. We can use better random functions to get a uniform randomization in order to not get stuck to a local best solution. The parallel artificial bee colony algorithm can be further modified, by using better techniques for the local search; hybridization with other algorithms can also help to get a better result.

REFERENCES

Balyan, A. K., Ahuja, S., Lilhore, U. K., Sharma, S. K., Manoharan, P., Algarni, A. D., Elmannai, H., & Raahemifar, K. (2022). A Hybrid Intrusion Detection Model Using EGA-PSO and Improved Random Forest Method. *Sensors (Basel)*, *22*(16), 5986. doi:10.339022165986 PMID:36015744

Brucker, P., & Schlie, R. (1990). Job-shop scheduling with multi-purpose machines. *Computing*, *45*(4), 369–375. doi:10.1007/BF02238804

Chong, C., Hean Low, M., Sivakumar, A., & Gay, K. (2006). A Bee Colony Optimization Algorithm to Job Shop Scheduling. *Proceedings of the 2006 Winter Simulation Conference*. 10.1109/WSC.2006.322980

Defersha, F. M., & Chen, M. (2009). A parallel genetic algorithm for a flexible job-shop scheduling problem with sequence dependent setups. *International Journal of Advanced Manufacturing Technology*, *49*(1–4), 263–279. doi:10.100700170-009-2388-x

El-Abd, M. (2010). A cooperative approach to The Artificial Bee Colony algorithm. *IEEE Congress on Evolutionary Computation.* 10.1109/CEC.2010.5586007

Ganesan, V.K., Sivakumar A.I., & Srinivasan, G. (n.d.). Heirarchical minimiation of completion time variance and makespan in job shops. *Computers and Operation Research.*

Gupta, N. E., Kumar, K., & Sinha, K. (2023). The Nexus of War, Violence, and Rights: A History of War-Torn Afghanistan. In Handbook of Research on War Policies, Strategies, and Cyber Wars (pp. 334-351). IGI Global.

Islam, M. S. U., Kumar, A., & Hu, Y.-C. (2021). Context-aware scheduling in Fog computing: A survey, taxonomy, challenges and future directions. *Journal of Network and Computer Applications, 180*, 103008. doi:10.1016/j.jnca.2021.103008

Jaiswal, G., Karmakar, M., & Sinha, K. (2023). Yoga: A Stress Removal Toolkit During War From the Women's Perspective. In Acceleration of the Biopsychosocial Model in Public Health (pp. 137-167). IGI Global.

Jaiswal, G., & Sinha, K. (2023). Yoga: An Ancient Healing Approach for Cyclical Mastalgia. In Perspectives on Coping Strategies for Menstrual and Premenstrual Distress (pp. 237-261). IGI Global.

Karaboga, D., & Basturk, B. (2008). On the performance of artificial bee colony (ABC) algorithm. *Applied Soft Computing*, *8*(1), 687–697. doi:10.1016/j.asoc.2007.05.007

Karaboga, N. (2009). A new design method based on artificial bee colony algorithm for digital IIR filters. *Journal of the Franklin Institute*, *346*(4), 328–348. doi:10.1016/j.jfranklin.2008.11.003

Karmakar, M., Priya, A., Sinha, K., & Verma, M. (2022, December). Shrinkable Cryptographic Technique Using Involutory Function for Image Encryption. In *International Conference on Advanced Network Technologies and Intelligent Computing* (pp. 275-289). Cham: Springer Nature Switzerland.

Kumar, K., Singhania, D., Singh, K. P., Mishra, P., & Sinha, K. (2023). Navigating the Economic Challenges of the Russia-Ukraine Conflict on India. In Handbook of Research on War Policies, Strategies, and Cyber Wars (pp. 218-238). IGI Global. doi:10.4018/978-1-6684-6741-1.ch012

Kumar, S., Jaiswal, G., & Sinha, K. (2023). Skin Cancer Lesion Detection Using Improved CNN Techniques. In Handbook of Research on Technological Advances of Library and Information Science in Industry 5.0 (pp. 355-377). IGI Global.

Li-Pei Wong, Low, & Chong. (2008). Bee Colony Optimization with local search for traveling salesman problem. *2008 6th IEEE International Conference on Industrial Informatics.* 10.1109/INDIN.2008.4618252

Priya, A., & Sahana, S. K. (2020). Multiprocessor Scheduling Based on Evolutionary Technique for Solving Permutation Flow Shop Problem. *IEEE Access : Practical Innovations, Open Solutions, 8*, 53151–53161. doi:10.1109/ACCESS.2020.2973575

Priya, A., & Sahana, S. K. (2020). Multi-Processor Job Scheduling in High-Performance Computing (HPC) Systems. *FPGA Algorithms and Applications for the Internet of Things*, 168–203. . doi:10.4018/978-1-5225-9806-0.ch009

Priya, A., & Sahana, S. K. (2020). Processor Scheduling in High-Performance Computing (HPC) Environment. *Emerging Trends and Impacts of the Internet of Things in Libraries*, 151–179. . doi:10.4018/978-1-7998-4742-7.ch009

Priya, A., Sharma, S., Sinha, K., & Yogesh, Y. (2023, March). Community Detection in Networks: A Comparative study. In *2023 International Conference on Device Intelligence, Computing and Communication Technologies (DICCT)* (pp. 505-510). IEEE. 10.1109/DICCT56244.2023.10110206

Sinha, K. (2023). The Metaverse and Digital Libraries: Ensuring Safe and Secure Access to Information. In Handbook of Research on Advancements of Contactless Technology and Service Innovation in Library and Information Science (pp. 1-22). IGI Global.

Wedde, H. F., Farooq, M., & Zhang, Y. (2004). *BeeHive: An Efficient Fault-Tolerant Routing Algorithm Inspired by Honey Bee Behavior, Ant Colony, Optimization and Swarm Intelligence*. Lecture Notes in Computer Science. Springer Berlin.

Xing, L.-N., Chen, Y.-W., Wang, P., Zhao, Q.-S., & Xiong, J. (2010). A Knowledge-Based Ant Colony Optimization for Flexible Job Shop Scheduling Problems. *Applied Soft Computing*, *10*(3), 888–896. doi:10.1016/j.asoc.2009.10.006

Zhang, J., Hu, X., Tan, X., Zhong, J. H., & Huang, Q. (2006). Implementation of an Ant Colony Optimization technique for job shop scheduling problem. *Transactions of the Institute of Measurement and Control*, *28*(1), 93–108. doi:10.1191/0142331206tm165oa

Zhang, R., & Wu, C. (2011). An Artificial Bee Colony Algorithm for the Job Shop Scheduling Problem with Random Processing Times. *Entropy (Basel, Switzerland)*, *13*(9), 1708–1729. doi:10.3390/e13091708

KEY TERMS AND DEFINITIONS

Ant Colony: An optimization algorithm inspired by the foraging behavior of ants, employed to solve complex problems by simulating the way ants find the shortest path to food sources.

Computing: The use of computers and algorithms to perform various tasks, including data processing, problem solving, and information retrieval, encompassing a wide range of applications from scientific research to everyday tasks.

FIFO (First-In-First-Out): A scheduling and data management strategy where the items or tasks are processed in the order they arrive, with the first item received being the first one to be processed.

Genetic Algorithm (GA): An optimization technique based on the principles of natural selection and genetics, used to find solutions to complex problems by evolving a population of potential solutions over multiple generations.

Job Shop Scheduling Problem (JSSP): A classic combinatorial optimization challenge where a set of jobs must be scheduled on a set of machines while minimizing makespan or other criteria.

Parallel Artificial Bee Colony: A parallel optimization algorithm inspired by the foraging behavior of honeybees, used for solving complex optimization problems by employing multiple simultaneous search agents.

Scheduling: The process of arranging and allocating tasks or jobs to resources (such as machines, workers, or time slots) in an efficient and optimal manner to meet specified objectives.

Shortest Processing Time (SPT): A scheduling rule used to prioritize tasks or jobs based on their processing time, with the shortest tasks being scheduled first to optimize throughput or minimize completion time.

Chapter 3
Digital Evidence Collection and Preservation in Computer Network Forensics

Rajdipsinh Vaghela
https://orcid.org/0009-0003-0790-0626
Parul Institute of Engineering and Technology, Parul University, Vadodara, India

V. Dankan Gowda
https://orcid.org/0000-0003-0724-0333
B.M.S. Institute of Technology and Management, Bangalore, India

Mohammad Taj
Aditya Engineering College, India

Annepu Arudra
https://orcid.org/0000-0001-5535-6045
Rajiv Gandhi Institute of Technology, India

Manoj Chopra
IES University, Bhopal, India

ABSTRACT

The growing integration of information and communication technology (ICT) in today's world has led to the rise of crimes in the digital realm, specifically those linked to networks and computers. This surge in cybercrime presents substantial hurdles for forensic evaluation. A pivotal evidence source in cyber forensic probes, especially when pinpointing potential threats to confidential data, stems from the extensive data produced by network nodes. The primary goal of cyber forensics is to offer clear, well-documented evidence that can stand up in a courtroom. This chapter intends to deliver a thorough overview of the current scholarly material, emphasizing diverse aspects of cyber forensic endeavors. It encompasses foundational theories, prior data analysis blueprints, and initiatives to refine methods, thereby augmenting the reach, proficiency, and precision of the network forensic structure.

DOI: 10.4018/979-8-3693-0807-3.ch003

INTRODUCTION

In an era where the digital domain permeates every aspect of our lives, the vast networks interconnecting devices serve as both a blessing and a curse. While they introduce conveniences, unparalleled speed, and a globalized lifestyle, they also bring inherent vulnerabilities. Malicious activities, from data breaches to cyber espionage, highlight the pressing need for vigilance and scrutiny within these networks. This is where computer network forensics steps in.

Computer network forensics, often referred to as 'digital forensics' in a wider context, is the meticulous process of capturing, analyzing, and interpreting the digital evidence left on computer networks. Much like a detective pieces together clues from a crime scene, digital forensic experts decode these digital trails, seeking answers to questions like "Who did this?", "How?", and "Why?".

As the scale and sophistication of cyber-attacks grow, the significance of computer network forensics rises in tandem. It not only aids in identifying and prosecuting cybercriminals but also provides organizations with insights to strengthen their security by learning from past vulnerabilities. Amidst the rapid pace of digital transformations, investing in network forensics today can prevent expensive repercussions in the future.

When addressing computer-related crimes, digital evidence is the linchpin of any investigation. These consist of bytes and bits, logs and packets, all acting as testimonies to a cyber event. Whether it's a timestamp in a log file indicating unauthorized access or a sequence of packets documenting data exfiltration, digital evidence is instrumental in piecing together the story behind the crime.

Figure 1. Transformation of confiscated material into evidence

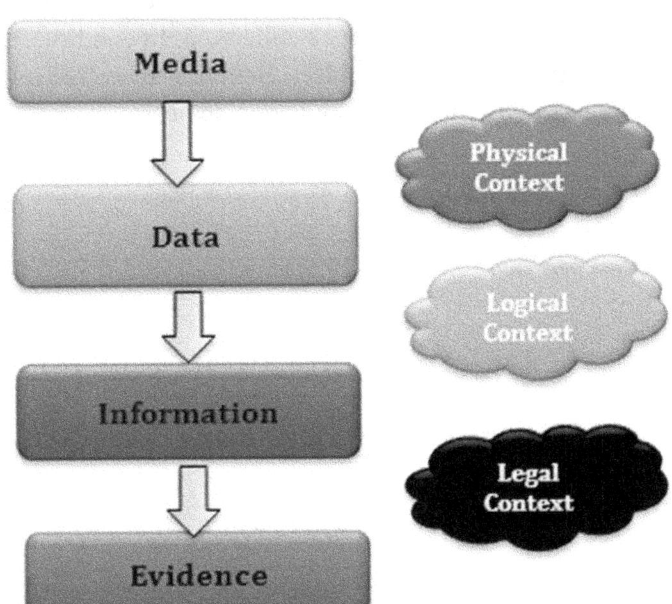

Cyber forensics is a rigorous investigative approach that produces evidence robust enough for legal proceedings. This methodical process involves the collection, processing, interpretation, and presentation of undeniable digital facts pertaining to online crimes in legal contexts. In the current age of ubiquitous computing, forensic methodologies have attracted attention from both researchers and professionals. Their evolving scope and consistent relevance over time is evident, as noted by S. Vinjosh Reddy, K. Sai Ramani, K. Rijutha, S. Mohammad Ali, and C. H. Pradeep Reddy in 2010. As the discipline expands, so too do the definitions and requirements for supportive tools and techniques. Approximately every few years, the procedural phases of network forensics experience revisions and updates.

Data undergoes significant transformation as it progresses through various stages: starting from raw data, evolving into processed information, then solidifying into concrete evidence, and ultimately reaching a form that's admissible in court, as depicted in Figure 1. Depending on the particular medium involved in cybercrime, cyber forensic terms can be categorized, as illustrated in Figure 2:

Network Forensics: The method entails systematically observing and analyzing network traffic to gather information, secure legal evidence, or detect intrusions. This perspective is supported by the findings of S. Almulla, Y. Iraqi, and A. Jones in 2013. Essentially, the process revolves around collecting and evaluating network-related data to identify security breaches.

Web Forensics: A variety of tools and technologies have been explored to facilitate effective responses based on evidence collection. The primary goal is to unearth digital evidence across the internet. When applied in an online context, this discipline is commonly termed Network Forensics.

E-mail Forensics: Examining electronic emails using a range of tools and methodologies reveals details and data associated with cybercrimes. The evidence obtained from this investigation is subsequently presented in court.

Enterprise Forensics: This category aims to protect the consistency and real-time integrity of information within an organization while preventing security breaches. It predominantly focuses on a proactive approach, with lesser emphasis on evidence collection. In contrast, System Forensics is used to gather and compile evidence from computing devices. Setting it apart from other forensic techniques, this method is invoked when an offense involves standalone devices.

Figure 2. Cyber forensics terminologies

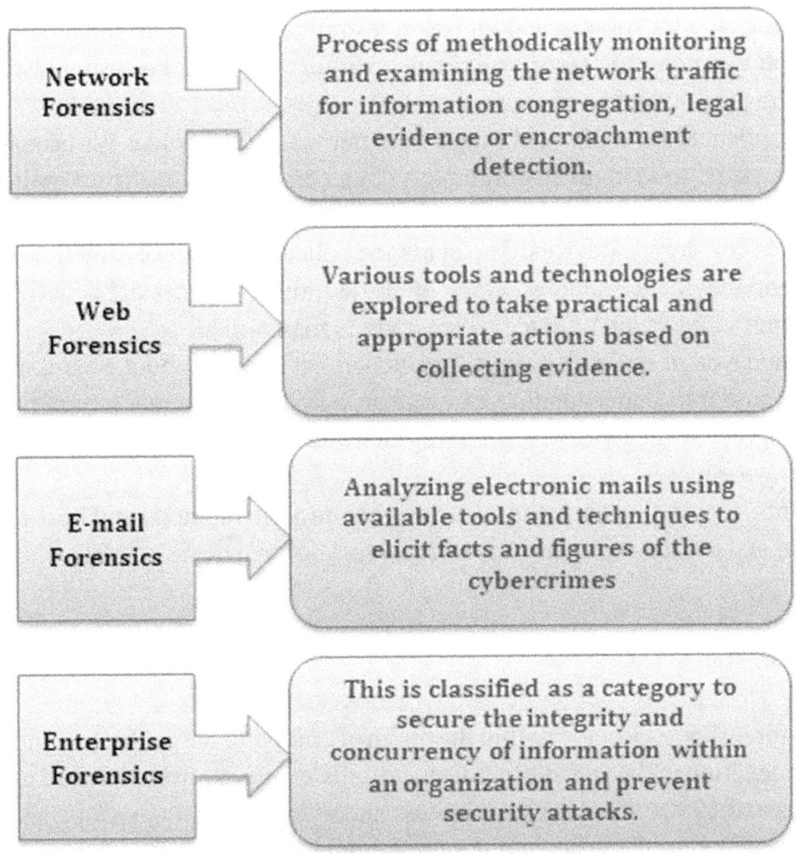

Understanding Digital Evidence: Digital evidence fundamentally encompasses a wide array of information in digital form, serving as a foundational pillar in today's legal and criminal landscapes. These digital traces—found in electronic documents such as PDFs, spreadsheets, system and application logs, email correspondences, multimedia files, or the organized data within databases—become the crux of contemporary investigations. When presented in court, such evidence can profoundly influence outcomes, wielding the potential to shape the direction of justice. Its significance is accentuated by its authenticity, precision, omnipresence, and accessibility. Not only is digital evidence time-stamped down to the millisecond, offering an exact timeline of events, but it also pervades almost every facet of our digital existence. This ready accessibility of data—be it for investigative scrutiny or enhancing cybersecurity—offers an unmatched advantage to organizations and legal bodies. In an age where traditional evidence is juxtaposed with digital variants, grasping the intricacies of digital evidence is crucial. This understanding paves the way for its proper collection, conservation, and subsequent deployment in legal arenas.

In digital forensics, the meticulous collection of electronic evidence serves as a linchpin, bridging specific incidents to a broader understanding. Digital evidence spans a wide range of sources, reflecting the expansive digital landscape. This encompasses network logs from firewalls, IDS/IPS systems, and routers, all of which document data flows and network interactions. Additionally, real-time data, such as packet captures and network traffic analyses, furnish pivotal insights into digital patterns. Large data repositories, including servers and databases, store transaction records, user activities, and system functions, all of which are ripe for forensic examination. Simultaneously, individual devices like desktops, laptops, and smartphones conceal extensive evidence within their files, browsing histories, and application logs, illuminating the sequence of events.

To collect this evidence, the tools used range from network sniffers like Wireshark, adept at recording transient data packets, to systems like Splunk, which consolidate logs from multiple sources into a unified platform. Further bolstering the forensic toolkit are disk imaging software solutions, capable of creating exact replicas of storage devices. The evidence collection process is methodical. It commences by identifying potential evidence sources. Once identified, these sources are accessed, data is securely replicated, and a continuous chain of evidence custody is maintained.

The intricate endeavor of collecting digital evidence isn't solely about possessing the right tools. It also demands an in-depth understanding of electronic systems. There's a paramount responsibility to maintain the integrity of the evidence, ensuring that the digital narrative remains untainted and its inherent veracity stays intact.

This chapter aims to provide comprehensive insights into the methods and best practices for digital evidence collection and preservation in computer network forensics.

BACKGROUND

The field of digital forensics, especially within the realm of computer networks, has undergone significant evolution since its inception in the late 20th century. Initially emerging from the need to address computer crimes in the 1970s and 1980s, the discipline has expanded dramatically in scope and complexity. This growth is largely attributed to the exponential increase in internet and network usage, which ushered in new forms of cybercrime and unique challenges. Network forensics, in particular, has had to adapt to the ephemeral nature of digital evidence, sophisticated encryption methods, and the sheer volume of data typical in modern networks. Concurrently, the legal landscape surrounding digital forensics has evolved, with regulatory frameworks like the Electronic Communications Privacy Act shaping methodologies and ethical practices in evidence collection. Technological advancements have been pivotal as well, with the development of specialized tools and techniques to efficiently collect and preserve digital evidence. Notably, the integration of artificial intelligence has begun to automate and refine forensic processes, pointing to a future where technology continues to shape the field. As digital forensics stands today, it is a dynamic and essential aspect of criminal investigation, navigating ongoing challenges while evolving with technological and regulatory developments.

FRAMEWORKS FOR BIG DATA FORENSICS

In a 2016 study, M. Uzun and O. Abul proposed an avant-garde method for big data analysis, focusing on the detection of anomalies in network traffic. They posited that the impacts of such irregularities could be swiftly mitigated by adjusting the network traffic distribution. This can be done by discerning the disparities between typical and aberrant traffic flows. The authors elaborated on their framework by dividing it into three distinct sub-models. The first, the Regular Traffic Selection Model, seeks to distinguish anomalies from standard data traffic, forgoing a focus on specific anomalous patterns. In contrast, the Abnormal Traffic Selection Model centers on maintaining a preponderance of standard traffic, rather than solely highlighting the anomalies. The Mixed Compensation Model amalgamates the insights from the preceding two models to render its final findings. It functions akin to the Regular Traffic Selection Model but encompasses both a Training and a Test phase.

Upon data analysis, several pivotal findings came to the fore. First, the Random Forest classification algorithm showcased a commendable capacity to adapt to shifts in traffic patterns. With the deployment of the recommended model, there was a notable reduction in false negative occurrences. Second, when there exists a pronounced difference in the volume of training data among distinct categories, a model anchored in the decision tree proves more apt, especially when navigating vast training datasets. Nevertheless, it's vital to exercise caution and avoid applying the decision tree model to anomalous traffic. Finally, to address the challenge of false positives, the k-means algorithm is employed. By adjusting the number of clusters in the regular traffic selection model, the model's efficacy in spotting anomalous behaviors significantly improves.

In a 2015 study by C. Wang, C. Chi, W. Zhou, and R. Wong, the authors unveiled a novel model leveraging big data analytics for the scrutiny of network traffic. This pioneering approach is tailored to identify anomalous behaviors and malevolent data transmissions within networks. The methodology consists of loading data into Hive databases housed within an HDFS framework. As illustrated in Figure 3, the model is segmented into five distinct stages. A standout benefit of this model lies in its ability to swiftly navigate vast data volumes. Its efficiency was gauged by running Hive queries and timing the duration needed to pinpoint anomalies. The team trialed three varied datasets: the first incorporated roughly 400,000 packets totaling 50 MB, the second had close to 3,100,000 packets, and the third dataset held around 1,200,000 packets, amounting to 131 MB.

Figure 3. Big data analysis model

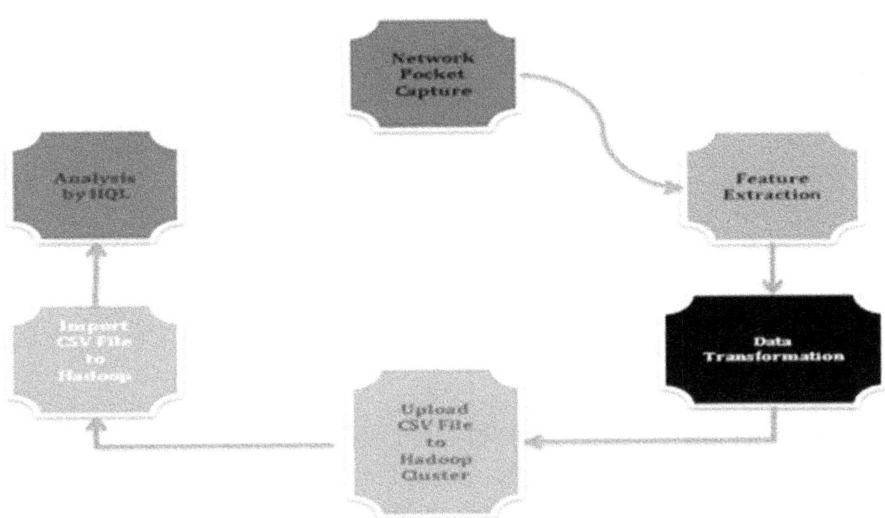

In their 2015 study, R. R. R. Robinson and C. Thomas advocated for the use of Hadoop in the development of a real-time Intrusion Detection System (IDS) tailored for high-speed data processing. The suggested IDS architecture is delineated into four distinct tiers: the data capture layer, the filtration and load balancing layer, the processing (specifically, the Hadoop) layer, and the decision-making tier. To infuse the system with machine learning capabilities, the authors employed Java, complemented by the WEKA 3.6.12 library.

Stage-1: For data captured in packets, the filtration process is executed at the Filtration and Load Balancing Server (FLBS). Once filtered, packets are then forwarded to non-intruder flows for further processing.

Stage-2: Check if the incoming packet is part of an existing flow. If not, register it as a new flow with unique entries consisting of four tuples: source IP, destination IP, source port, and destination port. This becomes the first line.

Stage-3: The master node continues to copy packet information into the sequence file until the duration threshold is reached. After this point, the sequence file is sent to one of the data nodes for computing flow parameters.

Stage-4: The data node employs MapReduce to compute the final values of each feature for intrusion detection. This information is then forwarded to the decision server, which determines whether the activity indicates an intrusion or a normal flow.

Figure 4. Real-time DDoS attack detection framework

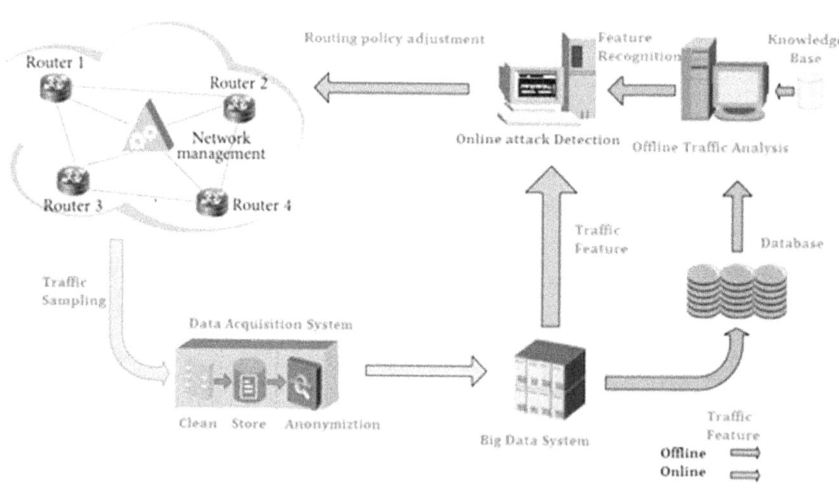

Jia, Bin, and their team introduced an advanced system designed to detect DDoS attacks in real-time amidst the vast landscapes of Big Data. Their pioneering method distinguishes malicious attack patterns from regular data flows by leveraging the capabilities of Multivariate Dimensionality Reduction Analysis (MDRA), as illustrated in Figure 4. The group employed Principal Component Analysis (PCA) to distill large datasets into representative and concise features. These refined dimensions, termed principal components, indicate different degrees of data variance. The foremost component embodies the maximum data variance. Should this component not fully capture the essence of the original data, an additional linear combination is introduced. The system's effectiveness hinges on two core algorithms: the Triangle Area Technique, which discerns geometric correlations between feature pairs in network traffic logs, and the Mahalanobis Distance (MD), used to gauge the similarity between individual traffic logs.

The ability to detect DDoS attacks is anchored in the integral use of Multivariate Correlation Analysis (MCA) to assess traffic features amidst the expansive terrain of Big Data. In the concluding phase of the procedure, the detection of attack traffic is executed using Mahalanobis Distance (MD) and a selected threshold, as highlighted by S. Reddy P and P. S. Patwal in 2022. This approach leverages a benchmark dataset defined by the covariance matrix, thereby reinforcing the basis upon which MD operates.

Preservation of Digital Evidence: In the realm of digital forensics, preservation acts as the steadfast guardian of truth, ensuring the integrity and authenticity of digital evidence. This stage grapples with the inherent volatility of data, a challenge unique to the digital landscape where information can evaporate in an instant. The threats of data modification or eradication, be they intentional or inadvertent, loom large. To combat these hazards, digital forensics deploys rigorous techniques. Foremost among these is the creation of forensic copies or images of the evidence, ensuring the primary source stays untarnished while inquiries unfold using replicas (S. R. Kawale, S. P. Diwan, 2022). Write blockers are instrumental, offering read-only access to original evidence, thereby thwarting any unintended alterations. Secure storage environments stand as the bulwark against unauthorized interference, ensuring digital evidence remains untouched. Integrity validation is achieved through checksums and cryptographic hashing, where digital imprints confirm the evidence's unchanged condition. Additionally, digital signatures certify both the integrity and authenticity of the evidence, underscoring its reliability. Within the intricate endeavor of preserving digital evidence, these strategies act as vigilant guardians, unwavering in their dedication to ensuring the truth embedded within digital data is preserved, symbolizing the uprightness of digital forensic investigations.

In the delicate dance between digital forensics and legal systems, the road to justice meanders through a maze of legal intricacies. The arena of search and seizure, underpinned by warrants and permissions, sets the stage for legitimate digital probes. As a bedrock principle of democratic societies, the mandate for warrants ensures that individual privacy rights are upheld even amidst digital advancements (B. Kameswara Rao, Naziya Hussain, 2022). Yet, the task of maneuvering through jurisdictional hurdles, amplified by the boundless reach of digital data, poses significant challenges. Court admissibility of digital evidence depends on strict adherence to established criteria, necessitating relevance, authenticity, unbroken integrity, and a well-documented chain of custody. The solidity of forensic probes can be put to the test with challenges and counterarguments cropping up frequently. On a broader scale, international collaboration becomes pivotal in addressing globally pervasive cybercrimes. In a world interwoven by digital threads, international frameworks and accords offer the structural support for nations to unite against cyber adversaries. Within this multifaceted legal landscape, digital evidence treads a fine line between upholding privacy and delivering justice, emphasizing an unwavering commitment to the law while navigating the ever-shifting terrain of the digital world.

BASIC ARCHITECTURE FOR BIG DATA ANALYTICS

In a 2014 study by G. Shrivastava and B. B. Gupta, a novel model was introduced, combining the advantages of cloud computing and machine learning to identify malicious traffic within vast real-time data streams. As illustrated in Figure 5, their anomaly detection module harnesses the power of HDFS, MapReduce, and Weka, blending Machine Learning (ML) and Cloud Computing. This fusion seeks to enhance the system's accuracy and efficiency across its various components. A central aspect of this system is data processing. To proficiently identify anomalous traffic patterns using machine learning, the algorithm requires pristine, high-caliber data. Once the data meets this benchmark, the algorithm, with slight tweaks, is primed for optimal performance, as noted by Namitha A R and Veera Sivakumar Chinamuttevi in 2022. Within the map function, two pivotal modules arise: the feature selection and the normalization modules.

Figure 5. Basic architecture for big data analytics using Hadoop and Weka

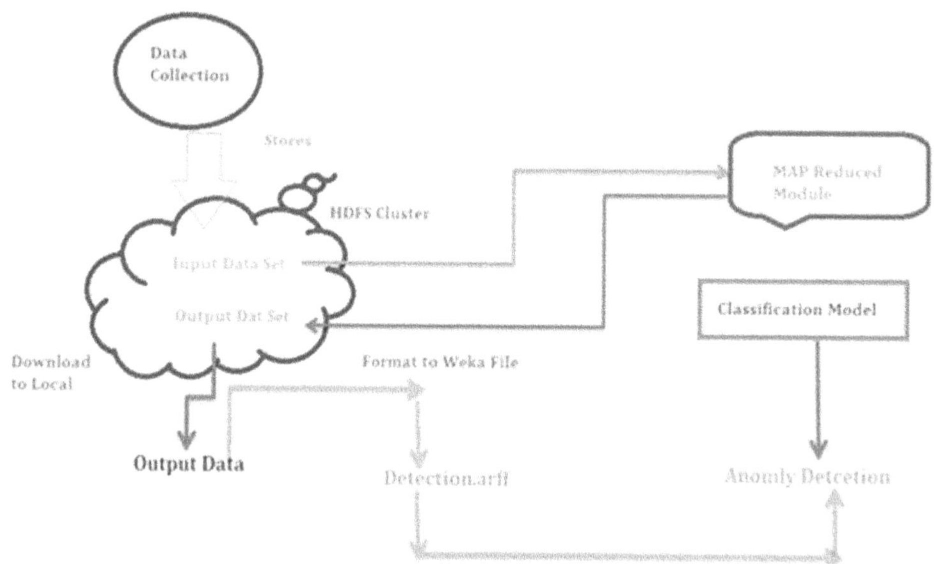

The latter ensures data's consistency and readability through measures like standardizing to the UTF-8 format, converting uppercase letters to lowercase, and excluding static input files such as ".jco", ".mp3", ".jpg", ".png", ".js", and ".gif". Conversely, the feature selection module uses machine learning to convert traffic data into multi-dimensional vectors. To obtain a global vector by pooling vectors from individual maps, the primary reduce function distributes input data among multiple nodes. This dispersion shrinks data volume, thereby enhancing processing speed. After duplication, data undergoes a log2 transformation to simplify numeric data management. Then, using labeled data, the detection model is crafted through the ML algorithm mining process, as discussed by P. Ramesh Naidu and N. Guruprasad in 2021. Evaluating three distinct machine learning models through the Weka platform, the decision tree was distinguished as the most efficient.

In their 2015 study, M. H. Mate and S. R. Kapse unveiled an avant-garde anomaly detection method termed the Adaptive Stream Projected Outlier detector (A-SPOT). This approach is tailored to pinpoint anomalous patterns within vast datasets by leveraging a distinct adaptive subspace analysis technique. To gauge the efficacy of A-SPOT, the researchers utilized the 1999 KDD CUP anomaly detection application as their experimental platform.

A standout aspect of this methodology is the introduction of the Sparse Subspace Template (SST). The formulation of SST is contingent upon the presence of a sizable labeled sample of anomalies. The SST is architecturally designed to integrate three primary components: the Supervised SST Subspace (SS), the Fixed SST Subspace (FS), and the Unsupervised SST Subspace (US).

The construction of the SS component within SST is steered by supervised learning techniques. In addition, the Multi-Objective Genetic Algorithm (MOGA) is utilized to identify anomalies belonging to a common category. This step aims to craft an SS tailored specifically to that category. With the SST meticulously assembled, the system pivots to generating Projected Cell Summaries (PCS) for each discrete subspace housed within the SST. The overarching objective of this process is to adeptly pinpoint and distinguish aberrant behavioral patterns.

It's imperative to understand that the data from the Projected Cell Summaries (PCS) remains static, with no updates. This choice is intentional, aimed at avoiding biases that lean towards anomalous data. Given that the foundational dataset encompasses both typical and atypical data, introducing such a bias could undermine the effectiveness of A-SPOT in detecting anomalies. Once the system pinpoints the outlying subspaces associated with all observed irregularities, a signature subspace lookup table is crafted. Additionally, the approach takes into account other essential aspects, such as minimizing false positives, generating training data, and classifying anomalies through the keen lens of outlying subspace analysis.

In a 2012 study, R. Hunt and S. Zeadally introduced a Real-Time Hybrid IDS (Intrusion Detection System) that leverages the robust features of Apache Storm, a renowned real-time and fault-tolerant big data stream processor. Their innovative approach utilizes hybrid detection techniques. Specifically, they integrate the Corner Classification 4 (CC4) neural network for identifying novel, uncharted attacks, while a Multi-Layer Perceptron (MLP) system targets the recognition of familiar, previously identified attacks.

Within the Apache Storm framework, the structure, or topology, is set up with an "Input file reader," also termed a spout. This spout acts as the data stream's genesis and directs streams of data packets to two unique components called bolts: the CC4 Launcher and the MLP Launcher. The MLP Launcher takes on the task of precisely extracting pertinent weights from trained signatures, channeling them to the subsequent MLP network. Simultaneously, the CC4 Launcher singles out the signatures that match the input from its training set, forwarding it to the specialized CC4 network bolt. Upon processing, the results from both the MLP and CC4 networks converge and are channeled to another bolt designated as the "Post-Process." Here, data is classified and tagged as either typical data, a known attack with an associated category, or an unfamiliar, newly emerging attack.

Opting for relevance, the authors bypassed older datasets like KDD '99 in favor of the contemporary ISCX Intrusion dataset for their tests. The neural network-based architecture of the IDS boasts a commendable average accuracy rate of 89%, complemented by a false positive rate of 4.32%. With its synergy with Apache Storm, renowned for its real-time processing capabilities in the face of extensive data volumes, this system is ideally tailored for contemporary network security landscapes, particularly for on-the-fly detection endeavors.

In a 2013 research article by Pallavi Asrodia and Vishal Sharma, the focus was on exploring diverse techniques tailored for anomaly-based intrusion detection, with a specific emphasis on campus network environments located at the network's periphery. Their study centered on a LAN setup within a campus, characterized by an expansive user community, with over 9,000 members, and a robust 90 Mbps internet connectivity. Given the scale and complexity of such a network, it became imperative to adopt fitting techniques that could effectively model user behaviors through the lens of big data analytics.

A notable feature of Asrodia and Sharma's approach was the segmentation of URLs into specific categories, such as entertainment and academic. This categorization was instrumental in understanding user behaviors. In line with this, models for these URLs were diligently crafted monthly, drawing data from proxy logs. Additionally, to bolster the intrusion detection system's effectiveness, users underwent weekly monitoring. This weekly observation period was chosen for its efficacy, offering a timely window to detect and analyze the activities of potentially malicious users.

Figure 6. Basic architecture of multi-level anomaly detection system

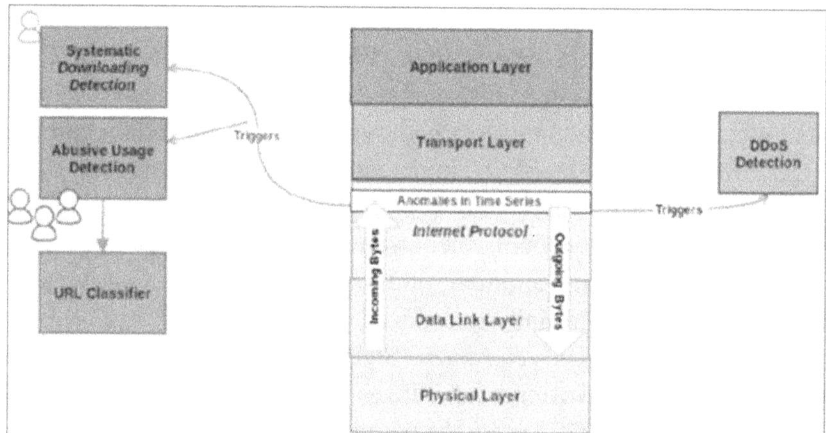

Pallavi Asrodia and Vishal Sharma introduced two distinct class labels for user categorization: usage-based and user-based. The former is instrumental in identifying abusive usage patterns, while the latter offers insights into the inherent characteristics of abusive users. Additionally, the study highlighted the value of time-series analysis in effective anomaly detection.

Machine learning, a cornerstone of their approach, was used to discern deviations in Internet usage patterns, indicating potential security threats. Interestingly, the method deployed at the campus edge was also integrated into the Network Intrusion Detection System (NIDS), showcasing its versatility across various scenarios. When applied to diverse and extensive datasets, the techniques demonstrated an impressive detection rate, nearing 100%, while maintaining a remarkably low false positive rate of just 0.9%.

In summary, the researchers employed a multifaceted approach, combining proxy server logs from a campus LAN, router traces, machine learning, and time-series analysis. This amalgamation of techniques facilitated the effective detection of anomalies stemming from the misuse of Internet access, DDoS attacks, and systematic downloading patterns.

In a study published in 2013, D. Merlette and D.P. Pruthi focused on the Adjustable Piecewise Entropy (APE) method as a tool to detect unusual driving patterns. They implemented this method using five servers situated on a college campus in a multi-node Hadoop environment. The research further explored the Adjustable Piecewise Shannon Entropy (APSE), a specific variant of APE, and executed it within the Hadoop environment.

To efficiently manage vast quantities of data in IPFIX format, a two-round MapReduce system was introduced. APSE value pairs were calculated for each designated time bin. In the first MapReduce round, algorithms were developed to extract essential flow features and count the cumulative occurrences within each time bin. The second round mirrored the first but incorporated both mapper and reducer algorithms.

A notable outcome was the ability of the proposed Adjustable Piecewise Entropy mode to capture the APE attributes inherent in conventional entropies. The Hadoop cluster's infrastructure consisted of five servers, all interconnected via a Gigabit Ethernet switch. Over the course of three days, flow data was systematically collected in the IPFIX traffic format from a single edge router.

The efficacy of the APSE was tested both theoretically and through hands-on experimentation. When compared with the Shannon entropy, it was evident that the APSE surpassed its counterpart, demonstrating superior efficiency in detecting traffic anomalies.

In a 2003 research paper by Shanmugasundaram K, Memon N, Savant A, and Bronnimann H, the authors explored the patterns of data acceleration used and delved deep into the analytics framework they adopted. The study illuminated the process of creating rich, interactive visualizations, vividly presenting the concept of a data acceleration pipeline and its associated analytics. Central to their proposal was a model designed to enhance security alerts. It does this by analyzing network agent behaviors and subsequently gauging the level of malice in the network. A data acceleration framework was foundational for analyzing these insights and for structuring the model in a distributed, parallel manner. The paper also offered a detailed overview of how machine learning algorithms were used to recognize typical behaviors. In this way, the machine autonomously formulates security protocols, applying them to large datasets. Yet, the path of data acceleration was not without its hurdles. The main challenges faced related to data movement, processing, and interactivity. Drawing from previous research in the field, the proposed model clearly delineated the algorithms and the setup, unveiling fresh insights. Additionally, it illuminated existing patterns, enriching the comprehension of the subject.

Figure 7. Illustration of Hashdoop architecture

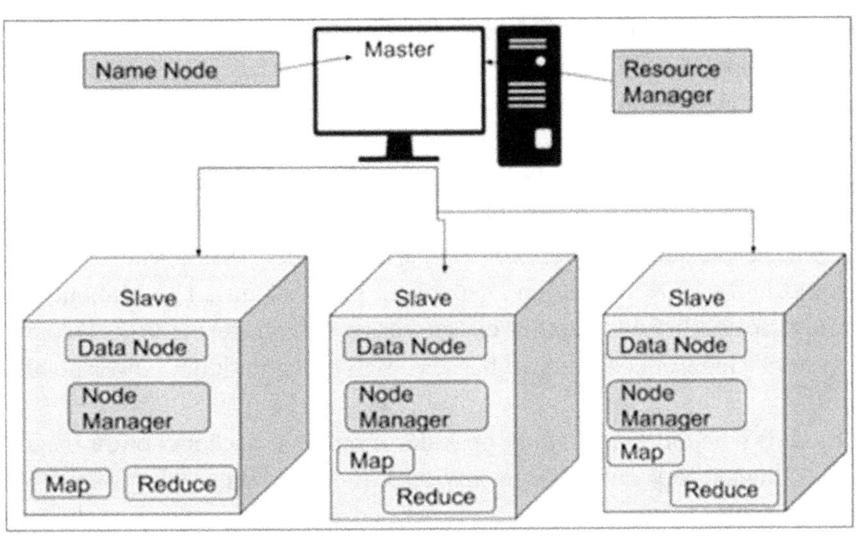

In a 2004 research study by Ren W., the emphasis was placed on "Hashdoop," a specialized MapReduce framework that uses a hash function to partition traffic while preserving its integral structures. This strategic partitioning aids in detecting anomalous traffic patterns by harnessing the power of distributed computing systems. Once partitioned, anomaly detectors evaluate these maintained spatial and temporal structures to pinpoint any irregularities.

The Hashdoop model is depicted in Figure 7. After the data undergoes hashing, the resulting smaller datasets, or partitions, are examined by the detectors. These detectors identify anomalies and then relay this information to network administrators for further action. A distinctive feature of this approach is its method of partitioning traffic traces. By utilizing the IP address as a key identifier, the data is divided longitudinally into specific buckets. Throughout this partitioning, the consistency of time and flow is meticulously maintained. To improve precision, the hashing process considers both the source and destination IP addresses, employed sequentially as keys. This guarantees that data from the same transmission is always grouped into one bucket. The hashing is performed using the CRC (Cyclic Redundancy Check) algorithm, a prevalent tool mainly used for traffic load balancing. Due to its straightforward design and proficient partitioning capabilities, the Hashdoop framework is a preferred choice for many Anomaly Detection Systems (ADS) in data mapping tasks.

The dataset used in this study comprised real-world data with an initial operational link speed of 18Mbps, later upgraded to 150 Mbps. With the integration of Hashdoop, there was a notable improvement in packet throughput. Specifically, throughput increased from 360 kpps (kilo packets per second) to an impressive 1.27 Mpps (million packets per second) and from 25 kpps to 375 kpps. This dramatic surge reduced the processing time by a factor of fifteen, underscoring the efficiency gains Hashdoop offers. One standout advantage of Hashdoop is its enhanced results in anomaly detection, largely due to its efficient mapping procedure. However, like all systems, Hashdoop has its limitations. A significant drawback relates to the data splitting process. Excessive segmentation can lead to the creation of very small data chunks in each bucket. Performing anomaly detection on these minute data fragments can become complex and less efficient.

In a 2015 publication by Jing YN, Tu P, Wang XP, and Zhang GD, the authors focused on leveraging tools such as Hadoop, Mahout, and Hive to develop a quasi-real-time Intrusion Detection System (IDS). The foundational technologies of this framework include MapReduce, Hadoop, Libpcap, and Mahout.

A fundamental component of this system is Tshark, which leverages the libpcap library to operate as a network protocol analyzer, allowing for data extraction from live networks. Notably, the captured packets can be customized, decoded, and then saved to a file. After the sniffer module completes which uses the Dumpcap tool for packet extraction from networks MapReduce takes on the crucial role of feature extraction. These packets are sent to Tshark, where pertinent fields for its features are extracted. These fields are then stored in the HDFS (Hadoop Distributed File System). The Mahout library, integrated with Hadoop, ensures scalability and handles classification and clustering tasks as part of MapReduce operations. The system's inherent capacity to harness high computational power results in remarkably efficient outcomes.

Notably, the module detailed in this study provides a scalable packet capture mechanism. It excels at processing data at high speeds and wide bandwidths, though with a delay varying between 5 to 30 seconds. The system features a dynamic feature extraction framework, enhancing the profiling of packet flows. Furthermore, it includes a peer-to-peer threat detection module adept at identifying unusual traffic. However, the model faces challenges. Using TCP relay has resulted in packet drops, prompting continued research efforts to address this problem. Currently, the system identifies anomalies in a timeframe of several seconds, but there's room for improvement. By adding more nodes and making strategic adjustments to the Hadoop cluster, it's conceivable to reduce the processing time to under 10 seconds.

The proposed Botnet framework offers improved fault tolerance and demonstrates adaptability to changing networks. This adaptability is realized through messages sent in the form of multiple short hops directed to each bot node. Intricately, these hops are structured based on the Degree Constrained Minimum Spanning Tree. It's important to highlight that many Intrusion Detection Systems, operating on the detection principle, have a predefined threshold value. As a result, intrusions occurring at a lower frequency may go undetected and be overlooked.

In the 2015 study by Tang Y and Daniels TE, the authors delve deeply into the analysis of extensive Netflow traffic using Hadoop. Their research emphasizes the combined advantages of MapReduce and SQL for standard analytical tasks. A notable technical breakthrough highlighted is the transformation of text to binary through Hadoop SequenceFiles. This change considerably saves storage space. Moreover, the MapReduce framework primarily uses SequenceFiles for its input/output operations. Given that SequenceFiles consist of key-value pairs, they facilitate a more straightforward parsing process.

A crucial analytical step emphasized is the conversion of data into basic computational statistics. This preliminary analysis can cover specific features or encompass the entire dataset. Central to obtaining these statistics are the tasks of filtering and counting. Pinpointing outliers becomes an essential part of this analysis. While the mapping algorithm remains largely consistent, the reduce algorithm introduces a distinct feature: it helps identify the Top-k records. These records are arranged in a list array, which is continuously updated during the mapping phase. Once the reduce function concludes, this Top-K list becomes the definitive array. This reduction procedure is repeated several times, managing an array of length 'k' (usually a small integer), and it both initializes and finalizes the list array.

The primary aim of this analytical effort was to detect specific cyberattacks, such as the watering hole, within the Netflow dataset. Successful detection relies on identifying unique patterns. To achieve this, a synchronized execution of several algorithms was essential, with Top-k operations like counting and aggregation taking center stage.

Hadoop's performance was evaluated against three critical benchmarks: SQL-based exploratory analysis on a public cloud, pattern recognition, and MapReduce-driven exploratory analysis on a multi-core server. The technical basis for this evaluation was a three-node cluster, with each node being an M1 large type, boasting four virtual cores and 15GB of memory. Apache Hadoop 2.2.0 was the software of choice, complemented by the standard configuration of Amazon Web Services (AWS). A significant optimization was the conversion of text to binary in the HDFS using the SequenceFile format, resulting in significant space and time savings. Highlighting shared state aggregation, it became clear that optimal efficiency required precise calibration of reducers to tasks. For data aggregation, combiners were seamlessly integrated into the MapReduce framework. Additionally, the synergy of AWS, HiveQL, and the RC File format stood out as a potent alternative to SequenceFiles, demonstrating Hadoop's versatility in various operational environments.

ANALYTICS STRATEGY

In a 2017 study by Wang D, Li T, Liu S, Zhang J, and Liu C, the authors introduced a novel framework tailored for forensics within Big Data contexts, as depicted in Figure 8. A primary challenge they addressed was reconciling the four V's characteristic of Big Data - Variety, Veracity, Volume, and Velocity - especially considering the foundational importance of Velocity, Veracity, and Volume. A key innovation was the transformation of unstructured data into a structured format, tackling the challenges posed by data Variety. Additionally, the authors emphasized the utility of Principal Component Analysis (PCA) in addressing issues related to Veracity.

Figure 8. Analytics strategy with methodology and tools

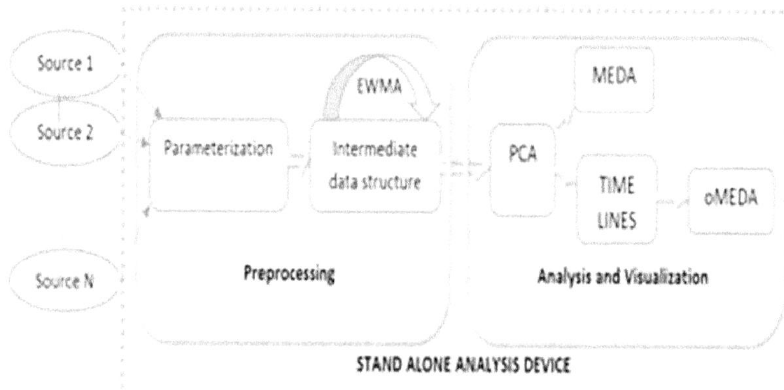

PCA excels at extracting features from high-dimensional datasets. Acknowledging the inherent constraints of traditional PCA, especially when dealing with large datasets, the authors adopted a kernel computation variant of PCA. This alternative outperforms the conventional approach by avoiding intensive computations and leveraging parallel processing, ensuring efficient management of vast datasets.

Wang D, Li T, Liu S, Zhang J, and Liu C's proposed framework was put to the test against the VAST 2012 challenge and successfully identified a growing botnet infection within the network. While both Minimum Entropy Deconvolution Adjusted (MEDA) and its variant Optimal Minimum Entropy Deconvolution Adjusted (oMEDA) detected background activities, oMEDA held a clear edge. It could pinpoint the exact location of the event on the timeline, enabling a more in-depth and detailed investigation. Thus, it's advisable to use MEDA and oMEDA in tandem when evaluating active network environments. The strength of the proposed framework stems from its ability to handle various data types directly and succinctly, making it highly compatible with security monitoring setups. Moreover, it effectively manages large data volumes, and intriguingly, as the amount of processed data increases, the system's performance improves. Another commendable feature is the framework's capacity to significantly reduce the number of events requiring analysis within Big Data, streamlining the investigative procedure.

The network analysis tool, Dumpcap, was instrumental in the sniffer module designed to extract packets from the network. Upon capturing these packets, Dumpcap relayed the data to Tshark, which diligently extracted specific fields based on their inherent features. This comprehensive set of fields was then stored in HDFS for subsequent processing. The Mahout library, a core component of Hadoop, was integrated to support this analytical journey. To evaluate the system's performance, the VAST 2012 mini challenge 2 dataset was used. The results were illuminating: the proposed framework surpassed other solutions presented during the VAST challenge in 2012, especially addressing the challenges of veracity, volume, and velocity typical of Big Data.

In a separate 2014 study by Kim JS, Kim M, and Noh BN, the emphasis shifted to creating a method specifically for investigating the Random-UDP flooding attack. This type of cyber-attack overwhelms target resources with a barrage of UDP packets. The authors introduced an innovative model to trace the origins of these malicious attacks. The model operated in three stages: it started with standard data transmission, then detected the flooding attack, and ultimately identified the precise source of the flood, offering a comprehensive approach to cyber forensics in this realm.

The framework operates in three distinct stages. First, it assesses the regular flow of User Datagram Protocol (UDP) traffic, illustrated by a user exploring a travel website featuring alluring and affordable travel packages. The situation turns malicious when the web server, unknown to the user, becomes compromised. This now-malicious server extracts user details, such as their IP address, and initiates a Distributed Denial of Service (DoS) attack using Random UDP flooding. As a result, the user's system is swamped with a deluge of UDP datagrams, effectively blocking their access to online resources or services. To analyze this attack, tools like Wireshark are invaluable. By recording the multitude of packets during the onslaught, Wireshark not only unveils the attack's intricacies but also crucially pinpoints its source, providing a comprehensive view of the entire attack progression.

In their 2015 research, Liu Z and Feng D introduced a novel model that employs a collection of Machine Learning (ML) classifiers. These classifiers rigorously examine the ongoing flow of sessions from a particular device to determine its type, be it a PC, a recognized IoT device, or a smartphone. For system training, traffic data was collected and labeled from a variety of devices, encompassing nine distinct IoT devices, PCs, and smartphones. This data was then subjected to supervised learning to create a multi-stage meta-classifier. The classifier's primary advantage is its proficiency in distinguishing between IoT-generated data and other types of data streams.

To evaluate this model, a sample data set was assembled by connecting the aforementioned devices to a WiFi access point. The resulting traffic was captured and saved in the pcap file format for detailed analysis. The device identification process was broken down into three stages: first, the implementation of binary classifiers designed for individual sessions; next, determining the ideal threshold for these classifiers; and finally, gauging their magnitude or size.

Results showed that the IP addresses of IoT and non-IoT devices exhibited distinct differences. The model demonstrated remarkable proficiency in identifying smartphones by analyzing the user agent property in HTTP, achieving a 100% accuracy rate. PCs were not far behind, with nearly impeccable detection efficiency using the single session classifier. As for IoT devices, the model identified them with an astounding 99.28% accuracy, discerning details such as the device's model and brand.

In essence, this groundbreaking model offers substantial promise for real-world applications, especially for organizations aiming to detect authorized as well as rogue IoT device connections within their network infrastructure.

In a 2019 study, Anaya EA, Nakano-Miyatake M, and Perez Meana HM introduced a pioneering traffic-aware system aimed at judiciously selecting crucial nodes for patching within an IoT-centric environment. This is particularly important considering the inherent constraints related to process durations and the limited resources available for patching. They tested their proposed framework using real-time traffic from a mobile social network that included 60 devices and a substantial 1750 Access Points (APs).

Within this network, users could communicate through two primary avenues. First is the "Infrastructure Link," where communication is facilitated through APs. Second is the "Direct Link," where communication occurs within a set transmission range without the intervention of APs.

While patching can enhance the security of the infrastructure links, the direct links still remain vulnerable. The innovative approach presented in this study deviates from the traditional methodology of patching compromised IoT devices directly. Rather, it suggests strategically patching key nodes based on the total amount of traffic they manage. By concentrating on specific areas, we can reduce the impact on a broader scale and confine the proliferation of threats to their initial entry points.

The efficacy of this innovative patching strategy was confirmed through comprehensive experimental testing. The research also illuminated various intriguing aspects of IoT security, paving the way for new methods of safeguarding these networks.

Despite enduring challenges, such as limited resources and a less intuitive user interface, new frameworks were developed based on a study aimed at preventing malware propagation. Yet, results from experiments using real-world datasets were promising, underscoring the potential of these innovative approaches.

In a 2018 paper by Rekhis S, Krichene J, and Boudriga N, a novel model named Stacked Auto Encoder (SAE) was introduced. Essentially comprised of multiple autoencoders, the SAE employs deep learning to predict traffic patterns. These autoencoders are pivotal to the model's intricate network design. The distinctive feature of this model is its layer-by-layer training, which facilitates a gradual understanding of traffic flow complexities. Additionally, the model's parameters are routinely fine-tuned to enhance its predictive accuracy.

The empirical data for this study was sourced from a motorway network with approximately 15,000 devices, each recording information every 30 seconds. However, the dataset was updated every five minutes. The collected data covered a span of three months. For training and validation purposes, the first two months of data were used for training, with the remaining data reserved for testing.

To benchmark the efficiency of the SAE model, its performance was compared with four other established models: Support Vector Machines (SVM), Radial Basis Function (RBF) Neural Network, Random Walk (RW) forecast, and Neural Network (NN). The comparative analysis highlighted the SAE model's superior predictive accuracy over its counterparts, demonstrating its potential in traffic flow prediction.

In 2019 research by Lin C, Zhitang L, Cuixia G, and Yingshu L, focus was given to a groundbreaking model in the Big Data domain termed Device to Device (D2D) Big Data. The primary aim of this model is to improve wireless inter-device connectivity, guaranteeing effective communication among users. It achieves this by efficiently promoting content and using intelligent offloading techniques. Previous models for short-range wireless device-to-device communication and content sharing mainly relied on limited-scale data and somewhat unrealistic assumptions. In contrast, the model by these authors broadens the application to extensive datasets, specifically around 3.5TB. This dataset originates from a popular device-to-device sharing app, capturing the interactions of nearly 850 million users over 13 weeks. A standout feature of their research was extracting diverse aspects like online behavior, geographic location, meeting dynamics, privacy protocols, and content sharing methods. After analyzing these facets, the D2D Big Data platform underwent thorough assessment, especially in terms of predicting content-sharing trends. A notable advantage of this model is its capacity to reduce mobile traffic using big data approaches, simultaneously supporting extensive content sharing. The authors highlighted the prospective advantages of their work, stressing the benefits of precisely predicting content sharing patterns and creating more user-aligned recommendations. They also pointed out the potential of collaborations between multidisciplinary organizations and Mobile Network Operators (MNOs) in the D2D Big Data sector. The model's utility extends beyond individual users; entities like government agencies, content providers, and various sectors can leverage its capabilities for a range of applications.

CHALLENGES AND FUTURE TRENDS

As digital forensics navigates an ever-changing landscape, it faces a mix of challenges and opportunities. The evolving nature of networked systems, characterized by the rise of IoT devices and edge computing, expands the scope of potential cyber threats and complicates investigations. While the increase in encrypted traffic enhances data security, it often masks digital evidence, presenting a formidable puzzle. Cloud-based infrastructures are redefining data storage paradigms, raising questions about access and challenging jurisdictional boundaries. Concurrently, the urgent need for updated laws and regulations resounds across the digital sphere, as technological progress frequently surpasses existing legal structures. Within this backdrop, digital forensics prepares for technology's transformative impact. Artificial Intelligence and machine learning offer to refine investigations, uncover data patterns, and forecast cyber threats. Quantum computing brings both challenges and potential, demanding new encryption standards while accelerating data processing. Decentralized systems and blockchain technology introduce fresh data patterns and cryptographic challenges for investigators to unravel. In a digital world without borders, strengthened cross-border collaboration becomes increasingly crucial, prompting countries to unify laws and procedures. As they strive to protect the digital domain, digital forensics experts find themselves at the nexus of obstacles and innovation, carving out new avenues and bolstering defenses against the relentless wave of cyber threats.

CONCLUSION

In the realm of digital forensics, change is the only constant. The continuous evolution of networked systems, the increasing prevalence of encryption, and the omnipresence of the cloud require us to be ever vigilant, adaptable, and proactive. Whether we're forensic investigators, cybersecurity specialists, or legal professionals, an unwavering commitment to ongoing learning is essential. It's not merely about keeping pace with technological innovations, but proactively outpacing those who aim to exploit them maliciously. Network and Computer Forensics has matured into an indispensable branch of cybersecurity. Its primary role is to sift through captured data, unveiling evidence robust enough to withstand legal scrutiny. However, forensics transcends mere data recovery or perpetrator identification; it entails the systematic collection, analysis, and presentation of data in ways that can be upheld in legal settings. Our modern digital era is marked by an explosive surge in data, often referred to as Big Data. Generated from countless sources, this vast reservoir of information offers both challenges and opportunities to forensic specialists. Traditional forensic approaches may stumble given the immense volume, diversity, and speed of this data. Consequently, forensic methodologies have been compelled to innovate and adapt.

The use of ontologies and associated technologies has grown increasingly prevalent in analyzing Big Data network traffic. Within computer and information sciences, ontologies refer to a structured representation, formal naming, and definition of the categories, properties, and relations among the concepts, data, and entities across one or multiple domains. At its core, ontology is about crafting a model to deepen our understanding of data. These models assist in systematically categorizing and analyzing data, simplifying the extraction of meaningful insights. Numerous researchers have highlighted the value of harnessing ontologies, particularly when navigating challenges such as scalability and distributed computing. As the globe becomes more interconnected and reliant on data, the need for sophisticated tools and methods in the field of Network and Computer Forensics intensifies. This chapter explores these complexities, spotlighting the pivotal role of ontologies and their promising future in digital forensics within a Big Data context.

In conclusion, the quest for justice in the digital domain rests squarely on the meticulous collection and preservation of digital evidence. As the boundaries of the digital frontier stretch ever outward, we bear a solemn duty: to stay vigilant, to evolve, and to ensure that the beacon of truth remains undimmed in this intricate and interconnected landscape.

ACKNOWLEDGMENT

We would like to acknowledge the support given by B.M.S.Institute Of Technolog and Mangement, Bangalore,Karnataka, India.

REFERENCES

Almulla, S., Iraqi, Y., & Jones, A. (2013). A distributed snapshot framework for digital forensics evidence extraction and event reconstruction from cloud environment. *Proceedings of the International Conference on Cloud Computing Technology and Science, CloudCom*, 1, 699–704. 10.1109/CloudCom.2013.114

Anaya, E. A., Nakano-Miyatake, M., & Perez Meana, H. M. (2019). Network forensics with Neurofuzzy techniques. *52nd IEEE international Midwest Symposium on Circuits and Systems (MWSCAS '19)*, 848–852.

Hunt, R., & Zeadally, S. (2012, December). Network Forensics: An Analysis of Techniques, Tools, and Trends. *Computer*, *45*(12), 36–43. doi:10.1109/MC.2012.252

Jing, Y. N., Tu, P., Wang, X. P., & Zhang, G. D. (2015). Distributed-log-based scheme for IP traceback. *The fifth international conference on Computer and Information Technology (CIT' 15)*, 711–715.

Kawale, S. R., & Diwan, S. P. (2022). Intelligent Breast Abnormality Framework for Detection and Evaluation of Breast Abnormal Parameters. *2022 International Conference on Edge Computing and Applications (ICECAA)*, 1503-1508.

Kim, J. S., Kim, M., & Noh, B. N. (2014). A fuzzy expert system for network forensics. In *Computational science and its applications* (Vol. 3043, pp. 175–182). Springer.

Lin, C., Zhitang, L., Cuixia, G., & Yingshu, L. (2019) Modeling and analyzing dynamic forensics system based on intrusion tolerance. *Ninth IEEE international conference on computer and information technology*, 230–235.

Liu, Z., & Feng, D. (2015). Incremental fuzzy decision tree-based network forensic system. In Y. Hao, J. Liu, Y. P. Wang, Y. M. Cheung, H. Yin, L. Jiao, J. Ma, & Y. C. Jiao (Eds.), *Computational intelligence and security* (Vol. 3802, pp. 995–1002). Springer. doi:10.1007/11596981_148

Mate, M. H., & Kapse, S. R. (2015). Network Forensic Tool — Concept and Architecture. *2015 Fifth International Conference on Communication Systems and Network Technologies*, 711-713. 10.1109/CSNT.2015.204

Merlette, D., & Pruthi, D. P. (2013). *Network security; NetDetector: Identifying real threats and securing your network.* Available: https://www.niksun.com/

Namitha, Manu, Rashmi, & Chinamuttevi. (2022). IOT Based Smart Health Care System to Monitor Covid-19 Patients. *IJEER, 10*(1), 36-40.

Pallavi Asrodia & Sharma. (2013). Network Monitoring and Analysis by Packet Sniffing Method. *International Journal of Engineering Trends and Technology.*

Ramesh Naidu, P., Guruprasad, N., & Dankan Gowda, V. (2021). A High-Availability and Integrity Layer for Cloud Storage, Cloud Computing Security: From Single to Multi-Clouds. *Journal of Physics: Conference Series*, *1921*(1), 012072. doi:10.1088/1742-6596/1921/1/012072

Rao, B. K., Chaturvedi, A., & Hussain, N. (2022). Industrial quality healthcare services using Internet of Things and fog computing approach, Measurement. *Sensors (Basel)*, *24*, 100517.

Reddy, S., & Patwal, P. P. S. (2022). Data Analytics and Cloud-Based Platform for Internet of Things Applications in Smart Cities. *2022 International Conference on Industry 4.0 Technology (I4Tech),* 1-6.

Rekhis, S., Krichene, J., & Boudriga, N. (2018). DigForNet: digital forensic in networking. In *IFIP TC-11 23rd international information security conference* (vol. 278). Springer.

Ren, W. (2004) On a network forensics model for information security. *3rd international conference on Information Systems Technology and its Applications (ISTA 2004)*, 229–234.

Robinson, R. R. R., & Thomas, C. (2015). *Ranking of machine learning algorithms based on the performance in classifying DDoS attacks. In 2015 IEEE Recent Advances in Intelligent Computational Systems*. RAICS.

Shanmugasundaram, K., Memon, N., Savant, A., & Bronnimann, H. (2003). ForNet: a distributed forensics network. In V. Gorodetsky, L. Popyack, & V. Skormin (Eds.), *Computer network security* (Vol. 2776, pp. 1–16). Springer. doi:10.1007/978-3-540-45215-7_1

Shrivastava, G., & Gupta, B. B. (2014). An Encapsulated Approach of Forensic Model for digital investigation. *2014 IEEE 3rd Global Conference on Consumer Electronics (GCCE)*, 280–284. 10.1109/GCCE.2014.7031241

Tang, Y., & Daniels, T. E. (2015) A simple framework for distributed forensics. *25th IEEE International Conference on Distributed Computing Systems Workshops (ICDCS 15),* 163–169.

Uzun, M., & Abul, O. (2016). End-to-end internet speed analysis of mobile networks with mapReduce. *2016 International Symposium on Networks, Computers and Communications, ISNCC 2016*. 10.1109/ISNCC.2016.7746114

Vinjosh Reddy, S., Sai Ramani, K., Rijutha, K., Mohammad Ali, S., & Pradeep Reddy, C. H. (2010). Wireless hacking-a WiFi hack by cracking WEP. *ICETC 2010 - 2010 2nd International Conference on Education Technology and Computer, 1*. 10.1109/ICETC.2010.5529269

Wang, C., Chi, C., Zhou, W., & Wong, R. (2015). Coupled Interdependent Attribute Analysis on Mixed Data. *Proc. Twenty-Ninth AAAI Conf. Artif. Intell. Coupled*, 1861–1867. 10.1609/aaai.v29i1.9480

Wang, D., Li, T., Liu, S., Zhang, J., & Liu, C. (2017). Dynamical network forensics based on immune agent. *Third International Conference on Natural Computation (ICNC 2017)*, 651–656.

KEY TERMS AND DEFINITIONS

Chain of Custody: Information that details every change in possession, access, and location of digital evidence is known as the chain of custody. It's essential for verifying the integrity of the evidence.

Computer Network Forensics: The process of capturing, recording, and analyzing network events to discover the source of security incidents or other problem events.

Digital Evidence: Information stored or transmitted in binary form that may be relied upon in court. It can be found on computer systems, networks, or digital devices and can be either volatile or persistent.

Disk Imaging: Creating an exact replica of a storage medium, preserving all its data and formatting.

File Carving: The process of extracting files from a larger dataset (typically unallocated space) based on their headers, footers, and structures.

Hashing: A procedure that ensures data integrity transforms a string into a unique number. Popular algorithms for this purpose include MD5, SHA-1, and SHA-256.

Live Acquisition: Live forensics involves obtaining information from an active, running computer system rather than from a dormant or powered-off one.

Log Files: Log files are utilized in forensic investigations to determine the actions performed on a system or network.

Packet Sniffer: A utility for network traffic collection and analysis was used to monitor and troubleshoot networks.

Preservation: It's imperative to keep digital evidence unaltered from the time it's collected until it's presented in court.

Timestamp: The metadata of digital files includes dates of creation, modification, and access.

Volatile Data: Data stored in volatile memory or temporary files is erased when a device is powered off. Specialized methods are necessary to safely collect this information.

Chapter 4
The Relevance of Knowledge and Information Management for Innovation Generation

Elaine da Silva
https://orcid.org/0000-0003-1449-354X
Sao Paulo State University, Brazil

Marta Lígia Pomim Valentim
https://orcid.org/0000-0003-4248-5934
São Paulo State University, Brazil

ABSTRACT

Recognizing that the sharing of information and knowledge is a preponderant factor for the generation of innovation and that innovative performance in a nation depends on the ability of innovation agents to share information and knowledge focusing on innovation, this chapter aims to highlight why and how information management (IG) and knowledge management (KM) processes constitute valuable subsidies for the generation of innovation. In addition, it presents and analyzes organizations whose purpose is the management of knowledge and information, such as archives, libraries, information/documentation centers, and museums seeking to show that these organizations have the potential to play an important role in the context of innovation systems.

INTRODUCTION

The systemic approach to innovation emphasizes the importance of information and knowledge sharing between various stakeholders within innovation systems (IS), identifying it as a predominant factor of innovation generation. This notion echoes the assertions of Lundvall (2002), who underscores knowledge as a fundamental element for innovation, and learning its core process. Similarly, Tidd, Bessant and Pavitt (2008) argue that innovation is a matter of knowledge.

DOI: 10.4018/979-8-3693-0807-3.ch004

Godin (2009) points out that innovative performance in a nation depends less on the performance of formal institutions (companies, research institutes, universities, etc.) individually, and more on the way they interact with each other. In other words, the success of an IS depends on the ability of its agents to share information and knowledge focusing on innovation. According to Lundvall and Johnson (1994), the scarcity does not lie in the existence of knowledge, but in the ability to utilize it.

Lundvall and Johnson's assertion is feasible as knowledge is too complex to be reduced to simpler concepts. Furthermore, knowledge cannot be managed in the same way as material resources already within the domain of organizational environments (MORIN, 1999). In this perspective, it is therefore necessary to understand the models, processes, and activities of Information and Knowledge Management (IKM), so that information and knowledge sharing within IS can be promoted.

A fundamental point is to understand the centrality of information and knowledge in today's society. To this end, Valentim (2008) emphasizes the importance of the interaction between society and organizations, given that individuals who share information and generate knowledge participate in both contexts. Therefore, the processes of information and knowledge management within organizations influence a nation's values and culture and, consequently, its potential for economic and social development.

In this context, it is pertinent to infer that an IS is characterized as a knowledge network, in which, as Morin (1999) points out, learning is not only about 'savoir-faire (knowing how to do something), but knowing what to do to acquire knowledge.

The area of Information Science has been concentrating efforts to demonstrate ways of how organizational subjects can effectively utilize information and create new knowledge, which, in turn, can form the foundation for generating innovative processes, products or methods. According to Fadel et. al. (2010), studies on information, knowledge and intelligence within organizational contexts are essential for shaping and understanding of policies, environments and informational flows. Therefore, it is crucial that these studies are grounded on information and knowledge management.

Tigre (2006) advocates on the importance of seeking development nationally, from the offer of products and services with high added value. Additionally, the author also highlights the role of information and knowledge in this context, and that the most developed countries among the indicated by the Global Economic Forum are those that maintain a policy of investing in education and innovation as the basis of economic growth.

The assertion that nations that establish innovation policies focused on issues related to information and knowledge become more innovative is ratified by the Global Innovation Index (GII). The GII measures and analyzes the innovative activity of around 98% of the Gross Domestic Product (GDP) worldwide, which constitutes a very comprehensive universe, both in the number of countries covered and in the percentage of world GDP (Cornell University, INSTEAD, WIPO, 2022).

From this perspective, it is essential for a country's public innovation policies to leverage IKM processes. Moreover, it falls to professionals studying societal phenomena to indicate the need for investments in educated human resources and infrastructure so that the Information Society becomes an actual reality, rather than just a governmental action plan or program (Valentim, 2008).

The literature presents management processes for both information and knowledge that become valuable subsidies for innovation generation, especially in the context of sharing and interaction advocated by the IS approach.

BACKGROUND

Information and Knowledge Management Models

In the 1990s, in a context when, as Drucker (1993, p.7) stated, "the basic economic resource – 'the means of production', is no longer be capital, nor natural resources, nor labor. It is and will be knowledge", the models of Information Management (IM), Knowledge Management (KM), or simply Information and Knowledge Management (IKM) arouse.

A key point that should be highlighted with regard to IKM is that they are connected and complementary, but distinct processes. The first (IM) is dedicated to formal information flows, and the second (KM) dedicated to informal flows.

Over the past few decades, authors have dedicated to establish IM models (McGee & Prusak, 1994; Davenport & Prusak, 1998; Beal, 2004; Valentim, 2004; Choo, 2006) and KM models (Stollenwerk, 2001; Terra, 2001; Probst et al., 2002; Valentim, 2004; Takeuchi & Nonaka, 2008) aimed at presenting and/or elucidating which processes, stages or phases comprise the management of these elements [information and knowledge]. Santos and Valentim (2014) understand that IM models are concerned, above all, with the information life cycle, and KM models demonstrate the activities that deserve the attention of organizations, especially in terms of informal flows and which are crucial to foster the dynamics between tacit and explicit knowledge (Santos & Valentim, 2014).

Among the existing models for IM and KM, the study selected the following for scope of this research: 'Information Management Processes' presented by Davenport and Prusak; 'The three Arenas of Information Use', model presented by Choo; and the 'SECI Model of Knowledge Conversion' advocated by Takeuchi and Nonaka. The first model is focused on IM, the second on KM, and the third model focuses on the conversion of tacit into explicit knowledge and vice versa, and its amplification in an organizational context. In addition, the 'Base Activities of IM and KM' listed by Valentim (2004) present the activities of IM and KM in a synthetic but complete way. The selection of models is supported by their breadth of scope and credibility, since they are fundamental sources in a wide range of studies related to IKM. However, this investigation emphasizes that the presented models do not constitute rules or standards to be implemented, nor do they represent superior models compared to others not detailed within the scope of this research.

Steps for Information Management

According to Davenport and Prusak (1998) information management is, like other organizational processes, constituted by sub-processes that can be enhanced or transformed. Specifically, IM is a structured set of activities distributed in sub-processes or steps described below and shown in Figure 1:

Step 1: Determination of information requirements – This involves the way organizational subjects perceive their information environment considering demands from political, psychological, cultural and strategic perspectives. It seeks to determine which structured and unstructured, formal and informal information is necessary to monitor and support the essential factors for the development of these subjects' activities.

Step 2: Obtaining information – This step involves a continuous system that encompasses exploring the information environment; classifying information into relevant structures; and formatting and structuring the information (DAVENPORT; PRUZAK, 1998). Effective exploration relies on a combination of both automated and human approaches for collecting and synthesizing information, which can then be classified into specific categories. The obtained and classified information is subsequently formatted and structured, typically through documents, which can be in various formats such as text, electronic or audiovisual, among others.

Step 3: Distribution of information – This step involves connecting the subject with the information he needs. Users can be privileged, assuming that they are able to assess what they want and need in terms of information, considering that users should be encouraged to seek and obtain it, without being passive recipients of data that another person considers important; or the dissemination strategy, when some providers decide what type of information should be distributed and to whom (Davenport & Prusak, 1998), with the argument that people would not know how to look for what they do not know. In addition, the adoption of combined dissemination and demand distribution strategies is also possible.

Step 4: Using information – The fourth step has a high degree of subjectivity, as the way organizational subjects appropriates information depends on their prior knowledge and their motivation for doing so. Davenport (1998) believes that organizations can employ some strategies that promote using information, such as: access estimates; symbolic actions such as recognition, rewards and awards granted as a result of ideas or proposals for innovation; institutional contexts such as presentation of various reports in meetings; and performance evaluations to promote using information.

Figure 1. Information management steps
Source: Davenport and Prusak (1998)

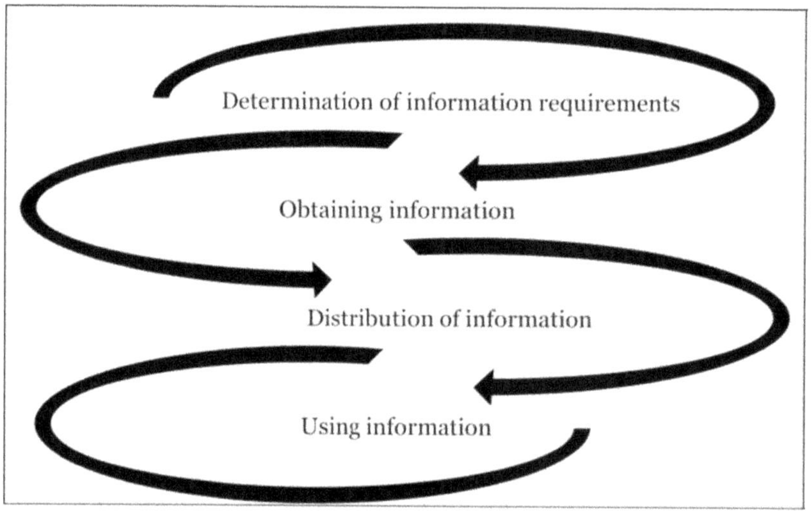

Davenport's four-step information management process, generally presented here, highlights the main sub-processes related to IM. The figure reveals that steps 1 (one) and 4 (four) are endowed with subjectivity, as the determination of information requirements and its use largely depend on the individuals. Steps 2 (two) and 3 (three), although more objective, contemplate a set of activities that contribute greatly for information appropriation, used to generate new and shared knowledge.

Three Arenas of Information Use

Choo (2006) understands that information creation and use play a strategic role in the organizational growth and adaptability. For this author, without a clear understanding of the organizational and human processes by which information is transformed into perception, knowledge and action, companies are not able to perceive the importance of their information sources and technologies (Choo, 2006). From this perspective, the author understands that organizations strategically use information in three arenas, as described below:

I. Sensemaking

Making sense of changes in the external environment is the focus of this arena. A context such as the current one, characterized by intense dynamism, requires constant attention to external relationships, as the messages and signs of occurrences and trends in the external environment are invariably ambiguous and subject to multiple interpretations (Choo, 2006), therefore, it is necessary to recognize and interpret the most significant changes. In this context, for the members of an organization, the immediate objective of sensemaking is to build consensus about what the organization is and what it is doing; the long-term goal is to ensure that the organization adapts and continues to thrive in a dynamic environment (Choo, 2006).

Sensemaking has, as a product, the reduction of uncertainties and ambiguities about the external environment. Ambiguity is reduced by executives and other members of the organization who exhaustively discuss ambiguous information and manage to reach a common interpretation of the external environment (Choo, 2006).

II. Knowledge Building

Creating, organizing and processing information aimed at generating new knowledge through learning. New knowledge enables organizations to develop new capabilities, create new products and services, enhance existing ones and improve organizational processes (Choo, 2006).

Knowledge building is important within organizational environments, especially those focused on innovation generation and management as they act in the conversion of tacit, personal knowledge, into explicit knowledge, capable of promoting innovation and the development of new products (Choo, 2006). Choo's knowledge building arena is in line with the SECI Model of Knowledge Conversion advocated by Takeuchi and Nonaka (2008). Thus, the product of the knowledge building process constitutes:

- Learning new skills through observation and training provided by socialization – converting tacit knowledge into tacit knowledge.
- Dialogue or collective reflection (through the use of metaphors, analogies and models) in which tacit knowledge is converted into explicit knowledge, characterizing externalization, a fundamental activity in the stages of conceptual creation and development of a new product, process or method.
- Gathering explicit knowledge from various sources by combining, converting explicit knowledge into explicit knowledge.

- Incorporation of explicit knowledge into the tacit knowledge repertoire by individuals through mental models or action routines; it occurs through internalization, which consists of converting explicit knowledge into tacit knowledge.

III. Decision Making

Strategically seeking and evaluating information for rational action in decision-making processes, so that decision making is grounded on information about feasible alternatives, probable outcomes and respective impacts of the outcomes for the organization constitute the center of this arena. This arena is important as every action of the company is provoked by a decision, and every decision is a commitment to action (Choo, 2006), therefore decision-making processes cannot be anchored in policies, interests, previous experiences and feelings; it is essential that internal and/or external information related to decision-making be used.

Premises that guide decisions and routines and that guide individual behavior in decision-making are characteristic of the decision-making process, as the decision-making model sees the organization as a rational decision-making system, in which decision-makers analyze the alternatives and assess the consequences based on the outcomes of what was built in the 'Sensemaking' and 'Knowledge building' arenas. As individuals are limited by their ability to process information, routines that guide the search for alternatives and decision-making simplify the decision-making process (Choo, 2006).

Choo (2006) suggests that efficient performance in the three arenas – sensemaking, knowledge building and decision making – can empower an organization to act with intelligence, creativity and even savvy, which outcomes in enhanced conditions for sustainability and growth in highly competitive markets. An organization's actions are based on an accurate understanding of the environment and its needs, leading to effective management of its resources and information processes. These processes facilitate the essential adaptability needed in response to constant changes in the current context, and they enable actions oriented towards mobilizing member learning for innovation generation, while focused on knowledge for rational and decisive actions.

A summarized view of the 'Arenas of Organizational Information Use' and their respective central idea; main process; actions and activities; outcomes and main concepts.

Table 1. The three arenas of organizational information use

Arena/Characteristic	Sensemaking	Knowledge Building	Decision Making
Central idea	Interpretive organization: environmental change - making sense of ambiguous data through interpretations.	Learning organization: existing knowledge - build knowledge through knowledge conversion and sharing.	Rational organization: problem - search for and select alternatives according to objectives and preferences.
Main process	Interpretation of news and messages.	Knowledge Conversion.	Information processing and analysis
Actions / activities	The members of the organization must decide which information is relevant and should receive attention. Starting from explanations of prior experiences, they exchange and negotiate their viewpoints until they arrive at a consensual interpretation.	Members share their knowledge and articulate what they intuitively know through metaphors, analogies, as well as more formal channels of communication.	Members search for and evaluate information guided by rules, routines, and preferences from the available alternatives, analyzing advantages and disadvantages.
Outcomes	Interpreted environments and shared interpretations to make sense	New explicit and tacit knowledge for innovation.	Decisions lead to rational behavior oriented towards objectives.
Main concepts	Interpretation, selection, retention.	Tacit knowledge. Explicit knowledge. Knowledge conversion.	Limited rationality. Decision-making premises. Rules and routines.

Source: by the authors, based on Choo – 2006.

The three arenas or ways of using information are complementary and interdependent. Environments interpreted through sensemaking motivate and guide the knowledge building process. Choo (2006) suggests that a clear idea of what the organization is and wants for its line of business, its market or its community helps to establish an agenda of learning and knowledge building. And this new knowledge grounds the decision-making process and, consequently, innovation generation.

Choo (2006) designates an organization that operates within the three arenas of information use as a 'Knowledge Organization', and postulates that such organization is efficient as it is continuously involved with its surrounding environment through sensemaking. It builds and renews knowledge and generates innovation, broadening the spectrum of choices, and guiding the decision-making process through established routines, rules and heuristic principles, which simplify and legitimize the actions of its executives.

From this perspective, the systemic approach to innovation benefits from knowledge organizations due to their emphasis on sharing information. At an organizational level, sensemaking and knowledge building form the foundation for the decision-making process, making it more assertive. When the knowledge built within these organizations is shared with other IS agents, it further boosts the capacity for knowledge building and the decision-making processes that promote innovation generation within the scope of the System.

SECI Model of Knowledge Conversion

According to Takeuchi and Nonaka (2008), in an economy of uncertainties, successful organizations are those capable of building new knowledge. This author highlights the Japanese management model, formed by companies that have become famous for their ability to respond quickly to customers, create new markets, quickly develop new products, and dominate emerging technologies (Takeuchi & Nonaka, 2008). These companies' secret to success is, according to the authors, the exclusive approach of managing the creation of new knowledge.

The creation of new knowledge begins with the individual and is amplified organizationally, fostering innovation generation – in products, services, processes or methods – capable of contributing to the development of the organization and the context in which it operates. Making personal knowledge available to others is the core activity of the knowledge-creating firm. This is maintained at all levels of the organization (Takeuchi & Nonaka, 2008).

The aforementioned authors indicate three terms to be used to describe the knowledge creation process:

- **Metaphor**: a differentiated method of perception; the creative process, the imagination is triggered through the use of images and symbols.
- **Analogy**: a process of reconciling potential contradictions arising from the use of metaphors. It acts as an intermediate step between pure imagination and logical reasoning;
- **Model**: capable of resolving contradictions and transferring concepts through logic.

Thus, firstly, the organization converts tacit into explicit knowledge by linking contradictory ideas and things through metaphors; then it solves the contradictions by analogy and, finally, it incorporates the knowledge created in a model and makes it available organizationally (Takeuchi & Nonaka, 2008).

The conversion of tacit knowledge into explicit knowledge is, according to Takeuchi and Nonaka (2008), one of the four forms of knowledge conversion that has been neglected in traditional Western models of organizational management. However, if knowledge is initially generated by the individual and then organizationally amplified, the company that does not promote or repress the creation of individual knowledge and its externalization at the organizational level is at risk of losing valuable contributions and possibilities for innovation.

From this perspective, the view of complementarity between tacit and explicit knowledge is crucial, presented in the dynamic model of knowledge creation advocated by Takeuchi and Nonaka (2008), which assumes the creation and expansion of human knowledge through social interaction between tacit knowledge and explicit knowledge. The authors designate this interaction, which occurs through four modes of conversion (Figure 2), as 'knowledge conversion'.

Figure 2. SECI knowledge conversion process
Source: Takeuchi and Nonaka (2008)

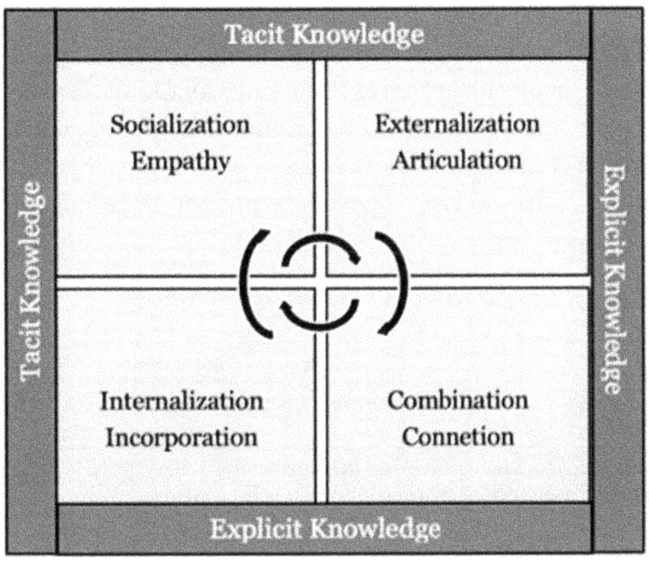

The presented conversion modes are known as the 'SECI Model of Knowledge Conversion', an acronym for the words: socialization, externalization, combination and internalization, described below:

a) **Socialization** – the conversion of tacit knowledge into tacit knowledge. It consists of a process of sharing experiences that results in the creation of knowledge through observation, imitation and practice. On-the-job training, activity tracking, and informal meetings are examples of potential situations for socialization.
b) **Externalization** – conversion of tacit knowledge into explicit knowledge. Triggered by dialogue or collective reflection, it can be presented through metaphors, analogies, concepts, hypotheses and models. It is especially important for knowledge creation as externalization creates new, explicit concepts from tacit knowledge (NONAKA; TAKEUCHI, 2008).
c) **Combination** – conversion of explicit knowledge into explicit knowledge; consists of the reconfiguration through the separation, combination, addition and classification of explicit knowledge into documents, meetings, telephone conversations, databases and others.
d) **Internalization** – conversion of explicit knowledge into tacit knowledge. Knowing subjects incorporate explicit knowledge to their collection of tacit knowledge, and as a result, new knowledge is generated.

The modes of knowledge conversion are not interdependent. 'New' knowledge, generated through internalization, is incorporated into the individual's tacit knowledge pool and can be subsequently socialized and/or externalized. The explicit knowledge resulting from this externalization can be merged with other explicit organizational knowledge and the result of this combination can, in turn, be internalized. Hence, the construction of organizational knowledge occurs in a spiraling motion (Figure 2), converting tacit knowledge into explicit knowledge and vice versa and, consequently, expanding organizational knowledge. Furthermore, for organizational knowledge to be created, it is essential that the tacit knowledge accumulated at the individual level be socialized with other organizational members, initiating a new spiral of knowledge creation (Nonaka & Takeuchi, 2008).

Nonaka and Takeuchi (2008) also consider that, for knowledge to be expanded from the individual to the organizational level, some factors identified as 'Enabling Conditions for Knowledge Creation' (Chart 2) should be observed. These conditions should be promoted by the organization in order to facilitate the creation and accumulation of individual knowledge, as well as group activities capable of promoting knowledge sharing, resulting in the modes of conversion and the knowledge spiral.

Table 2. Enabling conditions for organizational knowledge creation

Enabling Condition	Impact / Characteristic
Intention	The organization must express organizational standards and views, which can be used to evaluate and justify the knowledge created.
Autonomy	The autonomous action of individuals and teams allows the introduction of unexpected opportunities and increases the motivation of individuals to create new knowledge.
Fluctuation and creative chaos	The decomposition of habits, routines or cognitive structures leads organizational subjects to reflect on established assumptions and perspectives.
Redundancy	Information sharing beyond the immediate demand, or the rotation of subjects by various areas and processes in the organization, accelerates the knowledge creation process.
Requisite variety	Combining information in diverse ways that is flexible, fast, and equally accessible throughout the organization increases the potential for organizational knowledge creation.

Source: Takeuchi and Nonaka (2008)

Upon examining the conditions that foster organizational knowledge generation, and applying the process of knowledge conversion, a knowledge-creating company learns from the tacit knowledge held by its employees or external individuals (socialization); it then converts this tacit knowledge into explicit knowledge, so that the team can appropriate it (externalization or articulation); following, the team standardizes the newfound explicit knowledge and groups it with other existing explicit knowledge of the organization (combination). Finally, access and appropriation of explicit knowledge (combination outcome) by the knowing subject will allow the creation of new tacit knowledge (internalization) (Silva, 2013, pp. 68-69).

From the application of the SECI Model of Knowledge Conversion allied to the Enabling Conditions for Knowledge Creation, Takeuchi and Nonaka (2008) list five phases for knowledge creation within an organizational context:

I. **Sharing of tacit knowledge**: The individual knowledge of organizational subjects is amplified within the organization. Generically corresponds to socialization.
II. **Concept creation**: The knowledge shared in the previous phase is converted into explicit knowledge, creating a new concept. This corresponds to externalization.
III. **Concept justification**: The created concept is justified and accepted.
IV. **Construction of an archetype**: The concept is converted into a product prototype or an operational mechanism such as a new system, value or organizational structure;

V. **Knowledge Leveling**: Expands the knowledge created to other parts of the organization, as well as to external partner organizations.

The five phases for creating knowledge at the organizational level are presented (Figure 3).

Figure 3. Phases of the organizational knowledge creation process
Source: Nonaka and Takeuchi (2008)

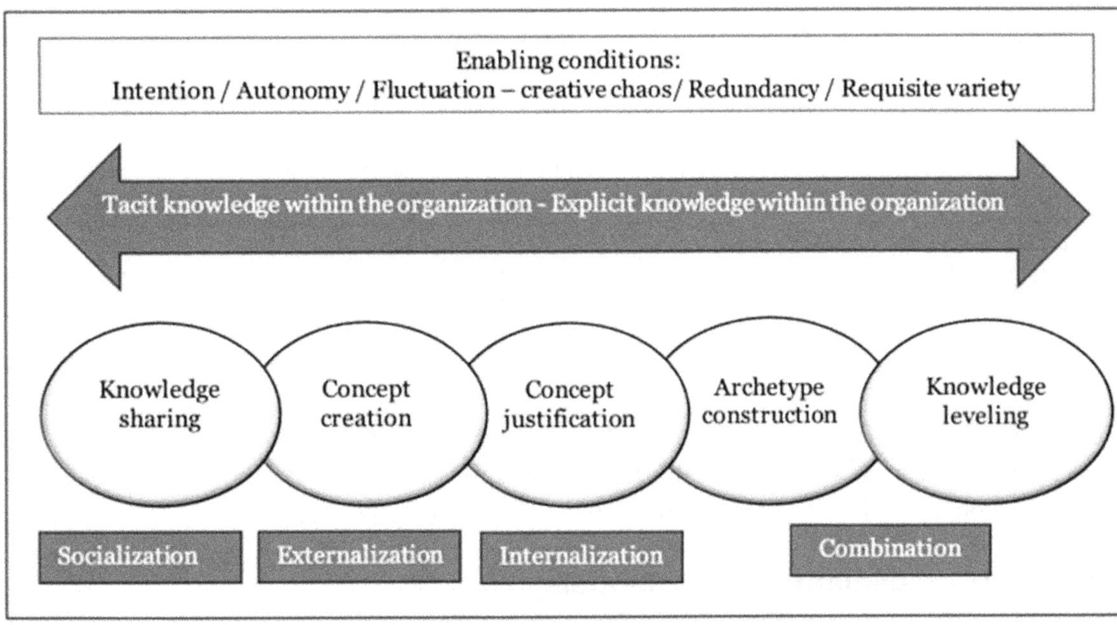

The five phases of the organizational knowledge creation process indicate how to enhance the generated individual knowledge from the ways of converting tacit to explicit knowledge and vice versa and considering the Enabling Conditions for Organizational Knowledge Creation. Emphasizing the importance of the individual's knowledge as the genesis of organizational knowledge creation is crucial. To amplify this knowledge at an organizational level, it is necessary to provide base conditions (Chart 2) that promote knowledge sharing. Furthermore, in line with the systemic approach to innovation, it is noteworthy that knowledge sharing extends beyond internal constituents of an organization. It may also encompass the knowledge from individuals within partner organizations, including suppliers, customers, universities and research institutes. Similarly, knowledge leveling is not limited to the originating organization, but impacts other organizations as well.

Base Activities of Information Management and Knowledge Management

In order to elucidate the intrinsic attributes of IM and KM, Valentim (2004) offers a systematization that underscores the scope, object and base activities to each approach (Chart 3). The author concretizes the IKM processes by correlating a set of activities specific to each management approach, enabling clear identification within the base activities.

Table 3. Base activities of information management and knowledge management

Information Management	Knowledge Management
Scope: Informal Flow	**Scope**: Informal Flow
Object: Explicit Knowledge	**Object**: Tacit knowledge
Base Activities	**Base Activities**
Identify information demands and needs. Map and recognize formal flows. Develop a positive organizational culture regarding information sharing/socialization. Provide informational communication efficiently, using information and communication technologies. Prospect and monitor information. Collect, select, and filter information. Treat, analyze, organize, store information, using information and communication technologies. Develop corporate systems of different nature, aiming at sharing and using information. Develop informational products and services. Establish guidelines and standards for systematizing information. Feed the cycle back.	Identify knowledge demands and needs. Map and recognize informal flows. Develop a positive organizational culture in relation to knowledge sharing/socialization. Provide information communication efficiently, using information and communication technologies. Enable creative spaces within the corporation. Develop skills and expertise focused on the organization's business. Create mechanisms for capturing knowledge generated by different people in the organization. Develop corporate systems of different nature, aiming at sharing and using knowledge. Establish guidelines and standards for systematizing knowledge. Feed the cycle back.

Source: Valentim (2004)

The systematization offered by Valentim (2004) highlights IM and KM specificities and convergences and provides a glimpse of the IM and KM processes presented by Davenport and Prusak (1998), Takeuchi and Nonaka (2008), and Choo (2006) in the described activities.

Knowledge Management Maturity Models

Identifying and analyzing IKM activities, sub-processes and processes constitute an important exercise to implement IKM within organizational environments, as the identification and analysis can signal fundamental IKM aspects that are or are not being contemplated within the organizational environment. Therefore, analyzing the level of IKM maturity within organizations is also crucial.

In this realm, the knowledge management maturity models emerge as notable tools. Generally, these models provide a means to measure KM in organizations (Borba et al., 2013). Originating in the 1990s, in view of the growing recognition of knowledge as a fundamental factor for organizational development and considering the existing models of IM and KM, these maturity models aim to illustrate the implementation of IKM processes, flows and activities within organizational environments.

According to Arias-Perez et al. (2016), KM in organizational environments faces constant challenges as such environments still lack clarity regarding the understanding of how processes, flows and activities can be implemented.

The KM maturity models (Ehms & Langen, 2002; Carvalho et al., 2006; Jiankang et al., 2011; Lin et al., 2012) are grounded on two fundamental axes: levels of KM maturity; and key areas of organizational KM.

With regard to maturity levels, it is recurrent to observe in the models, on average, five phases in these models. The first phase typically begins with a complete unawareness of KM, going through levels of initial implementation; expansion of activities; control and evaluation and, finally, they culminate in a level where KM is fully integrated into organizational processes. As an example, Chart 4 provides a summary of the maturity levels as described in the models: Knowledge Management Maturity Model (KMMM); Organizational Knowledge Assessment (OKA); and APO KM.

Table 4. Synthesis of knowledge management maturity levels

Phase	Description
Initial / Reaction / Unawareness	The organization is unaware of the importance of Knowledge Management (KM). It is likely that some KM activity or process exists within the organization, but they are not controlled;
Repetitive / Initiation / Planning	The organization recognizes the importance of Knowledge Management (KM) and initiates some KM activities, possibly within the scope of pilot projects;
Defined / Expantion / Initiation	The organization implements stable, well-defined Knowledge Management (KM) processes and activities;
Administrated / Control / Evaluation	The organization develops standardized KM approaches and applies and monitors efficiency indicators resulting from KM processes, aiming at continuous improvement of organizational processes;
Optimized / Maturity / Integration	The organization reaches a level where KM is fully integrated into the organizational processes.

Authors, 2023

In addition to providing an analysis of the KM maturity level an organization is positioned, the maturity models also aid in identifying the areas in which an organization should focus and invest, if it aims to advance further in KM maturity. These critical areas constitute the second fundamental axis of KM maturity models and, typically, are concentrated in four broad categories: technology; legal considerations; people and culture.

It is noteworthy that the two fundamental axes of KM maturity models interrelate and complement each other, while investing in key areas implies having more and better conditions to gather elements to advance in the maturity levels.

According to the Asian Productivity Organization (2010), maturity models aid in assessing progress in the implementation of KM in detail by describing the set of elements specific to each level of maturity. In this way, they contribute to organizations to carry out diagnoses regarding the level of KM maturity they are at and, thus, be able to assertively plan their actions towards the effective implementation and achievement of deeper levels of KM maturity. In addition, Ehms and Langen (2002) point out that maturity models promote improved communication and understanding of different perspectives on KM problems and solutions, resulting in gradual appreciation and consequent motivation of those involved in advancing in KM maturity levels.

KM maturity models are therefore effective tools for overcoming barriers and challenges inherent to the management of an element that, in addition to being complex and multifaceted, permeates the entire organization: its culture, policies, documents and employees (Lin et al., 2011).

Within the scope of NIS, as previously discussed (Section 3 'Innovation Systems), different types of organizations interact continuously, mainly through information and knowledge sharing aiming at generating innovation. In this context, it is important that all NIS agents utilize tools to enable them to identify their KM maturity level and respective key driving areas so that they can implement structured IKM processes to facilitate efficient interaction in the context of the NIS they belong.

Information Units and Action Centered on Knowledge Information Management

Considering the assumptions that innovation is a matter of knowledge; information and knowledge are fundamental elements in the systemic approach to innovation. As it is centered on the integrated action of the different IS agents and, this integration occurs through different arrangements between the agents, and is mainly guided information and knowledge sharing.

Knowledge is the object and objective of different areas such as Philosophy, Anthropology, Economics, Politics, Psychology, Cognitive Sciences, among others. Knowledge management, in turn, plays a central role within organizations of the most different segments, as knowledge is recognized as fundamental for organizational development and, consequently, its management is necessary. With regard to IS in particular, knowledge management – tacit and explicit – contributes to the development of individual organizations and enhances the knowledge sharing processes among IS agents. Certainly, the organization conceptualized by Choo (2006) as a 'Knowledge Organization' and characterized by being able to make sense, build knowledge and make decisions will be better able to share information and knowledge with other IS agents, which constitute other companies, customers, suppliers, universities, research centers, regulatory bodies and others.

Managing knowledge and information is relevant and appropriate to any type of organization, however, it is possible to identify institutions whose focus is on IKM, such as archival, information and museum institutions or, simply archives, libraries, information centers/documentation and museums.

This study does not suggest that only the aforementioned organizations have information and knowledge as their object, it confirms that knowledge is a complex phenomenon, object of different epistemological areas. The aim is to examine the role of archives, libraries, information/documentation centers and museums with regard to IKM. To this end, a brief account of the fields of Archival Science, Librarianship and Museology is presented below. It is noted that the purpose is not to contemplate the entire history of the referred fields, but rather to offer an overview for understanding the presence of these organizations in society over time.

Historical Perspectives of Archival Science, Librarianship, and Museology,and Information and Knowledge Management

Archival science, library and museum practices are known to accompany societies for thousands of years; however, it is from the Renaissance that the systematization of areas as fields of knowledge are observed. This subsection, based on the work by Araújo (2014) entitled 'Archival science, Librarianship, Museology and Information Science: the possible dialogue' seeks to gather elements for understanding the trajectory of the fields over time.

According to Araújo (2014) the disciplinary fields of Archival Science, Library Science and Museology were consolidated in the 19th century, in the wake of positivism, treatment techniques (description, inventory, classification, conservation, exhibition) of the collections held in the institutions were privileged, leaving the reflective dimension outside the core of the fields, which then corresponded to archival techniques – the principle of provenance, temporality tables, verification and authenticity rules of documents –; library techniques – bibliographic classification systems, cataloging rules –; and museum techniques – conservation, inventory and expography rules. Therefore, Archival Science, Librarianship and Museology emerged from a heritage perspective.

Criticisms started to emerge in the late 19th century against archives, libraries and museums for being overly focused on their collections and techniques. There were growing demands for these institutions to become more actively involved within the social contexts they were inserted, and thus expressions such as 'useful archive', 'living library', 'dynamic museum', among others, arose (Araújo, 2014). As a result, these demands for changes prompted the emergence of the functionalist perspective.

The functionalist perspective, a theoretical current that emerged late 19th century within the scope of Human and Social Sciences, is based on the identification of organic wholes (a society, a city, a company, a school), their parts and respective functions. Fundamental for the consolidation of scientific disciplines, this perspective also enabled an expansion of the research scope beyond the trinomial documents-institution-treatment, as it substantially transformed knowledge production in the three areas and sought to analyze the relationships between these institutions (and their collections and technical procedures) with the societies in which they operate, bringing a broader and more complex perspective to the fields of study (Araújo, 2014).

In this context, archives have become dynamic agents of culture; libraries played the role of instruments for knowledge propagation and, consequently, for progress within the society in which they are inserted (Araújo, 2014), and museums sought to build a deep relationship with the community they serve.

In the subsequent phase, viewed as the critical perspective, the roles of archives, libraries and museums in the dynamics of power and domination were scrutinized, primarily from the exposure of their ideological actions (Araújo, 2014), and no longer for the functions they should perform for the functioning of society.

Thus, during the 1960s and 1970s, discussions regarding information policies gained space, including archival issues such as, for example, the right to information as a cornerstone of citizenship in relation to the confidentiality parameters of state documents (Araújo, 2014). Concurrently, in the context of the Canadian Archival Science, Terry Cook proposed that archival science should contemplate notions such as authority, evidence and truth, a stance that profoundly impacted archivists' work. According to the author, archivists should scrutinize their actions, understanding that archives and their documents reflect power dynamics, and they are not merely passive deposits, but active arenas where societal powers are negotiated, challenged and reaffirmed (Araújo, 2014).

Within the realm of libraries, the prevailing passivity was criticized and a push for dynamism in the sense that libraries should contribute to enhancing the capacity of readers and students to influence their reality was taking place.

The prevalence of the critical perspective within museums has prompted approaches aligned more with the sociology of culture, aiming to discern the connections between museum actions and the preservation of cultural hierarchies. Notably, Pierre Bourdieu's work emerges in this context. Bourdieu posits that the act of museum visitation is, in itself, an agent of social distancing, a context which heightened focus on the ideological potency of museum exhibitions.

Finally, the contemporary perspective has added contributions for the last decades, resulting in new types of institutions, more concerned with information flows and focused on interaction and mediation, (Araújo, 2014).

In field of Archival Science, after a period closely associated with History and another with Administration, archives have evolved to be characterized as information systems. This shift is a consequence of the impact of Integrated Archival Science, which advocates against the separation of administrative archives from historical archives, information technologies and special records types. This stage has been termed as 'post-custodial'. In the same line, the systemic perspective of the 'total archive' was also developed.

In the contemporary approach to Librarianship, three distinct strands are highlighted. The first relates to mediation as the professional's intentional interference to facilitate information appropriation. Here, libraries begin to view their users or readers as active participants in the process, and are no longer mere tools for information transfer and evolve to constitute true "devices" that generate meanings (Araújo, 2014).

The second strand addresses information competence. Originally associated with the corporate environment as the ability to use of a broad array of information resources for solving problems, then associated with citizenship, correlated to decision-making practices related to social responsibility. In the field of education, it signifies an important shift in the librarians' role, transforming them into educational facilitators. Consequently, the library transitions from an information repository and service provider to a learning organization, inducing changes in institutions where it resides (Araújo, 2014).

The third strand involves electronic or digital libraries. In this environment, the library's role is no longer merely to provide information from its collection, but to enable everyone to participate in the construction of content that everyone will use (Araújo, 2014).

In Museology, models aimed at interaction and mediation have also emerged, systemic models seeking to integrate actions, collections and services. The concepts of ecomuseum and new Museology have been developed. This new paradigm proposes that the museum be understood as an instrument and agent of social transformation, integrating communities and stakeholders in their actions, that is, expanding beyond their traditional functions of identification, preservation and education (Araújo, 2014).

Today, it is observed that the three areas are dedicated to thinking about archives, libraries and museums as integrated with other human practices, with the dynamics of social and cultural life (Araújo, 2014). In this context, Archival Science, Librarianship and Museology characterize as fields which are less focused on their collections and techniques, as they incorporate more complex dimensions such as contexts, skills, interactions, the systemic, the immaterial and the virtual.

RECOMMENDATIONS AND FUTURE RESEARCH SUGGESTIONS

Reflections on the Relevance of Information and Knowledge Management for Innovation

Projects, actions and public policies developed to foster innovation generation are expected to address issues related to the promotion of information and knowledge sharing among NIS agents. However, to efficiently share information and knowledge, NIS agents need to include structured IKM processes withing their organizational processes.

The establishment of structured IKM processes can yield significant benefits within the NIS in terms of sharing, using and reusing information and knowledge among the various IS agents. In an organizational context, sensemaking and knowledge building underpin decision-making processes, enhancing their precision. When the knowledge built within organizations can be shared with other IS agents, it surely expands the scope of decision-making, potentially contributing to innovation generation.

Significant advances have been verified in organizational environments, regarding the implementation of IKM processes since the emergence of the first models in the 1990s. To illustrate, when Davenport and Prusak (1998) presented the model 'Four Steps for Information Management', the authors stated that

IKM processes were rarely focused on programs for organizational process improvement. According to these authors, organizational managers were unaware of the importance of IKM processes, consequently, they considered it a challenge to place these activities in the methodological scope, because their practitioners were autonomous and independent workers (Davenport & Prusak, 1998). Approximately 20 years after these authors' statement, it is believed that the inclusion of IKM in programs for organizational improvement is a reality. IKM importance is recognized by organizational managers and the professionals responsible for IKM are part of the organization's staff.

The assertion can be ratified with the popularization of KM maturity models. They have been discussed both in the academic and the organizational contexts. The implementation of KM maturity models indicates that IKM processes are a reality in organizational contexts that seek to advance to deeper levels of KM.

CONCLUSION

This chapter has presented a perspective which recognizes information and knowledge as fundamental elements for innovation generation and, therefore, the management of these elements as having a strong impact on the success of innovation systems. These must rely on agents that act in an integrated manner, sharing information and knowledge that, consequently, enhance the innovation generation and development. In this context, organizations focused on IKM for their actions, such as archives, libraries, information/documentation centers and museums, can offer a valuable contribution regarding the issues related to IKM and information and knowledge sharing, as these issues correspond to their base functions.

REFERENCES

Araújo, C. A. A. (2014). *Arquivologia, biblioteconomia, museologia e ciência da informação: o diálogo possível*. Briquet de Lemos.

Arias-Pérez, J., Tavera-Mesías, J., & Castaño-Serna, D. (2016). Construcción de un modelo de madurez de gestión del conocimiento para una multinacional de alimentos de una economía emergente. *El Profesional de la Información, 25*(1), 88-102. Disponível em: http://www.elprofesionaldelainformacion.com/contenidos/2016/ene/09.html

Asian Productivity Organization. (2010). *Knowledge management tools and techniques manual*. Tokyo: Asian Productivity Organization. Disponível em: https://www.apo-tokyo.org/publications/files/ind-43-km_tt-2010.pdf

Beal, A. (2004). *Gestão estratégica da informação: como transformar a informação e a tecnologia da informação em fatores de crescimento e de alto desempenho nas organizações*. Atlas.

Borba, F. R., Knoll, E. C., & Todescat, M. (2013). Diagnóstico de níveis de maturidade em gestão do conhecimento: centro de empreendedorismo inovador da Fundação CERTI. Navus - Revista de Gestão e Tecnologia, 3(2), 163-176.

Choo, C. W. (2006). *A organização do conhecimento: como as organizações usam a informação para criar significado, construir conhecimentos e tomar decisões. 2*. Editora SENAC.

Cornell University, INSTEAD, & WIPO. (2016). *The Global Innovation Index 2016: Winning with Global Innovation.* Geneva: WIPO. https://www.globalinnovationindex.org/gii

da Silva, E. (2013). *Gestão do conhecimento e da informação como subsídios para a geração de inovação* [Master's Dissertação]. Universidade Estadual Paulista. Disponível em: https://www.marilia.unesp.br/Home/Pos-Graduacao/CienciadaInformacao/Dissertacoes/SILVA_E_da_Dissertacao.pdf

Davenport, T. H., & Prusak, L. (1998). *Ecologia da informação: porque só a tecnologia não basta para o sucesso na era da informação.* Futura.

de Carvalho, R. B., Ferreira, M. A. T., & Silva, R. V. (2006). Análise da maturidade e do perfil de programas de gestão do conhecimento: pesquisa exploratória e comparativa em organizações brasileiras e portuguesas. *Revista Gestão Industrial, Ponta Grossa (PR), 2*(3), 15-28. Disponível em: https://periodicos.utfpr.edu.br/revistagi/issue/view/11

Drucker. (1993). *Sociedade pós-capitalista. 2* (M. J. Tradução de Nivaldo, Ed.). Pioneira.

Ehms, K., & Langen, M. (2002). *Holistic development of knowledge management with KMMM.* Siemens. Disponível em: http://www.kmmm.org/objects/kmmm_article_siemens_2002.pdf

Fadel, B. (2010). Gestão, mediação e uso da informação. In *Gestão, mediação e uso da informação.* São Paulo: Cultura Acadêmica. Disponível em: https://www.culturaacademica.com.br/catalogo-detalhe.asp?ctl_id=115

Godin, B. (2009, July). National Innovation System: The system approach in historical perspective. *Science, Technology & Human Values, 34*(4), 476–501. doi:10.1177/0162243908329187

Jiankang, W. (2011). Knowledge management maturity models: A systemic comparison. International Conference on Information Management, Innovation Management and Industrial Engineering (ICIII), 606-609. doi:10.1109/ICIII.2011.420

Lin, C., Wu, J. C., & Yen, D. C. (2012, January). Exploring barriers to knowledge flow at different knowledge management maturity stages. *Information & Management, 49*(1), 10–23. doi:10.1016/j.im.2011.11.001

Lundvall, B. A., & Johnson, B. (1994). The learning economy. *Journal of Industry Studies, 1*(2), 23–42. doi:10.1080/13662719400000002

Lundvall, B. A., Johnson, B., Andersen, E. S., & Dalum, B. (2002, February). National systems of production, innovation and competence building. *Research Policy, 31*(2), 213–231. doi:10.1016/S0048-7333(01)00137-8

Mcgee, J., & Prusak, L. (1994). *Gerenciamento estratégico da informação: aumente a competitividade e eficiência de sua empresa utilizando a informação como uma ferramenta estratégica.* Elsevier.

Morin, E. (1999). *O método 3: o conhecimento do conhecimento.* Sulina.

Probst, G., Raub, S., & Romhardt, K. (2002). *Gestão do conhecimento: os elementos construtivos do sucesso.* Bookman.

Santos, C. D., & Valentim, M. L. P. (2014). As interconexões entre a gestão da informação e a gestão do conhecimento para o gerenciamento dos fluxos informacionais. *Perspectivas em Gestão & Conhecimento, 4*(2), 19-33. Disponível em: http://hdl.handle.net/20.500.11959/brapci/49728

Stollenwerk, M. F. (2001). L. Gestão do conhecimento: conceitos e modelos. In *Inteligência organizacional e competitiva* (pp. 143–163). Editora UnB.

Takeuchi, H., & Nonaka, I. (2008). *Gestão do conhecimento*. Bookman.

Terra, J. C. C. (2001). *Gestão do conhecimento: o grande desafio empresarial. 3*. Negócio.

Tidd, J., Bessant, J., & Pavitt, K. (2008). *Gestão da Inovação. 3*. Bookman.

Tigre, P. B. (2006). *Gestão da inovação: a economia da tecnologia do Brasil*. Elsevier.

Valentim, M. L. P. (2008). Informação e conhecimento em organizações complexas. In *Gestão da informação e do conhecimento no âmbito da Ciência da Informação* (pp. 11–26). Polis/Cultura Acadêmica.

Valentim, M. L. P. (2013). *Gestão da informação e gestão do conhecimento: especificidades e convergências*. Infohome. Disponível em: https://www.ofaj.com.br/colunas_conteudo.php?cod=88

KEY TERMS AND DEFINITIONS

Base Activities of Information Management and Knowledge Management: Valentim model. highlights IM and KM specificities and convergences.

Information Units to Knowledge and Information Management: Institutions whose focus is on Knowledge and Information Management, such as archival, information and museum institutions or, simply archives, libraries, information centers/documentation and museums.

Innovative Performance in a Nation: Innovative performance in a nation depends on the ability of its agents to share information and knowledge focusing on innovation. In this approach, knowledge is the fundamental element for innovation, and learning its core process.

Knowledge and Information Management to Development and Innovation: The processes of information and knowledge management within organizations influence a nation's values and culture and, consequently, its potential for economic and social development.

Knowledge Management Maturity Models: Models with tools for overcoming barriers and challenges inherent to the knowledge management models.

SECI Model of Knowledge Conversion: Takeuchi and Nonaka model. Assumes the creation and expansion of human knowledge through social interaction between tacit knowledge and explicit knowledge.

Three Arenas of Information Use: Choo model. Understands that information creation and use play a strategic role in the organizational growth and adaptability. The strategic use of information requires sensemaking, knowledge building and decision making.

Chapter 5
The Herding Behavior of Investors in the Indian Financial Market:
An Insight Into the Influence of Social Media

L. G. Honey Singh
https://orcid.org/0009-0008-5455-5825
Ranchi University, India

Kishlay Kumar
https://orcid.org/0000-0001-9685-1798
Sarala Birla University, India

ABSTRACT

The study explores the phenomenon of herding behavior among investors in the Indian financial market with a specific focus on the influence of social media. Herding bias impacts the cognitive functions of the investor by inducing them to take decisions based on the decisions of the crowd. Social media platforms have gained significant popularity, becoming a prominent source of financial information and market sentiment for investors. The study analyses the impact based on the social media messages, news, and discussions on popular platforms. A sample of 215 investors was collected through a questionnaire via Google Form. The respondents were selected through purposive sampling technique. The hypothesis is primarily tested using PLS-SEM. The results of this study indicate that influencer credibility for the investors shows a significant positive impact on herd behaviour. Financial literacy had a detrimental effect on herding but became significant when risk perception was used as a mediator. Lastly, risk perception in isolation also showed a significant impact on herding behaviour.

DOI: 10.4018/979-8-3693-0807-3.ch005

INTRODUCTION

Comprehending how market participants make decisions has always been extremely difficult for academics and practitioners alike. Numerous studies have shown the efficient market theory's main limitations in simulating stock return patterns. According to behavioral financial theory, stock market actions can be influenced by an investor's feelings or ideas (Summers, 1986). According to the traditional finance theory, investors establish reasonable expectations of future prices and instantly discount all available market data into expected prices similarly. However, the rationality of investors has always been called into question by major investors, and this rationality and information access and discounting have formed reasons for the major criticism of the traditional theory of finance. Investors create homogeneous expectations based on all accessible information, are perfect rational utility maximizers, and know that others utilize this publicly available information the same way they do, according to the theory of efficient markets. One can find different schools of thought, disciplines, and subdisciplines to study money and investments in the past, present, and future. Numerous groundbreaking studies on stock returns have been done in modern finance, like Markowitz's Asset Pricing Theory (1952) and CAPM, The Capital Asset Pricing Model (1960s) were quantitative models for quantifying unsystematic risk. Sharpe (1964), and Lintner (1965), studied and introduced portfolio theory. Efficient Market Hypothesis (EMH) studied by (Fama 1965), the Modigliani-Miller (1988) approach for option pricing in investment decisions. All the above-mentioned theories discredit the fact that two investors having same set of data are still earning different returns. This was later explained by two renowned psychologists Kahneman & Tversky in their groundbreaking work. They claimed that the investors do not only exhibit rationality but there also exist psychological components of the investors (Priya et al., 2023). Contrary to traditional theories, traders are not always rational, and their decision making is often influenced by their belief system and information retention and processing powers. The Behavioural finance theory tries to explain the difference in returns for two identical investors as the emotional response to the information assimilated. The emotional response depends on various psychological aspects of investors, thereby leading to the impact on buying and selling decisions of the investors. Financial decision-making is influenced by investors' psychological makeup, according to behavioural finance (Sinha, 2023). We are aware that people make decisions based on their emotions. These judgments frequently have an inefficient and illogical nature and can result in stock market catastrophes. The most historic occurrence of these calamities is possibly documented by (Mackay, 2012) including the occurrence of Tulip Bubble. Market anomalies including speculative bubbles, overreaction to new information, and underreaction to it are evidence that there is more to financial decision-making than a cold, calculative rational agent. Thus, the necessity to comprehend these anomalies and the flaws in human judgment they involved gave rise to behavioural finance. Investors exhibit behavioural biases that fall short of perfect rationality (Jaiswal and Sinha, 2023). Their mood, market sentiment, and other seemingly unrelated external influences can all have an impact on their investment decisions. In the financial markets, herding is often defined as the propensity of an investor to mimic the behavior of others. Alternately, herding is a term frequently to describe the correlation in trades brought on by investor contacts. Since using their own information/knowledge would be more expensive, less experienced investors who try to emulate financial gurus or emulate the actions of successful investors are thought to be justified for engaging in this behavior. Consequently, this herding behavior is a note, ''a group of investors trading in the same direction over a period''. Empirically, this may result in observed behavior patterns that are associated across people and that cause entire groups to make systematically bad decision (Jaiswal et al., 2023). Investors must therefore choose a greater variety of securities with a lower degree of correlation to attain the same level of diversification. Additionally, investors' trading behavior may lead asset values to vary from economic fundamentals if market participants tend to herd around the market consensus. This behaviour has been identified as one of the major factors impacting the asset pricing and thus cannot be ignored. Investors, especially those having insufficient knowledge of the financial markets, are prone to get affected by this herd mentality (Gupta et al., 2023). The information gathering process by the investors tend to incline towards easily available mediums. With easy access to internets information disbursement and information gathering, both are equally seen on the social media platforms. It has become easier to gather information impacting the corporations and economy from these social media platforms than watching a full hour news. Platforms like Facebook, X (formerly Twitter) and Instagram have emerged as the most visited platforms. These mediums have become a storehouse of information about diverse topics (Kumar et al., 2023). An investor holding incomplete knowledge regarding trading and investment tends to gather information from these sources. Interactions on social media platforms have the potential to change people's information environments and trigger feedback cycles that could result in emotive hype. These effects may then have an impact on how investors trade, asset prices, and market efficiency.

BACKGROUND OF THE STUDY

Behavioural finance has been in competition with traditional finance in recent decades. While traditional finance focuses on rational analysis, behavioural finance takes psychological and behavioural elements into account while making investment decisions (Kumar et al., 2023). The focus of behavioural finance is on how people obtain and use information. Since not everyone can conceivably have and invest based on the same amount of information, this led to the conception of behavioural finance. Each person will read and observe various things, and each person will have a distinct perspective on what they see. This forms the central idea of several studies on behavioural biases in investing. In their article "An Exploratory Inquiry into the Psychological Biases in Financial Investment Behavior," (Sahi et al., 2013) sought to outline the mistakes investors frequently make. The authors identified a wide range of biases.

- Prefer known risks over unknown risks.
- Rely on a point of reference.
- Make investment decisions based on easily available information.
- Play it safe with regards to risk.
- Invest differently based on income source.
- Invest with a view of social responsibility.
- Invest in instruments which are familiar.
- Feel that past decisions could have been better or were inevitable.
- Be averse to losses.
- Feel regret.
- Be confident in one's own ability.
- Rely on family and friends.
- Follow trends.

Herding Bias

Amongst the various behaviour mentioned above, out study focuses on the behavioural aspect where the investors 'follow the trend'. Over the decades, herding has been defined differently by different scholars. Herding has been explained as the imitation of behaviour and decisions of other investors by the concerned investor (Karmakar et al., 2022). Herding as someone who follows what everyone else does even though their own personal data shows that they are acting in a very unnatural and harmful way. Herding behavior has been studied to understand how investors make investing decisions. Financial markets are significantly impacted by investors' willingness to imitate or follow other investors' activities. According to the herding behavior idea, investors who tend to herd would avoid utilising their own personal information for decision making, which would push prices further from their intrinsic value. This can make the markets volatile (Balcilar et al., 2013). Investors feel safer if they imitate and behave like other investors. However, whether the market is up or down, investors are now intensely focused on their private and personal details and information regarding their choices of investing methods, and they rely heavily on publicly available market data. Thus, herding will be more prevalent when the market is under pressure. Therefore, the existence of investor herding behavior would lead to market imbalances by causing the prices of the assets to be moved away from their intrinsic values. As a result, in this instance, the prices of the assets would represent both investors' rational and irrational expectations (Kataria & Choudhary, 2015).

Causes of Herding

Several reasons have been determined to cause investors to herd. Some of them are as follows:

- **Imperfect Information:** A positive investment signal from one trader frequently leads other investors to believe their information is unreliable. Investors mimic the behavior to acquire knowledge about everything.
- **Reputational Concerns:** Due to concerns over their reputation, investors may be hesitant to make independent trading decisions and instead opt to follow the group's collective trading decisions.
- **Compensation Structures:** Investor focuses on increasing principal as well as value while connecting it to the index's performance. The investor's ideal investment strategy moves in the direction of the benchmarks after observing the movements of the benchmarks.

Types of Herding

- **Intentional Herding:** Intentional herding involves imitating other market participants, which leads to identical buying or selling of comparable stocks regardless of prior beliefs or skill sets. This type of herding may lead to asset valuations that do not reflect fundamental information, increased volatility, and economic instability, all of which have the potential to lead to or at least be a contributing factor in financial market bubbles and crashes.
- **Unintentional or Spurious Herding:** In the study conducted by (Hirschleifer, 1994) Unintentional herding is primarily driven by fundamentals and develops because of organizations looking at the same factors and receiving cross-correlation private information, which causes them to come to

the same conclusions about specific stocks. This is mostly due to fund managers' incentives and specialists' same academic backgrounds, pertinent abilities, and similar information evaluation methods (Griffin et al., 2003).

FACTORS AFFECTING HERDING BEHAVIOR

The Effect of Stock Influencer Credibility on Herding

Influencers are people who regularly use their social media accounts, frequently participate in a particular topic, and constantly provide new information. Consumers seeking information about products or services often view influencers as credible sources of information. The role of an influencer in this regard is their credibility. Ascetic impact studies show that customers can positively perceive brands and products that they consider credible (Bergkvist & Zhou, 2016). Trustworthiness and expertise are two components of a person's credibility (Halder et al., 2021). The term "trustworthy" refers to the receiver's perception of authenticity, integrity, and trust, while the term "expertise" refers to the speaker's knowledge, competence, or experience (Erdogan, 1999). The reliability of the "influencer" is crucial to the success of "eWOM" in relation to consumer goods and purchases, according to research in the larger field of "electronic word of mouth" ("eWOM") (Reichelt et al., 2014), Erkan & Evans, (2016)). The data from earlier studies suggests a connection between the credibility of stock influencers and investors' propensity for herding behavior (Marietza et al.,2023), Chairunnisa et al, (2021)). Meanwhile, (Marietza et al., 2023) found that herding behavior is more prevalent among investors in sophisticated capital markets. While the investor in developing nations bases his or her selection on past prices. However, investors in emerging stock markets often become irrational in times of economic downturn, and the majority of them choose their positions by imitating other investors. According to (Marietza et al., (2023), many retail investors use well-known investors as references in that case. The investors' anxiety and desperation lead to this foolish deal. The (Trikonomika, 2021) study has also been successful in identifying variables that influence stock market herd behavior. (Trikonomika, 2021) asserts that monetary policies including interest rates, foreign investment, and currency rates significantly contribute to stock market herding. (Trikonomika, 2021) suggested that information or opinion circulated from a recognized authority in the field of monetary policy would result in a speculative stock market transaction. In contrast to wealthy countries, this phenomenon is easier to observe in emerging nations. The focus of the (Trikonomika, 2021) study, however, is solely on the impact of monetary policy on herding behavior and not the impact of information from sources with a strong reputation. The research done by (Chapple & Cownie, 2017) and (Djafarova & Rushworth, 2017) provides yet another hint that the influencers may have an impact on investor herd behavior. They contend that the reputation of influencers, who are well known for posting user-focused product reviews, suggestions, and personal experiences on their social media platforms, is essential in influencing purchasing decisions. Since prior research has so far continued to yield ambiguous and contradictory results, the following hypothesis is put forth.

H1: Stock influencer credibility has positively correlated with Investor herding behavior.

The Effect of Risk Perception on Herding Behavior

According to (Moreira, 2008), risk perception is a subjective evaluation of a particular accident type and the repercussions that people endure based on its characteristics and intensity. The evaluation of both the probability and the consequences is part of the risk perception process. "Risk perception is a method of evaluating risks that deviate from estimates, thoughts, or realities," according to (Rogers, 2017). Risk perception is encompassed by cognitive bias. The perception of risk decreases as human conduct becomes more biased. People sometimes misjudge the hazards involved with a particular activity due to their lack of relevant information. People who lack the necessary information or are uninformed may draw the wrong conclusions or judgments. Herding conduct is one of the psychological factors that might affect the decision-making process, according to (Mand et al., 2021). In particular, (Yang et al., 2022) made the case that investor risk tolerance, which is also one of the factors that influence investor behavior, has a beneficial impact on an investor's intention to invest in the stock market. Risk-takers are known to intend to invest in the stock market more frequently than risk-averse individuals. This is because risk-takers typically possess higher levels of confidence than risk-averse individuals. According to (Gul & Khan, 2019), herding behavior is significantly influenced by a number of attitude components, including choice conformity, rapid decision-making, mood, judgment correctness, and overconfidence. (Marietza et al.,2023) note that herding behavior can be viewed as an investor's attempt to manage the risk, and there is a link between investor risk perception and herding behavior. Additionally, according to (Marietza et al.,2023), pessimistic investors who wanted to avoid financial losses and had bad attitudes toward the market can cause herding behavior. This investor typically doesn't use reason when making investment judgments. This theory is further backed by (Lee at al., 2021), who discovered that risk may have a direct, beneficial impact on herding behavior.

H2: Investor risk perception is positively correlated with investor herding behavior.

The Effect of Financial Literacy on Investor Herding Behavior

According to (Moore, 2003), the fundamental principle of financial literacy is the capacity to be competent as well as the possession of a set of abilities and knowledge that empowers a person to make wise and informed financial decisions. This is because a trustee must be hired because financial literacy cannot be checked directly. Literacy is a practical skill that is attained via the active integration of knowledge. People become more economically sophisticated as they become more literate, and it is theorized that this may also imply that a person is more competent. Financial literacy was defined similarly by (Huston, 2010) as "the ability to assess new and sophisticated financial instruments and make informed decisions about which instruments to employ and how much to use that would be in their best long-term interests." The findings of earlier research indicate that academics agree about how financial literacy affects herding behavior. (Baker et al., 2019) discovered that the degree of financial literacy of investors had a negative impact on herding behavior. They claimed that more experienced or financially literate investors tend to be more confident than less literate investors. Similarly, (Sabir et al., 2019) claims that there is proof that financial literacy directly affects customer confidence. High financial literacy investors typically have higher confidence when choosing their investments. Furthermore, (Sabir et al., 2019) discovered that investors with strong financial literacy can do significantly better than investors with low financial literacy since they can conduct sound financial analyses. They also note that the degree of investor financial knowledge may have an impact on investor herding behavior. Additionally, a (Adil et al., 2021) study indicated that among female investors, financial literacy considerably attenuated the association between herding bias and investment decisions; however, the study was unable to demonstrate that this was also true of male investors. (Adil et al., 2021) concluded that female investors with high levels of financial capability typically use broker and friend recommendations as the primary factor when deciding on an investment. According to (Adil et al., 2021), investor behavior bias and financial literacy have a bad association. Investors who are more financially literate tend to be less behaviourally biased and are far less prone to make impulsive purchases. This conclusion is corroborated by (Baker et al., 2019), who discovered that while financial literacy has a detrimental impact on investor herding behavior, it positively influences mental bias. There is no evidence that financial literacy directly affects herding behavior, even though several earlier studies have provided evidence that investor financial literacy effects investment behavior. Therefore, we put up the following hypothesis in this study.

H3: Financial literacy is negatively correlated with investor herding behavior.

The Effect of Stock Influencer Credibility on Investor Risk Perception

Information asymmetry and information filtering have a significant impact on how people perceive danger, according to a study by (Singh & Bhattacharjee, 2019). The kind of information sources that investors will utilize in the investing decision-making process will depend on how much risk they consider themselves to be taking. Investor risk perception can be decreased with the help of reliable information (Weismueller et al., 2020). Meanwhile, there is a substantial body of evidence from the study of consumer behavior that suggests social media influencers have a significant influence on customer behavior (Sun, & Meng (2022); Sivaramakrishnan et al.,2017)). These studies suggest that a social media influencer's attractiveness, dependability, and expertise have a positive effect on a consumer's intention to make a purchase. Perhaps because consumers evaluate an influencer's credibility on a broad scale to determine the value of the product suggestion during the decision-making process. As a result, we also suggested the following.

H4: Stock influencer credibility is positively correlated with Investor risk perception.

The Effect of Financial Literacy on Investor Risk Perception

(Sivaramakrishnan et al., 2017) asserts that investor understanding of investment products and the market decreases people's reliance on information while simultaneously boosting their confidence in their ability to produce sound judgements. Financial literacy has been linked to improved financial planning, according to (Kanagasabai & Aggarwal, 2020). Risk-takers are more likely to hold a diversity of investments than conservative investors. (Kanagasabai & Aggarwal, 2020) also found that risk tolerance played a role in mediating the association between financial literacy, often known as the basic understanding of financial investments, and investment performance. (Prasad et al., 2020) conducted another earlier investigation that produced a comparable conclusion. Their research investigated how investors' financial literacy affected their level of risk tolerance. (Prasad et al, 2020) also investigate factors affecting investor demographics like age, gender, and educational attainment. This study showed that investor risk attitudes were influenced by both investor demographics and financial literacy. (Prasad et al., 2020) asserts that investors with high levels of financial awareness, education, and income generally do not hesitate to invest their money in a medium to high-risk instrument in an effort to receive a larger return. However, an investor's risk tolerance is negatively impacted by their age and the number of children they have. Since an improvement in financial literacy level enables people to make more thoughtful investing decisions, it follows that theoretically, risk tolerance of an individual should change (Prasad et al., 2020). The study found evidence of the impact of financial literacy on individual investors' risk tolerance (Nguyen et al., 2016), using data from 538 individuals. It was discovered that risk tolerance is positively impacted by financial literacy. Therefore, according to (Nguyen et al, 2016), wealth management companies and investment businesses should educate their clients to increase their financial literacy. Taking everything into account, we put forth a theory.

H5: Financial literacy has a positive relationship with investors' risk perception.

Social Media

Social media has been defined in a variety of ways. It is known as the colonization of the space between traditional broadcasting and private dyadic communication, providing individuals with a scale of group size as well as degrees of privacy that we have termed scalable sociality, in one sense. (Miller et al., 2016). A simpler explanation describes social media as internet platforms where information, viewpoints, thoughts, and media can be shared. It makes it possible for individuals and organizations to connect and encourages the development of partnerships. Some of the most visited sites that constitute social media include Twitter, Facebook, and YouTube (Nair, 2011). Another perspective presents social media as more than merely another form of media. It is described as "a movement where consumers and businesses engage in unstructured dialogue, discovery, and delivery of information, and make decisions to purchase". Organizations give this intricate synthesis of sociology and technology a lot of consideration because of how important it is to them and how it can change them (Nair, 2011). Investors rely on public news to keep up with new information, keep their expertise current, and make wise financial decisions (De Long et al., 1990). However, social media is now the main channel for disseminating information (Gan et al., 2020). While social media makes it easier for people to engage and links investors to financial markets, it can also encourage market players to act in concert when making investments (Bukovina, 2016). Investor sentiment consequently entangles with market quality, resulting in stock return continuations, escalating market frictions, and perhaps impacting the effectiveness of asset prices. Previous researches point to a possible connection between sentiment and informative effectiveness. On the one hand, emotion might increase effectiveness. Using Google searches to measure investor behaviour show that when investor attention increases, return predictability decreases, improving informational efficiency Vozlyublennaia, 2014). Gu and Kurov,2020) found that Twitter messages that have social media sentiment extracted from them reveal new data on analyst picks, analyst price targets, and quarterly profits. It is plausible to anticipate that social media sentiment may help to improve informational efficiency given that it may transmit firm-level information. Studies reveal that individual investors only have access to relatively basic information while institutional investors receive sophisticated information through specialist channels like Bloomberg (Da Z et al., 2011). To get around this, the individual investors share facts and ideas on social media. Retail investors are viewed as random, noise traders who make only modest investments in advanced fundamental analysis and generally lack professional knowledge. But research has shown that social media, where individual investors make up a significant share, is educational and not only explains the market but also has an impact on it (Antweiler & Frank, 2004). People with internet access can broadcast their opinions on business operations, make trade decisions, and share their predictions for future changes in stock price thanks to social media's characteristics that set it apart from more traditional media and make it a richer disclosure channel. It enables participants in the capital markets to openly discuss how they handle information (Cade, 2018). Investors can easily read all the posts relating to a certain publicly traded company or topic of interest since that shared material is also publicly accessible through the platform's search function. Additionally, social media has distinctive characteristics that present a wealth of data on various topics that may affect how investors view a company (Cade, 2018).

RESEARCH METHODOLOGY

Figure 1 represents the study's theoretical framework based on the goal of the current investigation. The evaluated material serves as the foundation for the expanded theoretical framework. Herding conduct in financial markets is used as the dependent variable in the current study. The influencer credibility and financial literacy of an individual investor, as well as risk perception, which is acknowledged as both an independent and dependent variable, operate as the independent variables and mediating variable in the framework.

Figure 1. Theoretical framework

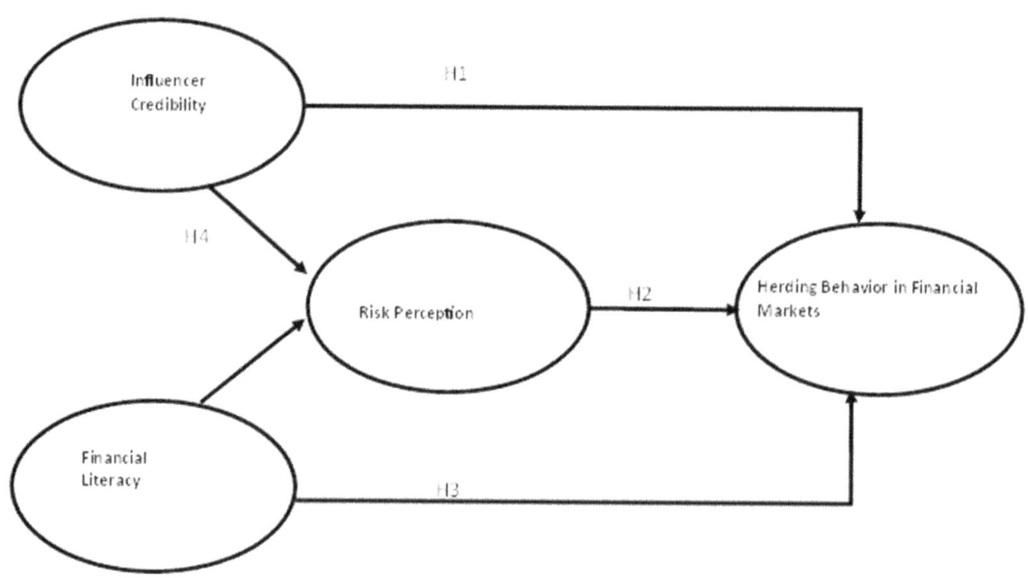

A quantitative research methodology was used in the research strategy. The numerical information was gathered quantitatively and statistically examined. Data for this study were gathered via an online questionnaire, which would then be given to the respondents. The data received from this online survey was then quantitatively evaluated. The research's goal is to explore the impact of financial literacy, influencer credibility, and risk perception on the herding behavior bias, notably in the financial market sector. The design is in line with this goal. Additionally, this study targeted Indian citizens with previous experience as private investors in the financial sector. Online surveys created with Google Forms were used to gather the study's main data. A minimum of 215 Indian residents who are at least 18 years old and have previous experience as individual investors in the financial market received this online questionnaire. To contact the intended responders, the author used a variety of social media and messaging platforms, including as Twitter(X), Instagram, Facebook, and LinkedIn and other. Distribution of the invitation to participate was done through the author's social media accounts and relationships. With the help of his co-workers, who shared the questionnaire on their own social media sites, the questionnaire was further disseminated. There were various sections to the questionnaire. The author introduces the research's context and goal in the cover letter, which is the opening portion of the report. For the benefit of the responders, a synopsis of the research topic was provided in the background section. The cover letter helps participants be sure that the data they provide is only used for this survey. Question filtering was a part of the initial component, and its goal is to weed out survey participants who are ineligible to participate. Age, Income, and other variables can affect respondents' experience as investors in the Indian financial market. The second component of the survey sought data on respondents' profiles and covered fundamental demographic information such gender, occupation, average monthly income, and engagement in the financial markets. The questionnaire then moved on to the sections that requested respondents to submit scores on a Likert scale that ranged from 1 to 5. The scale was created to measure how much people agreed or disagreed with the assertions. Respondents were specifically asked to rate their level of agreement with the given statements on a scale from "Strongly Disagree" (1) to "Strongly Agree" (5). The "Likert Scale" study measurement was adapted from (Hui et al, 2018), which examined "Herding Behavior in Indian Stock Market." To ensure the consistency and comparability of data, the measurement method employed in the study was also adopted/adapted from the validated scale as shown in Table 1. The resulting measurement tool has proven to be precise and reliable in capturing the subtleties of herding behavior, making it a good candidate for replication. This part will also help expose respondents' behavior prior to, during, and following their financial market activity. Strategic statistics show the respondents' financial market investment activity as well as their behavioural patterns over the course of making investment decisions. All of the factors used in this study were covered in this section, including stock influencer credibility, financial literacy, and risk perception. In this study, four variables—Influencer Credibility, Financial Literacy, Risk Perception, and Herding Behavior—were used to test five hypotheses. The antecedents of herding bias (influencer credibility, financial literacy, and risk perception) and individual "investors' herding behavior bias" in the financial market were examined in the hypothesis. Several methods were utilized in this study to assess whether the collection of observed values matches the anticipated relevant model, including; VIF (Variance Inflation Factor; "to measure the strength of the correlation between the independent variables in regression analysis"), Model-fit Testing ("to assess if a collection of observed values matches those anticipated by the relevant model"), R-Squared test ("to investigate the correlation which describes the strength of the link between independent and dependent variables in the study"), and F-Squared test ("to measure the effect size of the independent variables towards the dependent variable when exogenous constructs were removed"). Primarily, the author utilized hypothesis testing through the use of PLS-SEM, as remains to be the best option to estimate complex models containing many constructs/variables, indicators, and structural paths without imposing distributional assumptions on the data.

Table 1. Variable measurement

Variable	Definition	Sources	Number of Indicators	Measurement
Stock Influencer Credibility	The Extent of the believability of the provided information and in their providers.	Rebelo (2017)	8	Likert Scale of 1-5
Financial Literacy	"The ability to evaluate the new and complex financial instruments and make informed judgments in both choices of instruments and extent of use that would be in their own best long-run interests"	Mandell (2007)	9	
Risk Perception	"subjective assessment of the probability of a specified type of accident happening and how concerned we are with the consequences.	Moen et al., (2004)	10	
Herd Behavior	"The behavior of investors who tend to follow other investor in investing without conducting a fundamental analysis first so that the formed market becomes inefficient"	Fityani & Arfinto (2015)	8	

Results and Discussion

The descriptive statistics for the survey participants are depicted in Table 2. The research concluded 215 respondents submitted the Google Forms online questionnaire that the researcher distributed. Out of the 215 respondents that provided information, 165 (76.7%) were male and 50 (23.3%) were female, representing the gender distribution of the Indian population who responded to the survey. A notable portion of the respondents (67.4%) held postgraduate/master's qualifications. Most of the respondents are salaried person (39.5%). Out of total respondents, majority of respondents were earning between Rs25000 to Rs50000 (25.6%). In addition, 105 of the respondents were between 26 years to 35 years of age. Out of the 215 respondents whose information had been gathered, 61 respondents (31.6%) had received the survey from Facebook, 48 respondents (22.3%) from Instagram, 39 respondents (18.1%) from LinkedIn, 38 respondents (17.7%) from Twitter (X) and the final 22 respondents (10.2%) from other sources.

Table 2. Demographic details

Demographics	Category	Frequency	Percentage
Gender	Male	165	76.7
	Female	50	23.3
	Transgender	0	0.0
Age	Between 18-25	55	25.6
	26-35	105	48.8
	36-45	45	20.9
	46 and above	10	4.7
Education Level	Graduate	35	16.3
	Post Graduate/ Masters	145	67.4
	Professional Degree	30	14.0
	Others	5	2.3
Occupation	Student	25	11.6
	Salaried	85	39.5
	Professional	75	34.9
	Self Employed	30	14.0
	Other	0	0.0
Income	Below Rs 25,000	49	22.7
	Rs 25,000- Rs 50,000	55	25.6
	Rs 50,000- Rs 1,00,000	45	20.9
	Above Rs 1,00,000	60	27.9
Social Media Sites	Twitter (X)	38	17.7
	Facebook	68	31.6
	Instagram	48	22.3
	LinkedIn	39	18.1
	Other	22	10.2

Table 3. Validity and reliability

	Composite Reliability	AVE
FL	0.862	0.610
SIC	0.836	0.559
RP	0.869	0.624
HB	0.871	0.631

After collecting survey responses, a reliability test was conducted, with the research variables having a composite reliability above 0.708 as shown in Table 3. A total of 16 indicators were removed in accordance with (Hair et al, 2019)'s recommendation to remove from the construct any indicators with outside loadings between the range of 0.40 and 0.70. After 16 indications have been eliminated from the model, the PLS Algorithm is then run once more with the remaining indicators. The AVE values for the components risk perception (RP), stock influencer credibility (SIC), and herding behavior (HB), on the other hand, are sometimes insufficient or not at a satisfactory value. During the validity pre-testing phase, all three independent variables—financial literacy, stock influencer credibility, and risk perception—as well as the dependent variable in this study—herding behavior—scored above the 0.5 minimum value regarding AVE. This indicates that all the question items in these variables are valid for this study and that large-scale survey distribution can now begin. To increase the AVE values as the given threshold value, 3 indicators must be eliminated as a result, which results in the removal of 19 indicators from the study. Additionally, a validity test was carried out because, according to the reflective measurement paradigm, each indicator represents a different way to look at the same construct. (Fornell & Larcker, 1981) states that "0.4 or less can be acceptable" if the composite reliability is better than 0.60 but the AVE is less than 0.50, as long as the construct's convergent validity is still deemed sufficient. As a result, having AVE values of risk perception (RP), stock influencer credibility (SIC), and herding behavior (HB) that are greater than the 0.50 criterion and greater than the 0.60 threshold, respectively, is regarded sufficient. The study also generated collinearity statistics using the VIF method, which is used to assess the presence of any problematic high-multi collinearity (Schucmacker & Lomax, 2016). Financial Literacy (FL), Stock Influencer Credibility (SIC), and Risk Perception (RP) with Herding Behavior (HB) all had inner VIF values of 1.638, 1.227, and 1.368, respectively, showing no collinearity difficulties amongst the domains (not larger than 4). The study used model-fit testing via NFI to determine the suggested model's Chi-Square value and compare it to an appropriate benchmark. As a result, the NFI generates values between 0 and 1. The fit is better the higher the NFI. NFI values over 0.9 often signify a good match. The model-fit analysis score is only at 0.852, which is below the 0.9 standards. However, (Schucmacker & Lomax, 2016) notes that values close to 0.90 are a "good model fit" in their "Model-fit Criteria and Acceptable Fit Interpretation" section. To determine whether the study model was successful in capturing significant relationships between the variables, Model fit testing through SRMR was also computed. A more conservative definition of a good match is "a value less than 0.10 or 0.08" (Hu & Bentler, 1999). The Model Fit Analysis score is below the 0.08 cut off at 0.075, demonstrating that it is a decent fit for the study. The coefficient of determination (R2 Value), which is derived as the squared correlation between the actual and estimated values of a specific endogenous component, was used in the study to reflect a "structural model's prediction accuracy" (Hair et al., 2014). High prediction accuracy is shown by R2 values that are near to one (1). According to the study's R2 value of 0.313, the influence of all independent variables—financial literacy (FL), stock influencer credibility (SIC), and risk perception (RP)—could result in a variance in herding behavior (HB) of up to 31.3 percent. In order to evaluate the significant effects of removing the exogenous construct on the endogenous construct, the study also tested F-square to measure the change in R2 value [51], "comparing impacts of varying sizes, where 0.04, 0.16, and 0.34 represent the tiny, medium, and big effects of the exogenous latent variable, respectively." The study's f2 value ranged from 0.005 to 0.122, and it "shows small (0.15) effects on herding behavior (HB)".

Hypotheses Testing

Table 4, indicate that five hypotheses have been put out to examine the connection between the independent variables (financial literacy, trustworthiness of stock influencers, and risk perception) and the dependent variable (herding behavior). With a p value of 0.025, the path analysis result supports the validity of hypothesis 1, which states that "the stock influencer credibility has a positive relationship toward investor herding bias." The study found that among Indian investors, herding behavior bias and stock influencer believability have a positive association. Influencers who have a history of making credible suggestions and using the advised product—in this case, influencers who purchase the stock he or she recommended—may be trusted. In the setting of this study, the chance of Indian investors participating in herding behavior increased, as did the legitimacy of the influencers who advised the stocks. The statistical data validate hypothesis 2 of this study, which claimed that Indian investors exhibit herding behavior bias and risk perception are positively correlated (p = 0.012). This outcome supported a study by (Marietza et al, (2023) that found that investors who felt pessimistic about the market would take other investors' suggestions. Investors have a less positive attitude toward the market or have unfavorable feelings toward it when they think there is a large risk associated with participating in it. As a result of the path analysis, however, it is determined that hypothesis 3—according to which investor herding behavior is inversely correlated with financial literacy—is not true (p values of 0.429). According to this study, there is no connection between financial literacy and herding behavior among Indian stock market traders. The findings of the statistical study do not support the findings of the literature (Chairunnisa et al., 2021; Baker et al., 2019; Adil et al.,2021) that the credibility of an influencer has a substantial impact on investors' herding behavior. According to hypothesis 4 of this study, investors' perceptions of risk and the credibility of stock influencers differ in the Indian financial market. The finding that this hypothesis is invalid (p = 0.196) means that it fails to support the findings of [30], which found that the type of information is a factor in how investors perceive risk. The outcome of the hypothesis 5, revealed that there is a valid correlation between investor risk perception and financial literacy, with p = 0.009. The results of this study show that among Indian stock market participants, financial literacy and risk perception are positively correlated. This finding supports a study by (Schucmacker & Lomax, 2016) that indicated highly financially knowledgeable investors are more likely to put their money into high-risk investments to earn a better return. According to Prasad et al., (2020), investor's level of financial awareness affects their risk tolerance can also be confirmed.

Table 4. Summary of hypothesis

	Hypothesis	Path Coefficient	p-Value	Supported
H1	Investor herding behavior is positively correlated with stock influencer believability	0.197	0.023	Yes
H2	Investor risk perception is positively correlated with investor herding behavior	0.477	0.000	Yes
H3	Financial literacy is negatively correlated with investor herding behavior	0.085	0.429	No
H4	Stock influencer credibility is positively correlated with Investor risk perception	-0.110	0.196	No
H5	Financial literacy has a positive relationship with investors' risk perception	0.215	0.009	Yes

Path Coefficient

Table 5, show that risk perception (β=.215) has the strongest direct effect on herding behavior in terms of the route coefficients, highlighting its significant importance. Contrarily, compared to risk perception, Stock Influencer Credibility (β=0.197) shows a relatively less direct effect on herding behavior. Additionally, the analysis shows that stock influencer credibility (β =0.197) has an impact on herding behavior that is both substantial and favourable, with a p-value of 0.23 (α<0.05) showing a statistically significant association between the two variables. The "weakest direct path effects on herding behavior" are associated with financial literacy. Additionally, there is a relationship between financial literacy and herding behavior (β =0.085), although it is not substantial enough to affect it (p=0.429; α >0.05). According to Table 4, when an indirect path (β=0.101) is being taken, the independent variable financial literacy is observed to have a greater coefficient toward herd behavior. Additionally, the new p-value of 0.034 (α <0.05) shows that financial literacy is significant for herding behavior, but only when risk perception is a mediating factor. When mediated, the financial literacy "hypothesis testing" that predicted a "positive relationship with herding behavior" is found to have importance in this scenario. The results are in line with (Xia et al, 2014)'s study, which stated that "an investor with excessive self-confidence may disregard knowledge regarding other people's assets and feel that everything he or she has chosen or done must be genuinely based on his or her ability in financial literacy." This statement means that overconfident investors have a positive risk perception and a "risky" mentality, which leads them to pursue investments on their own accord and are therefore optimists in the financial market.

Table 5. Direct and Indirect relationship

	Direct Path	Indirect Path	p-Value
SIC -> HB	0.197		0.023
FL -> HB	0.085		0.429
RP -> HB	0.215		0.009
FL -> RP -> HB		0.101	0.034
SIC -> RP -> HB		-0.025	0.245

SOLUTION AND RECOMMENDATION

The study's findings may serve as a suggestion or direction for existing and potential investors. The research on herding behavior among Indian individual investors has important management repercussions, in the end. Managers and regulators should implement targeted investor education programs to boost financial literacy, put in place regulatory frameworks to support autonomous decision-making, and foster awareness of risk perception to fight herding behavior. These steps can strengthen investor power, improve the stability of the financial system, and lessen the potential long-term effects of herding behavior. Future researchers should continue using questionnaires to acquire quantitative data, increase the sample size and quantity used, and conduct their studies in every Indian state. Although the variable or construct of financial literacy has been explored in several previous works, this article was unable to identify any correlation between the two variables. Regarding the viability of the variable financial literacy as an independent variable against herding bias and revision of its indicators, more study should be conducted.

FUTURE RESEARCH

Future research should devote more time to examining the variables that affect investors' herding behavior, especially in the Indian stock market, by include additional elements that may skew herding behavior. In addition, several indicators were deleted, suggesting that future research projects may use different types of indicators or measurements. Researchers should think about examining other variables that might offer a completer and more sophisticated picture of investor herding behavior.

CONCLUSION

This study produced information that might be utilized to inform and advise individual investors in the Indian financial market. For both experienced and novice individual investors to understand the herding behavior bias that exists in the Indian financial market, several implications should be taken into account. Given that the main objective of this study is to "determine the relationship between the dependent variable, investors' herding behavior, and the independent factors, which include financial literacy, stock influencers' credibility, and risk perception" in India's financial market, questionnaires were given to respondents in India as part of this study's primary data collection using the author's social media platforms. The results of this study showed that stock influencer credibility is negatively related to Indian investors' perceptions of risk, but financial literacy is positively related to Indian investors' perceptions of risk. The results further confirm the significant and positive relationships between investor herding behavior and all independent variables (stock influencers' credibility and risk perception), except for financial literacy, which was negligible. However, when the path was mediated by the presence of risk perception, the association between financial literacy and herding behavior became substantial. Furthermore, it's critical to recognize that the results can be the result of the study's constraints regarding the questionnaire and its dissemination, the researcher's constrained time for data collection and analysis, and the study's small sample size. Furthermore, because the poll was largely closed-ended and respondents were not required to provide their own unique comments, the author was unable to determine whether this stock recommendation craze will be sustained over time or will simply be impulsive. The author felt that the small number of independent variables accounted indicated that it is not a good fit with the data received and that there is no way to ensure whether the respondents understood the questions or provided accurate answers. Additionally, several indicators were removed to improve reliability and validity.

ACKNOWLEDGMENT

I extend my thanks to Dr Nitu Singhi, Soil Institute of Design, for her hep and encouragement. She has held us in completing the research and study, which resulted in the completion of this chapter. I would also like to thank Dr Meghna Ghosh, BITS Mumbai, for her valuable support and guidance in writing and correction. Finally, I would also like to congratulate Ranchi University for supporting us with its vast collection of books and journals in its library.

REFERENCES

Adil, M., Singh, Y., & Ansari, M. S. (2021). Asian. *Journal of Accounting Research, 7*(1), 17–30. doi:10.1108/AJAR-09-2020-0086

Baker, H. K., Kumar, S., Goyal, N., & Gaur, V. (2019). How financial literacy and demographic variables relate to behavioral biases. *Managerial Finance, 45*(1), 124–146. doi:10.1108/MF-01-2018-0003

Balcilar, M., Demirer, R., & Hammoudeh, S. (2013). Investor herds and regime-switching: Evidence from Gulf Arab stock markets. *Journal of International Financial Markets, Institutions and Money, 23*, 295–321. doi:10.1016/j.intfin.2012.09.007

Bergkvist, L., & Zhou, K. Q. (2016). Zhou. *International Journal of Advertising, 35*(4), 642–663. doi: 10.1080/02650487.2015.1137537

Chairunnisa, A., & Dalimunthe, Z. (2021). Indonesian stock's influencer phenomenon: Did financial literacy on millennial age reduce herding behavior? *Jurnal Akuntansi Dan Keuangan, 23*(2), 62–68. doi:10.9744/jak.23.2.62-68

Chapple, C. (2017). *An Investigation into Viewers' Trust in and Response Towards Disclosed Paid-for-Endorsements by YouTube Lifestyle Vloggers*. https://www.semanticscholar.org/paper/An-Investigation-into-Viewers%E2%80%99-Trust-in-and-Towards-Chapple-Cownie/4ddff3c a932e45e225bdbcbe438546f85725cd14#citing-papers

Djafarova, E., & Rushworth, C. (2017). Exploring the credibility of online celebrities' Instagram profiles in influencing the purchase decisions of young female users. *Computers in Human Behavior, 68*, 1–7. doi:10.1016/j.chb.2016.11.009

Erdogan, B. Z. (1999). Celebrity Endorsement: A Literature Review. *Journal of Marketing Management, 15*(4), 291–314. doi:10.1362/026725799784870379

Erkan, I., & Evans, C. (2016). The influence of eWOM in social media on consumers' purchase intentions: An extended approach to information adoption. *Computers in Human Behavior, 61*, 47–55. doi:10.1016/j.chb.2016.03.003

Fama, E. F. (1965). The behavior of stock-market prices. *The Journal of Business, 38*(1), 34–105. doi:10.1086/294743

Fornell, C., & Larcker, D. F. (1981). Evaluating Structural Equation Models with Unobservable Variables and Measurement Error. *JMR, Journal of Marketing Research, 18*(1), 39–50. doi:10.1177/002224378101800104

Griffin, J. M., Ji, X., & Martin, J. S. (2003). Momentum investing and business cycle risk: Evidence from pole to pole. *The Journal of Finance, 58*(6), 2515–2547. doi:10.1046/j.1540-6261.2003.00614.x

Gul, F., & Khan, K. (2019). An Empirical Study of Investor Attitudinal Factors Influencing Herd Behavior: Evidence from Pakistan Stock Exchange. *Abasyn Journal of Social Sciences*, *12*(1), 1–11. doi:10.34091/AJSS.12.1.01

Gupta, N. E., Kumar, K., & Sinha, K. (2023). The Nexus of War, Violence, and Rights: A History of War-Torn Afghanistan. In Handbook of Research on War Policies, Strategies, and Cyber Wars (pp. 334-351). IGI Global.

Hair, J., Sarstedt, M., Hopkins, L., & Kuppelwieser, G. V. (2014). Article. *European Business Review*, *26*(2), 106–121. doi:10.1108/EBR-10-2013-0128

Hair, J. F., Risher, J. J., Sarstedt, M., & Ringle, C. M. (2019). When to use and how to report the results of PLS-SEM. *European Business Review*, *31*(1), 2–24. doi:10.1108/EBR-11-2018-0203

Halder, D., Pradhan, D., & Chaudhuri, H. R. (2021). Forty-five years of celebrity credibility and endorsement literature: Review and learnings. *Journal of Business Research*, *125*, 397415. doi:10.1016/j.jbusres.2020.12.031

Hirschleifer,J.(1994).Thedarksideoftheforce.*EconomicInquiry*,*32*(1),1–10.doi:10.1111/j.1465-7295.1994.tb01309.x

Hu, L. T., & Bentler, P. M. (1999). P. M. *Structural Equation Modeling*, *6*(1), 1–55. doi:10.1080/10705519909540118

Huston, S. J. (2010). Measuring Financial Literacy. *The Journal of Consumer Affairs*, *44*(2), 296–316. doi:10.1111/j.1745-6606.2010.01170.x

Jaiswal, G., Karmakar, M., & Sinha, K. (2023). Yoga: A Stress Removal Toolkit During War From the Women's Perspective. In Acceleration of the Biopsychosocial Model in Public Health (pp. 137-167). IGI Global.

Jaiswal, G., & Sinha, K. (2023). Yoga: An Ancient Healing Approach for Cyclical Mastalgia. In Perspectives on Coping Strategies for Menstrual and Premenstrual Distress (pp. 237-261). IGI Global.

Kanagasabai, B., & Aggarwal, V. (2020). The Mediating Role of Risk Tolerance in the Relationship between Financial Literacy and Investment Performance. *Colombo Business Journal*, *11*(1), 83–104. doi:10.4038/cbj.v11i1.58

Karmakar, M., Priya, A., Sinha, K., & Verma, M. (2022, December). Shrinkable Cryptographic Technique Using Involutory Function for Image Encryption. In *International Conference on Advanced Network Technologies and Intelligent Computing* (pp. 275-289). Cham: Springer Nature Switzerland.

Kataria, C. D., & Choudhary, S. (2015). Herding behavior in financial market: Critical literature review. *International Research Journal of Commerce Arts and Science*, *6*(12), 16–26.

Kumar, K., Singhania, D., Singh, K. P., Mishra, P., & Sinha, K. (2023). Navigating the Economic Challenges of the Russia-Ukraine Conflict on India. In Handbook of Research on War Policies, Strategies, and Cyber Wars (pp. 218-238). IGI Global. doi:10.4018/978-1-6684-6741-1.ch012

Kumar, S., Jaiswal, G., & Sinha, K. (2023). Skin Cancer Lesion Detection Using Improved CNN Techniques. In Handbook of Research on Technological Advances of Library and Information Science in Industry 5.0 (pp. 355-377). IGI Global.

Lee, Y., Wu, W., & Lee, C. (2021). How COVID-19 triggers our herding behavior? risk perception, state anxiety, and trust. *Frontiers in Public Health*, *9*, 587439. Advance online publication. doi:10.3389/fpubh.2021.587439 PMID:33659231

Mackay, C. (2012). *Extraordinary popular delusions and the madness of crowds*. Simon and Schuster.

Mand, A. A., Janor, H., Rahim, R. A., & Sarmidi, T. (2021). Herding behavior and stock market conditions. *PSU Research Review*, *7*(2), 105–116. doi:10.1108/PRR-10-2020-0033

Marietza, F., Ridwan, N., Santi, F., & Saiful, S. (2023). The Impact of Cultural Shocks on Investor Sentiment and Herding Behavior: An Evidence during COVID-19 Pandemic. *Asian Journal of Economics, Business and Accounting*, 30–50. . doi:10.9734/ajeba/2023/v23i5933

Monetary policy and herding behavior developed market and emerging market comparison. (2021). *Trikonomika Journal*. doi:10.23969/trikonomika.v20i1.1579

Moore, D. (2003). *Technical Report. 03-39*. Social and Economic Sciences Research Center, Washington State University.

Moreira, P. (2008). Stealth Risks and Catastrophic Risks. *Journal of Travel & Tourism Marketing*, *23*(2–4), 15–27. doi:10.1300/J073v23n02_02

Nguyen, L., Gallery, G., Newton, C., & Australasian Accounting, C. (2016). Article. *Business and Finance Journal*, *10*(3), 3–22.

Prasad, S., Kiran, R., & Sharma, R. K. (2020). Influence of financial literacy on retail investors' decisions in relation to return, risk and market analysis. *International Journal of Finance & Economics*, *26*(2), 2548–2559. doi:10.1002/ijfe.1920

Priya, A., Sharma, S., Sinha, K., & Yogesh, Y. (2023, March). Community Detection in Networks: A Comparative study. In *2023 International Conference on Device Intelligence, Computing and Communication Technologies (DICCT)* (pp. 505-510). IEEE. 10.1109/DICCT56244.2023.10110206

Reichelt, J., Sievert, J., & Jacob, F. (2014). Jacob. *Journal of Marketing Communications*, *20*(1–2), 65–81. doi:10.1080/13527266.2013.797758

Sabir, S. A., Mohammad, H. B., & Shahar, H. B. (2019). The Role of Overconfidence and Past Investment Experience in Herding Behaviour with a Moderating Effect of Financial Literacy: Evidence from Pakistan Stock Exchange. *Asian Economic and Financial Review*, *9*(4), 480–490. doi:10.18488/journal.aefr.2019.94.480.490

Sahi, S. K., Arora, A. P., & Dhameja, N. (2013). An exploratory inquiry into the psychological biases in financial investment behavior. *Journal of Behavioral Finance*, *14*(2), 94–103. doi:10.1080/15427560.2013.790387

Schucmacker, R. E., & Lomax, R. G. (2016). *A Beginner's Guide to Structural Equation Modeling* (4th ed.). Routledge.

Singh, R., & Bhattacharjee, J. (2019). Measuring Equity Share Related Risk Perception of Investors in Economically Backward Regions. *Risks*, *7*(1), 12. doi:10.3390/risks7010012

Sinha, K. (2023). The Metaverse and Digital Libraries: Ensuring Safe and Secure Access to Information. In Handbook of Research on Advancements of Contactless Technology and Service Innovation in Library and Information Science (pp. 1-22). IGI Global.

Sivaramakrishnan, S., Srivastava, M., & Rastogi, A. (2017). Attitudinal factors, financial literacy, and stock market participation. *International Journal of Bank Marketing*, *35*(5), 818–841. doi:10.1108/IJBM-01-2016-0012

Summers, L. H. (1986). Does the stock market rationally reflect fundamental values? *The Journal of Finance*, *41*(3), 591–601. doi:10.1111/j.1540-6261.1986.tb04519.x

Sun, R., & Meng, J. (2022). Looking at young millennials' risk perception and purchase intention toward GM foods: Exploring the role of source credibility and risk attitude. *Health Marketing Quarterly*, *39*(3), 263–279. doi:10.1080/07359683.2022.2053805 PMID:35343385

Weismueller, J., Harrigan, P., Wang, S., & Soutar, G. N. (2020). Influencer Endorsements: How Advertising Disclosure and Source Credibility Affect Consumer Purchase Intention on Social Media. *Australasian Marketing Journal*, *28*(4), 160–170. doi:10.1016/j.ausmj.2020.03.002

Xia, T., Wang, Z., & Li, K. (2014). Financial Literacy Overconfidence and Stock Market Participation. *Social Indicators Research*, *119*(3), 1233–1245. doi:10.100711205-013-0555-9

Yang, M., Mamun, A. A., Mohiuddin, M., Al-Shami, S. S. A., & Zainol, N. R. (2021). Predicting Stock Market Investment Intention and Behavior among Malaysian Working Adults Using Partial Least Squares Structural Equation Modeling. *Mathematics*, *9*(8), 873. doi:10.3390/math9080873

KEY TERMS AND DEFINITIONS

Credibility: It pertains to the perceived level of trust or expertise by an investor or individual of any particular disclosures which may impact decision making.

Financial Literacy: It means the skills, knowledge or behaviour that an individual exhibit and applies to various financial scenarios in order to effectively earn, save, invest and budget as well as borrow in terms of money.

Financial Market: Financial markets include any place or system that provides buyers and sellers the means to trade financial instruments, including bonds, equities, the various international currencies, and derivatives.

Herding Behaviour: It is the psychological influence on a person during decision making which influences them to follow the decision of the herd irrespective of their analysis and information.

Investor: Any individual or an organisation that keeps their savings in the safekeeping of another entity with an expectation of return for the risk undertaken.

Risk Perception: It is the individual subjective evaluation of any situation, scenario, or asset which an individual perceives and takes decision based on their risk-taking capabilities.

Social Media Platforms: It consists of those platforms on the internet which provides an individual to share their thoughts, ideas and information's among others and acts as a connection between individuals irrespective of the geographical location.

Chapter 6
Investigating Factors Affecting Artificial Intelligence (AI) Adoption by Libraries at Top-Rated Universities Worldwide

Daniel Tomiuk
University of Quebec in Montreal, Canada

Cataldo Zuccaro
University of Quebec in Montreal, Canada

Michel Plaisent
University of Quebec in Montreal, Canada

Aslı Gül Öncel
https://orcid.org/0000-0001-8740-7361
Galatasaray University, Turkey

Younes Benslimane
York University, Canada

Prosper Bernard
University of Quebec in Montreal, Canada

ABSTRACT

This chapter aims at understanding better the perceptions of academic libraries' top managers with regards to artificial intelligence (AI) and adoption decisions. Building on previous research, this study reports on the relationship between perceived familiarity with AI and the decision-makers' positive adoption attitude regarding AI in libraries. Results indicate that the main issues faced by senior-librarians when considering an AI implementation are the lack of maturity of the commercial solutions offered, security and privacy concerns, the library's core values, its funding capacity, and the need for technical expertise. The most popular AI applications currently implemented are natural language processing and virtual reference librarians (chatbots) while the least popular are robot guides and facial recognition.

DOI: 10.4018/979-8-3693-0807-3.ch006

INTRODUCTION

Economists from the 20th century predicted that emerging technologies would eventually replace labor in various sectors. Industry 4.0, introduced in 2011, reignited discussions with regard to increased automation and smart manufacturing. Current advancements in Artificial Intelligence (AI) are further fueling concerns about technological unemployment, profoundly impacting economies.

In parallel, the rapid advancement of AI has led to its widespread integration across various industries and sectors, including libraries, on a global scale that encompasses both developed and developing nations. While research-oriented institutions in more affluent countries are more likely to embrace AI due to their available resources, libraries worldwide are also undergoing an AI-driven transformation. This involves the utilization of IT tools like smart book chutes, intelligent bookshelves, mobile inventory systems, and self-check-in/out machines. AI's potential positive impacts for libraries are significant and includes virtual services, referencing, cataloguing, collection development, acquisition/technical services, and even instruction.

While the possibility of massive job displacement for librarians remains a topic of discussion, especially as smarter machines with human-like intelligence develop, current research has not extensively explored what other factors influencing decisions about AI adoption in university-libraries. Interestingly, senior librarians do not appear to be deterred by the potential job displacement, as many sources report a notable interest among library decision-makers in adopting AI. Librarians believe that AI may significantly transform their roles, but express little concern about job loss (e.g., Wood & Evans, 2018). The volume of research linking artificial intelligence (AI) to the field of librarianship is currently limited. In contrast to the rapid growth seen in AI research across other disciplines, the information sciences, including librarianship, have not experienced the same level of expansion (Wheatly and Hervieux, 2019).

To gain a deeper understanding of academic librarians' perceptions regarding AI adoption in libraries, an online questionnaire was administered to 106 chief librarians. This paper presents the analysis and findings from their responses.

BACKGROUND

The Economics of Artificial Intelligence

Keynes (1930) coined the term "technological unemployment" referring to the situation where advancements in technology would eventually lead to a reduction in the demand for labor, surpassing our ability to create new employment opportunities at the same pace. The year 2011 saw the introduction of Industry 4.0 by the German Industry-Science Research Alliance (Flynn et al., 2017) where increased automation and the use of smart factories and smart manufacturing processes reignited the conversation concerning technological unemployment. Moreover, current developments in Artificial Intelligence (AI), a rapidly emerging technology, are profoundly impacting economies and are contributing, yet again, in raising questions about technological unemployment.

Today, while technological development improves economies, it also replaces manpower-based jobs. This alters the very nature of employment not only by promoting the formation of new sectors and industries but also the types of jobs that are needed in existing ones. As mentioned by Acemoğlu and Restrepo (2020), Artificial Intelligence (AI) is considered to be among the most innovative of technologies now under development and has the potential to be used in a broad variety of jobs. While it promises to boost productivity, it is also very likely to replace more workers in order to cut expenses.

According to a Goldman Sachs report from July 2023, AI is expected to increase GDP by 7% annually within 10 years. A study conducted by PwC shows that AI is expected to increase global GDP by up to 14% by 2030. PwC expects AI to contribute $15.7 trillion to the global economy by the end of this decade. According to the same PwC report, among all of world's countries, China will achieve the biggest economic gains from AI with an estimated 26% growth in GDP, followed by North America with 14.5% growth (PwC Report, 2023). Acemoglu and Restrepo (2019) argue that technologies such as artificial intelligence are expected to have both displacement- and reinstatement-effects and do not threaten employment and wages. They distinguish between 'so-so' and 'brilliant' technologies, AI and automation being examples of the latter. 'So-so technologies' generate small productivity improvements and thus tend to primarily displace workers as very few new jobs are created. In contrast, AI has the potential to boost labor demand. The substitution of human labor by 'brilliant' technologies can result in significant improvements in productivity leading to new types of jobs (i.e., a reinstatement effect). In other words, contrary to 'so-so' technologies (providing limited productivity gains) which tends to replace workers, 'brilliant' technologies such as AI enabled automation counterbalance this displacement effect though major gains in productivity and the creation of new tasks. The growth in capital accumulation driven by increased AI automation can therefore contribute to a rise in the demand for labor (Acemoglu and Restrepo, 2019).

In the last years, some important studies were conducted to examine the effect of artificial intelligence on the economy. Aghion et al. (2019) explored the possible consequences of AI on the process of economic growth. They speculated on the effects of integrating AI with production technology for generating new ideas. There is a possibility that AI will progressively replace humans in processes requiring idea generation. During their analysis, they explored various aspects of market structure, sectoral reallocations, and firms' organizational structure. Among the insights gained, they observed that AI could potentially discourage future innovation by accelerating imitation processes. Graetz et al. (2022) conducted an analysis of the emerging labor market phenomena with a specific focus on the impact of Artificial Intelligence (AI). Their literature review shows that the influence of technology on the labor market goes beyond just a transformation of the production process. It can also alter the very nature of work by enabling firms and workers to establish new operational relationships.

AI is widely regarded as a driver of productivity and economic growth. Its potential to automate tasks, analyze vast amounts of data, and provide valuable insights has the capacity to enhance efficiency and innovation in various industries. As a result, AI is considered a transformative technology that can contribute significantly to economic development and progress. However, while AI has the potential to bring positive advancements and improvements to various sectors, it can also have a highly disruptive effect on the economy and society. The rapid development and widespread adoption of AI may lead to significant changes in industries, job markets, and even social dynamics, which could present challenges and require careful management and planning. According to a 2018 study conducted by the consulting company Accenture which focused on 12 developed economies representing over 0.5% of the world's economic output, it was projected that by the year 2035, the widespread adoption of AI could potentially lead to a doubling of annual global economic growth rates. This forecast highlights the significant impact that AI could have on the global economy, paving the way for substantial growth and progress (Szczepański, 2018).

However, with the development of technology, many studies show that people face the risk or fear of job loss (Rampersad, 2020; Pouliakas, 2018; Nedelkoska & Quintini, 2018; Brougham & Haar, 2020). Technological progress, including artificial intelligence, robotics, and automation, can have significant impacts on the job market, leading to certain jobs becoming replaced by machines. According to predictions, around 57% of jobs within the OECD could potentially be substituted with technology (Citi Bank, 2016). Using a mixed-method approach (i.e., a quantitative study supported by a subsequent case study), Koo et al. (2021) investigated AI in the hospitality industry. They looked at AI affected job insecurity perceptions using hotel employees in managerial and non-managerial positions. No statistically significant results were found between the two groups of respondents. Findings reveal that perceived job insecurity has a notable impact on perceived job engagement. Additionally, perceived job insecurity indirectly influenced turnover intention, with perceived job engagement acting as a mediator variable in this relationship.

After asking 60 leaders about AI, Krasadakis (2022) concludes that AI may (under some conditions) have an impact on unemployment but can also lead to some new forms of employment and prosperity.

According to Gursen et al (2023), the ongoing transformation of libraries using AI is not only a reality of developed countries but it is also a trend in developing countries as well. Countries such as Pakistan, Malaysia, United Arab Emirates, and Nigeria have all successfully adopted and are using AI for library services. Of course, the financial capacities of institutions in various countries are not equally distributed. Research-oriented universities in developed countries are more likely to adopt AI because such technology can help better address researchers' needs in terms of state-of-the-art tools. Nevertheless, the trend toward AI transformations in libraries is worldwide. In Caribbean libraries, AI will be used in conjunction with other IT tools such as smart book chutes, intelligent book shelves, mobile inventory system and self-check in/out machines, which promise to create new opportunities for improvement (Duncan, 2022).

Definitions and Components

Predictions indicate that AI is poised to permeate virtually all industries, including healthcare (e.g., early detection of diseases), customer service (e.g., personalized assistants), education (e.g., tailored teaching aids), and transportation (e.g., autonomous vehicles), among others. AI is projected to contribute approximately $15.7 trillion to the global economy by 2030 (Kelly et al., 2023).

Hervieux and Wheatley (2021) conducted a survey on how librarians perceive AI in both Canadian institutions (across 24 universities, with 42% of respondents) and top universities in the USA (15 institutions, with 55% of respondents). Their findings indicated that respondents' understanding of AI varies across regions, highlighting the need for better education about AI and additional training. Importantly, they noted a significant interest in AI among managers. As a result, they recommended further research in this area.

However, there is still a lack of agreement on a general definition of AI (Collins, 2021). In their review of past AI studies, Kelly et al. (2023) noted that many studies do not define AI in their papers and many do not even provide a definition of AI to their study's participants. Some authors describe AI as the capacity of a machine to perform tasks or behaviors that were believed to be of the exclusive resort of the human brain (Zhang, 2021; Finley, 2019). Moreover, AI is not static, but rather, adapts to the technological and economic environments. AI is able to learn new concepts/tasks, reason/draw useful conclusions and capable of performing tasks that traditionally required human intelligence (Asemi and Asemi, 2022). Through learning, different AI systems can develop the capacity to respond adequately to unpredictable conditions and events (Ali et al., 2021). Finally, Kelly et al. (2023) define AI "as an unnatural object or entity that possesses the ability and capacity to meet or exceed the requirements of the task it is assigned when considering cultural and demographic circumstances (p.2)".

In recent decades, AI development has continued to flourish because of continued technological advances, namely, improvements in software applications including big data, machine learning, natural language processing, and expert systems (Zhang & Lu, 2021). Improvements have also been made with hardware as well. Specifically, AI development has greatly benefitted from major enhancements in such areas as raw computer power, speech recognition capabilities, robotics, computer vision, grid computing, and the Internet of Things (IOT) (Li et al., 2019; Zhang & Lu, 2021). Other hardware improvements have also played an important role in AI, namely, pressure pad sensors, magic mirrors, and radio frequency identification (Gul & Bano, 2019).

According to Wheeler (2021), the progress of AI development has been rapidly accelerating, leading to its increased integration into various sectors. Notably, AI's presence has become especially pronounced in the domain of image recognition. The author highlights several key points:

i) Rapid Computing Capacity Growth: Before 2012, computing capacity for AI doubled every two years, but since 2012, this capacity has been doubling every three months;
ii) Increasing Adoption: Many companies are experiencing a significant annual increase of 10% in their adoption of artificial intelligence across various aspects of their operations; and
iii) Advancements in Image Recognition: The accuracy of machine-learned image recognition has notably improved, with a more than 20% increase in accuracy over the past six years. It is projected to exceed 90% accuracy in early 2021.

Ali et al. (2021) discuss AI technology from the point of view of library use. Accordingly, the term 'intelligent library' now describes any library that can use information systems to provide knowledge-based services to both library patrons and staff (Asemi & Asemi, 2022).

The idea of creating artificial intelligence systems
in libraries dates back to 1990. These intelligent library systems provide knowledge-
122
Artificial Intelligence in Libraries
based services to both the library staff and patrons (Asemi & Asemi, 2018).
Application of artificial intelligence in library system encompasses descriptive
cataloguing, subject indexing, reference services, technical services, shelf reading,
collection development, information retrieval system etc.

Okunlaya et al. (2022) propose a framework to integrate all aspects of AI relevant for libraries:

i) AI application and functionalities: Expert system (knowledge management), machine learning, robotic, natural language processing, machine vision and speech recognition;
ii) Digital transformation: Technology use (e.g., robotization, monitoring, etc), change of value creation, structural change and financial innovation (e.g., crowd funding); and
iii) Service innovation: Intelligent services offerings and delivery, new user interfaces and technological options.

Oyelude (2021) distinguishes three types of AI applications in libraries: (1) artificial narrow intelligence (ANI), (2) artificial general intelligence (AGI) and (3) artificial superintelligence (ASI). ANI is the type of AI mainly available today. It possesses a relatively weak/narrow range of capabilities (i.e., speech/facial recognition, self-driving vehicles). AGI aims at imitating the intellectual capacities and behaviors of humans (i.e., developing machines with the ability to see/understand/learn as humans do). ASI is still theoretical and encompasses areas of research into machines that surpass human intelligence and capabilities. It has the potential to drive groundbreaking discoveries across general, scientific, academic, creative, and social domains, possibly challenging the need for human involvement (Kelly et al., 2023).

Functionalities and Advantages

Bates (2019) suggests that AI in libraries can be used to reduce boring tasks and perform difficult tasks instead of challenging actual librarian jobs, a view shared by Ex Libris (2019).

One of the most famous developments in AI is ChatGPT, an application that has stoked the curiosity of many and quickly adopted by both private and public institutions and the general public. Lappalainen & Narayanan (2023) have developed a chatbot that promises personalized, fast and cheap support to end-users thus providing human-like dialogue, the ultimate criteria for intelligence according to Turing (1950). Moreover, Li et al (2019) believe that the development of 'Internet Plus' in China, which is analogous to the Information Superhighway and Industry 4.0 (represented by intelligent technologies and Big Data), will offer libraries new opportunities. They expect progress to occur in four (4) areas of personalized service: (i) Spatial integration and extension (where offline services will be expanded online resulting in savings by reducing unnecessary space and personnel cost), (ii) User driven and autonomic service (e.g., the development of more user-led self-services according to their own needs/interests), (iii) Personalized user service (e.g., providing each patron with a different views of the library, better corresponding to his/her needs) and (iv) Diversity of access (i.e., providing ubiquitous connections transcending time and space). Better integration with the Internet will be key in turning digital libraries into smarter environments, supporting several innovations such as innovative modes of book purchasing, Internet plus Maker Spaces, and Digital Service Centers.

According to two independent systematic reviews (Asemi et al., 2021; Collinset al., 2021), the areas of application for Expert systems available to libraries are: i) knowledge-based indexing; ii) natural language processing and abstracting; iii) reference work; iv) cataloging; v) online information retrieval; vi) intelligent interfaces in online information storage and retrieval systems; vii) information needs analysis and representation, including different services, such as classification, indexing and abstracting; viii) reference services; ix) Development of collection; and x) Hypertext and hypermedia. Moreover, Li et al. (2019) argue that AI is expected to enhance libraries in three areas: i) resource construction; ii) information organization; and iii) information services.

Cox et al. (2019) conducted interviews with 33 library managers, consultants, educators and experts from higher education and IT areas mostly from the UK. This work has been influential on many subsequent studies. Although their interviews were conducted in 2017 or five (5) years before the launch of ChatGPT (in November 2022), many of the benefits and capabilities of AI could already be foreseen such as AI's capacity to analyze huge amounts of data to discover patterns which human beings would find difficult to identify or that AI would change how scholarly communications would evolve, going from a decentralized set of journals and conferences to an online network of open services.

Cox & Mazumdar (2022) mention five (5) uses of AI that could be specifically beneficial to library: i) Application of AI to libraries' back-offices (i.e., administration and support) for facilitating routine, clerical and manual tasks (i.e., Robotic Process Automation); ii) library services for users/patrons: Knowledge discovery, collection management, chatbots; iii) Data scientist community creation and support; iv) Data and IA literacy and v) User management.

Harisanty et al. (2022) studied the benefits of AI perceived by 38 participants (11 leaders, 14 researchers and 13 librarians). They concluded that participants generally perceive AI as: i) some kind of a robot, mimicking human intelligence; ii) beneficial, namely for reducing routine and menial tasks; ii) useful in facilitating information search; iii) in providing information services to users; and iv) in supporting library management. The study also reveals that in order to truly benefit from AI, librarians must develop new and adequate skills, thus training is essential. There must also be vision and commitment from management in order to implement AI successfully, through the supply of sufficient budgets, the reduction of resistance to change, installations of updated technology infrastructures and by fostering a philosophy of ongoing and continuous improvement.

Among the chief benefits of AI for libraries, ExLibris (2019) mentions important cost savings and a more effective means of support for users. In a survey conducted by Wood & Evans (2018) with 341 professional librarians, results showed that 56% estimated that AI would have a transformational impact on their role, but were not concerned on its impact in terms of potential job loss. Participants responded that the library services that will reap the most benefits from AI include virtual services (78%), referencing (70%), cataloguing (52%), collection development (34%), acquisition/technical services (33%), and instruction (31%).

Potential Negative Aspects

An AI online generator (https://www.netvouchercodes.co.uk/blog/careers-at-risk-of-being-replaced-by-ai-or-automation#generator) was designed to evaluate whether a type of job is at low/medium/high risk of being replaced by AI and automation. Overall, librarians' jobs remain secure from the threat of AI/automation displacement. The current state of AI technology does not yet possess the sophistication needed to supplant the wisdom and expertise possessed by librarians. They excel in organizing and administering information, aiding patrons in their quest for specific information, supplying guidance for research, and educating users on effective library resource utilization. While AI can assist librarians with particular duties, such as book cataloging, as of now, it is still incapable of effectively substituting the comprehensive expertise and acumen found in the field of librarianship.

However, with continuous enhancements, AI will progressively think, behave and act like humans do (Omane & Alex-Nmecha, 2020). Although AI will definitely result in several improvements for libraries, it is also quite likely to generate new problems as libraires transition to greater reliance on AI. This includes: (i) the possibility of displacing workers by replacing jobs traditionally held by humans, (ii) the risk of propagating misinformation due to a malfunctioning algorithm, (iii) more impersonal service interactions due to a lack of human contact, and (iv) creating a huge dependency on AI for operational tasks such as cataloguing.

Moreover, even if massive job displacement for librarians is not likely to occur in the near future, AI and automation may lead libraries to lose that personal touch and human interaction that traditional libraries are known for. Some patrons (i.e., older, less tech-savvy) may simply prefer to turn to a human librarian for assistance. A research study conducted on AI by Forrester (2017) using a survey of 429 customer service and experience decision makers, found that human employees were still superior in understanding customer emotion and fostering trust in customers. Most respondents preferred hybrid-solutions combining AI technology with human agents allowing enterprises to harness the advantages of both approaches. The study reports that companies that have integrated AI alongside human representatives have observed that their customer service endeavors yielded higher levels of effectiveness in enhancing both customer satisfaction and employee satisfaction (Forrester, 2017). According to Bredeweg and Kragten (2022), hybrid intelligence unites human intelligence with machine intelligence to enhance human capabilities rather than replace them, while also unlocking the full potential of intelligent machines. However, some researchers have questioned whether intelligent machines are truly intelligent when used in practice or whether they are just well trained (Aicardi et al., 2020; Dekel, 2022; Marcus & Davis, 2019). Concerns about AI have been raised regarding the following: (i) specialization - AI systems are highly specialized and excel only in the specific tasks they were designed for and nothing beyond that; (ii) reliability/trustworthiness - software itself typically lacks self-awareness about its own competence, actions, and limitations. Therefore, can AI be trusted to behave ethically?; and (iii) transparency/explanation - can AI provide compelling arguments and insightful explanations for the correctness or viability of its results? Finding the right 'blend' in hybrid solutions can therefore be challenging and experimentation may be needed to achieve success. Additional challenges associated with AI are addressed in section 6 below.

User Acceptance, Utilization, and Attitude

AI acceptance depends on the context in which the AI is being utilized. Kelly et al. (2023) provide a review and synthesis of factors influencing participants' intentions to use AI systems across industries and sectors. Overall, researchers have employed various traditional models to understand user acceptance of AI technology (e.g., Alhashmi et al., 2020; Alzahrani et al., 2017; Andrews et al., 2021; Naidoo, 2023; Yu & Huang, 2020; Wang et al. 20211 Wang et al. 2023). Most frequently, this has included the original or some adaptation of TAM (Technology Acceptance Model - Davis, 1989), the Information Systems (IS) Success Model (Delone & McLean, 2003), and UTAUT (Unified Theory of Acceptance and Use of Technology - Venkatesh et al., 2003).

Yu and Huang (2020) investigated consumers' intentions to use smart libraries using TAM. They found that perceived ease of use positively influenced perceived usefulness and attitude. Perceived usefulness positively influenced attitude and behavioral intentions. Attitude, subjective norms (social influences or opinions), and perceived behavioral control impacted positively on behavioral intentions. Finally, perceived behavioral control behavioral intentions positively influenced actual behavior.

Yuan & Yang (2023) conducted a survey college students and educators across various provinces in China to study the factors that influence college users' readiness to engage with smart services offered by academic libraries. Their conceptual model was rooted in theories such as Uses and Gratifications, Social Cognition Theory, Innovation Diffusion Theory, and the Information Systems Success Model. They found that college users' willingness to participate in smart academic library services is positively influenced by several factors, including users' information needs, their innovative awareness, the performance of the service platform, user satisfaction, library promotion and guidance, as well as extrinsic incentives. Information quality, service platform performance, service quality, and service value also play a significant and positive role in shaping user satisfaction, indirectly affecting users' willingness to engage with smart library services through their impact on user satisfaction. Overall, the research reveals that the primary motivation for college students and teachers to participate in smart library services is to meet their information needs.

Andrews et al.'s (2021) study (based on UTAUT) demonstrated that the intention of librarians to embrace AI and related technologies was significantly influenced by their performance expectations (PE) and their attitudes towards using (ATU) these technologies. However, factors like social influence (SI) and effort expectations (EE) did not exhibit significant effects.

In response to several limitations of earlier technology acceptance models (TAM and UTAUT) when applied to AI technology, Gursoy et al. (2019) introduced the AI Device Use Acceptance model (AIDUA). It focuses on user acceptance of AI agents and involves three stages of users' AI experience assessment: primary appraisal, secondary appraisal, and the outcome stage. In the primary appraisal stage, consumers evaluate the importance of using the AI device, considering factors like social influence, hedonic motivation, and anthropomorphism. Hedonic motivation relates to the pleasure derived from using the AI device, while anthropomorphism concerns the human-like qualities the device may possess. Following this appraisal, users assess the AI device's benefits and costs based on perceived performance expectancy and effort expectancy, ultimately influencing their emotional response to the AI and the subsequent (un)willingness to use the AI.

Generally, AI is a broad and rapidly evolving field, and librarians may have different levels of expertise and awareness about its applications and implications. Ex Libris (2019) conducted a survey revealing that, despite 80% of librarians actively searching for information on how to effectively use AI, only 5% had or were currently implementing it in their workplace. Hervieux & Wheatley (2021) performed a study on the perception of librarians regarding AI. Respondents were from Canada (24 universities and 42% of respondents) and 15 top American universities (55% of respondents). They noted a great interest for the topic from managers. They also found that the concept of AI is not well understood by librarians and concluding that additional training would be needed and that more research should be conducted in this area.

Huang (2022) studied AI by surveying 472 academic Taiwan librarians. The main finding was that a positive relationship was identified between the degree of knowledge activities performed by the librarians and their attitude toward AI. Findings also revealed that, among AI applications in academic libraries, the three (3) most frequently adopted are automatic indexing and classification, intelligent data analysis for collection management, and intelligent data analysis for circulation management. Additionally, results indicate what AI-enabled applications that libraries are keen on implementing in the near future. These are guide-robots for libraries, intelligent analysis for circulation management, natural language processing, and machine learning tools to facilitate searching databases, and facial recognition technology for book borrowing and returns.

Huang's (2022) study also shows that librarians do not perceive AI as a threat to their jobs. Consequently, the primary impediments to the adoption of AI applications in academic libraries are seemingly rooted in factors other than job displacement concerns. These are discussed in the following section.

Challenges

Implementing AI in companies can offer numerous benefits, but it also comes with several challenges and considerations.

Dwivedi et al. (2021) distinguishes among many types of challenges: i) social, national and cultural; ii) ethical; iii) economic (affordability); iv) data related (namely bias); v) organizational and managerial; vi) technological (namely related to implementation and expertise); (vii) legal and/or political.

The first is data collection and data quality. AI systems rely on high-quality data for training and decision-making. Relevant data must be made readily available for AI to perform adequately. Some organizations wanting to implement AI may find it a struggle to collect, clean, and maintain large volumes of data (Khan et al., 2023). AI systems also require continuous learning and adaptation to remain effective. Organizations must allocate sufficient resources to monitor and update AI systems as needed.

There are also ethical concerns. If AI systems are trained on data containing biases, the systems themselves are likely to perpetuate those same biases through their search results and recommendations. AI algorithms trained on biased data may result in discrimination against marginalized communities and individuals of diverse backgrounds (Manyika et al., 2019).

Data privacy is also important. Customer and company data may be sensitive. Measures must be put in place to protect against data breaches and misuse (Huang, 2022). Compliance with data protection regulations such as GDPR in the EU, PIPEDA in Canada, and HIPAA in the US is essential.

Huang's (2022) results showed that librarians employed in libraries using AI applications identified information security and privacy concerns as significant concerns. Other concerns identified as possible obstacles to the advancement of AI applications in academic libraries include the scarcity of AI experts within library teams and the substantial development costs.

A lack of a skilled AI workforce, including software engineers, data scientists, machine learning engineers, and AI researchers is likely to cause organizations to fall behind in AI adoption. Finding and retaining skilled professionals can be challenging and costly (Owens, 2022). Omane & Alex-Nmecha (2020) mention that a lack of technical knowledge, namely the complexity of their development given the lack of experts and lack of adequate funding namely to develop and maintain AI systems are some of the most serious challenges that organizations face with implementing AI. Msauki (2021) examined how technology 4.0 can provides new opportunities for AI technologies but also recognizes the challenges it faces, namely funding, the capacities of communication infrastructures, and the lack of technical skills and the resistance to change. Indeed, the cost of developing and deploying AI systems can be expensive. Organizations must invest in infrastructure, software, hardware, and ongoing maintenance, which can strain budgets. Even a very basic version of an AI system for video/speech analysis can cost between $36 and $56 thousand USD (Likhadzed & Klubnikin, 2023). Costs may include integration with legacy systems, which can be complex. Ensuring that AI solutions work seamlessly with existing software and processes is a common challenge and may necessitate extensive modifications or even complete overhauls of the system and even the way the organization operates.

Change management is therefore also a concern. Implementing AI is likely to require changes in workflows and processes (Lemos et al., 2022). Employees and customers/patrons may resist such changes, and organizations need effective change management strategies to facilitate adoption of AI technologies.

Aside from technical skills, AI will also require new competencies. According to Gul et al. (2019), libraries play a new role in society which will necessitate new competencies such as procuring content (licensing), data quality control, data curation (preservation), teaching AI usage and information evaluation. Wheatly and Hervieux (2019) explored the role of librarians in a future dominated by AI. One significant aspect of this role is their involvement in educating and reaching out to their institutions' communities on AI-related subjects. While only a small number of libraries presently provide AI-focused programming or initiatives, such as speaker series and workshops, it is clear that AI will fundamentally alter how people seek information. Consequently, libraries have a valuable opportunity to position themselves as leaders in AI education (Wheatly and Hervieux, 2019).

Overcoming these challenges requires careful planning, a commitment to ongoing learning and improvement, and a clear understanding of the potential benefits that AI can bring to the organization.

ANALYSIS AND FINDINGS

Method and Data Collection

To understand better the perceptions of academic librarians with regards to AI adoption in libraries, an online questionnaire was developed composed of 27 questions covering the following areas:

i) Knowledge about the AI concept;
ii) Challenges/factors and their importance in the decision to adopt or not AI in the library; Huang (2022); Omame & Alex-Nmecha (2020);
iii) Actual state of adoption of AI and its potential applications: Huang (2022); Oyelude (2021); Asemi et al. (2019); ex Libris (2019); Omame & Alex-Nmecha (2020);
iv) Attitudes toward AI: Wheatley and Hervieux (2019); Zhang & Dafoe (2019).

The questions of the online questionnaire employed the same wording used Huang (2022) in order to facilitate the comparison results.

Email invitations to participate in the survey were sent to the first 1411 universities appearing on the list of QS World University Rankings and addressed to the chief manager of the library. These universities represent 109 countries and our sample was made up of 14% of respondents from US, 6% from the UK, 5% from China, 4% from Japan, 3.4% from Russia, and 3.3% from Germany. This accounted for about 35% of the overall sample. These universities were chosen because we expected them to be the ones with the greatest concern for AI applications. We compiled a list and proceeded with recruitment. Unfortunately, forty (40) solicitation emails did not reach their intended recipients among the 1411 schools we selected to contact. Due to the choice of highly-ranked universities (the best among the rankings), we recognize that our analysis and conclusions cannot be considered as representative of all universities but instead should be interpreted as the practices among the best universities worldwide.

We received 106 completed questionnaires which were used as the basis for the subsequent analyses. Thus, the response rate was 7.5% which is remarkable given that these universities are often solicited to participate in research studies and also because invitation emails were sent during the summer when many administrative staff are on holidays.

Profile of Respondents

The majority of the 106 respondents were working for medium-sized (55.7%) or large university (35.8%). The majority of respondents were women (52.4%). Of the remainder, less than half were men (46.7%) and 1% of respondents classified themselves as "other". By far, the largest age group (70% of respondents) was "middle-aged" (between 40 and 60) and 20% were over 60. Respondents' age demographics were not surprising given that they reflected the fact that respondents were supervisors (e.g., chief librarians, senior managers).

Interestingly, distributions along gender were similar, and more so for medium- and large-sized schools (see Table 1). Preliminary analysis showed that gender did not play a role according to university size. According to our sample, women and men share the same level of responsibility whatever the size of the university (X^2 = 1.919, sig. = .751).

Table 1. Gender of respondents and university size

	Gender of Respondent			
Size	Female	Male	Other	Total
Small	6	3	0	9
Medium	28	29	1	58
Large	21	17	0	38
Total	55	49	1	105

Data Analysis

Familiarity of Respondents With Artificial intelligence

Respondents' degree of familiarity is high. It can be seen that, except for about 7 respondents out of 106, mostly all respondents were familiar with AI (93.4%) and 43.4% described themselves as being very familiar with it.

The mean response for women on the familiarity scale (where 1 is not all familiar and 5 extremely familiar) The difference between the means for women and men is not statistically significant (t_0 = -.672, sig. =.252). We can thus conclude that there is no statistical difference between men and women with regards to their level of familiarity with AI.

Similarly, a one-way analysis of variance found no statistical difference between age groups and level of familiarity (Fo = 1.507, sig. = .206).

Attitude of Respondents Toward Artificial Intelligence

Attitude was measured on a continuum varying from 0 (entirely opposed to AI) to 100 (entirely positive attitude toward AI). The mean for our respondents was 76.41 (std. dev. = 15), indicating a very positive opinion among respondents towards AI. Men and women answered in a similar fashion, with women having a slightly more positive attitude towards AI but the difference is not significantly (t_0 = -.439; sig. Results of one-way analysis of variance also confirm that there are no statistical differences in attitudes towards AI and age (F_0 = .528, sig. .715). Similarly results of one-way analysis of variance also confirm that there are no statistical differences in attitudes towards AI and size of the organization (F_0 = 1.276, sig. = .715).

Finally, regression analysis was conducted on attitude towards AI (scale from 0 to 100) with level of familiarity with AI and usage volume as the independent variables. The results are presented in Table 2.

Table 2. Results of regression analysis

			Standardized Coefficients
Variables	**B**	**Std. Error**	**Beta**
(Constant)	53.431	7.417	
Familiarity with AI	5.793	2.219	0.277
Usage volume	1.465	0.974	0.016
r2= 1.31, F=6.491, sig=.002			

The model explains 13.1% (r^2) of the variability of attitude towards AI and it is statistically significant (sig. = .002). An analysis of the parameters of the model reveals that the level of familiarity with AI has a significant and positive effect on the attitude towards AI. The slope is 5.793 with a .001 level of significance. This means that for every additional level of familiarity with AI (from 1 not all familiar to 5 extremely familiar, the attitude towards AI increases by five points (on a scale from 0, extremely negative to 100, extremely positive). the slope of the variable, usage volume is 1.465 with a level of significance of .136. This means that there is no statistical dependence between usage volume and the attitude towards AI. Thus, one can conclude that the attitude towards AI reaches very quickly a level of positivity. Once the attitude is formed it does not improve as the volume of use though the introduction of new AI functions increases.

Challenge Factors and the Decision to Adopt AI in Libraries

Table 2 presents the main factors related to the decision to adopt AI. Accordingly, security of information and maturity of applications and the incorporation of library's core values were judged most important for adoption decisions, more important than cost or other technological considerations. Alignment with trends was judged to be least influential on chief librarians' decisions to adopt AI.

Table 3. Relative importance of the challenge factors in the decision to adopt AI

Factor (5=Very Important, 1=Not at All Important)	Median	Mode	Mean	Std. Deviation
Information security/privacy concerns	5	5	4.45	.855
Maturity and reliability of AI applications, complexity to operate	4	4	4.02	.836
Incorporating library core values	4	5	4.02	.971
Funding/cost associated with implementation	4	5	3.98	1.028
Expected labor, time and energy	4	4	3.91	.822
Acceptance by users (attractiveness, function, convenience)	4	5	3.89	1.059
Support and planning of the university	4	5	3.88	1.098
Lack of technological expertise	4	4	3.85	.988
Librarians' willingness and experience	4	5	3.71	1.051
Alignment with technological trends	4	3	3.59	1.011

Factor analysis is a statistical technique employed to condense a substantial set of variables into a smaller number of factors while maintaining as much of the original data's variability as possible. It is particularly useful in data reduction and simplification given that it helps researchers to identify patterns and relationships among variables. The identification of such relationships can help them gain insights into underlying constructs or dimensions within the data. In essence, factor analysis seeks to discover the latent/unobservable factors that contribute to the observed correlations or patterns among variables (Taherdoost et al., 2014). Researchers use this technique in various fields, including psychology, sociology, economics, and marketing to uncover underlying structures that drive observed behaviors or phenomena.

A factor analysis employing principal component extraction was conducted on ten challenge items or constraints in the decision to adopt AI in libraries. The rotated component structure contained important deviations from Thurstone's simple structure. The matrix possessed several items that loaded on serval components. To resolve this problem, it is suggested to remove the unstable items from the analysis. There is no consensus as to the appropriate cut-off value of the factor loading. Stevens (1992) recommends utilizing a cutoff value of 0.4 (in absolute value) for interpretive purposes regardless of sample size. Other researchers have proposed a cut-off value of .7 (in absolute value). Considering our sample, a cut-off value of .5 was employed. The final structure in presented in Table. 4

Table 4. Factorial analysis: Rotated matrix

	Component 1	Component 2
	Internal Issues	**External Issues**
Lack of technological expertise	0.775	0.125
Funding/cost associated with implementation	0.729	-0.122
Expected labor, time and energy	0.628	0.232
Information security / privacy concerns	0.212	0.695
Alignment with technological trends	-0.209	0.677
Maturity & reliability of applications, complexity to operate	0.178	0.604
Eignen value	1.815	1.223
Percentage of variance explained	**30.24**	**20.38%**
Extraction Method: Principal Component Analysis		
Rotation Method: Varimax with Kaiser Normalization		
a Rotation converged in 3 iterations.		

The rotated matrix shows two components (factors) that are conceptually related to the reality of AI in libraries. The first factor can be named "internal issues" since it groups the expected time and effort to choose among many technologies and implementation. This is not surprising given the lack of technical expertise in AI tools by the IT staff in even the largest universities. Also, one must also consider the fact that a transition to AI is costly and requires appropriate funding. This factor describes perfectly the internal issues or challenges that need to be addressed when introducing AI in libraries.

The second factor can be named "external issues" as they are not under the control of the library contrary to the previous factor (internal issues). This factor integrates several important elements such as the need to follow technological trends despite the relative immaturity of the technology, the complexity of operations of the AI products available (namely their capacity to respect confidentiality) and the need to guarantee the security of data.

These two factors describe eloquently the complex internal and external dynamics of adopting AI and related technologies in university libraries. These two internal and external pressures are real and have been considered important by the respondents of our study.

Current State of Adoption

This section presents the actual degree of implementation using the following scale (1=already implemented and operational, 2=implementation in progress, 3=not planned but keeping an eye, 4=not planned for now, 5=not considered at all). The lower the number, the most advanced the AI application at the respondent's library. Table 5 summarizes respondents' current state of AI adoption in libraries, by descending order. Results indicate that, in 2023, university libraries have already implemented or are implementing three AI applications: natural language processing (10.4%+15.1%), virtual reference librarians (9.5%+12.4%), and automatic indexing and classification (3.8%+13.5%).

Table 5. Summarizes respondents state of adoption for each application

For Each Possible Application: Number (and Valid %, i.e., Excluding Missing Observations) of Respondents	Already Implemented and Operational	Implementation in Progress	Not Planned for Now but Keeping an Eye on It	Not Planned for Now	Not at All Considered
Natural language processing and machine learning tools to improve database searches	11 (10.4%)	16 (15.1%)	56 (52.8%)	18 (17.0%)	5 (4.7%)
Virtual reference librarians (chatbots)	10 (9.5%)	13 (12.4%)	57 (54.3%)	18 (17.1%)	7 (6.7%)
Intelligent data analysis for collection management	5 (4.7%)	10 (9.4%)	61 (57.5%)	22 (20.8%)	8 (7.5%)
Automatic indexing and classification	4 (3.8%)	14 (13.5%)	51 (49.0%)	27 (26.0%)	8 (7.7%)
Intelligent data analysis for circulation management	4 (3.8%)	8 (7.6%)	53 (50.5%)	31 (29.5%)	9 (8.6%)
Intelligent search applications for use in an institutional depository	5 (4.8%)	11 (10.5%)	47 (44.8%)	23 (21.9%)	19 (18.1%)
Automatic navigation systems for libraries	6 (5.7%)	10 (9.4%)	38 (35.8%)	35 (33.0%)	17 (16.0%)
Other administrative work	6 (6.5%)	5 (5.4%)	25 (27.2%)	29 (31.5%)	27 (29.3%)
Intelligent applications for makerspaces	2 (1.9%)	3 (2.9%)	31 (29.5%)	37 (35.2%)	32 (30.5%)
Guide robot for the library	0 (0.0%)	5 (4.8%)	23 (21.9%)	40 (38.1%)	37 (35.2%)
Facial recognition for checking books in and out	2 (1.9%)	3 (2.9%)	18 (17.3%)	27 (26.0%)	54 (51.9%)

The first six applications were either already implemented or were being kept an eye on, while the five last were not planned and some (like facial recognition) were simply not being considered or are considered less pressing for immediate implementation in future projects.

FUTURE RESEARCH SUGGESTIONS

AI is a disruptive technology that is expected to transform many industries and libraries won't escape the movement. Most of the AI applications actually mentioned will make their way along with greater knowledge of these technologies by managers, availability of skilled technician and a new generation of fresh men from Libraries and Information Sciences Schools. Since all issues mentioned above won't get resolved immediately, more researches are needed on many aspects: what are the new tools to implement? What are the criteria who can help to choose? How to compute the benefits? how to implement these technologies? Is it only a question of funding or also some resistance to change as so often encountered by the replacement of old practices by new approaches, methods and tools. Despite AI can improve human work and speed it is there a lost of richness in the process? Clearly further research is needed.

CONCLUSION

Studies into whether AI adoption can beneficial to academic libraries have produced positive results. Additional studies now have to determine when and how to proceed. This paper presents the analysis and results of a survey conducted using 106 senior-librarians of the top 1400 universities around the world according to a 2023 survey. They show that decision-makers are relatively well-informed about AI and have a positive attitude toward implementing it in their libraries. A significant relationship was empirically demonstrated between these two constructs.

As of 2023, the two most popular AI applications that are already operational in university-libraries are natural language processing and virtual reference librarians (i.e., chatbots) while those considered to be the least urgent in terms of future implementation projects are facial recognition and robot-guides.

Our findings corroborate previous studies that find that library managers consider several factors before deciding whether or not to adopt AI. The first factor is related to internal (organizational) pressures; lack of technological expertise, high cost of funding AI implementation and time and costs of effort. The second factor is related to external pressure: issues with information security and privacy, alignment with technological trends and the lack of maturity of AI applications in university libraries.

This study suffers from several limitations. It is, of course, a reflection of the situation at one point in time. The state of affairs will change over time. Secondly, the definition and meaning of artificial intelligence is notoriously difficult to define as it is a general term which encompasses a broad spectrum of technologies, approaches and algorithms (some of which have not been invented yet). This study employed a rather general definition of the term.

Also, artificial intelligence (AI) has evolved (and will continue to do so) and will mean different things over time due to several factors including technological advancements, expanding subareas of study further broadening the range of applications and technologies associated with AI, changing societal expectations, and ethical considerations (e.g., whether "smart machines" are conscious and sentient and whether they should be afforded rights). If AI continues to evolve quickly (like Chat GPT did conquering the market in less than 3 years), the generalizability of the results from studies such as this one may be limited. Another limitation in terms of generalizability comes from the relatively limited number of participants in our study. The sample was collected from the top universities and it is possible that our findings are not applicable to smaller, less renowned universities. Nevertheless, AI adoption and AI applications in academic libraries are important areas of study that are currently under-researched. Libraries have been significantly affected by AI, and will continue to be. They are already experiencing important transformations as a result of artificial intelligence and related technologies.

REFERENCES

Acemoglu, D., & Restrepo, P. (2016). *The race between machine and man: Implications of technology for growth, factor shares and employment (No. w22252)*. National Bureau of Economic Research. doi:10.3386/w22252

Acemoglu, D., & Restrepo, P. (2019). *Artificial Intelligence, Automation, and Work*. University of Chicago Press. https://www.nber.org/chapters/c14027

Acemoglu, D., & Restrepo, P. (2020, March). The wrong kind of AI? Artificial intelligence and the future of labour demand. *Cambridge Journal of Regions, Economy and Society*, *13*(1), 25–35. doi:10.1093/cjres/rsz022

Aghion, P., Jones, B. F., & Jones, C. I. (2019). *Artificial Intelligence and Economic Growth*. University of Chicago Press. https://www.nber.org/chapters/c14015

Aicardi, C., Bitsch, L., Datta Burton, S., Evers, L., Farisco, M., & Mahfoud, T. (2020). *Trust and Transparency in Artificial Intelligence*. Technical report D12.5.4, Human Brain Project SGA2. Available at: https://www.humanbrainproject.eu/

Alhashmi, S. F. S., Salloum, S. A., & Abdallah, S. (2020). Document details - Critical Success Factors for Implementing Artificial Intelligence (AI) Projects in Dubai Government United Arab Emirates (UAE) Health Sector: Applying the Extended Technology Acceptance Model (TAM). *Advances in Intelligent Systems and Computing*, *1058*, 393–405. doi:10.1007/978-3-030-31129-2_36

Ali, M. Y., Naeem, S. B., & Bhatti, R. (2021). Artificial Intelligence (AI) in Pakistani University Library Services. *Library Hi Tech News*, *38*(8), 12–15. doi:10.1108/LHTN-10-2021-0065

Allison, D. (2012). Chatbots in the library: Is it time? *Library Hi Tech*, *30*(1), 95–107. doi:10.1108/07378831211213238

Andrews, J. E., Ward, H., & Yoon, J. (2021). UTAUT as a model for understanding intention to adopt AI and related technologies among librarians. *Journal of Academic Librarianship*, *47*(6), 102437. doi:10.1016/j.acalib.2021.102437

Asemi, A., & Asemi, A. (2018). Artificial Intelligence (AI) Application in Library Systems in Iran: A Taxonomy Study. *Library Philosophy and Practice (e-journal)*. Retrieved from digitalcommons.unl.edu/cgi/viewcontent.cgi?article=5134&context=libphilprac

Asemi, A., Ko, A., & Nowkarizi, M. (2020). Intelligent libraries: A review on expert systems, artificial intelligence, and robot. *Library Hi Tech, 39*(2), 412–434. doi:10.1108/LHT-02-2020-0038

Bates, M. E. (2019). *White paper: Insight as a service: Info pros and artificial intelligence.* Springer Nature. Available at: https://media.springernature.com/full/ springer-cms-preview/rest/v1/content/16773852/data/v1

Brougham, D., & Haar, J. (2020).Technological disruption and employment: The influence on job insecurity and turnover intentions: A multi-country study. *Technological Forecasting and Social Change, 161.* doi:10.1016/j.techfore.2020.120276

Citi Bank. (2016). *Technology At Work v2.0; The Future Is Not What It Used To Be.* Retrieved from https://www.oxfordmartin.ox.ac.uk/downloads/reports/Citi_GPS_Technology_Work_2.pdf

Collins, C., Dennehy, D., Conboy, K., & Mikalef, P. (2021). Artificial intelligence in information systems research: A systematic literature review and research agenda. *International Journal of Information Management, 60*, 102383. doi:10.1016/j.ijinfomgt.2021.102383

Cox, A. M., & Mazumdar, S. (2022). Defining artificial intelligence for librarians. *Journal of Librarianship and Information Science.*

Cox, A. M., Pinfield, S., & Rutter, S. (2019). The intelligent library: Thought leaders' views on the likely impact of artificial intelligence on academic libraries. *Library Hi Tech, 37*(3), 418–435. doi:10.1108/LHT-08-2018-0105

Davis, F. D. (1989). Perceived Usefulness, Perceived Ease of Use, and User Acceptance of Information Technology. *Management Information Systems Quarterly, 13*(3), 319–340. doi:10.2307/249008

Dekel, R. (2023). Despite How the Media Portrays It, AI Is Not Really Intelligent. Here's Why. *Entrepreneur – Science & Technology.* Available at: https://www.entrepreneur.com/science-technology/despite-how-the-media-portrays-it-ai-is-not-really/446894#:~:text=the%20training%20data.-,It%20is%20important%20to%20recognize%20that%20AI%20is%20not%20truly,decisions%20based%20on%20common%20sense

DeLone, W. H., & McLean, E. (2003). The Delone and McLean Model of Information Systems Success: A Ten-Year Update. *Journal of Management Information Systems, 19*(4), 9–30. doi:10.1080/07421222.2003.11045748

Duncan, A. S. P. (2022). The intelligent academic library: Review of AI projects & potential for Caribbean libraries. *Library Hi Tech News, 39*(5), 12–15. doi:10.1108/LHTN-01-2022-0014

Dwivedi, Y. K., Hughes, L., Ismagilova, E., Aarts, G., Coombs, C., Crick, T., . . . Williams, M. D. (2021). Artificial Intelligence (AI): Multidisciplinary perspectives on emerging challenges, opportunities, and agenda for research, practice and policy. *International Journal of Information Management, 57*, 101994.

Ex Libris. (n.d.). *Artificial Intelligence in the Library: Advantages, Challenges and Tradition.* An Ex Libris Whitepaper. Retrieved July 11, 2020 https://cdn2.hubspot.net/hubfs/2909474/Ex%20Libris%20Artificial%20Intelligence%20 White%20Paper.pdf

Finley, T. K. (2019). The democratization of artificial intelligence: One library's approach. *Information Technology and Libraries*, *38*(1), 8–13. doi:10.6017/ital.v38i1.10974

Flynn, J., Dance, S., & Dirk Schaefer, D. (2017)1 Industry 4.0 and its Potential Impact on Employment Demographics in the UK. *5th International Conference on Manufacturing Research (ICMR).*

Forrester. (2017). *Artificial Intelligence with the Human Touch - Blend AI with Human Agents to Improve Both Customer and Agent Satisfaction*. Retrieved September 15, 2023 from https://www.genesys.com/resources/artificial-intelligence-with-the-human-touch

Graetz, G., Restrepo, P., & Skans, O. N. (2022). Technology and the labor market. *Labour Economics*, *76*. doi:10.1016/j.labeco.2022.102177

Gul, S., & Bano, S. (2019). Smart libraries: An emerging and innovative technological habitat of 21st century. *The Electronic Library*, *37*(5), 764–783. doi:10.1108/EL-02-2019-0052

Gürsen, A. E., Öncel, A. G., Plaisent, M., Benslimane, Y., & Bernard, P. (2023). Artificial Intelligence Utilization in Libraries. *Athens Journal of Sciences, 10*(2), 83-94.

Harisanty, D., Anna, N. E. V., Putri, T. E., Firdaus, A. A., & Noor Azizi, N. A. (2022). Leaders, practitioners and scientists' awareness of artificial intelligence in libraries: A pilot study. *Library Hi Tech*. Advance online publication. doi:10.1108/LHT-10-2021-0356

Hervieux, S., & Wheatley, A. (2021). Perceptions of artificial intelligence: A survey of academic librarians in Canada and the United States. *Journal of Academic Librarianship*, *47*(1), 102270. doi:10.1016/j.acalib.2020.102270

Huang, Y. H. (2022). Exploring the implementation of artificial intelligence applications among academic libraries in Taiwan. *Library Hi Tech*. Advance online publication. doi:10.1108/LHT-03-2022-0159

Kelly, S., Kaye, S.-A., & Oviedo-Trespalacios, O. (2023). What Factors Contribute to the Acceptance of Artificial Intelligence? A Systemic Review. *Telematics and Informatics*, *77*, 101925. doi:10.1016/j.tele.2022.101925

Keynes, J. M. (1930). Economic Possibilities for our Grandchildren. Essays in Persuasion, 358-373.

Khan, B., Fatima, H., Qureshi, A., Kumar, S., Hanan, A., Hussain, J., & Abdullah, S. (2023). Drawbacks of Artificial Intelligence and Their Potential Solutions in the Healthcare Sector. *Biomedical Materials & Devices*, 1-8. doi:10.1007/s44174-023-00063-2

Koo, B., Curtis, C., & Ryan, B. (2021). Examining the impact of artificial intelligence on hotel employees through job insecurity perspectives. *International Journal of Hospitality Management*, *95*. doi:10.1016/j.ijhm.2020.102763

Krasadakis, G. (2022). *60 Leaders on Artificial Intelligence*. https://krasadakis.medium.com/60-leaders-on-artificial-intelligence-d1be5b27431b

Lappalainen, Y., & Narayanan, N. (2023). Aisha: A Custom AI Library Chatbot Using the ChatGPT API. *Journal of Web Librarianship*, *17*(3), 1–22. doi:10.1080/19322909.2023.2221477

Lemos, S.I.C., Ferreira, F.A.F., Zopounidis, C., Galariotis, E., & Ferreira, N.C.M.Q.F. (2022). Artificial Intelligence and Change Management in Small and Medium-Sized Enterprises: An Analysis of Dynamics Within Adaptation Initiatives. *Annals of Operations Research*, 1-27. . doi:10.1007/s10479-022-05159-4

Li, S., Hao, Z., Ding, L., & Xu, X. (2019). Research on the application of information technology of Big Data in Chinese digital library. *Library Management*, *40*(8/9), 518–531. doi:10.1108/LM-04-2019-0021

Libris, E. (2019). *How AI Can Enhance the Value of Research Libraries*. Retrieved from https://www.libraryjournal.com/story/how-ai-can-enhance-the-value-of-research-libraries

Likhadzed, V., & Klubnikin, A. (2023). *How Much does Artificial Intelligence Cost? Well, it Depends*. ItrexGroup.

Manyika, J., Silberg, J., & Presten, B. (2019). What do we do About the Biases in AI? *Harvard Business Review*. Available on: https://hbr.org/2019/10/what-do-we-do-about-the-biases-in-ai

Marcus, G., & Davis, E. (2019). *Rebooting AI: Building Artificial Intelligence We can Trust*. Pantheon Press.

Msauki, G. (2021). Library 4.0 and sustainable development: Opportunities and challenges. *Examining the impact of industry 4.0 on academic libraries*, 31-44.

Naidoo, D. T. (2023). Integrating TAM and IS Success Model: Exploring the Role of Blockchain and AI in Predicting Learner Engagement and Performance in E-learning. *Frontiers of Computer Science*, *18*(Sept), 5. doi:10.3389/fcomp.2023.1227749

Nedelkoska, L., & Quintini, G. (2018). *Automation, skills use and training*. OECD Social, Employment and Migration Working Papers, No. 202. Paris: OECD Publishing. http://dx.doi.org/ doi:10.1787/1815199X

Nelson, R. R., & Phelps, E. S. (1966). Investment in humans, technological diffusion, and economic growth. *The American Economic Review*, *56*(1/2), 69–75.

Okunlaya, R. O., Syed Abdullah, N., & Alias, R. A. (2022). Artificial intelligence (AI) library services innovative conceptual framework for the digital transformation of university education. *Library Hi Tech*, *40*(6), 1869–1892. doi:10.1108/LHT-07-2021-0242

Omame, I. M., & Alex-Nmecha, J. C. (2020). Artificial intelligence in libraries. In *Managing and adapting library information services for future users* (pp. 120–144). IGI Global. doi:10.4018/978-1-7998-1116-9.ch008

Owens, H. (2022). AI Experts are in Short Supply. That's Making the Skills Crisis Worse. *ZD Net/Business*. Available on: https://www.zdnet.com/article/ai-experts-are-in-short-supply-thats-making-the-skills-crisis-worse/

Oyelude, A. A. (2021). AI and libraries: Trends and projections. *Library Hi Tech News*, *38*(10), 1–4. doi:10.1108/LHTN-10-2021-0079

Pouliakas, K. (2018). *Determinants of automation risk in the EU labour market: A skills-needs approach*. IZA Discussion paper series, No. 11829. Bonn: Institute of Labor Economics (IZA). http://ftp.iza.org/dp11829.pdf

PwC Report. (2023). Retrieved from https://www.pwc.com/gx/en/issues/analytics/assets/pwc-ai-analysis-sizing-the-prize-report.pdf

Rampersad, G. (2020). Robot will take your job: Innovation for an era of artificial intelligence. *Journal of Business Research, 116*, 68–74. doi:10.1016/j.jbusres.2020.05.019

ReportG. S. (2023). Retrieved from https://www.goldmansachs.com/intelligence/pages/generative-ai-could-raise-global-gdp-by-7-percent.html

Stevens, J. P. (1992). *Applied Multivariate Statistics for the Social Sciences* (2nd ed.). Erlbaum.

Szczepański, M. (2018). *Economic impacts of artificial intelligence (AI)*. EPRS | European Parliamentary Research Service.

Taherdoost, H., Sahibuddin, S., & Jalaliyoon, N. (2014). Exploratory Factor Analysis; Concepts and Theory. Jerzy Balicki. *Advances in Applied and Pure Mathematics, 27*, 375-382. doi:10.1093/mind/LIX.236.433

Turing, A. (1950). Computing Machinery and Intelligence. *Mind, 59*(236), 433–460. doi:10.1093/mind/LIX.236.433

Venkatesh, V., Morris, M. G., Davis, G. B., & Davis, F. D. (2003). User Acceptance of Information Technology: Toward a Unified View. *Management Information Systems Quarterly, 27*(3), 425–478. doi:10.2307/30036540

Wang, C., Ahmad, S. F., Bani Ahmad Ayassrah, A. Y. A., Awwad, E. M., Irshad, M., Ali, Y. A., Al-Razgan, M., Khan, Y., & Han, H. (2023). An Empirical Evaluation of Technology Acceptance Model for Artificial Intelligence in E-commerce. *Heliyon, 9*(8), e18349. doi:10.1016/j.heliyon.2023.e18349 PMID:37520947

Wang, Y., Liu, C., & Tu, Y. F. (2021). Factors Affecting the Adoption of AI-Based Applications in Higher Education: An Analysis of Teachers Perspectives Using Structural Equation Modeling. *Journal of Educational Technology & Society, 24*(3), 116–129.

Wheatley, A., & Hervieux, S. (2019). Artificial Intelligence in Academic Libraries: An Environmental Scan. *Information Services & Use, 39*(4), 347–356. doi:10.3233/ISU-190065

Wheeler, A. R., & Buckley, M. R. (2021). The current and future states of automation, artificial intelligence, and machine learning. In *HR without People?* (pp. 29–44). Emerald Publishing Limited. doi:10.1108/978-1-80117-037-620211003

Wood, B. A., & Evans, D. (2018). Librarians' perceptions of artificial intelligence and its potential impact on the profession. *Computers in Libraries, 38*(1).

Yu, K., & Huang, G. (2020). Exploring Consumers' Intent to Use Smart Libraries with Technology Acceptance Model. *The Electronic Library, 38*(3), 447–461. doi:10.1108/EL-08-2019-0188

Yuan, J., & Yang, N. (2023). On factors affecting users' willingness to participate in the smart services of academic library. *Journal of Librarianship and Information Science, 0*(0). Advance online publication. doi:10.1177/09610006221146298

ZhangB.DafoeA. (2019). Artificial intelligence: American attitudes and trends. *Available at* SSRN 3312874.

Zhang, C., & Lu, Y. (2021). Study on artificial intelligence: The state of the art and future prospects. *Journal of Industrial Information Integration*, *23*, 100224. doi:10.1016/j.jii.2021.100224

KEY TERMS AND DEFINITIONS

Adoption: Decision to implement and therefore subsequently use a new product or service or IT application, often linked to a purchasing decision. Adoption can be temporary (trial) or permanent, timid, or ambitious.

Artificial Intelligence: This is a new field of study aimed at the simulation by computer means human cognitive faculties and intellectual capacities through combinations of hardware and software in order to carry out activities generally performed by humans. It is based to varying degrees on the use of statistics, vision, voice synthesis and other sciences such as robotics, expert systems, and big data.

Attitudes: Psychological disposition, often resulting from experience, which determines an individual's predisposition towards an object, a situation, an experience, a person, or a computer application. It is the degree of evaluation on a bipolar scale between favorability and non-favorability, mainly caused by beliefs towards the stimulus. It is deemed to condition or cause a certain behavior or action in this regard.

Challenges: A test in achieving a goal, a call to action or difficulties to overcome, a problem to solve, involving a certain degree of risk or unpredictability that hinders its success.

Familiarity: This term refers to the achievement of a level of knowledge regarding an object, a person, or a situation and usually with objects, people, situations or computer applications which makes an individual feel familiar comfortable after a given time.

High-Ranked: Comparative degree of value or importance (actual or presumed). In the case of universities, more or less scientific rankings are made annually to determine their relative value considering various and therefore partially subjective criteria.

Intention: The act of wanting; the exercise of this faculty, in particular to decide to do or not to do something (e.g.: create a legal act). It can also be the subjective probability of a certain behavior.

Library (Academic): Room, building (material or virtual) which acquires, classifies, and makes available documents (books, journals, daily newspapers, audio-visual materials and others) to a set of users. It is academic when it dedicates itself to the members of a university community.

Problem: This refers to a practical or theoretical question facing a situation while considering the uncertainty as to the means to be taken to resolve the difficulties which hinder its solution.

Success Factors: Important characteristics or decisive elements that must be present to determine the success of an activity, project, or company.

Chapter 7
Classification and Assessment of Visual Content of Medicinal Plants Using CNN

Priyanka Kumari
Yogoda Satsanga Mahavidyalaya, Ranchi, India

Piyush Ranjan
Jharkhand Rai University, India

Priyanka Srivastava
Sarala Birla University, Ranchi, India

ABSTRACT

Use of medicinal plants has a long history in traditional medicine around the world. It is critical to correctly identify medicinal plants in order to determine their therapeutic characteristics and prospective applications. However, due to the complexity of their appearance, it might be a challenging process. Variation in features of leaf restrict the use of existing plants identification methods. This research suggests a deep learning-based solution using VGG-19 model, which employs a convolutional neural network (CNN) that is capable of learning and encoding complex aspects of images, allowing it to recognize and classify medicinal plants with high accuracy. The experiment has been done with the help of Flavia dataset which complies 1000 images, and extracted features are classified using different classifiers. The research has the potential to provide a knowledge base for identifying herbal plants to healthcare providers and herbal medicine researchers.

INTRODUCTION

The plants are playing key role in constructing our ecosystem, which are present around us. a number of these plants give us food whereas there are a large range of plants that have found their use in medicine. Normally these medicinal plants are different from the non- medicinal plants. Ancient times people were excellent at spotting the medicinal benefits of those plants for curing the diseases. They were well-known

DOI: 10.4018/979-8-3693-0807-3.ch007

that within which plants have which kind of medicinal benefits. These plants were normally found in our homes or those that we discover within the roadsides. Because the days pass, for the people this is often becoming more complex to spot the medicinal plants. Many of us don't even realize this sort of plant has medicinal value. So, to identify a plant first we consider the leaves of that plant to classify them. Leaves may be classified supported various features like texture, shape, color and pattern. Plants are the backbone of all life on Earth and an essential resource for human well-being. Plant recognition is very important in agriculture for the management of plant species whereas botanists can use this application for medicinal purposes. Plants are essential to the balance of nature and in people's lives. They are the ultimate source of food and metabolic energy for nearly all animals, which cannot manufacture their own food. Thus, the study of plants is vital because they are a fundamental part of life on Earth and generate the oxygen and food that allow humans and other organisms to exist. A digital plant identification system can be used for quick characterization of plant species without requiring the expertise of botanists, thus automizing their task. Medicinal plants have played a significant role in healthcare throughout human history, providing a plethora of remedies for various ailments. Their importance in healthcare is undeniable, as they offer a natural and sustainable source of medicine. This brief overview will explore the historical context, cultural significance, scientific advances, and future potential of medicinal plants in healthcare.\

- **Historical Significance:** The use of medicinal plants dates back thousands of years, with evidence found in ancient civilizations like the Indian, Egyptians, and Chinese. In these cultures, healers relied on herbs, roots, and leaves to treat illnesses and injuries. The knowledge of medicinal plants was passed down through generations, forming the basis of traditional medicine systems worldwide.
- **Cultural Significance:** Different cultures have their own rich traditions of herbal medicine. In Ayurveda, the traditional medicine of India, and Traditional Chinese Medicine (TCM), plants are fundamental components of diagnosis and treatment. Native American tribes have an intricate understanding of regional plants for medicinal use. These cultural practices highlight the deep connection between communities and the natural world.
- **Scientific Advances:** In recent decades, scientific research has validated the efficacy of many medicinal plants. Active compounds found in plants have been isolated and synthesized to create modern medicines. For example, the pain-relieving properties of willow bark led to the development of aspirin, a widely used medication. Quinine, derived from the cinchona tree, revolutionized the treatment of malaria. These examples underscore the vital role of plants in drug discovery.
- **Biodiversity and Conservation:** The importance of conserving medicinal plants goes beyond healthcare. Biodiversity ensures a variety of genetic resources, which can lead to the discovery of new medicines. Destruction of natural habitats and overharvesting threaten many plant species. Conservation efforts not only preserve traditional knowledge but also protect potential cures for future diseases.
- **Alternative and Complementary Medicine:** Medicinal plants are integral to alternative and complementary medicine practices. Herbal supplements, acupuncture, and aromatherapy incorporate plant-based treatments. Many individuals prefer these therapies due to their holistic approach and fewer side effects, leading to a growing market for herbal products.
- **Challenges and Opportunities:** Despite their significance, challenges exist in integrating medicinal plants into mainstream healthcare. Standardization of herbal preparations, quality control,

and safety issues require stringent regulations. Additionally, there is a need for further research to understand the interactions between herbal remedies and conventional medicines.

However, these challenges also present opportunities. Collaboration between traditional knowledge holders and scientists can lead to the development of evidence-based herbal medicines. Integrative healthcare models, combining conventional and traditional approaches, provide comprehensive treatment options. The future of healthcare could be shaped significantly by medicinal plants. With advancements in biotechnology, scientists can explore plant genomes to understand their medicinal properties better. This knowledge can aid in genetic modification for enhanced therapeutic effects. The awareness of natural remedies and the shift toward sustainable practices align with global efforts for eco-friendly healthcare. Medicinal plants offer a renewable resource, reducing the environmental impact associated with synthetic drugs. but there is a challenge of accurately classifying and assessing medicinal plants. Figure 1 represents the visual representation of diseased image.

Figure 1. Leaf image

For accurately classifying and assessing medicinal plants can be a significant challenge due to several factors:

- **Taxonomic complexity:** Medicinal plants come from various species and genera, and they may have different subspecies or varieties. Accurate classification requires expertise in botany and taxonomy, and even experts may encounter difficulties when dealing with closely related species.
- **Morphological variability:** Plants of the same species can exhibit significant morphological variations, especially when grown in different geographic regions, climates, or under different environmental conditions. This can make it challenging to identify medicinal plants solely based on their physical characteristics.
- **Seasonal variations:** Medicinal plants can exhibit different traits, including color, size, and shape, depending on the season. This can lead to misidentification, as the same plant may appear quite different at different times of the year.
- **Confusion with similar-looking species:** Some medicinal plants closely resemble non-medicinal or even toxic plants. This can result in misidentification, which can have serious health consequences if the wrong plant is used for medicinal purposes.
- **Local and traditional knowledge:** Medicinal plant knowledge is often passed down through generations within specific communities. This knowledge may not always align with scientific

taxonomy, making it challenging to bridge the gap between traditional and scientific classification systems.

- **Preservation and documentation:** Proper preservation of plant specimens and accurate documentation of their characteristics are essential for accurate classification. However, these processes may not always be carried out consistently or effectively.

Aim of the Chapter: The chapter focuses on recent advancements in Classification methods for the classification of medicinal plants. In simpler terms, this research aims to assess the accuracy and efficiency of identifying and categorizing medicinal plants using Convolutional Neural Network (CNN) using VGG-19 based solution.

BACKGROUND

The introduction section highlights the significance of medicinal plants, particularly due to the increasing global population, the lack of expert support for research, insufficient government support for research activities, and limited awareness of medicinal plants. Many useful plants are at risk of being destroyed, and manual identification of these plants is time-consuming and often requires expert assistance. To address these challenges, there is a growing need for automated identification and classification of medicinal plants. The field of Convolutional Neural Network (CNN) technique plays a crucial role in automating the identification and classification of medicinal plants. Key developments in this area include feature extraction and classification methods, which significantly impact the overall accuracy of systems designed for scientific categorization. Here are some key concepts and aspects related to Computer Vision and CNNs:

- **Image Processing:** Computer Vision often involves preprocessing and enhancing images to make them more suitable for analysis. Techniques like blurring, sharpening, and filtering are commonly used for this purpose.
- **Feature Extraction:** One of the fundamental tasks in computer vision is feature extraction, where meaningful information is derived from images. Features can be edges, corners, textures, colors, or any other patterns that help distinguish objects.
- **Convolutional Neural Networks (CNNs):** CNNs are a class of deep neural networks designed for processing grid-like data, such as images and videos. They consist of multiple layers of interconnected neurons and utilize convolutional layers to automatically learn hierarchical features from the input data.
- **Convolution:** In a CNN, convolution is the primary operation. It involves sliding a small filter (kernel) over the input image to extract features. Convolution allows the network to recognize patterns irrespective of their location in the image.
- **Pooling:** After convolution, pooling layers are often used to reduce the spatial dimensions of the feature maps and make the network more robust to variations in the input.
- **Fully Connected Layers:** These are conventional neural network layers at the end of the CNN, which are responsible for making predictions or decisions based on the extracted features.

- **Training:** CNNs are trained using labeled datasets, where the network learns to map input images to specific categories or labels. Common optimization techniques like stochastic gradient descent are used to adjust the network's weights during training.
- **Transfer Learning:** Transfer learning is a technique where a pre-trained CNN, often on a large dataset like ImageNet, is fine-tuned for a specific task. This is a practical approach when you have limited data or computational resources.
- **Object Detection:** CNNs are commonly used for object detection tasks, where the goal is to identify and locate objects within an image. Popular algorithms for object detection include Faster R-CNN and YOLO.
- **Image Classification:** CNNs are also used for image classification tasks, where the goal is to assign a label or category to an entire image. Common datasets for image classification include CIFAR-10, MNIST, and ImageNet.
- **Segmentation:** Image segmentation involves partitioning an image into meaningful regions or segments. CNNs, particularly fully convolutional networks (FCNs), are used for this purpose.
- **Ethical Considerations:** The use of computer vision in surveillance, facial recognition, and other applications raises ethical concerns related to privacy and bias. Computer Vision and CNNs have revolutionized many industries and continue to play a significant role in the advancement of technology and automation. They have the potential to transform the way we interact with and interpret visual information.

Convolutional Neural Network (CNN)

CNNs are a class of Deep Neural Networks that can recognize and classify particular features from images and are widely used for analyzing visual images. Their applications range from image and video recognition, image classification, medical image analysis, computer vision and natural language processing. CNN has high accuracy, and because of the same, it is useful in image recognition. Image recognition has a wide range of uses in various industries such as medical image analysis, phone, security, recommendation systems, etc. The term 'Convolution" in CNN denotes the mathematical function of convolution which is a special kind of linear operation wherein two functions are multiplied to produce a third function which expresses how the shape of one function is modified by the other. In simple terms, two images which can be represented as matrices are multiplied to give an output that is used to extract features from the image. There are three main parts to CNN architecture.

(i). A convolution tool that separates and identifies the various features of the image for analysis in a process called Feature Extraction.
(ii). The network of feature extraction consists of many pairs of convolutional or pooling layers.
(iii). A fully connected layer that utilizes the output from the convolution process and predicts the class of the image based on the features extracted in previous stages.
(iv). This CNN model of feature extraction aims to reduce the number of features present in a dataset. It creates new features which summarize the existing features contained in an original set of features.

Convolutional Layer

This layer is the first layer that is used to extract the various features from the input images. In this layer, the mathematical operation of convolution is performed between the input image and a filter of a particular size MxM. By sliding the filter over the input image, the dot product is taken between the filter and the parts of the input image with respect to the size of the filter (MxM). The output is termed as the Feature map which gives us information about the image such as the corners and edges. Later, this feature map is fed to other layers to learn several other features of the input image. The convolution layer in CNN passes the result to the next layer once applying the convolution operation in the input. Convolutional layers in CNN benefit a lot as they ensure the spatial relationship between the pixels is intact.

Pooling Layer

In most cases, a Convolutional Layer is followed by a Pooling Layer. The primary aim of this layer is to decrease the size of the convolved feature map to reduce the computational costs. This is performed by decreasing the connections between layers and independently operates on each feature map. Depending upon method used, there are several types of Pooling operations. It basically summarizes the features generated by a convolution layer. In Max Pooling, the largest element is taken from feature map. Average Pooling calculates the average of the elements in a predefined sized Image section. The total sum of the elements in the predefined section is computed in Sum Pooling. The Pooling Layer usually serves as a bridge between the Convolutional Layer and the FC Layer. This CNN model generalizes the features extracted by the convolution layer and helps the networks to recognize the features independently. With the help of this, the computations are also reduced in a network.

Fully Connected Layer

The Fully Connected (FC) layer consists of the weights and biases along with the neurons and is used to connect the neurons between two different layers. These layers are usually placed before the output layer and form the last few layers of CNN Architecture. In this, the input image from the previous layers is flattened and fed to the FC layer. The flattened vector then undergoes few more FC layers where the mathematical functions operations usually take place. In this stage, the classification process begins to take place. The reason two layers are connected is that two fully connected layers will perform better than a single connected layer. These layers in CNN reduce human supervision.

VGG-19

VGG stands for Visual Geometry Group; it is a standard deep Convolutional Neural Network (CNN) architecture with multiple layers. The "deep" refers to the number of layers with VGG-16 or VGG-19 consisting of 16 and 19 convolutional layers. The VGG architecture is the basis of ground-breaking object recognition models. Developed as a deep neural network, the VGG Net also surpasses baselines on many tasks and datasets beyond ImageNet. Moreover, it is now still one of the most popular image recognition architectures. The concept of the VGG19 model (also VGGNet-19) is that it supports 19 layers. The "16" and "19" stand for the number of weight layers in the model (convolutional layers). This means that VGG19 has three more convolutional layers than VGG16.

LITERATURE REVIEW

In this section, we present the various authors' work in terms if methods used, and findings from the papers. Tan et al. 2018, used the method DLeaf utilized CNN for highlight extraction and ANN for characterization. Sobel edge location calculation is utilized for venation division from the resized leaf pictures. Finding: D-Leaf model achieved a classification accuracy of 94.88% for plant species classification using leaf vein morphometrics. Gopal et al. (2012), method Used: Proposed an automatic identification system for selected medicinal plant leaves using boundary-based features, moment features, and color features. Finding: The software exhibited a classification efficiency of 92% when trained with 100 leaves and tested with 50 leaves. Janani and Gopal (2013), method Used: Developed an ANN-based model to classify medicinal plant species using color, texture, and shape of leaves. Minimal prominent features were identified. Finding: This method achieved an accuracy of 94.4%. Venkataraman and Mangayarkarasi (2016), method Used: Proposed a computer vision-based approach for identifying medicinal plant leaves and retrieving their medicinal details using a Probabilistic Neural Network classifier. Finding: The method involves preprocessing, feature extraction, classification, and retrieval of medicinal values. Prasad and Singh (2017), method Used: Presented an efficient technique for leaf acquisition and feature extraction using VGG-16 and PCA methods, achieving an accuracy of 97.6% for VGG-16 and 98.2% for l-VGG-16 with PCA. Sabu et al. (2017), method Used: Employed a machine learning and computer vision-based method to classify medicinal plants using SURF and HoG features. Finding: The k-NN classification algorithm was used, and the method achieved an accuracy of more than 96%, but feature extraction was computationally expensive. Kumar et al, (2017), method Used: Proposed a method to find the optimum combination of features for classifying medicinal leaves using geometric, color, texture, HU invariant moments, and Zernike moments. Finding: The maximum accuracy of 99% was obtained on MLP classifier for Geometric-Colour-Texture Zernike combination with 38 features. Salima et al., (2015), method Used: Implemented a Hessian matrix-based leaf vein segmentation. Finding: The segmentation scoring techniques were applied, and a certain percentage of leaf images attained different segmentation scores. Grinblat et al. (2016), Method Used: Proposed a deep Convolutional Neural Network model for plant classification using leaf venation. Finding: The study employed the Support Vector Machine, Penalized Discriminant Analysis, and Random Forests for classification. Pvloiu et al. (2017), method Used: Proposed a method to extract shape features of medicinal leaves using RELIEF feature selection algorithm. Finding: The MLP NN classifier achieved an accuracy of 47.08%. Ghazi et al. (2017), Method Used: Used deep convolutional neural networks to identify plant species and conducted a comparative study on popular CNNs. Finding: Finetuned VGGNet achieved the highest performance with an overall accuracy of 78.44%. Hajam et al. (2023), Method Used: Leveraged the power of deep convolutional neural networks (VGG16, VGG19, and DenseNet201) to identify medicinal plant leaf images. Finding: The ensemble of VGG19+DenseNet201 with fine-tuning outperformed standalone models with an accuracy of 99.12%. Krizhevsky et al. (2012), Method Used: Proposed a deep Convolutional Neural Network model for plant classification using leaf venation. Finding: The 5-layer CNN outperformed the 6-layer CNN with an average accuracy of 96.9%. Wu et al. (2007), method Used: Neural network approaches for leaf recognition using RGB to GRAY conversion, boundary enhancement, PCA for feature extraction, and Probabilistic Neural Network (PNN) for classification. Finding: Achieved 90% accuracy on 32 plant species with 1800 leaf samples. Priya et al. (2012), method Used: Proposed image preprocessing techniques and feature extraction for leaf recognition using Support Vector Machine (SVM) classification. Finding: Extracted 12 leaf functions and achieved efficient leaf recognition. Kumar et al., (2017), method Used: Dealt with Ayurveda plant identification using Support Vector Machine and Multilayer Perceptron. Finding: Achieved a high accuracy of 94.5% with Multilayer Perceptron after preprocessing and feature extraction. VijayaLakshmi and Mohan, (2016), Method Used: Suggested a classification method based on shape, color, and texture properties for leaf type detection. Finding: Employed various techniques, including KNN, PNN, fuzzy vector machine, and SVM for classification. These papers cover a wide range of methods and techniques for plant species and leaf identification, including deep learning, feature extraction, and classification algorithms.

METHODOLOGY

Pre-Processing

Plant identification heavily relies on analyzing leaves, a prominent distinguishing characteristic. To begin this process, digital images of plant leaf segments are used as input data. Preprocessing is vital to eliminate extraneous disturbances and enhance the image, making it easier to identify key features. The primary objective of preprocessing is to improve image quality by accentuating details. This clarity is essential for identifying distinct features crucial for subsequent analysis. By enhancing image quality, preprocessing ensures that the analysis is based on accurate and reliable information. One critical preprocessing step is the conversion of color leaf images into grayscale. Grayscale images simplify feature extraction. They represent the leaf's varying shades of gray, simplifying the image for analysis. This step eliminates complexities associated with handling color variations, providing a consistent representation of the leaf. A consistent representation is essential for reliable analysis. Another significant preprocessing step is the identification of the leaf's contour using edge detectors. Edge detection algorithms highlight boundaries and edges in the leaf image. This process significantly improves the delineation of the leaf's shape and boundaries, providing more precise information for further analysis. Various edge detection techniques, such as Sobel, Canny, and Prewitt operators, help identify abrupt changes in intensity that correspond to edges in the image. These algorithms create an edge map, making the leaf's boundaries stand out, facilitating feature extraction and enhancing accuracy.

In conclusion, preprocessing plays a pivotal role in plant identification based on leaves. It ensures the removal of disturbances, enhances image quality, and simplifies subsequent feature extraction. The conversion to grayscale and the identification of leaf contours are integral steps that enable precise and reliable analysis, ultimately contributing to the accurate identification of plant species based on their leaves.

Feature Extraction

Feature extraction is a fundamental step in plant classification and identification, as it helps distinguish one plant from another based on specific characteristics. These features are typically categorized into shape, color, and texture, each of which plays a significant role in plant recognition.

- **Shape:** Plant leaves come in a variety of shapes, such as oval, lanceolate, oblong, or elliptical. The overall contour and the presence of lobes or serrations on the leaf margin can be essential distinguishing features. Leaf shape can be quantified by measuring parameters like length, width, aspect ratio, and circularity. These geometric attributes help in numerical representation and differentiation.

- **Color:** Leaf color is a crucial feature for classification. Different plant species exhibit distinctive color variations, including shades of green, red, yellow, or brown. Color features are quantified by using color spaces such as RGB, HSV, or LAB. Metrics like mean color intensity, color histograms, or color distribution statistics provide valuable information.
- **Texture:** Texture refers to the visual patterns and structures present on the leaf surface. It includes features like venation patterns, surface roughness, and patterns of hair or scales. Texture analysis involves techniques like texture co-occurrence matrices (GLCM), fractal dimension, and local binary patterns (LBP), which capture the fine-grained details on the leaf surface.

Figure 2 represents the classification of these features into the mentioned categories. It is a visual representation of how shape, color, and texture are the primary attributes used to differentiate and classify plants. Utilizing these features, computational algorithms and machine learning models can be trained to recognize and classify plant species accurately. In practice, combining these features is common to improve the accuracy of plant classification systems. For instance, shape features can help distinguish between broad categories, while color and texture details can further refine the identification process, making it possible to discriminate between closely related species. Overall, feature extraction is a crucial aspect of plant classification, as it provides the necessary data for automated systems to identify and differentiate plants, whether for ecological research, agricultural purposes, or plant conservation efforts.

Figure 2. Features of leaf

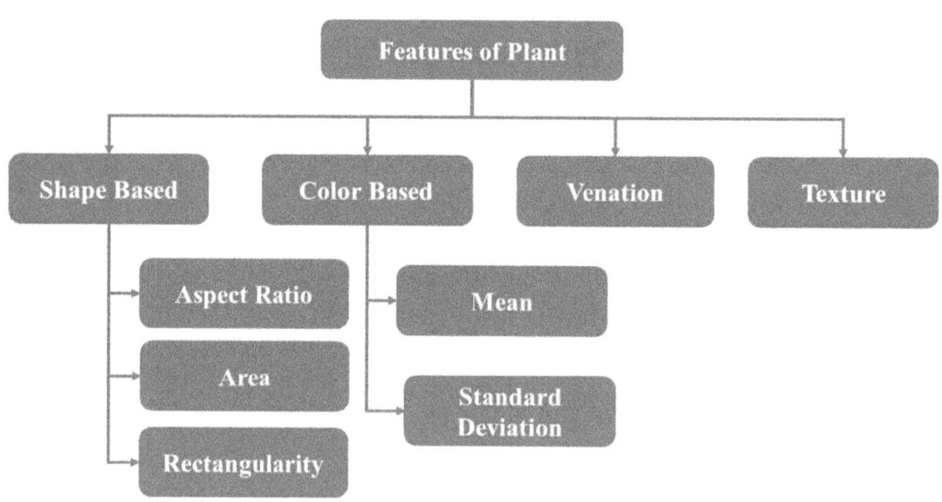

Shape Features

Shape features play a pivotal role in the field of leaf analysis, as they enable researchers and botanists to glean essential insights into the structural characteristics of leaves. These features are primarily derived from the geometric properties of leaves, helping distinguish and identify various plant species. Leaf length, a fundamental measure, is determined by calculating the Euclidean distance between the tips situated on opposite sides of the leaf's central axis. In contrast, leaf breadth is assessed by measuring the length of the minor axis. The aspect ratio, derived from the comparison between leaf length and breadth, offers crucial information about a leaf's shape. This ratio encapsulates the proportion between the two dimensions and serves as a distinctive marker for different plant species. These shape features are indispensable in botanical research, aiding in the identification and classification of plants. They are especially valuable for discriminating between species with similar overall appearances but distinct leaf shapes. Additionally, these features find applications in diverse fields, including ecology, agriculture, and environmental science, enhancing our understanding of plant diversity, adaptations, and ecosystem dynamics by leveraging the unique fingerprints encoded in leaf morphology. As a result, shape features have become essential tools for researchers, facilitating more accurate and efficient botanical investigations and contributing to a broader understanding of our natural world.

Color Features

Color features encompass essential statistical metrics, such as mean and standard deviation, which play a pivotal role in image analysis and understanding the color characteristics of objects, particularly leaves. The mean value in this context signifies the arithmetic average of the pixel color values throughout the entire leaf image. This average serves as a representative measure of the overall color content present within the leaf. Meanwhile, standard deviation offers insight into the degree of color variation within the leaf. It quantifies how much individual pixel color values deviate from the mean. Higher standard deviation values indicate a broader range of colors and, consequently, greater color diversity within the leaf. These color features hold significance across various applications, from botany to computer vision. They aid in distinguishing and classifying different objects or regions based on their color profiles. In the case of leaves, these metrics can help identify and characterize plant species, assess their health, and study environmental factors affecting coloration. Moreover, the mean and standard deviation values are fundamental in image processing, enabling the development of algorithms and techniques that rely on color information for tasks such as object recognition, segmentation, and quality control. Ultimately, these color features are essential tools for understanding and working with digital images in a multitude of fields.

Venation Features

Venation features, found within the intricate network of veins in plant leaves, offer a distinctive means of identifying and distinguishing various plant species. These vein patterns are unique and characteristic for each plant, making them a valuable tool in botanical classification and ecological research. To extract and emphasize these venation features, image processing techniques, specifically morphological operations, are employed. One common method involves using morphological opening, where a structuring element is applied to the leaf image. The structuring element is a small binary matrix that defines the operation's behavior. By performing an opening operation, the background information in the image is subtracted, leaving behind the prominent vein patterns. This process effectively isolates the vein network from the rest of the leaf, enhancing their visibility and making them more accessible for analysis and feature extraction. Researchers and botanists can then use these vein patterns to create characteristic profiles for different plant species. Additionally, this method is instrumental in various applications, including plant identification, disease diagnosis, and the study of plant adaptations, as it highlights a key botanical trait that is both species-specific and ecologically significant. In summary, the application of morphological operations to leaf images unveils distinctive venation features, providing a valuable resource for plant scientists and enthusiasts alike.

Classification

Classification is the method of determining classes based on certain attributes. It defines the position of the unidentified image of the leaf in a specific class, described objectively. A Convolutional Neural Network (CNN) Using VGG19 architecture is a powerful deep learning model used primarily for image classification tasks. VGG19 is an extension of the VGG family of CNN architectures, known for its depth and impressive performance.

- **Architecture:** VGG19 is composed of 19 layers, including 16 convolutional layers and 3 fully connected layers. It's known for its uniform structure - using 3x3 convolutional filters and 2x2 max-pooling layers. This consistent architecture makes it easier to train and fine-tune for various image classification tasks.
- **Convolutional Layers:** In CNN, convolutional layers are responsible for extracting features from the input image. VGG19 uses a series of convolutional layers with different depths, followed by rectified linear unit (ReLU) activation functions. These layers help the network learn various hierarchical features from simple edges and textures to complex object parts.
- **Max-Pooling Layers:** After convolution, max-pooling layers are employed to down-sample the spatial dimensions of the feature maps while retaining the most important information. In VGG19, 2x2 max-pooling layers are inserted between convolutional layers to reduce the computational load and prevent overfitting.
- **Fully Connected Layers:** Towards the end of the network, VGG19 includes three fully connected layers that take the high-level features from the convolutional layers and use them to classify the input image into different classes. These layers are connected in a traditional neural network architecture.
- **Classification:** For image classification tasks, the last fully connected layer of VGG19 is typically a softmax layer. This layer assigns probabilities to different classes based on the features learned throughout the network. The class with the highest probability is considered the final prediction.
- **Pretrained Model:** VGG19, like other deep neural networks, can be pre-trained on a large dataset such as ImageNet. Pretraining helps the model learn useful features from a wide range of images. After pretraining, the final classification layer can be fine-tuned on a specific dataset to adapt the network to the target classification task.
- **Transfer Learning:** One of the strengths of VGG19 is its suitability for transfer learning. You can take a pretrained VGG19 model and fine-tune it for specific tasks with a relatively small dataset. This is particularly useful when you have limited data to train a CNN from scratch.

VGG19 has been successfully used in various computer vision tasks, including image classification, object detection, and segmentation. Its ability to learn complex features makes it valuable in tasks where detailed feature extraction is essential.

SOLUTION AND RECOMMENDATIONS

Pre-Processing

Effective pre-processing of plant leaf images is essential for accurate and reliable plant identification. Converting color leaf images to grayscale simplifies subsequent analysis. It's recommended to use established algorithms for grayscale conversion, ensuring consistent representations for leaves. Utilize edge detection algorithms like Sobel, Canny, or Prewitt operators to enhance the delineation of leaf shape and boundaries. Ensure that the chosen algorithm is suitable for your specific dataset and image characteristics. Apply noise reduction techniques to eliminate unwanted disturbances from the images. This can include median filtering, Gaussian blurring, or other denoising methods. Employ techniques to enhance image quality, such as contrast adjustment, histogram equalization, or gamma correction. Enhanced images provide clearer details for feature extraction. Consider implementing automated pre-processing pipelines to streamline the process and ensure consistency. Automation can save time and minimize errors.

Feature Extraction

Effective feature extraction is crucial for distinguishing and classifying plant species. For shape features, consider using standard geometric parameters such as length, width, aspect ratio, and circularity. These parameters provide numerical representations of leaf shape and are valuable for distinguishing different plant species. Utilize color spaces like RGB, HSV, or LAB to extract color features. Metrics like mean color intensity and standard deviation can be used to quantify the color characteristics of leaves. Ensure color features capture the distinctive variations in leaf color. For texture analysis, explore methods like texture co-occurrence matrices (GLCM), fractal dimension, and local binary patterns (LBP). These techniques capture fine-grained details on the leaf surface, which can be valuable for species differentiation. To improve accuracy, consider combining shape, color, and texture features in your classification model. Combining features allows for a more comprehensive analysis and can help discriminate between closely related species.

Venation Features

Venation features offer a unique way to identify plant species. Apply morphological operations, such as morphological opening, to isolate vein patterns from leaf images. This step enhances the visibility of vein networks, making them accessible for analysis. Once vein patterns are isolated, extract relevant features from the veins, such as vein density, branching patterns, and vein curvature. These features can be incorporated into your classification model for enhanced accuracy. Develop characteristic profiles for different plant species based on their vein patterns. These profiles serve as valuable references for species identification and classification.

Classification

Effective classification is essential for plant identification. Employ the VGG19 architecture for its depth and performance in image classification tasks. It provides a consistent structure with 16 convolutional layers, 2x2 max-pooling layers, and 3 fully connected layers. Consider pretraining your VGG19 model on a large dataset like ImageNet. Pretraining allows the model to learn useful features from a wide range of images, which can be valuable for fine-tuning on your specific dataset. Take advantage of VGG19's suitability for transfer learning. Fine-tune the model with your dataset, adapting it to the target classification task. Transfer learning is particularly useful when you have limited data. Ensure that the last fully connected layer of your VGG19 model is a softmax layer for image classification. This layer assigns probabilities to different classes based on the learned features. Combine shape, color, texture, and venation features to provide a comprehensive set of inputs for your CNN model. This can enhance the accuracy of plant classification by considering multiple distinguishing characteristics. Use appropriate validation techniques, such as cross-validation, to evaluate the performance of your classification model. Thoroughly test the model on a separate testing dataset to assess its accuracy and generalization. Experiment with different hyperparameters, such as learning rates and batch sizes, during the fine-tuning process. Fine-tune the model iteratively to optimize its performance. Apply data augmentation techniques to increase the diversity of your training dataset. Techniques like rotation, scaling, and flipping can help improve the model's robustness.

FUTURE RESEARCH DIRECTIONS

In the field of plant identification and classification based on leaves involves several exciting opportunities for research and development. Here are some potential directions for future work:

- Explore the use of more advanced deep learning architectures beyond VGG19. Investigate the effectiveness of newer architectures like ResNet, Inception, and EfficientNet for plant identification.
- Develop lightweight deep learning models optimized for deployment on resource-constrained devices, such as smartphones and embedded systems.
- Investigate novel approaches to transfer learning. This may include pretraining on botanical or ecological datasets specific to plant identification tasks.
- Develop methods to adapt pretrained models to various plant species and different geographic regions, enabling more generalized plant recognition.
- Explore advanced data augmentation techniques to generate synthetic leaf images for model training. This can help address data scarcity issues and improve model robustness.
- Investigate the use of generative adversarial networks (GANs) for generating realistic synthetic leaf images.
- Extend plant identification to the fine-grained level, focusing on distinguishing between closely related plant species or even subspecies.
- Develop specialized models for identifying rare or endangered plant species, contributing to conservation efforts.
- Combine leaf image analysis with other modalities, such as leaf spectroscopy, to improve plant identification accuracy. Multi-modal approaches can provide complementary information for more reliable identification.
- Implement semantic segmentation techniques to identify different parts of a leaf, such as veins, stomata, and margins. This detailed analysis can enhance the understanding of leaf characteristics.

- Develop user-friendly mobile applications that enable individuals, including researchers, botanists, and nature enthusiasts, to identify plants in the field using smartphone cameras.
- Explore cloud-based solutions that leverage the processing power of remote servers for plant identification.
- Extend plant identification systems to detect and diagnose diseases, pests, and environmental stressors affecting plant health. Early detection can aid in agricultural management and plant protection.
- Collaborate with ecologists and environmental scientists to integrate plant identification tools into ecological studies and biodiversity monitoring.
- Use plant identification data to assess the impact of climate change on plant populations and distributions.
- Apply plant identification technology to ethnobotanical research, enabling the identification of medicinal plants and the study of traditional knowledge related to plant use.
- Collaborate internationally to create comprehensive plant datasets representing diverse ecosystems and plant species from around the world.
- Encourage data sharing and cooperation among researchers and organizations involved in plant identification and conservation.

CASE STUDY: QUESTIONS RELATED TO CLASSIFICATION AND ASSESSMENT OF MEDICINAL PLANTS

Q.1 How can CNNs be employed to differentiate between various species of medicinal plants based on their visual characteristics?

Sol. CNNs can be employed by training on a large dataset of images of medicinal plants, where each image is labeled with the corresponding plant species. The network learns to recognize unique visual patterns and features that distinguish one species from another. This can be achieved by passing the images through several convolutional layers, which automatically extract hierarchical features.

Q.2 What challenges and limitations exist when using CNNs to classify medicinal plants, and how can they be addressed?

Sol. Challenges include the need for a large and diverse dataset, potential overfitting, and model interpretability. These challenges can be addressed by collecting a representative dataset, using data augmentation, implementing regularization techniques, and utilizing interpretability tools like Grad-CAM.

Q.3 How can CNN-based systems be utilized to assess the quality and potency of different plant parts used in traditional medicine?

Sol. CNN-based systems can assess the quality and potency by recognizing visual cues associated with these attributes. For instance, they can analyze the color, texture, and shape of plant parts. The system can be trained on labeled images of plant parts with known quality and potency to make predictions.

Q.4 What data sources and databases are most valuable for training CNNs to identify and classify medicinal plant species accurately?

Sol. Valuable data sources include botanical databases, herbarium collections, and expert-annotated datasets. These sources provide accurate and diverse information for training the CNN model effectively.

Q.5 Can CNNs assist in identifying counterfeit or adulterated medicinal plant products in the market, and how reliable is this technology?

Sol. CNNs can assist in identifying counterfeit or adulterated products by comparing the visual characteristics of a product with those of the genuine plant. The reliability depends on the quality of the training data and the extent of variation in the counterfeit products.

Q.6 How can CNNs be integrated into field research for rapid botanical surveys and biodiversity monitoring of medicinal plants?

Sol. In field research, CNNs can be deployed through mobile applications. These apps can identify plant species based on photos taken in the field, enabling rapid data collection and species identification for biodiversity monitoring.

Q.7 What implications does the use of CNNs for medicinal plant classification have for the conservation of endangered plant species?

Sol. CNNs can aid in the conservation of endangered plant species by providing accurate identification and monitoring. This information can guide conservation efforts and help prevent the illegal trade of endangered plants.

Q.8 In traditional medicine, how can CNNs help validate the traditional uses of medicinal plants based on visual characteristics?

Sol. CNNs can provide visual evidence to support traditional knowledge. By correlating the visual characteristics of plants with their traditional uses, these systems can offer a scientific basis for traditional medicine.

Q.9 Are there any ethical concerns or cultural considerations when using CNNs for the assessment of medicinal plants in traditional medicine contexts?

Sol. Ethical concerns may involve respecting indigenous knowledge, seeking consent, and protecting cultural heritage. It's important to engage with local communities and indigenous knowledge holders in a respectful and collaborative manner.

Q.10 What impact does the use of CNNs in plant classification and assessment have on the development of new pharmaceutical drugs from natural sources?

Sol. CNNs can accelerate drug discovery by identifying potential sources of bioactive compounds in medicinal plants. This can lead to the development of new pharmaceutical drugs and therapies.

Q.11 How can CNNs assist in predicting the potential medicinal properties of newly discovered plant species or compounds?

Sol. CNNs can analyze the visual characteristics of newly discovered plant species or compounds and correlate them with known medicinal properties, aiding in predictions about their potential uses.

Q.12 What are the key steps in building a CNN model for the classification of medicinal plants, and how can researchers with limited technical knowledge implement them?

Sol. Key steps include data collection, preprocessing, model selection, and evaluation. Researchers with limited technical knowledge can use user-friendly machine learning platforms or seek collaboration with experts.

Q.13 What applications and user-friendly tools are available for botanists and traditional medicine practitioners to access CNN-based plant classification and assessment?

Sol. User-friendly apps like PlantSnap and Seek can provide botanists and traditional medicine practitioners with access to CNN-based plant identification tools.

Q.14 How can the reliability and accuracy of CNN-based assessments be validated and improved in the context of medicinal plants?

Sol. Continuous refinement through expert validation and feedback, along with the collection of more diverse data, can improve the reliability and accuracy of CNN-based assessments.

Q.15 What role can CNNs play in public education and awareness about the importance of medicinal plants in traditional medicine and pharmaceutical research?

Sol. CNN-based apps and educational resources can raise public awareness by making information about medicinal plants easily accessible and engaging.

These detailed answers provide a comprehensive understanding of the applications, challenges, and ethical considerations of using CNNs for the classification and assessment of medicinal plants.

CONCLUSION

Plant identification is a critical component in the realms of both medicinal plants and botanical research. In our study, we harnessed the formidable capabilities of deep learning convolutional neural network (CNN) models, namely VGG19, These models were employed in conjunction with the VNPlant-200 dataset, a rich source of information comprising 200 distinct leaf layers. Through the implementation of a pre-trained model, we succeeded in significantly elevating the accuracy of our classification system.

ACKNOWLEDGMENT

I would like to express my heartfelt gratitude to all those who contributed to the completion of this book chapter. First and foremost, I am deeply thankful to my guide, Dr. Piyush Ranjan, Dr. Priyanka Srivastava & the editor of this volume, for providing me with the opportunity to contribute to this collection. I'm obligated to my associates for their significant direction and keen input all through the research and writing process. Their mastery has been instrumental in forming the thoughts introduced in this part. I'm likewise grateful to my loved ones for their steady help and consolation. Their confidence in my capacities kept me propelled during testing times, and for that, I am genuinely thankful. Lastly, I am very grateful to Dr. Keshav Sinha who generously shared their experiences and insights, without whom this work would not have been possible.

REFERENCES

Barré, P., Stöver, B. C., Müller, K. F., & Steinhage, V. (2017, July). LeafNet: A computer vision system for automatic plant species identification. *Ecological Informatics*, *40*, 50–56. doi:10.1016/j.ecoinf.2017.05.005

Bertrand, S., Ben Ameur, R., Cerutti, G., Coquin, D., Valet, L., & Tougne, L. (2018, July). Bark and leaf fusion systems to improve automatic tree species recognition. *Ecological Informatics*, *46*, 57–73. doi:10.1016/j.ecoinf.2018.05.007

Chaki, J., Parekh, R., & Bhattacharya, S. (2015). Plant leaf recognition using texture and shape features with neural classifiers. *Pattern Recognition Letters*, *58*, 61–68. doi:10.1016/j.patrec.2015.02.010

Chollet. (2017). Xception: Deep Learning with Depthwise Separable Convolutions. In *2017 IEEE Conference on Computer Vision and Pattern Recognition (CVPR)* (pp. 1800–1807). IEEE.

Fekri-Ershad, S. (2020, November). Bark texture classification using improved local ternary patterns and multilayer neural network. *Expert Systems with Applications*, *158*, 113509. doi:10.1016/j.eswa.2020.113509

Geetharamani & Pandian. (2019). Identification of plant leaf diseases using a nine-layer deep convolutional neural network. *Computers & Electrical Engineering*, *76*, 323–338.

Ghazi, M. M., Yanikoglu, B., & Aptoula, E. (2017). Plant identification using deep neural networks via optimization of transfer learning parameters. *Neurocomputing*, *235*, 228–235. doi:10.1016/j.neucom.2017.01.018

Gopal, A., Prudhveeswar Reddy, S., & Gayatri, V. (2012). Classification of selected medicinal plants leaf using image processing. *2012 International Conference on Machine Vision and Image Processing (MVIP)*, 5–8. 10.1109/MVIP.2012.6428747

Guillermo, L. (2016). Deep learning for plant identification using vein morphological patterns. *Computers and Electronics in Agriculture*, *127*, 418–424. doi:10.1016/j.compag.2016.07.003

Haralick, R. M., Shanmugam, K., & Dinstein, I. H. (1973). Textural features for image classification. *IEEE Transactions on Systems, Man, and Cybernetics*, *SMC-3*(6), 610–621. doi:10.1109/TSMC.1973.4309314

He, Zhang, Ren, & Sun. (2016). Deep Residual Learning for Image Recognition. In *2016 IEEE Conference on Computer Vision and Pattern Recognition (CVPR)* (pp. 770–778). IEEE.

Howard, Zhu, Chen, Kalenichenko, Wang, Weyand, Andreetto, & Adam. (2017). *MobileNets: Efficient Convolutional Neural Networks for Mobile Vision Applications*. arXiv: 1704.04861.

Hu, R., Jia, W., Ling, H., & Huang, D. (2012). Multiscale distance matrix for fast plant leaf recognition. *IEEE Transactions on Image Processing*, *21*(11), 4667–4672. doi:10.1109/TIP.2012.2207391 PMID:22875247

Huang, Liu, Van Der Maaten, & Weinberger. (2017). Densely Connected Convolutional Networks. In *2017 IEEE Conference on Computer Vision and Pattern Recognition (CVPR)* (pp. 2261–2269). IEEE.

Janani, R., & Gopal, A. (2013). Identification of selected medicinal plant leaves using image features and ann. *2013 International Conference on Advanced Electronic Systems (ICAES)*, 238–242. 10.1109/ICAES.2013.6659400

Joly, Goeau, Bonnet, Bakic, Barbe, Selmi, Yahiaoui, Carre, Mouysset, Molino, Boujemaa, & Barthelemy. (2014, September). Interactive ´ plant identification based on social image data. *Ecological Informatics*, *23*, 22–34.

Kadir, A., Nugroho, L. E., Susanto, A., & Santosa, P. I. (2013). *Leaf classification using shape, color, and texture features*. arXiv preprint arXiv:1401.4447.

Kebapci, H., Yanikoglu, B., & Unal, G. (2011). Plant image retrieval using color, shape and texture features. *The Computer Journal*, *54*(9), 1475–1490. doi:10.1093/comjnl/bxq037

Kingma & Ba. (2017). *Adam: A Method for Stochastic Optimization*. arXiv: 1412.6980.

Krizhevsky, A., Sutskever, I., & Hinton, G. E. (2017, May). ImageNet classification with deep convolutional neural networks. *Communications of the ACM*, *60*(6), 84–90. doi:10.1145/3065386

Krizhevsky, A., Sutskever, I., & Hinton, G. E. (2012). Imagenet classification with deep convolutional neural networks. In *Proceedings of the 25th International Conference on Neural Information Processing Systems* (vol. 1, pp. 1097–1105). Curran Associates Inc

Kumar, N., Belhumeur, P. N., Biswas, A., & Jacobs, D. W. W. (2012). Computer Vision System for Automatic Plant Species Identification. In Computer Vision – ECCV 2012 (vol. 7573, pp. 502–516). Springer Berlin Heidelberg.

Kumar, P. M., Surya, C. M., & Gopi, V. P. (2017, November). Identification of ayurvedic medicinal plants by image processing of leaf samples. In *2017 Third International Conference on Research in Computational Intelligence and Communication Networks (ICRCICN)* (pp. 231-238). IEEE. 10.1109/ICRCICN.2017.8234512

Kumar, P. M., Surya, C. M., & Gopi, V. P. (2017). Identification of ayurvedic medicinal plants by image processing of leaf samples. *2017 Third International Conference on Research in Computational Intelligence and Communication Networks (ICRCICN)*, 231–238. 10.1109/ICRCICN.2017.8234512

Larsson, Maire, & Shakhnarovich. (2017). *FractalNet: Ultra-Deep Neural Networks without Residuals.* arXiv: 1605.07648.

Lee, Chan, Mayo, & Remagnino. (2017). How deep learning extracts and learns leaf features for plant classification. *Pattern Recognition, 71*, 1–13.

Lee, Chan, Wilkin, & Remagnino. (2015). Deep-plant: Plant identification with convolutional neural networks. *2015 IEEE International Conference on Image Processing (ICIP),* 452–456.

K. Mao, & X. Jiang (Eds.). Local binary pattern based on image gradient for bark image classification. In *Tenth International Conference on Signal Processing Systems* (p. 39). SPIE.

Mostajer Kheirkhah, F., & Asghari, H. (2019, June). [Plant leaf classification using GIST texture features. *IET Computer Vision*, *13*(4), 369–375. doi:10.1049/iet-cvi.2018.5028

Munisami, T., Ramsurn, M., Kishnah, S., & Pudaruth, S. (2015). Plant leaf recognition using shape features and colour histogram with K-nearest neighbour classifiers. *Procedia Computer Science*, *58*, 740–747. doi:10.1016/j.procs.2015.08.095

Olsen, Konovalov, Philippa, Ridd, Wood, Johns, Banks, Girgenti, Kenny, Whinney, Calvert, Azghadi, & White. (2019, December). DeepWeeds: A Multiclass Weed Species Image Dataset for Deep Learning. *Scientific Reports*, *9*(1), 2058. PMID:30765729

Pawar, M. S., Perianayagam, L., & Rani, N. S. (2017, June). Region based image classification using watershed transform techniques. In *2017 International Conference on Intelligent Computing and Control (I2C2)* (pp. 1-5). IEEE. 10.1109/I2C2.2017.8321839

Pearline, S. A., Kumar, V. S., & Harini, S. (2019). A study on plant recognition using conventional image processing and deep learning approaches. *Journal of Intelligent & Fuzzy Systems*, (Preprint), 1-8.

Prasad, S., Kumar, P., & Tripathi, R. C. (2011, September). Plant leaf species identification using curvelet transform. In *2011 2nd International Conference on Computer and Communication Technology (ICCCT-2011)* (pp. 646-652). IEEE. 10.1109/ICCCT.2011.6075212

Prasad, S., & Singh, P. P. (2017). Medicinal plant leaf information extraction using deep features. TENCON 2017 - 2017 IEEE Region 10 Conference, 2722–2726. doi:10.1109/TENCON.2017.8228324

Priya, C. A., Balasaravanan, T., & Thanamani, A. S. (2012, March). An efficient leaf recognition algorithm for plant classification using support vector machine. In *International conference on pattern recognition, informatics and medical engineering (PRIME-2012)* (pp. 428-432). IEEE. 10.1109/ICPRIME.2012.6208384

Pvloiu, Ancuceanu, Enache, & Vasileanu. (2017). Important shape features for romanian medicinal herb identification based on leaf image. *2017 E-Health and Bioengineering Conference (EHB),* 599–602.

Quoc & Hoang. (2020). Vnplant-200–a public and large-scale of Vietnamese medicinal plant images dataset. In *International Conference on Integrated Science* (pp. 406–411). Springer.

Russakovsky, Deng, Su, Krause, Satheesh, Ma, Huang, Karpathy, Khosla, Bernstein, Berg, & Fei-Fei. (2015, December). ImageNet Large Scale Visual Recognition Challenge. *International Journal of Computer Vision, 115*(3), 211–252.

Sabu, A., Sreekumar, K., & Nair, R. R. (2017). Recognition of ayurvedic medicinal plants from leaves: A computer vision approach. *2017 Fourth International Conference on Image Information Processing (ICIIP),* 1–5. 10.1109/ICIIP.2017.8313782

Salima, A., Herdiyeni, Y., & Douady, S. (2015). Leaf vein segmentation of medicinal plant using hessian matrix. *2015 International Conference on Advanced Computer Science and Information Systems (ICACSIS),* 275–279. 10.1109/ICACSIS.2015.7415152

Simonyan & Zisserman. (2015). *Very Deep Convolutional Networks for Large-Scale Image Recognition.* arXiv: 1409.1556.

Soderkvist. (2001). *Computer Vision Classification of Leaves from Swedish Trees* [Dissertation].

Szegedy, Ioffe, Vanhoucke, & Alemi. (2017). Inception-v4, inception-resnet and the impact of residual connections on learning. In *Proceedings of the Thirty-First AAAI Conference on Artificial Intelligence, AAAI'17* (pp. 4278–4284). AAAI Press.

Szegedy, Liu, Jia, Sermanet, Reed, Anguelov, Erhan, Vanhoucke, & Rabinovich. (2015). Going deeper with convolutions. In *2015 IEEE Conference on Computer Vision and Pattern Recognition (CVPR)* (pp. 1–9). IEEE.

Venkataraman, D., & Mangayarkarasi, N. (2016). Computer vision based feature extraction of leaves for identification of medicinal values of plants. *2016 IEEE International Conference on Computational Intelligence and Computing Research (ICCIC),* 1–5. 10.1109/ICCIC.2016.7919637

VijayaLakshmi, B., & Mohan, V. (2016). Kernel- based PSO and FRVM: An automatic plant leaf type detection using texture, shape, and color features. *Computers and Electronics in Agriculture, 125,* 99–112. doi:10.1016/j.compag.2016.04.033

Wei Tan, J., Chang, S. W., Abdul-Kareem, S., Yap, H. J., & Yong, K. T. (2018). Deep learning for plant species classification using leaf vein morphometric. *IEEE/ACM Transactions on Computational Biology and Bioinformatics, 17*(1), 82–90. PMID:29994129

Wu, S. G., Bao, F. S., Xu, E. Y., Wang, Y. X., Chang, Y. F., & Xiang, Q. L. (2007, December). A leaf recognition algorithm for plant classification using probabilistic neural network. In *2007 IEEE international symposium on signal processing and information technology* (pp. 11-16). IEEE.

Wu, Bao, Xu, Wang, Chang, & Xiang. (2007). A Leaf Recognition Algorithm for Plant Classification Using Probabilistic Neural Network. In *2007 IEEE International Symposium on Signal Processing and Information Technology* (pp. 11–16). IEEE.

Xiao, Q., Li, G., Xie, L., & Chen, Q. (2018, November). Real-world plant species identification based on deep convolutional neural networks and visual attention. *Ecological Informatics, 48,* 117–124. doi:10.1016/j.ecoinf.2018.09.001

Yao, Y., Rosasco, L., & Caponnetto, A. (2007, August). On Early Stopping in Gradient Descent Learning. *Constructive Approximation*, *26*(2), 289–315. doi:10.100700365-006-0663-2

Yigit, E., Sabanci, K., Toktas, A., & Kayabasi, A. (2019). A study on visual features of leaves in plant identification using artificial intelligence techniques. *Computers and Electronics in Agriculture*, *156*, 369–377. doi:10.1016/j.compag.2018.11.036

Zhang, S., Zhang, C., & Huang, W. (2018, December). Integrating leaf and flower by local discriminant CCA for plant species recognition. *Computers and Electronics in Agriculture*, *155*, 150–156. doi:10.1016/j.compag.2018.10.018

Zhang, S., Zhang, C., Wang, Z., & Kong, W. (2018, June). Combining sparse representation and singular value decomposition for plant recognition. *Applied Soft Computing*, *67*, 164–171. doi:10.1016/j.asoc.2018.02.052

KEY TERMS AND DEFINITIONS

Biodiversity Monitoring: It facilitates biodiversity monitoring by automating the identification of plant species, aiding in ecological studies and conservation strategies. Continuous biodiversity monitoring is crucial for tracking changes in plant populations and ecosystems.

Conservation Efforts: CNNs aid in conservation efforts by accurately identifying and monitoring endangered plant species, contributing to their protection. Effective conservation strategies rely on data-driven insights and technology like CNNs for plant species assessment.

Convolutional Neural Networks (CNN): It is deep learning model uniquely suited for tasks like medicinal plant classification due to their ability to learn hierarchical features from images. The versatility and accuracy of CNNs make them indispensable in a wide range of applications beyond plant classification.

Ethnobotany: It benefits from CNNs by enabling the systematic documentation and validation of traditional plant uses. The integration of AI in ethnobotanical research enhances our understanding of the cultural significance of medicinal plants.

Medicinal Plants: It is a vital source of natural remedies, and CNNs can help unlock their potential through image analysis. Research on medicinal plants is advancing with the aid of AI, improving the discovery and validation of their therapeutic properties.

Pharmaceutical Research: CNNs play a pivotal role in pharmaceutical research, accelerating the discovery of bioactive compounds within medicinal plants. AI-driven drug discovery from natural sources relies on CNNs to identify potential candidates for pharmaceutical development.

Plant Species Identification: It works of botanists and ecologists, ensuring accurate and rapid classification. Accurate plant species identification is essential for ecological studies, conservation efforts, and pharmaceutical research.

Traditional Medicine Validation: The validation with CNNs involves scientific analysis of plant properties, bridging traditional knowledge with modern research. This approach helps preserve traditional practices while ensuring the safety and efficacy of medicinal plant use.

VGG-19: VGG-19 is a popular CNN architecture known for its deep and complex network structure, making it effective for fine-grained image classification. Researchers often employ VGG-19 as a pre-trained model for transfer learning in medicinal plant classification.

Visual Feature Extraction: It is a critical step in CNNs, allowing them to identify and differentiate plant species based on their visual characteristics. CNNs excel at visual feature extraction, enabling them to recognize intricate details in medicinal plants' images.

Chapter 8
Leading the Library Revolution With FOLIO:
A Cutting-Edge Open Source Library Service Platform

Subhajit Panda
https://orcid.org/0000-0002-1578-1159
Chandigarh University, India

Navkiran Kaur
Punjabi University, India

ABSTRACT

This chapter delves into the evolution of library management systems (LMS) and the emergence of library services platforms (LSP) with a focus on FOLIO, an innovative open-source solution. Beginning with the historical context of open-source software in libraries, it dissects the architectural nuances between monolithic and micro-services systems in LMS development. The discussion shifts to a comprehensive understanding of FOLIO, exploring its installation, specialized apps, and pivotal features. Addressing challenges in FOLIO implementation, the chapter offers practical insights and best practices. It emphasizes enhancing user experience through accessibility and personalized options and elucidates FOLIO's robust security measures and data privacy in the open-source realm. Furthermore, it illuminates the thriving FOLIO community, encouraging active participation and collaboration. The chapter concludes by contemplating FOLIO's transformative impact on the future landscape of library management.

INTRODUCTION

Libraries have always been dynamic institutions, continuously evolving to meet the growing expectations of users. While financial constraints pose challenges, embracing new technologies and software solutions becomes crucial to surpass user demands. Open-source options have proven particularly beneficial for nonprofit organizations like libraries. As libraries undergo digital transformation, traditional

DOI: 10.4018/979-8-3693-0807-3.ch008

Integrated Library Systems (ILS) are becoming outdated, and Library Services Platforms (LSPs) offer enhanced flexibility and functionality within a unified framework (Grant, 2013; Paulderscheid, 2021). Among emerging LSPs, FOLIO (Future of Libraries is Open) has shown rapid progress, with its microservices architecture and emphasis on apps over modules, providing a multitasking app environment, an intuitive Dashboard, and efficient data management (Chauhan et al., 2023). This user-friendly approach sets FOLIO apart from conventional ILS systems. Notwithstanding its abundant features and potential benefits, FOLIO has yet to gain widespread recognition, particularly within the library community in India, where its adoption remains rare. This chapter, therefore, endeavors to heighten awareness among library professionals about this cutting-edge LSP and encourage them to embrace it for their libraries' advancement. By exploring FOLIO's distinctive capabilities and highlighting its transformative impact, this chapter aims to inspire librarians to consider FOLIO as a promising solution to enhance their library services and meet the evolving needs of their patrons in the digital age.

Overall these study highlighted that, FOLIO, as an open-source library management system, presents a promising alternative to conventional proprietary systems. Its modular design, API integration, and collaborative community approach empower libraries to innovate and adapt. While challenges exist, FOLIO's potential to revolutionize library services is evident. Continued research, development, and global collaboration will further enhance FOLIO's role in shaping the future of libraries.

STUDY OBJECTIVES

The primary objectives of the study is to,

1) Understand architectural paradigms in ILS development.
2) Differentiate between Library Management Software and Library Services Platforms.
3) Explore FOLIO's architecture, installation, features, and specialized apps.
4) Overcome challenges, adopt best practices, and prepare for FOLIO adoption.
5) Enhance user interactions, ensure accessibility, and gather feedback.
6) Understand FOLIO's security, open-source data privacy, and collaborative measures.
7) Explore collaboration opportunities, contribute to growth, and grasp FOLIO's impact on library management.

STUDY BACKGROUND

Timeline of Open Source Software (OSS) Development in Libraries

In the 21st century, managing libraries effectively and meeting the ever-changing needs of patrons are paramount (Momoh & Folorunso, 2019). With time and changing users' need libraries must evolve and synchronize with technology to thrive. However, limited funds often hinder library progress. Open-Source Software (OSS) emerges as a solution (Velmurugan & Kannan, 2012). Richard Stallman initiated the open-source movement in 1985, emphasizing community support, cost-effectiveness, and flexibility (Nduta, 2023). Following are the benchmarks of the timeline of OSS development in libraries (Figure 1):

Figure 1. Evolution of open-source software in libraries (chronological overview)
Source: Chauhan et al. (2023)

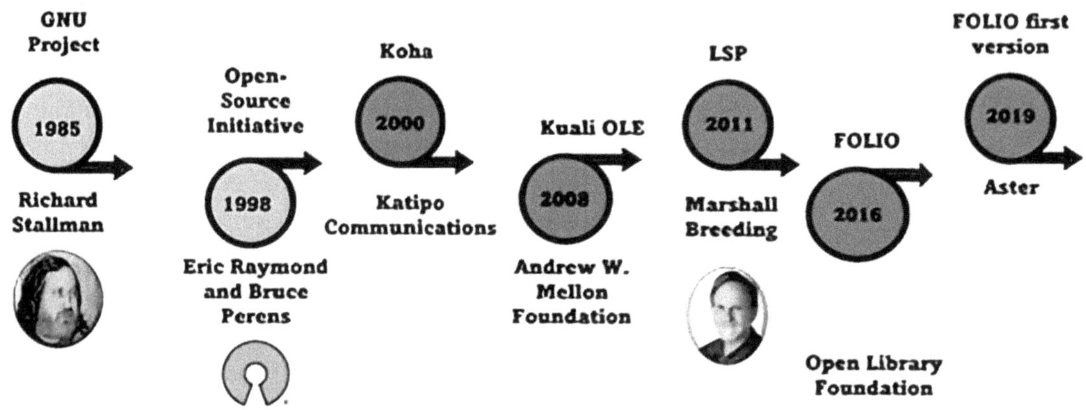

1985: The open-source movement begins with Richard Stallman's GNU Project, laying the foundation for community-driven software development.

1998: The Open Source Initiative (OSI) is established by Bruce Perens and Eric S. Raymond, emphasizing the importance of open-source principles and collaboration.

2000: Koha, a pioneering open-source Integrated Library System (ILS), is introduced by Karipo Communications, marking a significant leap in library technology.

2008: Kuali OLE, an open-source library management system, is launched with support from the Andrew W. Mellon Foundation, emphasizing collaborative development.

2011: Library Services Platforms (LSPs) emerge, led by Marshall Breeding, introducing a unified platform to manage various types of library resources.

2016: FOLIO, a revolutionary open-source Library Services Platform, is initiated, signaling a new era in library automation.

2019: FOLIO's first version, developed by Aster, is released, showcasing the practical implementation of the innovative FOLIO platform.

Libraries, driven by the digital revolution, face challenges managing non-physical resources like electronic materials. Legacy of Integrated Library Systems (ILS) become obsolete, necessitating specialized E-Resources Management systems (ERM). While ERM software like CORAL and Alma ERM exists, they function independently, demanding separate maintenance and costs (Fournie, 2020). To bridge these gaps, Library Services Platforms (LSPs) emerged. Powered by micro-service architecture, LSPs offer a unified solution for managing diverse resources, overcoming the limitations of traditional ILS, and embracing cloud computing, revolutionizing the library landscape.

Literature Review

The FOLIO Library Services Platform (LSP) is an open-source initiative revolutionizing library management systems globally. Despite being in continuous development, recent studies shed light on FOLIO's evolution, challenges, and transformative potential in the library landscape.

FOLIO's Development Odyssey

Owens and Thomas (2019) underscored FOLIO's flexibility, crucial for adapting to the uncertain future of cataloging. Taylor (2021) emphasized FOLIO's modular design, allowing libraries to actively participate and tailor modules to their unique needs, fostering a vibrant, community-driven approach.

Navigating Implementation Challenges

The successful transition of Cornell University from a vended application to FOLIO (Colt and Howell, 2021) highlighted FOLIO's adaptability, making it a versatile solution for libraries of varied scales and structures. Shanghai Library's implementation journey (Zhou et al., 2023) illustrated collaborative problem-solving within the Chinese library network, marking a milestone in FOLIO's global implementation.

Empowering Libraries Through Technical Advancements

Dobson (2021) spotlighted FOLIO's prowess in API integration, facilitating seamless data transfer and enabling enhanced functionality. This aligns with Liu's (2021) forward-thinking perspective, emphasizing FOLIO's ability to meet librarians' expectations through cutting-edge API-driven solutions.

FOLIO's Vision in Smart Libraries

W. Liu (2021) delved into FOLIO's potential in shaping Smart Libraries in China, championing its open and adaptable service platform. Kulkarni et al. (2023) provided an insightful panorama of FOLIO, highlighting its affordability, usability, and transformative impact on library services, setting the stage for a progressive library era.

WHAT IS MONOLITHIC AND MICRO-SERVICES ARCHITECTURE IN ILS DEVELOPMENT?

In the context of Integrated Library Systems (ILS) development, a monolithic architecture refers to a traditional approach where all components and features of the system are tightly interconnected and interdependent. On the other hand, a microservices architecture is a more modern and flexible approach to software development, including ILS. In this architecture, the system is broken down into smaller, independent services, each serving a specific function or process. Following are some main features of monolithic and micro-services architecture (Harris, n.d.) (Raman, 2020):

Table 1. Monolithic vs. micro-services architecture in ILS development

Monolithic Architecture	Micro-Services Architecture
1. Unified Codebase: Monolithic ILS systems have a single, interconnected codebase where all functions are tightly integrated. **2. Interdependent Modules:** Changes or updates in one module can affect the entire system due to the tight coupling between components. **3. Complexity:** Monolithic architectures tend to be large and intricate, making them challenging to modify or scale. **4. Limited Flexibility:** It is difficult to add new features or adapt to changing needs without significant system-wide changes. **5. Maintenance Challenges:** Maintenance can be cumbersome as modifications need careful consideration to avoid disrupting other modules.	**1. Modular Approach:** Micro-services ILS systems consist of independent, modular services, each serving specific functions. **2. Decentralized Services:** Each micro-service operates independently, communicating with others through well-defined APIs. **3. Scalability:** Micro-services allow for individual components to be scaled independently based on demand, enhancing system efficiency. **4. Flexibility:** Libraries can easily add, modify, or remove specific services without impacting the entire system, ensuring adaptability to changing requirements. **5. Ease of Maintenance:** Maintenance is streamlined as modifications can be made to individual services without disrupting the entire system, leading to quicker updates and reduced downtime.

Figure 2. Monolithic architecture

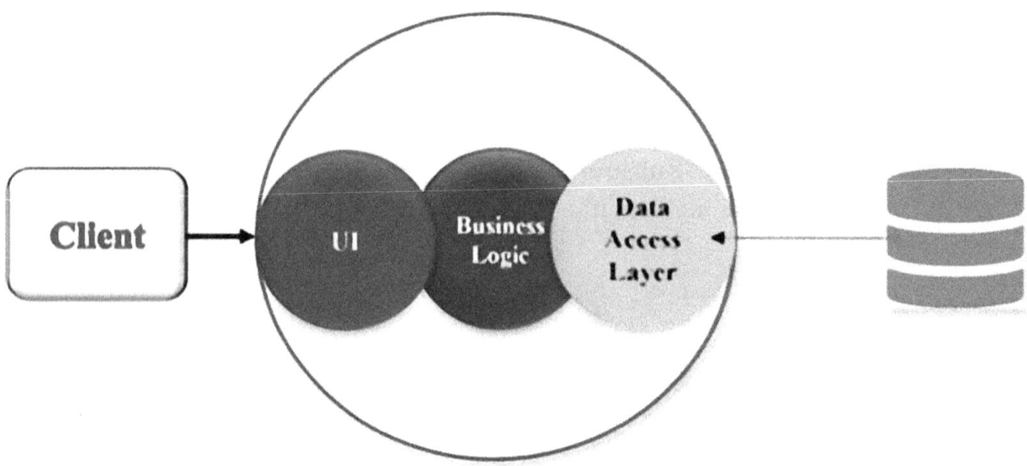

Figure 3: Micro-services architecture

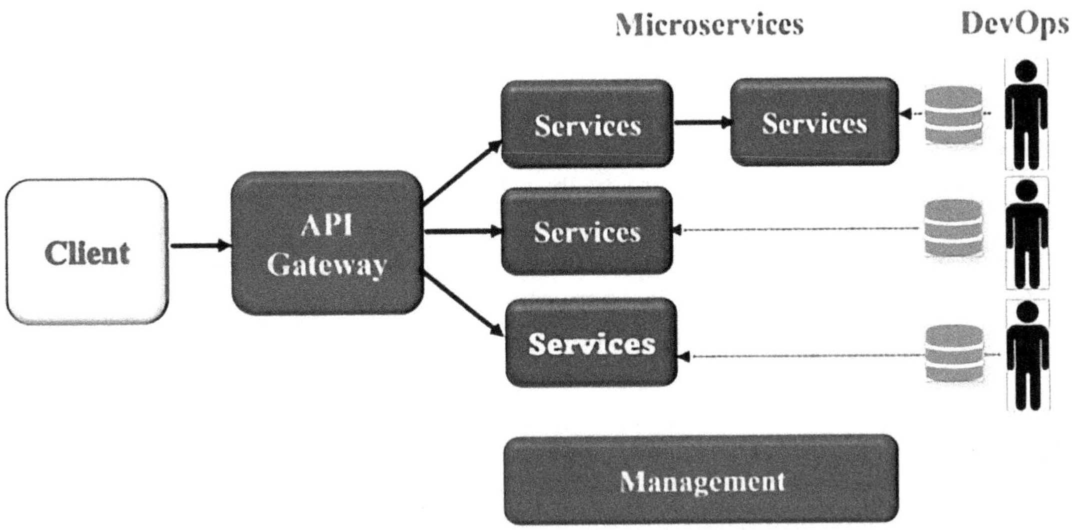

UNDERSTANDING LIBRARY MANAGEMENT SOFTWARE (LMS) AND LIBRARY SERVICES PLATFORM (LSP)

Library Management Software (LMS) and Library Services Platform (LSP) are both types of software systems used by libraries to manage their resources, streamline operations, and enhance user experiences. While they serve similar purposes, there are differences in their scope and functionality.

Library Management Software (LMS)

Library Management Software, often referred to as an LMS, is a comprehensive software solution designed to automate and manage the day-to-day operations of a library (Anurag, 2020). It helps librarians and library staff in tasks such as cataloging, circulation (loans and returns), acquisitions (ordering and receiving materials), serials management, and patron management (keeping track of library members). LMS also typically includes modules for generating reports, managing fines, and sometimes even for online public access catalogs (OPACs), enabling patrons to search for library materials remotely (Ferguson & Hebels, 2003).

Key features of LMS include:

- **Cataloging:** Creating and managing the library's catalog, including details of books, journals, multimedia, and other resources.
- **Circulation:** Managing the borrowing and returning of materials by patrons.
- Acquisitions: Handling the process of ordering, receiving, and paying for new materials.
- **Patron Management:** Managing user accounts, including membership details and borrowing history.
- **Serials Management:** Tracking and managing periodicals, journals, and other recurring publications.

- **Reporting:** Generating various reports related to library usage, inventory, and finances.

Library Services Platform (LSP)

Library Services Platform (LSP) is an evolved form of Library Management Software. It includes all the functionalities of an LMS but goes a step further by providing a unified, integrated platform that supports a broader range of library services (Pradhan, 2021). LSPs are designed to be more flexible, allowing libraries to customize and extend the system based on their specific needs. They often emphasize openness, allowing integration with other systems and services. LSPs also typically leverage modern technologies like cloud computing and APIs (Application Programming Interfaces) for seamless interaction with various library applications and databases.

Key features of LSP include:

- **Modular Architecture:** LSPs are built on a modular architecture, allowing libraries to add or remove modules based on their requirements. Each module serves a specific purpose, like cataloging, acquisitions, or analytics.
- **Flexibility:** LSPs are highly flexible, enabling libraries to tailor the system to their unique workflows and processes.
- **Interoperability:** LSPs can integrate with other library systems, databases, and external services, creating a more interconnected library ecosystem.
- **User Experience:** LSPs often focus on providing a seamless and user-friendly experience for both library staff and patrons. This may include intuitive interfaces and enhanced search capabilities.
- **Data Analytics:** Many LSPs incorporate advanced analytics tools, allowing libraries to gain insights into patron behavior, resource usage, and other important metrics.

Overall, while Library Management Software primarily focuses on automating core library functions, Library Services Platforms offer a more dynamic and integrated approach, allowing libraries to adapt and expand their services in response to changing user needs and technological advancements.

THE FOLIO REVOLUTION: OVERVIEW OF THE CORE CONCEPTS

Early Development

A roadmap functions as a strategic blueprint outlining goals and essential steps to achieve them. It not only communicates the 'why' behind the objectives but also serves as a tool for articulating strategic plans. For FOLIO, this roadmap amalgamates priorities defined by the FOLIO Project and Community, aligning them with development capacities to establish goals and milestones for upcoming releases (Figure 4). It aids the community in planning releases, resource coordination, and communicating project goals, encompassing software development from platforms to apps and third-party integrations (Figure 5). Essentially, the roadmap acts as a bridge between strategic vision and actual development, ensuring alignment. An update shared official Twitter account of FOLIO, on October 23, 2019, highlighted FOLIO's progress, showcasing successful library implementations, ongoing testing, and adoption efforts (FOLIO-Open Libraries, 2023).

Figure 4. FOLIO milestones (ver. 2)
Source: Murray and Martin (2022)

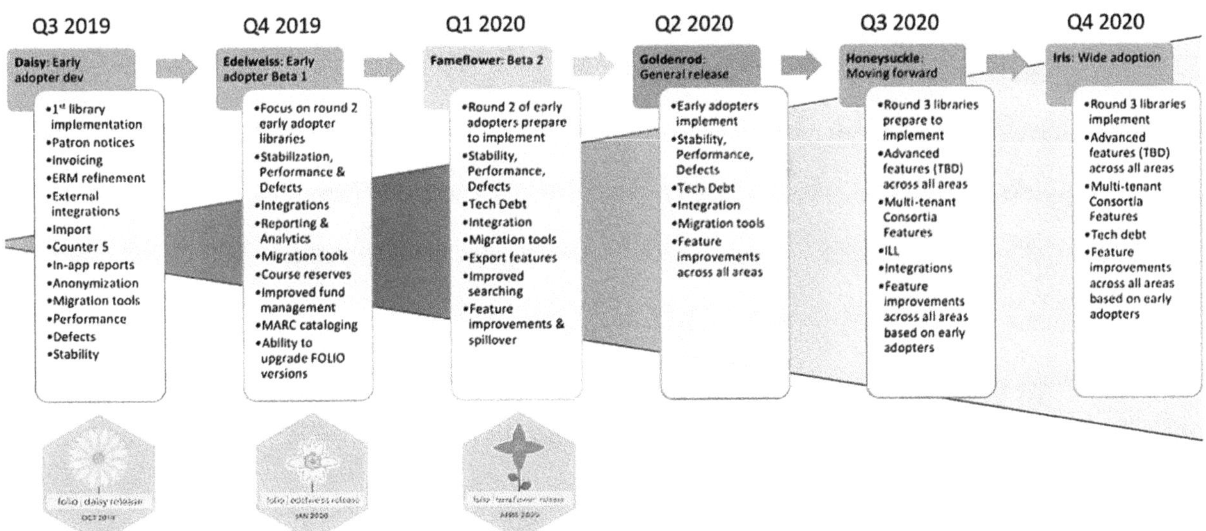

Figure 5. FOLIO software relese milestones
Source: Murray and Martin (2022)

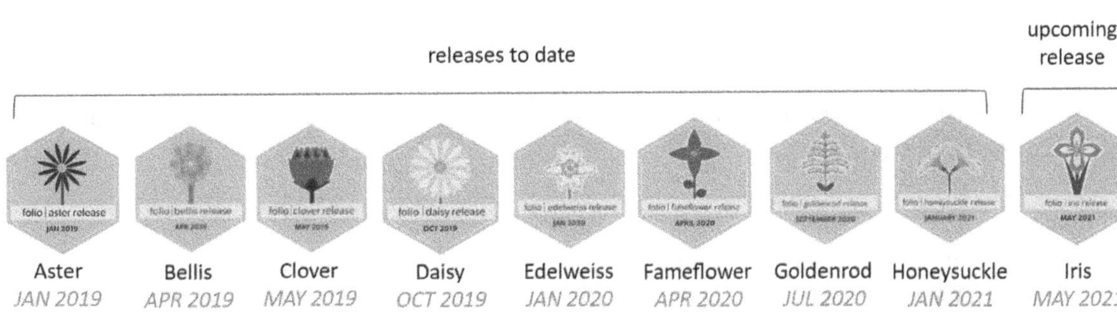

FOLIO Architecture

At the heart of FOLIO lies its innovative modular architecture, a design that fosters seamless interoperability and communication among its various components. Central to this architecture is the Okapi gateway (Figure 6), a pivotal component enabling integration with loosely coupled apps, often referred to as micro-services (McNally & Kuss, 2020).

Figure 6. Folio platform architectural diagram
Source: McNally and Kuss (2020)

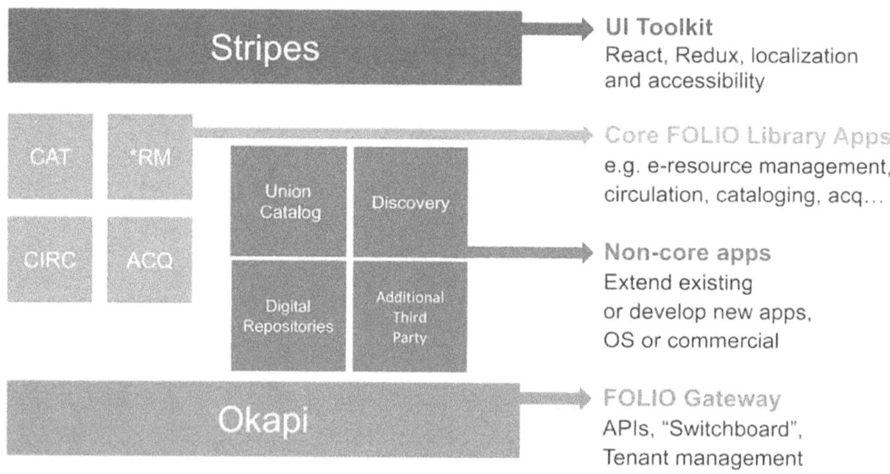

These micro-services exhibit functional cohesion, providing a rich array of features such as analytics, circulation, acquisitions, and inventories (Murray & Colt, 2023). This well-crafted architecture forms the backbone of FOLIO, ensuring a dynamic and adaptable platform that meets the diverse needs of modern libraries.

Installation of FOLIO (Pre-Built Vagrant Boxes)

FOLIO offers multiple installation methods, including pre-built vagrant boxes, single-server deployment, and Kubernetes deployment. For a hassle-free trial, individuals can opt for the pre-built vagrant box installation. Here's how:

Prerequisites:

- **Vagrant:** Ensure you have the latest version installed.
- **VirtualBox:** Match the version of VirtualBox with your Vagrant version.

Installation Steps:

1. **Folder Setup:** Create a new folder. Open it, then right-click to open the terminal. Paste the following commands in sequence:

Figure 7. Code for folder setup

```arduino
vagrant init --minimal folio/release-core
```

2. **Create VagrantFile:** Within the same folder, create a file named VagrantFile and add the following code:

Figure 8. Code to create VagrantFile

```ruby
Vagrant.configure("2") do |config|
  config.vm.box = "folio/snapshot"
  config.vm.provider "virtualbox" do |vb|
    vb.memory = 24576
    vb.cpus = 2
  end
end
```

3. **Start the Installation:** In your browser, access localhost:3000 (initial credentials: diku_admin/admin).

Having explored this Library Services Platform (LSP) hands-on, it becomes evident that FOLIO's micro-services architecture, or 'apps,' represents a significant advancement from traditional ILS modules. These apps offer enhanced efficiency and user-friendliness. The interface is both simple and impressive, featuring a customizable dashboard with quick access options and widgets. FOLIO's integrated Electronic Resource Management (ERM) system reduces reliance on external software. Its multitasking app environment enhances accessibility, while specialized tools like the courses app facilitate streamlined course reserves management. Additionally, FOLIO supports an open-source reporting project named LDP (Library Data Platform), functioning as a relational database capable of creating custom tables for importing non-FOLIO data. Despite its strengths, certain limitations include potential challenges in production-level implementation due to technical complexities. Furthermore, the involvement of commercial vendors might pose a risk to FOLIO's open-source status in the future. Additionally, meeting the platform's minimum requirements could be a hurdle for some libraries. Overall, FOLIO's pre-built vagrant boxes offer a convenient entry point, allowing users to experience its advanced features without the complexities of a full installation.

Features of FOLIO

FOLIO, as a cutting-edge Library Services Platform (LSP), boasts a range of distinctive features that elevate its status in the realm of library technology. Below are the key aspects that define its prowess:

User Interface/User Experience (UI/UX)

FOLIO's User Interface (UI) stands as a cornerstone of its design philosophy. Guided by the MOTIF design system, FOLIO ensures consistency and user-friendliness across its apps. Implemented using Stripes, a dedicated front-end framework, developers can create FOLIO apps with minimal coding. The system offers reusable UI components and modules, simplifying tasks like data gathering, routing, authentication, and localization. Resources on the FOLIO UX website, including interactive prototypes, design documentation, and downloadable assets, empower developers and designers to craft FOLIO apps in alignment with MOTIF guidelines (FOLIO Project, n.d.).

API Support

FOLIO's robust Application Programming Interface (API) facilitates seamless interactions with external systems. Built on REST principles, it uses common HTTP methods like GET, POST, PUT, and DELETE, communicating with the FOLIO server through JSON. The Okapi, an API Gateway, manages various modules such as acquisitions, circulation, and analytics. It categorizes web service endpoints into core APIs for general module and tenant management and business-logic-specific interfaces for modules like circulation or patron management. FOLIO's flexible API allows libraries to modify and enhance the platform according to their needs (Figure 9). It also enables integration with external systems like discovery layers and digital repositories, ensuring versatility.

Figure 9. Working pattern of a FOLIO API

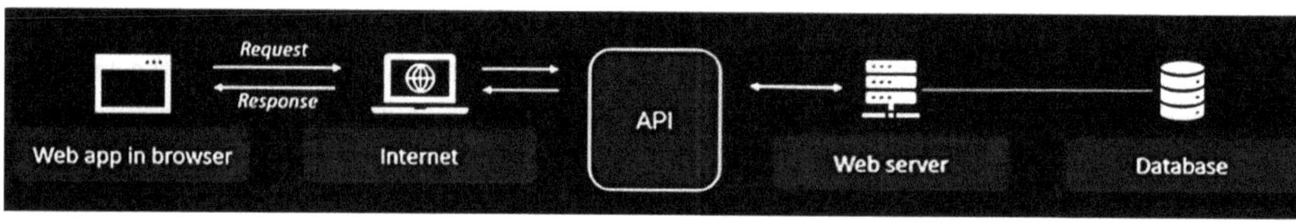

FOLIO Community

FOLIO's active and expansive community is a testament to the strength of open-source collaboration. This vibrant community encourages innovation, offering feedback, support, and suggestions that enhance the software's quality and efficiency. Governed by three distinct councils—Community, Product, and Technical—FOLIO hosts Special Interest Groups (SIGs) focused on specific functional areas. These SIGs, such as the App Interaction SIG and ERM SIG, involve library practitioners who contribute to the platform's development and improvement (Gorrell & Colt, 2023).

Choice-Oriented Services

FOLIO empowers libraries with choice-oriented services, allowing them to tailor their offerings based on patron preferences. The platform's flexibility enables libraries to select modules and applications that align with their workflows and objectives. This freedom gives libraries control over their future, ensuring adaptability and scalability in response to changing needs.

FOLIO Codex

FOLIO's microservices architecture communicates with various apps, managing metadata and diverse formats through what is known as the Codex. This collection of metadata, with its normalization and virtualization layers, allows FOLIO to incorporate metadata from multiple resources regardless of format, storage location, or encoding (Figure 10).

Figure 10. FOLIO codex
Source: Bareau and Nettifee (2023)

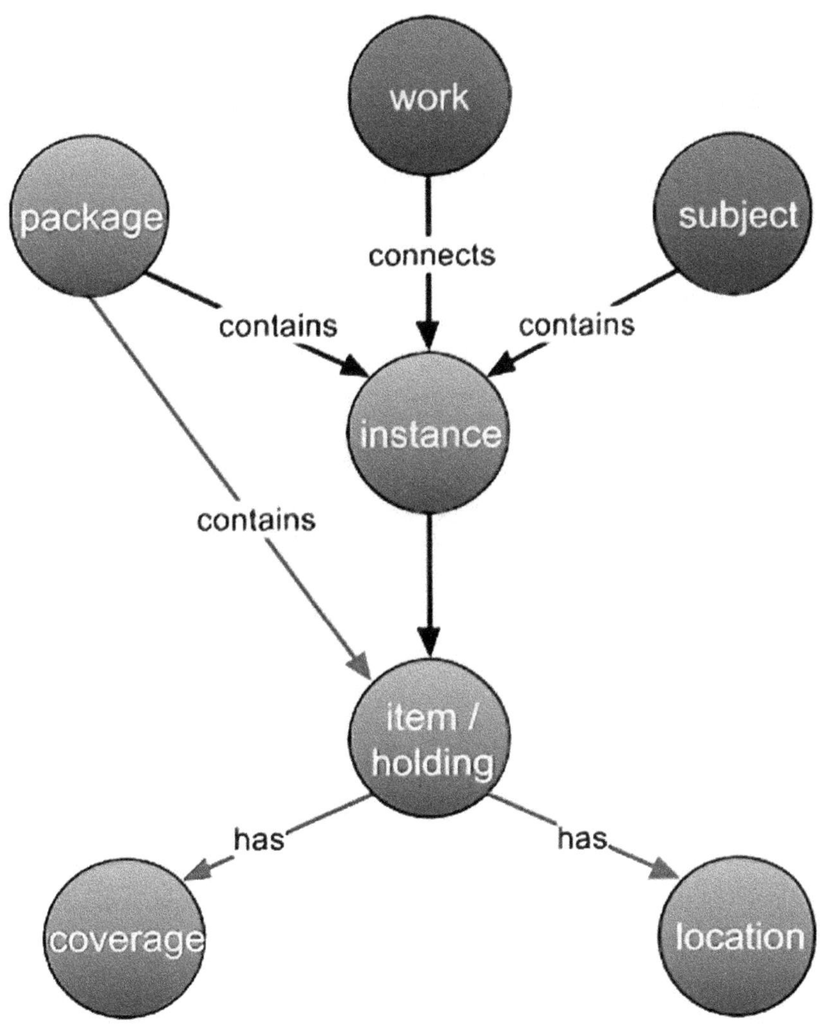

The Codex utilizes a simplified metadata schema that can accommodate widely used models like MARC, Dublin Core, MODS, and BIBFRAME. It facilitates "cataloguing-by-reference" and enhances efficiency compared to traditional copy cataloguing methods. The Codex Search app, a prominent FOLIO Codex application, enables users to search for resources across multiple apps, including institutional repositories and inventory management systems (Bareau & Nettifee, 2023).

FOLIO With Cloud

FOLIO's futuristic vision includes its integration with cloud-based infrastructure. By leveraging cloud services, FOLIO gains maximum uptime, elasticity, resilience, and security. Moving to the cloud enhances FOLIO's services, aligning it with contemporary standards of efficiency and adaptability.

Overall, FOLIO's features not only reflect its technological prowess but also underscore its commitment to user-centric design, community collaboration, and adaptability in the evolving landscape of library services.

FOLIO's Specialized Apps for Various Library Functions

FOLIO, as a versatile Library Services Platform, offers a range of specific apps tailored to diverse library functions.

Figure 11. FOLIO's specialized apps
Source: FOLIO (2023j)

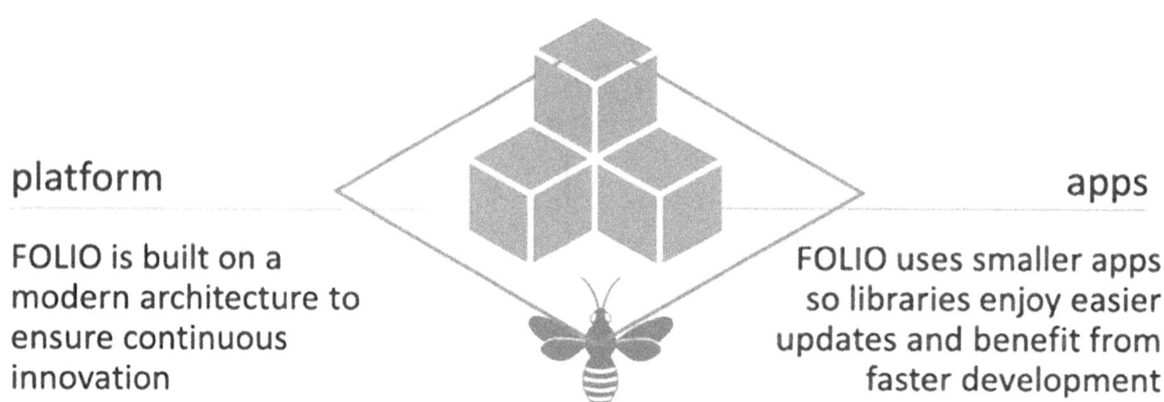

These apps are designed to cater to various aspects of library management and user experience. Some specific FOLIO apps include (Murray, 2023):

Bulk Edit

The Bulk Edit app enables simultaneous modifications across various records (FOLIO, 2022b).

Supported Record Types: In Nolana, bulk edits are supported for three records types,

- Users: Edit user records through FOLIO's CSV or In-App methods. CSV involves downloading, editing, and uploading user records, while In-App utilizes identifiers for batch edits.
- Inventory Items: Modify item records by uploading identifiers and applying changes using the In-App method within the Inventory app.
- Inventory Holdings: Edit holdings records by employing identifiers and In-App changes within the Inventory app.

Note: Future releases may include additional record types.

Permissions:

- Define access with permissions in the Users app:
  - Bulk Edit (CSV) Delete: Delete multiple user records using CSV.
  - Bulk Edit (CSV) Edit: Edit fields in multiple user records via CSV.
  - Bulk Edit (CSV) View: View identified user records using CSV.
  - Bulk Edit (In App - Delete: Delete multiple inventory records within the Bulk Edit app.
  - Bulk Edit (In App - Edit: Modify fields in multiple inventory records within the Bulk Edit app.
  - Bulk Edit (In App - View: View inventory records within the Bulk Edit app.
- Additional permissions may be required based on the library's bulk edit processes in modules like Export Manager, Inventory, Users, and Settings.

Editing Methods:

- CSV Approach: Utilize .csv files for record editing, allowing modifications based on Record identifiers. Changes are saved in the .csv file and uploaded to commit edits. Caution is advised, especially with Excel, to prevent unintended alterations.
- In-App Approach: Search for and modify multiple records directly within the browser window using the In-App method.

Check Out

The Check Out application enables you to lend items to patrons. To complete the process, begin by finding the relevant patron in the system and then scan or manually input the item for borrowing (FOLIO, 2023f).

Permissions:

- Check Out: All Permissions: Allows creating new loans, viewing open loans, and loan details. Does not provide full access to the user record.
- Check Out: Circulating Items: Enables item checkouts but doesn't override non-circulating loan policies.

Upcoming Permissions (In Development):

- View Fees/Fines: Permits users to view a patron's fees/fines in the Users app via a link in the Scan patron card pane.
- View Loans: Grants access to view a patron's current loans in the Users app through a link in the Scan patron card pane.

- View Requests: Allows users to view a patron's current requests in the Requests app via a link in the Scan patron card pane.

Circulation Log

The Circulation Log app enables viewing and searching for various circulation actions, including those from Check In, Check Out, Requests, as well as notices and fee/fine actions (FOLIO, 2023e).

Permissions:

Circulation Log: All Permission: Users require this permission to access the Circulation Log. It allows filtering of all log actions and data within the app. No other permissions are available for the Circulation Log app. Access is granted through assignment in the Users app.

Courses

The Courses app facilitates the creation and management of course reserves (FOLIO, 2023a).

Note: To make courses discoverable by patrons, integration with an external interface or discovery layer interacting with FOLIO is necessary.

Permissions:

- Courses: All Permissions: Enables full maintenance (view, add, edit, delete) of courses, items, instructors, and cross-listed courses.
- Courses: Read, Add, Edit Courses: Allows viewing, adding, and editing courses but prohibits deletion.
- Courses: Add, Edit Courses' Reserved Items: Permits addition and editing of items associated with a course but not removal.
- Courses: Add, Edit, Remove Courses' Reserved Items: Provides complete control, allowing viewing, adding, editing, and removal of items linked to a course.
- Courses: Read All: Grants access to view all course and item information.
- Settings (Courses): Create, Edit, Delete Course Settings: Allows maintenance (view, add, edit, delete) of all course settings.

Invoices

Manages payment for library-ordered materials. Allows searching and editing of existing invoices (FOLIO, 2023g).

Definitions:

- Accounting Code: Library's code referencing an organization in their payment system.
- Acquisition Unit: Restricts user interaction with acquisitions records; defined by the library in Settings.
- Adjustments: Additional charges on an invoice (e.g., shipping costs).
- Batch Group: Invoices processed together, usually from the same library.
- Funds: Specific money allocations within a ledger.

- Invoice Lines: Individual line items in an invoice, comprising materials description, costs, and vendor reference number.
- Organizations: Institutions interacting with the library, may not be material vendors.
- Vendor: Institution from which the library purchases materials.
- Vendor Invoice Number: Number provided by the vendor for an invoice.
- Voucher Number: System-generated number to identify payment requests exported from FOLIO.

Permissions:

- Approve Invoices: Allows invoice approval.
- Assign Acquisition Units: Permits assigning acquisition units to new invoices.
- View and Edit Invoices and Invoice Lines: Enables viewing and editing of invoices and invoice lines.
- View Invoices and Invoice Lines: Allows viewing of invoices and invoice lines.
- View, Edit, and Create New Invoices and Invoice Lines: Enables viewing, editing, and creating new invoices and invoice lines.
- View, Edit, and Delete Invoices and Invoice Lines: Allows viewing, editing, and deletion of invoices and invoice lines.
- Cancel Invoice: Permits invoice cancellation.
- Download Batch File from Invoice Record: Allows downloading batch voucher files from an invoice record.
- Export Search Results: Enables exporting files containing invoice information for specific invoices.
- Manage Acquisition Units: Permits changing acquisition unit assignments for an invoice.
- Pay Invoices: Allows approving invoices for payment.
- Voucher Export: Permits running voucher exports from the Invoices app Actions menu.

Licenses

The Licenses app facilitates the creation and management of your library's licenses, which can be linked to agreements in the Agreements app (FOLIO, 2023k).

Definitions:

- Agreement: Specifies accessible content for the library.
- License: Contract detailing content usage terms.
- Organization: Institutions interacting with the library, often licensors or consortiums.

Permissions:

- Search & View Licenses: Allows searching and viewing existing licenses and amendments, accessing the License app.
- Edit Licenses: Grants all "Search & View Licenses" permissions, enabling license and amendment editing, document management, and tag modification.
- Delete Licenses: Grants all "Search & View Licenses" permissions, enabling license and amendment deletion.
- File Download: Permits document downloads (not uploads).
- Manage Pick Lists and Values: Access to License settings, managing pick lists and values.

- Manage License Terms: Access to License settings, managing available terms and viewing pick list information (necessary for managing license terms using pick lists).

Additional Permissions (for linking/viewing organizations and internal contacts in a license record):

- View Organizations: Allows searching and viewing organization records and settings, accessing Contacts and Interfaces (excluding Interface usernames and passwords).
- View Interface Usernames and Passwords: Permits viewing usernames and passwords in the Interface section.
- View User Profile: Allows viewing user profiles.

Local KB Admin

The Local KB admin app in FOLIO manages the importation of data in KBART and JSON formats, integrating it into FOLIO's local knowledgebase (KB). It also monitors harvest jobs from external sources of e-resource metadata. These imported e-resources are accessible in the Agreements app's E-resources tab and can be linked to agreements as agreement lines. The app's use is optional if you're using the eHoldings app, which relies on EBSCO's knowledgebase; you can hide the Local KB by activating the "Hide internal agreements knowledgebase" checkbox in Settings > Agreements > Display settings (FOLIO, 2022a).

Key Terms Defined:

- E-resource: Electronic resources organized into packages and titles.
- Provider: The vendor or publisher supplying the e-resource.
- Package: A bundled collection of e-resources.
- Title: An individual e-resource like an e-book, e-journal, or database.
- Package Title: A title within a specific package-platform combination.
- Knowledgebase (KB): A comprehensive database containing information about electronic resources, maintained by a knowledge base supplier.
- Local Knowledgebase: FOLIO's internal system for managing packages and e-resources.
- Proxy Server: A service used to proxy requests for e-resources to minimize authentication issues.
- Platform: A provider's infrastructure allowing access to e-resources.

Permissions:

- Local KB admin: Create jobs: Allows adding new import jobs.
- Local KB admin: Delete jobs: Permits deletion of existing import jobs.
- Local KB admin: Manage proxy server configuration: Allows creating, editing, and deleting proxy server settings.
- Local KB admin: Manage remote KB configuration: Enables creating, editing, and deleting external data sources.
- Local KB admin: View jobs: Allows viewing existing jobs and access to the Local KB admin app in the FOLIO interface.

Organizations

The Organizations app in FOLIO enables the management of information about libraries' associated organizations. Records include contact details, websites, interfaces, and accounts, shared across various FOLIO apps (FOLIO, 2023b). Key terms include:

- Acquisition Units: Additional layers in acquisitions records restricting user interactions, defined in the Settings app.
- Organization: Any institution the library interacts with, whether purchasing materials or not.
- Vendor: Institutions selling materials to the library.
  Permissions for Organizations:
- Assign Acquisition Units: Assign units when creating a new organization record.
- Integration Usernames and Passwords (View): View usernames and passwords in FTP section.
- Integration Usernames and Passwords (View, Edit): Edit usernames and passwords in FTP details section.
- Interface Usernames and Passwords (View): View usernames and passwords in the Interface section.
- Interface Usernames and Passwords (View, Edit, Create, Delete): Create, edit, and delete usernames and passwords in the Interface section (requires View, Edit, Create or View, Edit, Delete permissions).
- Manage Acquisition Units: Change unit assignments when editing an organization record.
- View Organizations: Search and view organization records and settings. Access Contacts and Interfaces (excluding Interface usernames and passwords).
- View, Edit Organizations: Edit and view organizations. Access Contacts (excluding Interface usernames and passwords).
- View, Edit, Create Organizations: Create, edit, and view organizations. Access Contacts (excluding Interface usernames and passwords).
- View, Edit, Delete Organizations: View, edit, and delete organizations. Access Contacts (excluding Interface usernames and passwords).

Receiving

The Receiving app in FOLIO allows the confirmation of materials ordered through purchase order lines in the Orders app (FOLIO, 2023h). Key terms include:

- Package: A purchase order representing multiple titles.
- Piece: A subsection of a receiving title (e.g., a journal volume).
- Receive: Confirming the delivery of part or all of an order.
- Receiving Title: The title of the ordered material, potentially with multiple associated pieces.
- Unreceive: Indicating that a previously marked "received" order has not been delivered.
  Permissions for Receiving App:
- Export Search Results: Export receiving search results in .csv format.
- View Receiving Information: View receiving details for orders.
- View and Edit Pieces: Receive and edit pieces associated with a purchase order line.

- View, Edit, Create Pieces: View, edit, and create piece records (creation depends on Receiving workflow settings).
- View, Edit, Delete Pieces: View, edit, and delete pieces in the Receiving app.

Requests

The Requests app in FOLIO allows the creation and management of requests (FOLIO, 2023c).

There are two types of requests: item level (individual items) and title level (requests made at the instance level, allowing FOLIO to select available items).

Title level requests can be enabled in Settings > Circulation > Title level requests.

Considerations for title-level requests:

- Once activated, title-level requesting cannot be turned off without removing existing title level requests.
- Existing open item level requests should be closed before enabling title level requests to avoid queue ordering issues.
- Title level requests are not supported for multi-volume sets; such requests must be handled as item-level requests.

New items added to FOLIO need to be checked in to potentially fill open title level requests.

Permissions for Requests App:

  - All Permissions: Allows all request functions.
  - Move Requests: Enables moving requests from one item to another (subject to request policies).
  - Access Request Queue: Grants access to the request queue page with reorder capabilities. Needed only for users reordering the queue.
  - View Requests: Allows searching and viewing request records.
  - Create, Edit, Cancel Requests: Permits creating new requests and editing or canceling existing requests.

Settings (Some Areas)

In FOLIO, the Settings app allows libraries to customize apps based on their unique requirements. Most apps have specific settings, both required and optional. While some apps lack explicit settings, others have settings meant to support FOLIO's overall configuration. Certain settings impact multiple apps; for instance, inventory settings like material types affect circulation rules and are visible in loan records in apps like Check Out and Users (FOLIO, 2023d).

Users

Manage user information for patrons and library staff in the Users app, where both user records are stored. Library staff users differ from patrons as they have FOLIO permissions, a username, and password (FOLIO, 2023i).

Users App Terms:

- User: Any person using FOLIO.
- User Record: Contains contact details and identifiers for individuals, available for both patrons and library staff.
- Permission: Assigned value granting access or specific tasks in FOLIO.
- Permission Set: Group of permissions enabling specific tasks, defined in Settings > Users > Permission sets.

User App Permissions:

- User Import: Import user records.
- Can Override Item Blocks: Override item blocks in Check Out.
- Can Override Patron Blocks: Override patron blocks for borrowing, requesting, or renewing in Check Out.
- Assign/Unassign Permissions to Users: Manage permissions for other users.
- Assign/Unassign Service Points: View and edit service points assigned to users.
- Check Open Transactions: Verify open transactions on a user record.
- Create New User: Create new user records.
- Manage Fees/Fines: Create, edit, remove, and view user fees/fines.
- Manage Patron Blocks: View, edit, create patron blocks.
- Manage Proxies: View and edit proxies assigned to a user.
- Delete User Profile: Delete user profiles without open transactions (must be used with Users: Can check open transactions).
- Edit User Profile: Edit user record sections.
- Process Lost Items: Bill for lost items (actual cost processing not fully implemented in Nolana).
- View Fees/Fines and Loans: View user fees/fines and loans.
- View Permissions: View permissions assigned to other users.
- View Proxies: View but not edit proxies assigned to a user.
- View Service Points: View but not edit service points assigned to a user.
- Search and View User Records: Basic user information search.
- Cash Drawer Reconciliation Report: Create and download the report.
- Financial Transaction Detail Report: Create and download the report.
- Refunds to Process Manually Report: Create and download the report.
- Create/Reset Password: Send password reset emails or copy reset links for users.
- Anonymize User Loans: Remove user details from a loan.
- Change Due Date: Change due dates of loans on other users' records.
- Claim Returned: Change loaned items' status to Claim Returned.
- Declare Lost: Change loaned items' status to Declared Lost.
- Mark Claimed Returned Missing: Change status of loaned, claim returned items to Missing.

- Renew Loans: Renew loans based on loan policy.
- Renew Through Override: Override failed renewals.
- View Loans: View the Loans section on a user record, including loan details.
- View Loans, Change Due Date, Renew: View loans, change due dates, and renew loans.
- View Requests: View the Requests section on a user record.

Several applications maintain official documentation on docs.folio.org, complemented by additional informal resources linked below.

IMPLEMENTING FOLIO: CHALLENGES AND BEST PRACTICES

Preparing for FOLIO Adoption: Infrastructure and Data Migration Considerations

Implementing FOLIO, a comprehensive library services platform, involves meticulous planning and strategic considerations. Here's a detailed exploration of the crucial aspects associated with preparing for FOLIO adoption, focusing on infrastructure and data migration:

Infrastructure Evaluation

Prior to FOLIO adoption, a thorough assessment of the existing infrastructure is imperative. Libraries need to evaluate their servers, networks, and hardware to ensure they meet the specifications and requirements laid out by FOLIO. This evaluation forms the foundation for a seamless integration process.

Data Migration Strategy

One of the central challenges during FOLIO implementation is migrating data effectively. Libraries must devise a comprehensive data migration strategy. This involves identifying critical data sets, cleaning and refining the data, and formatting it to align with FOLIO's standards. Engaging data migration experts or specialized tools may be necessary to ensure accurate and efficient data transfer.

Integration Planning

Libraries typically operate a range of systems beyond the core library management, such as databases, authentication systems, or external service providers. Integrating these systems with FOLIO is vital for uninterrupted operations. FOLIO offers robust Application Programming Interfaces (APIs) that enable seamless communication between different applications. Planning these integrations meticulously ensures that FOLIO operates cohesively within the existing technological ecosystem.

Backup and Disaster Recovery

Implementing a robust backup and disaster recovery plan is non-negotiable. Libraries deal with vast amounts of sensitive data, and ensuring its safety is paramount. Libraries should establish regular backup protocols and develop comprehensive disaster recovery strategies to safeguard data integrity and availability.

Scalability Considerations

Libraries should anticipate future growth and scalability requirements. FOLIO's flexibility allows libraries to expand their services and collections. Therefore, planning for scalability in terms of hardware, software, and network resources is essential to accommodate future demands seamlessly.

Security Measures

With the digital landscape evolving, security is a top concern. Libraries must implement robust security measures to protect user data, transactions, and system integrity. This involves deploying firewalls, encryption protocols, and access control mechanisms to safeguard against potential cyber threats.

User Accessibility

Ensuring that FOLIO is accessible to all users, including those with disabilities, is vital for inclusive library services. Libraries should evaluate the platform's user interfaces and experiences to guarantee they comply with accessibility standards, ensuring equal access and usability for everyone.

Addressing Common Challenges During the Implementation Process

Implementing FOLIO, like any major software transition, comes with its set of challenges. Addressing these common issues effectively is key to ensuring a smooth and successful implementation. Here's a breakdown of strategies to tackle the challenges faced during the implementation process:

Change Management

Resistance to change among staff members is a common hurdle. Implementing comprehensive change management strategies, including training sessions, workshops, and open communication channels, helps staff adapt to the new system smoothly. Involving employees in the transition process and addressing their concerns fosters a positive attitude toward the change.

Data Integrity

Maintaining data integrity during migration is critical. Libraries must conduct rigorous data audits, ensuring accurate mapping, cleansing, and validation processes. Regular checks and validation routines post-migration are essential to identify and rectify any discrepancies promptly.

Customization and Configuration

Libraries often require specific customizations to align FOLIO with their unique workflows. Balancing these customizations without overcomplicating the system is crucial. Libraries should prioritize essential customizations, considering long-term maintenance and system stability. Adopting FOLIO's best practices and industry standards can guide effective configuration decisions.

Integration Challenges

Integrating FOLIO with existing library systems and third-party applications can be complex. Libraries should collaborate closely with FOLIO's support teams and utilize available documentation and resources. Conducting rigorous testing during the integration phase helps identify and resolve compatibility issues early.

Staff Training

Inadequate training can hinder the adoption process. Libraries should invest in comprehensive training programs tailored to different user roles. Training should be ongoing, covering not just the initial implementation phase but also providing continuous support as staff members encounter new challenges or updates.

Performance Optimization

Libraries must continuously monitor FOLIO's performance to identify and resolve bottlenecks promptly. Regular performance audits, load testing, and system optimization measures are essential to ensure FOLIO operates efficiently, especially during peak usage periods.

User Feedback Mechanisms

Establishing feedback mechanisms is crucial for continuous improvement. Libraries should create avenues for users and staff to report issues, suggest enhancements, and provide feedback. Regular feedback analysis informs necessary system modifications and updates, enhancing user satisfaction and system efficiency.

Budget and Resource Management

Effective budgeting and resource allocation are vital. Libraries should anticipate unforeseen expenses and allocate resources for ongoing maintenance, updates, and support services. Proper budgeting ensures that the system remains sustainable and up-to-date.

Best Practices for a Seamless Transition to FOLIO

Transitioning to FOLIO requires careful planning and execution. By adhering to best practices, libraries can ensure a seamless migration process and optimize the benefits of the new system. Here are key best practices for a successful transition:

Comprehensive Needs Assessment

Conduct a thorough assessment of your library's requirements. Identify specific features, workflows, and integrations needed. Understanding your unique needs forms the foundation for a tailored FOLIO implementation.

Engage Stakeholders

Involve all stakeholders, including library staff, users, and IT personnel, early in the planning phase. Encourage open discussions to gather insights and address concerns. Inclusivity fosters a sense of ownership and collective responsibility for the transition's success.

Expert Consultation

Collaborate with FOLIO experts and consultants. Leverage their experience to design a customized implementation plan. Expert guidance ensures that your library maximizes FOLIO's potential and avoids common pitfalls.

Data Migration Strategy

Develop a meticulous data migration strategy. Cleanse and validate existing data, ensuring accuracy before migration. Create backup plans and conduct extensive testing to prevent data loss or corruption during the migration process.

Effective Training Programs

Invest in comprehensive training programs for all users. Tailor training sessions to different user roles within the library. Continuous training and refresher courses help staff adapt to the new system's functionalities and workflows.

Gradual Implementation

Consider a phased approach to implementation. Start with a pilot phase involving a smaller subset of users. Gather feedback, address issues, and refine the system before expanding the implementation to the entire library. Gradual adoption minimizes disruptions and allows for fine-tuning.

Robust Support Mechanism

Establish a robust support system. Provide channels for users to seek assistance, report issues, and access resources. Timely and efficient support services enhance user confidence and satisfaction during the transition.

Documentation

Develop comprehensive documentation for users and administrators. Clear, user-friendly guides and manuals facilitate self-help and empower users to navigate FOLIO effectively. Regularly update documentation to reflect system changes and new features.

Quality Assurance

Implement rigorous quality assurance processes. Conduct thorough testing of all modules, integrations, and workflows. Identify and address bugs, glitches, or inconsistencies before they impact users. Regular updates and patches should undergo similar testing before deployment.

Continuous Feedback Loop

Establish a continuous feedback loop between users and developers. Encourage users to provide feedback on their experiences. Regularly assess user satisfaction and address concerns promptly. Feedback informs ongoing improvements and ensures FOLIO evolves to meet changing library needs.

Sustainability Planning

Develop a long-term sustainability plan. Allocate resources for ongoing maintenance, updates, and staff training. Stay informed about FOLIO's roadmap and updates to align your library's services with the platform's latest advancements.

Strategies for Maximizing User Adoption and Staff Training

Implementing FOLIO successfully not only requires technical proficiency but also effective strategies for user adoption and staff training. Libraries can employ several strategies to maximize user adoption and ensure staff are proficient with the new system:

User-Centric Design

Prioritize user experience in the FOLIO interface design. Ensure the system is intuitive, responsive, and aligns with user expectations. User-centric design promotes natural interaction and encourages adoption.

User Feedback Sessions

Organize regular feedback sessions with users during the implementation and after the system goes live. Actively listen to their concerns, suggestions, and challenges. Addressing user feedback promptly fosters a sense of ownership and engagement.

Customized Training Modules

Develop tailored training modules for different user roles within the library. Offer role-specific training to staff, covering essential workflows and functionalities relevant to their responsibilities. Customization enhances relevance and improves retention.

Hands-On Workshops

Conduct hands-on workshops and interactive training sessions. Allow users to explore FOLIO features in a controlled environment. Encourage active participation, questions, and practical exercises. Hands-on experience enhances confidence and proficiency.

Online Learning Platforms

Utilize online learning platforms to provide self-paced training modules. Create video tutorials, interactive quizzes, and documentation accessible to users anytime, anywhere. Online resources cater to diverse learning styles and schedules.

Peer Mentoring

Establish a peer mentoring program where experienced staff assist newcomers and provide guidance. Peer mentors can share best practices, shortcuts, and practical tips, easing the learning curve for new users.

Regular Training Refreshers

Offer periodic refresher courses and advanced training sessions. Staff may not absorb all information during initial training. Refreshers reinforce knowledge, introduce new features, and address common challenges that arise with system usage.

Gamified Learning

Introduce gamified elements to training programs. Use quizzes, challenges, and rewards to make learning engaging. Gamification enhances motivation and encourages healthy competition among staff, promoting active participation.

Continuous Support Channels

Maintain various channels for ongoing support, such as dedicated helplines, chat support, and email assistance. Provide timely responses to user queries. A responsive support system enhances user confidence and encourages them to explore the system.

Recognize and Reward Proficiency

Acknowledge and celebrate staff members who exhibit exceptional proficiency in using FOLIO. Recognitions, certificates, or small rewards create a positive incentive for staff to master the system and share their knowledge with peers.

Encourage Knowledge Sharing

Organize knowledge-sharing sessions and forums where staff can share their FOLIO experiences and insights. Peer-to-peer learning encourages collaboration, fosters a sense of community, and enhances overall expertise.

Continuous Assessment

Regularly assess user satisfaction and proficiency levels. Gather feedback about training programs and user experiences. Use assessment results to make necessary adjustments and improvements to training strategies.

By implementing these strategies, libraries can ensure a smooth transition to FOLIO, maximize user adoption, and empower staff with the skills and confidence needed to leverage the system effectively in their daily tasks.

FOLIO AND LIBRARY USER EXPERIENCE

Implementing FOLIO offers libraries the opportunity to significantly enhance the user experience. Libraries can provide seamless access to resources, streamline services, and engage users effectively. Here's how FOLIO can elevate the library user experience:

Personalization and Customization Options for Patrons

User Profiles

FOLIO allows patrons to create personalized profiles where they can save preferences, reading history, and favorite materials. Personalized profiles enable customized recommendations and tailored user experiences.

Alerts and Notifications

Patrons can set preferences for alerts related to due dates, new arrivals, or specific genres. Customized notifications keep users informed and engaged, ensuring they never miss important updates.

Reading History and Recommendations

FOLIO tracks users' reading history and recommends materials based on their preferences. Personalized recommendations enhance user engagement and encourage exploration of diverse content.

Accessibility and Inclusivity Considerations

Screen Reader Compatibility

FOLIO prioritizes accessibility by ensuring compatibility with screen readers and assistive technologies. This inclusivity feature enables patrons with visual impairments to independently navigate the platform.

Language Options

FOLIO supports multiple languages, catering to diverse user demographics. Patrons can choose their preferred language, fostering inclusivity for non-native speakers and multilingual communities.

Alt Texts and Descriptions

Images and multimedia content within FOLIO are accompanied by descriptive texts (alt texts). Descriptive content ensures that visually impaired users receive comprehensive information, promoting equal access to resources.

Gathering User Feedback and Continuous Improvement

Feedback Surveys

Libraries can conduct regular surveys to gather feedback on FOLIO's usability, features, and overall user experience. Insights from surveys help libraries understand user preferences and areas needing improvement.

User Testing Sessions

Organize user testing sessions where patrons interact with FOLIO under observation. Observations provide firsthand insights into user behavior and pain points, guiding refinements in the platform's design.

Iterative Development

FOLIO developers can employ an iterative approach, releasing updates based on user feedback and evolving needs. Regular updates ensure the platform remains dynamic, addressing emerging challenges and aligning with user expectations.

By focusing on these aspects, libraries can leverage FOLIO to create a user-centric environment, fostering engagement, accessibility, and inclusivity for all patrons. Continuous feedback mechanisms enable libraries to adapt, ensuring FOLIO aligns seamlessly with users' evolving needs and expectations.

FOLIO SECURITY AND DATA PRIVACY

FOLIO prioritizes robust security protocols to safeguard sensitive library and user data. The platform employs advanced encryption methods, secure data transmission, and authentication mechanisms to ensure data integrity and user privacy. Key security measures include:

Understanding FOLIO's Security Measures

Data Encryption

FOLIO encrypts data both in transit and at rest. Encryption protocols secure data during transmission over networks and when stored in databases, safeguarding it from unauthorized access.

Authentication Protocols

FOLIO implements multi-factor authentication and strong password policies to verify user identities. Authentication measures prevent unauthorized access, ensuring that only authorized personnel can access sensitive information.

Regular Security Audits

FOLIO conducts regular security audits and vulnerability assessments. These evaluations identify potential weaknesses, allowing for proactive measures to enhance the platform's security posture.

Data Privacy and Compliance in an Open-Source Environment

Compliance Standards

FOLIO adheres to international data privacy standards, such as GDPR (General Data Protection Regulation), ensuring that libraries using the platform are compliant with global data protection regulations.

User Data Anonymization

FOLIO incorporates features for anonymizing user data when needed. Libraries can manage patron data responsibly, ensuring privacy while retaining essential statistical information.

Transparency and Consent

FOLIO emphasizes transparency regarding data usage. Libraries using the platform are encouraged to inform users about how their data will be utilized and seek appropriate consent, promoting ethical data practices.

Collaboration and Shared Security Responsibilities

Community Collaboration

FOLIO operates in a collaborative ecosystem. Libraries, developers, and the FOLIO community work together to identify security risks and share best practices. Collective knowledge enhances the overall security awareness of the platform.

Shared Security Responsibilities

While FOLIO provides a secure foundation, libraries also play a crucial role in maintaining security. Regular staff training, secure user behaviors, and adherence to established security protocols contribute significantly to the overall security posture.

Incident Response

FOLIO provides guidelines for incident response protocols. Libraries are encouraged to have clear procedures in place to address security incidents promptly. Timely reporting and collaborative efforts help in mitigating potential risks effectively.

By understanding these aspects, libraries can confidently utilize FOLIO, knowing that the platform's security and data privacy measures align with global standards. Additionally, active collaboration and shared responsibilities within the FOLIO community ensure a collective effort toward maintaining a secure, reliable, and privacy-conscious library management platform.

FOLIO COMMUNITY AND FUTURE DEVELOPMENTS

FOLIO boasts a vibrant and diverse community of contributors, including libraries, developers, and organizations worldwide. These contributors actively collaborate to enhance FOLIO's features, security, and user experience. Libraries share insights, developers contribute code, and institutions offer resources, fostering a dynamic environment of mutual learning and growth.

Libraries of all sizes and backgrounds have the opportunity to actively shape FOLIO's future. By contributing code, sharing expertise, participating in SIGs (Special Interest Groups), and engaging in discussions, libraries can directly influence the platform's development. FOLIO's collaborative nature encourages libraries to voice their requirements, enabling tailored solutions that address diverse challenges.

FOLIO represents a pivotal evolution in the realm of library management, reshaping the traditional paradigms in profound ways. Its influence extends across several crucial facets, heralding a new era for libraries:

Enhanced Accessibility

FOLIO's user-centric design and intuitive interfaces ensure seamless accessibility, empowering patrons of all backgrounds and abilities to navigate library resources effortlessly.

Streamlined Workflows

FOLIO optimizes internal processes, simplifying tasks such as cataloging, acquisitions, and circulation. Automation and intelligent algorithms reduce manual efforts, allowing library staff to focus on higher-value services and interactions.

Personalized User Experiences

FOLIO enables libraries to tailor their services to individual preferences. From customized reading recommendations to personalized notifications, patrons experience a library ecosystem curated specifically for their needs and interests.

Data-Driven Decision Making

FOLIO's robust analytics and reporting tools provide libraries with deep insights into user behavior and resource usage. This data-driven approach facilitates informed decision-making, enabling libraries to allocate resources effectively and enhance user satisfaction.

Interconnected Library Ecosystem

FOLIO's modular architecture fosters seamless integration with third-party applications and services. Libraries can effortlessly connect with diverse digital platforms, expanding their offerings and creating a holistic, interconnected information environment.

Community Collaboration

FOLIO's collaborative ethos encourages libraries to share knowledge, codes, and best practices. This collaborative synergy cultivates a rich ecosystem of ideas, innovations, and problem-solving approaches, benefitting all participating institutions.

Global Standardization

FOLIO establishes a global standard for library management, ensuring consistency and compatibility across institutions and geographical boundaries. Libraries adopting FOLIO become part of a worldwide network, fostering collaboration and resource sharing on an unprecedented scale.

In essence, FOLIO transcends the conventional boundaries of library management. It transforms libraries into dynamic hubs of knowledge, accessibility, and tailored experiences. By embracing FOLIO, libraries are not merely adapting to the future but actively shaping it, redefining the very essence of what a library means in the digital age.

CONCLUSION

In the ever-evolving landscape of library sciences, FOLIO stands as a beacon of transformative change. Its open-source ethos, modular architecture, and user-centric design have ushered libraries into an era of unparalleled innovation and adaptability. As we conclude this exploration into FOLIO, it becomes evident that it is not merely a software platform; it is a paradigm shift, a catalyst for redefining the very essence of libraries in the digital age.

FOLIO empowers libraries to become dynamic, interconnected hubs of knowledge, breaking free from the constraints of traditional systems. Through seamless workflows, personalized user experiences, and data-driven insights, FOLIO enriches every facet of library services. It promotes collaboration, both within library communities and on a global scale, fostering a spirit of collective progress and shared knowledge.

The journey to adopting FOLIO is not merely a technological transition; it is a commitment to shaping the future of libraries. It is about embracing change, about making information accessible to all, and about crafting library experiences that resonate with every patron. It signifies a dedication to inclusivity, innovation, and the unwavering belief in the transformative power of libraries.

As libraries around the world integrate FOLIO into their core, they do more than upgrade their systems; they embark on a voyage towards a more vibrant, responsive, and engaged future. FOLIO is not just a platform; it is a movement, an embodiment of the spirit of libraries to evolve, adapt, and thrive.

In closing, as libraries embrace FOLIO, they are not merely adopting software; they are embracing a vision. A vision of libraries that are not confined by the physical constraints of their buildings but are boundless realms of knowledge in the digital sphere. With FOLIO, libraries are not just preserving their legacy; they are shaping a legacy of innovation, accessibility, and community.

In the world of libraries, FOLIO isn't just the next chapter; it's the beginning of a new book, one where the story of libraries is rewritten, not in ink and paper, but in code and connectivity. It's a story where every library, every patron, and every community is an active participant, shaping the narrative of libraries in the 21st century. The story of FOLIO is, ultimately, a story of libraries realizing their fullest potential, a story that continues to unfold with each new chapter written.

REFERENCES

Anurag. (2020, December 21). *Library Management System | Library Management Software in India*. https://www.skoolbeep.com/blog/library-management-system/

Bareau, V., & Nettifee, E. (2023, April 10). *The Codex Metadata Model. - FOLIO Platform - FOLIO Wiki*. https://wiki.folio.org/pages/viewpage.action?pageId=1415393

Chauhan, S., Kandhasamy, K., & Sakthivel, N. (2023). FOLIO: The Future of Library is Open. *SRELS Journal of Information Management, 60*(3), 150–156. doi:10.17821rels/2023/v60i3/171035

Colt, J., & Howell, D. (2021). Cornell Library FOLIO Case Study. *International Journal of Librarianship, 6*(2), 13–20. doi:10.23974/ijol.2021.vol6.2.205

Dobson, G. (2021). Lessons Learned about FOLIO's APIs. *International Journal of Librarianship, 6*(2), 30–39. doi:10.23974/ijol.2021.vol6.2.206

Ferguson, S., & Hebels, R. (2003). Library management systems. In Computers for Librarians: An Introduction to the Electronic Library (pp. 111–142). Woodhead Publishing Limited. doi:10.1016/B978-1-876938-60-4.50010-0

FOLIO. (2022a, April 7). *Local KB Admin | FOLIO Documentation.* https://docs.folio.org/docs/erm/local-kb-admin/

FOLIO. (2022b, December 6). *Bulk Edit | FOLIO Documentation.* https://docs.folio.org/docs/bulk-edit/

FOLIO. (2023a, February 9). *Courses | FOLIO Documentation.* https://docs.folio.org/docs/access/courses/courses/

FOLIO. (2023b, February 9). *Organizations | FOLIO Documentation.* https://docs.folio.org/docs/acquisitions/organizations/

FOLIO. (2023c, February 9). *Requests | FOLIO Documentation.* https://docs.folio.org/docs/access/requests/requests/

FOLIO. (2023d, February 18). *Settings | FOLIO Documentation.* https://docs.folio.org/docs/settings/

FOLIO. (2023e, February 23). *Circulation log | FOLIO Documentation.* https://docs.folio.org/docs/access/circulation-log/circ_log/

FOLIO. (2023f, February 28). *Check out | FOLIO Documentation.* https://docs.folio.org/docs/access/check-out/checkout/

FOLIO. (2023g, March 31). *Invoices | FOLIO Documentation.* https://docs.folio.org/docs/acquisitions/invoices/

FOLIO. (2023h, April 18). *Receiving | FOLIO Documentation.* https://docs.folio.org/docs/acquisitions/receiving/

FOLIO. (2023i, May 2). *Users | FOLIO Documentation.* https://docs.folio.org/docs/users/

FOLIO. (2023j, May 2). *Welcome | FOLIO Documentation.* https://docs.folio.org/docs/

FOLIO. (2023k, July 27). *Licenses | FOLIO Documentation.* https://docs.folio.org/docs/erm/licenses/

FOLIO-Open Libraries. (2023, October 23). https://twitter.com/FOLIO_LSP/status/1187025363836297219?s=20

FOLIO Project. (n.d.). *Welcome to MOTIF: The FOLIO design system · FOLIO UX docs · UX prototypes, guidelines & assets.* FOLIO UX. Retrieved October 16, 2023, from https://ux.folio.org/docs/

Fournie, J. (2020). Managing Electronic Resources Without Buying into the Library Vendor Singularity. *The Code4Lib Journal, 47.* https://journal.code4lib.org/articles/14955

Gorrell, M., & Colt, J. (2023, March 6). *FOLIO Governance Model - Community - FOLIO Wiki.* https://wiki.folio.org/display/COMMUNITY/FOLIO+Governance+Model

Grant, C. (2013). The Future of Library Systems: Library Services Platforms. *Information Standards Quarterly, 24*(4), 1–13. https://www.niso.org/sites/default/files/stories/2017-09/FE_Grant_Future_Library_Systems_%20isqv24no4.pdf

Harris, C. (n.d.). *Microservices vs. monolithic architecture*. https://www.atlassian.com/microservices/microservices-architecture/microservices-vs-monolith#:~:text=A%20monolithic%20application%20is%20built

Kulkarni, A. M., Pandiyan, M., & Sonawane, C. S. (2023). An overview of FOLIO: An open-source library management system. *Library Hi Tech News*. Advance online publication. doi:10.1108/LHTN-08-2023-0138

Liu, T. (2021). How is FOLIO different from its predecessors? *International Journal of Librarianship, 6*(2), 40–48. doi:10.23974/ijol.2021.vol6.2.207

Liu, W. (2021). FOLIO and Smart Libraries: Meeting the future needs of Chinese Libraries. *International Journal of Librarianship, 6*(2), 73–83. doi:10.23974/ijol.2021.vol6.2.213

McNally, C., & Kuss, I. (2020, March 6). *Deployment Environments (general overview) - System Operations and Management SIG - FOLIO Wiki*. https://wiki.folio.org/pages/viewpage.action?pageId=7832871

Momoh, E. O., & Folorunso, A. L. (2019). The Evolving Roles of Libraries and Librarians in the 21st Century. *Library Philosophy and Practice (E-Journal)*, 1–11. https://digitalcommons.unl.edu/libphilprac/2867

Murray, P. (2023, August 17). *Information and User Guides for FOLIO Apps*. https://wiki.folio.org/display/FOLIOtips/Information+and+User+Guides+for+FOLIO+Apps

Murray, P., & Colt, J. (2023, August 14). *Welcome to the FOLIO Wiki - Community - FOLIO Wiki*. https://wiki.folio.org/

Murray, P., & Martin, K. (2022, March 3). *FOLIO Roadmap (2019-2020) - Product Council - FOLIO Wiki*. https://wiki.folio.org/pages/viewpage.action?pageId=1410538

Nduta, A. (2023, April 3). *A Brief History of Open Source*. https://www.freecodecamp.org/news/brief-history-of-open-source/

Owens, N., & Thomas, C. (2019). The Future of Cataloging in a FOLIO Environment. *The Serials Librarian, 76*(1), 66–71. doi:10.1080/0361526X.2019.1579692

paulderscheid. (2021, September 15). *Implications of the transition towards library services platforms*. https://medium.com/@paulderscheid/implications-of-the-transition-towards-library-services-platforms-7ad7f62034d6

Pradhan, P. (2021). Library Services Platform (LSP): An Overview. *INFLIBNET, 26*(1), 12–22. https://www.researchgate.net/publication/333816851

Raman. (2020, March 24). *Monolithic vs Microservices architecture*. GeeksforGeeks. https://www.geeksforgeeks.org/monolithic-vs-microservices-architecture/

Taylor, M. P. (2021). Modularity in FOLIO: Principles, techniques and tools. *International Journal of Librarianship*, *6*(2), 3–12. doi:10.23974/ijol.2021.vol6.2.208

Velmurugan, C., & Kannan, M. (2012). Recent Growth and Developments in Open-Source Software on Digital Libraries in India. *Pearl. Journal of Library and Information Science*, *6*(4), 173–178. doi:10.5958/j.0973-7081.6.4.019

Zhou, G., Zhang, C., Ji, T., Zhou, J., & Zhang, Z. (2023). FOLIO Successfully Goes Alive in the Largest Public Library in China. *International Journal of Librarianship*, *8*(1), 3–10. doi:10.23974/ijol.2023.vol8.1.288

ADDITIONAL READING

Breeding, M. (2015). Library Technology Library Services Platforms: A Maturing Genre of Products. *Library Technology Reports*, *51*(4). https://journals.ala.org/ltr/issue/download/509/259

Busch, H., & Li, H. (2023). Pivoting to FOLIO: Our migration experience to a new LSP. *Journal of Electronic Resources Librarianship*, *35*(1), 67–74. doi:10.1080/1941126X.2023.2165265

KEY TERMS AND DEFINITIONS

Future of Library Is Open (FOLIO): FOLIO is a leading open-source Library Services Platform (LSP) designed for modern libraries, offering flexibility, modularity, and a collaborative environment. It revolutionizes library management, enabling efficient digital resource handling, streamlined workflows, and enhanced user experiences. FOLIO's innovative architecture and specialized apps, combined with strong community support, make it a transformative solution for libraries, ensuring optimal resource management and user satisfaction.

Library Management Systems (LMS): LMS are integrated software solutions designed for libraries to efficiently manage cataloging, circulation, acquisitions, and user interactions, enhancing overall library operations and user experiences.

Library Services Platform (LSP): A LSP is an all-in-one software solution that revolutionizes library management. It integrates various functions like cataloging and user services into a seamless, customizable platform, enhancing both user experience and library efficiency.

Micro-Services Architecture: A modern software design approach where applications are divided into smaller, loosely coupled services, allowing for flexibility, scalability, and independent development, deployment, and maintenance of each service.

Monolithic Architecture: A traditional software design where all components are tightly integrated into a single unit, limiting flexibility and scalability due to lack of modularity.

Open Source Software (OSS): OSS refers to software with freely accessible and modifiable source code, promoting collaborative development, innovation, and user freedom.

User Experience (UX): UX in library services through an LSP refers to patrons' satisfaction and ease of interaction with digital resources. It emphasizes seamless navigation, accessibility, and effective use of the platform, enhancing overall user satisfaction.

Chapter 9
Thirty Years of Digital Technologies in the Field of Cultural Heritage

Fatma Sezin Dogruer
Ministry of Culture and Tourism, Turkey

ABSTRACT

Digital technologies promoted innovation and proposed unprecedented opportunities to the sectors, one of which is cultural heritage. There are many benefits of digitization such as rapid access of data, cost-effectiveness according to benefit and loss assessment in a long term, and rapid identification of cultural heritage and risks. This study is the comprehensive bibliometric analysis that ensures statistical and all-embracing understanding in the digital technologies in cultural heritage literature, which was carried out in Web of Science between 1993 and 2022. The study is expected to spur scholars to perform more studies on digital technologies in cultural heritage. The analysis embodied 1826 publications written by 200 authors from 98 countries. Italy produced 24.20% of the world's publications on digital technologies in cultural heritage, which has the highest number of publications with 442 documents. The most used keywords in this literature are cultural heritage, virtual reality, and augmented reality.

INTRODUCTION

With the rapid rise of digital technologies, cultural heritage studies have not remained a spectator to these developments, and the use of digital technologies in the protection, documentation and exhibition of cultural heritage has become widespread. Digital technologies promoted innovation and proposed unprecedented opportunities to the sectors. Among these, digital transformation has reflections in the cultural heritage studies. There are many benefits of the digitization and AI such as collection of large scale of digital shared knowledge, rapid access of data, cost-effectiveness according to benefit and loss assessment in a long term and rapid identification of cultural heritage and risks.

Developing or adjusting geographic information system (GIS) tools for analysis of data and monitoring of affected areas is crucial for more efficient and cost-effective urban planning in the historical

DOI: 10.4018/979-8-3693-0807-3.ch009

texture. Such digital infrastructure can help ensure participatory, accountable and transparent governance mechanisms in recovery and reconstruction. GIS will give opportunity to present the mapping data, current situation and damage level of the immovable cultural properties after the damage assessment studies and also the unique architectural elements or movable cultural properties found in the removal works of culture debris with the right locations on the maps, what is more, about the number of the structures studied on. Building Information Modelling (BIM) can be used as a digital representation of physical and functional characteristic of a facility. Also, photogrammetric range imaging techniques such as Structure from motion (SFM) estimate three dimensional structures from two-dimensional image sequences coupled with local motion signals.

A range of changes are proposed in standards and regulatory policies to ensure that cultural properties are resilient to earthquakes and other disasters. In long term, making a visual documentation of immovable cultural assets, with the earthquake-prone provinces being of top priority, and keep their digital data available and keeping inter-institutional digital data sharing up-to-date and available for sharing, in this regard is essential. The focus must be on increasing the digitalization level of these studies and benefitting from the latest digital solutions. Dynamic measurements with non-invasive techniques can be used to obtain relevant information.

Intelligent systems based on artificial intelligence and machine learning methods that can continuously improve themselves should be supported. These systems facilitate the identification of visual funds in collections with object recognition features in archaeological areas. With the ability to integrate the works carried out in the field under the ability to collect data from the field with automatic mapping into the system instantly with their locations, it enables the on-site recording of the finds made especially in the excavation areas.[1]

Digitalization is important for preventing the deterioration of heritage data that need to be protected by transferring them to digital media, increasing access to these materials, and thus for sustainable documentation and presentation (Halaç and Öğülmüş, 2021, 524). With an application that will be developed to share these digital data, it is thought that restitution data on cultural assets that have been demolished during on-site inspection or excursion by researchers or visitors can be obtained. Three-dimensional modelling of the restitution of the assets and even animations showing the old life can be prepared and presented together with historical information. In order to prevent damage to our social memory and to achieve the highest level of social benefit, open access to resources that aim to protect cultural heritage should be supported and encouraged.

Being the base of this study, bibliometrics ensures statistical and integrated information of scientific literature in a topical working area. The aim of these studies is to produce consequential information from data stacks. There is a popularity in the bibliometric techniques in various disciplines. Bibliometrics is a subject that is becoming widespread in the previous decades, a total number of 24203 documents have been prepared at the date of June 2023, when 'bibliometric analysis', 'bibliometric analyses', bibliometric* or 'bibliometric study' were searched in the WoS database. *Digital technologies in cultural heritage* contains limited bibliometric analysis, one of which is restricted with museum studies: "The Use of Technologies in Museums: A Bibliometric Analysis Based on the Web of Science Database". The study is a review that includes the adaptation of museums toward digital transformation (Sousa, Cordeiro and Cunha, 2022). The other bibliometric study is entitled as "Bibliometric Analysis on the Implementation Digitization Technologies in Cultural Heritage in Malaysia", which is restricted with the country of Malaysia (Salleh, S.Z. and Bushroa, A.R., 2022). However, our study, which is the first bibliometric study on digital technologies in cultural heritage aims to offer data of a comprehensive bibliometric analysis of the topic.

This study embraces the bibliometric analysis of the documents on *digital technologies in cultural heritage* which are indexed in Web of Science Core Collection, within a period between 1993 and 2022. In the exploration process, a total of 1826 publications were achieved in the database. The analysis includes 1826 publications written by 200 authors from 98 countries, where *computer science interdisciplinary applications, computer science information systems, computer science theory methods, imaging science photographic technology* and *information science library science* are the main research areas.

Materials and methods are going to be stated in the following section. The results section constitutes from the analysis on the general feature of the literature, outputs according to countries, authors, journals and organizations, and analyses of citations, keywords and bibliometric network. "Digital technologies in the field of cultural heritage" and "studies in Türkiye about use of digital technologies in the field of cultural heritage" are discussed in the next parts. Finally, conclusion section take part with brief overview and future implications of the study.

The data have been gathered from SCI-Expanded, SSCI, A&HCI, emerging sources citation index (ESCI), conference proceedings (CPCI-S, CPCI-SSH) and book citation index (BKCI-S, BKCI-SSH) in the database of Web of Science Core Collection (WoS) that uses multiple databases on different academic disciplines to obtain reliable and holistic database service. "Digital technolog*" or digitalization or digitization or digitisation or "artificial intelligence" or AI or machine learning or ML or "virtual reality" or VR or "augmented reality" or AR; and "cultural heritage" or "cultural propert*" were used as the pivotal keywords to topic search; and "heritage or museum* or historic* or cultur* were used as the keywords to title search in the WoS Database. The star symbol (*) characterized the letters like -y or -ies or -s or -al. Web of Science categories that are *biodiversity conservation, engineering biomedical, food science technology, biotechnology applied microbiology, oceanography, agricultural economics policy, cell biology, oceanography, engineering ocean, medicine research experimental, pharmacology pharmacy, forestry, mathematical computational biology* are excluded. All the documents published on digital technologies in cultural heritage between 1993 and 2022 were analyzed in this study. As an article on digital technologies in cultural heritage was firstly published in the index in 1993, it is chosen as the initial year of the analysis.

The most contributing authors, organizations and countries were classified from the database. The study involves author-dependent and keyword-dependent distributions via a bibliometric analysis tool called VOSviewer that is the freeware analysis application for data visualizing, bibliometric analysing and creating bibliometric networks (VOSviewer, 2023). It is a text mining application showing the relationship between components. The clustering method that is formed in the VOSviewer application concentrates on the total level of items and clusters (Artsın, 2020, 344, 351). VOSviewer is a software tool to support bibliometric analysis designed by Van Eck and Waltman, which is useful for showing bibliometric maps in an understandable way and addresses the graphical depiction of bibliometric maps (Aria and Cuccurullo, 2017, 962). United Nations (UN) system was utilized for the country classification of the studies on digital technologies in cultural heritage (UN, 2022). A global productivity map was produced in order to show the publication density of the world countries by Microsoft Excel.

This study is the first bibliometric study on *digital technologies in cultural heritage* that aims to reveal data about the comprehensive bibliometric analysis on the topic, which are indexed in Web of Science Core Collection, within a period between 1993 and 2022. This data analysis is essential in the academic literature in order to completely utilize from the studies on *digital technologies in cultural heritage*.

BACKGROUND

Bibliometric analysis is a way of summarizing large amounts of bibliometric data in order to present the condition of intellectual structure and emerging trends of a specified field of research in the case that the scope of the review is broad and the dataset is immense for manual review (Donthu and others, 2021, 287). In order to find relevant information, support judgments, and support decision-making, data analysis is the process of analyzing, purifying, manipulating, and modeling data. Descriptive analysis and network extraction are components of data analysis. Various methods have been developed to extract networks using various analytical units. Co-word analysis creates semantic mappings of a field that make its cognitive structure easier to comprehend. Co-author analysis, which looks at writers and their affiliations to evaluate the social structure and collaboration networks, is another typical bibliometric approach. Citation analysis is the most typical bibliometrics analysis. It uses citation counts as a metric for document, author, and journal similarity. Bibliographic coupling and co-citation analysis are two subfields of citation analysis (Aria and Cuccurullo, 2017, 961).

Researchers utilize bibliometric analysis for a variety of purposes, including to study the intellectual framework of an existing field and to identify developing trends in article and journal performance, collaboration patterns, and research constituents. The fact that bibliometrics was first discussed in the 1950s implies that the methodology is not brand-new (Donthu and others, 2021, 285-286).

Bibliometric studies include the methodological steps of study design, bibliometric data collection, analysis, visualization and interpretation (Espina-Romero and Guerrero-Alcedo, 2022, 2). The main steps for the bibliometric analysis are as follows:

- Defining the aims and scope.
- Choosing the technique.
- Collecting data.
- Running the analysis and reporting the findings (Donthu and others, 2021, 294).

Regardless of the nature of the fields, digitalization has impacted several of these fields. Its advancement follows the sustainability movement, which has the benefit of reducing a field's environmental impact (Espina-Romero and Guerrero-Alcedo, 2022, 1).

Digital technologies have transformed all the current works, promoted innovation, proposed new opportunities to the sectors. One area where digitalization is being used is in cultural heritage. Digital technologies can be served in several ways to aid the conservation of movable and immovable cultural heritage. There are many benefits and opportunities of the digital technologies such as 3D modelling, artificial intelligence, virtual and augmented reality, robotics, satellite imagery, motion technology and so on. Among these, there are predictive maintenance, mapping and modelling. Recognizing the cultural properties or specific objects/structures in cultural heritage sites can be succeeded by AI, by this way any changes in the condition of them can be realized and need of restoration, cleaning etc. can be identified. Algorithms of AI can be used to monitor and predict potential damages on the cultural heritage, so that conservationists take preventive measures before deteriorations. Mapping technology supports to create digital archives of cultural heritage sites, structures and objects, which can help researchers to better understand the significance of these, identify potential damages and plan restoration projects. What is more, machine learning help scholars to gain new insights into the historical and cultural aspects of these sites and objects, and to identify new areas of research. Virtual reality and augmented reality experiences provide interactive ways to experience cultural heritage sites and artifacts in museums. These experiences provide virtual access to the ancient and current condition of the objects or sites, and raise awareness of the meaning and importance of cultural heritage. Image processing can be used to analyze photographs of cultural assets. Laser Scanning can be used to create 3D models of cultural assets. Laser scanning technology scans the surfaces of objects in the form of high-resolution point clouds and produces 3D models from this data. Drone technology, which can be used for aerial photography and video recording of cultural assets, provides fast and wide-area covering documentation and speed up the process. Image processing technology is used to process photographs and provide important information on issues such as the condition of structures and damage detection.

Today, the terms "digital heritage", "digital cultural heritage" or "new heritage" are used as interchangeable terms and are represented as one common theme in different research fields. A similar trend can be seen in traditional arts, design, humanities and social sciences, which are developing towards digitisation on a large scale. Thus, there is a growing accumulation of data through new digital tools. New principles of digital preservation have emerged from the need to acquire, store, research, disseminate and display cultural heritage data. Although digital possibilities contribute to heritage studies, it is important to find effective methods of utilisation in order to transfer this information to various users in the most comprehensive way (Varinlioğlu and others, 2019).

Complete digital recording, whose first step is 3D digitization, addresses all facets of this new digital content management, representation, and reproduction, not just the issue of the three-dimensional digitalization of objects and monuments (Pavlidis and others, 2007, 93).

As one of the technologies of digitization, digital twin technology is a simulation of physical assets that uses real-time data to create a virtual representation of the asset in the form of a digital model. This technology can be used to track and analyze the state of a physical asset over time, allowing a better understanding of how it changes and how it is affected by its environment. Digital twin technology can be used to create detailed 3D models of cultural artefacts and monuments, providing valuable information about their architecture and structure. These 3D models can be used to track and monitor the deterioration of cultural artefacts over time, making it easier to identify areas of damage and prevent further damage. Digital twins can also be used to create virtual exhibitions and galleries, allowing people to interact with cultural heritage artefacts in a virtual environment. This can help increase public engagement with cultural heritage, as well as provide an opportunity to educate people about the history and significance of these artefacts.[2]

International organizations are making efforts to develop and control this issue through various legal regulations in the recent years. Leveraging Digital technologies for the promotion and protection of cultural heritage is addressed in international meetings and endeavors to incorporate it into national and international legislation such as G20 Leaders' Ministerial Declarations. The G20 supports promoting digital technologies, equal access to affordable connectivity and technology devices, narrowing the digital divide between and within countries as well as the gender digital divide and data divide, and enhancing digital inclusion through literacy, vocational skills, and competency development programs. Recognizing that digital transformation and data advances are important instruments that can help advance, support, and accelerate the achievement (G20, 2023, 3).

Some of the existing normative instruments related to culture in the digital environment are 2017 Operational Guidelines on the Implementation of the UNESCO 2005 Convention in the Digital Environment and the culture-related provisions of the 2021 UNESCO Recommendation on the Ethics of Artificial Intelligence.

On its official website, the European Union emphasizes the special significance and importance of digitizing cultural goods because doing so gives them a new lease on life. By this way, citizens now have unprecedented access to cultural material, and institutions and state actors have a variety of options for handling and disseminating this data and digital products. The General European Commission Directorate for Communications Networks, Content & Technology has coordinated policies extensively and provided funds for initiatives to support Member States' cultural policies in the fields of digitization, online access to cultural content, and digital preservation (Chroni, 2018).

Some examples of digitalization studies in cultural heritage will be presented as follows. Photographing the structures using drones and analyzing the problems with artificial intelligence are among the method suggestions that can use advanced technology. In this way, the images of structures located in difficult-to-access geographies or in earthquake debris can be analyzed and three-dimensional modelled with an artificial intelligence algorithm. Technology companies such as Microsoft and Intel have projects related to the Great Wall of China and the immovable properties in the ancient city of Olympia in Greece.[3 4]

In the study conducted at Princeton University, a solution was sought by developing a genetic algorithm for the estimation and reconstruction of the direction and rotation of the motifs after taking 3D surface scans of the frescoes in archaeological areas, and a 90% compatible result was achieved (Kayıkçı, 2019, 14).

Transparent, immutable and traceable blockchain technology, combined with other technologies such as facial recognition and artificial intelligence for authentication, will be able to regulate the digital market and protect the intellectual property of digital products by providing a verifiable audit trail of transactions. China has launched a cultural heritage digital platform powered by blockchain technology to share digital images of six thousand-year-old cave sites in Gansu Province in the northwest of the country with people around the world. The Dunhuang Academy has begun a digitization project in the 1990s to create digital versions of the Mogao Grottoes and other cave temples, accumulating vast digital cultural resources and making the first batch of these definitive materials publicly available for download for the first time. The platform invites people to participate in cultural and creative product design with these cultural resources and share the profits from their creations.[5]

Museums, which are institutions open to change and transformation, benefit from technological innovations such as visitor interactive applications. In Türkiye, which is very rich in terms of archaeological finds, studies on the digitization of museum collections have been obtained after a long period of research and preparation, and a system entitled Museum National Inventory System (MUES) has been prepared in detail.

MUES, which is developed as a complete local and national project with the Turkish Ministry of Culture and Tourism and TÜBİTAKBİLGEM as solution partner, is a project that is conscious of the universal trust in museums and aims to pass on the cultural assets of many civilizations in Türkiye. To carry this legacy into the future, technology is used to transfer inventory information to electronic media in a more qualified manner. Using artificial intelligence and deep learning techniques, the project includes many modules and details ranging from visual information on artifacts to anti-smuggling and commission operations, excavation sites to laboratory processes, private museums to collectors. By this system, it is planned to conduct general quality surveys and inventory scientific studies by museum professionals to provide a means of obtaining large quantities of artifacts and their visual representations as part of the MUES project. This prevents the original artifact from being constantly moved, damaged, worn or stolen. Risk factors are eliminated. The MUES project aims to form a national database containing detailed information on all museum artefacts, to search visual content based on artificial intelligence; to help detect contraband and counterfeit goods; to accelerate of the decision-making process as a decision support system; to use digital media to protect artifacts from harm and risk; and to provide a national and standardized metadata model for artifacts and museums.[6]

The use of artificial intelligence in portable cultural assets can be utilized in the context of restoration, conservation, tourism and anti-smuggling. For example, "Weary Herakles" named Herakles statue in the Antalya Museum, was scanned by a Breuckmann optoTOP-HE system. 3D object modeling was formed via digitization, registration, surface triangulation, editing, texture mapping and visualization (Akça ve diğerleri, 2006, 14). Prior to the return of the half of the Tired Heracles Statue in Antalya Museum from the USA in 2011, a 3D modelling of the piece in Türkiye was prepared in 2006.

Within the scope of the "3D Scanning of Cuneiform Tablets in the Museum of Anatolian Civilisations and Reading of Boğazköy Tablets by Artificial Intelligence Project" carried out by the Ministry of Culture and Tourism and Ankara University, over 70 thousand tablets in Istanbul Archaeological Museums, around 40 thousand tablets in Ankara Museum of Anatolian Civilisations and around 4 thousand tablets in Boğazkale will be scanned and read. In this way, studies are carried out much faster and with a low margin of error compared to manual decipherment studies. In this learning process, artificial intelligence will analyze the Hittite language through algorithms taught to it with image processing technology.[7]

Issues, Controversies

The research produced in the database of Web of Science Core Collection is composed of 1826 articles in the literature of digital technologies in cultural heritage between 1993 and 2022. 719 of the documents were open access. The number of publications demonstrates that the peak year was 2022 with 248 articles (Fig.1). English is the main language used in the *digital technologies in cultural heritage* literature with 1683 articles followed by Spanish, Italian, Russian and Croatian (n=45, 24, 17 and 11, respectively; Table.1).

Figure 1. Number of the publications on digital technologies in cultural heritage by year[8]

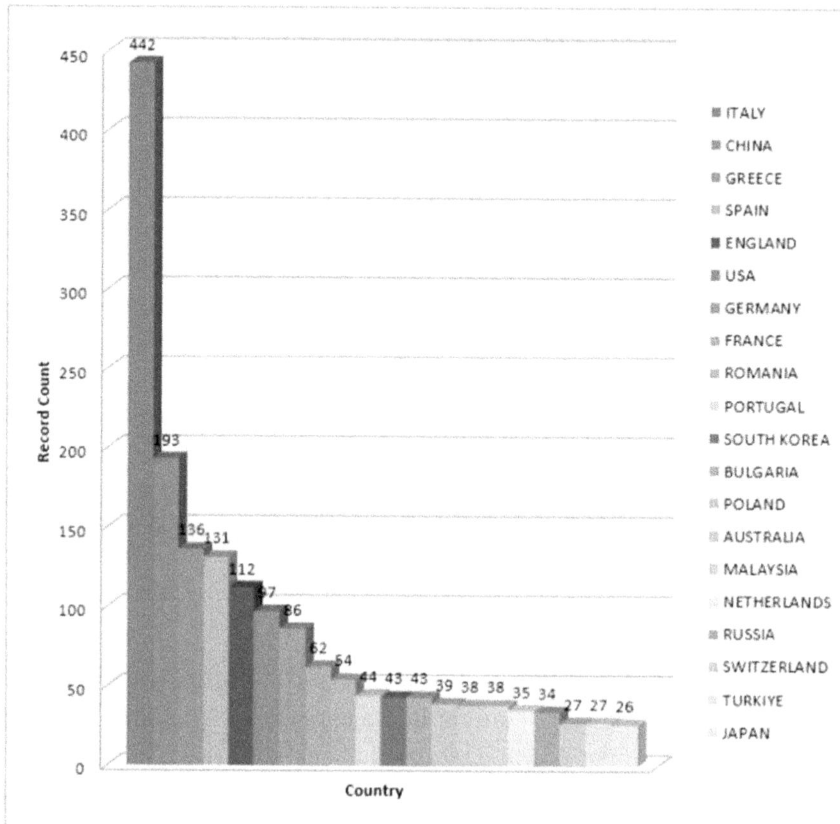

Table 1. Languages used on digital technologies in cultural heritage between 1993 and 2022

Language	Record Count	% of the 1826 Articles
English	1683	92.17
Spanish	45	2.46
Italian	24	1.31
Russian	17	0.93
Croatian	11	0.60
German	10	0.55
Portuguese	8	0.44
Slovak	8	0.44
French	5	0.27
Turkish	5	0.27

The most studied categories are Computer Science Interdisciplinary Applications, Computer Science Information Systems, Computer Science Theory Methods, Humanities Multidisciplinary and Information Science Library Science (15.12, 14.73, 14.68, 12.32 and 10.73%, respectively; Table.2). Of the *digital technologies in cultural heritage* documents published between 1993 and 2022 in the WoS database, the most common document types were articles, proceeding papers, book chapters, review articles, and editorial materials (n=969, 815, 30, 30 and 17; respectively) (Figure 2).

In 2022, the most common document types were articles, proceeding papers, review articles editorial materials and meeting abstracts (n=172, 62, 11, 2 and 2; respectively) on mostly computer science, art humanities, engineering, chemistry and material science (n=92, 53, 47, 38 and 37; respectively).

Table 2. The most 20 studied categories in the digital technologies in cultural heritage literature between 1993 and 2022

Research Area	Record Count	% of the 1826 Articles
Computer Science Interdisciplinary Applications	276	15.12
Computer Science Information Systems	269	14.73
Computer Science Theory Methods	268	14.68
Humanities Multidisciplinary	225	12.32
Information Science Library Science	196	10.73
Imaging Science Photographic Technology	194	10.62
Archaeology	185	10.13
Computer Science Artificial Intelligence	182	9.97
Engineering Electrical Electronic	158	8.65
Remote Sensing	154	8.43
Computer Science Software Engineering	140	7.67
Materials Scince Multidisciplinary	126	6.90
Architecture	125	6.84
Geography Physical	95	5.20
Art	85	4.65
Chemistry Analytical	81	4.43
Geosciences Multidisciplinary	81	4.43
Computer Science Cybernetics	80	4.38
Engineering Multidisciplinary	70	3.83
Environmental Sciences	68	3.72

Figure 2. Distribution of document types on digital technologies in cultural heritage published between 1993 and 2022

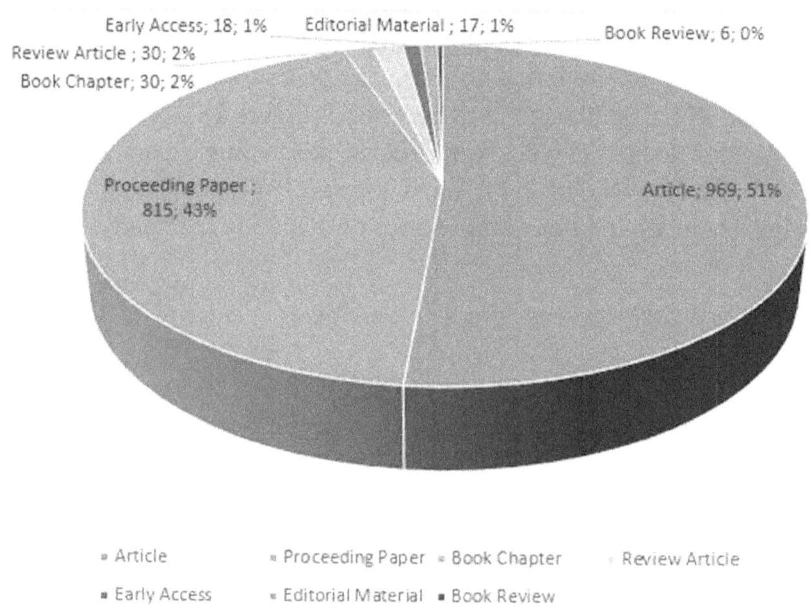

Outputs According to Countries, Authors, Journals, and Organizations

Regarding the publication statistics, Italy produced 24,20% of the world's publications on 'digital technologies in cultural heritage', which is the first country with the highest number of publications with 442 documents and followed by China, Greece and Spain (n=193, 136 and 131, respectively; Fig.3). China, which is among the developing countries according to the UN classification, is the second country of all with 193 documents (10.58%) and first of the developing countries followed by South Korea, Malaysia, Türkiye, India and Taiwan (n=43, 38, 27, 23 and 20, respectively). Russia among the economies in transition take place in the most productive 20 countries list with 34 documents. The countries that contribute to the literature the most are in the continents of Europe and America (Fig.4).

In 2022, Italy produced 59 documents of the world's publications (Total=248) on 'digital technologies in cultural heritage', which is the first country with the highest number of publications and followed by China, Greece, Spain and England (n= 53, 23, 19 and 12; respectively).

Figure 3. Top 20 countries on digital technologies in cultural heritage between 1993 and 2022

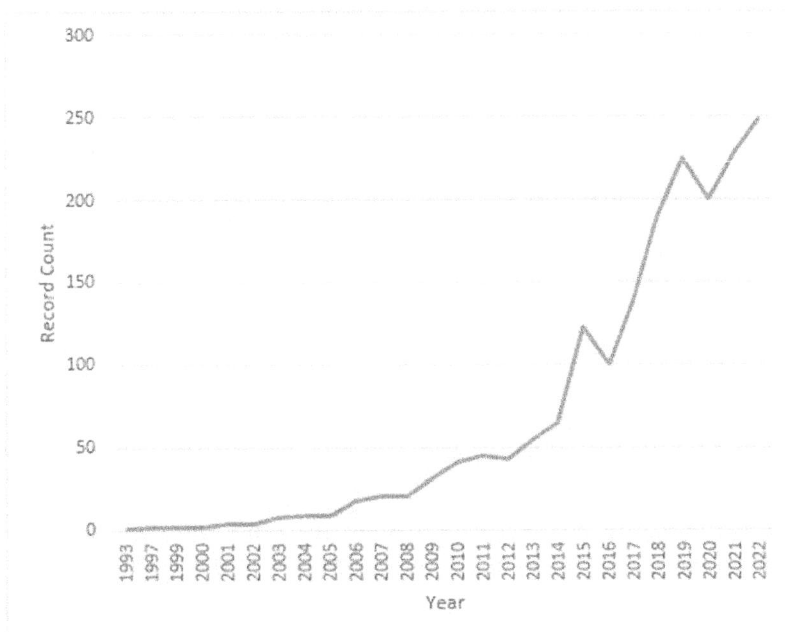

Figure 4. Publication density of the world countries in the field of digital technologies in cultural heritage between 1993 and 2022

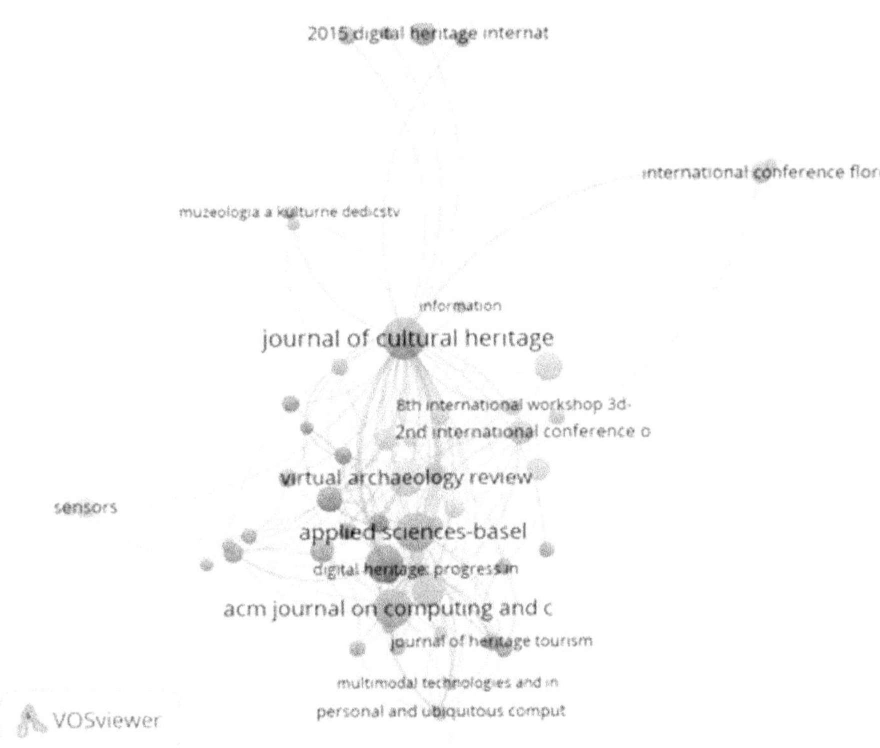

Pierdicca, Roberto is the most prolific author of the *digital technologies in cultural heritage* literature between 1993 and 2022 with 12 documents (0.66%) followed by Remondino, Fabio; Carrozzino, Marcello; Belhi, Abdelhak; Rizvic, Selma and Bouras, Abdelaziz (n=12, 10, 10, 10 and 10; Table.3). Remondino, F is the most prolific editor of the selected period with 68 articles (3.72%, Table.4) followed by Ionnides, M; Brumana, R, Depaolis, LT and Martins, J (n=50, 32, 27 and 26). IEEE, IOP, ACM, ASSOC COMP Machinery and IEEE COMP SOC are the group of authors who have studied the *digital technologies in cultural heritage* between 1993 and 2022 (n=96, 19, 18, 12 and 10, respectively; Table.5).

The publications with the most contributions to the literature of *digital technologies in cultural heritage* were Lecture Notes in Computer Science, International Archives of the Photogrammetry Remote Sensing and Spatial Information Sciences, Journal of Cultural Heritage, ACM Journal on Computing and Cultural Heritage and Applied Sciences Basel (n=136, 94, 47, 40 and 40, respectively; Table.6). *Journal of Archaeological Science* is the earliest publication on the *digital technologies in cultural heritage* literature. On the other hand, no article has been published on *digital technologies in cultural heritage* in this publication between 1994 and 1996, and the year of 1998. The results show that the 10 most productive publications have great number of documents on *digital technologies in cultural heritage* in 2022 as well except *Virtual Archaeology Review*, *Heritage* and the proceedings. *Lecture Notes in Computer Science,* which has the most contributions in the literature in 2022, has published on the literature since 2004. The most contributive book series to the *digital technologies in cultural heritage* literature between 1993 and 2022 were *Lecture Notes in Computer Science, International Archives of the Photogrammetry Remote Sensing and Spatial Information Sciences, Communications in Computer and Information Science, IOP Conference Series Materials Science* and *Engineering and Proceedings of Spie* (n=136, 94, 38, 17 and 15, respectively; Table.7).

Table 3. The 20 most prolific authors of the digital technologies in cultural heritage literature between 1993 and 2022

Author	Record Count	% of the 1826 Articles
Pierdicca, Roberto	12	0.66
Remondino, Fabio	12	0.66
Carrozzino, Marcello	10	0.55
Belhi, Abdelhak	10	0.55
Rizvic, Selma	10	0.55
Bouras, Abdelaziz	10	0.55
Thwaites, Harol	9	0.49
Woo, Woontack	9	0.49
Frontoni, Emanuele	9	0.49
Barrile, Vincenzo	9	0.49
Chng, Eugene	8	0.44
Terras, Melissa	8	0.44
Foufou, Sebti	8	0.44
Marto, Anabela	8	0.44
Fotia, Antonino	7	0.38
Caggianese, Giuseppe	7	0.38
Montusiewicz, Jerzy	7	0.38
Quintero, Mario Santana	7	0.38
Goncalves, Alexandrino	7	0.38
Di Giulio, Roberto	7	0.38

Table 4. The 20 most prolific editors of the digital technologies in cultural heritage literature between 1993 and 2022

Editor	Record Count	% of the 1826 Articles
Remondino, F	68	3.72
Ionnides, M	50	2.74
Brumana, R	32	1.75
Depaolis, LT	27	1.48
Martins, J	26	1.42
Barcelo, J	25	1.37
Brunet, P	25	1.37
Duranti, L	25	1.37
Georgopoulos, A	25	1.37
Graf, H	25	1.37
Guidi, G	25	1.37
Hazan, S	25	1.37
Scopigno, R	25	
Torres, JC	25	1.37
Doulamis, A	24	1.31
Fink, E	23	1.26
Rinaudo, F	22	1.20
Scaioni, M	22	1.20
Thwaites, H	20	1.10
Chova, LG	18	0.99

Table 5. The 10 most prolific group authors in the digital technologies in cultural heritage literature between 1993 and 2022

Group Author	Record Count	% of the 1826 Articles
IEEE	96	5.26
IOP	19	1.04
ACM	18	0.99
IEEE Computer Society	15	0.82
ASSOC Comp Machinery	12	0.66
Informat Resources management Assoc	4	0.22
SGEM	4	0.22
ASME	2	0.11
IS T	2	0.11
Creative Research Team	1	0.06

Table 6. The publications with the most contributions to the digital technologies in cultural heritage between 1993 and 2022

Sources	Record Count	% of the 1826 Articles
Lecture Notes in Computer Science	136	7.45
International Archives of the Photogrammetry Remote Sensing and Spatial Information Sciences	94	5.15
Journal of Cultural Heritage	47	2.57
ACM Journal on Computing and Cultural Heritage	40	2.19
Applied Sciences Basel	40	2.19
Communications in Computer and Information Science	38	2.08
Sustainability	37	2.03
Virtual Archaeology Review	33	1.81
Heritage	28	1.53
Digital Presentation and Preservation of Cultural and Scientific Heritage	22	1.20
2015 Digital Heritage International Congress Vol.2 Analysis Interpretation Theory Methodologies Preservation Standarts Digital Heritage Projects Applications	18	0.99
IOP Conference Series Materials Science and Engineering	17	0.93
Remote Sensing	17	0.93
2nd International Conference of Geomatics and Restoration Geores 2019	16	0.88
Disegnarecon	16	0.88
Heritage Science	16	0.88
Proceedings of SPIE	15	0.82
ISPRS International Journal of Geo Information	14	0.77
International Conference Florence Heri Tech The Future of Heritage Science and Technologies	13	0.71
Scires It Scientific Research and Information Technology	13	0.71

Table 7. The book series with the most contributions to the digital technologies in cultural heritage between 1993 and 2022

Book Series	Record Count	% of the 1826 Articles
Lecture Notes in Computer Science	136	7.45
International Archives of the Photogrammetry Remote Sensing and Spatial Information Sciences	94	5.15
Communications in Computer and Information Science	38	2.08
IOP Conference Series Materials Science and Engineering	17	0.93
Proceedings of Spie	15	0.82
Fabbrica Della Conoscenza	12	0.66
Advances in Social Science Education and Humanities Research	10	0.55
Iceri Proceedings	9	0.49
Proceedings of the International Conference on Virtual Systems Multimedia Vsmm	9	0.49
Procedia Social and Bhevioral Sciences	7	0.38
Advances in Intelligent Systems and Computing	6	0.33
Inted Proceedings	6	0.33
International Symposium on Mixed and Augmented Reality	6	0.33
Isprs Annals of the Photogrammetry Remote Sensing and Spatial Information Sciences	6	0.33

The conferences in which the number of the presented documents on *digital technologies in cultural heritage* was the most were "Digital Heritage International Congress", "2nd International Conference of Geomatics and Restoration Geores", "7th European Mediterranean International Conference Euromed ", "2nd International Conference on Florence Heri Tech the Future of Heritage Science and Technologies" and "26th International Symposium of ICOMOS ISPRS International Scientific Committee on Heritage Documentation CIPA on Digital Workflows for Heritage Conservation" (n=25, 16, 16, 13, 11, 10, respectively; Table.8). RLUK Research Libraries (UK) is the most productive organization of the *digital technologies in cultural heritage* literature between 1993 and 2022 with 60 documents, followed by Consiglio Nazionale Delle Ricerche CNR (Italy), Polytechnic University of Milan (Italy), University of Naples Federico II (Italy) and Polytechnic University of Turin (Italy) were the most productive organizations (n=56, 36, 31 and 28, respectively; Table.9).

Table 8. The conferences in which the number of the presented documents on digital technologies in cultural heritage was the most, between 1993 and 2022

Meeting Title	Record Count	% of the 1826 Articles
Digital Heritage International Congress	25	1.37
2nd International Conference of Geomatics and Restoration Geores	16	0.88
7th European Mediterranean International Conference Euromed	16	0.88
2nd International Conference on Florence Heri Tech the Future of Heritage Science and Technologies	13	0.71
26th International Symposium of ICOMOS ISPRS International Scientific Committee on Heritage Documentation CIPA on Digital Workflows for Heritage Conservation	11	0.60
27th CIPA International Symposium on Documenting the Past for a Better Future	10	0.55
8th International Workshop on 3D Virtual Reconstruction and Visualization of Complex Architectures 3D Arch	10	0.55
3rd Digital Heritage International Congress Digital Heritage 24th International Conference on Virtual Systems and Multimedia VSMM	9	0.49
2nd International Conference TMM CH	8	0.44
Conference of the Marie Sklodowska Curie Initial Training Network For Digital Cultural Heritage ITN DCH	8	0.44

Table 9. The 10 most productive affiliations of the digital technologies in cultural heritage literature between 1993 and 2022

Organization-Enhanced	Country	Record Count	% of the 1826 Articles
RLUK Research Libraries UK	UK	60	3.29
Consiglio Nazionale Delle Ricerche CNR	Italy	56	3.07
Polytechnic University of Milan	Italy	36	1.97
University of Naples Federico II	Italy	31	1.70
Polytechnic University of Turin	Italy	28	1.53
Marche Polytechnic University	Italy	26	1.42
University of Aegean	Greece	23	1.26
Sapienza University Rome	Italy	20	1.10
Cyprus University of Technology	Cyprus	18	0.99
University of Bologna	Italy	18	0.99

Analyses of Citations, Keywords, and Bibliometric Network

The metric value calculated to measure productivity and citation impact (h-index) in the digital technologies in cultural heritage literature is found as 42. The total number citations are 12535 (10343 without self-citations) and the average number of citations is 6.86 per item, as of the date of May 2023.

The most cited document was an original article published in 2009 and entitled "State-of-The-Art and Applications of 3D Imaging Sensors in Industry, Cultural Heritage, Medicine, and Criminal Investigation" by Sansoni, G; Trebeschi, M and Docchio, F (Table.10). It was cited 383 times. The study is about 3D imaging sensors for the acquisition of for the optical 3D measurement of surfaces in various sectors including cultural heritage applications. The study emphases that the future of 3D systems is promising, since the applications of 3D acquisition are increasing and 3D imaging is a main part of automation, 3D modeling, robotics and of Rapid Prototyping (Sansoni and others, 2009).

Among the publications of 2022, the most cited article was "3D Technologies For Intangible Cultural Heritage Preservation-Literature Review For Selected Databases" regarding the general state of use of 3D digital technologies in intangible cultural heritage, most of which are 3D visualization, 3D Modelling, Augmented Reality, Virtual Reality and motion capture systems (Skublewska-Paszkowska and others, 2022).

Table 10. The most cited articles published in the digital technologies in cultural heritage literature between 1993 and 2022[9]

Article	Author(s)	Year	Total Citation	Average per Year
State-of-The-Art and Applications of 3D Imaging Sensors in Industry, Cultural Heritage, Medicine, and Criminal Investigation	Sansoni, G; Trebeschi, M and Docchio, F	2009	383	25.53
Methods for 3D digitization of Cultural Heritage	Pavlidis, G; Koutsoudis, A; (...); Chamzas, C	2007	275	16.18
A Survey of Augmented, Virtual, and Mixed Reality for Cultural Heritage	Bekele, MK; Pierdicca, R; (...); Gain, J	2018	274	45.67
Beyond virtual museums: Experiencing immersive virtual reality in real museums	Carrozzino, M and Bergamasco, M	2010	251	17.93
Learning cultural heritage by serious games	Mortara, M; Catalano, CE; (...); Petridis, P	2014	242	24.2
Developing serious games for cultural heritage: a state-of-the-art review	Anderson, EF; McLoughlin, L; (...); de Freitas, S	2010	164	11.71
Virtual museums, a survey and some issues for consideration	Sylaiou, S; Liarokapis, F; (...); Patias, P	2009	151	10.07
The Role of Augmented Reality for Experience-Influenced Environments: The Case of Cultural Heritage Tourism in Korea	Chung, N; Lee, H; (...); Koo, C	2018	127	21.17
Value of augmented reality at cultural heritage sites: A stakeholder approach	Dieck, MCT and Jung, TH	2017	125	17.86
3D reconstruction methods for digital preservation of cultural heritage: A survey	Gomes, L; Bellon, ORP and Silva, L	2014	121	12.1

Bibliometric networks of the citation of the authors and sources and citations among organizations in the *digital technologies in cultural heritage* literature are gathered from Vosviewer (2023) and shown in Figures 5-7.

Figure 5. Bibliometric network of the citation of the authors in the digital technologies in cultural heritage literature
Source: VOSviewer (2023)

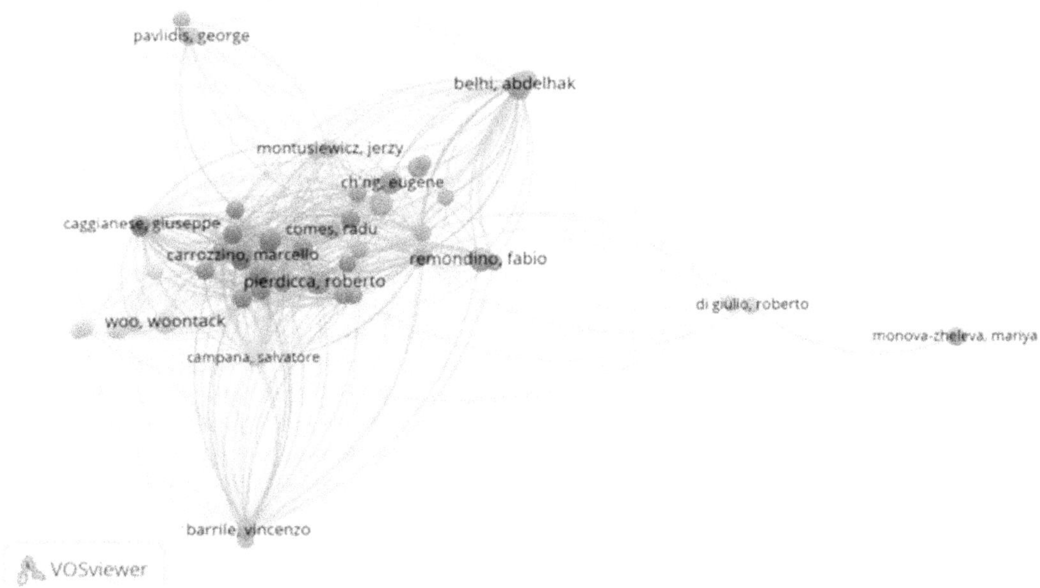

Figure 6. Bibliometric network of the citations of the sources in the digital technologies in cultural heritage literature
Source: VOSviewer (2023)

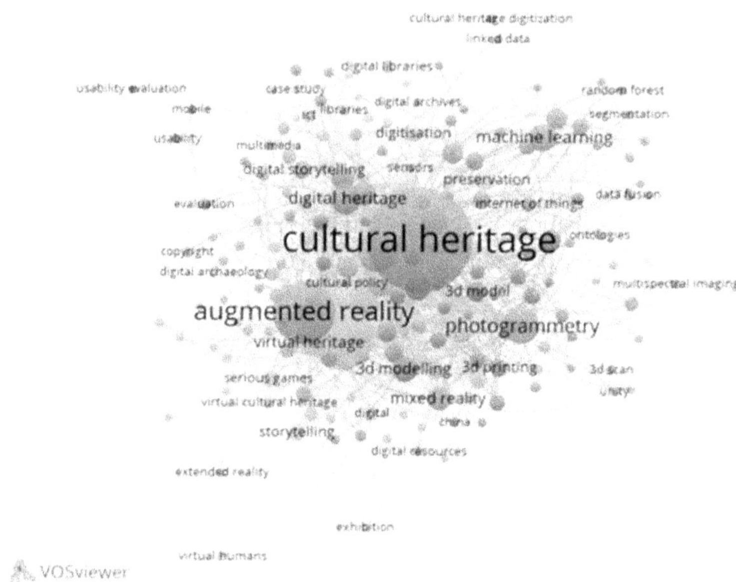

Figure 7. Bibliometric network of the citations among organizations in the digital technologies in cultural heritage literature
Source: VOSviewer (2023)

The most used keywords on *digital technologies in cultural heritage* are cultural heritage, virtual reality and augmented reality (Table 11; Figure 8). When analyzing the co-authorship among organizations, the most collaborative ones are identified as Politechnic University of Milan, Politechnic University of Turin, Consiglio Nazionale Delle Ricerche CNR and University of Naples Federico II (Figure 9).

Table 11. The co-occurrence of the author keywords with minimum two occurrences in the digital technologies in cultural heritage literature between 1993 and 2022

Keywords		Total Link Strength	Keywords		Total Link Strength
1	Cultural Heritage	1184	**6**	Digital Heritage	134
2	Virtual Reality	476	**7**	3D Reconstruction	113
3	Augmented Reality	444	**8**	Documentation	102
4	Photogrammetry	215	**9**	Museums	102
5	Digitization	141	**10**	Virtual Museum	98

Figure 8. Bibliometric network of the co-occurrence of the author keywords in the digital technologies in cultural heritage literature
Source: VOSviewer (2023)

Figure 9. Bibliometric network of the co-authorship among organizations in the digital technologies in cultural heritage literature
Source: VOSviewer (2023)

SOLUTIONS AND RECOMMENDATIONS

It is shown in the study that 90% of the top ten countries by total number of publications on *digital technologies in cultural heritage* between 1993 and 2022 are from the countries in developed category. The countries that contribute to the literature the most are in the continents of America and Europe. China, which is among the developing countries according to the UN classification, is the second country of all with 193 documents and first of the developing countries followed by South Korea, Malaysia and Türkiye. Russia among the economies in transition take place in the most productive 20 countries list with 34 documents. The academic studies on *digital technologies in cultural heritage* should be supported in the underdeveloped and developing countries besides developed countries, too.

FUTURE RESEARCH DIRECTIONS AND CONCLUSION

Digital technologies help to engage people with cultural heritage, attract visitors, help scholars to make use of knowledge and collect data. Technical infrastructure, capacity, knowledge and skills are the basic needs for this digital transformation. Future needs for the use of digitalization are the repositories of archaeological/cultural digital documentation; reliable access point to digital heritage, automated systems of documentations and monitoring, promoting digital reconstruction in cultural heritage areas, facilitating digital popularization of the cultural properties. Besides these, there are some challenges of the digitalization in the field of cultural heritage. These are legislations that does not recognize digital data on cultural heritage; need to develop digital skills within the administration; need of manually recording prone to error; technological challenges; lack of standards and high costs.

Bibliometrics is the way of analyzing in order to provide quantitative and qualitative data on a definite subject in the literature (Van Eck and Waltman, 2010). Document analysis is said to be a method of analyzing the documents on a particular topic extensively without interviews or observations (Yıldırım and Şimşek, 2018). It is a summarizing method by assessing the certain indicators (Thelwall, 2008). The statistical analysis is made in the matters of author, subject, research areas, countries, keywords and cited authors and sources to expose the general structure (Zan, 2012). The bibliometric studies display the development process of the topic (Deng, Tian and Zhang, 2009).

The discipline of bibliometrics has enhanced and increased in number since 1993. There is a total of approximately 25000 bibliometric studies published in the time period of this study according to the WoS databases. The number of bibliometrics studies have an increasing trend through years [n(2018-2022)=1344, 1880, 2652, 3814 and 5134, respectively]. However there are limited bibliometric studies, literature on digital technologies in cultural heritage does not contain any comprehensive bibliometric analysis.

Data mining research showed that there has been a regular increase in annual paper production on *digital technologies in cultural heritage* on the WoS from the starting date to 2022. Despite this trend of growth in the numbers, there was a decrease in the number of publications in the years of 2016 and 2020. To conclude, the research outputs about the publications on *digital technologies in cultural heritage* are conducted by retrieving bibliometric data from WoS database in the study. This study is expected to urge scholars to implement more studies on this definite topic and stimulate growth on the academic studies.

REFERENCES

G20 Ministers of Culture. (2023). *Outcome Document and Chair's Summary*. G20 Development Ministerial Meeting Varanasi.

Akça, D., Grün, A., Alkis, Z., Demir, N., Breuckmann, B., Erduyan, İ., & Nadir, E. (2006). 3D modeling of the Weary Herakles statue with a coded structured light system. *IAPRS*, (5), 46.

Anadolu Ajansı. (2023). *Hitit tabletleri yapay zeka ile analiz ediliyor.* https://www.aa.com.tr/tr/kultur/hitit-tabletleri-yapay-zeka-ile-analiz-ediliyor/2779718

Aria, M., & Cuccurullo, C. (2017). Bibliometrix: An R-tool for comprehensive science mapping analysis. *Journal of Informetrics*, *11*(11), 959–975. doi:10.1016/j.joi.2017.08.007

Arkeolojik Haber. (2023). *Çin Seddi yapay zeka ile restore edilecek.* https://www.arkeolojikhaber.com/haber-cin-seddi-yapay-zeka-ile-restore-edilecek-11684/

Artsın, M. (2020). A text mining application: Vosviewer. *Eskişehir Teknik Üniversitesi Bilim ve Teknoloji Dergisi B-Teorik Bilimler*, *8*(2), 344–354.

Lab. (2023). *MUES (Museum National Inventory System) Project.* https://b3lab.org/en/sayfa/mues_museum_national_inventory_system_project-32

Bozdoğan, K. (2020). A bibliometric analysis of educational studies about museum education. *Participatory Educational Research*, *7*(3), 161–179. doi:10.17275/per.20.40.7.3

Chroni, A. (2018). Cultural Heritage Digitization and Copyright Issues. *Euro-Mediterranean Conference, Digital Heritage. Progress in Cultural Heritage: Documentation, Preservation and Protection*, 396-407. 10.1007/978-3-030-01762-0_34

Cumhuriyet (2023). *Blockchain teknolojisi, bin yıllık mağaraları daha erişilebilir kılıyor.* https://www.cumhuriyet.com.tr/bilim-teknoloji/blockchain-teknolojisi-bin-yillik-magaralari-daha-erisilebilir-kiliyor-2010544

Deng, S., Tian, Y., & Zhang, H. (2009). Using the bibliometric analysis to evaluate global scientific production of data mining papers. *2009 First International Workshop on Database Technology and Applications*, 233-238. 10.1109/DBTA.2009.157

Donthu, N., Kumar, S., Mukherjee, D., Pandey, N., & Lim, W. M. (2021). How to conduct a bibliometric analysis: An overview and guidelines. *Journal of Business Research, 133*, 285–296. doi:10.1016/j.jbusres.2021.04.070

Espina-Romero, L., & Guerrero-Alcedo, J. (2022). Fields touched by digitalization: Analysis of scientific activity in Scopus. *Sustainability (Basel), 2022*(14), 1–16. doi:10.3390u142114425

Halaç, H.H., & Öğülmüş, V. (2021). Kültürel miras verilerinin dijital olarak depolanması: OpenHeritage3D Örneği. *The Turkish Journal of Design, Art and Communication, 11*(2), 521–540.

Kayıkçı, D. (2019). Arkeoloji ve müzeolojide yapay zeka / derin öğrenme: 3B parça eşleştirme sistem modeli önerisi. *Proceedings of the 2nd International Conference on Technology and Science.*

Kultur Limited. (2023). *Kültürel miras için yapay zekâ tabanlı arşiv otomasyon sistemi: GAMOS.* https://kulturlimited.com/kulturel-miras-icin-yapay-zeka-tabanli-arsiv-otomasyon-sistemi-gamos/

NTV. (2023). *Microsoft'tan tarihi ve yapay zekayı bir araya getiren proje.* https://www.ntv.com.tr/galeri/teknoloji/microsofttan-tarihi-ve-yapay-zekayi-bir-araya-getiren-proje-ilk-olimpiyatlara-katilmak-artik-mumkun,oAjB-S_jPkm86F_m8WF 7Lw

Pavlidis, G., Koutsoudis, A., Arnaoutoglou, F., Tsioukas, V., & Chamzas, C. (2007). Methods for 3D Digitization of Cultural Heritage. *Journal of Cultural Heritage, 8*(1), 93–98. doi:10.1016/j.culher.2006.10.007

Salleh, S. Z., & Bushroa, A. R. (2022). Bibliometric analysis on the implementation digitization technologies in cultural heritage in Malaysia. *Geografia : Malaysian Journal of Society and Space, 18*(2), 287–300. doi:10.17576/geo-2022-1802-22

Sousa, J. P., Cordeiro, P., & Cunha, C. R. (2022). The use of technologies in museums: A bibliometric analysis based on the Web of Science database. *Advanced Research in the Technologies, Information Innovation and Sustainability, 1676*(PT II), 269–282.

Thelwall, M. (2008). Bibliometrics to webometrics. *Journal of Information Science, 34*(4), 605–621. doi:10.1177/0165551507087238

United Nations. (2022). *World Economic Situation and Prospects 2022.* https://www.un.org/development/desa/dpad/wp-content/uploads/sites/45/WESP2022_ANNEX.pdf

Van Eck, N. J., & Waltman, L. (2010). Software survey: Vosviewer, A computer program for bibliometric mapping. *Scientometrics, 84*(2), 523–538. doi:10.100711192-009-0146-3 PMID:20585380

Varinlioğlu, G., Alankuş, G., Aslankan, A., & Mura, G. (2019). Oyun Tabanlı Öğrenme ile Dijital Mirasın yaygınlaştırılması. *METU JFA*, *36*(1), 23–40.

Vosviewer. (2023). *Visualizing scientific landscapes.* https://www.vosviewer.com/

Yıldırım, A., & Şimşek, H. (2018). *Qualitative research methods in the social sciences* (11th ed.). Seçkin Publishing.

Zan, B. U. (2012). *A comparative bibliometric analysis study in scientific disciplines at Türkiye* [Doctorate Dissertation]. Ankara University Social Sciences Institute.

KEY TERMS AND DEFINITIONS

Artificial Intelligence: Simulation of human intelligence by a computer or computer-controlled robot to perform tasks.

Bibliometrics: The way of analyzing in order to provide quantitative and qualitative data on a definite subject in the scientific literature.

Building Information Modelling: Digital representation and process of managing information used in architecture, engineering and construction.

Digitization: A process of converting data into a digital format.

Geographic Information System: A system for storing, displaying and analyzing geographically referenced data.

Mapping: A methodological tool used in data collection and analysis on projects.

Virtual Reality: A simulated experience of virtual world by giving the user an immersive feeling.

ENDNOTES

1 Kultur Limited (2023). *"Kültürel miras için yapay zekâ tabanlı arşiv otomasyon sistemi: GAMOS"*. Accessed on April 7, 2023 https://kulturlimited.com/kulturel-miras-icin-yapay-zeka-tabanli-arsiv-otomasyon-sistemi-gamos/

2 TS2. (2023). *"Kültürel Mirasın Korunması ve Analizi İçin Üretim İçin Dijital İkiz"*. Accessed on August 29, 2023 https://ts2.space/tr/kulturel-mirasin-korunmasi-ve-analizi-icin-uretim-icin-dijital-ikiz/

3 Arkeolojik Haber (2023). *"Çin Seddi Yapay Zeka İle Restore Edilecek"*. Accessed on April 7, 2023 https://www.arkeolojikhaber.com/haber-cin-seddi-yapay-zeka-ile-restore-edilecek-11684/

4 NTV. (2023). "*Microsoft'tan Tarihi Ve Yapay Zekayı Bir Araya Getiren Proje*". Accessed on April 7, 2023 https://www.ntv.com.tr/galeri/teknoloji/microsofttan-tarihi-ve-yapay-zekayi-bir-araya-getiren-proje-ilk-olimpiyatlara-katilmak-artik-mumkun,oAjB-S_jPkm86F_m8WF 7Lw

5 Cumhuriyet (2023). *"Blockchain teknolojisi, bin yıllık mağaraları daha erişilebilir kılıyor"*. Accessed on April 7, 2023 https://www.cumhuriyet.com.tr/bilim-teknoloji/blockchain-teknolojisi-bin-yillik-magaralari-daha-erisilebilir-kiliyor-2010544

6 B3Lab (2023). *"MUES (Museum National Inventory System) Project"*. Accessed on April 7, 2023 https://b3lab.org/en/sayfa/mues_museum_national_inventory_system_project-32

7 Anadolu Ajansı (2023). *"Hitit Tabletleri Yapay Zeka İle Analiz Ediliyor"*. Accessed on April 7, 2023 https://www.aa.com.tr/tr/kultur/hitit-tabletleri-yapay-zeka-ile-analiz-ediliyor/2779718

8 All of the figures and tables are prepared by the author.

9 The data is gathered from WoS in the end of May 2023.

Chapter 10
Fortifying Data Security in the Evolving Digital Landscape:
Challenges and Solutions

Naman Srivastava
https://orcid.org/0009-0000-4742-4423
University of Petroleum and Energy Studies, Dehradhun, India

Harshita Sharma
https://orcid.org/0009-0005-2232-4393
University of Petroleum and Energy Studies, Dehradhun, India

Akshita Maliyal
https://orcid.org/0009-0001-4741-7650
University of Petroleum and Energy Studies, Dehradhun, India

Madhav Verma
Birsa Institute of Technology, Sindri, India

Keshav Sinha
https://orcid.org/0000-0003-1053-3911
University of Petroleum and Energy Studies, Dehradhun, India

ABSTRACT

Data security presents significant concerns for organizations and individuals in today's evolving digital landscape. Prominent challenges include sophisticated cyberattacks, remote work vulnerabilities, cloud security, phishing, insider threats, data privacy, encryption, and identity and access management. In addressing diverse challenges, a range of solutions can be implemented, such as using multi-factor authentication (MFA) to enhance user authentication. At the same time, zero trust networking (ZTN) ensures continuous authentication and authorization. Dynamic data masking (DDM) alters sensitive data during transit to thwart unauthorized access. Regular security training, cloud security tools, and insider threat prevention measures further bolster data security. Techniques like data backup, encryption, and disaster recovery plan are used to safeguard against data loss and breaches. Organizations can strengthen their data security and protect sensitive information by adopting these solutions.

DOI: 10.4018/979-8-3693-0807-3.ch010

INTRODUCTION

Security encompasses a multi-layered approach to protect individuals, organizations, and data from threats. It includes physical security measures, such as access control systems and surveillance cameras, to safeguard tangible assets. Information security, also known as cybersecurity, focuses on protecting digital data through strategies like encryption, firewalls, and secure coding practices. Network security secures computer networks with measures like network segmentation and intrusion prevention systems (Rawat and Singh, 2019). Operational security ensures business continuity and minimizes vulnerabilities in supply chains and incident response. Personnel security involves background checks, access controls, and ongoing training to mitigate insider threats. Additionally, security awareness programs address social engineering tactics and educate individuals about potential threats and best practices. By implementing these various security measures, individuals and organizations can effectively mitigate risks and protect against many threats in today's complex and evolving threat landscape.

Data Security

Data security is evolving to meet the challenges and opportunities of the future. It includes adopting advanced encryption techniques, such as quantum-resistant algorithms, to ensure the confidentiality and integrity of data (Sinha et al., 2021). Stricter data privacy regulations and growing consumer awareness emphasize the need for organizations to prioritize data protection. Integrating artificial intelligence and machine learning enables faster threat detection and response (Sinha et al., 2018). Cloud computing, IoT devices, and emerging technologies like blockchain require robust access controls, encryption, and monitoring to safeguard data. Addressing challenges like deepfakes, biometric data protection, and decentralized technologies will be crucial. By embracing innovation and staying proactive, individuals and organizations can navigate the changing landscape and effectively protect sensitive data.

The chapter is structured to provide a comprehensive overview of the various data security challenges faced in today's evolving digital landscape. It begins by introducing the significance of data security concerns for organizations and individuals. The chapter then delves into the prominent challenges data security professionals and stakeholders encounter, such as sophisticated cyberattacks, remote work vulnerabilities, cloud security, phishing, insider threats, data privacy, encryption, and identity and access management (Sinha et al., 2020). The chapter follows a logical flow, systematically addressing each challenge and presenting potential solutions to combat them effectively. The chapter explores relevant concepts, methodologies, and best practices for each challenge, making it an informative and practical resource for readers seeking to enhance data security in their organizations.

This chapter's structure strives to provide a complete overview of the various data security concerns encountered in today's fast-evolving digital realm. It starts by emphasizing the significance of data security problems for enterprises and people. The chapter then explores the major challenges data security professionals and stakeholders face, such as complex cyberattacks, vulnerabilities associated with remote work, cloud security, phishing, insider threats, data privacy, encryption, and identity and access management. The chapter follows a logical structure, addressing each difficulty in turn and proposing alternative solutions to meet them effectively. Relevant concepts, approaches, and best practices are addressed concerning each obstacle, making the chapter an instructional and practical guide for readers looking to improve data security inside their businesses.

MOTIVATION

This chapter addresses the urgent requirement for effective solutions in data security within the ever-evolving digital context. The widespread adoption of technology and the increasing dependence on digital platforms have yielded notable advantages, yet they have also introduced inherent risks and vulnerabilities. In this environment, organizations and individuals are confronted with an array of data security threats that are progressively intricate and challenging to manage. Cybercriminals persist in exploiting weaknesses in systems, while the emergence of remote work and cloud-based services has opened novel avenues for attacks. Moreover, the growing emphasis on data privacy and compliance regulations has elevated the responsibility of organizations to protect sensitive information. The chapter aims to cultivate a proactive data security culture by underscoring the significance of consistent security training, utilizing cloud security tools, and establishing disaster recovery plans. Organizations can alleviate the impact of data breaches and potential losses by adopting these measures. The chapter aims to function as a valuable resource that provides a comprehensive perspective on data security challenges in the contemporary digital landscape. It offers actionable strategies to counter cyber threats, safeguard sensitive data, and reinforce overall data security for organizations and individuals.

RESEARCH BACKGROUND

Securing data is critical to modern applications to protect against security breaches and maintain customer trust. Figure 1 presents the categorized data security techniques for safeguarding data in the realms of (i) Distributed Data, (ii) Internet of Things (IoT) Devices, and (iii) Cloud Data (Sinha et al., 2022).

Figure 1. Data security in different environments

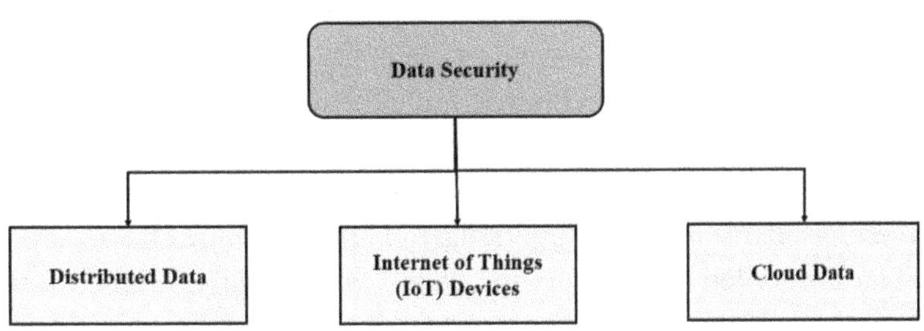

Securing Data in a Distributed Environment

Distributed data security is critical in today's interconnected and data-driven world. With the exponential growth of data and the increasing reliance on distributed computing systems, ensuring data privacy, integrity, and availability has become paramount. Ensuring data security in distributed systems involves several best practices, such as (i) securing the environment by controlling application access and securing file paths that could expose sensitive data is essential, (ii) Data should be encrypted both at rest and during transit, employing protocols like TLS over SSL for communication channels and encrypting disk volumes or application databases. Implementing an authentication and authorization layer with multi-factor authentication helps verify user identities and control data access based on roles and permissions. Privatizing system schemas and separating roles and duties within the organization also enhance data security by restricting access to sensitive information. By adopting these practices, organizations can establish robust data security measures in their distributed systems. We aim to identify critical methodologies, challenges, and advancements in distributed data security (Rawat and Singh, 2023).

Gu et al. (2017) introduce the distributed privacy utility using distributed lossy source coding. The essence of this approach lies in its utilization of foundational concepts from source coding theory and distributed source coding with side information. Here, the authors introduce a coding scheme to quantify the relationship between source coding rate, privacy leakage, and distortion. A pivotal aspect of their work is the establishment of two significant regions: the Rate-Distortion-Equivocation (RDE) region and the Rate-Distortion-Leakage (RDL) region, tailored explicitly for distributed data sources with side information. The practical implementation of the method could encounter real-world challenges arising from data heterogeneity, varying levels of trust among data participants, and compatibility issues. In conclusion, the research paper contributes to data privacy, offering valuable insights and methodologies applicable in diverse distributed settings, thereby advancing our understanding and management of the delicate privacy-utility trade-off.

Xu et al. (2005) proposed distributed device networks with Security Constraints. In this paper, they adopt a descriptive and explanatory approach to present the design of distributed device control systems that incorporate essential security features. Subsequently, the authors propose a design framework that combines the IEC61499 architecture with security modules to tackle the identified security challenges. They elucidate the three logical domains of the system architecture: (i) the client domain, (ii) the repository domain, and (iii) the device domain. It delves into secure clients, repositories, and device control gateways' functionalities and responsibilities. Advantages of the proposed design include increased interoperability, as using the IEC61499 specification facilitates the exchange of control components between different tools and suppliers, enabling devices from multiple vendors to collaborate effectively.

Moreover, the design framework offers portability by allowing control components and codes to be stored and retrieved by authorized users or devices from anywhere, thus ensuring adaptability across diverse devices and software tools. While acknowledging the need for further research and development to address the challenges of running a distributed device control system in open and dynamic environments, the paper does not extensively discuss specific issues related to storing, retrieving, and protecting components in such settings. It discusses the functional modules of secure clients, repositories, and device control gateways but lacks detailed implementation details or practical examples of the proposed design.

Thuraisingham and Ford (1995) present an integrated architecture for effectively managing security constraints in a multilevel, secure, distributed environment. By categorizing various security constraints and adapting existing techniques from non-multilevel relational databases, the authors introduce an approach that ensures enhanced data security, flexibility, and fine-grained control over access. Additionally, processing constraints during query execution and database updates may introduce performance overhead, necessitating careful consideration during implementation.

El-Zoghdy and Ghoneim (2016) propose a novel strategy to optimize task scheduling in a heterogeneous distributed computing system with high-speed network connectivity. The approach utilizes a First-Come-First-Serve (FCFS) scheduling policy for task queues. It aims to minimize the per-class average response time while maximizing the average computing node utilization. The comprehensive evaluations would be beneficial to validate the practical applicability and performance of the proposed multi-class task scheduling strategy for heterogeneous distributed computing systems.

Zeng et al. (2012) present a novel data storage scheme using wireless sensor networks. The system model consists of strategically deployed sensor nodes that generate and distribute data blocks to storage nodes. Random Byzantine failures and malicious attacks are the main threats and aim to ensure data availability, integrity, and efficiency in computational and communication overheads. The scheme's advantages include data integrity, availability, fault, intrusion tolerance, efficiency, and extensive security analysis. However, the work lacks specific details, performance evaluations, scalability considerations, and practical implementation insights, requiring further exploration and validation for real-world deployment.

Zubi (2009) explores the advantages and disadvantages of distributed database systems. It highlights scalability, enhanced accessibility, flexibility, and high availability. Disadvantages include more complexity, higher expenses, network reliance, data consistency difficulties, and security risks. Additionally, optimizing performance through query optimization, indexing, caching, and load balancing is crucial for maximizing system efficiency and minimizing response times in distributed computing environments.

Dardzinska-Glebocka (2007) presents a comprehensive methodology to address crucial challenges in Distributed Information Systems (DIS). It highlights a rule-discovery method that resolves semantic inconsistencies between distributed sites, manages null values, and reconstructs hidden attributes. The proposed approach is effective, and practicality in real-world settings becomes essential for a holistic understanding of its potential impact on distributed information systems.

Matousek (2008) presents a comprehensive methodology for addressing security and reliability in developing distributed software systems in healthcare. The methodology involves identifying and discussing key components related to system security, asset protection, threats, security awareness, reliability requirements, and security infrastructure. The advantages of the paper include its focus on the healthcare domain, emphasizing the importance of risk analysis, and recognizing the need for both security and reliability in healthcare systems. The paper lacks specific implementation details, may not cover recent technological developments, and provides limited discussion on legal and regulatory aspects, warranting further exploration in these areas to ensure comprehensive security and reliability in distributed healthcare systems.

Ruminski (2007) presents a pioneering methodology that harnesses Jini technology for distributed processing. The paper delves into creating a distributed system by capitalizing on the power of Jini network technology and JavaSpaces. The work underscores various advantages, including amplified computational power, streamlined workflow management, scalability, and robust security implementation. It simultaneously navigates the intricacies of ensuring privacy, security, and efficiency in a distributed healthcare landscape.

Grabis et al. (2020) unveil a compelling methodology centered around the development and execution of MyDataExperience. This innovative personal data storage and sharing solution harmoniously integrates distributed storage, blockchain technology, smart contracts, and a knowledge base. The methodology encapsulates diverse data management facets, including secure asset storage, nuanced data sharing bolstered by access controls, and facilitating data searches within the shared repository. The inherent latency of blockchain transactions, sometimes spanning several minutes, might hinder real-time data management objectives. Lastly, the imposition of costs associated with blockchain technology and transactions introduces a factor to be reckoned with, constraining the system's scalability and accessibility, particularly in frequent transactions.

Securing Data on IoT Devices

The Internet of Things (IoT) has changed how we interact with our surroundings by linking everyday objects and devices to the internet and allowing them to communicate and exchange data. As the Internet of Things grows in popularity, securing its security, dependability, and efficiency becomes increasingly important. Here, we hope to better grasp critical topics, advancements, and challenges in IoT. Securing sensitive data on IoT devices requires taking several essential steps. First, it is crucial to identify the number and types of IoT devices connected to the network and catalog potential security vulnerabilities. Secondly, implementing strict password policies with complex passwords that are regularly updated helps mitigate the risk of compromised credentials. Keeping all devices updated with the latest security patches is essential, as many IoT devices often lack regular updates. It is advisable to assess the usefulness of each connected device and disconnect any that do not bring tangible benefits to the business. Monitoring the behavior of connected devices, preferably with a comprehensive Data Security Platform, enables effective oversight of sensitive data usage, ensuring knowledge of its location, authorized access, and user activities. By following these steps, organizations can enhance the security of sensitive data on IoT devices.

Zhang et al. (2020) introduce a novel approach to enhance IoT network security by integrating virtualization into edge computing and addressing the vulnerability of edge devices in conventional IoT setups due to limited computing power and security measures. STEC-IoT introduces a virtualization layer that effectively isolates hardware resources from software applications on IoT devices. They mitigate the risks of data breaches, unauthorized access, and device compromises while providing to the unique security challenges inherent in IoT devices operating at the network's edge.

Chen and Giannakis (2019) focus on enhancing Secure Mobile Edge Computing (MEC) on the Internet of Things (IoT) through Collaborative Online Learning (COL). As the IoT expands, MEC offers computational services at the network edge, but security challenges arise. This combined approach offers benefits like reduced latency, improved efficiency, enhanced security, privacy preservation, and adaptive learning.

Li et al. (2021) presents the concept of Location-Enabled IoT (LE-IoT) involving the integration of location-awareness capabilities into IoT systems, enabling applications like asset tracking and location-based services. Strategies such as sensor fusion, machine learning, map matching, signal monitoring, and collaborative positioning are employed to mitigate errors, with the choice guided by application needs.

Ortigueira et al. (2021) focus on addressing the demands of direct-to-satellite IoT applications. The RESS-IoT (Reliable and Energy-Efficient Scalable MAC Protocol for Direct-to-Satellite IoT) protocol is tailored to ensure scalability, energy efficiency, and reliable communication for IoT devices directly communicating with satellites. Distributed channel access mechanisms, such as CSMA/CA and adaptive backoff mechanisms, reduce contention and delays. RESS-IoT's design is geared toward scalability, using efficient signaling and resource allocation to support many IoT devices.

Said et al. (2020) introduce a specialized framework known as EMS (Energy Management Scheme) aimed at fostering energy efficiency and sustainability within the realm of the Internet of Things (IoT). It employs strategic task scheduling, adaptive duty cycling, machine learning algorithms, and predictive analytics to optimize energy consumption while maintaining system functionality. Moreover, EMS encourages the integration of renewable energy sources and prioritizes energy-aware communication protocols to minimize energy consumption associated with data transmission.

Samaila et al. (2020) present a comprehensive framework to address the security challenges of IoT devices and applications. With IoT's rapid growth, ensuring secure design practices has become crucial. IoT-HarPSecA promotes security by design, embedding security from the start to preempt vulnerabilities.

Verma et al. (2021) present an approach to enhance the security of IoT devices on IPv6-enabled WLANs. Security concerns rise as IoT devices become more prevalent due to their vulnerabilities and limited resources. This research contributes to creating a more secure IoT environment by improving device configurations and developing effective mitigation strategies.

Hwang et al. (2021) explore two vital strategies within edge computing to enhance IoT application efficiency and performance. IoT service slicing involves partitioning applications into independent service slices with dedicated resources optimizing resource management and customization.

Lee et al. (2022) introduces an innovative approach to enhance IoT services' energy efficiency and reliability in Wi-Fi networks. The proposed energy-conscious access point (eAP) system adopts a cross-layer design strategy, considering interactions across the network stack layers. The system aligns with IoT-specific characteristics like intermittent connectivity and diverse application needs, offering a comprehensive solution to enhance the performance and sustainability of IoT services within Wi-Fi networks.

Nguyen et al. (2021) delve into the intricate process of creating a comprehensive model and conducting a thorough analysis of data trading within a blockchain-based market in IoT networks. This endeavor entails designing a conceptual model that encapsulates the market's components and interactions, followed by detailed mapping of the data trading process, identification of performance metrics, and simulations to assess system behavior and performance. The analysis examines potential benefits like data security and transparency and challenges like scalability and privacy concerns, leading to informed recommendations for refining market design and operation.

Securing Data on Cloud

Cloud computing has revolutionized businesses and individuals to manage and store data. However, data security has become paramount with the increasing reliance on cloud-based services. The background delves into cloud data security, presenting a comprehensive review of ten research reports that explore various aspects of securing data in the cloud computing environment (Butt et al., 2023). We aim to understand better key threats, countermeasures, encryption techniques, and governance approaches to safeguarding data in the cloud (Mallisetty et al., 2023). Data protection is a crucial concern for organizations in the cloud, and implementing effective security measures is vital to safeguard sensitive information. Several proven techniques, such as authentication and identity verification, access control, encryption, and secure data deletion and recovery strategies, can be employed. Authentication involves verifying the identity of individuals accessing the system through multi-factor authentication. Access control ensures that users have appropriate access levels to company data, employing models such as role-based or attribute-based access control. Encryption is crucial in protecting data at rest in the cloud, while secure data deletion techniques prevent unauthorized access to deleted data. Implementing regular data backups and testing data recovery procedures are essential for rapid data restoration in case of disruptions. Compliance with regulatory standards is also critical when migrating to a secure and compliant cloud environment. Organizations can enhance their data security and minimize risks by adopting these data protection techniques and following best practices for cloud migration.

Achar et al. (2022) investigates the critical subject of cloud data security, analyzing risks and emphasizing protective measures. It underscores the shared responsibility model between cloud service providers and clients, spotlighting security standards and compliance support by CSPs. Future research areas span advanced threat detection, cloud provider assessments, data privacy compliance, security best practices, and emerging technology implications. It underscores the importance of embracing cloud-native security methods to navigate data security during cloud migration, harnessing advanced features, economic benefits, and streamlined operations.

Ghosh et al. (2023) presents a robust data security strategy for cloud computing by integrating random salting, padding, encryption, and hashing techniques. This approach enhances data security by making encryption more resistant to unauthorized access. The approach offers improved data protection through a sophisticated encryption model despite increased processing time. However, longer encryption and decryption times could impact system performance and require further optimization for real-time applications. In conclusion, the proposed approach offers enhanced cloud data security through innovative encryption techniques, though careful consideration of processing times and potential optimization is advised for practical implementation.

Alghofaili et al. (2021) introduce an innovative approach centered on an independent cryptographic service provider. This study aims to establish a public cloud storage system that ensures the integrity of stored data and safeguards user privacy during the auditing process. The research addresses a critical concern in cloud computing by enabling third-party auditors (TPAs) to efficiently verify data authenticity without compromising user data privacy.

Tyagi et al. (2021) delve into the intricate landscape of cloud computing's application in the banking sector. The methodology proposed involves harnessing a combination of RSA, SHA, and Twofish algorithms to fortify data transmission security in cloud-based banking environments. Banks can harness cloud technology while upholding customer trust and confidentiality by ensuring data integrity, authenticity, and confidentiality.

Madhava et al. (2023) navigate the intricacies of securing data in cloud-based ERP, specifically emphasizing SAP S/4HANA cloud (Public edition). The paper underscores the significance of cloud computing in the banking industry, highlighting its advantages, yet recognizes that robust security measures are imperative. This methodology empowers banks to harness cloud technology while maintaining data security and customer trust. The study delves into security concerns in cloud-based ERP, examines SAP HANA's security features, and offers insights into elevating data protection in Cloud ERP implementations.

Hasan et al. (2023) examine the paramount aspects of cloud technology. The paper illuminates the challenges encompassing unauthorized access and data accuracy. The research's strengths lie in fortified data reliability, remote integrity checks, and enhanced data security while acknowledging complexities in implementation and overhead.

Dibetle and Kalema (2023) embark on crafting a data security governance model tailored for the Software-as-a-Service (SaaS) cloud computing landscape, particularly within South African financial institutions. The study underscores the necessity of robust security measures and governance processes. Rooted in the Technology-Organization-Environment (TOE) model, information security theory, risk management theory, and control and audit theory, the research employs a quantitative methodology, surveying IT professionals from selected financial institutions.

Chatterjee et al. (2023) investigate the pivotal role of cloud-based Learning Management Systems (LMS) in modern education, particularly during global challenges like the COVID-19 pandemic. The proposed methodology offers efficient encryption, improved file decryption, and addresses cloud storage concerns. However, potential challenges include longer decryption times with the hybrid approach and algorithm complexity. Future work could involve hybrid Lightweight Cryptosystem Execution to fortify data security in cloud-based LMS platforms further.

Sambyal and Arora (2023) address the pressing concern of safeguarding electronic health records (EHRs) and medical databases, particularly within cloud environments. As digitization of medical data rises, so do the risks of cyberattacks targeting patient information. The HSMDC model employs a step-by-step encryption process, utilizing algorithms such as blowfish, AES, and ECC for secure transmission over the network. Decryption is performed in reverse order to retrieve the original data.

THEORETICAL FRAMEWORK FOR DATA SECURITY

Figure 2 presents the theoretical framework to secure the data in different environments. Data security is selected based on the research hypothesis and the identity of the various challenges.

Figure 2. Theoretical framework for data security

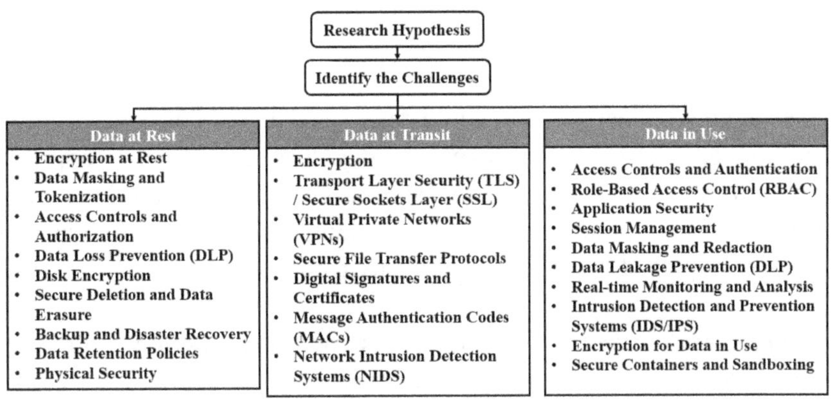

Security measures applied to data kept or at rest on physical or digital storage devices are called in rest. When not utilized or sent, these strategies protect the data's confidentiality and integrity (Karmakar et al., 2022). Here are some common strategies for "at rest" data security:

(i). ***Encryption at Rest***: Encryption at rest involves encrypting data stored on storage devices. It prevents unauthorized access to the data even if the physical storage device is compromised. Encrypted data can only be accessed with the appropriate decryption key or credentials.

(ii). ***Data Masking and Tokenization***: Data masking involves replacing sensitive information with fictional data, while tokenization replaces sensitive data with unique tokens. These techniques help protect sensitive data while allowing applications to function with the substituted values.

(iii). ***Access Controls and Authorization***: Implementing access controls ensures that only authorized individuals or processes can access and modify data stored in a system. It includes role-based access control (RBAC), permissions, and user authentication.

(iv). ***Data Loss Prevention (DLP)***: DLP solutions monitor and prevent unauthorized movement of sensitive data within an organization. They can detect and block attempts to copy, transfer, or email sensitive data to unauthorized recipients (Rawat and Singh, 2019).

(v). ***Disk Encryption***: Disk encryption involves encrypting the entire storage device, such as a hard or solid-state drive. It protects all data stored on the device and requires decryption before the data can be accessed.

(vi). ***Secure Deletion and Data Erasure***: When data is no longer needed, secure deletion methods ensure that the data is effectively erased and cannot be recovered using conventional methods. It is crucial to prevent data leakage when devices are retired or reused.

(vii). ***Backup and Disaster Recovery***: Regular data backups and well-defined disaster recovery plans are important for data resilience. These techniques ensure that data can be restored in case of accidental deletion, hardware failure, or other data loss events.

(viii). ***Data Retention Policies***: Establishing data retention policies helps organizations manage the data lifecycle. It defines how long data should be kept, when it should be deleted, and when it can be archived.

(ix). ***Physical Security***: Physical security measures include locking server rooms, using access control systems, monitoring for unauthorized access, and preventing unauthorized physical access to storage devices.

These "in rest" techniques collectively safeguard data stored on various devices and systems, mitigating the risk of unauthorized access, data breaches, and data loss. Data "in use" approaches are security measures applied to data while it is actively processed, accessed, or altered by applications, users, or systems. These strategies aim to protect the data's confidentiality, integrity, and availability while it is in use. Here are some examples of "in-use" data security techniques:

(i). ***Access Controls and Authentication*****:** Strong access controls ensure only authorized users or processes can interact with the data. Multi-factor authentication (MFA) and strong user authentication methods help prevent unauthorized access.

(ii). ***Role-Based Access Control (RBAC)*****:** RBAC assigns permissions and access rights to users based on their roles within an organization. It ensures that users can only access the data and perform necessary actions for their responsibilities.

(iii). ***Application Security***: Ensuring the security of the applications that handle data is crucial. It includes secure coding practices, regular security testing, and patch management to address vulnerabilities that attackers could exploit.

(iv). ***Session Management***: Proper session management ensures that authenticated users remain securely connected to the application while interacting with the data. It prevents session hijacking and unauthorized access during active user sessions.

(v). ***Data Masking and Redaction***: Data masking involves hiding sensitive data within an application so only authorized users can see the complete information. Redaction involves selectively hiding portions of data, such as personal information, before displaying it to users.

(vi). ***Data Leakage Prevention (DLP)***: DLP solutions can monitor outgoing data flows and prevent sensitive data from leaving the organization's network or systems. It helps to prevent accidental or intentional data leaks.

(vii). ***Real-time Monitoring and Analysis***: Monitoring data in real-time allows for detecting abnormal activities or anomalies. It includes detecting unusual patterns of data access or unexpected system behavior.

(viii). ***Intrusion Detection and Prevention Systems (IDS/IPS)***: IDS and IPS solutions monitor network traffic and system activity in real-time to identify and block suspicious activities or attacks that could compromise data during its use.

(ix). ***Encryption for Data in Use***: In some cases, encryption can also be applied to data while it's actively used within applications or systems. It involves techniques like memory encryption to protect data from unauthorized access in volatile memory.

(x). ***Secure Containers and Sandboxing***: Secure containers and sandboxes isolate applications or processes, ensuring they cannot interact with other processes or access data outside their designated boundaries.

These "in use" solutions operate together to keep data private and secure while it is processed or accessed by authorized users and applications. Data "in transit" procedures are security measures applied to data while it is being sent over networks or communication channels. The fundamental purpose is to protect the data's secrecy, integrity, and authenticity as it travels from one site to another. Here are some examples of "in transit" data security techniques:

(i). ***Encryption***: Encryption involves encoding data so only authorized parties can decipher using a specific key. It ensures that even if an unauthorized entity intercepts the data during transmission, it won't understand its contents without the proper decryption key. Common encryption protocols include SSL/TLS (for web traffic) and VPN (Virtual Private Network) encryption.

(ii). ***Transport Layer Security (TLS) / Secure Sockets Layer (SSL)***: TLS and its predecessor SSL are cryptographic protocols that provide secure communication over a computer network. They establish an encrypted connection between the client and the server, ensuring that data exchanged between them is protected from eavesdropping and tampering.

(iii). ***Virtual Private Networks (VPNs)***: VPNs create secure "tunnels" over public networks, allowing data to be transmitted between remote locations as if on a private network. VPNs encrypt the data and route it through secure servers, making it difficult for unauthorized parties to intercept or manipulate the transmitted data.

(iv). ***Secure File Transfer Protocols***: SFTP (Secure File Transfer Protocol) and SCP (Secure Copy Protocol) are designed to transfer files over a network securely. They use encryption and authentication mechanisms to protect the data being transferred.

(v). ***Digital Signatures and Certificates***: Digital signatures and certificates help ensure the authenticity and integrity of data in transit. Certificates issued by trusted Certificate Authorities (CAs) verify the parties' identity in the communication, and digital signatures ensure that the data hasn't been tampered with.

(vi). ***Message Authentication Codes (MACs)***: MACs are cryptographic hashes that provide a way to verify the integrity of a message or data. They use a shared secret key to create a unique hash for the data, allowing the recipient to confirm that the data hasn't been altered during transit.

(vii). ***Network Intrusion Detection Systems (NIDS)***: NIDS monitor network traffic to detect and alert suspicious or malicious activities in real time. They can help identify unauthorized access attempts, malware propagation, and other network-based attacks.

These "in transit" techniques ensure that data remains secure between devices, servers, or networks, preventing unauthorized access, interception, and tampering during transmission. Policies are collections of rules, guidelines, and procedures that define how specific actions or behaviors inside an organization should be carried out. Policies are created in the context of data security to define clear expectations. Figure 3 presents the data security policies for preserving sensitive information, avoiding security breaches, and responding to security incidents.

Figure 3. Data security policies

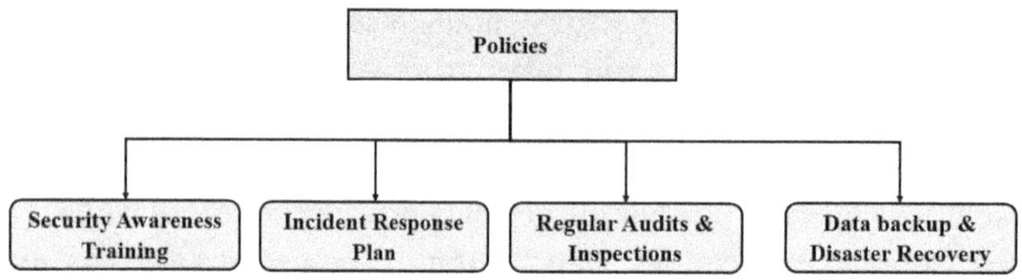

Now, let's look at how the techniques you mentioned help enhance data security:

(i). ***Security Awareness Training***: This technique involves educating employees and users about best practices and potential security threats and recognizing and responding to security incidents. By providing security awareness training, organizations empower their staff to identify phishing emails, avoid risky online behaviors, and understand the importance of strong passwords. It increases the organization's overall security posture and helps prevent accidental data breaches caused by human error.

(ii). ***Incident Response Plan***: An incident response plan outlines the steps to be taken when a security incident occurs, such as a data breach or cyberattack. It includes a well-defined process for detecting, containing, mitigating, and recovering from incidents. A well-prepared incident response plan minimizes the impact of security breaches, reduces downtime, and ensures that the organization responds swiftly and effectively to incidents, thus preserving data integrity.

(iii). ***Regular Audits & Inspections***: Regular audits and inspections involve systematic reviews of an organization's security practices, policies, and technical controls. It helps to identify vulnerabilities, non-compliance with security policies, and potential weaknesses in the data security infrastructure. By conducting audits and inspections, organizations can proactively address security gaps and ensure that security measures are up-to-date and effective.

(iv). ***Data Backup & Disaster Recovery***: Data backup and disaster recovery strategies involve creating duplicate copies of important data and planning to restore data in case of data loss or system failures. Regularly backing up data to secure locations and having a well-defined disaster recovery plan ensures that data can be recovered and systems can be restored quickly during data breaches, hardware failures, or natural disasters. This technique minimizes data loss and ensures business continuity.

These strategies greatly contribute to data security by establishing a comprehensive and proactive strategy to protect sensitive information. Security awareness training teaches users how to avoid common security traps, and incident response plans provide timely and effective responses to security issues, audits assure security compliance, and data backup and disaster recovery plans reduce data loss and downtime. Implementing these strategies together strengthens an organization's ability to protect its data and maintain its stakeholders' trust.

CASE STUDY 1: INTELLIGENT VIDEO DATA SECURITY: A SURVEY AND OPEN CHALLENGES

It is a comprehensive survey work that explores the field of intelligent video data security. Figure 4 presents the video data in various domains, such as surveillance, healthcare, and social media.

Figure 4. Video data security and cyber law

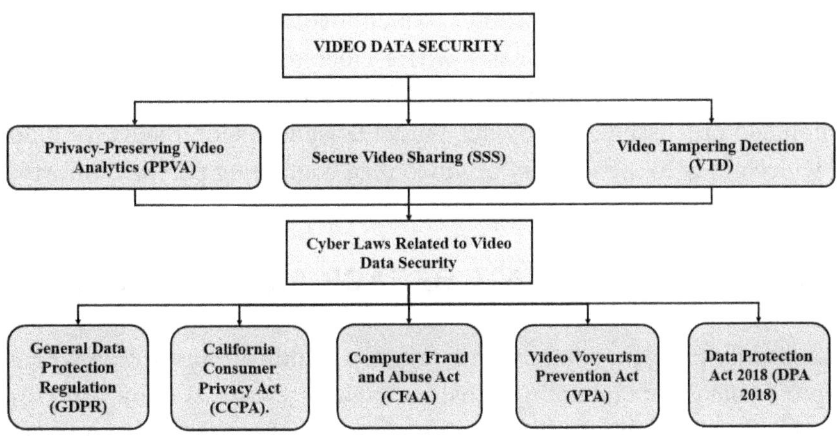

The current state-of-the-art video data security technique highlights encryption, watermarking, and authentication techniques commonly used to protect video data from unauthorized access and manipulation. The challenges and open research areas in intelligent video data security are:

(i). ***Privacy-Preserving Video Analytics (PPVA):*** The goal is to extract meaningful insights from video data while respecting individuals' privacy rights. It involves developing techniques to analyze video content without compromising the privacy of individuals captured in the video.

(ii). ***Secure Video Sharing (SSS):*** The security mechanism is developed to securely share video data between authorized parties while preventing unauthorized access or tampering.

(iii). ***Video Tampering Detection (VTD):*** As video data can be easily manipulated or altered, it is crucial to develop techniques to detect and identify tampering attempts, ensuring the integrity and authenticity of the video content. It involves advanced algorithms and machine learning approaches to detect subtle changes or manipulations in video data.

Intelligent video data security is required in today's data-driven world. Advanced security techniques and algorithms protect video data from unauthorized access, tampering, and privacy breaches.

Cyber Laws Related to Video Data Security

(i). ***General Data Protection Regulation (GDPR):*** GDPR is a regulation that governs the data protection and privacy of individuals within the European Union (E.U.). It includes provisions for the secure processing and storage of personal data relevant to video data security and its associated privacy concerns.

(ii). ***California Consumer Privacy Act (CCPA):*** CCPA is a state-level law in California, United States, which grants consumers specific rights regarding their personal information. It requires businesses to disclose collecting and sharing personal data, which can be relevant to video data security.

(iii). ***Computer Fraud and Abuse Act (CFAA):*** CFAA is a federal law in the United States criminalizes computer-related activities, including unauthorized access to computer systems. This law can apply when video data security breaches involve unauthorized access to protected systems.

(iv). ***Video Voyeurism Prevention Act (VPA):*** VPA is a U.S. federal law prohibiting the capture and distribution of voyeuristic video recordings, which involve the invasion of privacy. It is relevant to video data security, particularly in cases where video recordings are obtained without consent.

(v). ***Data Protection Act 2018 (DPA 2018):*** DPA 2018 is a United Kingdom law governing personal data protection and processing. It provides guidelines and requirements for data controllers and processors, which apply to the security of video data containing personal information.

CASE STUDY 2: HEALTHCARE DATA BREACH AND GDPR COMPLIANCE

A significant data security problem emerged in a primary healthcare institution when a cybercriminal accessed the hospital's database containing sensitive patient records. Figure 5 presents vulnerability in the hospital's network, allowing it to infiltrate the system and extract a vast amount of patient data, including names, addresses, medical histories, and insurance information.

Figure 5. GDPR compliance for medical data

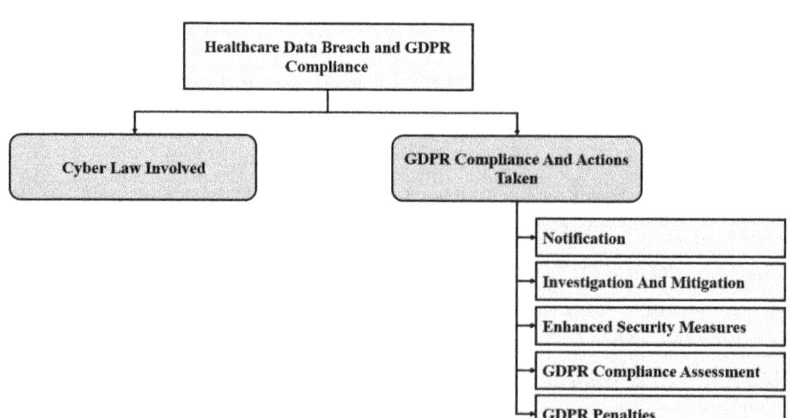

The breach severely threatened patient privacy and raised concerns about potential identity theft and medical fraud.

(i). *Cyber Law Involved:* The General Data Protection Regulation (GDPR), enacted in May 2018, is a comprehensive data protection regulation applicable to all European Union (E.U.) Member states and any organization processing the personal data of (E.U.) residents. The GDPR was directly involved as the healthcare institution collected and processed patients' data in the E.U.

(ii). *GDPR Compliance and Actions Taken:* Upon discovering the data breach, the healthcare institution had to immediately comply with GDPR and protect the affected patients' privacy rights. Step-by-step procedures are:

- ***Notification:*** According to GDPR, the institution must notify the appropriate data protection authority within 72 hours of becoming aware of the breach. The affected individuals get informed about the incident and its potential impact on their data.
- ***Investigation and Mitigation:*** A thorough investigation was conducted to identify the scope of the breach and the extent of the data compromised. Measures were taken to mitigate the impact and prevent any further unauthorized access.
- ***Enhanced Security Measures:*** The healthcare institution implemented more robust security measures to fortify its data infrastructure, ensuring that similar breaches would be less likely to occur.
- ***GDPR Compliance Assessment:*** The institution comprehensively assessed data processing practices and privacy policies to ensure compliance with all GDPR requirements. It includes reviewing consent mechanisms, data retention policies, and access controls.
- ***GDPR Penalties:*** The GDPR imposes significant penalties for non-compliance, including fines of up to 4% of the organization's global annual revenue or €20 million, whichever is higher. The healthcare institution had to consider this while addressing the breach and ensuring they met all GDPR obligations.

This case study demonstrates the critical importance of data security, particularly in the healthcare sector, where sensitive personal information is at risk of unauthorized access and exploitation. The involvement of GDPR in this real-time data security problem highlights the need for organizations to comply with data protection laws and prioritize safeguarding personal data. GDPR's stringent requirements emphasize the accountability of data controllers and processors in securing data and promptly reporting any breaches to the relevant authorities and affected individuals. Adhering to cyber laws such as GDPR is crucial in building trust with customers and stakeholders while protecting individuals' privacy rights in the digital era.

CASE STUDY 3: E-COMMERCE WEBSITE DATA BREACH AND CCPA COMPLIANCE

In this case study, an e-commerce company experienced a significant data breach, where hackers gained unauthorized access to the company's customer database. It exposed sensitive customer information such as names, addresses, payment card details, and purchase history. Figure 6 presents the CCPA compliance for millions of customers' privacy, and financial security were at risk, leading to public outrage and damage to the company's reputation.

Figure 6. CCPA compliance for e-commerce data breach

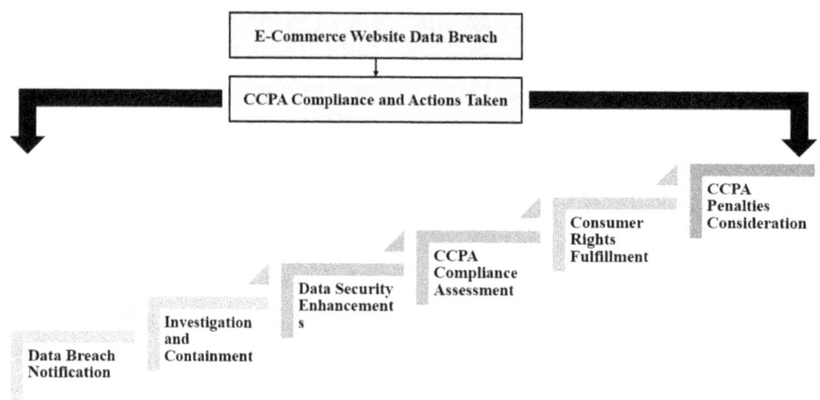

The California Consumer Privacy Act (CCPA) is used to protect the privacy rights of California residents. In this case, the e-commerce company was required to comply with CCPA regulations as it collected and processed the personal data of California consumers.

CCPA Compliance and Actions Taken

In response to the data breach and to ensure CCPA compliance, the e-commerce company took the following measures:

(i). ***Data Breach Notification:*** The company promptly informed the affected California residents about the data breach, as required by CCPA. They disclosed the nature of the incident, the categories of personal information exposed, and the company's response measures.
(ii). ***Investigation and Containment:*** A thorough investigation was conducted to identify the cause and extent of the breach. The company took immediate steps to contain the breach and prevent further unauthorized access.
(iii). ***Data Security Enhancements:*** The company implemented enhanced data security measures, such as encryption, multi-factor authentication, and access controls, to fortify its systems against future cyberattacks.
(iv). ***CCPA Compliance Assessment:*** The company conducted a comprehensive review of its data processing practices, privacy policies, and data handling procedures to ensure compliance with CCPA requirements.
(v). ***Consumer Rights Fulfillment:*** Under CCPA, California residents have certain rights, including access to their data, request deletion, and opt-out of data sales. The company established a mechanism to handle these consumer requests promptly.

(vi). ***CCPA Penalties Consideration:*** CCPA imposes penalties for non-compliance, including statutory damages ranging from $100 to $750 per California resident per incident. The company considered this while addressing the breach and implementing CCPA-compliant measures.

This case study highlights the severe consequences of a data breach in an e-commerce setting, where sensitive customer data is compromised. It emphasizes the importance of complying with data protection laws such as CCPA to effectively protect consumers' privacy rights. The company's response to the breach, including timely notification, investigation, and containment, demonstrates the significance of taking immediate action to mitigate the impact on affected individuals. Adhering to CCPA requirements, such as fulfilling consumer rights and implementing robust data security measures, is vital in maintaining consumer trust and adhering to legal obligations in data security and privacy.

SOLUTION AND RECOMMENDATION

Data Security

(i). ***Encryption:*** Implement strong encryption algorithms to protect data at rest and in transit. Utilize technologies such as SSL/TLS for securing network communications and disk encryption for data storage.

(ii). ***Access Controls:*** Enforce strict access controls to limit data access to authorized individuals. Use role-based access control (RBAC) mechanisms and regularly review and update user privileges.

(iii). ***Data Classification:*** It classifies the data based on its sensitivity level. Apply appropriate security measures based on the classification, such as access restrictions and data masking.

(iv). ***Firewalls:*** They serve as protective measures that oversee, sift through, and regulate both inbound and outbound network traffic, adhering to pre-established security protocols. Their role is to act as barricades, demarcating trusted internal networks from potentially untrusted external ones like the Internet. The significance of firewalls lies in their ability to thwart unauthorized entry, cyber assaults, and data breaches by scrutinizing network packets and implementing security guidelines. The deployment of firewalls can occur at various junctures within a network:

- ***Network-Level Firewalls***: Positioned at the network perimeter, typically between an internal network and the internet, these firewalls analyze traffic based on IP addresses, port numbers, and protocols. They are the initial defense line, often shielding against known threats and malicious traffic trying to infiltrate the network.
- ***Host-Based Firewalls***: Installed on individual machines or devices, host-based firewalls regulate incoming and outgoing traffic at a per-device level. It allows users to dictate rules and limitations for network communication, adding an extra layer of security to devices linked to potentially insecure networks.
- ***Application-Level Firewalls***: Concentrating on supervising and managing traffic at the application layer firewalls that can assess packet content and discern the context of the employed application. Their efficacy shines in their ability to spot and obstruct attacks targeting specific application vulnerabilities.

To reinforce security protocols of firewalls, adopt a range of techniques:

- ***Packet Filtering***: Scrutinizing individual data packets, firewalls decide whether to grant passage or hinder them in line with predefined criteria.
- ***Stateful Inspection***: Monitoring ongoing connections to ensure that solely valid and expected traffic gains access.
- ***Proxy Services***: Acting as intermediaries between internal users and external resources that conceal internal IP addresses, appending an extra layer of anonymity and safeguarding.
- ***Deep Packet Inspection (DPI)***: Beyond examining header information, this technique involves scrutinizing packet content in-depth. DPI can recognize and obstruct specific content types or applications.
- ***Intrusion Detection and Prevention***: Certain firewalls incorporate capabilities for identifying and obstructing established attack patterns and behaviors through intrusion detection and prevention features.

In a holistic sense, firewalls constitute a pivotal facet of network security. They empower organizations to exert authority over their network traffic, thus safeguarding sensitive data against unauthorized entry and potential cyber hazards.

(v). ***Data Masking***: It suppresses or anonymizes high-value data by replacing sensitive information with random characters. You can also substitute data with a low-value representative token; this method is called tokenization.

(vi). ***Data Erasure*** involves cleaning your repository if stored data is no longer used or active.

(vii). ***Data Resilience***: involves full, differential, and incremental backups of your critical data. Storing your valuable data in different locations helps to make it recoverable and resilient to different cybersecurity threats.

Schemes and Techniques

(i). ***Two-Factor Authentication (2FA)***: Implement 2FA for user accounts and systems to provide an additional layer of security. It involves using something the user knows (password) and something they have (e.g., a mobile app-generated code).

(ii). ***Secure Coding Practices***: To reduce vulnerabilities, teach developers to adopt secure coding approaches to mitigate security problems. Apply secure coding rules, perform regular code reviews, and employ automated testing techniques.

(iii). ***Regular Updates and Patches***: Stay updated with the latest security patches and updates for all software and systems. Vulnerabilities in schemes and techniques are often discovered and addressed through patches (Rawat and Singh, 2023).

Policies

(i). ***Security Awareness Training***: Conduct regular security awareness training for all employees to educate them about best practices, social engineering risks, and identifying and reporting security incidents.
(ii). ***Incident Response Plan***: Develop an incident response plan outlining the steps to be taken in case of a security breach or incident. Test and update this plan regularly.
(iii). ***Regular Audits and Assessments***: Perform security audits and assessments to identify vulnerabilities, ensure compliance with security policies, and address any weaknesses in your security infrastructure.
(iv). ***Data Backup and Disaster Recovery***: Implement robust data backup and disaster recovery processes to ensure that critical data can be restored during a security incident or system failure.

FUTURE RESEARCH DIRECTIONS

In the ever-evolving digital technology landscape, pursuing data security remains an ongoing endeavor with promising future scopes. As we navigate the complexities of data protection, several avenues offer opportunities for further advancement:

(i). ***Advanced Encryption Techniques***: While encryption is a cornerstone of data security, continued research into quantum-resistant encryption methods is essential. As quantum computing evolves, encryption mechanisms must adapt to ensure data remains impervious to emerging threats.
(ii). ***Machine Learning and AI Integration***: Machine learning and artificial intelligence can play a pivotal role in identifying and mitigating security risks. These technologies can enhance anomaly detection, predictive threat modeling, and real-time response to rapidly evolving threats.
(iii). ***Blockchain for Data Integrity***: Blockchain technology can potentially ensure data integrity and transparency. Implementing blockchain in data storage and transactions can establish immutable records, reducing the risk of unauthorized alterations.
(iv). ***IoT Security Enhancements***: With the proliferation of Internet of Things (IoT) devices, bolstering security for interconnected devices becomes paramount. Future research can focus on developing standardized security protocols and frameworks to protect against IoT-based cyber threats.
(v). ***Privacy-Preserving Techniques***: As data collection and analysis expand, privacy-preserving techniques gain importance. Homomorphic encryption, differential privacy, and federated learning are areas with the potential to enhance data security while still allowing meaningful insights to be gleaned from collected data.
(vi). ***Zero Trust Architecture***: The Zero Trust model treats every user and device as a potential threat and promises to minimize data exposure. Further research can refine and implement Zero Trust principles to secure data across networks, applications, and user interactions.
(vii). ***Ethical Data Usage***: The ethical collection, storage, and usage of data are gaining prominence. The future calls for establishing ethical guidelines and ensuring data security aligns with individual rights and societal values.
(viii). ***Multi-Factor Authentication Innovations***: As cyber threats become more sophisticated, continuous advancements in multi-factor authentication methods are necessary. Biometric authentication, behavioral analytics, and adaptive authentication can enhance user access security.

(ix). ***Regulatory Compliance Adaptation***: With evolving data protection regulations like GDPR and CCPA, organizations must remain vigilant in adapting their data security practices to meet new compliance requirements.

(x). ***User-Centric Security***: Future data security efforts should focus on user-centric approaches, empowering individuals to control their data more. Decentralized identity systems and consent management tools can empower users while enhancing security.

Data security holds immense potential for growth and innovation. By exploring advanced encryption, harnessing the power of AI, embracing emerging technologies like blockchain, and prioritizing user privacy, we can collectively shape a more secure and resilient digital future. Ongoing research, collaboration, and adaptation to evolving threats are the keystones of ensuring data security remains robust and effective in the face of dynamic challenges.

CONCLUSION

Data security is a pivotal concern for modern applications in the contemporary digital landscape. Safeguarding data across its distinct states—in transit, at rest, and in use—demands a strategic fusion of techniques and policies to establish a robust and comprehensive data security framework. As data traverses networks, it faces vulnerabilities that encryption can mitigate. Encryption transforms data into unintelligible forms during transmission, ensuring its confidentiality and thwarting unauthorized access. Transport Layer Security (TLS) fortifies data integrity during transit. Virtual Private Networks (VPNs) carve secure pathways for data to evade potential eavesdropping. Embracing secure file transfer protocols and employing digital signatures bolsters data authenticity and tamper resistance. The security of data at rest, residing on storage devices, is paramount. Encryption at rest is a protective barrier, rendering data inaccessible without decryption keys even if storage is compromised.

Data masking conceals sensitive information, while access controls add an extra layer of defense. Technologies that prevent data loss monitor and counteract unauthorized data movements, preempting inadvertent leaks. The active utilization of data necessitates stringent security measures. Robust access controls and fortified authentication mechanisms are pivotal to curbing unauthorized access. Elevating application security is instrumental in thwarting potential vulnerabilities and ensuring data integrity. Technologies that avert data leakage actively identify and impede unauthorized data flows, heightening security during data utilization. The underpinning policies serve as navigational guides for effective data security practices. Security awareness training is an initial defense, enlightening users about security nuances and fostering responsible behavior—the incident response plan charts a blueprint for coordinated actions during security breaches, minimizing damage. Regular audits and inspections maintain vigilance, pinpointing vulnerabilities and expediting mitigation. Data backup and disaster recovery strategies ensure data resilience, countering breaches and system failures. Organizations construct a fortified data security posture by harmonizing these techniques and policies. This posture extends beyond compliance, engendering customer trust and stakeholder assurance. The collective impact of these measures reverberates in the broader realm of cybersecurity, contributing to a safeguarded digital environment. Amid the intricate interconnectivity defining the contemporary digital landscape, these measures emerge as a holistic shield against breaches, an advocate for resilience, and a guardian of trust.

ACKNOWLEDGMENT

I want to thank our mom and dad for encouraging and motivating us. Secondly, I thank UPES, Dehradun, for providing the necessary resources.

REFERENCES

Achar, S., Patel, H., & Hussain, S. (2022). Data Security in Cloud: A Review. *Asian Journal of Advances in Research*, 1099-1106.

Alghofaili, Y., Albattah, A., Alrajeh, N., Rassam, M. A., & Al-Rimy, B. A. S. (2021). Secure cloud infrastructure: A survey on issues, current solutions, and open challenges. *Applied Sciences (Basel, Switzerland)*, *11*(19), 9005. doi:10.3390/app11199005

Butt, U. A., Amin, R., Mehmood, M., Aldabbas, H., Alharbi, M. T., & Albaqami, N. (2023). Cloud security threats and solutions: A survey. *Wireless Personal Communications*, *128*(1), 387–413. doi:10.100711277-022-09960-z

Chatterjee, P., Bose, R., Banerjee, S., & Roy, S. (2023). Enhancing Data Security of Cloud Based LMS. *Wireless Personal Communications*, *130*(2), 1123–1139. doi:10.100711277-023-10323-5 PMID:37168441

Dardzinska-Glebocka, A. (2007). Optimization Algorithm and Data Security Problem in Distributed Information Systems. *2007 Third International IEEE Conference on Signal-Image Technologies and Internet-Based System*. 10.1109/SITIS.2007.136

DibetleM.KalemaB. M. (2023). *Data security governance for Software-as-a-Service Cloud computing environment: A South African perspective*. doi:10.21203/rs.3.rs-3040096/v1

El-Zoghdy, S. F., & Ghoneim, A. (2016). A Multi-Class Task Scheduling Strategy for Heterogeneous Distributed Computing Systems. *KSII Transactions on Internet and Information Systems*, *10*(1), 117–135.

GhoshS.VermaS. K.GhoshU. (2023). *An Improved End-to-End Data Security Approach for Cloud Computing*. doi:10.36227/techrxiv.23553489.v1

Grabis, J., Stankovski, V., & Zariņš, R. (2020, April). Blockchain enabled distributed storage and sharing of personal data assets. In *2020 IEEE 36th International Conference on Data Engineering Workshops (ICDEW)* (pp. 11-17). IEEE. 10.1109/ICDEW49219.2020.00-13

Gu, Y., Wang, Y., Yang, Z., & Gao, Y. (2017). A Distributed Privacy-Utility Trade-off Method Using Distributed Lossy Source Coding with Side Information. *KSII Transactions on Internet and Information Systems*, *11*(5), 2778–2791.

Hasan, M. Z., Hussain, M. Z., Mubarak, Z., Siddiqui, A. A., Qureshi, A. M., & Ismail, I. (2023, January). Data security and Integrity in Cloud Computing. In *2023 International Conference for Advancement in Technology (ICONAT)* (pp. 1-5). IEEE. 10.1109/ICONAT57137.2023.10080440

Hwang, J., Nkenyereye, L., Sung, N., Kim, J., & Song, J. (2021). IoT service slicing and task offloading for edge computing. *IEEE Internet of Things Journal*, *8*(14), 11526–11547. doi:10.1109/JIOT.2021.3052498

Karmakar, M., Priya, A., Sinha, K., & Verma, M. (2022, December). Shrinkable Cryptographic Technique Using Involutory Function for Image Encryption. In *International Conference on Advanced Network Technologies and Intelligent Computing* (pp. 275-289). Cham: Springer Nature Switzerland.

Lee, S., Choi, H., Kim, T., Park, H. S., & Choi, J. K. (2022). A Novel Energy-Conscious Access Point (eAP) System with Cross-Layer Design in Wi-Fi Networks for Reliable IoT Services. *IEEE Access : Practical Innovations, Open Solutions*, *10*, 61228–61248. doi:10.1109/ACCESS.2022.3181304

Li, B., Chen, T., & Giannakis, G. B. (2019). Secure mobile edge computing in IoT via collaborative online learning. *IEEE Transactions on Signal Processing*, *67*(23), 5922–5935. doi:10.1109/TSP.2019.2949504

Li, Y., Zhuang, Y., Hu, X., Gao, Z., Hu, J., Chen, L., He, Z., Pei, L., Chen, K., Wang, M., Niu, X., Chen, R., Thompson, J., Ghannouchi, F. M., & El-Sheimy, N. (2021). Toward Location-Enabled IoT (LE-IoT): IoT Positioning Techniques, Error Sources, and Error Mitigation. *IEEE Internet of Things Journal*, *8*(6), 4035–4062. doi:10.1109/JIOT.2020.3019199

Madhava Varma, K., Chowdary, N. D., Chandra, P. P., & Kumar, G. P. (2023). Cloud based ERP systems and Data Security for Cloud based ERP Applications - SAP S/4HANA. *International Journal Of Scientific Research In Engineering And Management*, *07*(02). Advance online publication. doi:10.55041/IJSREM17828

Mallisetty, S. B., Tripuramallu, G. A., Kamada, K., Devineni, P., Kavitha, S., & Krishna, A. V. P. (2023, January). A Review on Cloud Security and Its Challenges. In *2023 International Conference on Intelligent Data Communication Technologies and Internet of Things (IDCIoT)* (pp. 798-804). IEEE. 10.1109/IDCIoT56793.2023.10053520

Matousek, K. (2008). Security and reliability considerations for distributed healthcare systems. *2008 42nd Annual IEEE International Carnahan Conference on Security Technology*. 10.1109/CCST.2008.4751326

Nguyen, L. D., Leyva-Mayorga, I., Lewis, A. N., & Popovski, P. (2021). Modeling and analysis of data trading on blockchain-based market in IoT networks. *IEEE Internet of Things Journal*, *8*(8), 6487–6497. doi:10.1109/JIOT.2021.3051923

Ortigueira, R., Fraire, J. A., Becerra, A., Ferrer, T., & Cespedes, S. (2021). RESS-IoT: A scalable energy-efficient MAC protocol for direct-to-satellite IoT. *IEEE Access : Practical Innovations, Open Solutions*, *9*, 164440–164453. doi:10.1109/ACCESS.2021.3134246

Rawat, G. S., & Singh, K. (2019). Detection and prevention of vulnerabilities in open source software: An experimental study. In *Communication and Computing Systems* (pp. 297–303). CRC Press. doi:10.1201/9780429444272-48

Rawat, G. S., & Singh, K. (2019). Beacon inter-reception time based adaptive beaconing (BIRA) for congestion-aware vehicular networks. *Journal of Discrete Mathematical Sciences and Cryptography*, *22*(8), 1477-1487.

Rawat, G. S., & Singh, K. (2023). Evaluation and Optimization of a Congestion Control Scheme for Vanets. In *Advanced Computer Science Applications* (pp. 351–363). Apple Academic Press. doi:10.1201/9781003369066-29

Rawat, G. S., & Singh, K. (2023). A bayesian-based distributed trust management scheme for connected vehicles' security. *Peer-to-Peer Networking and Applications*, *16*(5), 1–17. doi:10.100712083-023-01515-8

Ruminski, J. (2007). Security of Distributed Processing of Medical Image Data Using JINI Technology. *2007 29th Annual International Conference of the IEEE Engineering in Medicine and Biology Society*. 10.1109/IEMBS.2007.4353630

Said, O., Al-Makhadmeh, Z., & Tolba, A. M. R. (2020). EMS: An energy management scheme for green IoT environments. *IEEE Access : Practical Innovations, Open Solutions*, *8*, 44983–44998. doi:10.1109/ACCESS.2020.2976641

Samaila, M. G., Sequeiros, J. B., Simoes, T., Freire, M. M., & Inacio, P. R. (2020). IoT-HarPSecA: A framework and roadmap for secure design and development of devices and applications in the IoT space. *IEEE Access : Practical Innovations, Open Solutions*, *8*, 16462–16494. doi:10.1109/ACCESS.2020.2965925

SambyalS.AroraB. (2023). Hybrid Security Model for Securing Healthcare Data on Cloud. https://doi.org/ doi:10.21203/rs.3.rs-2908979/v1

Sinha, K., Choudhary, S., Paul, S., & Paul, P. (2018, September). Security of Multimedia in Cloud using Secret Shared Key. In *2018 International Conference on Computing, Power and Communication Technologies (GUCON)* (pp. 908-912). IEEE. 10.1109/GUCON.2018.8675031

Sinha, K., & Paul, P. (2021). Randomized Block Size (RBS) Model for Secure Data Storage in Distributed Server. *KSII Transactions on Internet and Information Systems*, *15*(12).

Sinha, K., & Paul, P. (2022). An Improved Pseudorandom Sequence Generator and its Application to Image Encryption. *KSII Transactions on Internet and Information Systems*, *16*(4).

Sinha, K., Priya, A., & Paul, P. (2020). K-RSA: Secure data storage technique for multimedia in cloud data server. *Journal of Intelligent & Fuzzy Systems*, *39*(3), 3297–3314. doi:10.3233/JIFS-191687

Thuraisingham, B., & Ford, W. (1995). Security constraint processing in a multilevel secure distributed database management system. *IEEE Transactions on Knowledge and Data Engineering*, *7*(2), 274–293. doi:10.1109/69.382297

Tyagi, K., Yadav, S. K., & Singh, M. (2021). Cloud data security and various security algorithms. *Journal of Physics: Conference Series*, *1998*(1), 012023. doi:10.1088/1742-6596/1998/1/012023

Verma, S., Kawamoto, Y., & Kato, N. (2021). A Network-Aware Internet-Wide Scan for Security Maximization of IPv6-Enabled WLAN IoT Devices. *IEEE Internet of Things Journal*, *8*(10), 8411–8422. doi:10.1109/JIOT.2020.3045733

Xu, Y., Song, R., Korba, L., Wang, L., Shen, W., & Lang, S. (2005). Distributed device networks with security constraints. *IEEE Transactions on Industrial Informatics*, *1*(4), 217–225. doi:10.1109/TII.2005.843826

Zeng, R., Jiang, Y., Lin, C., Fan, Y., & Shen, X. (2012). A Distributed Fault/Intrusion-Tolerant Sensor Data Storage Scheme Based on Network Coding and Homomorphic Fingerprinting. *IEEE Transactions on Parallel and Distributed Systems*, *23*(10), 1819–1830. doi:10.1109/TPDS.2011.294

Zhang, P., Jiang, C., Pang, X., & Qian, Y. (2020). STEC-IoT: A security tactic by virtualizing edge computing on IoT. *IEEE Internet of Things Journal*, *8*(4), 2459–2467. doi:10.1109/JIOT.2020.3017742

Zubi, Z. S. (2009). On distributed database security aspects. *2009 International Conference on Multimedia Computing and Systems.* 10.1109/MMCS.2009.5256696

KEY TERMS AND DEFINITIONS

Blockchain Technology: A decentralized, tamper-resistant ledger for secure data storage and transactions.

Data Security: Ensuring protection against unauthorized access and breaches of sensitive information.

Encryption Techniques: Encoding data to prevent unauthorized access, enhancing confidentiality.

Ethical Data Usage: Adhering to responsible practices when collecting, storing, and using data.

Internet of Things (IoT) Security: Safeguarding connected devices and networks from cyber threats.

Machine Learning: Utilizing algorithms to detect patterns and anomalies, enhancing threat detection.

Privacy-Preserving Methods: Techniques to analyze and share data while preserving individual privacy.

Zero Trust Architecture: A security model that verifies every access request, regardless of location.

Chapter 11
Developing an IoT Adoption Framework for Library Management for Public Tertiary Institutions in Ghana

Frank Boateng
https://orcid.org/0000-0002-8786-7269
Durban University of Technology, South Africa

Oluwasegun Julius Aroba
Durban University of Technology, South Africa

Sulaiman Saleem Patel
https://orcid.org/0000-0003-3557-3645
Durban University of Technology, South Africa

ABSTRACT

The chapter presents an IoT adoption framework for improving library management practices in Ghana's public tertiary institution. The internet of things (IoT) has revolutionized various industries, including libraries. The chapter aims to define a comprehensive framework that addresses the challenges and needs of Ghana's public higher education institution. Key areas where IoT integration can benefit library operations include resource monitoring, security, user experience, and data analytics. The framework also addresses potential obstacles and concerns related to privacy, security, and infrastructure limitations in the Ghanaian context. The chapter provides valuable insights for academic and administrative stakeholders on using IoT technologies to improve library services and knowledge dissemination in Ghana's public tertiary institution.

DOI: 10.4018/979-8-3693-0807-3.ch011

INTRODUCTION

The Internet of Things (IoT) has revolutionized various industries, particularly in educational institutions, such as public tertiary institutions (Phung *et al.*, 2022). These institutions play a crucial role in molding the future of most countries by providing students and other stakeholders with access to quality education and resources. However, traditional library management systems face obstacles in adapting to the changing demands of the digital age, such as manual processes, limited data analytics, and inefficient resource allocation (Maharaja, Iyer and Ye, 2020). Consequently, the adoption of IoT technology offers a promising solution for overcoming these obstacles and realizing the full potential of public tertiary institutions' libraries. For this reason, the study proposed an IoT adoption framework customized for library management in public tertiary institutions. The framework sought to enhance library services, increase resource utilization, and provide data-driven insights for informed decision-making (Babiceanu and Seker, 2019). The framework aims to equip library administrators, librarians, and stakeholders with the necessary tools to adjust to the shifting educational landscape and cultivate a culture of innovation within these institutions. The objectives of the IoT adoption framework include enhancing accessibility and availability, optimizing resource management, personalizing user experiences, fostering data-driven decision-making, strengthening security and safety, and promoting collaborative learning. By integrating IoT sensors, the framework enables real-time monitoring and tracking of library assets, resulting in efficient resource allocation, and reduced operational costs (Yeh, Arthaud-Day and Turvey-Welch, 2021).

Figure 1. Application areas of IoT adoption in library management
Source: Khan et al. (2021)

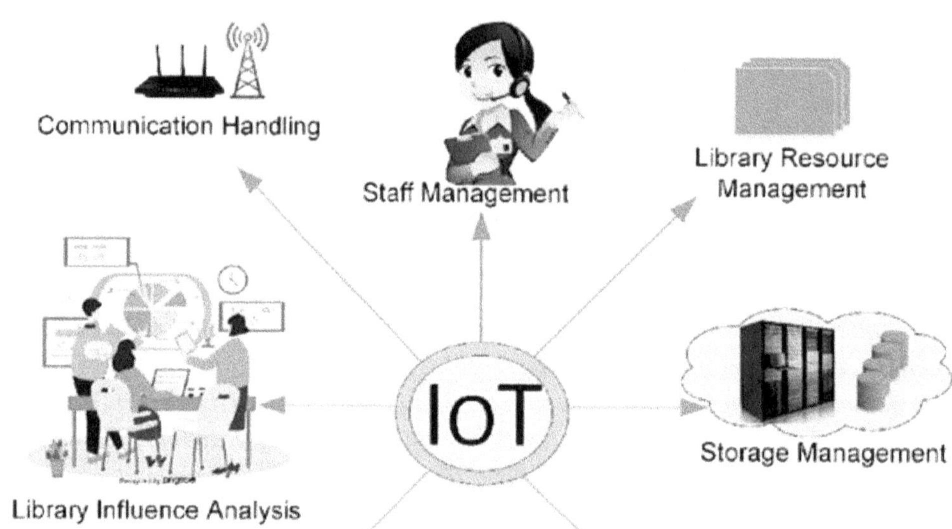

Similarly, literature has proven that tertiary institutions are made up of systems which further consider the interplay between social and technical components (Hogarth & Wójcik 2016). This study further gives credence to situate the overall study within the context of Davis' socio-technical systems analytical framework or thinking (STS).

According to Khan et al., (2021) IoT technology in libraries enhances user experience by providing real-time library resource availability information, helping users find books, and offering personalized recommendations (Bashir et al., 2022). This further enhances security by protecting valuable materials and enabling access control. The vast data generated by IoT can provide insights into patron behavior, resource utilization, and library operations, enabling more informed decision-making (Ojha et al., 2023).

Similarly, IoT technology also enables personalized user experiences, allowing for personalized recommendations and support for individual learning needs (Jagatheesaperumal et al., 2023). Moreover, these personalized recommendations are achieved through data collection and analytics, the IoT framework offers valuable insights into library usage patterns, enabling data-driven decision-making for future improvements and enhancements (Islam et al., 2021). Additionally, IoT-enabled security systems can enhance the safety of library users and protect valuable resources, reducing instances of theft and damage (Migabo, Djouani and Kurien, 2020) in Figure 1.

The overarching aim of this book chapter was to develop a framework for IoT adoption in library management through a strategic roadmap with the following breakdown of the objectives:

[RO1]: Review the existing literature on IoT adoption in library management.
[RO2]: Identify and analyze the key factors that influence IoT adoption in library management, based on the reviewed literature.
[RO3]: Design and develop a framework for IoT adoption in library management based on the key factors identified, which is contextualized to the Ghana Public Tertiary Institution landscape.
[RO4]: Explore the benefits and challenges associated with IoT adoption in Ghana Public Institutional libraries.
[RO5]: Provide recommendations for Ghana Public Institutions looking to adopt IoT technologies based on the findings and the developed framework.

BACKGROUND / LITERATURE REVIEW

This chapter thoroughly examines the existing literature and delves into several key aspects. It discusses the general understanding of digital transformation and explores both its advantages and disadvantages, particularly in relation to the adoption of the Internet of Things (Qazi et al., 2022). Additionally, it investigates the potential applications of IoT in the academic sphere, with a specific focus on library management. In addition to the key aspects this chapter also critically assesses the feasibility of implementing IoT in these contexts (Alahi et al., 2023). Moreover, the chapter offers a comprehensive review of the shift from traditional methods of data capture, storage, processing, and presentation to the contemporary paradigm of fulfilling public demands within the value chain (Bayanati, 2023). This transformation builds upon the established socio-technical systems analytical thinking framework, providing essential context for the chapter's background (Davis et al., 2014).

Digital Transformation

Digital transformation has become a niche process that involves countries and organizations such as education, health, engineering, manufacturing, entertainment, and others integrating digital technologies and data-driven strategies into their operations, products, and services (Demuyakor, 2020; Aroba

& Abayomi, 2023). This transformation is driven by the need to adapt and thrive in the ever-evolving digital landscape of the modern era. The modern world is marked by rapid technological advancements, such as artificial intelligence, big data analytics, cloud computing, and the Internet of Things, which allow businesses to operate more efficiently, make informed decisions, and stay competitive (Moumtzidis et al., 2022).

Similarly, in most reviewed literature (Maimun et al., 2022), digital transformation enables organizations to deliver seamless, personalized, and convenient experiences by using data to understand customer behavior and preferences. With globalization and the ease of market entry provided by the internet, competition has become fiercer, and digital transformation can give companies an edge by optimizing operations and reaching a wider customer base (Samuel, 2022; Diaz & Montalvo, 2022).

According to Emmert-Streib (2021), data-driven decision-making is essential in the digital age, allowing organizations to make informed decisions, predict trends, and adapt to changing market conditions. Automation, machine learning, and other digital tools can streamline processes, reduce manual labor, and enhance productivity.

In a similar vein, further studies continue to promote the processing of digital transformation as a developmental agenda in modern economies that leads to enhanced agility, cost reduction, sustainability, global connectivity, and regulatory compliance (Pratono et al., 2023; Yao et al., 2022). By optimizing operations, reducing manual errors, and implementing robust security measures, digital transformation helps organizations comply with increasing regulations related to data protection and privacy (Nwaiwu & Mbelu, 2020).

Literature has proven that, moving further into the regime of Industry 4.0, which talks more about the 4th industrial revolution, the digital transformation is a strategic process organizations engage in to integrate digital technologies and data-driven capabilities across multiple business functions (Jeong, 2023; Bettin, 2023). Further studies have posited that this change in the digital space intends to boost operations, enhance customer interactions, and stimulate innovation. It entails a fundamental shift in how companies run their operations, frequently with a focus on how to use technology to create value and stay competitive in the digital age.

Digital Transformation in Libraries

Digital transformation in libraries involves integrating technology and digital solutions to optimize functions and services, adapting to user preferences in the digital age (Bettin, 2023). This involves implementing digital tools, automation, and data utilization to improve efficiency, accessibility, and user experience in library operations (Mangalaraj, Nerur and Dwivedi, 2023). This includes converting collections into digital format, improving accessibility and remote services, managing and analyzing data, and incorporating emerging technologies like artificial intelligence, augmented reality, virtual reality, and machine learning (Venkatesh & Singhal, 2022). In addition to technology integration it includes library management systems, collection conversion, automation of procedures, and software for cataloging, circulation, and data management (Yang, 2023).

While these present several benefits to the discourse, digitization enables broader accessibility, conservation of fragile artifacts, and remote availability for users (Venkatesh & Singhal, 2022). Data management and analytics aid in making informed decisions on resource allocation, collection development, and service enhancement (Chen et al., 2021). Educational activities include technology training, digital literacy programs, and workshops (Chubko et al., 2020). Library spaces are modified for digital activities and collaborative work, with technology-friendly areas and maker spaces (Bessadok et al., 2021). Partnerships and collaborations are encouraged to enhance resource availability. A user-centric approach is adopted, prioritizing user needs and expectations, and addressing security and privacy concerns. This is again, supported by other literature that the digital transformation of libraries, driven by the adoption of Internet of Things (IoT) technologies, has revolutionized their functions and services (DeFranco and Voas, 2023). Benefits of digital transformation include enhanced accessibility and convenience, improved resource management, personalized user experience, data-driven decision making, and collaboration and connectivity (Attaran and Attaran, 2020).

However, challenges include infrastructure and cost, privacy and security concerns, technical expertise and training, compatibility and integration, and user acceptance and digital divide (Qian *et al.*, 2022). IoT-based solutions can automate inventory management, track user behavior, and suggest relevant books, articles, or research materials based on individual interests (Thomasian and Adashi, 2021).

Again, some practitioners make the point that libraries must ensure robust data protection measures and technical expertise to set up, maintain, and troubleshoot complex interconnected devices (Ahmad *et al.*, 2021). Additionally, ensuring seamless compatibility and smooth integration is crucial to avoiding disruptions in library operations and the user experience.

In Ghana's public tertiary institutions, addressing these challenges will help libraries adapt their services to better meet user needs and foster a more inclusive and efficient digital environment (Falayi *et al.*, 2023). However, in the face of the myriad benefits possessed by the digital transformation agenda in many areas of the global economy, including the West African sub-region, specifically Ghana, there is seemingly opposition from some sections of the population. That notwithstanding, the government is poised to transition into digitalization and to make sure the agenda of digital transformation succeeds.

Internet of Things (IoT)

Lee, (2020) defines the Internet of Things (IoT) as a network of interconnected physical devices with sensors and software that allows them to collect, communicate, and analyze data over the internet. These devices can communicate with one another and with central systems to perform automated actions and provide real-time insights (Maharaja, Iyer and Ye, 2020; Phung *et al.*, 2022). IoT technologies have been adopted in several areas and have returned some positive results (Allioui & Mourdi, 2023).

IoT Adoption

According to Almugari *et al.*, (2020); Gabryelczyk *et al.*, (2022) IoT Adoption involves integrating IoT technologies into existing systems to improve efficiency, data collection, automation, and performance. In public tertiary institutions, IoT adoption involves leveraging devices, sensors, and data analytics to enhance library operations, including inventory management, resource utilization, user experience, security, and maintenance (Schuster and Habibipour, 2022). The Internet of Things (IoT) has revolutionized various sectors, including education and libraries. Public tertiary institutions, implementing IoT in library management can improve efficiency, resource optimization, user engagement, and overall library service quality (Agyemang, 2020). IoT technologies, such as RFID tags and sensors, enable efficient tracking and management of library assets, reducing operational costs and improving user experience. Smart space utilization is achieved through real-time data on space usage, enhancing study environments and reducing overcrowding (Sharma and Hashmi, 2021).

Additionally, personalized user experience is achieved through the collection of user data, fostering engagement and increased usage of library resources (Maresova *et al.*, 2020). Remote access to resources is also possible, enhancing the reach and availability of digital content. Data-driven decision-making is achieved through data analytics, enabling better resource allocation and cost optimization (Sharma and Hashmi, 2021). Other indicators of the energy efficiency is achieved through IoT-based energy management systems, regulating lighting, heating, and cooling systems based on occupancy data. With successful implementation requires careful planning, investment, and training to ensure seamless integration and maximize the advantages of IoT in the library context (Zhang *et al.*, 2020).

On the other hand, the adoption of IoT in public tertiary institutions in developing countries like Ghana faces challenges such as cost, budget constraints, security, privacy, interoperability, network infrastructure limitations, data management, analytics, user training, regulatory compliance, maintenance, environmental impact, and vendor selection (Schuster and Habibipour, 2022). These challenges may vary depending on the context and objectives of IoT adoption in library management, and a lack of expertise in handling IoT security can exacerbate these concerns (Sharma and Hashmi, 2021).

Smart Libraries

Smart Libraries, also known as IoT-enabled or connected libraries, utilize IoT technology to enhance library administration and user experience (Maharaja, Iyer and Ye, 2020). These modernized environments utilize IoT devices, sensors, and data analytics to optimize operations, enhance services, and provide innovative solutions (Lohiya and Thakkar, 2021). IoT implementation leads to increased efficiency, resource utilization, and user engagement. Smart libraries, powered by the Internet of Things (IoT), have gained attention for their potential to transform traditional library management systems (Yeh, Arthaud-Day and Turvey-Welch, 2021). In Ghana's public tertiary institutions, the adoption of IoT-based smart libraries can offer several benefits, including enhanced library services, efficient resource management, data-driven decision-making, personalized learning experiences, remote access, and increased security and safety (Farjana, Fahad, Alam & Islam 2023). However, challenges include infrastructure and connectivity, cost and budget constraints, data privacy and security concerns, staff training and skills, interoperability and standards, and user acceptance and adoption (Schuster and Habibipour, 2022). Inadequate training may hinder the full realization of the benefits of smart libraries, while standardized protocols can pose integration challenges (Lee, 2020).

Similarly, several other scholars highlight the benefits of smart libraries, digital transformation, and the Internet of Things in the global dimension (Gul & Bano, 2019). Accordingly, the Chong & Wan, (2018) in literature also makes the point that the benefits include increased accessibility, efficiency, personalized user experiences, cost savings, and data-driven decision-making. However, obstacles like infrastructure limitations, data privacy concerns, digital divide, technical expertise requirements, and initial implementation costs must be addressed to maximize IoT adoption (Alshohoumi & Sarrab, 2020).

SOLUTIONS AND RECOMMENDATIONS

Factors Influencing the IoT Adoption in Library Management in Public Tertiary Institutions

The development and adoption of the Internet of Things (IoT) framework in library management significantly impacts Ghana's public tertiary institutions. Key factors include the availability of reliable internet connectivity, cost and budget constraints, skill and knowledge gaps, security and data privacy, stakeholder buy-in, and regulatory and compliance issues. IoT technologies can enhance the user experience by enabling remote access to resources, personalized recommendations, and streamlined services. They can optimize library operations, automate routine tasks, and reduce administrative burdens on staff. Improved inventory management and resource allocation can lead to better resource utilization and cost savings. IoT-generated data can offer insights into user behavior and preferences, facilitating evidence-based decision-making. Remote accessibility can also be achieved through IoT-enabled libraries, offering resources and services to a wider audience, including distance learners. However, challenges such as data security, privacy, and ongoing maintenance and upgrades must be addressed for successful implementation. All in all, the success of IoT in library management in Ghana's public tertiary institutions depends on addressing these factors.

The development of an IoT framework for library management in public tertiary institution in Ghana and the global economy is compared. As Ghana faces resource constraints, such as budget and infrastructural issues, which can hinder the adoption of IoT technologies. The framework may require additional training and skill development. Local relevance is also crucial, as IoT applications need to be tailored to address local challenges like access to resources and language barriers. Collaboration among institutions and government bodies is essential for pooling resources and expertise.

On the other hand, the global economy benefits from advanced technology infrastructure, more financial resources, access to skilled professionals, standardization, and greater scale and scope. Global institutions often adhere to international standards, making it easier to integrate IoT technologies with other systems and libraries worldwide. Overall, the global economy offers a more flexible and adaptable approach to IoT implementation in libraries.

Methodology

The decision to use socio-technical systems analytical thinking as a strategic roadmap for developing, adopting, and implementing IoT in library management is a deliberate and well-thought-out approach. This approach recognizes the interdependence of technology and humans while dealing with the intricacies of adopting IoT (Baxter & Sommerville, 2011; Kumar et al., 2019).

Additionally, it takes into account the specific geographical and cultural circumstances, placing importance on the user's involvement and the influence of the Internet of Things on library patrons. Furthermore, in the development of this roadmap, this chapter tackles regulatory and compliance factors, guaranteeing the lawful and moral deployment of IoT (Sony & Naik, 2020).

The methodology additionally facilitates flexibility and adaptation, fostering methodical troubleshooting and innovation. It promotes a comprehensive perspective on implementation, taking into account technical, social, economic, and cultural factors while avoiding narrow-mindedness and oversights (Davis, Hughes, McKay, Robinson, & van der Wal 2019). Furthermore, it facilitates stakeholder interaction, encouraging a sense of ownership and participation in the process of adopting IoT technology (Quazi & Patel, 2023).

The Essence of the Socio-Technical Systems Framework for IoT Adoption in Library Management

According to Shin (2014), Socio-Technical systems provide a holistic framework for the seamless integration of Internet of Things (IoT) technology within the context of library management. The authors emphasize the significance of considering social, human, and organizational variables to augment consumer pleasure (Davis et al., 2014) in Figure 1.

As an aspect of the public tertiary institutional factor, the assessment of the influence of IoT on library services is of utmost importance to properly comprehend its potential benefits (Schroeder, Naik, Ziaee Bigdeli & Baines 2020; Davis, Hughes, McKay, Robinson & van der Wal 2019). Achieving effective implementation depends on active engagement, comprehensive training, and adequate support from the employees.

Consequently, to safeguard customers, privacy and ethical concerns should be addressed with explicit policies (Heidari & Jabraeil Jamali, 2022). The adoption of innovative Internet of Things (IoT) services and events serves as a means for libraries to actively involve the community, ensuring their continued relevance (Liang & Chen, 2018; Yoon, 2020). As the Internet of Things (IoT) continues to advance, it is imperative for libraries to adapt their systems and engage in interdisciplinary collaboration (Tariq et al., 2023).

Continuous review and feedback play a crucial role in ensuring that the IoT continues to be in line with the library's goal of efficiently serving its community. Socio-technical systems offer a comprehensive approach to integrating IoT, with the aim of optimizing advantages and tackling obstacles in alignment with the library's core objectives.

Figure 2. Socio-technical systems analytical framework
Source: Davis et al. (2014)

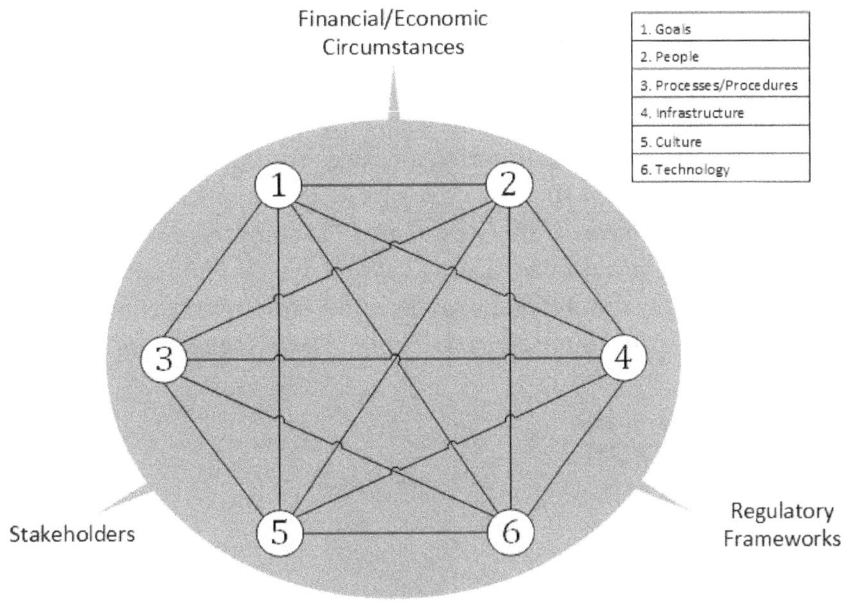

Determinants for Socio-Technical Systems Analytical Framework

May (2022) posits that the choice of Socio-Technical Systems (STS) Analytical Framework is a useful tool for researchers in a variety of fields who want to study the complex interactions between people and technology, and this is corroborated in literature and the larger organizational or societal context (Aldriweesh, Zakuan, Hafiz Bajuri, & Mufareh Alshammakh 2022). Additionally, in providing the strategic roadmap for the IoT adoption framework for library management and practice the Socio-Technical Systems (STS) thinking which underpins the development of the framework coupled with several determinants this could be considered when examining the digital transformation and IoT adoption in library management. These determinants cover both the social and technical aspects of the system and aid in assessing the transformation's impact on various levels (Quazi & Patel 2023; Ali, Aboelmaged, Govindan & Malik 2023).

Data Sources

This chapter's analysis takes into consideration information derived from the following sources:

- Reviewed journal articles,
- commercial white papers and reports, and
- government reports and policy documents

Data Analysis

When examining the data, the authors employed the document analysis approach. This methodology offers advantages such as minimal interference when studying social communities, reliability, and non-intrusiveness in relation to social communities, precision, and effectiveness (Cardno, 2019). However, certain drawbacks of the document analysis method emerge when documents are unavailable or inaccessible, when documents lack sufficient information, and in situations where a biased selection of documents leads to partiality (Bowen, 2009).

For this research, the authors have carefully examined the analyzed documents and confirmed that the available documents possess an adequate quality to yield meaningful results. The integration of IoT technology into library management and operations was analyzed and by the consideration of the roadmap each of the six fundamental system components within the Davis socio-technical system framework.

ANALYSIS AND DISCUSSION

Goals

The goal of adopting IoT (Internet of Things) in library and information science in public tertiary institutions, using a socio-technical systems and analytical framework, can be multifaceted (Gkrimpizi et al., 2023). Further to that, it is also argued that the integration of IoT in public tertiary institution libraries offers several benefits, including enhancing user experience with real-time access to resources, optimizing resource management, ensuring security, and enabling data-driven decision-making (Farias-Gaytan et al., 2023). This integration aligns with the institution's mission and requires interdisciplinary collaboration, clear privacy policies, and continuous improvement to adapt to evolving needs and technology trends in library and information science (Chan & Chan, 2018).

People and Culture

According to Altawalbeh (2023), the success of digital transformation, particularly IoT adoption in libraries, depends on how well the staff, including librarians, administrators, and support personnel, accept and embrace modern technologies. Additionally, capacity-building in the form of training, education, and ongoing support is essential to ensure that library staff members can effectively use these tools and understand their benefits as far as user acceptance and adoption (people) are concerned. In the same way, Wedajo & Chekole (2020) argue that introducing digital technologies and IoT into the library ecosystem can result in significant changes to workflows and operations. Besides the point, the fear of job loss or unfamiliarity with the new systems may cause individuals to oppose these changes. Appropriate change management strategies that address concerns and actively involve employees in decision-making can foster a positive attitude towards the transformation. However, some institutions' library cultures may be risk-averse, which can inhibit the implementation of modern technologies (Peng & Potipiroon 2022). Nonetheless, creating an environment in which experimentation and failure are viewed as opportunities for growth and improvement is necessary to overcome this cultural barrier (Meskó 2022).

Processes and Procedures

The STS framework details how libraries can adopt digital transformation and the Internet of Things. It places an emphasis on service design, automation, data collection, and the end user (Smith II 2023). With digital transformation in mind, it is important to evaluate current procedures, pinpoint problem areas, and develop solutions. As noted by Quazi & Patel (2023), automating mundane tasks and freeing up workers' time allows them to focus on more intricate projects. Collecting data, storing it, and analyzing it for insights are all parts of data analysis that preserve the anonymity and confidentiality of library patrons and their personal information (Quazi & Patel 2023; Xashimov & Khaydarova 2023).

Ghaffari, Lagzian, Kazemi & Malekzadeh (2019) describes process and procedure in the context of IoT (Internet of Things) adoption, socio-technical systems involve the integration of social and technical components to effectively implement IoT solutions. Stakeholder analysis involves involving all relevant stakeholders, considering both technical and social factors.

However, the process involves a collaborative, interdisciplinary design, and development process, including user-centered design principles. Testing and prototyping involve rigorous testing with users, while privacy and security measures are implemented. Training and support for users are provided, and deployment and integration ensure seamless transitions (Narang 2022). These processes must be tailored to the unique context, domain, and objectives, requiring flexibility, adaptability, and continuous engagement with stakeholders for successful implementation in a socio-technical system setting (Cimini & Cavalieri 2022).

Infrastructure and Technology

In the context of the framework for digital transformation through IoT adoption in library management and information science, infrastructure and technology play a crucial role as they are reviewed in literature and adapted from Davis framework (Quazi & Patel 2023). The Socio-Technical Systems conceptual framework emphasizes the interaction between social and technical elements within an organization, which is highly relevant in the context of libraries embracing digital transformation (Lima, Neto, Santos & Caiado 2023). In the same way Infrastructure in an organization is critical as is the backbone that enables connectivity and data administration in libraries. It involves the hardware, software, networking, and data storage capabilities necessary for IoT devices and other technologies to function effectively (Maftei, Lavric, Petrariu & Popa 2023; Shram 2021). Libraries need robust infrastructure to support the implementation and management of IoT devices, as well as to handle the vast amount of data generated by these devices. IoT devices, such as sensors, beacons, and RFID tags, enhance the user experience in libraries (Marin, Pawlowski & Jara 2015). They enable features like real-time location tracking of resources, personalized recommendations, and self-checkout systems. These devices collect data that can be leveraged for data-driven decision-making, allowing libraries to gain insights into usage patterns, resource popularity, and user preferences (Xu, Xu, Ling & Zhang 2022).

The External Circumstances

The external environment of a socio-technical system framework considers multiple stakeholder groups, the financial & economic and regulatory frameworks, its proper context, as shown in Figure 2 of the Davis framework. The chapter presents the following effects of an effective framework implementation.

Financial and Economic Circumstances

The development of IoT adoption in library management for public tertiary institutions in Ghana requires careful consideration of the financial and economic circumstances within the sociotechnical system (Pedersoli & Presbitero, 2023; Uryadova & Leshcheva, 2022). Therefore, analyzing the current financial and economic landscape in Ghana, such as GDP growth rate, inflation, exchange rates, and government policies, can help determine potential funding sources for IoT adoption (Mazikana, 2023). Nonetheless, others are of the view that a comprehensive cost-benefit analysis is necessary to evaluate the economic viability of IoT adoption, including initial setup costs, ongoing operational expenses, and potential returns in terms of efficiency gains, improved user services, and cost savings over time (Mazikana, 2023; Koelmel et al., 2023; Ugwuanyi et al., 2021; Fotouhi et al., 2021).

According to Ali et al., (2023) Return on Investment (ROI) projections are also crucial, considering how IoT adoption will impact library efficiency, user satisfaction, and the institution's overall performance. However, Masadeh & El-Haggar, (2023) argues that human resources and skill gaps must be identified, and the legal and regulatory framework in Ghana, especially regarding data privacy and security, must be considered. Risk assessments should be conducted to develop risk mitigation strategies and allocate resources for risk management (Dramani et al., 2022; Ameyaw & Frempong-Kore, 2021).

Community and Stakeholder Engagement

Community and stakeholder engagement is essential, as the library's user community and other stakeholders should be involved in the decision-making process to ensure IoT solutions align with their expectations and requirements (Martínez-Peláez et al., 2023). Whiles long-term sustainability of IoT adoption should be considered, with an expected lifespan of devices and technologies and a plan for upgrades and replacements. Performance metrics and monitoring should be established to measure the economic and operational impact of IoT adoption, and scalability and future expansion should be considered to accommodate the institution's growth and evolving needs.

Regulatory and Compliance Readiness

Regulatory and compliance issues must be taken into account when analyzing a Davies sociotechnical system for IoT adoption in library management at a public tertiary institution in Ghana (Quazi & Patel 2023).

This is necessary for the system to be used successfully and ethically. This involves understanding the sociotechnical system, which refers to the interconnectedness of technology, people, processes, and the environment within which the library operates (Dadzie & Mensah, 2022; Zakaria & Mohd Yusof, 2016).

The benefits of adopting IoT in library management include enhanced operations, improved user experiences, and contributing to the institution's overall goals. The regulatory framework in Ghana, including data protection laws, intellectual property regulations, and specific regulations related to IoT devices and data, should be provided (Morol, 2022).

Compliance considerations include adhering to local and international compliance standards, data privacy and security regulations, procurement and vendor assessment, user consent and data control, training and awareness, case studies and best practices, a collaborative approach with relevant regulatory bodies, legal experts, and industry associations, continuous monitoring and adaptation, and ethical considerations (Lartey, 2012).

By integrating these considerations, libraries can ensure that IoT adoption in library management aligns with local regulations, maintains data privacy and security, and fosters ethical practices. This approach helps create a robust, compliant, and sustainable sociotechnical system for the betterment of library services and user experiences in Ghana.

In the case of Ghana, all tertiary education institutions are required to obtain approval and clearance from the Ghana Tertiary Education Commission (GTEC). GTEC is the sole regulatory body mandated to oversee the activities of tertiary institutions in the country, as stipulated in the "Education Regulatory Bodies Act 2020, Act 1023" (Coverghana.com.gh, 2022). This process fulfils the requirement of assessing the library's regulatory environment, including any legal or compliance obligations. Furthermore, it outlines the specific regulations or standards that must be followed when implementing any policy or a framework of a kind, hence the adoption and implementation of IoT in library management. Adhering to these regulations ensures compliance with relevant data protection, privacy, and security measures for IoT technologies (Selam and Ababu, 2021). Using Davies' socio-technical systems framework, organizations can assess and resolve the regulatory/compliance readiness aspects of IoT adoptions in a systematic manner. This includes considering social, technical factors, organizational processes, and the need for continuous adaptation. This strategy ensures that compliance requirements are incorporated into the design and implementation of IoT systems, thereby promoting the responsible and secure use of IoT technologies while meeting regulatory requirements (Kirsch 2000).

Perceived Ease of Use

Taqi et al., (2023) argues that when examining the sociotechnical systems environment, it also requires examining IoT instruments' interactions with users and the broader social and organizational context to gauge the users' perceptions. Thus Perceived simplicity of use can be integrated into the environment (Aronson & LaFont 2020).

Nonetheless, one must conduct user surveys or usability tests to determine the perceived usability of IoT library management systems among library staff and users. Evaluate the user interface, interaction design, and overall user experience of the library management solution for the Internet of Things. In other words, identify any pain points or areas for improvement to increase the system's usability and adoption (Chen & Aklikokou 2019).

Once you have evaluated these variables, you can use the resulting insights to make informed decisions and devise IoT library management implementation strategies (Yang, Li, and Qi, 2023). This may involve addressing infrastructure deficiencies, revising policies, offering training and support, and ensuring regulatory compliance. Regular monitoring and evaluation of these variables will contribute to the ongoing enhancement of the IoT library management system (Ali & Warraich 2023).

FUTURE RESEARCH DIRECTION BASED ON SOCIO-TECHNICAL SYSTEMS ANALYTICAL THINKING

Taqi et al., (2023), have identified the continuous engagement with the stakeholders of public tertiary institutions and, in particular, the provision of a strategic roadmap for the IoT adoption framework for institutions of higher learning and have again suggested the following for further studies as depicted in Figure 3:

- Implementing a socio-technical systems framework in library management can open up multiple avenues for study to enhance the application and comprehension of IoT in Ghana.
- Looking at what makes an implementation successful, studying the sociocultural effects, long-term viability and scalability, security and privacy issues, analyzing how people and machines interact, adapting IoT solutions for educational settings, integrating IoT with current library management systems, examining change management techniques, figuring out what the effects will be on the economy and resources, and looking into how institutions can work together.
- The socio-cultural impact studies will concentrate on how local preferences and cultural norms influence the adoption and application of IoT technologies in libraries. An evaluation will be conducted to determine the long-term viability and scalability of IoT systems. The exploration of security and privacy problems will be undertaken due to the involvement of data gathering and sharing in IoT. The study will focus on analyzing the dynamics of human-machine interaction and developing Internet of Things (IoT) solutions specifically designed for the educational environment. An evaluation will be conducted on the integration of current library management systems as well as the implementation of change management methods, economic and resource analysis, collaborative networks, and policy and regulatory analysis.
- The Internet of Things (IoT) has the potential to improve the learning and research experience in libraries by utilizing data analytics, providing research support, and enabling digital scholarship. The exploration will encompass ethical aspects such as the utilization of data, the availability of information, and the fairness of distribution. The research will focus on IoT-enabled learning spaces, with a continuous collection and analysis of user feedback and experience to guide iterative improvements and addition.

Figure 3. IoT adoption strategic roadmap for library management

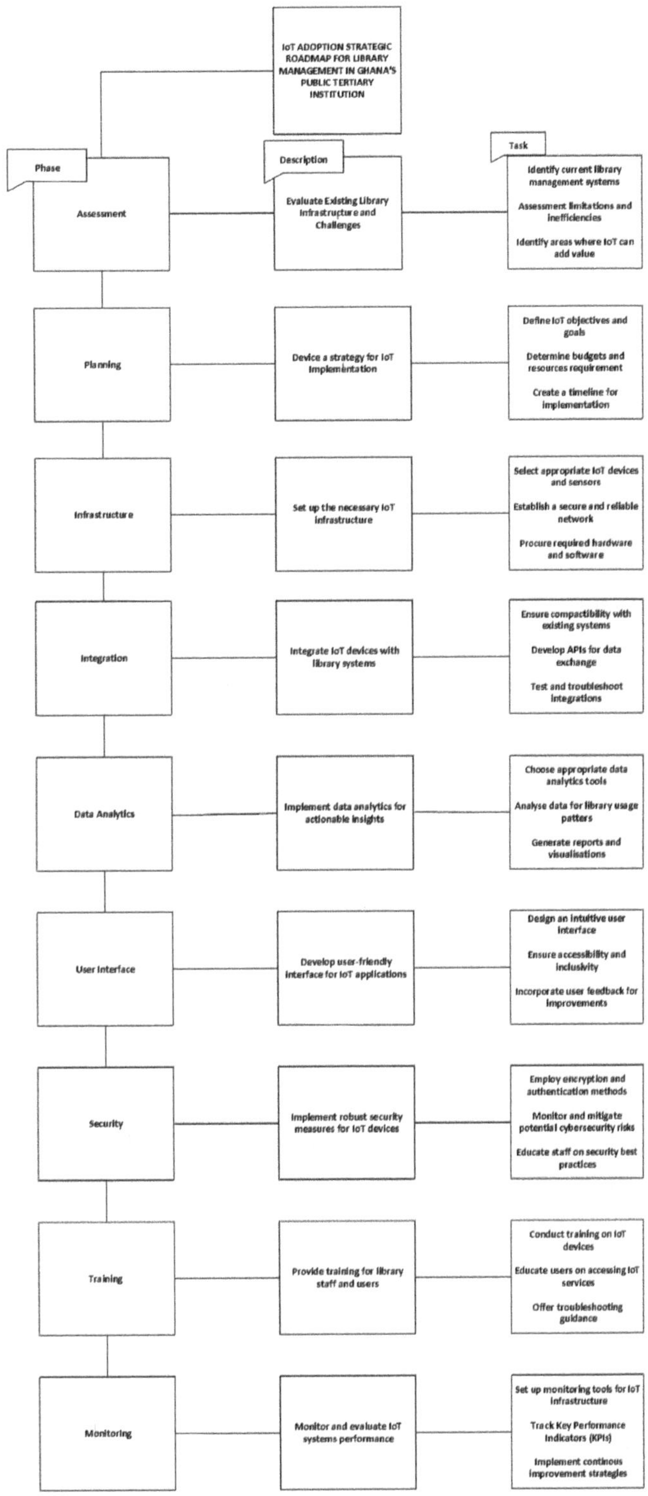

Limitations of Work

Socio-technical analyses are inherently influenced by their specific context. In this research, we focused on library within Ghana's public tertiary institution, which means that certain findings may not directly apply to different settings. Nevertheless, the research methodology employed in this study can be modified and utilized in other contexts. Subsequent studies could explore similar contextualized investigations in alternative environments.

CONCLUSION

This socio-technical analysis offers a distinctive viewpoint on Ghana's public tertiary institutions' library systems and offers insightful observations. The researcher's methodology particularly used in this study can serve as a framework for researchers undertaking analogous investigations in diverse contexts, including both social and technical elements. The present study establishes a fundamental basis for subsequent research endeavors, facilitating a more comprehensive comprehension of socio-technical processes inside library environments on a global scale. Adapting policies and solutions to align with unique conditions is of greatest significance for policymakers, library administrators, and stakeholders, as the implementation details are subject to variation. The results obtained from this investigation ought to serve as a foundation for ongoing enhancements, guaranteeing the efficacy and adaptability of libraries' systems and services in meeting customer requirements. The ever-changing nature of technology and society requires continuous assessment and adjustment.

REFERENCES

Aboelmaged, M., Govindan, K., & Malik, M. (2023). Understanding the key determinants of IOT adoption for the digital transformation of the food and beverage industry. *Industrial Management &amp. Data Systems*, *123*(7), 1887–1910. doi:10.1108/imds-02-2022-0082

Adamova, A. D., Zhukabayeva, T. K., & Ven-Tsen, K. (2021). Development of a digital educational platform using augmented reality and Gamification Technologies to intensify learning and cognitive activities of students in the course of studying the subject. *BULLETIN of L.N. Gumilyov Eurasian National University. Technical Science and Technology Series*, *137*(4), 39–47. doi:10.32523/2616-7263-2021-137-4-39-47

Adashi, E. Y. (2021). Cybersecurity in the internet of medical things. *Health Policy and Technology*, *10*(3), 100549. doi:10.1016/j.hlpt.2021.100549

Agyemang, F. G. (2019). From classroom to library: What are the transferable knowledge and skills teachers bring to library work. *Journal of Librarianship and Information Science*, *52*(3), 659–670. doi:10.1177/0961000619856401

Ahmad, R., Alsmadi, I., Alhamdani, W., & Tawalbeh, L. (2021). Models versus datasets: Reducing bias through building a comprehensive ids benchmark. *Future Internet*, *13*(12), 318. doi:10.3390/fi13120318

Alahi, M. E., Sukkuea, A., Tina, F. W., Nag, A., Kurdthongmee, W., Suwannarat, K., & Mukhopadhyay, S. C. (2023). Integration of IOT-enabled technologies and Artificial Intelligence (AI) for Smart City Scenario: Recent advancements and future trends. *Sensors (Basel)*, *23*(11), 5206. doi:10.339023115206

Aldriweesh, E., Zakuan, N., Hafiz Bajuri, N., & Mufareh Alshammakh, A. (2022). The moderating role of organizational culture on the relationship between enterprise risk management dimensions and financial performance in manufacturing companies: A theoretical framework. *International Journal of Academic Research in Accounting. Finance and Management Sciences*, *12*(4). Advance online publication. doi:10.6007/ijarafms/v12-i4/15810

Ali, J., Madni, S. H., Jahangeer, M. S., & Danish, M. A. (2023). IOT adoption model for e-learning in higher education institutes: A case study in Saudi Arabia. *Sustainability*, *15*(12), 9748. doi:10.3390u15129748

Allioui, H., & Mourdi, Y. (2023). Exploring the full potentials of IOT for better financial growth and stability: A comprehensive survey. *Sensors (Basel)*, *23*(19), 8015. doi:10.339023198015

Almugari, F., Bajaj, P., Tabash, M. I., Khan, A., & Ali, M. A. (2020). An examination of consumers' adoption of internet of things (IOT) in Indian Banks. *Cogent Business &amp. Management*, *7*(1), 1809071. doi:10.1080/23311975.2020.1809071

Alshohoumi, F., & Sarrab, M. (2020). Privacy concerns in IOT a deeper insight into privacy concerns in IOT based healthcare. *International Journal of Computing and Digital Systems*, *9*(3), 399–418. doi:10.12785/ijcds/090306

Altawalbeh, M. A. (2023). Adoption of academic staff to use the Learning Management System (LMS): Applying extended technology acceptance model (TAM2) for Jordanian universities. *International Journal on Studies in Education*, *5*(3), 288–300. doi:10.46328/ijonse.124

Ameyaw, S., & Frempong-Kore, A. (2021). Records management practices in Ghanaian tertiary institutions: A case study of ghana technology university college. *UDS International Journal of Development*, *7*(2), 461–472. doi:10.47740/503.udsijd6i

Aroba, O. J., & Abayomi, A. (2023). An implementation of SAP Enterprise Resource Planning – A Case Study of the south african revenue services and taxation sectors. *Cogent Social Sciences*, *9*(1). Advance online publication. doi:10.1080/23311886.2023.2228060

Attaran, M., & Attaran, S. (2020). Digital Transformation and economic contributions of 5G networks. *International Journal of Enterprise Information Systems*, *16*(4), 58–79. doi:10.4018/ijeis.2020100104

Babiceanu, R. F., & Seker, R. (2019). Cyber Resilience Protection for Industrial Internet of Things: A Software-defined networking approach. *Computers in Industry*, *104*, 47–58. doi:10.1016/j.compind.2018.10.004

Bashir, M. R., Gill, A. Q., & Beydoun, G. (2022). A reference architecture for IOT-enabled smart buildings. *SN Computer Science*, *3*(6). Advance online publication. doi:10.100742979-022-01401-9

Baxter, G., & Sommerville, I. (2011). Socio-technical systems: From design methods to systems engineering. *Interacting with Computers*, *23*(1), 4–17. doi:10.1016/j.intcom.2010.07.003

Bayanati, M. (2023). Business model of internet of things and blockchain technology in developing countries. *International Journal of Innovation in Engineering, 3*(1), 13–22. doi:10.59615/ijie.3.1.13

Bessadok, A., Abouzinadah, E., & Rabie, O. (2021). Exploring students digital activities and performances through their activities logged in learning management system using educational data mining approach. *Interactive Technology and Smart Education, 20*(1), 58–72. doi:10.1108/itse-08-2021-0148

Bettin, A. (2023). Digital transformation for the water industry: How a data-driven business intelligence platform can improve operations. *Water Practice &amp. Technology, 18*(7), 1599–1607. doi:10.2166/wpt.2023.091

Blockchain technology to enhance the public service capability of Digital Government. (2023). *Eurasian Law Journal, 6*(181). https://doi.org/ doi:10.46320/2073-4506-2023-6-181-507-508

Bowen, G. A. (2009). Document analysis as a qualitative research method. *Qualitative Research Journal, 9*(2), 27–40. doi:10.3316/qrj0902027

Budu, K. W., Yinping, M., & Mireku, K. K. (2018). Investigating the effect of behavioral intention on e-learning systems usage: Empirical study on Tertiary Education Institutions in Ghana. *Mediterranean Journal of Social Sciences, 9*(3), 201–216. doi:10.2478/mjss-2018-0062

Cardno, C. (2019). Policy Document Analysis: A practical educational leadership tool and a qualitative research method. *Educational Administration: Theory and Practice, 24*(4). Advance online publication. doi:10.14527/kuey.2018.016

Chan, H. C., & Chan, L. (2018). Smart Library and smart campus. *Journal of Service Science and Management, 11*(06), 543–564. doi:10.4236/jssm.2018.116037

Chen, C.-L., Lin, Y.-C., Chen, W.-H., Chao, C.-F., & Pandia, H. (2021). Role of government to enhance digital transformation in small service business. *Sustainability, 13*(3), 1028. doi:10.3390u13031028

Chong, S. L., & Wan, R. (2018). Technological Infrastructure and Human Culture: Appropriating innovative teaching methods to 21st century classrooms. *SHS Web of Conferences, 53*, 05001. https://doi.org/10.1051hsconf/20185305001

Choudhary, H. (2023). Building Bridges to digital inclusion: Implications for curriculum development of digital literacy training programs. *International Journal of Technology Enhanced Learning, 1*(1). Advance online publication. doi:10.1504/ijtel.2023.10059464

Chubko, N., Morris, J. E., McKinnon, D. H., Slater, E. V., & Lummis, G. W. (2020). Digital Storytelling as a disciplinary literacy enhancement tool for EFL students. *Educational Technology Research and Development, 68*(6), 3587–3604. doi:10.100711423-020-09833-x

Cimini, C., & Cavalieri, S. (2022). Industrial Smart Working: A Socio-technical model for enabling successful implementation. *IFAC-PapersOnLine, 55*(2), 505–510. doi:10.1016/j.ifacol.2022.04.244

Dadzie, P. S., & Mensah, M. (2022). Change management in libraries: The case of the university of ghana library system (UGLS). *Library Leadership &amp. Management, 36*(1). Advance online publication. doi:10.5860/llm.v36i1.7496

Davis, M. C., Challenger, R., Jayewardene, D. N. W., & Clegg, C. W. (2014). Advancing Socio-Technical Systems thinking: A call for bravery. *Applied Ergonomics*, *45*(2), 171–180. doi:10.1016/j.apergo.2013.02.009

Davis, M. C., Hughes, H. P., McKay, A., Robinson, M. A., & van der Wal, C. N. (2019). Ergonomists as designers: Computational Modelling and simulation of complex socio-technical systems. *Ergonomics*, *63*(8), 938–951. doi:10.1080/00140139.2019.1682186

DeFranco, J. F., & Voas, J. (2023). Thoughts on automotive IOT. *Computer*, *56*(3), 13–18. doi:10.1109/mc.2022.3219637

Demuyakor, J. (2020). Ghana Go Digital Agenda: The Impact of Zipline drone technology on Digital Emergency Health Delivery in Ghana. *Shanlax International Journal of Arts. Science and Humanities*, *8*(1), 242–253. doi:10.34293ijash.v8i1.3301

Diaz, R., & Montalvo, R. (2022). Digital Transformation as an enabler to become more efficient in sustainability: Evidence from five leading companies in the Mexican market. *Sustainability*, *14*(22), 15436. doi:10.3390u142215436

Dramani, I. E., Tang, Z., & Coffie, C. P. (2022). Usage intention of e-learning systems in Ghanaian tertiary institutions: A case study of the university for development studies. *Sustainability*, *14*(12), 7360. doi:10.3390u14127360

Elsafty, A., & Yehia, A. (2023). Digital Transformation Challenges for Government Sector. *Business and Management Studies*, *9*(1), 11. doi:10.11114/bms.v9i1.6160

Emmert-Streib, F. (2021). From the Digital Data Revolution toward a digital society: Pervasiveness of Artificial Intelligence. *Machine Learning and Knowledge Extraction*, *3*(1), 284–298. doi:10.3390/make3010014

Falayi, A., Wang, Q., Liao, W., & Yu, W. (2023). Survey of distributed and decentralized IOT Securities: Approaches using Deep Learning and blockchain technology. *Future Internet*, *15*(5), 178. doi:10.3390/fi15050178

Farias-Gaytan, S., Aguaded, I., & Ramirez-Montoya, M.-S. (2023). Digital Transformation and digital literacy in the context of complexity within Higher Education Institutions: A systematic literature review. *Humanities & Social Sciences Communications*, *10*(1). Advance online publication. doi:10.105741599-023-01875-9

Florio, M., Morretta, V., & Willak, W. (2018). Cost-benefit analysis and European Union Cohesion Policy: Economic Versus Financial returns in Investment Project Appraisal. *Journal of Benefit-Cost Analysis*, *9*(1), 147–180. doi:10.1017/bca.2018.4

Fotouhi, A., Oudi, M., Gueni, B., & Mabrouk, M. B. (2021). User behavior analysis using IOT Data. *Nordic and Baltic Journal of Information &amp. Tongxin Jishu*. Advance online publication. doi:10.13052/nbjict1902-097x.2020.011

Ghaffari, K., Lagzian, M., Kazemi, M., & Malekzadeh, G. (2019). A socio-technical analysis of internet of things development: An interplay of technologies, tasks, structures and actors. *Foresight*, *21*(6), 640–653. doi:10.1108/fs-05-2019-0037

Gkrimpizi, T., Peristeras, V., & Magnisalis, I. (2023). Classification of barriers to digital transformation in Higher Education Institutions: Systematic Literature Review. *Education Sciences*, *13*(7), 746. doi:10.3390/educsci13070746

Gohari, A., Ahmad, A. B., Rahim, R. B., Supa'at, A. S., Abd Razak, S., & Gismalla, M. S. (2022). Involvement of surveillance drones in Smart Cities: A systematic review. *IEEE Access : Practical Innovations, Open Solutions*, *10*, 56611–56628. doi:10.1109/access.2022.3177904

Gul, S., & Bano, S. (2019). Smart libraries: An emerging and innovative technological habitat of 21st century. *The Electronic Library*, *37*(5), 764–783. doi:10.1108/el-02-2019-0052

Heidari, A., & Jabraeil Jamali, M. A. (2022). Internet of things intrusion detection systems: A comprehensive review and Future Directions. *Cluster Computing*, *26*(6), 3753–3780. doi:10.100710586-022-03776-z

Hogarth, J., & Wójcik, D. (2016). An evolutionary approach to adaptive capacity assessment: A case study of soufriere, Saint Lucia. *Sustainability*, *8*(3), 228. doi:10.3390u8030228

Islam, N., Altamimi, M., Haseeb, K., & Siraj, M. (2021). Secure and sustainable predictive framework for IOT-based multimedia services using machine learning. *Sustainability*, *13*(23), 13128. doi:10.3390u132313128

Jagatheesaperumal, S. K., Rajkumar, S., Suresh, J. V., Gumaei, A. H., Alhakbani, N., & Uddin, Md. Z., & Hassan, M. M. (2023). An IOT-based framework for Personalized Health Assessment and recommendations using Machine Learning. *Mathematics*, *11*(12), 2758. doi:10.3390/math11122758

Jeong, Y. (2023). Digitalization in production logistics: How ai, Digital Twins, and simulation are driving the shift from model-based to data-driven approaches. *International Journal of Precision Engineering and Manufacturing-Smart Technology*, *1*(2), 187–200. doi:10.57062/ijpem-st.2023.0052

Khan, A. U., Zhang, Z., Chohan, S. R., & Rafique, W. (2021). Factors fostering the success of IOT services in academic libraries: A study built to enhance the library performance. *Library Hi Tech*, *40*(6), 1976–1995. doi:10.1108/lht-06-2021-0179

Khaydarova, G. (2023). Thermal characteristics of compositions of polyvinyl chloride with flame retardants. *Universum:Technical Sciences*, *107*(2). Advance online publication. doi:10.32743/unitech.2023.107.2.15077

Kirsch, C. (2000). MTO contingency model for the transferability of socio-technical methods - the Swiss KOMPASS method applied to the design and implementation of Advanced Manufacturing Systems in Australia. *Proceedings of the Human Factors and Ergonomics Society Annual Meeting*, *44*(36), 497–500. doi:10.1177/154193120004403612

Koelmel, B., Borsch, M., Bulander, R., Waidelich, L., Brugger, T., Kuehn, A., Weyer, M., Schmerber, L., & Krutwig, M. (2023). Quantifying the economic and financial viability of Nb-IOT and Lorawan Technologies: A comprehensive life cycle cost analysis using Pragmatic Computational Tools. *FinTech*, *2*(3), 510–526. doi:10.3390/fintech2030029

Kumar, S., Tiwari, P., & Zymbler, M. (2019). Internet of things is a revolutionary approach for future technology enhancement: A Review. *Journal of Big Data*, *6*(1). Advance online publication. doi:10.118640537-019-0268-2

Lartey, R. (2012). The banking regulatory and Market Framework in Ghana: Strengths, weaknesses, opportunities and threats. SSRN *Electronic Journal*. https://doi.org/ doi:10.2139/ssrn.2083237

Lee, I. (2020). Internet of things (IOT) cybersecurity: Literature review and IOT cyber risk management. *Future Internet*, *12*(9), 157. doi:10.3390/fi12090157

Liang, X., & Chen, Y. (2018). Libraries in internet of things (IOT) era. *Library Hi Tech*, *38*(1), 79–93. doi:10.1108/lht-11-2017-0233

Lima, B. F., Neto, J. V., Santos, R. S., & Caiado, R. G. (2023). A socio-technical framework for LEAN project management implementation towards sustainable value in the digital transformation context. *Sustainability*, *15*(3), 1756. doi:10.3390u15031756

Lohiya, R., & Thakkar, A. (2021). Application domains, evaluation data sets, and research challenges of IOT: A systematic review. *IEEE Internet of Things Journal*, *8*(11), 8774–8798. doi:10.1109/jiot.2020.3048439

Maftei, A. A., Lavric, A., Petrariu, A. I., & Popa, V. (2023). Massive data storage solution for IOT devices using Blockchain Technologies. *Sensors (Basel)*, *23*(3), 1570. doi:10.339023031570

Maharaja, R., Iyer, P., & Ye, Z. (2019). A hybrid fog-cloud approach for securing the internet of things. *Cluster Computing*, *23*(2), 451–459. doi:10.100710586-019-02935-z

Maimun, A., Siow, C. L., Khairuddin, J., & Hiekata, K. (2022). Digital transformation through data-driven and data-centric approaches with Artificial Intelligence. *ICCAS, 2022*. Advance online publication. doi:10.3940/rina.iccas.2022.19

Mangalaraj, G., Nerur, S., & Dwivedi, R. (2022). Digital transformation for agility and resilience: An exploratory study. *Journal of Computer Information Systems*, *63*(1), 11–23. doi:10.1080/08874417.2021.2015726

Maresova, P., Krejcar, O., Barakovic, S., Barakovic Husic, J., Lameski, P., Zdravevski, E., Chorbev, I., & Trajkovik, V. (2020). Health–related ICT solutions of smart environments for elderly–systematic review. *IEEE Access : Practical Innovations, Open Solutions*, *8*, 54574–54600. doi:10.1109/access.2020.2981315

Marin, L., Pawlowski, M., & Jara, A. (2015). Optimized ECC implementation for secure communication between heterogeneous IOT devices. *Sensors (Basel)*, *15*(9), 21478–21499. doi:10.3390150921478

Martínez-Peláez, R., Ochoa-Brust, A., Rivera, S., Félix, V. G., Ostos, R., Brito, H., Félix, R. A., & Mena, L. J. (2023). Role of digital transformation for achieving sustainability: Mediated role of stakeholders, key capabilities, and Technology. *Sustainability*, *15*(14), 11221. doi:10.3390u151411221

Masadeh, S. A., & El-Haggar, N. (2023). Analyzing factors influencing IOT adoption in higher educational institutions in Saudi Arabia using a modified TAM model. *Education and Information Technologies*. Advance online publication. doi:10.100710639-023-12039-2

May, C. K. (2022). Complex adaptive governance systems: A framework to understand institutions, organizations, and people in socio-ecological systems. *Socio-Ecological Practice Research*, *4*(1), 39–54. doi:10.100742532-021-00101-7

Mazikana, A. T. (2023). How inflation, GDP growth, unemployment, interest rates and exchange rates affect an organisation. SSRN *Electronic Journal*. https://doi.org/ doi:10.2139/ssrn.4377852

Meskó, B. (2022). Covid-19's impact on digital health adoption: The growing gap between a technological and a cultural transformation. *JMIR Human Factors*, *9*(3). Advance online publication. doi:10.2196/38926

Migabo, E. M., Djouani, K. D., & Kurien, A. M. (2020). The narrowband internet of things (NB-IOT) resources management performance state of art, challenges, and opportunities. *IEEE Access : Practical Innovations, Open Solutions*, *8*, 97658–97675. doi:10.1109/access.2020.2995938

Moore, S. (2019). Digital Government, public participation and service transformation: The impact of virtual courts. *Policy &amp. Politics*. Advance online publication. doi:10.1332/030557319x1558603936750

Morol, Md. K. (2022). Data Security and privacy in cloud computing platforms: A comprehensive review. *International Journal of Current Science Research and Review*, *05*(05). Advance online publication. doi:10.47191/ijcsrr/v5-i5-09

Moumtzidis, I., Kamariotou, M., & Kitsios, F. (2022). Digital transformation strategies enabled by internet of things and Big Data Analytics: The use-case of telecommunication companies in Greece. *Information (Basel)*, *13*(4), 196. doi:10.3390/info13040196

Narang, N. K. (2022). Mentor's musings on standardization imperatives for the connected vehicles for seamless integration in sustainable mobility. *IEEE Internet of Things Magazine*, *5*(2), 4–8. doi:10.1109/miot.2022.9889259

Nwaiwu, F., & Mbelu, S. (2020). Digital transformation in healthcare and surveillance capitalism: Comparative assessment of data and Privacy Protection Compliance across the European Union. SSRN *Electronic Journal*. https://doi.org/ doi:10.2139/ssrn.3643838

Ojha, A., Jindal, A., & Chanak, P. (2023). An intelligent indoor emergency evacuation system using IOT-enabled WSNS for smart buildings. *IEEE Internet of Things Journal*, •••, 1–1. doi:10.1109/jiot.2023.3321646

Pedersoli, S., & Presbitero, A. F. (2023). Public Debt Management and private financial development. *Economic Systems*, *47*(1), 101010. doi:10.1016/j.ecosys.2022.101010

Peng, B., & Potipiroon, W. (2022). Fear of losing jobs during COVID-19: Can psychological capital alleviate job insecurity and job stress? *Behavioral Sciences (Basel, Switzerland)*, *12*(6), 168. doi:10.3390/bs12060168

Phung, K. A., Kirbas, C., Dereci, L., & Nguyen, T. V. (2022). Pervasive Healthcare internet of things: A survey. *Information (Basel)*, *13*(8), 360. doi:10.3390/info13080360

Pratono, A. H., Nawangpalupi, C. B., & Sutanti, A. (2023). Achieving Sustainable Development Goals through digitalising creative works: Some evidence from social enterprises in Indonesia. *Digital Economy and Sustainable Development*, *1*(1). Advance online publication. doi:10.100744265-023-00011-4

Qazi, S., Khawaja, B. A., & Farooq, Q. U. (2022). Iot-equipped and AI-enabled Next Generation Smart Agriculture: A Critical Review, current challenges and future trends. *IEEE Access : Practical Innovations, Open Solutions*, *10*, 21219–21235. doi:10.1109/access.2022.3152544

Qian, C., Liu, X., Ripley, C., Qian, M., Liang, F., & Yu, W. (2022). Digital Twin—cyber replica of Physical Things: Architecture, applications and future research directions. *Future Internet*, *14*(2), 64. doi:10.3390/fi14020064

Quazi, T. A.-M., & Patel, S. S. (2023). Socio-Technical Systems Engineering Perspectives towards a South African halaal blockchain system. *Advances in Logistics, Operations, and Management Science*, •••, 287–309. doi:10.4018/978-1-6684-7455-6.ch014

Samuel, K. C. (2022). Optimizing the internet despite threat to IP: How Fashion Designers in Nigeria are leveraging digital media platforms for market entry and growth. *Advanced Journal of Social Science*, *10*(1), 1–13. doi:10.21467/ajss.10.1.1-13

Schroeder, A., Naik, P., Ziaee Bigdeli, A., & Baines, T. (2020). Digitally enabled advanced services: A socio-technical perspective on the role of the internet of things (IOT). *International Journal of Operations &amp. Production Management*, *40*(7/8), 1243–1268. doi:10.1108/ijopm-03-2020-0131

Schuster, F., & Habibipour, A. (2022). Users' privacy and security concerns that affect IOT adoption in the home domain. *International Journal of Human-Computer Interaction*, •••, 1–12. doi:10.1080/10447318.2022.2147302

Selam, M. N., & Ababu, A. (2021). Extemporaneous Compounding Practice for dermatologic preparations in Ethiopian Public Hospitals: Regulatory Requirements and quality concerns. *Risk Management and Healthcare Policy*, *14*, 1933–1938. doi:10.2147/rmhp.s300906

Sharma, V., & Hashmi, M. (2021). On the seamless integration and co-existence of chipless RFID in broad IOT framework. *IEEE Access : Practical Innovations, Open Solutions*, *9*, 69839–69849. doi:10.1109/access.2021.3078318

Shin, D. (2014). A socio-technical framework for internet-of-things design: A human-centered design for the internet of things. *Telematics and Informatics*, *31*(4), 519–531. doi:10.1016/j.tele.2014.02.003

Shram, M. M. (2021). Data Processing by end devices in IOT Systems. *Connectivity*, *153*(5). Advance online publication. doi:10.31673/2412-9070.2021.052428

Sony, M., & Naik, S. (2020). Industry 4.0 integration with socio-technical systems theory: A systematic review and proposed theoretical model. *Technology in Society*, *61*, 101248. doi:10.1016/j.techsoc.2020.101248

Taqi, F., Batool, S. H., & Arshad, A. (2023). Examining differences in perceived usability of Google Drive among Public Library Users. *Library Hi Tech*. Advance online publication. doi:10.1108/lht-05-2022-0275

Tariq, U., Ahmed, I., Bashir, A. K., & Shaukat, K. (2023). A critical cybersecurity analysis and future research directions for the internet of things: A comprehensive review. *Sensors (Basel)*, *23*(8), 4117. doi:10.339023084117

Thomasian, N. M., & Adashi, E. Y. (2021). Cybersecurity in the internet of medical things. *Health Policy and Technology*, *10*(3), 100549. doi:10.1016/j.hlpt.2021.100549

Ugwuanyi, S., Paul, G., & Irvine, J. (2021). Survey of IOT for developing countries: Performance analysis of lorawan and cellular Nb-IOT Networks. *Electronics (Basel)*, *10*(18), 2224. doi:10.3390/electronics10182224

Uryadova, T., & Leshcheva, M. (2022). Analytical tools to justify investment decisions. *Research of Economic and Financial Problems*, (3), 1–10. doi:10.31279/2782-6414-2022-3-7-1-10

Venkatesh, R., & Singhal, T. K. (2022). Articulating Business Model Innovation, Digital Transformation and managed services: Case of Digital Transformation as a Service. *International Journal of Business and Globalisation*, *31*(4), 1. doi:10.1504/ijbg.2022.10040365

Wedajo, M., & Chekole, B. (2020). Attitude of employees towards change initiatives as influenced by commitment and job satisfaction: The case of selected higher education institutions in Ethiopia. *Journal of Process Management. Nuclear Technology*, *8*(3), 42–52. doi:10.5937/jouproman8-25868

Wicaksana, S. A., Purwoko, B., & Sihite, M. (2022). Role of organization culture on organizational agility for digital transformation in XYZ Government organization. *International Journal of Business Management and Economic Research*, *05*(03), 70–83. doi:10.35409/ijbmer.2022.3391

Xu, Z., Xu, L., Ling, X., & Zhang, B. (2022). Data-driven hierarchical learning and real-time decision-making of equipment scheduling and location assignment in automatic high-density storage systems. *International Journal of Production Research*, *61*(21), 7333–7352. doi:10.1080/00207543.2022.2148011

Yao, Q., Tang, H., Boadu, F., & Xie, Y. (2022). Digital transformation and firm sustainable growth: The moderating effects of cross-border search capability and managerial digital concern. *Journal of the Knowledge Economy*. Advance online publication. doi:10.100713132-022-01083-x

Yeh, S.-T., Arthaud-Day, M., & Turvey-Welch, M. (2021). Propagation of Lean Thinking in academic libraries. *Journal of Academic Librarianship*, *47*(3), 102357. doi:10.1016/j.acalib.2021.102357

Yoon, J. (2020). Deep-learning approach to attack handling of IOT devices using IOT-enabled network services. *Internet of Things : Engineering Cyber Physical Human Systems*, *11*, 100241. doi:10.1016/j.iot.2020.100241

Zakaria, N., & Mohd Yusof, S. A. (2016). Understanding Technology and people issues in Hospital Information System (his) adoption: Case study of a tertiary hospital in Malaysia. *Journal of Infection and Public Health*, *9*(6), 774–780. doi:10.1016/j.jiph.2016.08.017

Zhang, W., Zhang, B., Zhou, Y., He, H., & Ding, Z. (2020). An IOT honeynet based on multiport honeypots for capturing IOT attacks. *IEEE Internet of Things Journal*, *7*(5), 3991–3999. doi:10.1109/jiot.2019.2956173

ADDITIONAL READING

Agyemang, F. G. (2019, July 7). From classroom to library: What are the transferable knowledge and skills teachers bring to library work. *Journal of Librarianship and Information Science*, *52*(3), 659–670. doi:10.1177/0961000619856401

Elsafty, A., & Yehia, A. (2023, July 3). Digital Transformation Challenges for Government Sector. *Business and Management Studies*, *9*(1), 11. doi:10.11114/bms.v9i1.6160

Moore, S. (2019). Digital government, public participation and service transformation: The impact of virtual courts. *Policy and Politics*, *47*(3), 495–509. Advance online publication. doi:10.1332/030557319X15586039367509

KEY TERMS AND DEFINITIONS

Digital Transformation: Digital transformation involves utilizing digital technologies to improve various sectors of the economy and society, including government services, business operations, education, and healthcare.

Digital Transformation in Libraries: Digital transformation in libraries involves modernizing services, operations, and resources through digital technologies. Key aspects include expanding digital collections, improving library management systems, enhancing online catalogues and discovery services, developing user-friendly websites, investing in digital preservation, transforming physical spaces, offering data management services, promoting open access, offering digital literacy programs, improving user experiences, and ensuring inclusivity and accessibility.

Ghana: Ghana, a country with unique characteristics, challenges, and opportunities, is used as a case study in the development of the Internet of Things (IoT) framework in public tertiary institutions.

Internet of Things (IoT): In this book chapter the Internet of Things is a fourth-industrial revolution (4IR) technology that refers to mass-deployed, large scale networks of embedded systems that communicate over the Internet. Typically, IoT systems have a backbone of cloud technology.

IoT Adoption Framework: The IoT adoption framework in this context is a standardized strategy for integrating IoT technologies into library management systems, guiding institutions on requirements, hardware selection, compatibility, security, privacy, and efficacy.

Public Tertiary Institutions: Public tertiary institutions are government-funded institutions offering post-secondary education, including universities, colleges, and vocational training, typically open to the public.

Smart Libraries: Smart libraries utilize digital technologies like IoT, artificial intelligence, and data analytics to improve services, resources, and operations. They offer innovative features like self-checkout systems, digital catalogs, personalized recommendations, and remote access, aiming to provide a more intelligent and integrated library experience.

Socio-Technical Systems Analytical Thinking: Socio-technical systems analytical thinking relies on considering technology and society holistically, such that due consideration is paid to how technology must be shaped by social influences, as well as the impacts of technology on society.

Chapter 12
Growth and Poverty:
Estimating Regional Dimensions With Unit-Level Data

Meghna Ghosh
https://orcid.org/0000-0002-9739-6181
BITS Law School, Mumbai, India

ABSTRACT

This study estimates poverty in India across the different states in terms of incidence, depth, and severity by using different rounds of household level unit data provided by the National Sample Survey Office (NSSO). In this study, the authors have estimated the different measures of both absolute and relative poverty, such as the poverty rate, depth, and severity of poverty across the 22 major states of India, separately for the rural and urban regions. Apart from this, the authors have made a regression analysis to estimate the growth elasticity of poverty (GEP) in India. The panel regression analysis has been carried out over the five rounds of the NSSO, i.e., the 50th (1993-94), 55th (1999-2000), 61st (2004-05), 66th (2009-10), and the 68th rounds. The analysis showed that the urban sector has a significant GEP. A detailed analysis of poverty creates an environment conducive for the poor to improve their living standards in the future. This research, if made available across all public libraries, will play an important role in that direction.

INTRODUCTION

Growth of per capita domestic product is a primary determinant affecting the capacity of an economy to reduce poverty. However, the effect of economic growth on poverty levels depends to a considerable degree on the relationship between growth and economic inequality (Datt and Ravallion, 1992). Rising inequality in an economy nullifies the poverty-decreasing effects of growth. One can define growth as pro-poor if the elasticity of poverty reduction with respect to growth is positive, or alternatively, if the poor benefit more proportionally from growth than do the non-poor. In India, there has been a sharp reduction in public investment in infrastructure and services in the rural areas during the post-reform period (Priya et al., 2023). State support to farmers and agricultural production including formal bank

DOI: 10.4018/979-8-3693-0807-3.ch012

credits and extension services also fell down. Moreover, there was the issue of structural deficiencies in planning which led to the successive plans failing to alleviate poverty and income inequality at regional and interpersonal levels. Agriculture was neglected and industry, particularly the capital goods production, was given excessive importance during the plan period. There was complete absence of any specific poverty alleviation programme till the launching of the seventh five-year plan (1974-79). Even after the reforms took place and state-control was lessened, the advantages of growth did not reach the low-income groups. Owing to the fact that the elasticity of poverty to non-farm output has been found to be high in all the states in India (Datt and Ravallion,2002), the traditionally backward states like Bihar, Uttar Pradesh, Madhya Pradesh, Orissa did not exhibit pro-poor growth due to their slow pace of growth of non-farm output. Another proof of structural deficiency can be found in the fact that employment shares of agriculture declined at a much lower pace as compared to its income share in most of the states over the years (Sinha, 2023). Against this backdrop this study looks into the poverty situation across major states in India by considering both absolute and relative measures with the help of unit level data from different rounds of survey by National Sample Survey Office (NSSO). We have also attempted to focus on the nature of relationship between economic growth and poverty in India during the high growth regime since the early 1990s. A detailed study of the actual poverty scenario of India, to supplement the official poverty figures reported by the government, will be a valuable addition to the data and literature repository across all libraries in the country. The chapter is structured as follows: Section 1 describes the introduction of the chapter. Section 2 deals with the motivation of the study. Section 3 presents the background of the study which explains the different ways in which poverty is measured, in the context of the Indian economy. This section also discusses the data and methodology and section 4 analyses all the estimated results. Section 5 describes the future research directions and section 6 concludes the study.

MOTIVATION OF STUDY

India has achieved high rates of economic growth during the post-reform period, but the number of poor remains high even today (Jaiswal and Sinha, 2023). The challenge of poverty reduction still remains a key policy concern. Official measures of poverty in India estimate absolute poverty in terms of Head-Count Ratio (HCR) of poverty. However, HCR, as a measure of poverty, as we elaborate later on in the methodology section, has a number of drawbacks. In this study, therefore, we make use of official poverty lines to calculate not only the rate of poverty but also the depth and severity of poverty in India across the major states (Jaiswal et al., 2023). We have also attempted to estimate the relative poverty across the same states and population sub-groups. In this particular study, we will look whether the claim by the Government that poverty has substantially decreased in the post-reform period is actually true in terms of the relative poverty measures.

BACKGROUND OF THE WORK

Measuring Poverty

Poverty is conventionally defined as “pronounced deprivation in well-being.” There are two broad concepts of poverty that are being utilized by researchers around the world. One is the concept of absolute poverty, which is the lack of one or more basic needs over a period long enough that it endangers one's life. It is the absence of financial resources required to maintain a certain minimal standard of living (Fields, 2000). The other is the concept of relative poverty. It is concerned with how well-off an individual is, with respect to others in the same society. Absolute poverty is characterized by a sharp division of the income status of the poor and the non-poor. It also accepts income or consumption as being central to the concept of poverty. On the other hand, a relative poverty line is set at a constant proportion of the mean or median income in a country (Gupta et al., 2023). Each country has its own individual relative poverty line, in terms of its own currency which changes as income changes. Relative poverty lines thus classify people in society into two groups, those who are relatively disadvantaged to the rest of the population. A minimum threshold variable is fixed below which people are considered to be poor. If the income of every person in a society increases homogenously, relative poverty does not change since the poverty threshold will increase, but the proportion of poor will remain the same. Relative poverty lines, therefore, do not consider any biological norm to estimate poverty. Rather, they give more importance to the income distribution pattern prevalent in a society. The poverty line is conventionally measured in terms of biological considerations related to the requirements of survival. This approach to poverty measurement relates primarily to the concept of absolute poverty (Kumar et al., 2023). Poverty is defined based on the basic needs a person has to meet in order to survive adequately in a society. Basic needs are defined in several countries in terms of the minimum intake of calories and proteins a person needs to survive. However, this approach has been recently criticized. There are several technical problems with this approach. The biological approach defines poverty in terms of minimum nutritional requirements. When the nutritional requirements are translated into food requirements, it depends on the choice of commodities. Choosing a minimum cost diet for meeting specified nutritional requirements from food items, which are sold at different prices, is a difficult exercise (Karmakar et al., 2022). Actual incomes at which the nutritional requirements are met depends on the consumption habits of the people. Minimum consumption requirements are difficult to specify for non-food requirements. Physical features, climatic conditions and work habits vary among people. Nutritional requirements are also difficult to define precisely. Therefore, the concept of minimum nutritional requirement is arbitrary and varies between groups and regions. Despite these drawbacks, the biological approach cannot be discarded altogether. According to Sen (1993), nutritional standards are vague, but the concept of poverty is also vague itself. Also, to check whether an individual is meeting the required minimum nutritional standard, one just needs to examine the direct nutritional information obtained from the sample surveys of consumption bundles without collecting any information about the income level. This means that the measurement of poverty by this method is not that tedious a task. Moreover, since malnutrition is one of the key elements of poverty, the biological approach of measuring poverty is hard to ignore. In India, there has been great debate in methodological issues in the estimation of poverty, particularly in selecting the poverty line accurately (Sinha, 2022). The initiative in estimating poverty in a comprehensive manner by the Planning Commission was taken first during the formulation of the third five-year plan in 1962. Since then, the Planning Commission has constituted a number of Expert Groups and Working Groups to review the methodological issues in estimating poverty in India. In 1962, the Working Group recommended a consumption expenditure of Rs.100 per month in rural areas and Rs. 125 per month at 1960-61 prices in urban areas at the national level for a household of five persons to maintain the minimum balanced diet calculated by the Nutrition Advisory Group of the Indian Council of Medical Research (ICMR) in 1958. In this formulation of fixing the poverty line, expenditures on health and education were excluded. In July 1977, the Planning Commission constituted the Task Force on "Projections of Minimum Needs and Effective Consumption Demand" under the Chairmanship of Alagh. The Task Force estimated the poverty line separately for the rural and urban areas at the national level in terms of average calorie requirement as a population weighted average of the all-India average of the age-gender-activity specific calorie allowances recommended by the Nutrition Expert Group (1968) by taking the 1971 population census as reference. The estimated calorie norm was calculated at 2400 kcal per capita per day in rural areas and 2100 kcal per capita per day in urban areas. In monetary terms, the estimated average consumption expenditure was Rs.49.09 per capita per month in rural areas and Rs.56.64 per capita per month in urban areas. The 28th Round (1973-74) NSS data relating to household consumption was used to convert the calorie requirements into monetary units. For later years, the poverty line was estimated by updating the poverty lines for the 1973-74 prices. To estimate the percentage of persons living below the poverty line, the Task Force used the percentage distribution of persons in different expenditure classes in the NSS data on household consumption expenditure. Then, the NSS distribution of private consumption was adjusted pro- rata to correspond to the consumption estimates of National Accounts Statistics (NAS) made by the Central Statistical Organization (CSO). The poverty line was defined at the national level separately for rural and urban areas. However, the adjustment between the NSS and NAS data on a pro-rata basis across all expenditure classes has been debated mainly because of the discrepancy between NSS and NAS estimates. Also, applying a single poverty line for all the states assumes the absence of price differentials across the states. This methodology also assumed a fixed consumption basket of the poor overtime and a uniform consumption basket for all the states. As a result, the Planning Commission constituted an Expert Group under the Chairmanship of Prof. D.T. Lakdawala to revisit the method of poverty estimation. The Expert Group retained the poverty line at the national level in the rural and urban division but disaggregated these poverty lines into the state-specific poverty lines by taking inter-state price differentials measured by the Fisher's Index. These state-specific poverty lines of base (1973-74) were updated for the later years by taking weighted average of the commodity group-wise Consumer Price Index for Agricultural Labourers (CPIAL) (for rural) and Consumer Price Index for Industrial Workers (CPIIW) (for urban). The distribution of consumption expenditure from the NSS survey was used to calculate the state-specific distribution of persons by expenditure groups, without adjustment to the NAS. The Planning Commission estimated poverty by using the Lakdawala methodology until January 2011. However, the poverty line used in this methodology was estimated using data from a survey of consumer behavior conducted in 1973-74 by the NSSO and updating it with price indices for latter periods. The poverty lines obtained in this way have been criticized for being too low and for focusing exclusively on food consumption norms with no allowance being made for expenditure on, inter alia, health, education and other basic needs. Now, recognizing the need to address the issues of insufficiency of official poverty estimates, the Planning Commission in December,2005, appointed an Expert Group under the Chairmanship of Late Prof. Suresh D. Tendulkar to review the alternate concepts of poverty lines and to recommend changes in the existing procedure used for estimating poverty. The Expert Group, however, did not construct a new poverty line but converted the officially measured poverty line of 2004-05 by the Lakdawala methodology by taking relevant information on the basis of Mixed Recall Period (MRP) consumption, where unlike the Uniform Recall Period (30 days recall periods for all items of consumption), consumption expenditure data are collected using 365-day recall period for five non-food items and 30- day recall period for remaining items. The Tendulkar methodology took an indirect approach of fixing the poverty line. It did not peg the poverty line to a calorie norm. Rather, it started with the official urban poverty ratio of 25.7 derived using the Lakdawala methodology as an agreed upon incidence of poor in the urban areas. Then, it worked backwards and estimated the MRP based poverty line as the level of per capita consumption expenditure that corresponds to the bottom 25.7 of the population. One important criticism of this methodology is that the Expert Group claimed that the people around the poverty line can afford a consumption expenditure which is equal to 2100 calorie per capita but their observed calorie intake is around 1776 calorie per capita, which is very close to a norm of 1770 calorie recommended by the Food and Agriculture Organization (FAO) for 2003-05. However, the standards for energy requirement released by the FAO are the minimum dietary energy requirement which is the amount of energy needed to perform light and sedentary activities. Anyone who has seen how hard the poor toil for their paltry wages will see the absurdity of this assumption. However, discontinuing the norm of anchoring poverty lines to calorie intake requirements went against an established view and there was a huge controversy that many people who deserve public support would remain excluded, particularly in urban areas, if the Planning Commission used the Tendulkar estimates to calculate the number of people who are entitled to government benefits. As a result, the Planning Commission constituted another expert committee to deal with the crisis. The Rangarajan Committee was constituted in May,2012 with C. Rangarajan as Chair to revisit the issue of poverty measurement. The Rangarajan methodology discards the approach of starting with a poverty ratio and then arriving at a commodity basket. Rather, it marks a return to a calorie-anchored commodity basket norm. A novelty of the Rangarajan methodology is computing the poverty line commodity basket by combining items from two fractile groups- one set is determined from a fractile group associated with the average calorie, protein and fat requirements and the other set consists of four essential non-food items, based on a relative norm (behavior of the median fractile group. Also, this methodology computes poverty by making use of the modified mixed recall period (MMRP) for various items of consumption. Under the MMRP, data was collected on the basis of weekly recall for some high frequency food items, annual recall for five low frequency items and monthly recall for all other items of consumption. Experts are of the view that the mix of reference periods for different items under the MMRP estimates may be expected to yield estimates that are closer to their "true value". These factors made the choice of recall period in favour of MMRP by the Rangarajan Expert Group. However, the Rangarajan method also has its own share of criticisms. The treatment of the non-food items is problematic conceptually. It causes the norm poverty line basket to differ from the actual and also impairs the welfare proposition implied by the Tendulkar methodology that poverty lines in different places should allow the same poverty line basket to be affordable everywhere. The restoration of the link between poverty line and calorie norm is a positive step forward but the committee does not provide any justification regarding lowering the rural daily calorie requirement from 2400 kcals to 2155 kcals. It cites changing lifestyle as the sole reason. Sen (2005), however, argues that the intensity of labour effort has not changed for the people close to the poverty line. Therefore, lowering calorie requirements may have led to a significant understatement of poverty figures (Ray and Sinha, 2014). The period from 2004-05 to date has witnessed a severe financial crisis and global recession with a rapid rise in international and local food prices. India has also faced a moderately severe drought in 2009-10. Given this adverse situation, poverty was expected to worsen. However, the official figures claim an altogether different picture. These estimates show that poverty has declined, in both urban and rural areas, between 2004-05 and 2009-10. Official poverty lines have, over the years, underestimated the true poverty lines, permitting access to a level of nutritional intake which is continuously declining over the years. Krishnaji (2012) says that the estimated poverty rates derived from the consumer e expenditure data are arbitrary since it depends upon who is constructing the poverty line. These so-called poverty lines do not focus on the different dimensions of poverty. So, a better solution is to abolish the poverty line altogether and collect disaggregated information on parameters such as education, health, clothing, etc. which can lead to better allocation of resources for poverty alleviation programmes. In this study, we have tried to estimate relative poverty by setting the poverty line at a threshold of 70 percent of the median MPCE of the distribution of per capita expenditure of the respective social and religious population groups. People whose income falls below this poverty line face the risk of being poor. They do not have to be poor in terms of conventional calorie intake, but they find themselves placed in the lowest income group compared to the population at large. Then, we compared the figures with the official poverty figures which use an absolute poverty line to estimate poverty.

Measures To Estimate Poverty

The official measures of poverty in India focus only on the concept of absolute poverty and the measure used to estimate poverty is the Head-Count Ratio of poverty (HCR). However, there are other ways of measuring poverty too, such as Poverty Gap (PG), Squared Poverty Gap (SPG), the Foster-Greer Thorbecke (FGT) measure of poverty and Sen's index(S)[1]. The HCR measures the rate of poverty or the incidence of poverty i.e. the share of the population whose income or expenditure falls below the defined poverty line. It is defined as:

$$HCR=H/P \quad \text{(i)}$$

Here H: number of people below the poverty line and P: total population. Despite being simple to construct and interpret, it suffers from the disadvantage of being insensitive to changes in income below the poverty line. Poverty Gap, on the other hand, shows the depth of poverty.

$$PG = 1/N\left\{\sum_{i=1}^{H}\left(\left(Y_p - Y_i\right)/Y_p\right)\right\} \quad \text{(ii)}$$

where Y_i: income of the ith poor, Y_p: poverty line, N= total population

It shows the average, over the entire population, of the proportionate gaps between poor people's income and the poverty line. However, PG as an indicator of poverty is not perfect. It ignores the inequality among the poor themselves, which implies that it does not indicate the severity of poverty. Squared Poverty Gap is a normalized weighted sum of squares of the poverty gaps of the population. It gives the highest weightage to the largest poverty gaps and helps in calculating the inequality among the poor. In spite of being the most superior of all the three poverty indices that are mentioned above, SPG is not very widely used since it lacks intuitive appeal and is not very easy to interpret. It can be estimated in the following way:

$$SPG = 1/N\left[\sum_{i=1}^{H}\left\{\frac{\left(Y_p - Y_i\right)}{Y_p}\right\}^2\right] \quad \text{(iii)}$$

All the three indices of poverty mentioned above are the first three measures of the Foster-Greer-Thorbecke (FGT) class of poverty measures. The general formula for this class of poverty measure depends on a parameter α.

$$\text{FGT} = 1/N\left[\sum_{i=1}^{H}\left\{\frac{(Y_P - Y_i)}{Y_P}\right\}^{\alpha}\right] \text{(iv)}$$

α takes a value of 0 for HCR, 1 for PG and 2 for SPG in the above equation. α can be interpreted as an indicator of poverty aversion and also as the elasticity of individual poverty with respect to the normalized poverty gap, so that a percent increase in the poverty gap of a poor person leads to α percent increase in the individual's level of poverty. The most important advantage of FGT as a measure of poverty is that larger values of α place higher weight on the poverty gaps of poor people. In this case, it overcomes the most important drawback of the poverty gap index of not reflecting the severity of poverty among the poor. The FGT Index has sound axiomatic properties such as:

- **Additivity:** By additivity, we mean that the poverty measure for the entire population is equal to the weighted sum of the poverty measures for the population sub-groups. Here the weights are equal to their proportionate share of the total population. The property of additivity makes it feasible to analyze the contribution of each sub-group to the overall poverty situation.
- **Monotonicity:**_The decomposition property shows that the FGT index also satisfies the property of monotonicity. Monotonicity implies that a fall in a poor person's income, keeping other peoples' incomes constant, increases the poverty index.

Since we intend to estimate relative poverty levels across the various groups of population, a measure satisfying the property of additive decomposability is very much applicable and will assist us in identifying the factors that contribute to poverty. Moreover, the FGT measure also satisfies the property of subgroup monotonicity or subgroup consistency. Sen's index violates this property while all of the FGT measures satisfy both the properties of additivity and subgroup consistency. There have been very few studies that have focused on the concept of relative poverty and have estimated poverty rates by using the relative poverty lines. Das (2015), by using the 61st and 66th round NSS data, has focused on the incidence, depth and severity of poverty, on the basis of relative poverty lines at 75 and 50 percent of the median value of the distribution of per capita expenditure of the respective population sub-groups. On the basis of his findings, he has concluded that inequality in the urban regions of India has increased post the economic reforms that took place in 1991. Sharpe (2001) has estimated relative poverty for the working population in the OECD countries. Working poor households are defined as those with at least one member reporting some kind of labour income during an accounting year. To the best of our search, we have found no study in the Indian context, that has estimated all the three different measures of poverty, using both absolute and relative poverty lines.

DATA AND METHODOLOGY

The study is based mainly on unit level data from household consumer expenditure survey conducted by the NSSO. For our analysis, we have used data from Schedule 1 from 50th (July,1993-June,1994), 55th (July,1999-June,2000), 61st (July 2004-June 2005), 66th (July, 2009-June, 2010) and the 68th (July,2011-June,2012) NSSO rounds. The NSSO has been conducting all-India surveys quinquennially on consumer expenditure and employment and unemployment. The results of these surveys are released under different reports. The information reported under these surveys is collected under different reference periods according to which the reports are divided under two schedules. In this study, we have made use of Type I information which uses the last 30 and 365-days reference period for clothing, other durable goods, bedding, education and medical expenses and a 30 day reference period for all other expenses. For the purpose of our analysis, we have estimated the FGT index for each of India's 22 major states at α=0, 1 and 2 separately, for the rural and urban regions in India. The index has been calculated for both the official poverty lines and the poverty lines at 70 percent median expenditure of the respective population group. We make a comparison of the relative poverty estimates with the estimates calculated with the help of the official absolute poverty lines. We have gone a little beyond the head count ratio (HCR) and calculated the poverty gap (PG) and the squared poverty gap index (SPG) as well, for both the absolute and the relative poverty lines. Moreover, the official estimates have used the Tendulkar methodology which uses a Mixed Reference Period (MRP). This implies that our estimates may differ a little from the official ones (absolute estimates) at the value of α=0 since we have considered the value of MPCE, estimated on the basis of a uniform recall period (URP). Data on per capita net state domestic product (PNSDP) is collected from the Handbook of Statistics on the Indian economy published by the Reserve Bank of India (RBI).

RESULTS AND ANALYSIS

Poverty estimates across the major 22 states of India have been calculated, separately for the urban and the rural areas. Prices differ across states and also between rural and urban regions within the same state. Therefore, we have separate poverty lines for each state, for the urban and the rural regions. The results are given in the tables below.

Table 1. Comparison of absolute poverty estimates in the rural areas by states

State	1993-94			1999-2000			2011-12		
	HCR	PG	SPG	HCR	PG	SPG	HCR	PG	SPG
Jammu & Kashmir	0.32	0.07	0.02	-	-	-	0.11	0.02	**0**
Himachal Pradesh	0.41	0.09	0.03	0.8	0.01	0	0.11	0.01	**0**
Punjab	0.2	0.06	0.02	0.06	0.01	0	0.08	0.01	**0**
Uttaranchal	-	-	-	-	-	-	0.12	0.02	**0**
Haryana	0.44	0.12	0.05	0.08	0.01	0	0.1	0.02	**0**
Delhi	0.15	0.03	0.01	0.01	0	0	0.12	0.01	**0**
Rajasthan	0.4	0.12	0.04	0.13	0.02	0.01	0.16	0.04	**0.01**
Uttar Pradesh	0.52	0.15	0.06	0.31	0.06	0.02	0.3	0.06	**0.02**
Bihar	0.69	0.2	0.08	0.44	0.09	0.03	0.3	0.06	**0.02**
Assam	0.63	0.15	0.05	0.4	0.08	0.03	0.34	0.06	**0.02**
West Bengal	0.43	0.1	0.03	0.32	0.06	0.02	0.24	0.04	**0.01**
Jharkhand	-	-	-	-	-	-	0.39	0.08	**0.02**
Orissa	0.63	0.17	0.07	0.48	0.12	0.04	0.37	0.08	**0.03**
Chattisgarh	-	-	-	-	-	-	0.49	0.12	**0.04**
Madhya Pradesh	0.49	0.16	0.06	0.37	0.08	0.02	0.33	0.08	**0.03**
Gujarat	0.53	0.14	0.05	0.12	0.02	0.01	0.24	0.03	**0**
Maharashtra	0.61	0.2	0.09	0.23	0.04	0.01	0.26	0.05	**0.02**
Andhra Pradesh	0.5	0.13	0.05	0.11	0.02	0.01	0.12	0.02	**0**
Karnataka	0.61	0.18	0.07	0.17	0.03	0.01	0.28	0.05	**0.01**
Goa	0.26	0.08	0.03	-	-	-	0.01	0	**0**
Kerala	0.38	0.1	0.03	0.09	0.01	0	0.12	0.02	**0**
Tamil Nadu	0.54	0.15	0.06	0.2	0.04	0.01	0.18	0.03	**0**
All-India	**0.55**	**0.16**	**0.06**	**0.27**	**0.05**	**0.02**	**0.25**	**0.05**	**0.02**

According to the absolute poverty estimates in Table 1, there has been a decrease in the rate of poverty across all the states taken into consideration during the given period of time. The most drastic declines have been in Gujarat, Tamil Nadu, Bihar, Karnataka, Maharashtra and Uttar Pradesh where the poverty head-count has dropped to almost half the initial number. According to our estimates, the depth and severity of poverty has also decreased over the years. Karnataka, Maharashtra and Andhra Pradesh have experienced the sharpest fall in the poverty gap over the period of survey. The absolute estimates point out that the severity of poverty has also declined in the rural areas for all the states. Now, we need to see whether a similar scenario is replicated in the urban areas as well. Also, there is a need to compare these absolute declines in poverty rates with the relative rates.

Table 2. Comparison of absolute poverty estimates in the urban areas by states

State	1993-94			1999-2000			2011-12		
	HCR	PG	SPG	HCR	PG	SPG	HCR	PG	SPG
Jammu & Kashmir	0.09	0.01	0	-	-	-	0.09	0.01	**0**
Himachal Pradesh	0.16	0.04	0.01	0.05	0.1	0	0.05	0.01	**0**
Punjab	0.3	0.06	0.02	0.06	0.01	0	0.12	0.02	**0.01**
Uttaranchal	-	-	-	-	-	-	0.15	0.02	**0.01**
Haryana	0.27	0.06	0.02	0.1	0.02	0.01	0.1	0.02	**0**
Delhi	0.17	0.04	0.02	0.09	0.02	0	0.1	0.02	**0**
Rajasthan	0.32	0.09	0.03	0.19	0.03	0.01	0.1	0.02	**0**
Uttar Pradesh	0.41	0.11	0.04	0.31	0.07	0.02	0.26	0.06	**0.02**
Bihar	0.46	0.11	0.04	0.33	0.07	0.02	0.29	0.07	**0.02**
Assam	0.28	0.06	0.02	0.07	0.02	0	0.2	0.04	**0.01**
West Bengal	0.31	0.08	0.03	0.15	0.03	0.01	0.16	0.03	**0.01**
Jharkhand	-	-	-	-	-	-	0.24	0.06	**0.02**
Orissa	0.34	0.09	0.03	0.44	0.11	0.04	0.2	0.04	**0.01**
Chattisgarh	-	-	-	-	-	-	0.3	0.06	**0.02**
Madhya Pradesh	0.36	0.09	0.03	0.38	0.1	0.03	0.2	0.04	**0.01**
Gujarat	0.34	0.08	0.03	0.15	0.02	0.01	0.11	0.02	**0**
Maharashtra	0.33	0.1	0.04	0.27	0.07	0.02	0.1	0.02	**0**
Andhra Pradesh	0.38	0.09	0.03	0.27	0.06	0.02	0.07	0.01	**0**
Karnataka	0.39	0.1	0.03	0.25	0.06	0.02	0.17	0.04	**0.01**
Goa	0.18	0.03	0.01	-	-	-	0.02	0	**0**
Kerala	0.24	0.06	0.02	0.2	0.04	0.01	0.07	0.02	**0**
Tamil Nadu	0.35	0.09	0.03	0.22	0.05	0.02	0.07	0.01	**0**
All-India	**0.35**	**0.09**	**0.03**	**0.24**	**0.05**	**0.02**	**0.14**	**0.03**	**0.01**

Table 2 shows the rates of absolute poverty across the states in the urban areas. In the urban areas too, HCR has reduced in most of the states. The southern states of Kerala, Tamil Nadu and Andhra Pradesh have performed really well in terms of reduction in the headcount ratio of poverty. In absolute terms, most of them have recorded a fall in the depth and the severity of poverty as well. However, there are some exceptions as well. In Karnataka, the depth of poverty has risen with time, but the severity has decreased. On the other hand, in Kerala, although the severity of poverty has remained unchanged over the years, the poverty gap has widened. In Jammu and Kashmir, all the three poverty measures have remained approximately the same. This shows that growth has not driven substantial reduction in absolute poverty rates in the urban regions of the state. Another reason might be the political situation in Kashmir, which is always in a state of turmoil. Uttar Pradesh and Bihar are the two states which have performed extremely well in the period between 1999-2000 to 2011-12. Absolute poverty rates have dipped drastically between these years. On the other hand, West Bengal has not been able to perform up-to- the-mark between 1999-2000 to 2011-12. Not only has the poverty gap and the squared poverty gap remained the same, but the headcount ratio has also increased slightly. At the all-India level, all the three poverty estimates have experienced a fall from their initial levels. Now, we will compare the relative estimates of poverty across the states over the same period of time.

Table 3. Comparison of relative poverty estimates in the rural areas by states

State	1993-94			1999-2000			2011-12		
	HCR	PG	SPG	HCR	PG	SPG	HCR	PG	SPG
Jammu &Kashmir	0.17	0.03	0.01	-	-	-	0.19	0.04	**0.01**
Himachal Pradesh	0.18	0.03	0.01	0.16	0.02	0.01	0.21	0.04	**0.01**
Punjab	0.17	0.03	0.01	0.18	0.03	0.01	0.18	0.03	**0.01**
Uttaranchal	-	-	-	-	-	-	0.16	0.02	**0**
Haryana	0.25	0.05	0.02	0.22	0.04	0.01	0.22	0.05	**0.02**
Delhi	0.2	0.05	0.02	0.18	0.03	0.01	0.25	0.06	**0.02**
Rajasthan	0.18	0.03	0.01	0.14	0.02	0.01	0.17	0.04	**0.01**
Uttar Pradesh	0.21	0.04	0.01	0.16	0.02	0.01	0.18	0.03	**0.01**
Bihar	0.15	0.02	0.01	0.13	0.02	0	0.16	0.03	**0.01**
Assam	0.11	0.01	0	0.15	0.03	0.01	0.11	0.02	**0**
West Bengal	0.14	0.02	0.01	0.17	0.03	0	0.17	0.03	**0.01**
Jharkhand	-	-	-	-	-	-	0.15	0.02	**0.01**
Orissa	0.16	0.03	0.01	0.18	0.03	0.01	0.17	0.03	**0.01**
Chattisgarh	-	-	-	-	-	-	0.15	0.02	**0.01**
Madhya Pradesh	0.19	0.04	0.01	0.17	0.03	0.01	0.21	0.04	**0.01**
Gujarat	0.18	0.03	0.01	0.18	0.03	0.01	0.2	0.03	**0.01**
Maharashtra	0.22	0.05	0.02	0.2	0.03	0.01	0.18	0.04	**0.01**
Andhra Pradesh	0.19	0.04	0.01	0.15	0.02	0.01	0.19	0.03	**0.01**
Karnataka	0.19	0.04	0.01	0.16	0.03	0.01	0.15	0.02	**0.01**
Goa	0.24	0.05	0.01	-	-	-	0.26	0.04	**0.01**
Kerala	0.22	0.04	0.01	0.19	0.04	0.01	0.25	0.05	**0.02**
Tamil Nadu	0.2	0.04	0.01	0.19	0.04	0.01	0.19	0.03	**0.01**
All-India	**0.2**	**0.04**	**0.01**	**0.19**	**0.03**	**0.01**	**0.21**	**0.04**	**0.01**

Table 3 shows that the relative estimates, unlike the absolute ones, record a rise during the same time period. Although the all-India HCR has remained unchanged, the incidence of poverty has increased in states such as West Bengal, Bihar, Kerala and Gujarat among others. In the other states, HCR has either reduced or remained unchanged. The performance of Kerala and Gujarat is really surprising. Kerala is one of the states where the literacy rate is quite high, and Gujarat is one of the states which has a high economic growth rate. Growth and education are the two prime factors which can contribute immensely to reducing poverty. So, there is definitely a need to identify the factors which have contributed to an increasing relative poverty in these two states. The depth of relative poverty has increased, and the severity has remained unchanged in most of the states. In spite of a reduction in the rate of poverty in the rural areas of Haryana, the poverty gap and the severity of poverty have remained unchanged. Quite similar is the case of Rajasthan. HCR has decreased slightly but the depth of poverty has increased, and its severity has remained the same. The rural regions of Gujarat remain unaffected by the growth that has taken place in the state and the country as a whole, which implies that the poverty rates have not changed much in the state. Maharashtra is the only state where all the three relative rates have reduced over the years.

Table 4. Comparison of relative poverty estimates in the urban areas by states

State	1993-94			1999-2000			2011-12		
	HCR	PG	SPG	HCR	PG	SPG	HCR	PG	SPG
Jammu & Kashmir	0.18	0.03	0.01	-	-	-	0.25	0.05	**0.02**
Himachal Pradesh	0.24	0.05	0.01	0.22	0.05	0.02	0.27	0.08	**0.03**
Punjab	0.24	0.04	0.01	0.24	0.04	0.01	0.26	0.07	**0.02**
Uttaranchal	-	-	-	-	-	-	0.3	0.06	**0.02**
Haryana	0.19	0.03	0.01	0.24	0.06	0.02	0.31	0.07	**0.03**
Delhi	0.34	0.1	0.04	0.25	0.07	0.02	0.28	0.07	**0.03**
Rajasthan	0.21	0.04	0.01	0.17	0.03	0.01	0.21	0.05	**0.01**
Uttar Pradesh	0.24	0.05	0.02	0.24	0.05	0.01	0.24	0.05	**0.01**
Bihar	0.18	0.04	0.01	0.2	0.04	0.01	0.27	0.06	**0.02**
Assam	0.22	0.03	0.01	0.26	0.05	0.02	0.24	0.06	**0.02**
West Bengal	0.04	0.05	0.02	0.24	0.04	0.01	0.3	0.08	**0.03**
Jharkhand	-	-	-	-	-	-	0.3	0.08	**0.03**
Orissa	0.26	0.06	0.02	0.22	0.04	0.01	0.3	0.07	**0.02**
Chhattisgarh	-	-	-	-	-	-	0.31	0.07	**0.02**
Madhya Pradesh	0.23	0.05	0.01	0.24	0.05	0.01	0.24	0.05	**0.01**
Gujarat	0.2	0.04	0.01	0.21	0.04	0.01	0.26	0.06	**0.02**
Maharashtra	0.28	0.08	0.03	0.26	0.06	0.02	0.23	0.05	**0.02**
Andhra Pradesh	0.22	0.05	0.01	0.23	0.04	0.01	0.26	0.06	**0.02**
Karnataka	0.26	0.06	0.02	0.25	0.06	0.02	0.3	0.07	**0.03**
Goa	0.24	0.04	0.01	-	-	-	0.22	0.06	**0.02**
Kerala	0.22	0.05	0.02	0.25	0.05	0.02	0.28	0.06	**0.02**
Tamil Nadu	0.22	0.05	0.02	0.25	0.06	0.02	0.26	0.06	**0.02**
All-India	**0.24**	**0.05**	**0.02**	**0.25**	**0.06**	**0.02**	**0.28**	**0.07**	**0.03**

According to Table 4, in the urban areas, the relative poverty incidence has increased in all the states except Delhi, Maharashtra and Goa, where it has decreased and in Rajasthan and Uttar Pradesh, where the HCR has remained unchanged. The poverty gap too, has increased with time in most of the states. However, between 1999 and 2012, the poverty gap increased again. Bihar and Haryana are two of the worst performing states. They have not only recorded a high increase in relative HCR but an increase in the poverty gap as well as the squared poverty gap. Jammu and Kashmir and Haryana have experienced massive increases in relative incidence of poverty. In the urban areas, Madhya Pradesh has shown no substantial rise or fall in poverty rates. On the other hand, Karnataka, which performed really well in the urban areas in terms of absolute estimates, shows a rise in all the relative measures of poverty. Also, unlike the absolute estimates, at the all-India level, relative poverty increases within the stipulated time period.

Estimating the Growth Elasticity of Poverty

Debates over the effect of growth on poverty have been going on for many years. This debate originated when Chenery and Ahluwalia (1974) criticized the trickle-down hypothesis, according to which, the positive effects of growth of an economy benefits the poorest of the population. However, back in the 1970s, adequate cross-country data was not available. In the 1990s, when cross-country data again became available, it revived the interest around the question of when and how growth can benefit the poor and its policy implications. Majority of the empirical evidence suggests that there is ample variation in poverty reducing the effect of a given growth rate across countries. A widely used measure used in the growth-poverty literature is the Growth Elasticity of Poverty (GEP). This measure gives the percentage change of a selected poverty measure in response to a percentage change in GDP or mean income. If the growth elasticity of poverty is negative, it implies that the poor people are benefitting more proportionally from growth, the process of growth will be pro-poor. If the absolute value of the elasticity is quite high, then poverty reduction strategies relying on economic growth are more justified. Otherwise, poverty reduction strategies might need a balanced combination of both growth and redistribution. Mathematically,

$$\text{GEP} = -\left[\frac{\%change\ in\ PR}{\%change\ in\ y}\right] \text{(v)}$$

where PR is the poverty measure and y is the per capita income. There are three approaches of estimating the GEP. The first approach is to use the information on poverty, inequality and per capita income and run the regressions on the log variables to extract the elasticities. The co-efficients of the regression analysis give the required elasticities. This method is generally used in cross-country studies. The second method uses the ratios of changes in poverty to changes in growth over a given period as a measure of the elasticity of poverty with respect to growth (Ravallion, 2000). Another approach is based on the decomposition of a poverty measure into two elements, namely, growth and inequality (Datt and Ravallion, 1992; Bourguignon, 2004). The last method provides a measure of point elasticity while the other two methods provide an average measure of elasticity. The fragmentation of a poverty measure into the components of growth and inequality that proposed by Datt and Ravallion (1992) was further developed by Kakwani (1993). He gave importance to percentage changes in poverty and income and ignored the absolute changes. In this case, its relative contribution could be interpreted as elasticities of poverty with respect to a one percentage change in growth. This measure aimed at analyzing how pro-poor a certain growth process was, rather than determining if a growth process was actually pro-poor or not. Assuming a log-normal distribution, Klassen and Misselhorn (2008) investigated the mathematical relation between economic growth and change in income distribution on absolute changes in the measures of poverty (HCR, PG and SPG). They coined the relation as semi-elasticity of growth and distribution change on poverty. They also tested the empirical relationship of the estimated semi-elasticities and found them to be better at explaining poverty changes than the concept of growth elasticity of poverty. In our study, we have used monthly per capita expenditure as a proxy for poverty rate and carried out a panel regression analysis. We have tried to show the effect that a growth in the per capita NSDP value has on the consumption expenditure. In this study, the growth poverty relationship has been estimated in a panel data frame with data from 25 Indian states for 5 different year's corresponding to NSS rounds on household consumer expenditure survey. The panel data provides more variability, more degrees of freedom and lesser collinearity. The model used for this study is:

$$\log P_{it} = \mu_i + \beta \log y_{it} + \varepsilon_{it} \text{ (vi)}$$

Here, P_{it} is the poverty ratio taken from official estimates in state i (1, 2,…25) and time t (1993. 1999, 2004, 2009, 2011), y_{it} denotes per head net state domestic product at constant price, μi is unobserved heterogeneous state specific fixed effect. The fixed effect measures the impact of other unobserved factors (other than economic growth) on poverty reduction. The coefficient β measures growth elasticity of poverty. We have selected the fixed effect model by carrying out Hausman test. The Hausman test is a useful device for determining the preferred specification of the common effects model. It is used to test the orthogonality of the common effects and the regressors. The Hausman test tests whether the random effect estimates would be appropriate for a model and data in which fixed effect estimates are applicable. In this particular test, the null hypothesis is that μi are distributed independently of yit. If the null hypothesis is true, then both the random and fixed effect estimates are considered to be consistent. However, fixed effect will be inefficient. If the null hypothesis is incorrect, the random effect estimates will face unobserved heterogeneity bias and will thus differ from the fixed effect estimates. The results are specified below:

Table 5. Regression results

Estimated Co-Efficient	Rural Poverty	Urban Poverty	Combined Poverty
β	-0.21	-0.09**	-0.28
Fixed Effect			
Andhra Pradesh	4.97	3.88	5.73
Arunachal Pradesh	5.74	3.64	6.34
Assam	5.71	3.59	6.30
Bihar	5.80	4.43	6.39
Goa	4.28	3.38	5.35
Gujarat	5.33	3.82	5.95
Haryana	5.03	3.71	5.74
Himachal Pradesh	4.79	1.66*	5.45
Jammu & Kashmir	4.49	2.87	5.10
Karnataka	5.42	4.12	6.09
Kerala	4.82	3.60	5.52
Madhya Pradesh	5.78	4.36	6.38
Maharashtra	5.67	4.02	6.25
Manipur	5.80	3.89	6.32
Meghalaya	5.20	3.47	5.86
Mizoram	5.66	3.02	5.82
Nagaland	5.32	3.26	5.94
Orissa	5.88	4.35	6.50
Punjab	4.63	3.41	5.36
Rajasthan	5.20	3.95	5.86
Sikkim	5.39	3.01	5.99
Tamil Nadu	5.37	3.80	5.94
Tripura	5.51	3.22	6.06
Uttar Pradesh	5.78	4.40	6.45
West Bengal	5.57	3.88	6.13
No. of Observations	125	125	125
R^2	0.98	0.96	0.98
Adjusted R^2	0.98	0.95	0.98

Note: *,** and *** indicate significance at the 10%, 5% and 1% level respectively.

The figures shown in the lower panel of Table 5 are useful to judge the goodness of fit of the model we have used in our empirical exercise. The value of adjusted R^2 is very high for urban, rural as well as combined poverty. This means that the explanatory variables significantly explain the variation in the poverty rates. As is evident, the growth elasticity of poverty is insignificant in rural areas while it is significant in urban areas. The negative sign of the coefficient of yit implies that the higher the economic growth, lower will be the incidence of poverty. One percent growth in per capita

NSDP does not make any significant dent on rural poverty. However, the same amount of growth has a considerable effect on poverty reduction in the urban areas as well as on poverty in the entire state. We have estimated the unobservable state-specific effects by applying the least square dummy variable (LSDV) model. The fixed effect captures the impact of other unobserved factors, other than the growth rate, on poverty. Unobserved factors are those which are not used in this model. They may be state specific or household specific. The state level factors that have effect on poverty are the literacy rate, rural infrastructure like irrigation, other infrastructures like road density, availability of power and so on. The effects vary across the states in India over the period from 1993 to 2011.

FUTURE RESEARCH DIRECTIONS

Our future course of study would be in the direction of exploring the concept of growth elasticity of poverty further. A study based on the country-wise comparison along with an investigation into the preconditions that determine the value of the elasticity will have important policy implications. Economists and policymakers will be able to devise and implement better pro-poor growth strategies if they are able to analyse the actual factors that contribute to poverty reduction.

CONCLUSION

This study is an attempt to investigate how poverty levels, both absolute and relative, in the major states of India, have responded to the economic growth that took place following the reforms of the 1990s. The official statistics only give us information on the incidence of poverty across the states. They do not enlighten us on the depth and severity of poverty in the country. Moreover, official poverty measures are absolute measures. We have shed light upon the relative poverty situation in the country too. Apart from this, we have also estimated the relation between growth and poverty through a regression analysis and arrived at the conclusion that growth in NSDP has failed to reduce poverty in the rural regions substantially.

ACKNOWLEDGMENT

I would like to express my gratitude to Dr. Panchanan Das, Associate Professor of Economics, University of Calcutta, whose guidance, encouragement and support was of immense help to me. I am very grateful to my friends at the Department of Economics, University of Calcutta, for their immense help in dealing with the software packages used in the due course of my research work. Finally, I would like to thank my family. Had it not been for their encouraging words, I would not have been able to deal with the immense pressure that any research work demands.

REFERENCES

Ahluwalia, M. S., & Chenery, H. (1974). Redistribution with Growth: The Economic Framework. In *Milestones and Turning Points in Development Thinking* (pp. 135–147). Palgrave Macmillan UK.

Bourguignon, F. (2004). *The poverty-growth-inequality triangle* (No. 125). Working Paper.

Das, P. (2015). Non-income Dimensions, Prevalence, Depth and Severity of Poverty: Spatial Estimation with Household-Level Data in India. In A. Heshmati, E. Maasoumi, & G. Wan (Eds.), *Economic Studies in Inequality, Social Exclusion, and Well-Being, Poverty Reduction Policies and Practices in Developing Asia* (pp. 187–203). Springer. doi:10.1007/978-981-287-420-7_10

Datt, G., & Ravallion, M. (1992). Growth and redistribution components of changes in poverty measures: A decomposition with applications to Brazil and India in the 1980s. *Journal of Development Economics*, *38*(2), 275–295. doi:10.1016/0304-3878(92)90001-P

Fields, G. S. (2000). The dynamics of poverty, inequality and economic well-being: African economic growth in comparative perspective. *Journal of African Economies*, *9*(Supplement_1), 45–78. doi:10.1093/jafeco/9.Supplement_1.45

Foster, J., Greer, J., & Thorbecke, E. (1984). A class of decomposable poverty measures. *Econometrica*, *52*(3), 761–766. doi:10.2307/1913475

Government of India. (2009). *Report of the Expert Group to Review the Methodology for Estimation of Poverty, Press Information Bureau, Planning Commission Government of India (2012), Press Notes on Poverty Estimates 2009-10*. Press Information Bureau.

Gupta, N. E., Kumar, K., & Sinha, K. (2023). The Nexus of War, Violence, and Rights: A History of War-Torn Afghanistan. In Handbook of Research on War Policies, Strategies, and Cyber Wars (pp. 334-351). IGI Global.

Jaiswal, G., Karmakar, M., & Sinha, K. (2023). Yoga: A Stress Removal Toolkit During War From the Women's Perspective. In Acceleration of the Biopsychosocial Model in Public Health (pp. 137-167). IGI Global.

Jaiswal, G., & Sinha, K. (2023). Yoga: An Ancient Healing Approach for Cyclical Mastalgia. In Perspectives on Coping Strategies for Menstrual and Premenstrual Distress (pp. 237-261). IGI Global.

Kakwani, N. (1993). Poverty and economic growth with application to Côte d'Ivoire. *Review of Income and Wealth*, *39*(2), 121–139. doi:10.1111/j.1475-4991.1993.tb00443.x

Karmakar, M., Priya, A., Sinha, K., & Verma, M. (2022, December). Shrinkable Cryptographic Technique Using Involutory Function for Image Encryption. In *International Conference on Advanced Network Technologies and Intelligent Computing* (pp. 275-289). Cham: Springer Nature Switzerland.

Klasen, S., & Misselhorn, M. (2008). *Determinants of the growth semi-elasticity of poverty reduction* (No. 176). IAI Discussion Papers.

Krishnaji, N. (2012). Abolish the poverty line. *Economic and Political Weekly*, 10–11.

Kumar, K., Singhania, D., Singh, K. P., Mishra, P., & Sinha, K. (2023). Navigating the Economic Challenges of the Russia-Ukraine Conflict on India. In Handbook of Research on War Policies, Strategies, and Cyber Wars (pp. 218-238). IGI Global. doi:10.4018/978-1-6684-6741-1.ch012

Planning Commission Government of India. (2013). *Press Notes on Poverty Estimates 2011-12*. Press Information Bureau, Planning Commission.

Priya, A., Sharma, S., Sinha, K., & Yogesh, Y. (2023, March). Community Detection in Networks: A Comparative study. In *2023 International Conference on Device Intelligence, Computing and Communication Technologies (DICCT)* (pp. 505-510). IEEE. 10.1109/DICCT56244.2023.10110206

Ravallion, M. (2000). What is needed for a more pro-poor growth process in India? *Economic and Political Weekly*, 1089–1093.

Ravallion, M., & Datt, G. (2002). Why has economic growth been more pro-poor in some states of India than others? *Journal of Development Economics*, *68*(2), 381–400. doi:10.1016/S0304-3878(02)00018-4

Ray, R., & Sinha, K. (2014). Rangarajan committee report on poverty measurement: Another lost opportunity. *Economic and Political Weekly*, 43–48.

Sen, A. (1993). Capability and well-being. *The Quality of Life, 30*, 270-293.

Sen, A. (2005). Human rights and capabilities. *Journal of Human Development*, *6*(2), 151–166. doi:10.1080/14649880500120491

Sharpe, A. (2001). Estimates of relative and absolute poverty rates for the working population in developed countries. In Meeting of the Canadian Economics Association, Montreal, Canada.

Sinha, K. (2022). *Development of Enhanced Cryptography Based Model for Multimedia Security in Distributed Environment*. Academic Press.

Sinha, K. (2023). The Metaverse and Digital Libraries: Ensuring Safe and Secure Access to Information. In Handbook of Research on Advancements of Contactless Technology and Service Innovation in Library and Information Science (pp. 1-22). IGI Global.

KEY TERMS AND DEFINITIONS

Absolute Poverty: Absolute poverty refers to a condition where individuals or households do not have the minimum income or resources necessary to meet their basic needs for survival, such as food, shelter, and healthcare. It is typically defined by a specific income threshold.

Growth Elasticity of Poverty: The growth elasticity of poverty is a measure of how changes in economic growth impact poverty rates. It indicates the percentage reduction in poverty for each percentage point increase in economic growth. A higher growth elasticity of poverty suggests that economic growth is more effective in reducing poverty.

Head Count Ratio: The head count ratio, often referred to as the poverty headcount index, is a measure that calculates the proportion of a population living below the poverty line. It provides a straightforward percentage of people in poverty within a given population.

NSSO Data: The National Sample Survey Office (NSSO) is a government agency in India responsible for conducting large-scale household surveys and collecting socio-economic data. NSSO data provides valuable insights into various aspects of the Indian population, including poverty, employment, consumption, and more. These surveys are crucial for policy formulation and research in India.

Poverty Gap: The poverty gap is a measure that quantifies the depth of poverty. It reflects the average income or resources required to bring those living below the poverty line up to the poverty threshold. In essence, it measures the extent to which the income of the poor falls below the poverty line.

Relative Poverty: Relative poverty is a relative measure of poverty within a specific society or context. It is determined based on a person or household's income or resources relative to the overall living standards in their society. People are considered relatively poor if their living standards fall significantly below the average in their community.

ENDNOTE

1 $S(x, Y_p) = HCR(I+ (1-I)Gp)$ where x: income distribution, I: income-gap ratio and Gp: Gini Coefficient among the poor.

Chapter 13
Electronic Health Records (EHR) and Clinical Decision Support Systems:
Integrating AI Solutions

G. U. Vasanthakumar
Nitte Meenakshi Institute of Technology, Bengaluru, India

V. Dankan Gowda
https://orcid.org/0000-0003-0724-0333
Department of Electronics and Communication Engineering, BMS Institute of Technology and Management, India

Prabhakar S. Manage
KLE Technological University's MSSCET Belagavi Campus, Belagavi, India

K. D. V. Prasad
https://orcid.org/0000-0001-9921-476X
Symbiosis Institute of Business Management, Symbiosis International University, India

Venkatesan Hariram
https://orcid.org/0000-0003-2237-7071
Vinayaka Mission's Homoeopathic Medical College and Hospital, Salem, India

ABSTRACT

The extensive use of clinical decision support systems (CDSS) and electronic health records (EHR) has significantly altered the landscape of healthcare. Medical professionals now have access to priceless tools that transform patient data management and help them make wise clinical judgments. However, as we seamlessly incorporate artificial intelligence (AI) solutions into EHR and CDSS, a new era of healthcare is beginning. The incorporation of AI technologies is thoroughly explored in this chapter, shedding light on how they might improve clinical operations and patient outcomes. The chapter opens by emphasizing the crucial role played by EHR in centralizing medical records, digitizing patient data, and enabling effective data sharing between healthcare providers. The chapter conducts an in-depth exploration of how machine learning algorithms are applied to unearth patterns in patient data, identify disease risks, and provide personalized treatment recommendations.

DOI: 10.4018/979-8-3693-0807-3.ch013

1. INTRODUCTION

Within the ever-evolving healthcare landscape, technological advancements serve as pivotal catalysts, profoundly influencing the manner in which medical professionals engage with patient data. Central to this transformation is the concept of Electronic Health Records (EHRs) and Clinical Decision Support Systems (CDSS). As we venture further into the era of data-driven healthcare, it becomes pivotal to understand these systems and the transformative potential of integrating Artificial Intelligence (AI) into them.

Electronic Health Records (EHRs): EHRs, at their core, are digital versions of a patient's paper chart. They encapsulate a patient's medical history, diagnoses, medications, treatment plans, immunization dates, allergies, radiology images, and laboratory and test results. Gone are the days where patient files were stacked in towering shelves; modern healthcare necessitates instant access to patient information to deliver timely and effective care (R. Kishore Kumar and M. S. C. Senthil Kamalesh, 2023). EHRs streamline this process, allowing healthcare providers to swiftly make decisions based on comprehensive patient data. Moreover, they enhance the continuity of care since the data is easily shared across different healthcare settings, from specialists to labs, and even pharmacies(B. Ram Vishal and K. A. M, 2023).

Electronic Health Records (EHRs) digitally catalog patient or population health data in a systematic manner. They serve as lifelong health documentation, aggregating diverse forms of health-related information for easy access. EHRs encompass data from various healthcare sectors like administration, pharmacy, clinical, radiology, laboratory, and nursing, as illustrated in Figure.1. The information within an EHR can be neatly organized, semi-organized, freeform, or a mix of these categories(D. Palanikkumar, A. Y. Begum, 2023). For instance, EHR content might include plain text, basic data types like state variables or Boolean values, timestamps, coded information, embeddable data like multimedia or readable content, quantified measurements with their respective units, URLs, and grouping structures like sets or lists.

Figure 1. Block diagram of electronic health records

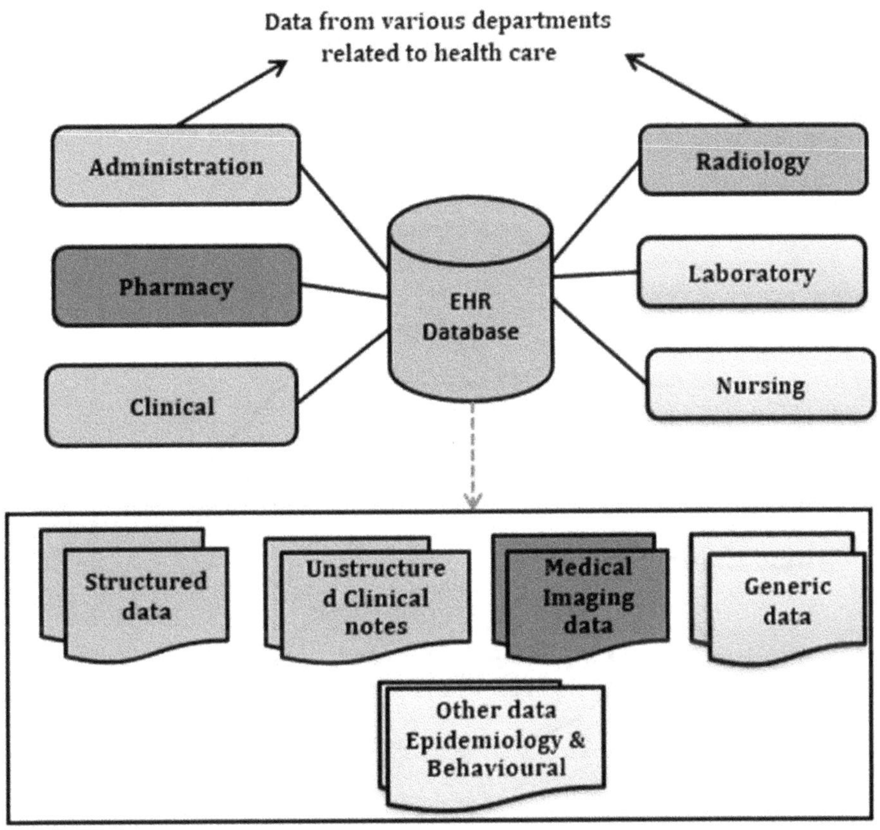

In the past, health records primarily existed in paper form, comprised of various prescriptions, X-ray findings, and laboratory results (A. Nareshkumar and B. Gururaj, 2022). These paper-based records, however, are cumbersome to manage. EHRs provide a streamlined solution by housing comprehensive patient health histories electronically. Furthermore, EHRs simplify the electronic transfer of medical information between hospitals, alleviating the need for patients to transport physical documents and reports. To truly harness the advantages of EHRs, institutions should implement an information system adept at storing, organizing, and transmitting these electronic records(R. Kavitha, and V. Hariram, 2023). Yet, a proficient information system must also be paired with a robust data management strategy. This strategy should address and rectify the challenges inherent in EHRs, which we'll discuss in the subsequent section.

Clinical Decision Support Systems (CDSS): Guiding Clinical Decisions: While EHRs fundamentally changed the way patient information is stored and accessed, CDSS took it a step further by aiding clinicians in their decision-making process. CDSS provides healthcare professionals with knowledge and patient-specific information, intelligently filtered and presented at appropriate times, to enhance health and medical care(S. Archana Shreee, G. Jeevitha Sai, 2023). Whether it's reminding a physician about a patient's allergy before prescribing medication or recommending a specific test based on symptoms, CDSS ensures that clinical decisions are rooted in evidence-based medicine, thereby potentially reducing errors.

When it comes to storing data, several significant challenges tied to EHRs emerge. These include issues of complexity, semantic interoperability, and the evolution of knowledge. Addressing these concerns is essential for effective EHR data management (M. Kranthi, and R. C. Tanguturi, 2023). EHRs are typically documented during a clinical examination. The process by which a clinical investigator captures this data encompasses four iterative steps, as depicted in Figure 2.

Figure 2. Clinical decision support systems

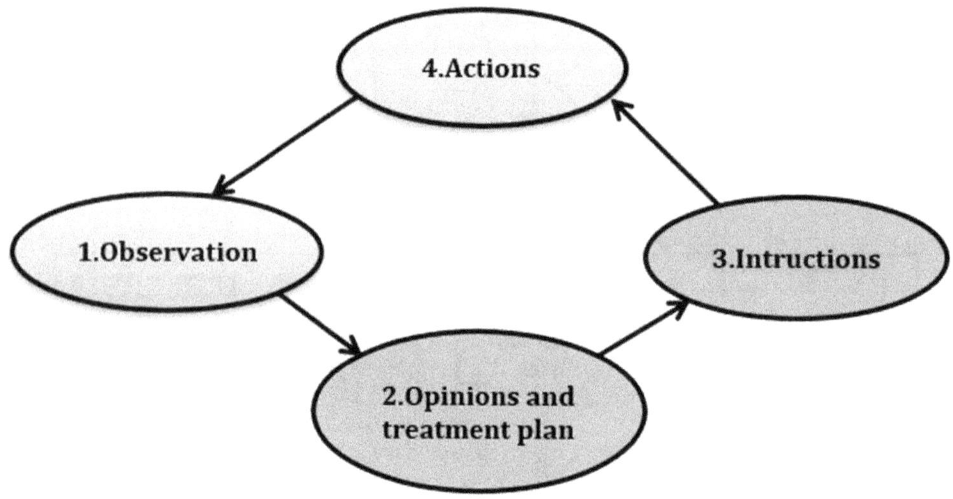

In the initial step, patients present with various symptoms. Based on these observations, a medical specialist formulates a diagnosis and crafts a corresponding treatment plan (R. C. Tanguturi, and V. C. H, 2023). This plan is then translated into specific instructions, leading to actionable medical interventions. Once these actions are executed, the cycle resumes with new observations, and this iterative process continues (R. V. Mailapur and M. K, 2023). This cyclical approach allows healthcare professionals to monitor a patient's health evolution and adjust treatments as necessary (S. Venkatakiran and N. S. Reddy, 2023). The information gathered during each cycle should be interconnected when stored, necessitating a tiered storage framework to encapsulate the data from multiple iterations. Consequently, the repetitive nature of the clinical recording process adds to the intricacy of EHRs. Furthermore, the IEEE Standard 1073 defines semantic interoperability as encompassing shared coding, data types, and terminology (Sadashiva V. Chakrasali, A. Azhagu Jaisudhan Pazhani, 2023). The frequent exchange of EHRs facilitates the provision of healthcare services to patients anytime, anywhere. Yet, in the realm of healthcare, the interpretation of a term can vary across different hospitals involved in these exchanges (Hombalimath, and N. Patwari, 2023). Take, for instance, a scenario where one hospital (let's call it MAX) records a patient's body temperature in Fahrenheit. In contrast, another hospital (let's name it AIIMS) records the same patient's temperature in Celsius. If data from MAX is transferred to AIIMS without appropriate context or conversion, the Fahrenheit measurement might be mistakenly interpreted as Celsius. Such discrepancies in data interpretation can lead to grave consequences for the patient (Namitha A R, and Veera Sivakumar Chinamuttevi 2022). Therefore, to ensure that EHRs convey consistent meanings across all healthcare institutions, achieving semantic interoperability is paramount.

The BIG model approach's inflexibility has led to the proposal of the generic model approach. This strategy emphasizes the creation of a "universal set of data structures." This set is crafted to be robust enough to capture any shifts or advancements in existing knowledge (P. Ramesh Naidu and N. Guruprasad, 2021). Unlike the earlier method where each medical concept had a dedicated class, with the generic model, any medical concept can be mapped using these universal structures, as illustrated in Figure.3. Such a model greatly augments adaptability, making it receptive to new knowledge.

However, this flexibility comes at a cost. In striving to provide a one-size-fits-all data structure set, constraints are often sacrificed, leading to diminished data quality. The lack of rigid boundaries and checks means there's no guarantee of data accuracy. Additionally, the model does not inherently support semantic interoperability (G. A, A. B. Naik and N. HG, 2021). Given its universal structure, different clinical entities can derive varying definitions for a single medical concept, relying on this generic structure, potentially leading to inconsistencies and misinterpretations.

Figure 3. Generic method of data storage

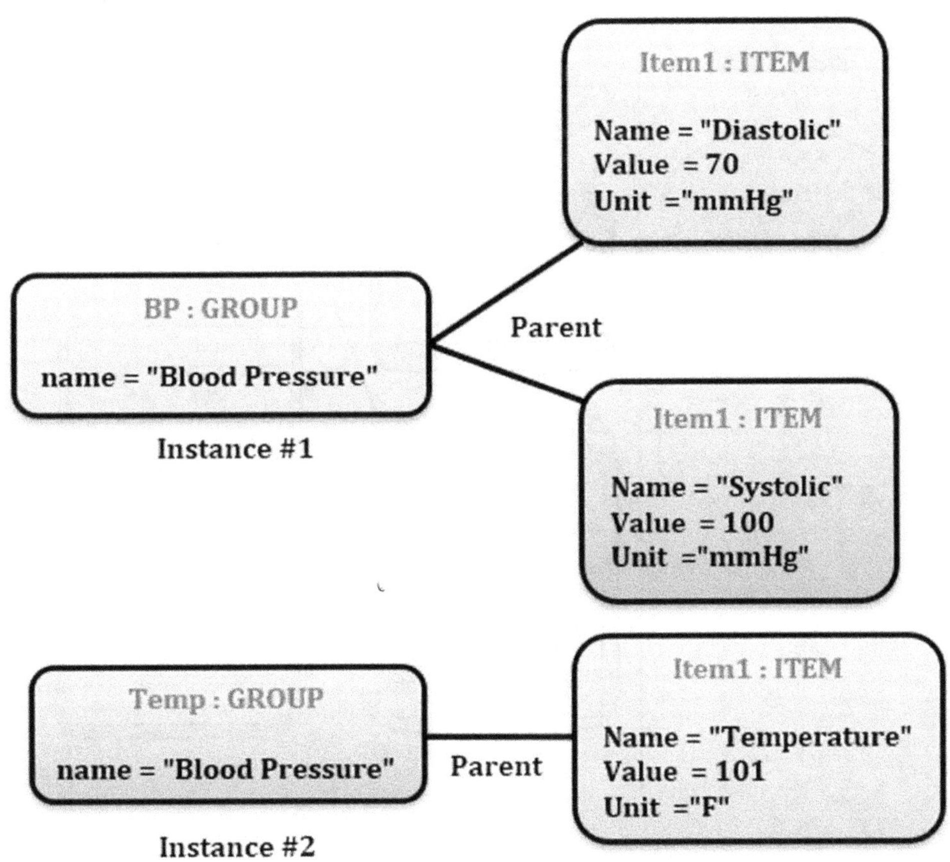

RM, inspired by the generic model approach, emphasizes the flexibility and interoperability intrinsic to generic data structures. This foundation paved the way for the creation of the first layer, or RM, in the dual model approach. RM establishes a set of versatile classes that are equipped to encapsulate any form of medical information. For instance, referring to Figure.4, an IT specialist might set up two data structures: Quantity and Text, to represent data that's quantifiable and purely textual, respectively (K. Jeevan and B. M. Sathisha, 2020). The classes within RM, as defined by openEHR, are the culmination of over two and a half decades of meticulous research. Consequently, RM provides the necessary framework for constructing a database environment prepared for any future shifts or advancements in medical knowledge. The stability and resilience of RM make it an ideal cornerstone for a system that's future-proof.

Figure 4. Dual model approach

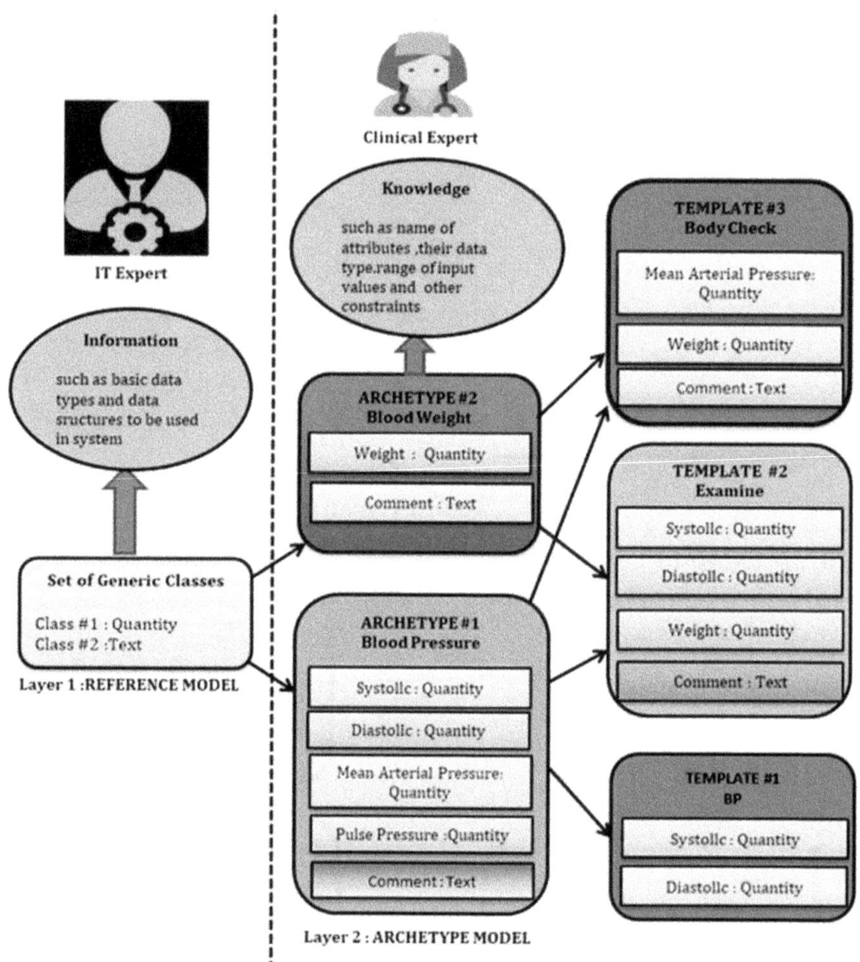

Moreover, addressing the cyclical nature of the clinical investigator recording process, RM is structured hierarchically. Data can manifest as individual values, lists, tables, or even intricate trees of values (U. K N and R. V M, 2022). This data structure is broken down further into either compound components or singular elements. These compound components can subsequently be dissected further into either more compound elements or individual elements.

The second layer of the dual model approach, known as AM, is designed to address the issue of low data quality that arises from the generic model approach. AM focuses on maintaining knowledge in terms of constrained specifications based on the structures defined in RM. It provides a framework for defining constraints such as the name of the medical parameter, acceptable range of values for the parameter, and the cardinality of the parameter (i.e., how many instances are required). AM delivers these constraints in the form of archetypes and templates. An archetype serves as a meta-description of structured clinical records, providing a computable formalism (M. R. G. and H. Anandaram, 2022). In this context, "computable formalism" refers to a formal, implementable object that conveys the same information to anyone using it. The meta-description includes details about each component within the archetype, such as its name, cardinality, multiplicity, domain, and data type (Revanna C and Parismita Sarma, 2022). The structured clinical records, as governed by the archetype's constraints, ensure that data quality is maintained.

Figure 5. Blood pressure archetype

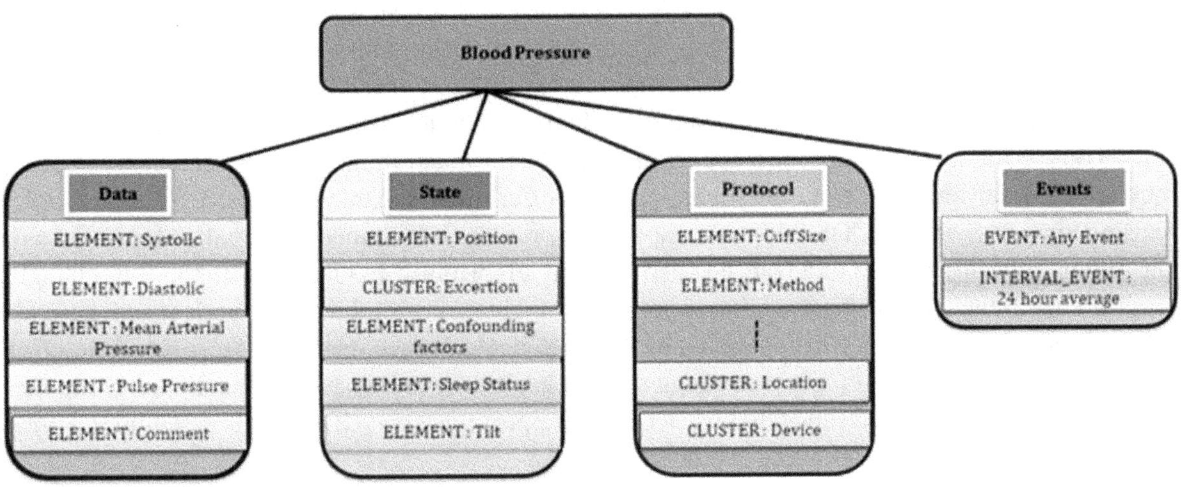

Clinical experts utilize the classes defined in RM to create archetypes or templates within AM. For instance, in the scenario depicted in Figure.4, clinical experts define two archetypes: "Blood Pressure" and "Body Weight," each comprising a specific set of attributes. Archetypes provide a comprehensive definition of every possible parameter related to a particular medical concept, offering maximal detail. Figure.5 provides an example of a blood pressure archetype, illustrating how it captures various parameters (e.g., systolic, position, and cuff size) across different dimensions (data, state, protocol, and event) within a clinical data recording system (S. Reddy P, P. S. Patwal, 2022). Knowledge residing within various archetypes can be effectively consolidated to create templates, which are specialized components of the dual model approach (S. R. Kawale, S. P. Diwan, 2022). Templates inherit knowledge from various archetypes to cater to specific organizational needs. Organizations have the flexibility to tailor templates according to their unique data requirements using a tool like the Template Designer (B. Kameswara Rao and Naziya Hussain, 2022). For example, in Figure.4, three templates (BP, Examine, and Body Check) are defined by selectively inheriting the desired set of attributes from existing archetypes. Typically, a template is directly linked to a graphical user interface designed for data entry, ensuring that the collected data aligns with the predefined constraints and structures (M. Swathi Pai and B. Naveen K, 2020). To define these archetypes and templates within AM, a specialized language known as Archetype Definition Language (ADL) is employed. ADL serves as the foundational framework for articulating the intricacies of archetypes and templates within an archetype editor. It offers a standardized methodology for crafting and overseeing these vital elements, essential to the dual model approach.

By creating linkages to widely used medical terminologies like SNOMED-CT and LOINC, openEHR archetypes play a crucial role in developing clear data interchange and attaining semantic interoperability (K. B. Naveen and G. N. Pai, 2020). This connection ensures that data sent corresponds to widely accepted terms, reducing the possibility of misunderstandings or misinterpretations. Adopting archetypes improves structural interoperability by enabling healthcare systems to communicate data while having a common understanding of the data's meaning and structure(P. Ramesh Naidu, N. Guruprasad, 2020) . This harmonious integration enhances the overall effectiveness and efficiency of healthcare information exchange. This harmonization of data structures and terminologies across different healthcare organizations and systems contributes to more effective and efficient healthcare data exchange and utilization.

The Intersection of AI, EHRs, and CDSS: Artificial Intelligence, with its capability to sift through vast datasets and draw meaningful insights, stands as a promising tool to further enhance EHRs and CDSS. Imagine a system where a patient's symptoms are instantly matched against millions of clinical cases to suggest potential diagnoses or where predictive analytics flags potential health risks before they become critical (K. Prasad and G. Poornima, 2022). By integrating AI, EHRs can be transformed from mere digital repositories to intelligent systems offering actionable insights. Likewise, Clinical Decision Support Systems (CDSS) have the capacity to provide finely-tuned, personalized recommendations through the application of advanced deep learning algorithms. In tandem with the ever-changing healthcare landscape, the methods of documenting, analyzing, and administering patient care have also undergone a profound transformation driven by technological advancements (H. Anandaram, and B. K. Verma, 2023). To gain insight into the present state of healthcare and its reliance on systems like Electronic Health Records (EHRs) and Clinical Decision Support Systems (CDSS), it is essential to embark on a journey tracing their origins and evolutionary path.

History of EHRs

From Paper to Pixels: The Shift in Record Keeping

Healthcare organizations have traditionally relied mostly on paper-based records for the purpose of managing patient information. The major method of keeping a patient's medical history was tangible records, often housed in large physical file systems. The individuals were kept inside these systems. Notwithstanding this, the medical sector saw the emergence of the computer era and the ascent of digitalization as a noteworthy chance for profound change in the latter part of the 20th century. The shift from physical paper records to electronic records not only represented a significant advancement in technology, but it also marked the start of a new era in the management, retrieval, and dissemination of patient data.

Benefits of Digital Transformation

The use of electronic health records (EHRs) has ushered in a transformative phase in the medical field, characterized by heightened efficiency and improved availability. The use of electronic health records has resulted in notable advancements in the administration and retrieval of data, obviating the need for large physical storage facilities and arduous searches through patient files. Due to the ability of healthcare staff to access patient data from several places, essential information remained readily available, irrespective of the time or place it was required. The revolutionary nature of electronic health records has been attributed to this factor (Prasad & Ashreetha, 2023). Electronic health records (EHRs) have also facilitated interoperability, so enhancing the ease with which healthcare practitioners from various backgrounds may interchange data. This improved coordination and comprehensive approach to patient care signified a substantial change from the previous, disjointed methods.

Challenges in the Digital Realm

However, the transformational move towards Electronic Health Records (EHRs) in healthcare was not without its share of difficulties. Data security was one of the main issues that surfaced, since the digital environment increased the possibility of breaches that may endanger private patient data. While interoperability was a significant benefit, it paradoxically presented challenges of its own, with different EHR systems often grappling with compatibility issues that hindered seamless data exchange. Another pressing issue was the perceived loss of the personal touch in patient care; with physicians increasingly engaged with screens, there were concerns that valuable face-to-face interactions with patients were dwindling, potentially impacting the quality of care. These challenges underscored the complex and evolving nature of the healthcare technology landscape, necessitating ongoing efforts to strike a balance between innovation and the preservation of essential aspects of patient care.

2. THE RISE OF AI IN HEALTHCARE

As technology continues its relentless march forward, its integration into various sectors becomes an inevitable and transformative process. Among these advancements, Artificial Intelligence (AI) stands out as a game-changer. With its remarkable ability to emulate human intelligence and swiftly analyze immense datasets, AI has initiated a paradigm shift in numerous industries, healthcare being no exception. This chapter embarks on a journey to elucidate the mounting relevance of AI in the medical sector, shedding light on its current applications within Electronic Health Records (EHRs) and Clinical Decision Support Systems (CDSS). As we delve deeper, we uncover the profound impact that AI is exerting on the landscape of healthcare, paving the way for more precise diagnoses, data-driven insights, and ultimately, improved patient care.

2.1 Why AI in Healthcare?

The Capabilities of AI Across Sectors

AI's remarkable capabilities have left an indelible mark across a spectrum of sectors, from its role in financial forecasting within the banking industry to its ability to provide personalized content recommendations in the realm of entertainment. Its core capability lies in recognizing patterns from massive datasets, learning from them, and making decisions or predictions based on this learned information. The ability to continuously evolve and adapt makes AI not just a tool but an ever-growing repository of knowledge.

Benefits of AI in Healthcare

Accuracy: With AI algorithms, there's a significant reduction in human errors, especially in tasks like diagnosing diseases from medical images or predicting patient trajectories based on historical data.

Speed: AI can quickly analyze large datasets. For instance, reading and interpreting a radiological image, which might take a human expert several minutes, can be done in mere seconds by a trained AI model.

Predictive Analysis: AI can forecast potential health risks, allowing for timely interventions. For example, by analyzing a patient's medical history and real-time data, AI might predict the onset of a chronic disease or the likelihood of hospital readmission.

Scalability: AI systems, once trained, can be scaled to cater to larger populations, ensuring that high-quality care and insights are not restricted by the number of available human experts.

2.2 Current AI Applications in EHRs and CDSS

Natural Language Processing (NLP) for Patient Notes

Doctors and healthcare professionals often jot down their observations, diagnoses, and treatment plans in patient notes. These unstructured data sets, while invaluable, were previously challenging to analyze systematically. With NLP, a subset of AI, these notes can be parsed, understood, and converted into structured data. This allows for better trend analysis, understanding patient trajectories, and even automatic coding for billing purposes.

Predictive Analytics for Patient Outcomes

AI's predictive capabilities are being harnessed to forecast patient outcomes. By analyzing a combination of historical patient data, current vitals, and other relevant parameters, AI models can predict risks like potential ICU transfers, sepsis onset, or even readmission risks after discharge.

Image Recognition in Radiology and Pathology

One of the most celebrated applications of AI in healthcare is in the domain of image recognition. AI models trained on vast datasets of radiological or pathological images can detect anomalies, from tumors in MRI scans to abnormalities in pathology slides. These systems, when used in conjunction with human experts, ensure higher accuracy, faster results, and the possibility of catching conditions that might be overlooked by the human eye.

In conclusion, the intersection of AI with EHRs and CDSS is paving the way for a new era in healthcare. An era where technology augments human expertise, ensuring that patient care is more accurate, timely, and personalized than ever before.

3. INTEGRATING AI WITH EHR

The promise of AI-enhanced healthcare is compelling, but integrating AI with Electronic Health Records is not a mere plug-and-play operation. It demands careful consideration of various challenges and a structured approach to integration.

3.1 Challenges of Integration

Data Privacy and Security Concerns

As we venture deeper into the digital age, data privacy and security remain paramount. With EHRs containing sensitive patient information, integrating AI poses potential risks:

Data Breaches: AI integration often requires data to be moved or accessed by new systems, which can become potential points of vulnerability.

Unauthorized Access: AI algorithms, especially those leveraging cloud computing, might be susceptible to unauthorized data access if not adequately protected.

Interoperability of Different EHR Systems

Different healthcare institutions often use different EHR systems. These systems, while functional on their own, might not be inherently compatible with each other or with new AI solutions. The challenge lies in:

Data Standardization: Different EHRs might store data in varied formats, making it challenging for an AI system to process data consistently.

System Communication: For seamless AI integration, EHR systems need to "talk" to the AI algorithms and vice-versa. Ensuring this communication without data loss or misinterpretation is crucial.

Over-reliance on AI and Reduced Human Intervention

While AI offers numerous advantages, there's a genuine concern about over-relying on it:

Loss of Human Touch: Excessive reliance on AI might reduce face-to-face interactions between healthcare providers and patients.

Potential Errors: No AI system is infallible. Over-reliance might lead to missed diagnoses or treatment opportunities if the system makes a rare error.

4. DATABASE APPROACHES

The database approach indeed plays a critical role in the efficiency of an information system, particularly when dealing with the unique characteristics of Electronic Health Records (EHRs) data. EHRs present several specific challenges that a suitable database approach must address:

Sparseness: EHRs often contain a vast amount of data, but not all data points are populated for every patient or encounter. A good database approach should efficiently handle sparse data by optimizing storage and retrieval mechanisms to avoid wasting resources on empty fields.

Frequent Evolution: EHRs are subject to constant updates and changes due to advancements in medical knowledge and healthcare practices. The database approach should support versioning and allow for seamless updates to the data structure without disrupting existing records.

Query Efficiency: Effective querying is essential for swiftly locating pertinent patient data, making quick clinical judgments, and advancing research. To ensure quick and effective data retrieval, the database must use strong indexing and optimization algorithms.

Mining Support: Data mining techniques are often used in the healthcare industry to glean significant insights from Electronic Health Records (EHR) data. The database must enable sophisticated data analytics and data mining functions so that useful information may be extracted from these entries.

The choice between these database approaches hinges on the specific requirements of the healthcare organization, the inherent characteristics of the EHRs data, and the envisaged patterns of data usage. Some organizations may opt for a hybrid approach that seamlessly combines elements of both schema-based and schema-less databases, thereby striking a delicate balance between enforcing data structure and accommodating flexibility. Ultimately, the selection of the database approach should harmonize with the overarching goals of the organization in terms of data management, analysis, and interoperability within the intricate healthcare landscape.

Figure 6. Transforming unstructured data into relational table

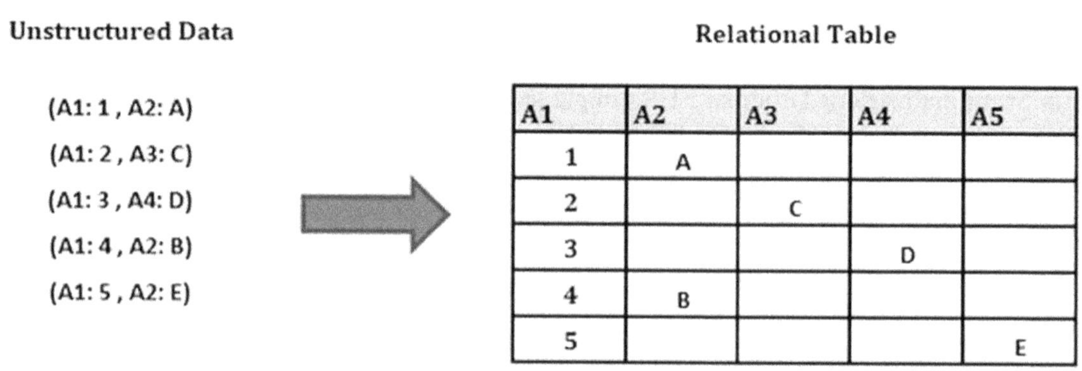

Indeed, when grappling with unstructured data within a Relational Database Management System (RDBMS), the common approach involves a transformation process that molds it into a structured format with a predefined schema, as illustrated in Figure 6. This schema serves as a blueprint, defining a comprehensive set of attributes capable of accommodating diverse types of data.

However, this approach comes with its share of inherent challenges. First and foremost is the Data Transformation Overhead; converting unstructured data into a structured schema demands significant effort in terms of data preprocessing, parsing, and mapping. This undertaking can be particularly time-consuming and intricate, especially when confronted with substantial volumes of unstructured data.

Another issue to contend with is the prevalence of Sparse (Null) Values. As previously mentioned, the structured schema may lead to numerous instances of sparse or null values, wherein many attributes contain no data for a specific record. This can lead to inefficient storage utilization and heightened query complexity. Furthermore, there is a risk of Loss of Information during the transformation process. Simplification or omission of certain aspects of unstructured data can potentially result in the loss of valuable information or contextual insights. Organizations frequently look towards alternate strategies in light of these difficulties, with NoSQL databases emerging as a possible remedy. NoSQL databases were created with the specific intent of handling semi- and unstructured data with increased flexibility. They are the best options for situations when the data structure is not predetermined and may change often since they may store data without using a schema or with a flexible schema. This method efficiently reduces the issue of sparse values, makes data intake and searching for unstructured data easier, and reduces the possibility of losing important information.

The individual use case, the qualities of the data in issue, and the organizational needs ultimately determine whether to convert unstructured data into a structured schema within an RDBMS or utilize a NoSQL database. In certain cases, a hybrid strategy combining unstructured and structured data processing and storage approaches could be the most practical and flexible answer to the organization's particular problems.

5. DATABASE APPROACHES FOR STANDARDIZED EHR

In the domain of modeling Electronic Health Records (EHRs) data, standard-based systems have devised a pragmatic approach that combines both schema-less and schema-based database methodologies to accommodate the multifaceted nature of EHRs data. EHRs data can be incredibly diverse, encompassing structured, semi-structured, and unstructured information. To effectively manage this data heterogeneity, healthcare systems employ distinct database strategies tailored to the specific characteristics of each data type. For structured data within EHRs, where the format is well-defined, a schema-based approach prevails, employing relational tables hosted in databases like PostgreSQL or MySQL. These relational databases excel at enforcing data consistency and maintaining relationships, making them a natural fit for structured information such as patient demographics and lab results.

Semi-structured EHRs data, which often possesses a flexible or evolving structure, finds its home in databases leveraging XML. XML offers a hierarchical structure capable of adapting to changing data elements, a feature highly valued in healthcare systems for managing semi-structured clinical data.

Healthcare systems often employ a judicious combination of these storage technologies, with structured data typically residing in relational databases, while clinical narratives and documents are housed in XML or NoSQL databases. Moreover, the concept of polyglot persistence allows healthcare organizations to employ multiple storage approaches within the same system, optimizing data management, retrieval, and overall system performance to meet the diverse and evolving demands of modern healthcare.

This approach takes advantage of the strengths of each storage technology for different types of data. In the context of EHRs, a polyglot storage architecture may involve using a relational database like

PostgreSQL for structured data, an XML database for semi-structured data, and one or more NoSQL databases like MongoDB and Neo4j for unstructured data. This approach optimizes data storage and retrieval according to the specific characteristics and needs of each data type, ultimately enhancing the efficiency and scalability of EHRs systems.

XML has indeed been a popular choice for storing frequently evolving Electronic Health Records (EHRs) data due to its flexibility and extensibility. It has served as the foundation for several studies on healthcare data management and is a common component of standard-based EHR systems:

Application Integration and Data Interoperability: Researchers like Catley et al. have taken advantage of XML's advantages for data exchange and application integration. Because of its organized nature, XML may be used to represent and exchange medical data between various systems and organizations.

The introduction of XML (Extensible Markup Language) has sparked significant developments in the healthcare industry. One such innovation is the suggestion of Medical Markup Language (MML), an XML extension made specifically for constructing information systems in hospitals engaged in the transmission of data from Electronic Health Records (EHRs). MML acts as a standardized channel for organizing and making it easier for medical data to be exchanged throughout various healthcare organizations, hence fostering smooth interoperability.

To optimize the efficiency of XML-based queries, researchers have introduced various XML databases engineered to handle XML data efficiently. These databases employ techniques such as indexing to expedite query processing. However, it's worth noting that XML databases may face performance limitations, especially in attribute-centric query scenarios, where relational databases often excel due to their finely-tuned indexing and query optimization capabilities.

Additionally, XML's synergy with the openEHR framework is reinforced through XML specifications and tools, simplifying the serialization of openEHR objects into XML format. This integration bolsters interoperability and streamlines data exchange within the openEHR ecosystem, promoting standardized data representation and ensuring a cohesive healthcare data landscape.

The choice between XML and relational databases for EHRs data storage depends on the specific requirements of the healthcare system, including data complexity, query patterns, and interoperability needs. In practice, some organizations opt for hybrid solutions that combine the strengths of both XML and relational databases to strike a balance between flexibility and performance.

It's interesting to note that while the openEHR standard provides flexibility in data modeling and storage, many existing openEHR-based systems have been built using the relational model, which represents a schema-based approach. These systems often adopt various schema-based database strategies to manage standardized EHRs data following the openEHR standard. Here, we'll briefly examine three of these approaches: Object Relational Mapping (ORM), Node+Path (based on EAV), and Archetype Relational Mapping (ARM), as presented in Figure.7.

Figure 7. Model based storage approaches for standardized HER

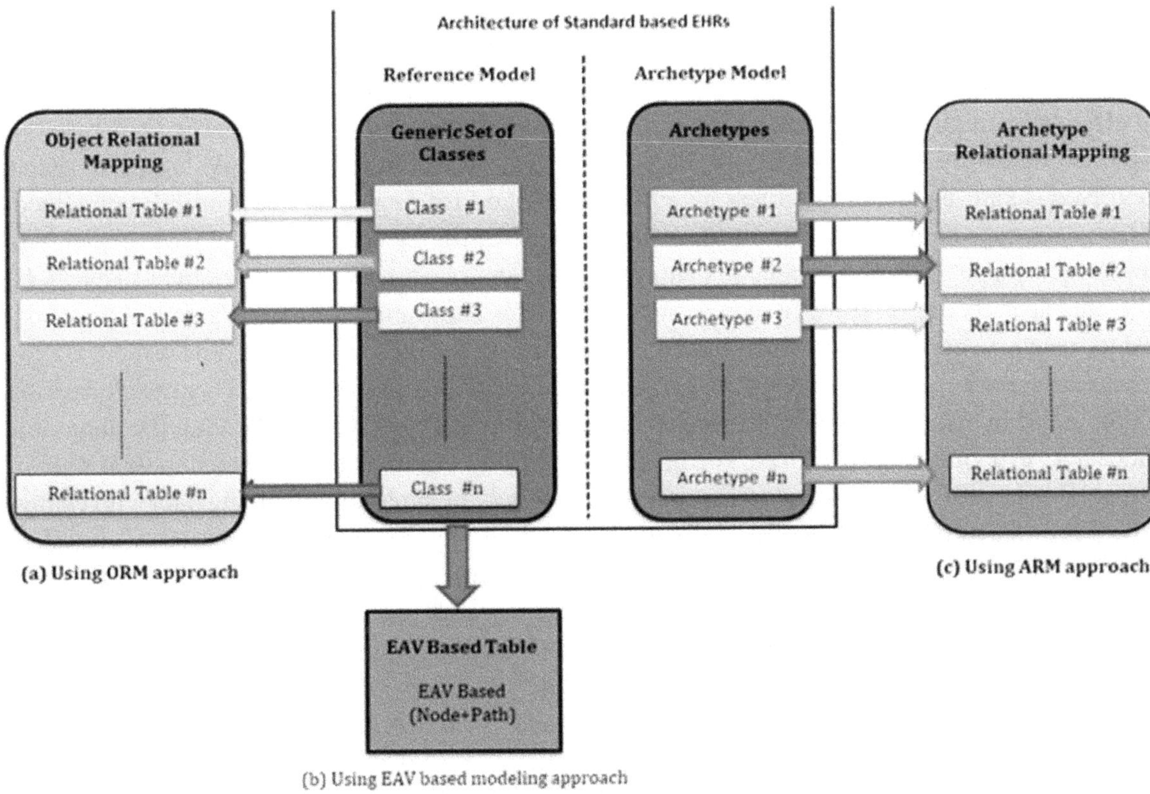

Object-Relational Mapping (ORM) is a key method that connects relational databases with object-oriented programming languages, and it is crucial in the creation of software. ORM plays an essential part in the configuration of openEHR since it simplifies the process of translating openEHR archetypes and templates into the more structured world of relational database tables.

One of the most significant benefits of ORM is its capacity to assist in the coordination of a seamless integration of data from Electronic Health Records (EHRs) into software applications. This connection is made feasible by empowering developers with the capacity to operate in an object-oriented fashion with electronic health record data. In its most basic form, object-relational mapping (ORM) enables programmers to manage electronic health record (EHR) data by using the same object-oriented ideas and coding standards that direct the development of their programs. The central tenet of ORM revolves around establishing a correspondence between the objects in the application code and the tables in the relational database. Typically, this mapping is defined through configuration or annotation mechanisms. ORM frameworks, such as Hibernate (for Java) and Entity Framework (for .NET), substantially automate this mapping process, simplifying the developer's task of working with data as objects.

In essence, ORM serves as a linchpin in modern software development, facilitating the harmonious coexistence of object-oriented application logic and relational database structures. This synergy not only streamlines the development process but also enhances the maintainability and flexibility of software systems, making it an indispensable tool in the realm of openEHR and beyond.

By adopting ORM in openEHR-based systems, developers can harness the benefits of structured relational databases while seamlessly incorporating the flexibility and complexity of openEHR archetypes and templates. The combination of relational databases and object-oriented programming improves the manageability, scalability, and maintainability of EHR systems, which ultimately aids in the effective and efficient archiving and retrieval of patient data in healthcare applications.

(Based on Entity-Attribute-Value, or EAV) Node+Path The Entity-Attribute-Value (EAV) model-based Node+Path methodology offers an attractive method for managing Electronic Health Records (EHRs) data, especially when working with variable and semi-structured data. The EAV model, which is renowned for its lack of a schema, is an appropriate option in situations when data displays flexibility and sparsity, traits typically seen in healthcare data. The Entity-Attribute-Value (EAV) model is used to transform complicated, structured Electronic Health Records (EHR) data into a more flattened and tabular format using the Node+Path technique in the context of openEHR. This transformation is accomplished by using hierarchical routes to link characteristics to entities, allowing the depiction of changeable, evolving data structures. The inherent flexibility of the Node+Path technique is one of its most notable benefits. As a result, it is especially well-suited for situations involving data with changing properties or situations where the data structure is not entirely established. This flexibility proves to be a key benefit in the dynamic healthcare scene, which is defined by the ongoing appearance of new data pieces and variances in information. Node+Path-based systems efficiently adapt to changing requirements and shifting data structures while handling the storage and retrieval of EHR data. The Node+Path technique is a suitable option for managing EHRs data since it is naturally varied, prone to frequent updates and additions, and necessitates a strong and adaptable data representation mechanism due to these adaptabilities and its schema-less nature. Essentially, the Node+Path strategy is in line with the dynamic nature of healthcare data and is an effective option for businesses looking for a compromise between organized storage and the adaptability to handle constantly changing EHR data.

Archetype Relational Mapping (ARM): In the world of openEHR-based systems for handling Electronic Health Records (EHRs) data, the Archetype Relational Mapping (ARM) method stands as a specialized and personalized solution. It has been specifically created to follow the archetype-based data modeling principles of openEHR and to guarantee the integrity and semantics of these archetypes inside a relational database structure. In essence, ARM acts as a link between the complex and flexible openEHR archetypes and the structured world of relational databases. The main goal of the Archetype-Relational Mapping (ARM) technique is to make sure that the semantics and detailed data models described in openEHR archetypes are accurately represented inside a relational database architecture. This is accomplished by carefully mapping relational database tables into openEHR archetypes and templates. The structure, restrictions, and relationships outlined by the archetypes are painstakingly preserved by these mappings, guaranteeing that the underlying data continues to adhere to the exacting criteria of openEHR. The outstanding capacity of the ARM technique to accept complicated, archetype-based Electronic Health Records (EHR) data while resolutely sustaining data consistency is one of its most salient features. These methods highlight the relational model's extraordinary flexibility to managing Electronic Health Records (EHRs) data based on openEHR standards. It is important to keep in mind, nevertheless, that openEHR's intrinsic flexibility might be problematic when attempting to translate its data structures to a structured database architecture. The decision between these strategies depends on a number of variables, such as the complexity of the data, necessary performance criteria, and the necessity to follow openEHR standards.

Each of these strategies aims to achieve a careful balance between the relational databases' built-in structure and openEHR's data modeling's inherent flexibility. By doing this, they ensure strict adherence to the demanding regulations governing healthcare data while facilitating the effective storage and retrieval of EHR data. In the end, choosing the best strategy is a complex choice driven by the unique requirements and limitations of the healthcare data environment as well as the objective of integrating structured database storage with openEHR's flexible data representation.

An inventive method for splitting a relational database into many attribute tables and a separate binary table for each one is the Multi-database Entity-Attribute-Value (MTEAV) technique. All of the original relational table's attributes—aside from the main key—are covered by this decomposition. Each attribute table essentially functions as a binary table, signifying its capability to distinguish between non-null and null values. Precisely, it focuses on capturing the non-null values of the corresponding attribute while retaining the associated primary key values. In addition to these attribute tables, the MTEAV approach introduces another pivotal binary table known as the Entity Attribute (EA) table. The primary function of this table is to maintain an inventory of non-null attributes for all entities present in the dataset. These entities are uniquely identified by their primary key values. To efficiently store blood pressure data within a hospital setting, a thoughtfully designed relational (n-ary) table can effectively fulfill the intended purpose. In this particular scenario, the table should be structured to accommodate various parameters inherently linked with blood pressure measurements, as depicted in Figure 8. This approach ensures a systematic and comprehensive representation of blood pressure data, enabling efficient storage and retrieval within the healthcare environment.

Figure 8. Parameters of blood pressure

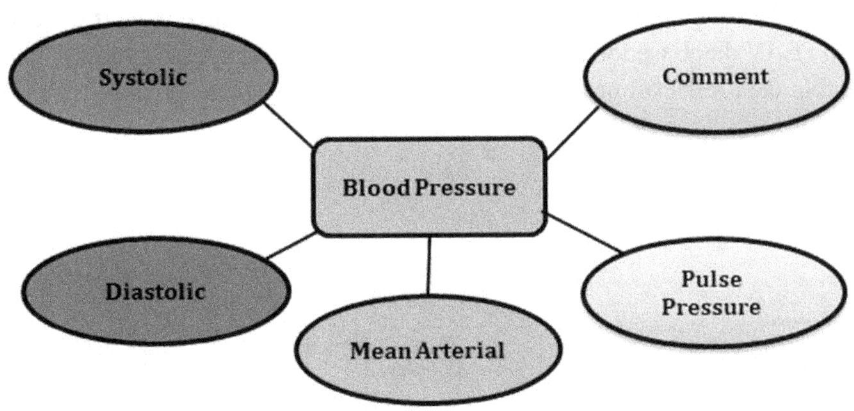

Blood pressure data indeed encompasses several parameters, and the selection of which parameters to document may vary among healthcare practitioners. For instance, while some doctors may opt to record the fundamental systolic and diastolic pressure values, obtained directly from a medical device, others may choose to include additional derived parameters like mean arterial pressure (MA) or pulse pressure (PP). These derived values are typically computed using predefined mathematical formulas that involve the systolic and diastolic pressure readings. Furthermore, it's common practice to include a comment section (CO) in the record, which serves as a valuable space for providing contextual information or describing the patient's condition during the measurement process. This comment section offers a crucial narrative element that augments the quantitative data, allowing for a more comprehensive and nuanced understanding of the patient's health status during the blood pressure assessment. By structuring the data in this relational table with these six attributes, the hospital can effectively store and manage blood pressure data in a structured and organized manner. This approach enables flexibility in recording various parameters while maintaining data integrity and associating measurements with specific patients.

6. TRANSLATIONS

The need for translating SQL queries to align with the Multi-Table Entity-Attribute-Value (MTEAV) structure is evident to query the MTEAV database effectively. Since there is currently no specialized database system designed explicitly for MTEAV, the adaptability of MTEAV relies on leveraging existing Relational Database Management Systems (RDBMS) to provide SQL support.

MTEAV represents a logical modification of the traditional Nested Set Model (NSM). While NSM users are accustomed to crafting SQL queries based on the conventional NSM structure, transitioning to MTEAV's different architecture can be challenging and may disrupt user habits and workflows.

To mitigate this discomfort and to ensure a smooth transition, a translation layer is proposed to sit atop existing RDBMS systems, as depicted in Figure.9. The translation layer serves as a vital intermediary bridging the gap between users familiar with NSM-style queries and the MTEAV database structure. The integration of the MTEAV database and the NSM-style query language enables users to effectively retrieve and manipulate data. This integration promotes smooth communication and interaction between these distinct components. This is achieved by the facilitation of communication and interaction between the two components. The inclusion of an intermediary layer is crucial in enhancing the accessibility and usability of the MTEAV database for a broader spectrum of users, as it facilitates a more user-friendly and easily navigable data retrieval procedure. This objective may be achieved by simplifying the data retrieval mechanism.

Figure 9. MTEAV structure

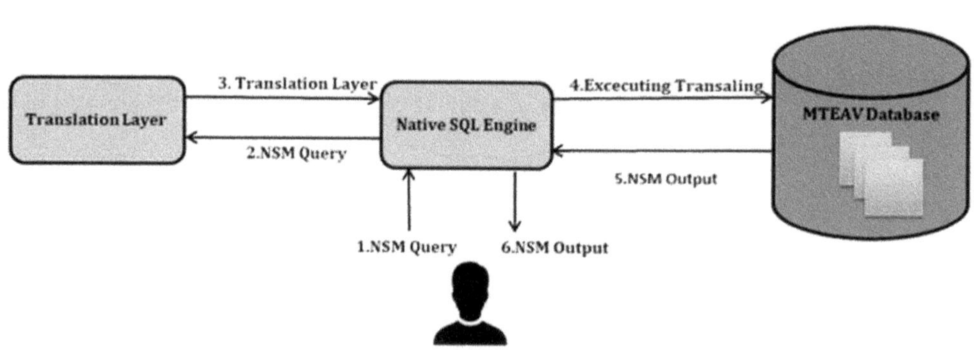

The use of the Multi-Table Entity-Attribute-Value (MTEAV) format entails some intrinsic adjustments to the query structure. The main purpose of the translation layer is to obscure or hide these modifications.

The achievement of this task is facilitated by providing users with the capability to submit SQL queries that adhere to the well-known Nested Set Model (NSM) structure. It then takes on the essential process of translating these queries into the appropriate MTEAV query format in order to successfully retrieve data from the MTEAV database. Only then is it able to successfully get data. By ensuring that users can continue to interact with the database using their known query habits and patterns, this translation procedure makes the switch to MTEAV easier.

In essence, the translation layer acts as a link between the intricate MTEAV database and the user expectations, which are accustomed to NSM query formats. This essential middleman enables businesses to take use of MTEAV's benefits without interfering with current workflows or requiring users to learn query formats all over again. Consequently, when querying data stored in the MTEAV format while adhering to an NSM paradigm, a specialized workflow comes into play. Users compose their queries based on their familiarity with NSM data structures, creating queries in the NSM format as they usually would. These NSM-style queries are then routed to the native SQL engine, which serves as the initial interface for query processing. However, the SQL engine is cognizant of the transition to MTEAV and acknowledges the need for a translation layer to bridge the gap effectively. This is precisely where the translation layer assumes a pivotal role.

The user's NSM-style query is transformed inside of the translation layer. In order to assure effective data retrieval from the MTEAV database, it is painstakingly rebuilt into an analogous MTEAV query syntax. This translation layer serves as an essential intermediary, ensuring that user expectations and queries are perfectly in line with the subtleties of the MTEAV database structure, allowing for a seamless transition and unbroken query operations.

Following the translation of the query, it proceeds to execution within the SQL engine. The SQL engine then establishes communication with the Multi-Table Entity-Attribute-Value (MTEAV) database, initiating the retrieval of pertinent data in accordance with the MTEAV query structure. Subsequently, the retrieved data is subjected to processing as per the query's instructions. What sets this process apart and makes it particularly unique is that the query meticulously constructed by the translation layer is explicitly designed to generate output in the familiar Nested Set Model (NSM) format. As a result, when the data is extracted from the MTEAV database, it is seamlessly presented to the user by the SQL engine in the format they are accustomed to – the NSM format. This distinctive feature ensures that users can continue to work with the data in a manner consistent with their established practices and expectations, despite the underlying transition to MTEAV. The process, therefore, optimally balances the benefits of MTEAV with user familiarity, promoting a smooth and user-friendly experience in querying and handling data.

In summary, this approach allows users to continue using their preferred NSM-style query format while benefiting from the advantages of MTEAV for data storage and management. The translation layer acts as a bridge, ensuring a smooth and familiar query experience while accommodating the structural differences between NSM and MTEAV.

In our proposed architecture, a sample dataset containing standardized blood pressure data has been meticulously organized, consisting of a total of 5,000 instances. This dataset adheres to the architecture we've discussed earlier. It encompasses various attributes, including Systolic Pressure, Diastolic Pressure, Mean Arterial Pressure, and Pulse Pressure, all in line with the specifications outlined in the Blood Pressure archetype. Additionally, a parameter labeled 'Comment' is recorded in the dataset, allowing for observations related to the patient's health status. Currently, the 'Comment' parameter includes one value among six possible observations, namely, Hypotension, Normal, Prehypertension, Hypertension Stage 1, Hypertension Stage 2, and Hypertension Crisis. To derive actionable insights and build a decision support system from this dataset, we applied a range of data mining techniques. These techniques include JRIP, BayesNet, PART, Decision Tree, OneR, Random Tree, LMT, Multilayer Perceptron, Random Subspace, KStar, SMO, REP Tree, J48, Simple Logistic, Random Forest, and IBk.

Figure 10. Blood pressure dataset

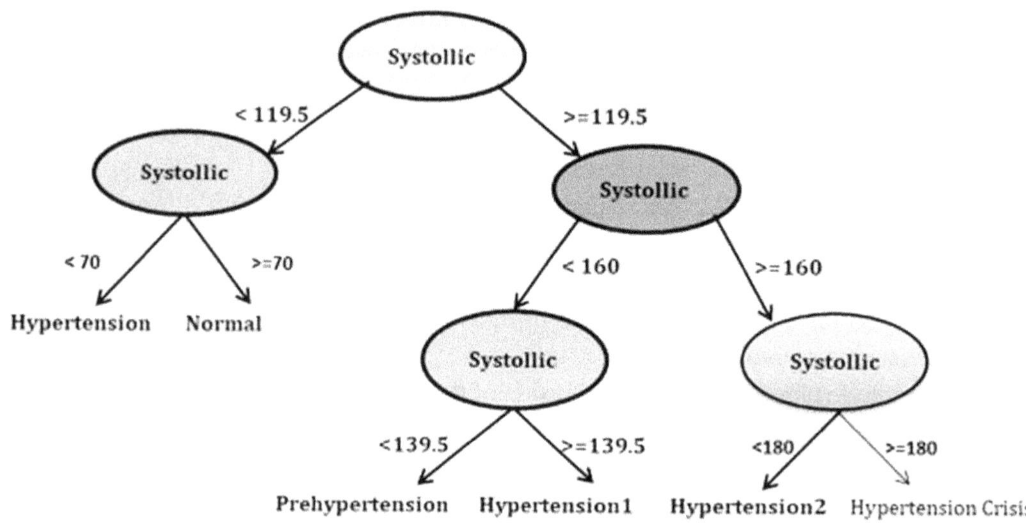

The application of these mining algorithms was facilitated using the WEKA tool, a widely used platform for data mining and machine learning. Among the various mining algorithms considered, it was observed that the Random Tree algorithm yielded the most accurate and efficient results. This algorithm not only provided high accuracy in its predictions but also exhibited faster performance compared to the other algorithms in the evaluation. As a result of the Random Tree mining algorithm's effectiveness, Figure.10. showcases the resultant decision tree generated by this algorithm. This decision tree represents the structure that allows us to make informed decisions and predictions based on the blood pressure data and 'Comment' parameter, contributing to a robust and effective decision support system in the healthcare domain. Standard-based Electronic Health Records (EHRs) present unique challenges, including issues related to data sparseness, frequent updates, and the need for efficient querying. Medical professionals often recommend visualizing EHRs as a collection of attribute-value pairs, which provides a structured way to represent patient information. However, any alterations to the data model or attribute-value representation can introduce incompatibilities with existing data mining tools available in the market. Data mining plays a crucial role in uncovering hidden patterns and valuable insights within healthcare data, leading to important discoveries. Therefore, making standard-based EHRs, especially those stored as Entity-Attribute-Value (EAV) representations, amenable to existing data mining tools becomes essential. This chapter introduces an architecture designed to organize standard-based EHRs modeled as EAV representations. This architecture's main goal is to successfully solve the problems caused by data sparsity, frequent updates, and query efficiency. A careful and effective data structure makes the data far more receptive to data mining and analysis, releasing its full potential for study and informed decision-making.

To evaluate the performance of this architecture, a series of experimental studies were conducted. These experiments involved the manipulation of the dataset size, varying the number of instances, to assess the impact of dataset scale on the architecture's performance. Significantly, the results demonstrated that the proposed architecture excels in efficiently organizing Entity-Attribute-Value (EAV)-based data, accomplishing this task within a matter of seconds. It's important to note that analytical queries conducted on Electronic Health Records (EHRs) data often do not necessitate real-time responses. Given this consideration, the time taken by the proposed architecture is deemed highly acceptable, especially when weighed against the considerable advantages it brings in terms of improved data organization and readiness for data mining. This readiness empowers healthcare organizations to harness the full potential of their EHRs data, ultimately fostering a richer understanding of patient health, facilitating informed decision-making, and facilitating valuable research initiatives in the healthcare sector.

7. FUTURE SCOPE

Acknowledging the pivotal role of data mining in revealing valuable insights within the vast realm of healthcare data, this chapter introduces an innovative architecture tailored to meet the unique demands of organizing standard-based Electronic Health Records (EHRs). These EHRs frequently use the Entity-Attribute-Value (EAV) paradigm to describe data, which presents unique issues because of data sparsity, the dynamic nature of healthcare datasets, and the requirement for quick query processing. An extensive set of tests were carefully carried out to evaluate the effectiveness of this unique architecture. These experiments systematically varied dataset sizes to gauge the architecture's performance under different scales. Remarkably, the outcomes of these experiments underscored the architecture's exceptional efficiency, demonstrating its capacity to efficiently organize EAV-based data within mere seconds. This architectural innovation stands as a testament to the commitment to enhancing the management and utilization of healthcare data. It equips healthcare organizations with a powerful tool to navigate the complexities of data sparsity and evolving datasets, thereby fostering the discovery of valuable insights and ultimately advancing the quality of healthcare services and research. Furthermore, it's important to highlight that analytical queries on EHRs data often do not demand real-time responses, making the architecture's processing time not only acceptable but also highly valuable in optimizing data organization. This chapter underscores the significance of harmonizing EHRs data models with data mining tools to unlock the full potential of healthcare data. By effectively addressing the challenges associated with EHRs, this architecture empowers healthcare organizations to harness the wealth of information embedded within their data, facilitating informed decision-making, groundbreaking research, and ultimately, the advancement of healthcare outcomes. The future scope of research and development in the field of Electronic Health Records (EHRs) and healthcare data management is promising and holds the potential for numerous advancements. Here are some key areas of future scope:

Interoperability Standards: Enhancing and standardizing interoperability protocols and standards will remain a critical focus. Future efforts should concentrate on developing universally accepted standards that facilitate seamless data exchange among healthcare systems and organizations. This will enable comprehensive patient care and improve data sharing across borders.

The future of Electronic Health Records (EHRs) and healthcare data management is poised for remarkable advancements across various fronts. Data security and privacy will remain paramount, driving the adoption of robust encryption methods, stringent access controls, and compliance with evolving regulations such as GDPR and HIPAA. Blockchain-based solutions and other innovations in safe data exchange will help strengthen the security of sensitive patient data.

Furthermore, the integration of AI and ML into EHRs will keep developing, enabling predictive analytics, early illness identification, individualized treatment plans, and improved natural language processing for better data extraction and interpretation. Future improvements will concentrate on seamless integration with EHRs, providing real-time updates and effective use of remote healthcare services. The rising acceptance of telemedicine and remote patient monitoring will lead to an increased number of digital health data.

Additionally, the move toward patient-centered treatment will provide people more access to and control over their health data. Future EHR systems are anticipated to have more user-focused features such secure patient portals, mobile applications, and seamless wearable device integration. Last but not least, the importance of big data analytics will grow as the healthcare industry produces enormous volumes of data. Healthcare professionals will be able to gain insightful data from EHRs with the use of advanced analytics tools, which will result in more efficient treatments, lower costs, and better population health management.

In conclusion, there is enormous potential for game-changing developments in the future of EHRs and healthcare data management. It will be crucial to seize these chances if we want to enhance patient care, cut costs, and advance the healthcare industry as a whole.

8. CONCLUSION

In conclusion, this book chapter offers a thorough investigation of the complicated world of standard-based Electronic Health Records (EHRs), providing insightful information about the numerous difficulties they inevitably pose. These challenges encompass issues of data sparseness, the dynamic and frequent evolution of healthcare data, and the critical necessity for efficient query processing within this evolving landscape. By addressing these challenges and proposing innovative solutions, the chapter contributes to the ongoing development and enhancement of EHR systems, ultimately fostering the improvement of healthcare data management and delivery for the benefit of patients and healthcare providers alike. The medical community's preference for visualizing EHRs as attribute-value pairs adds a layer of complexity, particularly when it comes to compatibility with existing data mining tools. The intersection of healthcare and technology has historically been a fertile ground for innovation, and the advent of Artificial Intelligence (AI) has ushered in a new era of boundless possibilities. Several key themes have emerged as we've worked through the challenging process of integrating AI into Clinical Decision Support Systems (CDSS) and Electronic Health Records (EHRs). First and foremost, it is plainly obvious that the incorporation of AI into these systems marks a transformational leap rather than merely an incremental advance. EHRs, which have previously simplified and digitalized patient data, are now reaching new heights because to AI's amazing capacity to quickly evaluate and extract insightful knowledge from massive amounts of data. Contrarily, CDSS is going through a significant transformation, moving from rule-based systems that provide general guidance to intelligent systems that may provide individualized, real-time suggestions. Numerous advantages are anticipated as a result of this integration of AI with EHRs and CDSS. These advantages include a wide range of topics, such as improved patient safety, individualized treatment regimens, precise diagnostics, and increased healthcare productivity. The advantages of AI also extend to data management, enabling improved healthcare data organization and usage for research and population health management. Furthermore, these systems will only improve with continued usage since AI is capable of adapting and learning from data over time. In conclusion, the integration of AI into CDSSs and EHRs is a noteworthy development that might fundamentally change the healthcare sector. It enhances patient care, provides fresh perspectives to medical practitioners, and may hasten important advancements in medical research. This marks a turning point for the healthcare sector as artificial intelligence (AI) and data systems continue to evolve together. This confluence might bring about a profound change in the healthcare industry by revolutionising the provision and use of healthcare services. Artificial intelligence (AI) has great promise for revolutionising the healthcare sector via its capacity to improve diagnostic accuracy, facilitate personalised treatment plans, enable real-time patient monitoring, and provide predictive analytics. Artificial intelligence (AI) has the potential to empower patients as well as help healthcare practitioners by giving them the knowledge and resources they need to take an active role in their own treatment. As with any innovative inventions, there are still problems. Potential biases, data privacy, system interoperability, and ethical issues are major concerns. A balanced strategy that incorporates strong legal frameworks, ethical standards, and technology improvements is needed to address these issues. However, the potential is definitely amazing going forward. We are at the beginning of a time when patient-centered, proactive, and accurate healthcare will be the norm. a time when artificial intelligence (AI) technology collaborates with human knowledge to guarantee the best possible results for patients. The vision of a highly technologically sophisticated and profoundly compassionate healthcare system is becoming a reality as we develop and improve these linkages.

REFERENCES

Anandaram, Gupta, & Verma. (2023). IoT Wearable Breast Temperature Assessment System. *2023 7th International Conference on Computing Methodologies and Communication (ICCMC)*, 1236-1241.

Archana Shreee, S., Maheshwari, B., & Jeevitha Sai, G. (2023). A Novel Method of Identification of Delirium in Patients from Electronic Health Records Using Machine Learning. *2023 World Conference on Communication & Computing (WCONF)*, 1-6.

Chakrasali, S. V., Kumar, C., Chaturvedi, A., & Jaisudhan Pazhani, A. A. (2023). Computer vision based healthcare system for identification of diabetes & its types using AI, Measurement. *Sensors (Basel)*, *27*, 10075.

G. A., Naik, & HG. (2021). Covid-19 Prevention Kit Based on an Infrared Touchless Thermometer and Distance Detector. *2021 5th International Conference on Electronics, Communication and Aerospace Technology (ICECA)*, 358-362.

Hombalimath, Palanikkumar, & Patwari. (2023). Symmetrized Feature Selection with Stacked Generalization based Machine Learning Algorithm for the Early Diagnosis of Chronic Diseases. *2023 5th International Conference on Smart Systems and Inventive Technology (ICSSIT)*, 838-844.

Jeevan, K., & Sathisha, B. M. (2020). Implementation of IoT Based Wireless Electronic Stethoscope. *2020 Third International Conference on Multimedia Processing, Communication & Information Technology (MPCIT)*, 103-106.

Kavitha, R., Kumar, A., Kalpana, V., & Hariram, V. (2023). Artificial Intelligence based Health Monitoring System on IoTH platform. *2023 Second International Conference on Augmented Intelligence and Sustainable Systems (ICAISS)*, 1458-1463.

Kawale, S. R., & Diwan, S. P. (2022). Intelligent Breast Abnormality Framework for Detection and Evaluation of Breast Abnormal Parameters. *2022 International Conference on Edge Computing and Applications (ICECAA),* 1503-1508.

Kishore Kumar, R., Pandidurai, M., & Senthil Kamalesh, M. S. C. (2023). Design of IoT based Rural Health Helper using Natural Language Processing. *2023 4th International Conference on Electronics and Sustainable Communication Systems (ICESC)*, 328-333.

Kranthi, M., & Tanguturi, R. C. (2023). Design of Intelligent Medical Integrity Authentication and Secure Information for Public Cloud in Hospital Administration. *2023 2nd International Conference on Edge Computing and Applications (ICECAA),* 256-261.

M. R. G. & Anandaram. (2022). Extraction of Fetal ECG Using ANFIS and the Undecimated-Wavelet Transform. *2022 IEEE 3rd Global Conference for Advancement in Technology (GCAT),* 1-5.

Mailapur & M. K. (2023). Implementation of GUI based Vital Track Ambulance for Patient Health Monitoring. *2023 8th International Conference on Communication and Electronics Systems (ICCES),* 1417-1424.

Namitha, Manu, Rashmi, & Chinamuttevi. (2022). IOT Based Smart Health Care System to Monitor Covid-19 Patients. *IJEER, 10*(1), 36-40.

Nareshkumar, A., & Gururaj, B. (2022). An Integrated IoT Technology for Health and Traffic Monitoring System with Smart Ambulance. *2022 IEEE North Karnataka Subsection Flagship International Conference (NKCon),* 1-6.

Naveen, K. B., Ramesha, M., & Pai, G. N. (2020). Internet of things: Internet revolution, impact, technology road map and features. *Adv. Math. Sci. J.*, *9*(7), 4405–4414. doi:10.37418/amsj.9.7.11

Palanikkumar, D., Mary, P. A., & Begum, A. Y. (2023). A Novel IoT Framework and Device Architecture for Efficient Smart city Implementation. *2023 7th International Conference on Trends in Electronics and Informatics (ICOEI),* 420-426.

Prasad, K., Anil Kumar, N., Reddy, N. S., & Ashreetha, B. (2023). Technologies for Comprehensive Information Security in the IoT. *2023 International Conference for Advancement in Technology (ICONAT),* 1-5.

Prasad, K., Dekka, S., Tanguturi, R. c., & Poornima, G. (2022). An Intelligent System for Remote Monitoring of Patients Health and the Early Detection of Coronary Artery Disease. *2022 International Conference on Smart Generation Computing, Communication and Networking (SMART GENCON),* 1-6.

Ram Vishal, Shankar, & K. A. M. (2023). Cardiovascular Disease Prediction Using LSTM Algorithm based On Cytokines. *2023 4th International Conference for Emerging Technology (INCET),* 1-5.

Ramesh Naidu, P., Guruprasad, N., & Dankan Gowda, V. (2020). Design and implementation of crypt-cloud system for securing files in cloud. *Adv. Math. Sci. J.*, *9*(7), 4485–4493. doi:10.37418/amsj.9.7.17

Ramesh Naidu, P., Guruprasad, N., & Dankan Gowda, V. (2021). A High-Availability and Integrity Layer for Cloud Storage, Cloud Computing Security: From Single to Multi-Clouds. *Journal of Physics: Conference Series*, *1921*(1), 012072. doi:10.1088/1742-6596/1921/1/012072

Rao, B. K., Chaturvedi, A., & Hussain, N. (2022). Industrial quality healthcare services using Internet of Things and fog computing approach, Measurement. *Sensors (Basel)*, *24*, 100517.

Reddy, S., & Patwal, P. P. S. (2022). Data Analytics and Cloud-Based Platform for Internet of Things Applications in Smart Cities. *2022 International Conference on Industry 4.0 Technology (I4Tech)*, 1-6.

Revanna, Kameswara Rao, & Sarma. (2022). Enhanced Diagnostic Methods for Identifying Anomalies in Imaging of Skin Lesions. *IJEER 10*(4), 1077-1085.

Swathi Pai, Shruthi, & Naveen. (2020). Internet of Things: A Survey on Devices, Ecosystem, Components and Communication Protocols. *2020 4th International Conference on Electronics, Communication and Aerospace Technology (ICECA)*, 611-616.

Tanguturi, S. R. C. K., & V. C. H. (2023). Implementation of Machine Learning Approach for Detecting Cardiovascular Diseases. *2023 3rd International Conference on Intelligent Technologies (CONIT)*, 1-6.

U. K. N., & R. V. M. (2022). Arduino based COVID-19 Suspect Detection Device. *2022 6th International Conference on Electronics, Communication and Aerospace Technology,* 158-163.

Venkatakiran, S., Ashreetha, B., & Reddy, N. S. (2023). Implementation of a Machine Learning-based Model for Cardiovascular Disease Post Exposure prophylaxis. *2023 International Conference for Advancement in Technology (ICONAT),* 1-5.

KEY TERMS AND DEFINITIONS

Artificial Intelligence (AI): A field in computer science that aims to build robots that can replicate cognitive processes like language comprehension, learning, reasoning, and problem-solving.

Clinical Decision Support Systems (CDSS): Computer programmes that assist in decision-making in healthcare settings, interpreting clinical data and offering advice to medical personnel.

Electronic Health Records (EHR): A digital copy of a patient's medical history that is kept up to date over time by the provider and contains all of the essential clinical information necessary for that person to receive care from that particular provider, such as demographics, progress notes, issues, medications, vital signs, previous medical history, immunisations, laboratory results, and radiology reports.

Health Informatics: The multidisciplinary study of how IT-based innovations are designed, developed, adopted, and used in the management, planning, and provision of healthcare services.

Interoperability: The capacity of various devices, applications, or information systems to communicate, share information, and work together in a coordinated way.

Machine Learning (ML): A branch of AI that focuses on the use of statistical models and techniques to enable computers to become better at tasks over time.

Natural Language Processing (NLP): A branch of artificial intelligence that focuses on how people and computers interact, particularly on how to teach computers to handle and analyse large volumes of natural language input.

Predictive Analytics: Estimating future outcomes' probability using data, statistical algorithms, and machine learning methods based on past performance.

Chapter 14
Assessment of Machine Learning Techniques for Improving Agriculture Crop Production

Jayanti Kumari
Ranchi University, India

Khushbu Kumari
Yogoda Satsanga Mahavidyalaya, Dhurwa, India

Ashish Sinha
Sarala Birla University, India

ABSTRACT

In an agricultural country like India, planning and execution play an essential role in upsurging productivity with minimal cost. Crop production is based on different parameters like soil, moisture, temperature, rainfall, seeds, seasons, and crop production planning. Various parameters play crucial roles in crop production and in improving farmer economic situations. The data mining concept has come into the picture for a better understanding of the crop market. In this chapter, different machine learning methods are being analyzed to showcase the application and importance of applying machine learning tools in the improvement of crop production. The research continues with the requirement of kinds of fertilizers and pesticides, types of crops produced as per the soil type, and Rabi and Kharif crops distinction for different seasons. The chapter critically examines the machine learning techniques for crop production. The research will provide a framework for researchers in the agricultural and technology sectors to understand crop production.

DOI: 10.4018/979-8-3693-0807-3.ch014

INTRODUCTION

Agriculture is a critical sector in India, providing livelihoods to a substantial portion of the population. While the sector faces various challenges, it continues to be a backbone of the Indian economy and plays a pivotal role in ensuring food security for the nation. The cultivating and farming area give significant establishments to the Indian economy. Disregarding the way that India has accomplished self-maintainability in food staples its rural efficiency is low. Efforts to modernize farming practices, improve infrastructure, and enhance the well-being of farmers remain ongoing priorities in the agricultural sector in Indian economy (Wagh, 2016; Bais & Bahadur, 2023). The cultivating and farming area give significant establishments to the Indian economy. Disregarding the way that India has accomplished self-maintainability in food staples its rural efficiency is low. India because of its changed actual elements has assortment of soil which is extraordinarily ideal for developing various harvests and it is powerful country for rice creation everywhere. To obtain wanted result farmers should definitively know when to plant the seeds. Also, India encounters shifted precipitation at better places which straightforwardly influences the harvest on the grounds that both low and extreme precipitation will make harm crops; thus, genuine precipitation is wanted for better yield creation. Many factors, for example, temperature, humidity likewise influence the harvest yield. Farming results depend upon geographical, climatic circumstances and season. The horticultural yield gives one of the quantifiable boundaries that contribute towards the real pay of the country. This is still up in the air based on developed regions and harvest creation of whole country. To get further developed monetary results we ought to concentrate on the agrarian information base comprising information about crops, season, region, creation, and so forth. Study and examination of such enormous rural data set is brought out using different information mining strategies. Information mining is the most common way of dissecting enormous informational indexes to decide helpful examples and removing significant data, this cycle is otherwise called information extraction. Information extraction from enormous informational index is finished by applying different information mining procedures. There are number of public area associations which comprise of exhaustive hotspot for farming information, either for instructive reasons or different practices connected with horticulture. This information is generally accessible on Indian sites. Many open-source devices for mining information are accessible to decide patterns and expectations connected with agrarian results and harvest yield. Today, Data mining plays a significant role in agriculture by helping farmers, researchers, and agricultural organizations make informed decisions, optimize processes, and enhance overall productivity which ultimately improve the farmer's economical condition which is the most concerned goal of agriculturally based economy (Raorane & Kulkarni, 2013; Macuácua et al., 2023; Medar & Rajpurohit, 2014; Li et al., 2023; Paul et al., 2015; Hira & Deshpande, 2015). Here are some ways data mining is used in agriculture:

- **Crop Yield Prediction:** Data mining techniques can analyse historical weather data, soil information, and crop yield data to predict future yields. This helps farmers plan planting and harvesting schedules and make informed decisions regarding crop management.
- **Pest and Disease Detection:** Data mining can be used to identify patterns and anomalies in crop health data. By analyzing data from sensors, satellite imagery, or drones, it's possible to detect early signs of pest infestations or diseases. This allows for timely interventions to minimize crop losses.

- **Soil Analysis:** Data mining can help analyze soil data to determine its nutrient content, pH levels, and other properties. This information aids in making decisions about soil management, such as the types of crops to plant and the need for fertilizers or soil amendments.
- **Precision Agriculture:** Data mining, combined with technologies like GPS and drones, enables precision agriculture. Farmers can collect data on soil quality, moisture levels, and other variables at a fine-grained level. This information is then used to optimize the use of resources, such as water and fertilizers, reducing waste and improving yields.
- **Supply Chain Optimization:** Data mining can be used to analyze supply chain data in agriculture. This includes tracking the movement of products from farm to market, optimizing transportation routes, and managing inventory. It helps reduce waste and improve the efficiency of the agricultural supply chain.
- **Market and Price Analysis:** Data mining can analyze market data, including historical prices and demand trends. Farmers can use this information to make decisions about what crops to plant, when to sell, and where to sell their products.
- **Livestock Management:** Data mining can be used to track and manage livestock health and performance. For example, sensors and data analysis can help monitor the health of animals, optimize feed, and predict disease outbreaks.
- **Weather Forecasting:** Accurate weather forecasts are crucial for agriculture. Data mining can be used to improve weather prediction models, helping farmers make more informed decisions about planting and harvesting times.
- **Machine Learning for Crop Identification:** Machine learning models can be trained to identify specific crop types and their growth stages using image and sensor data. This helps with monitoring crop health and automating tasks like weed control.
- **Research and Genetic Improvement:** Data mining can be used in genomic analysis to identify genetic traits in crops and livestock that are associated with desirable characteristics, such as resistance to diseases or high yield. This information can guide breeding programs.
- **Decision Support Systems:** Data mining can be integrated into decision support systems that provide farmers with actionable insights and recommendations based on data analysis. These systems can help with day-to-day farm management decisions.

Nowadays, Machine learning has the potential to significantly improve crop production by helping farmers make data-driven decisions and optimize various aspects of their farming operations (Prema et al., n.d.; Benos et al., 2021; Jagtap et al., 2022; McQueen et al., 1995). Machine learning is one of the tools of data mining and currently outperforming in comparison to traditional methods since it is based on learning scenarios or real time data of the concerned field. Machine learning algorithms can be trained on data collected from different regions to classify soil types based on their features. Features could include soil texture, pH levels, organic matter content, moisture, and mineral composition. Once classified, this information can help farmers and agronomists make informed decisions about crop selection and soil management. Soil plays a crucial role in agriculture, and understanding the various types of soil and their characteristics is essential for successful crop cultivation. Here are some key applications of machine learning in agriculture to enhance crop production:

- **Crop Yield Prediction:** Machine learning models can analyze historical data on weather patterns, soil conditions, and crop yields to make predictions about future yields. This information helps farmers plan their planting, harvesting, and resource allocation more effectively.
- **Disease and Pest Detection:** Machine learning algorithms can analyze images or sensor data to detect signs of crop diseases, pests, or stress in plants. Early detection allows for timely intervention to prevent or minimize crop losses.
- **Weed Management:** Machine learning can be used to distinguish between crops and weeds in images, enabling precision herbicide application and reducing the need for chemicals, ultimately saving costs and reducing environmental impact.
- **Irrigation Management:** Machine learning models can analyze soil moisture data and weather forecasts to optimize irrigation schedules. This helps conserve water resources and prevents over-irrigation, which can damage crops and degrade soil quality.
- **Nutrient Management:** Machine learning can analyze soil data to determine nutrient levels and recommend precise fertilizer application, minimizing waste and reducing environmental pollution.
- **Crop Health Monitoring:** Remote sensing data from satellites or drones can be analyzed using machine learning to monitor the overall health of crops. This includes detecting nutrient deficiencies, water stress, and other factors affecting crop growth.
- **Weather Forecasting:** Accurate weather predictions are crucial for farming. Machine learning can help improve weather forecasting models, enabling farmers to plan and make decisions based on accurate weather information.
- **Genetic Improvement:** Machine learning can assist in genetic research by analyzing genomic data to identify genes associated with desirable crop traits. This information can guide crop breeding programs to develop more resilient and high-yielding varieties.
- **Predictive Analytics for Disease Outbreaks:** Machine learning models can analyze historical disease and weather data to predict disease outbreaks. Farmers can use this information to implement preventive measures.
- **Market and Price Analysis:** Machine learning can process market data to help farmers make informed decisions about what crops to plant, when to sell, and where to sell their products. This information can also aid in price negotiation and market strategies.
- **Robotic Farming:** Machine learning algorithms are used to control agricultural robots and autonomous machinery, such as autonomous tractors and robotic harvesters, which can perform various tasks more efficiently and with precision.
- **Decision Support Systems:** Machine learning can be integrated into decision support systems that provide real-time insights and recommendations for farmers, assisting them in managing their operations effectively.
- **Smart Farming and IoT Integration:** Machine learning can be used to analyse data from Internet of Things (IoT) devices and sensors, allowing farmers to monitor various factors like temperature, humidity, and soil conditions in real-time.
- **Crop Rotation and Planning:** Machine learning can help in optimizing crop rotation strategies, which can improve soil health and reduce the risk of pests and diseases.
- **Resource Allocation:** Machine learning can assist in managing resources such as labour, machinery, and equipment more efficiently, reducing operational costs.

Thus, by applying machine learning to agriculture, farmers can enhance their decision-making processes, improve resource management, reduce environmental impact, and ultimately increase crop yields and profitability while contributing to sustainable and efficient farming practices.

BACKGROUND OF THE WORK

This part endeavors to characterize a rundown of models or methodologies that are examined comparable to proposed work. furthermore, how to build the harvest yield in view of a few elements. The K-Means clustering is usage of spatial temporal cluster data mining techniques provides changes report of the dataset. Using clustering analysis is the process of discovering groups. The FT is used to filter the data season wise and found maximum production of rice occurrence district report (Shettar & Angadi, 2016). Research showcases the status of IOT and working of smart agriculture using IOT. This research explains about completely robotize the framework; this exploration is essentially center around improving the adequacy of the current harvest yield Forecast. The harvest yield forecast cautiously screens the harvest yield level. The sensor empowers the camera to refresh the noticeable worth and save it to the cloud as the harvest yield level raises (Sharma et al., 2020). In order to choose the strategy that would produce the highest results, decision tree regression and random forest regression techniques are both applied to the input data. Performance indicators are used to compare these strategies. Both techniques appear to be effective based on metrics studies, but Random Forest regression provides a higher accuracy score on test data than Decision tree regression. The suggested study can be expanded to analyse the crop's climatic circumstances and other aspects in order to boost crop productivity (Vanitha et al., 2019). Crop yield expectation and proficient utilization of the manure is effectively anticipated and furthermore tracked down the productive calculation from both the calculation and got the most proficient result of the yield. In future fostering the web application in light of this belief system and make the client utilize this effectively and help the client to comprehend the yield of the harvest, he will trim in that season (Bhanumathi et al., 2019). There are many reasons given for farmer suicides like inadequate monsoon rainfall, interest rates are high, certain government policies are not in welfare, mental health issues, personal and family problems. It is also noticed that even the states are responsible for manipulating certain statistics. this research work uses data mining clustering technique to group attributes that results in low crop production. Case studies are conducted to map and co-relate the low crop production, monsoon factors along with farmer suicidal data (Sharma & Sabitha, 2019). Day by day environment is changing and is not stable at various places. It is very important for the farmer to cultivate their farm in good climatic conditions, under such conditions they need technology that predicts the environment. In such cases data mining is the apt technology for prediction (Venkaiah & Sunitha, 2019). Numerous associations are tracking agrarian practices and their results and information being created by such associations is expanding dramatically. Thus, this rural information should be examined to notice helpful patterns and data. In our review we are utilizing fast digger apparatus for executing information mining strategies to examine accessible informational collection, mining valuable examples and getting expectations utilizing summed up direct model, profound learning, choice tree, irregular backwoods, and slope helped trees and backing vector machine calculation (Jambekar et al., 2018). Farmers would profit from precise forecasts of different harvest yields all through various areas. This assists with supporting the Indian economy by expanding crop yield rates (Bhosale et al., 2018). This horticultural information should be investigated to notice valuable patterns and data. In review we are utilizing fast digger device for executing information mining procedures to dissect accessible informational collection, mining valuable examples and getting expectations utilizing summed up straight model, profound learning, choice tree, irregular woods, and slope helped trees and backing vector machine calculation (Kaur & Attwal, 2017). Soil information investigation is typically connected with training in farming creation the board or then again revelation in agro-biological system process, so it isn't not difficult to acquire named information that requires human intercession, and it is additionally not sensible to set determined design ahead of time. It is attractive to audit the examination work on soil information investigation utilizing spatial grouping procedures in setting of rural applications, which is the object of this study. Soil properties (counting physical, synthetic, also organic properties) and the attributes of the spatial soil information are first presented. Spatial bunching strategies are then, at that point, summed up in five unique classes. Soil information investigation utilizing spatial bunching is explored in four classifications of agrarian applications: horticultural creation the board drafting, exhaustive appraisal of soil and land, soil and land order, and connection study for agro-environment. The customary grouping calculations for the most part function admirably, and model based bunching strategies are more liked practically speaking. Some AI models can be additionally brought into the spatial bunching calculations for better convenience to different qualities of soil dataset (Majumdar et al., 2017). GATree, Fuzzy Classification rules and Fuzzy C - Means calculation for arranging soil surface in farming soil information. The soil information utilized in this paper comprises of 111 examples with 8 ascribes like (i.e., Profundity, Sand, Sediment, Mud, Sand by silt, Sand by clay, Sand bysiltclay, Texture Class). The paper clearly examines the effectiveness of Genetic algorithm, Fuzzy Classification Rules and Fuzzy C- Means on the basis of supervised and unsupervised soil data. Where Fuzzy Classification is recorded better than Genetic Algorithm. The GA-Tree achieved 46.67% accuracy and Fuzzy Classification rules achieved 99% classification accuracy (Bhargavi & Jyothi, 2011). The uses of convolutional neural network-based supervised learning (CNN-SL), Transfer learning (TL), and few-shot learning (FSL) in crop detecting at land, field, covering, and leaf scales are the focal point of this survey. this work can go about as a source of perspective for the worldwide rural local area with respect to Deep Learning for precision Agriculture can further used for more extensive exploration to advance the development of present-day farming (Wang). Machine Learning is the most common way of separating helpful data from different sorts of information. The characterization of items is a significant region inside the field of data mining, and its application reaches out to various regions, whether in the area of science. Albeit k-Nearest Neighbor classification algorithm is a simple and powerful method. A data set of 500 pictures of yields was used for performing study. In trial examination, three order calculations in particular, SVM-Support Vector Machine, C 4.5 and ID3 classifiers are applied. The machine learning based classifiers classifies different crop images. This will help in identification of crop diseases prediction (Jagtap et al., 2022). The created picture detecting techniques are considered as sensors in an agrarian digital actual framework in which huge information on the development status of horticultural plants and natural data (e.g., climate, temperature, mugginess, sun-oriented radiation, soil condition, and so on) are examined to dig helpful guidelines for suitable development. The proposed picture detecting strategies are developed by joining a few picture handling and AI methods. The bloom discovery is acknowledged in light of a coarse-to-fine methodology where up-and-comer areas of blossoms are first identified by SLIC and tint data, and the acknowledgment of blossoms is chosen by CNN (Yahata et al., 2017).

MACHINE LEARNING ALGORITHMS

Machine learning encompasses a wide range of algorithms and techniques used to enable computers to learn and make predictions or decisions based on data. These algorithms are classified into various categories based on their characteristics and the types of problems they are designed to solve. Here are some common machine learning algorithms:

Supervised Learning Algorithms

- **Linear Regression:** Used for regression problems to model the relationship between a dependent variable and one or more independent variables (Su et al., 2012).
- **Logistic Regression:** Suitable for binary classification problems, it models the probability that an instance belongs to a particular class (Gasso, 2019).
- **Support Vector Machines (SVM):** Effective for classification and regression, SVM aims to find a hyperplane that best separates data points of different classes (Suthaharan & Suthaharan, 2016).
- **Decision Trees:** Used for classification and regression, decision trees represent decisions and their consequences in a tree-like structure (Kotsiantis, 2013).
- **Random Forest:** An ensemble method that combines multiple decision trees to improve predictive accuracy and reduce overfitting (Rigatti, 2017).
- **Gradient Boosting (e.g., XGBoost, LightGBM):** Ensemble methods that build decision trees sequentially, learning from the errors of previous trees to improve prediction (Bentéjac et al., 2021).
- **K-Nearest Neighbours (KNN):** A simple instance-based classification algorithm that assigns a class label based on the majority class among its k-nearest neighbours (Guo et al., 2003).

Unsupervised Learning Algorithms

- **K-Means Clustering:** Used for clustering data into k clusters based on similarity (Na et al., 2010).
- **Hierarchical Clustering:** Builds a tree-like structure of clusters that can be used for hierarchical data analysis (Nielsen & Nielsen, 2016).
- **Principal Component Analysis (PCA):** A dimensionality reduction technique used to reduce the number of features while preserving the most important information (Bro & Smilde, 2014).
- **Autoencoders:** Neural networks used for unsupervised learning and feature extraction (Bank et al., 2023).
- **DBSCAN:** Density-based spatial clustering of applications with noise (Schubert et al., 2017).

Reinforcement Learning Algorithms

- **Q-Learning:** A model-free reinforcement learning algorithm used to make decisions based on trial and error.
- **Deep Q-Networks (DQN):** Combines Q-learning with deep neural networks for more complex tasks (Huang).
- **Policy Gradient Methods:** Directly optimize the policy of an agent in reinforcement learning.

Natural Language Processing (NLP) Algorithms

- ◦ **Word2Vec:** Used for word embeddings to represent words as dense vectors.
- ◦ **Recurrent Neural Networks (RNNs):** Designed for sequence data and used for tasks like text generation and sentiment analysis (Grossberg, 2013).
- ◦ **Long Short-Term Memory (LSTM) Networks:** A type of RNN with improved handling of long sequences (Graves & Graves, 2012).
- ◦ **Transformer Models (e.g., BERT, GPT-3):** State-of-the-art models for NLP tasks, capable of understanding context and generating human-like text.

Deep Learning Algorithms

- ◦ **Convolutional Neural Networks (CNNs):** Specialized for image analysis and computer vision tasks (O'Shea & Nash, 2015).
- ◦ **Recurrent Neural Networks (RNNs):** Designed for sequential data analysis, including text and time series (Grossberg, 2013).
- ◦ **Deep Neural Networks (DNNs):** General-purpose deep learning models used in various applications, such as image and speech recognition (Montavon et al., 2018).

Ensemble Methods

- ◦ **Bagging:** Combining multiple models to reduce variance (e.g., Random Forest).
- ◦ **Boosting:** Combining multiple models to reduce bias (e.g., AdaBoost, Gradient Boosting).
- ◦ **Stacking:** Building a meta-model that combines predictions from multiple base models.

These are just a few examples of machine learning algorithms, and there are many more specialized algorithms and techniques for specific tasks. The choice of algorithm depends on the problem you are trying to solve, the nature of your data, and the resources available for training and deployment (Dietterich, 2000; Zhou, 2012).

APPLICATION OF MACHINE LEARNING TECHNIQUES FOR IMPROVING CROP PRODUCTION

Machine learning techniques have shown significant promise in improving crop production, but like any technology, they come with their own set of advantages and challenges. Here's a critical review of machine learning techniques in the context of crop production and agricultural sector. Machine learning classifiers are algorithms used to categorize or label data into predefined classes or categories. These classifiers are namely Logistic Regression, K-Nearest Neighbors (KNN), Support Vector Machines (SVM), Random Forest, Decision Tree, Gradient Boosting, Artificial Neural Network etc. as an essential part of directed AI, and they are utilized in a great many applications, including picture acknowledgment, spam email separating, clinical conclusion, and the sky is the limit from there. The decision of classifier relies upon the idea of the information, the issue's intricacy, and the particular prerequisites of the application. It's generally expected to explore different avenues regarding various classifiers to figure out which one performs best for a given errand. Also, troupe techniques like Arbitrary Backwoods, Inclination Supporting, and AdaBoost are in many cases used to consolidate numerous classifiers for further developed execution and heartiness. Table 1 comprises different machine learning techniques used in improving agricultural production and allied activities.

Table 1. Different machine learning techniques used for agricultural and allied activities

Article	Method Used	Dataset/Research Testbed	Outcome/Result
A Machine Learning-Based Comparative Approach to Predict the Crop Yield Using Supervised Learning With Regression Models (Panigrahi et al., 2023)	Six Different Regression Model Namely Linear Regression, Decision Tree Regression, Gradient Boosting Regression, Random Forest Regression, XGBoot Regression, Voting Regression were used for experimentation.	A two-year data (2016 to 2018) of Groundnut, Bengal Gram and Maize crop production data have been taken from Telangana State of India.	This examination intensely underlined the adaption of the AI (ML) procedures and prepared on six different directed based learning relapse models to assess the crop yield. Outcome recorded through Random Forest Regression and XGBoost Regression were more accurate than other comparatively used methods. The three metrics namely Mean Absolute Error (MAE), R2 score, and Cross-Validation score were used for testing accuracy of these techniques. Additionally, with a MAE score of 468.16, MSE score of 825.29, R2 score of 0.7952 and a Cross-Approval score of 0.6087 is recorded where Random Forest Regression model outperformed the XGBoost Regression model after parameter tuning.
Prediction of major crop yields of Tamilnadu using K-means and Modified KNN (Suresh et al., 2018)	K-Means Clustring, Fuzzy System & K-Nearest Neighbour (KNN) and Modified KNN are used for performing the research.	The five important crops of Tamilnadu state for the year 2005-2010 was taken for performing the test. These are Rice, Sugarcane, Maize, Ragi, and Tapioca.	The research has expressed the forecast of significant harvest yields of Tamilnadu utilizing K-Means and Modified KNN. The Investigation has been performed on three sorts of calculations fuzzy System, KNN and Modified KNN out of which the modified KNN has ended up being awesome of all the three calculations with 95.3% of accuracy which was comparatively better than the other two used methods.
Precision Sugarcane Monitoring Using SVM Classifier (Kumar et al., 2017)	K-Nearest Neighbour (KNN) and Support Vector Machine (SVM) classifiers have been used for performing the test on 200 images taken from camera along with sensor data of Sugarcane crop.	Research experiment includes information from sensors and Pictures from camera. Sensors utilized are temperature, Humidity and Moisture.	Accuracy agribusiness techniques with brilliant calculations are the need of hour to meet current and future necessities of agricultural crop production. The precision accomplished is 96% on example of 200 pictures, the model was tried at Lolai, close to Malhaur, Gomti Nagar Augmentation.

Continued on following page

Table 1. Continued

Article	Method Used	Dataset/Research Testbed	Outcome/Result
Improved CNN Method for Crop Pest Identification Based on Transfer Learning (Liu et al., 2022)	Convolutional Neural Network (CNN) based VGG16 and Inception-ResNet-v2 transfer learning techniques are used for experimentation.	The dataset applied in this trial comes from the Image Data set for Agricultural Disease and Pests Research (IDADP). IDADP contains countless picture assets of harvest infections like rice, wheat, and corn. In the experimentation, the rice and wheat are chosen as the exploration objects. Each examination object chooses three normal Pests classes, a sum of six classifications, in particular, rice bacterial scourge, rice flax spot, rice impact, wheat fine mold, wheat scab, and wheat leaf rust, including 600 pictures of rice also, 400 pictures of wheat. A sum of 3,000 pictures were utilized for preparing and confirmation, and one more 300 were utilized for testing.	CNN series bug picture acknowledgment and examination models are successfully intertwined to work on the precision of the model for acknowledgment and grouping of crop pest. The results show that the accuracy of the proposed strategy for crop pest identification proof is 97.71%, which is improved in order to current techniques.
Soil Classification Using Data Mining Techniques: A Comparative Study (Bhargavi & Jyothi, 2011)	GATree, Fuzzy Classification rules and Fuzzy C - Means calculation for arranging soil surface in farming soil information	The soil information utilized in this paper comprises of 111 examples with 8 ascribes like (i.e., Profundity, Sand, Sediment, Mud, Sand by silt, Sand by clay, Sand bysiltclay, Texture Class)	This paper clearly examines the effectiveness of Genetic algorithm, Fuzzy Classification Rules and Fuzzy C- Means on the basis of supervised and unsupervised soil data. Where Fuzzy Classification recorded better than Genetic Algorithm. The GA-Tree achieved 46.67% accuracy and Fuzzy Classification rules achieved 99% classification accuracy.

Continued on following page

Table 1. Continued

Article	Method Used	Dataset/Research Testbed	Outcome/Result
Crop Prediction using Machine Learning Approaches (Nischitha et al., 2020)	For Rainfall prediction SVM algorithm are used. And for Crop prediction Decision tree algorithm are used.	The dataset includes the following details about crop production: i)Soil PH ii) Temperature iii) Mugginess iv) Precipitation v) Harvest information vi) NPK values, For the yearly precipitation expectation, we gather earlier year precipitation information.	As of now our farmers are not actually utilizing innovation and investigation, so there might be an opportunity of wrong determination of yield for development that will lessen their pay. To lessen those kind of loses we have fostered a farmers cordial framework with GUI, that will foresee which would be the best reasonable yield for specific land and this framework will likewise give data about expected supplements to add up, required seeds for development, expected yield and market cost. Along these lines, this makes the farmers to take right choice in choosing the harvest for development to such an extent that horticultural area will be created by inventive thought.
An Effective Crop Prediction Using Random Forest Algorithm (Geetha et al., 2020)	Random Forest Algorithm is a corps research philosophy for managed learning for parting, affiliation, relapse, and other tasks are set off by affecting various trees at preparing and testing process then, at that point, dissecting which class is addressing the method of the characterization or prescient relapse of choice trees. The random forest classifiers are reasonable for individual trees over fitting to their preparation and testing set of tests.	The online dataset is gathered which incorporates states and regions names, development year of harvests, climatic circumstances, locale, mass creation and which harvest must be developed.	The precision level for proposed framework is a high contrasting with exactness level in existing framework. The precision level of random forest algorithm is high since it is a stowing method. This strategy decreases the complexity of the model that over fit the preparation information where choice tree is a supporting method that increments the complexity of the model that prompts under fitting the preparation information. To defeat this the random forest algorithm was presented. In existing framework, the naïve bayes classifier precision level is less since it is a likelihood-based calculation.

Continued on following page

Table 1. Continued

Article	Method Used	Dataset/Research Testbed	Outcome/Result
Hybrid Deep Learning-based Models for Crop Yield Prediction (Oikonomidis et al., 2022)	A Hybrid Method XGBoost were applied which comprises Convolutional Neural Network (CNN) and Deep Neural Network (DNN) methods based on Neural Network Algorithm, they were both built with stacked convolutional and dense layers.	The dataset that Khaki and Wang, and Khaki, Wang, Along with Archontoulis accumulated, analysed, and used in for performing the test. The review region for this dataset alludes to the soybean crop in 9 conditions of the United State of America (USA). The dataset comprises of climate, soil, and the management data. Specifically, there are data of regular experimental soyabean crop through the time period of 1980 to 2018.	The hybrid CNN-DNN model outflanked all the others methods, having R2 = 0.87, RMSE = 0.266, MSE = 0.071, and MAE = 0.199. A hybrid technique named XGBoost with a Deep Learning algorithm like RNN or LSTM, joined with a consideration component might give better execution in crop yield forecast utilizing consecutive information of dates, this is a future work we might examine. Ultimately, Transfer learning can be utilized with a pre-trained CNN model on a comparable regression task for crop yield forecast. This technique can save a great deal of computational assets.
A GNN-RNN Approach for Harnessing Geospatial and Temporal Information: Application to Crop Yield Prediction (Fan et al., 2022)	A graph-based framework have been used which comprises Graph Neural Networks along with Recurrent Nural Network (GNN-RNN).	Crop yield labels for corn and soybean data are used which have been taken from USDA Crop Production Reports (USDA 2013) for numerous counties in the US.	A novel GNN-RNN system were proposed in this research to creatively integrate both geospatial and transient information into crop yield forecast, through graph based deep learning techniques. This paper is the first to exploit the spatial construction in the information while making crop yield prediction, instead of past methodologies which accept that neighbouring provinces are independent examples. The research direct perform experimentation on huge scope datasets covering 41 US states and 39 years, and show that the proposed methodology considerably beats a large number existing best in class AI strategies across numerous datasets.
Application of Hybrid Data Mining Model (Genetic Algorithm-Wavelet-Deep Neural Network-Monte Carlo Method) for Forecasting the Price of Agricultural Products: A Case Study of Future Price of Saffron in Agricultural Commodity Exchange (Heydari & Haj Seyed Javady, 2023)	Data mining model for exact value determining of agrarian items, including nonlinear models of wavelet change, Genetic algorithm, Deep Neural Network and Monte Carlo strategy. This proposed model included a two-stage hybrid model and the base model of nonlinear. The Genetic algorithm and wavelet function are used for price prediction fo agricultural crop.	Secondary data collected from Agricultural sector.	proposed model had the essential effectiveness and high exactness for transient anticipating representing things to come cost of saffron. Hence, the current review has a decent situation in accomplishing the record of most extreme precision, situation making of future cost patterns, responsiveness examination of parts influencing the cost lastly, determining the future cost. Appropriately, the utilization of the proposed model to gauge the cost of agrarian items is suggested.

CASE STUDY: ENHANCE AGRICULTURAL CROP PRODUCTION USING MACHINE LEARNING

The application of data mining using machine learning methods for soil classification can indeed enhance agricultural crop production in several ways. Here are some keyways this approach can be leveraged, and the potential challenges and opportunities associated with it:

Benefits and Opportunities

- **Improved Crop Selection:** Machine learning models can analyze historical data on soil composition, climate, and crop performance to suggest the most suitable crop varieties for specific regions. Farmers can make informed decisions to maximize yield and quality by planting crops that are well-suited to the soil conditions and climate.
- **Optimized Fertilization:** Machine learning can analyze soil nutrient levels, pH, and crop requirements to recommend precise fertilization strategies. This reduces over-fertilization, minimizes nutrient runoff, and leads to cost savings for farmers.
- **Pest and Disease Management:** Machine learning can identify patterns in soil data that are correlated with pest and disease outbreaks. Farmers can then implement targeted preventive measures such as crop rotation or the use of natural predators, reducing the need for chemical pesticides.
- **Water Management:** Machine learning can analyze soil moisture data and weather forecasts to optimize irrigation schedules. This conserves water, reduces energy costs, and minimizes the risk of overwatering or underwatering crops.
- **Predictive Analytics:** By analyzing historical soil data, machine learning models can predict soil degradation, erosion, and nutrient depletion. Farmers can take proactive steps, such as implementing cover cropping or conservation tillage, to preserve soil quality.
- **Precision Agriculture:** The combination of data mining and machine learning supports precision agriculture, where every action in farming is optimized. This can lead to increased productivity, reduced resource use, and better environmental sustainability.

FUTURE RESEARCH

- **Data Quality and Availability:** Soil data might be sparse or outdated in certain areas, making it challenging to develop accurate models. Collaboration between government agencies, research institutions, and technology companies is needed to improve data quality and accessibility.
- **Model Complexity:** Developing machine learning models for soil classification requires domain expertise and data science skills. Collaboration between agricultural experts and data scientists is crucial for success.
- **Interpretability:** Many machine learning models are considered black boxes, which can be a barrier for adoption. Efforts should be made to develop interpretable models or provide clear explanations for model recommendations to build trust among users.

- **Integration with Existing Practices:** Farmers may be hesitant to adopt new technologies and practices. Education and training programs can help bridge the gap and show farmers the benefits of data-driven approaches.
- **Costs:** Setting up the necessary infrastructure and collecting high-quality data can be expensive. Governments and organizations may need to provide financial support, subsidies, or grants to make these technologies more accessible to all farmers.
- **Security and Privacy:** Storing and managing sensitive soil and farm data raises concerns about security and privacy. Robust security measures, data encryption, and clear data-sharing policies can address these concerns and build trust.

The benefits of data mining and machine learning in agriculture are substantial, but addressing challenges related to data quality, model complexity, transparency, adoption, costs, and security is crucial to realizing the full potential of these technologies in enhancing crop production and sustainability. Collaborative efforts among various stakeholders are key to overcoming these challenges.

- **Data Collection and Standardization:** Efforts should be made to collect and standardize soil data. Governments, agricultural institutions, and technology companies can collaborate on this.
- **Education and Training:** Farmers and agricultural professionals should be provided with training and support to help them understand and use the technology effectively.
- **Open Data Sharing:** Encouraging open data sharing can promote innovation and research in this field, benefiting farmers and the agricultural sector as a whole.
- **Model Transparency:** Develop models that are interpretable and provide clear explanations for their recommendations. This can help build trust among users.
- **Cost Mitigation:** Explore ways to reduce the costs associated with technology adoption, perhaps through subsidies or grants for small-scale farmers.
- **Security Measures:** Implement robust security and privacy measures to protect sensitive data and build trust with farmers.

Data mining and machine learning for soil classification in agriculture offers tremendous potential for improving crop production and sustainability. However, it also comes with challenges related to data, technology adoption, and privacy that need to be addressed for its widespread and successful implementation.

SOLUTION AND RECOMMENDATION

Addressing the provokes of conventional strategies a progress to additional manageable and mechanically advanced agricultural practices, frequently alluded to as "modern" or "smart" farming. Such strategies might integrate accuracy cultivating, agtech, and feasible cultivating practices to upgrade efficiency, moderate assets, and work on the livelihoods of farmers. Regardless, the progress to present day agribusiness should be executed cautiously, considering the particular requirements and conditions of individual cultivating networks to guarantee food security, financial dependability, and natural supportability. Machine learning techniques hold enormous potential in further developing yield creation, upgrading assets for the executives, and decreasing environmental effect. Notwithstanding, addressing difficulties connected with quality of information, privacy, and implementation are significant for the broad and manageable execution of these advances in agribusiness. Moreover, guaranteeing that AI models are dependable, interpretable, and versatile to different rural settings stays a key test. Machine learning empowers information driven dynamic in horticulture. By investigating enormous datasets, it assists farmers with pursuing better decisions about crop planting, asset allotment, and reaping. Thus, by applying machine learning in agricultural sector, farmers can enhance their decision-making processes, reduce resource wastage, enhance crop yields, and improve the overall sustainability and profitability of agricultural operations. Machine learning, when combined with accurate data collection and analysis, is a valuable tool for modernizing and optimizing agriculture.

CONCLUSION

Farming exploration has profited from innovative headways, especially by integrating modern technologies into a maintainable horticulture creation framework. By zapping each cultivating system, innovation has changed cultivating into a suitable business. This sets aside the farmer cash and wipes out the go between who purchases low from farmers and offers high to end buyers. Late utilizations of computational knowledge procedures (like neural network, learning based algorithms etc.) give answers for decision modelling issues in agricultural framework. Farming is critical to the country's economy since it takes care of the entire populace. It connects and collaborates with the nation's all's pertinent endeavors along these lines. A nation is thought to be socially and monetarily prosperous in the event that it has adequately enormous farming premise. In most nations, horticulture is the essential wellspring of work. Enormous homesteads typically require the employing of additional specialists to assist with planting and livestock care. The greater part of these immense ranches has close handling plants where their agrarian items are handled and created. Farmers face numerous challenges in the agricultural sector, which can vary depending on their location, type of farming, and the specific agricultural practices they employ. The problems are mainly associated to environment concern, proper crop identification and planning seeds according to the seasons and resources, finding perfect market for their product, analyzing market and improve the production accordingly etc. To address these challenges and improve the economic conditions of farmers, it is essential to adopt sustainable and innovative farming practices, invest in rural infrastructure, provide education and training, improve access to financing and markets, and develop supportive policies that prioritize the well-being and prosperity of the farming community. For dealing with all these concerned problems the idea of machine learning has come in the picture. Machine learning applications can significantly contribute to improving farmers' economic conditions by enhancing various aspects of agriculture. leveraging machine learning applications, farmers can enhance their decision-making, reduce costs, minimize risks, and improve crop productivity, all of which contribute to improving their economic condition and the overall sustainability of agricultural practices. Machine Learning versatility, advancement, and diminished costs helps in evaluating the confounded connection between the info and result of agrarian frameworks using scientific methodologies that are described by non-linearity, time variable highlights, and various obscure components. This paper gives a survey of different machine learning based techniques that can be utilized in farming for undertakings like crop production, identification of yield disease recognition, savvy water system, soil characterization, observing previous case base scenarios, identifying better market for agricultural product, understanding different perspective of agriculture from planning to execution and so on for providing a database to future researchers. The paper clearly concluded that the diverse application and versatility of machine learning methods would improve the crop production with implementing better planning and execution approaches of crop production which will be helpful improve farmers economic condition by providing better market to their products.

ACKNOWLEDGMENT

I would like to express my heartfelt gratitude to all those who contributed to the completion of this book chapter. First and foremost, I am deeply thankful to my guide, Dr. Ashish Sinha & the editor of this volume, for providing me with the opportunity to contribute to this collection. I'm obligated to my associates, Khushbu Kumari, Saroj Kumari & Priyanka Kumari for their significant direction and keen input all through the research and writing process. Their mastery has been instrumental in forming the thoughts introduced in this part. I'm likewise grateful to my loved ones for their steady help and consolation. Their confidence in my capacities kept me propelled during testing times, and for that, I am genuinely thankful. Lastly, I am very grateful to Dr. Keshav Sinha who generously shared their experiences and insights, without whom this work would not have been possible.

REFERENCES

Bais, P., & Bahadur, P. S. (2023). Agriculture in Indian Economy and Contribution of Science and Technology. *Asian Journal of Applied Science and Technology*, *7*(1), 167–176. doi:10.38177/ajast.2023.7116

Bank, D., Koenigstein, N., & Giryes, R. (2023). Autoencoders. *Machine Learning for Data Science Handbook: Data Mining and Knowledge Discovery Handbook*, 353-374.

Benos, L., Tagarakis, A. C., Dolias, G., Berruto, R., Kateris, D., & Bochtis, D. (2021). Machine learning in agriculture: A comprehensive updated review. *Sensors (Basel)*, *21*(11), 3758. doi:10.339021113758 PMID:34071553

Bentéjac, C., Csörgő, A., & Martínez-Muñoz, G. (2021). A comparative analysis of gradient boosting algorithms. *Artificial Intelligence Review*, *54*(3), 1937–1967. doi:10.100710462-020-09896-5

Bhanumathi, S., Vineeth, M., & Rohit, N. (2019, April). Crop yield prediction and efficient use of fertilizers. In *2019 International Conference on Communication and Signal Processing (ICCSP)* (pp. 769-773). IEEE. 10.1109/ICCSP.2019.8698087

Bhargavi, P., & Jyothi, S. (2011). Soil classification using data mining techniques: A comparative study. *International Journal of Engineering Trends and Technology*, *2*(1), 55–59.

Bhosale, Thombare, Dhemey, & Chaudhari. (2018). Crop Yield Prediction Using Data Analytics and Hybrid Approach. In *Proceedings of the 4th International Conference on Computing, Communication Control and Automation*. IEEE.

Bro, R., & Smilde, A. K. (2014). Principal component analysis. *Analytical Methods*, *6*(9), 2812–2831. doi:10.1039/C3AY41907J

Dietterich, T. G. (2000, June). Ensemble methods in machine learning. In *International workshop on multiple classifier systems* (pp. 1-15). Springer Berlin Heidelberg.

Fan, J., Bai, J., Li, Z., Ortiz-Bobea, A., & Gomes, C. P. (2022, June). A GNN-RNN approach for harnessing geospatial and temporal information: Application to crop yield prediction. *Proceedings of the AAAI Conference on Artificial Intelligence*, *36*(11), 11873–11881. doi:10.1609/aaai.v36i11.21444

Gasso, G. (2019). Logistic regression. INSA Rouen-ASI Departement Laboratory: Saint-Etienne-du-Rouvray, France.

Geetha, V., Punitha, A., Abarna, M., Akshaya, M., Illakiya, S., & Janani, A. P. (2020, July). An effective crop prediction using random forest algorithm. In *2020 International Conference on System, Computation, Automation and Networking (ICSCAN)* (pp. 1-5). IEEE. 10.1109/ICSCAN49426.2020.9262311

Graves, A., & Graves, A. (2012). Long short-term memory. *Supervised sequence labelling with recurrent neural networks*, 37-45.

Grossberg, S. (2013). Recurrent neural networks. *Scholarpedia Journal*, *8*(2), 1888. doi:10.4249cholarpedia.1888

Guo, G., Wang, H., Bell, D., Bi, Y., & Greer, K. (2003). KNN model-based approach in classification. In *On The Move to Meaningful Internet Systems 2003: CoopIS, DOA, and ODBASE: OTM Confederated International Conferences, CoopIS, DOA, and ODBASE 2003, Catania, Sicily, Italy, November 3-7, 2003. Proceedings* (pp. 986-996). Springer Berlin Heidelberg. 10.1007/978-3-540-39964-3_62

Heydari, R., & Haj Seyed Javady, S. M. R. (2023). Application of Hybrid Data Mining Model (Genetic Algorithm-Wavelet-Deep Neural Network-Monte Carlo Method) for Forecasting the Price of Agricultural Products: A Case Study of Future Price of Saffron in Agricultural Commodity Exchange. Agricultural Economics and (Wagh, 2016). *Development*, *30*(4).

Hira, S., & Deshpande, P. S. (2015). Data analysis using multidimensional modeling, statistical analysis and data mining on agriculture parameters. *Procedia Computer Science*, *54*, 431–439. doi:10.1016/j.procs.2015.06.050

Huang, Y. (2020). Deep Q-networks. *Deep Reinforcement Learning: Fundamentals, Research and Applications*, 135-160.

Jagtap, S. T., Phasinam, K., Kassanuk, T., Jha, S. S., Ghosh, T., & Thakar, C. M. (2022). Towards application of various machine learning techniques in agriculture. *Materials Today: Proceedings*, *51*, 793–797. doi:10.1016/j.matpr.2021.06.236

Jambekar, S., Nema, S., & Saquib, Z. (2018). Prediction of crop production in India using data mining techniques. *Fourth International Conference on Computing Communication Control and Automation (ICCUBEA)*. 10.1109/ICCUBEA.2018.8697446

Kaur, K., & Attwal, K. S. (2017). Effect of temperature and rainfall on paddy yield using data mining. *7th International Conference on Cloud Computing, Data Science & Engineering*. 10.1109/CONFLUENCE.2017.7943204

Kotsiantis, S. B. (2013). Decision trees: A recent overview. *Artificial Intelligence Review*, *39*(4), 261–283. doi:10.100710462-011-9272-4

Kumar, S., Mishra, S., Khanna, P., & Pragya. (2017). Precision sugarcane monitoring using SVM classifier. *Procedia Computer Science*, *122*, 881–887. doi:10.1016/j.procs.2017.11.450

Li, D., Nanseki, T., Chomei, Y., & Kuang, J. (2023). A review of smart agriculture and production practices in Japanese large-scale rice farming. *Journal of the Science of Food and Agriculture*, *103*(4), 1609–1620. doi:10.1002/jsfa.12204 PMID:36069313

Liu, Y., Zhang, X., Gao, Y., Qu, T., & Shi, Y. (2022). Improved CNN method for crop pest identification based on transfer learning. *Computational Intelligence and Neuroscience*, *2022*, 2022. doi:10.1155/2022/9709648 PMID:35341164

Macuácua, J. C., Centeno, J. A. S., & Amisse, C. (2023). Data mining approach for dry bean seeds classification. *Smart Agricultural Technology*, *5*, 100240. doi:10.1016/j.atech.2023.100240

Majumdar, Naraseeyappa, & Ankalaki. (2017). Analysis of agriculture data using data mining techniques: application of big data. *Journal of Big Data.*

McQueen, R. J., Garner, S. R., Nevill-Manning, C. G., & Witten, I. H. (1995). Applying machine learning to agricultural data. *Computers and Electronics in Agriculture*, *12*(4), 275–293. doi:10.1016/0168-1699(95)98601-9

Medar, R. A., & Rajpurohit, V. S. (2014). A survey on data mining techniques for crop yield prediction. *International Journal of Advance Research in Computer Science and Management Studies*, *2*(9), 59–64.

Montavon, G., Samek, W., & Müller, K. R. (2018). Methods for interpreting and understanding deep neural networks. *Digital Signal Processing*, *73*, 1–15. doi:10.1016/j.dsp.2017.10.011

Na, S., Xumin, L., & Yong, G. (2010, April). Research on k-means clustering algorithm: An improved k-means clustering algorithm. In *2010 Third International Symposium on intelligent information technology and security informatics* (pp. 63-67). IEEE.

Nielsen, F., & Nielsen, F. (2016). Hierarchical clustering. *Introduction to HPC with MPI for Data Science*, 195-211.

Nischitha, K., Vishwakarma, D., Ashwini, M. N., & Manjuraju, M. R. (2020). Crop prediction using machine learning approaches. *International Journal of Engineering Research & Technology (Ahmedabad)*, *9*(8), 23–26.

O'Shea, K., & Nash, R. (2015). *An introduction to convolutional neural networks*. arXiv preprint arXiv:1511.08458.

Oikonomidis, A., Catal, C., & Kassahun, A. (2022). Hybrid deep learning-based models for crop yield prediction. *Applied Artificial Intelligence*, *36*(1), 2031822. doi:10.1080/08839514.2022.2031823

Panigrahi, B., Kathala, K. C. R., & Sujatha, M. (2023). A machine learning-based comparative approach to predict the crop yield using supervised learning with regression models. *Procedia Computer Science*, *218*, 2684–2693. doi:10.1016/j.procs.2023.01.241

Paul, M., Vishwakarma, S. K., & Verma, A. (2015, December). Analysis of soil behaviour and prediction of crop yield using data mining approach. In *2015 International Conference on Computational Intelligence and Communication Networks (CICN)* (pp. 766-771). IEEE. 10.1109/CICN.2015.156

Prema, P., Veeramani, A., & Sivakumar, T. (n.d.). Machine Learning Applications in Agriculture. *Journal of Agriculture Research and Technology*, 126.

Raorane, A., & Kulkarni, R. (2013). Role of data mining in Agriculture. *International Journal of Computer Science and Information Technologies*, *4*(2), 270–272.

Rigatti, S. J. (2017). Random forest. *Journal of Insurance Medicine (New York, N.Y.)*, *47*(1), 31–39. doi:10.17849/insm-47-01-31-39.1 PMID:28836909

Schubert, E., Sander, J., Ester, M., Kriegel, H. P., & Xu, X. (2017). DBSCAN revisited, revisited: Why and how you should (still) use DBSCAN. *ACM Transactions on Database Systems*, *42*(3), 1–21. doi:10.1145/3068335

Sharma & Sabitha. (2019). Identification of influential factors for productivity and sustainability of crops using data mining techniques. *6th International Conference on Signal Processing and Integrated Networks (SPIN)*.

Sharma, A., Jain, A., Gupta, P., & Chowdary, V. (2020). Machine learning applications for precision agriculture: A comprehensive review. *IEEE Access : Practical Innovations, Open Solutions*, *9*, 4843–4873. doi:10.1109/ACCESS.2020.3048415

Shettar & Angadi. (2016). Efficient data mining algorithms for agriculture data. *International Journal of Recent Trends in Engineering and Research, 2*(9).

Su, X., Yan, X., & Tsai, C. L. (2012). Linear regression. *Wiley Interdisciplinary Reviews: Computational Statistics*, *4*(3), 275–294. doi:10.1002/wics.1198

Suresh, A., Kumar, P. G., & Ramalatha, M. (2018, October). Prediction of major crop yields of Tamilnadu using K-means and Modified KNN. In *2018 3rd International conference on communication and electronics systems (ICCES)* (pp. 88-93). IEEE.

Suthaharan, S., & Suthaharan, S. (2016). Support vector machine. *Machine learning models and algorithms for big data classification: Thinking with examples for effective learning*, 207-235.

Vanitha, C. N., Archana, N., & Sowmiya, R. (2019). Agriculture analysis using data mining and machine learning techniques. In *5th International Conference on Advanced Computing & Communication Systems (ICACCS)*. IEEE.

Venkaiah & Sunitha. (2019). A new approach for predicting crop yield prediction using data mining techniques. *International Journal of Engineering, IT and Scientific Research, 3*(1).

Wagh, R., & Dongre, A. P. (2016). Agricultural sector: Status, challenges and it's role in Indian economy. *Journal of Commerce and Management Thought*, *7*(2), 209–218. doi:10.5958/0976-478X.2016.00014.8

Wang, D., Cao, W., Zhang, F., Li, Z., Xu, S., & Wu, X. (2022). A review of deep learning in multiscale agricultural sensing. *Remote Sensing (Basel)*, *14*(3), 559. doi:10.3390/rs14030559

Yahata, S., Onishi, T., Yamaguchi, K., Ozawa, S., Kitazono, J., Ohkawa, T., ... Tsuji, H. (2017, May). A hybrid machine learning approach to automatic plant phenotyping for smart agriculture. In *2017 International Joint Conference on Neural Networks (IJCNN)* (pp. 1787-1793). IEEE. 10.1109/IJCNN.2017.7966067

Zhou, Z. H. (2012). *Ensemble methods: Foundations and algorithms*. CRC Press. doi:10.1201/b12207

KEY TERMS AND DEFINITIONS

Agricultural Production: Data-driven strategies increase yields and reduce waste in agricultural production. Precision agriculture transforms farming into an efficient, sustainable practice.

Crop Prediction: Machine learning aids in accurate crop prediction for better harvest planning. Data mining reveals hidden insights for precise crop yield forecasts.

Crop Selection Optimization: Optimization tools help farmers choose the best crops for specific soil and climate conditions. This leads to increased yields and improved financial outcomes.

Data Mining: Data mining uncovers valuable insights for informed soil classification and crop choices. It identifies trends, such as soil characteristics' impact on crop yield.

Machine Learning: Machine learning optimizes tasks like irrigation and pest control in agriculture. Real-time decisions benefit agricultural production through adaptable machine learning models.

Precision Agriculture: Precision agriculture optimizes farming with technology and data for efficiency and sustainability. Resource use is fine-tuned, reducing environmental impact and boosting productivity.

Soil Classification: Soil classification aids crop selection by understanding unique soil properties. Machine learning identifies suitable crops for different soil types.

Soil Data Analysis: Soil data analysis provides crucial insights for effective soil and crop management. Machine learning interprets soil data, supporting data-driven farming decisions.

Chapter 15
Applications, Challenges, and Future Directions of Cybersecurity Surveillance Systems

Saptarshi Kumar Sarkar
Brainware University, India

Piyal Roy
Brainware University, India

Shivnath Ghosh
Brainware University, India

Amitava Podder
Brainware University, India

ABSTRACT

Systems for monitoring cybersecurity are now crucial instruments for safeguarding digital assets and fending off numerous attacks. This chapter covers the various uses, challenges, and new developments of using surveillance systems in order to enhance cybersecurity. Discussion themes include threat detection, incident response, insider threat identification, and vulnerability management. The primary challenges—including data overload, false positives, privacy concerns, skill gaps, regulatory compliance, adaptive threats, and cultural acceptance—are also exhaustively examined. The report also covers recent advancements, such as the use of zero trust architectures, the development of behavioral analytics, and the blending of AI and ML technologies. By addressing these problems and implementing these trends, organizations can strengthen their entire cybersecurity posture.

DOI: 10.4018/979-8-3693-0807-3.ch015

INTRODUCTION

It is impossible to exaggerate the critical necessity of cybersecurity in the fast changing digital environment of the twenty-first century. Fortifying digital environments against harmful actions has become a necessity due to expanding interconnectedness, technological advancement, and cyberthreat sophistication (Cybersecurity, 2018). Systems for surveillance, which act as watchful defenders in this digital world, have become crucial elements of all-encompassing cybersecurity plans.

In-depth analysis of the complex environment of surveillance systems created specifically to support cybersecurity measures is provided in this review paper. These defense-leading technologies offer a holistic security approach that includes continuous monitoring in real time, early threat identification, and quick incident response (Mekala & Vennila, 2018). They are important because they can spot, evaluate, and stop cyber threats before they become full-fledged breaches, which is essential for maintaining the integrity of digital records and defending the virtual spaces on which we are becoming more and more reliant.

An important place to start is how surveillance systems are categorized. There are three main varieties of these systems, each with a distinct emphasis and range. Utilizing advanced tools like intrusion detection and prevention systems (IDS and IPS), network surveillance involves the ongoing monitoring along with analysis of network traffic. These systems carefully examine data packets as they go via networks, compared them to known signatures of attacks or behavioral norms. Alerts are set off or automated responses are performed to neutralize possible dangers when deviations from the usual are found. Endpoint surveillance, on the other hand, focuses on specific networked devices. Computers, servers, and Internet of Things (IoT) gadgets are among these items, and they act as the first line of defense against online attacks. These devices' activities are tracked and analyzed by endpoint detection and response, or EDR, systems, which give cybersecurity personnel immediate knowledge of potential intrusions. Due to the ability to quickly respond to threats, hostile actions can be contained and stopped before they have a chance to do serious harm. The third sort of technology, behavioral surveillance, ushers machine learning and artificial intelligence into the field of cybersecurity (Drewek-Ossowicka et al., 2021). For consumers, devices, and networks, these systems provide baselines of typical behavior that allow them to identify variations that could be signs of unauthorized activity. For instance, User and Entity Behavior Analytics (UEBA) systems make use of advanced analytics to spot anomalies and new dangers, empowering cybersecurity teams to proactively handle internal and external security breaches.

Data gathering, analysis, and response are the three main building blocks of surveillance systems. In the data collecting phase, information is gathered from a variety of sources, such as network activity, log files, as well as user activity. In order to find trends, abnormalities, and potential risks, this data is then put into analytical pipelines that make use of cutting-edge machine learning algorithms. Automated measures can be triggered in response to suspicious activity, from isolating infected devices to notifying cybersecurity experts for human intervention. The variety of uses that surveillance systems have within the cybersecurity field demonstrate their adaptability. These systems stand out in the field of threat detection (Asif et al., 2021). Surveillance systems may quickly identify both known and unidentified risks by evaluating real-time data and compared it to predetermined baselines, enabling prompt countermeasures to be taken. These systems are also essential resources for incident response. Rapid and focused measures are necessary after a cyberattack to reduce damage. Systems for surveillance provide the tools needed to evaluate the severity and impact of an occurrence, allowing for efficient containment and mitigation measures.

However, surveillance systems have uses that go beyond protecting against external dangers. Insider threats, in which authorized people carry out hostile actions, pose a serious problem. With its emphasis on unusual behavior and departures from predetermined norms, behavioral surveillance is ideally suited to spot and neutralize these insider threats. Additionally, surveillance systems are essential for managing vulnerabilities since they help businesses find potential flaws and security holes in their own software and systems (Mekala & Vennila, 2018). This makes it possible to undertake preventative patching and mitigation steps, strengthening the overall cybersecurity posture. While there is no denying that monitoring systems have advantages, there are also drawbacks. Privacy issues are quite important, particularly so when it includes tracking user actions and behaviors (Probst et al., 2010). Careful study and clearly defined procedures are required to strike the correct balance between personal privacy rights and cybersecurity requirements. The problem of false positives as well as false negatives also presents a difficult hurdle. Finding the appropriate balance is crucial because too many false positives might cause alert fatigue while too many false negatives can let threats slip by unnoticed. Another urgent concern is the performance and scalability of surveillance systems. These systems must scale effortlessly to manage the growing load without sacrificing performance in an era of unheard-of data quantities and network complexity.

The development of surveillance systems is expected to undergo some exciting changes in the future. Innovation is anticipated to be sparked by the combination of artificial intelligence along with machine learning, which will enable predictive analytics that make use of past data to foresee and stop potential risks. Furthermore, the combination of surveillance data and intelligence on threat feeds promises to improve threat detection accuracy and thus increase the usefulness of these systems. In our digital age, surveillance systems are at the forefront of cybersecurity efforts. In order to recognize and counteract cyber risks, their contributions to proactive threat detection, quick responses to incidents, and behavioral surveillance are essential. These systems will develop as technology progresses to meet the difficulties faced by more capable cyber attackers. In the end, they want to make sure that digital assets are safeguarded and that a safe and robust digital ecosystem is maintained.

This chapter introduces the importance of cybersecurity in present days digital landscape, focusing on surveillance systems' role in threat detection, incident response, and vulnerability management. It discusses key categories, functions, and challenges associated with surveillance systems, such as privacy concerns, false positives, resource intensity, and skilled personnel. The chapter also hints at future developments and innovations in the field, providing a foundation for further exploration and analysis in the subsequent sections of the paper.

BACKGROUND

Surveillance systems act as the vigilant defenders that allow businesses to identify, evaluate, and effectively address possible threats in the complicated world of cybersecurity. These technologies are divided into three main categories: network surveillance, endpoint surveillance, along with behavioral surveillance, each geared to handle particular aspects of the cybersecurity landscape.

NETWORK SURVEILLANCE

One of the most important aspects of cybersecurity is network monitoring, which acts as the first layer of defense against outside influences that aim to undermine digital infrastructures. This type of surveillance entails the ongoing observation and evaluation of network traffic in order to spot trends that may point to unauthorized actions or potential security breaches. The essential elements that define network monitoring are intrusion detection systems (IDS) and intrusion prevention systems (IPS).

Intrusion Detection Systems (IDS)

In order to function, IDS carefully examines arriving network traffic in real time. It contrasts the traffic's characteristics with a vast dataset of recognized attack signatures. If a match is found, an alarm is set off to warn of the possibility of a security breech. IDS serves as a form of early warning system, allowing cybersecurity professionals to react quickly and implement the necessary countermeasures when the threat worsens.

Intrusion Prevention Systems (IPS)

Intrusion Prevention Systems (IPS), which expand upon IDS's capabilities, adopt a more proactive stance. These technologies not only identify possible dangers but also act quickly to stop them. Incoming data packets are analyzed by IPS using specified rules or policies, and when necessary, suspect traffic is blocked or redirected. By eliminating risks at the point of entry, this real-time intervention aims to stop possible breaches before they reach the network.

Network surveillance is important because it can act as a first line of protection against a variety of external threats. These technologies protect network integrity and thwart unwanted access attempts by tracking traffic and spotting recognized attack patterns. This kind of surveillance is especially skilled at fending off threats that aim to exploit network weaknesses, like malware infections and Distributed Denial of Service (DDoS) attacks. To enable reliable threat detection, attack signature databases must be continuously updated in response to the growing sophistication of cyberattacks. Additionally, the sheer amount of network data can produce a lot of noise and false positives, which must be properly controlled to prevent alert fatigue among cybersecurity professionals. In conclusion, network monitoring serves as the first line of protection against external threats and is a fundamental component of cybersecurity. The monitoring of network traffic, the detection of potential breaches, and the facilitation of quick response measures are all made possible by intrusion detection systems (IDS) along with intrusion prevention systems (IPS). It is impossible to exaggerate the significance of network monitoring in this era of growing cyberthreats because it is a crucial part of a comprehensive cybersecurity strategy.

ENDPOINT SURVEILLANCE

Modern cybersecurity tactics must include endpoint surveillance, which focuses on the observation and defense of specific networked devices. Computers, servers, and Internet of Things (IoT) devices all fall under this category and are frequently used as entry points for cyberattacks. Endpoint detection and response (EDR) systems enable endpoint monitoring by enabling real-time insight into the actions of these devices, facilitating quick threat identification, analysis, and response.

Endpoint Detection and Response (EDR)

EDR solutions are made to work at the level of the device, recording and examining endpoint activity within a network. These systems use sophisticated analytics, such as machine learning techniques, to define baselines of typical endpoint behavior. Processes, file actions, and system configurations are continuously monitored by EDR systems, allowing them to quickly spot any changes that might be signs of malicious activity.

Endpoint surveillance is important because it may give precise information about potential risks at the device level. Endpoint surveillance provides a thorough view of individual activities as opposed to network surveillance, which tracks traffic and patterns throughout the whole network. This allows security experts to tailor responses that lessen the effect of an attack by locating the precise device with activity that could be compromised. Endpoint monitoring is particularly helpful when thwarting threats that aim to take advantage of flaws in software or hardware. EDR systems can identify potential breaches in their early stages by keeping an eye out for strange behaviors or unauthorized access attempts. The lateral migration of threats inside the network is prevented by this proactive strategy, which also improves incident response times.

Even with its benefits, endpoint surveillance has drawbacks. Creating thorough behavioral baselines is difficult due to the huge diversity of devices on a network, from conventional computers to IoT devices. EDR systems must also strike an agreement between gathering enough data for analysis and preserving device performance, particularly for devices with limited resources. In conclusion, endpoint monitoring, which offers immediate insight into the behavior of specific devices within a network, is essential for modern cybersecurity. EDR systems make it possible to quickly identify and respond to potential risks at the device level, which helps to contain and mitigate cyberattacks. Endpoint surveillance is becoming more and more crucial for protecting digital assets and averting breaches as devices become more interconnected.

BEHAVIORAL SURVEILLANCE

A cutting-edge method of cybersecurity is behavioral monitoring, which uses artificial intelligence (AI) as well as machine learning to identify and counteract complex threats that frequently elude more conventional techniques. This type of surveillance focuses on comprehending typical user, device, and system behavior patterns inside a network, enabling the identification and analysis of deviations from pre-established baselines. Systems that use User and Entity Behavior Analytics (UEBA) best illustrate the effectiveness of behavioral monitoring.

User and Entity Behavior Analytics (UEBA)

UEBA systems use sophisticated analytics as well as machine learning algorithms to build profiles of typical user and entity behavior inside a network. UEBA systems create baselines for behavior by gathering and analyzing enormous volumes of data, such as login behaviors, system interactions, and data access activities. Alerts that identify potential dangers or malicious activity are set off when these baselines are deviated, such as odd login times or illegal access attempts (Khaliq et al., 2020).

The advantage of behavioral surveillance is its ability to spot both insider risks and newly emerging unknown dangers. Authorized individuals that commit malevolent acts, frequently evading perimeter protections, are considered insider threats. An insider threat can be discovered using behavioral monitoring, which is excellent at spotting irregularities in user behavior such unexpected transmissions of data or privilege escalation.

The excellent effectiveness of this strategy also extends to sophisticated threats that may do not match predetermined attack signatures. Because behavioral surveillance may identify departures from accepted standards, it enables firms to quickly respond to fresh and developing risks as cyber attackers modify their tactics. Implementing behavioral surveillance, though, is not without difficulties. Extensive data gathering and processing are needed to create precise behavioral profiles, which could cause privacy issues. It is difficult to strike a balance between the necessity for reliable danger detection and each person's right to privacy (Tipton & Krause, 2006). To avoid alert fatigue and ensure effective incident response, the system must also be tuned to reduce false positives and negatives.

The three different kinds of surveillance systems—network, endpoint, and behavioral—combine to provide the essential elements of a thorough cybersecurity approach. Network surveillance keeps an eye on traffic and spots recognized attack patterns to protect against external threats. Endpoint surveillance focuses on specific devices, offering in-the-moment information about potential risks and facilitating quick action. The use of behavioral monitoring ensures the detection of insider threats and sophisticated, evolving cyberattacks by utilizing AI and machine learning to spot anomalies and deviations from regular behaviors. These surveillance systems work as a dynamic protection system against the always changing and prevalent cyber threat scenario.

COMPONENTS OF SURVEILLANCE SYSTEMS

Cybersecurity surveillance systems are made up of interconnected parts that work together to effectively identify, analyze, and respond to threats (Jang-Jaccard & Nepal, 2014). These elements are essential for gathering, analyzing, and acting on data in order to protect digital assets and lessen potential cyber risks.

Data Collection

The initial stage of any surveillance system used for cybersecurity is data collection (Chander et al., 2022). In order for the ensuing analysis along with response phases to function properly, it entails obtaining a variety of relevant information from a variety of sources (Zawali et al., 2021). Organizations can proactively identify potential cyber risks thanks to data collecting techniques that make sure that real-time insights into user behaviors, system events, and network activities are gathered (Jang-Jaccard & Nepal, 2014).

Sources of Data

To keep an eye out for anomalies, unwanted access, and potential breaches, surveillance systems record network traffic statistics, including packets sent between devices.

Log files: These records of system events, mistakes, and actions are produced by operating systems, programs, and network hardware. Log data analysis might reveal strange behavior and unwanted access attempts.

User behaviors: Keeping track of user behaviors like login times, data access, as well as system interactions can reveal insider threats or other illegal activity.

Device incidents: Data from servers, routers, and Internet of Things (IoT) devices is used to identify anomalous device activity, potential security flaws, and security incidents.

Methods of Data Collection

Agents: Installed software agents on hardware gather and send information to centrally located servers for analysis. Agents are able to keep an eye on endpoint activity and offer current insights on how devices behave.

Network Sensors: By monitoring incoming and outgoing traffic at key locations throughout the network, network sensors enable the analysis of data trends and behaviors.

Data gatherers: Data gatherers compile information from numerous sources and direct it toward the analysis stage. They guarantee effective and thorough data collection.

Table 1. Sample sources and methods for data collection

Data Source	Methods of Data Collection
Network Traffic	Network Sensors
Log Files	Agents
User Activities	Agents
Device Events	Data gatherers

CHALLENGES AND CONSIDERATIONS

There are difficulties with data collection in terms of quantity, quality, and privacy. Modern networks generate a rising amount of data, which can overwhelm systems; hence, effective data collection along with processing are required. Accurate threat detection depends on the obtained data being accurate and relevant. Additionally, it is important to respect people's privacy and data protection laws, particularly when keeping an eye on user actions and conduct (Scheibner et al., 2020).

Effective surveillance systems are built on data collecting, which provides the foundation for later analysis and reaction. Organizations can improve their overall level of cybersecurity by taking proactive steps to identify and combat possible cyber attacks by gathering insights about network activities, user behavior, including system events.

Analysis

An essential step in surveillance systems used for cybersecurity is the analysis stage, where the data gathered is processed, patterns are found, and possible dangers are found (Golovko & Kochurko, 2005).

The goal of this stage is to find anomalies, deviations, and behaviors that could point to malicious activity or security breaches. To do this, we use advanced analytics, machine learning algorithms, including artificial intelligence (Goodfellow et al., 2016). Effective analysis turns unactionable data into insights that can be put into practice, enabling quick reactions to new cyberthreats.

Recognition of patterns: Analysis entails locating patterns and actions that differ from predetermined norms. The system can recognize anomalous actions that could be signs of possible hazards by recognizing what regular activity entails.

Machine Learning Algorithms: Complex patterns and relationships in the data are found using cutting-edge machine learning methods like neural networks. These algorithms can adapt to changing threat environments and learning from historical data.

Behavioral analytics: Analysis frequently focuses on behavioral anomalies, when deviations from typical user, device, or network behavior are found. This is particularly helpful in spotting insider risks and newly emerging unknown dangers (Bin Sarhan & Altwaijry, 2022).

Table 2. Sample approaches to data analysis

Analysis Technique	Description
Signature based Analysis	Collects data and compares it to known attack signatures to find recurring threat patterns.
Anomaly Detection	Detects departures from predetermined baselines and signals abnormal behavior.
Machine Learning	Uses AI algorithms to find intricate patterns and connections in the data.
Behavioral Analytics	Concentrates on locating changes from typical user, device, or network behavior.

Data gathered from multiple sources is analyzed in the graphical structure to find patterns and anomalies. Machine learning along with behavioral analytics approaches must be used in this situation. As a result of the analysis phase, actionable insights including threat visualizations are produced, which direct further reaction procedures.

Figure 1. Data analysis stages

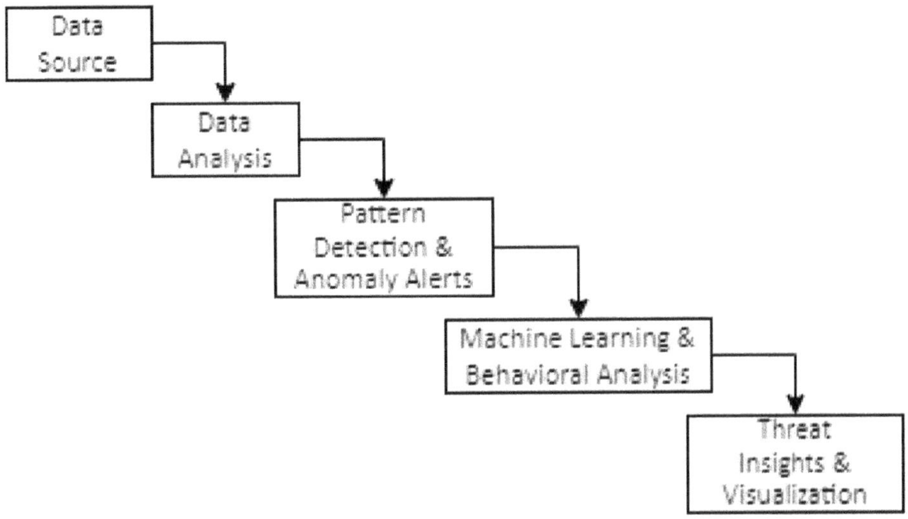

The analysis stage is an important part of surveillance systems since it converts gathered data into insightful knowledge. This phase, which makes use of modern analytics as well as machine learning, pinpoints possible cyber risks so that businesses may react quickly and successfully. Analysis improves the ability to reduce risks and defend digital assets from changing cyber threats by spotting trends and behavioral anomalies (Antonakakis et al., 2017).

Response

The critical final step in cybersecurity surveillance systems is the response phase, where risks are handled, contained, and mitigated (Schneier, 2015). This phase includes a variety of automatic and manual procedures targeted at lessening the effects of online dangers and regaining the network or system's security. For limiting downtime, mitigating possible damage, and stopping threats from spreading further, effective reaction techniques are crucial.

Automated Responses: When possible dangers or abnormalities are found during the analysis stage, automated responses are activated. These procedures may involve blocking malicious IP addresses, isolating infected devices, or launching established security mechanisms. Automated responses guarantee quick answers to new hazards, preventing them from immediately harming people.

Manual Intervention: Cybersecurity experts must manually intervene when complex scenarios develop or when automated operations could have unexpected repercussions. In a manual response, the situation is evaluated, the threat is verified, and the best plan of action to successfully reduce risks is chosen.

Table 3. Sample response actions

Response Action	Description
Isolation of Devices	Isolates infected devices from the network automatically to stop lateral migration.
Blocking Malicious IP	Automatically obstructs traffic coming from shady IP addresses to stop illegal access.
Incident Investigation	Manual investigation to confirm the threat, gauge the effect, and collect data.
Containment and Mitigation	Manual steps to neutralize the threat's effects on the network and confine it.

Developing efficient response tactics is essential to reducing the potential harm and disruption brought on by cyber threats. Threats can be quickly identified and mitigated, allowing firms to quickly resume normal business activities.

Finally, in cybersecurity surveillance systems, the response phase serves as the vital connection between threat detection along with mitigation. This stage makes sure that possible dangers are dealt with quickly and successfully by combining automatic actions and manual interaction. Cyber risks are lessened by a well-implemented response strategy, which also increases the general resilience of digital assets and networks (Haghtalab et al., 2022).

SYSTEMS OF SURVEILLANCE FOR USE IN CYBERSECURITY

Cybersecurity surveillance systems have a wide range of applications in a number of different fields and are essential for improving threat detection, incident response, including overall cybersecurity posture. To protect digital assets and guarantee the integrity of digital ecosystems, these systems make use of data collecting, analysis, and reaction mechanisms.

Threat Detection

Threat detection is one of the most important and fundamental uses of surveillance systems in cybersecurity (Thakur et al., 2015). Systems of surveillance act as watchful sentinels that constantly scan digital environments for indications of potential cyberthreats. These systems quickly detect and eliminate diverse threats by combining data collecting, cutting-edge analytics, and automated reactions.

Key Aspects of Threat Detection

Early Detection: Surveillance systems are made to spot hazards early on, before they have a chance to do much harm. These systems are able to identify patterns and anomalies that could point to unauthorized access attempts or harmful activities by keeping an eye on network traffic, user habits, and system operations (Sarkar et al., 2023).

Known Threats: By comparing acquired data to recognized attack signatures, surveillance systems excel at recognizing known dangers. These signatures capture the characteristics of well-known cyberattacks, allowing systems to identify risks and send out notifications for quick action.

Unknown Threats: In addition to spotting known dangers, surveillance systems are essential in spotting unknown or zero-day threats. These systems can detect departures from established baselines even in the absence of known threat signatures because to the use of behavioral analytics, machine learning, along with anomaly detection approaches.

Rapid Response: As soon as a possible threat is identified, surveillance systems can start automating reactions to stop or lessen the danger. Using automated processes, unlawful activities might be stopped, malicious IP addresses blocked, and hacked devices isolated. Insider threats are situations in which authorized personnel participate in hostile activity. Surveillance technologies play a vital role in identifying these situations. These systems can spot anomalies that can point to data exfiltration, unlawful access, or other questionable conduct by studying user activities and data access patterns.

Incident Validation: Incident validation is a component of effective threat detection. The information needed to evaluate the size and impact of an occurrence is provided through surveillance systems. This helps cybersecurity professionals assess the threat's seriousness and facilitates the right course of action.

False Positive Mitigation: While identifying threats is essential, it is also critical to reduce false positives in order to keep cybersecurity workers from being overly alert. Advanced analytics are used by surveillance systems to improve threat identification algorithms and lower false positive rates. Figure 2 represents some of the key aspect of Threat Detection.

Figure 2. Threat detection

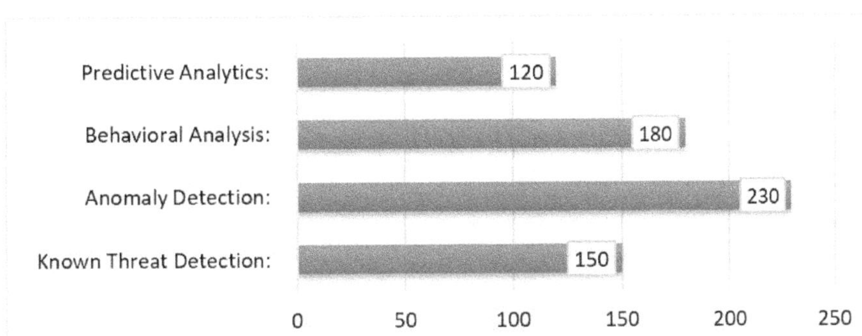

A crucial use of surveillance systems in cybersecurity is threat detection (Narayanan et al., 2018). These systems detect and react to potential cyber threats in real time by continually monitoring network activities, user behaviors, and system events. The entire cybersecurity posture is improved by their capacity to identify both known and unknown threats in combination with quick response mechanisms, ensuring that new threats are found and dealt with before they can cause major harm.

Incident Response

An essential use of surveillance systems in the field of cybersecurity is incident response. This element focuses on the methodical strategy used to deal with and mitigate cyber assaults, security breaches, and other unfavorable situations that could endanger an organization's digital assets. In order to respond to incidents, surveillance systems are essential since they offer real-time insights, assist quickly and effectively in danger assessment, and enable quick and effective countermeasures.

Key Aspects of Incident Response

Real-time Visibility: Surveillance systems provide real-time observation and analysis of user actions, network activity, and system events. With constant visibility, security personnel can monitor issues as they develop and take appropriate action to lessen their potential damage.

Threat Validation: During an incident, surveillance systems support the verification of the type and gravity of the danger. These systems aid in establishing the existence of a security breach and its possible effects by evaluating data gathered from multiple sources, such as network traffic and user activities.

Automated Containment: When surveillance systems spot known threat patterns, automated containment procedures may be triggered. To stop the problem from spreading further, these steps can include isolating infected devices, blocking malicious IP addresses, or launching security protocols.

Manual investigation: Surveillance systems offer detailed information that supports manual inquiry for more complex situations. Security experts can examine the information produced by these systems to gain an understanding of the attack paths, methods, and potential vulnerabilities employed by attackers.

Evidence gathering: Forensic investigation and legal considerations are frequently involved in incident response. By gathering pertinent data that can be used for forensic investigations, reporting, and prospective legal actions, surveillance systems aid in the gathering of evidence.

Figure 3 represents some of the key aspect of Incident Response.

Figure 3. Incident response

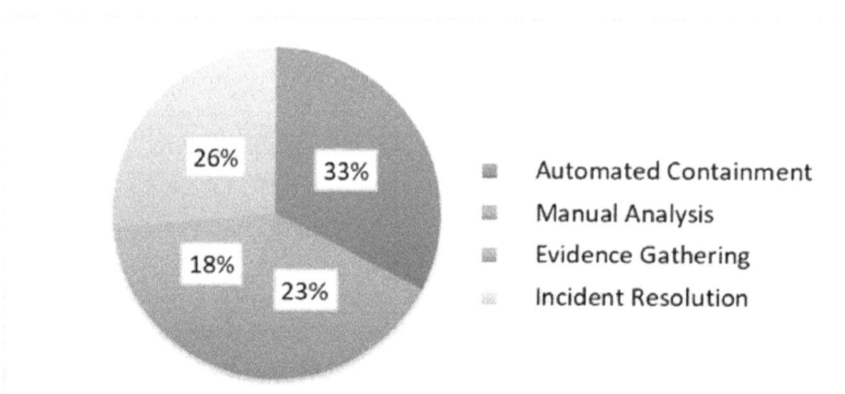

Figure 4. Process used in incident response with surveillance systems

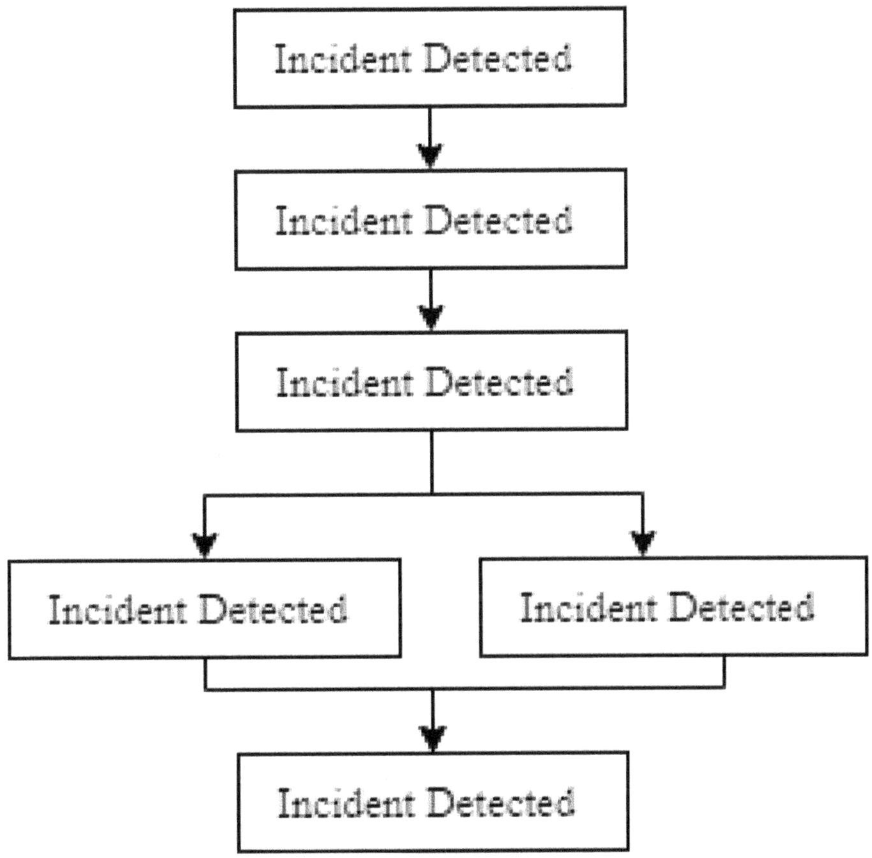

The process of incident response with the integration of surveillance systems is shown in Figure 4. Threat assessment is sparked by incident detection, and real-time information gleaned from surveillance is used to assess the situation. Automated containment techniques stop the spread of the problem, while manual analysis along with evidence gathering aid in a thorough inquiry. Finally, a combination of automated as well as manual procedures are used to remedy the situation. Incident response is a crucial use of surveillance systems because it gives users the information and resources they need to successfully handle and defend against cyberattacks. Surveillance systems improve the incident response procedure and add to the overall robustness of cybersecurity strategies by providing real-time visibility and assisting in threat validation.

Insider Threat Detection

Insider threat detection, which focuses on locating potential security concerns coming from within an organization, is a crucial application of surveillance systems in cybersecurity (Jang-Jaccard & Nepal, 2014). This feature addresses the dangers posed by authorized individuals who participate in nefarious or inadvertent behaviors that can jeopardize data integrity along with organizational security.

Key Aspects of Insider Threat Detection

Behavioral analysis: Monitoring systems keep track of system usage, user interactions with digital assets, along with user behavior. These systems can identify anomalies that could be an indication of illicit actions or departures from standard usage by creating baseline behavior patterns.

Monitoring User Activity: Surveillance systems keep tabs on user activity such data access, system logins, as well as file interactions. By keeping an eye out for unusual or suspicious behavior, insider risks can be identified.

Data Transfer Analysis: Monitoring systems examine data transfers that take place both inside and outside the company. This analysis assists in identifying data exfiltration that is not authorized because it could be an indication of insider threat activity.

Monitoring of access privileges: Surveillance systems make sure that users are only gaining access to the information and resources necessary for their responsibilities. Alerts are set off by any unauthorized efforts to access sensitive information or carry out actions outside of their scope.

Behavioral Anomaly Alerts: Surveillance systems that detect departures from expected behavior patterns produce alerts to let cybersecurity teams know about possible insider threats. These notifications encourage additional research and reactionary measures.

Profile Development: Surveillance systems develop behavioral profiles of users and entities. The systems can identify odd actions that can indicate insider threats by evaluating real-time behaviors against these profiles.

Some of the key aspect of Insider Threat Detection is represented as a chart in Figure 5.

Figure 5. Insider threat detection

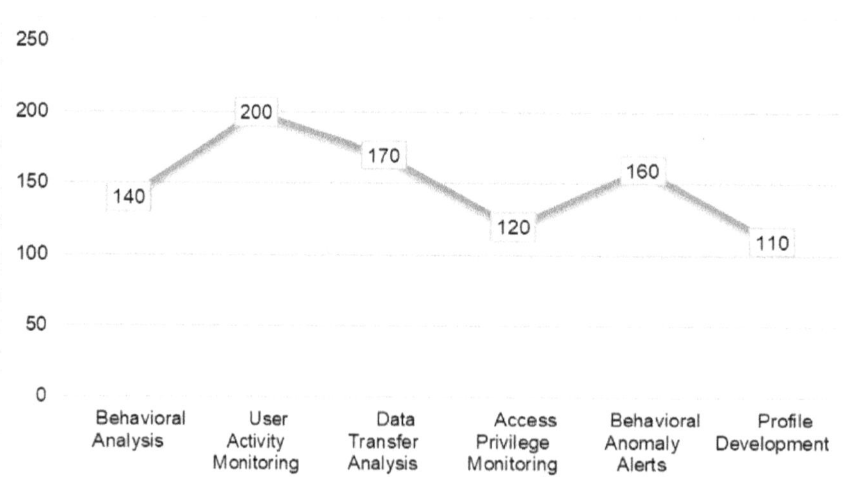

Detecting insider threats is a crucial feature of cybersecurity, along with surveillance systems improve this aspect by constantly observing user behaviors and actions. These technologies assist in reducing the risks posed by insiders including preventing potential security breaches coming from within the business by spotting anomalies and deviations from typical behavior.

Vulnerability Management

An important use of surveillance systems in cybersecurity is vulnerability management, which seeks to find, evaluate, and fix potential holes in a company's digital infrastructure. The monitoring of activities, behaviors, as well as system configurations by surveillance systems helps identify potential security flaws that might be exploited by hacker groups.

Key Aspects of Vulnerability Management

Monitoring of Configuration: Security surveillance systems keep an eye on system configurations along with settings to make sure they adhere to best practices. The identification and correction of any deviations or setup errors that can reveal vulnerabilities.

Software and Patch Management: These programs monitor the updates and patches made to systems and devices. A potential entry point for attackers is outdated or missing patches, therefore monitoring systems make sure that software is always current.

Strange Activity Detection: Surveillance systems identify strange behaviors or actions that may be attempts to take advantage of security flaws. This includes actions like unauthorized login tries or port scanning.

Network Vulnerability Scanning: These programs run routine checks on the network to find exposed services, open ports, and possible points of entry for hackers. The findings aid in deciding which vulnerabilities need to be fixed first.

Risk Assessment: By finding vulnerabilities, evaluating their possible effects, and offering information on the likelihood of exploitation, surveillance systems help with risk assessment.

Integration of threat intelligence: Surveillance systems improve their precision in discovering vulnerabilities that are currently being targeted by online attackers by comparing information from vulnerability scans with external threat intelligence feeds.

Some of the key aspect of Vulnerability Management is represented in Figure 6.

Figure 6. Vulnerability management

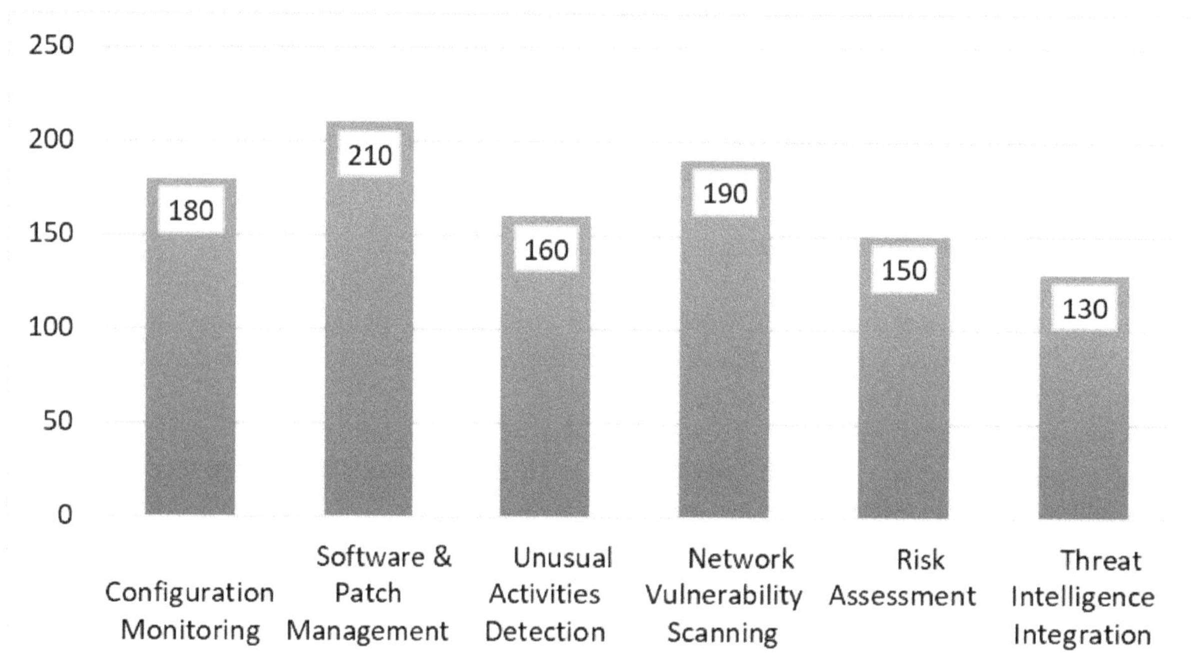

Cybersecurity must include vulnerability management, and monitoring systems are essential in spotting and correcting possible flaws. These systems improve an organization's capacity to proactively manage vulnerabilities and decrease the attack surface, thereby increasing the overall security posture. They do this by continually monitoring system configurations, behaviors, as well as network activity.

CHALLENGES AND CONSIDERATIONS

Organizations must face several issues and concerns that arise with the adoption of surveillance systems for cybersecurity reasons in order to maintain the efficacy as well as the integrity of their security strategy. These difficulties result from the complexities of contemporary cyber threats, the complexity of monitoring technology, and the necessity to strike a balance between security, user privacy, and regulatory compliance.

Data Overload

The concept of data overload is one of the major obstacles to putting cybersecurity surveillance systems into place. Large volumes of data are produced by contemporary surveillance systems from a variety of sources, including network traffic, user activity, system logs, and more. While managing and processing this data in real-time can be daunting for enterprises, it is essential for recognizing and responding to cyber threats.

Key Aspects of Data Overload Challenge

Volume of Data: Continuous data collection by surveillance systems from a variety of endpoints produces a flood of data that needs to be handled and processed effectively.

Processing in real-time: Cyberthreats demand quick reactions, necessitating analysis of gathered data in real-time. To meet the increased needs for data processing, organizations must invest in a strong infrastructure.

Resource Allocation: If computing resources are not managed effectively, the vast amounts of data produced by surveillance systems could impose a pressure on other corporate processes.

Analytical Complexity: This difficulty is further increased by the need for sophisticated analytics software and knowledgeable staff when analyzing massive databases for patterns, abnormalities, and dangers.

Mitigation Strategies

Data Prioritization: Use techniques to prioritize data such that crucial information is processed more quickly than less important data.

Automated Processing: The use of machine learning and automation algorithms to preprocess along with filter data, freeing security analysts to concentrate on high-priority risks.

Scalable Infrastructure: To accommodate peak data loads without affecting system performance, invest in scalable computer infrastructure.

Data Retention Policies: Use data retention policies to preserve only pertinent information, hence decreasing the amount of data that must be processed and kept.

Impact and Significance

The effective detection and reaction to threats might be hampered by data overload. If not controlled, it may cause false negatives, longer response times, and delays in spotting crucial threats. By addressing the data overload issue, surveillance systems can work at their peak efficiency, allowing for the quick identification and reduction of cyber risks.

Controlling the problem of data overload is crucial even though data is a useful asset for cybersecurity. To preserve the effectiveness of their surveillance systems and their capacity to react quickly to new cyber threats, organizations must implement techniques for processing, analyzing, and prioritizing data with efficiency.

False Positives

The problem of false positives is a serious obstacle in the field of cybersecurity monitoring systems. When the system raises alerts for behaviors or occurrences that aren't genuinely security dangers, this is known as a false positive. Although surveillance systems are intended to be proactive and vigilant, a high number of false positives can cause alert fatigue, which can cause security staff to become overburdened and potentially miss real threats. Addressing false positives is essential because it prevents security personnel from being diverted by non-threatening incidents and allows them to concentrate their attention on real threats. To reduce false positives, it is crucial to effectively fine-tune surveillance system algorithms, use cutting-edge machine learning approaches to improve threat detection accuracy, and incorporate context-based analysis. Organizations may improve their incident response efforts, manage resources more effectively, and preserve the legitimacy of their monitoring systems by minimizing false positives.

Privacy Concerns

Privacy issues are a crucial component of the difficulties and factors to consider while putting cybersecurity surveillance systems into place. Organizations must strike a difficult balance between protecting digital assets and upholding people's right to privacy as they work to strengthen their security postures.

Key Aspects of Privacy Concerns

Employee Privacy: Since many surveillance methods entail watching employees' online behavior, privacy concerns may be raised. Employee morale may suffer as a result of employees' concerns that their online interactions will be examined.

Transparency in Data Collection: Poor data collection procedures might damage confidence. Employees must be informed in full about the categories of data gathered, why it is being collected, and the way it will be used.

Consent and Legal Compliance: It is important to make sure that data collection along with surveillance procedures abide by applicable privacy laws (Cybersecurity, 2018) (such the GDPR, HIPAA, etc.). Prior to monitoring someone's activity, explicit consent must be obtained from that person.

Data minimization: It is critical to just gather the data that is required for cybersecurity. Reduced data collecting lowers the risk of abuse and aids organizations in upholding privacy norms.

Secure Data Storage: It is crucial to protect gathered data from unauthorized access. If data breaches happen and private data is exposed, privacy concerns grow.

User Monitoring Scope: In order to prevent overreach, organizations must specify the scope of user monitoring, including whether communications or personal devices are monitored.

Mitigation Strategies

Organizations can use several techniques to solve privacy issues while maintaining strong cybersecurity:

Clear Policies: Create thorough and open surveillance policies that specify the goals, parameters, and restrictions of monitoring activities.

Explicit Consent: Ensure that employees or people under surveillance understand and agree to monitoring activities by obtaining their explicit consent.

Anonymization: To protect individual identities while still gathering insight, anonymize or pseudonymize data that has been acquired.

Privacy Impact Assessments: To examine the potential dangers and advantages of surveillance methods and make wise judgments, conduct privacy impact assessments.

Third-party Audits: Involve auditors from a third party to evaluate the organization's surveillance operations and confirm that privacy laws are being followed.

Impact and Significance

Inaction on privacy issues can result in legal liability, reputational harm, and strained relations between staff and management. To promote a culture of trust, assure ethical behavior, and achieve a healthy balance between cybersecurity along with individual privacy rights, organizations must prioritize privacy considerations.

Insider Threat Detection

A major issue and consideration in the field of cybersecurity surveillance systems is insider threat detection (Khaliq et al., 2020). Although these systems are intended to protect against external threats, it might be difficult to spot internal hazards because of their complexity. Differentiating between user actions that are legitimate and those that indicate malevolent intent or unintentional security flaws is difficult. It is crucial to strike a balance between extensive surveillance and regard for employees' privacy.

Complexities of Identifying Insider Threats

Behavioral analysis: Monitoring systems must be able to differentiate between typical employee behavior and anomalies that can point to criminal activity. Extensive algorithms and machine learning methods are needed to create precise behavior profiles and identify discrepancies.

User Activity Monitoring: It can be difficult to strike a balance between monitoring and protecting employees' privacy. A refined strategy that eliminates pointless scrutiny is required to spot anomalous activity, such as excessive data access or unexpected logins.

Data Transfer Analysis: Monitoring data flows while maintaining data privacy and confidentiality is necessary in order to detect unlawful data transfers, whether they are purposeful or unintentional.

Access Privilege Monitoring: It might be challenging to spot people who are using resources outside of their scope without compromising productivity.

Behavioral Anomaly Alerts: It takes a subtle technique to create alerts for potential insider threats without swamping security staff with unfounded positives.

Profile Development: To create thorough behavioral profiles for users, a wide range of data points must be analyzed to build a baseline and spot deviations.

Impact and Significance

Due to the inherent access that authorized individuals have, insider threats can be highly harmful. Ineffective threat detection can result in data breaches, the theft of intellectual property, and the compromise of sensitive information. Organizations may strengthen the security of their digital assets and promote a security-conscious culture while upholding employee privacy and trust by tackling the problems associated with detecting insider threats.

Resource Intensity

Implementing surveillance systems for cybersecurity is a significant difficulty and consideration related to resource intensity. A large amount of hardware, software, staff, and ongoing maintenance resources must be allocated for surveillance systems to operate well. Striking a balance between guaranteeing strong security and controlling the expenses and efforts involved in surveillance activities presents a problem.

Key Dimensions of Resource Intensity Challenge

Infrastructure Requirements: To manage the constant influx of data from many sources, such as network traffic, logs, and user actions, surveillance systems need a lot of computational power and storage.

Processor Speed: When it comes to processing power, real-time data analysis and threat detection put a burden on already-stretched resources.

Skilled Workforce: Cybersecurity experts with knowledge of data analysis, threat detection, incident response, and system administration are required to operate surveillance systems successfully. The difficulty with resources might be made worse by a lack of qualified workers.

Financial Expenses: Investing in surveillance technologies, hardware, software licensing, and qualified employees entails financial expenses, which must be justified in terms of the value they add to the organization.

Maintenance and Updates: To remain successful against new threats, surveillance systems need constant maintenance, updates, and patches, adding to ongoing resource needs.

Impact and Significance: The number of resources an organization has at its disposal can affect its capacity to continue running effective surveillance activities and counter rising threats. Poor resource management can result in decreased system performance, missed chances to detect threats, and increased susceptibility. By addressing this issue, surveillance systems will run as efficiently as possible, strengthening the cybersecurity posture and reducing any potential security breaches caused by resource limitations.

Skill and Expertise Gap

The lack of necessary skills and knowledge makes putting in place surveillance systems for cybersecurity extremely difficult. Cybersecurity experts with understanding in data analysis, threat detection, and incident response are needed to operate and manage these systems effectively. The lack of qualified workers in the cybersecurity sector, however, may prevent businesses from making the most of surveillance technology's potential. To ensure correct system usage, precise threat assessment, and efficient incident response—all of which improve an organization's overall security posture—bridging the skill and expertise gap is crucial.

Data Quality

When installing cybersecurity surveillance systems, data quality is a serious problem that must be considered. The correctness, completeness, and trustworthiness of the data gathered from multiple sources, including network traffic, user activity, and system logs, are crucial for these systems' success. False positives and inaccurate threat assessments can result from poor data quality, which also makes it more difficult to identify and address cyber attacks. It takes careful data collection, validation, and cleansing procedures, as well as ongoing monitoring to spot abnormalities or inconsistencies that could compromise the correctness of the system, to ensure data quality. Organizations may improve the integrity of their surveillance systems, enable more accurate threat identification, and enable informed decision-making in cybersecurity operations by solving the data quality challenge.

Regulatory Compliance

Regulatory compliance is a major obstacle and factor to be considered when putting cybersecurity surveillance systems into place. The complicated web of data protection and privacy laws, including the GDPR, HIPAA, and industry-specific requirements, must be navigated by organizations. To prevent legal obligations, reputational harm, and potential financial penalties, it is crucial that monitoring activities comply with these laws. Understanding the precise requirements of pertinent legislation, developing open data usage rules, getting the required consents from people being watched, and putting strong security measures in place to protect acquired data are all crucial for achieving regulatory compliance. It can also be necessary to conduct regular audits and evaluations to guarantee continued compliance. Organizations can use the advantages of surveillance systems for improved cybersecurity while maintaining the confidence of stakeholders, protecting sensitive data, and operating within the law by addressing regulatory compliance concerns.

Adaptive Threats

Implementing cybersecurity surveillance systems presents a considerable challenge and consideration for adaptive threats. Cyber attackers constantly improve their strategies, techniques, and procedures to avoid discovery while corporations use surveillance technologies to strengthen their defenses. Traditional surveillance techniques are less effective at spotting sophisticated and targeted attacks because these adaptive threats can get through them. In order to stay up with these changing risks, organizations must be proactive in updating their monitoring techniques. This calls for a thorough awareness of new attack pathways, sophisticated threat intelligence integration, and the adaptability to change surveillance tactics as necessary. Organizations may strengthen their ability to recognize and respond to new cyber risks by staying ahead of adaptive threats. This will strengthen their cybersecurity posture and reduce the chance of a breach or compromise.

Cultural Acceptance

Cultural acceptance is a complex issue and a key one to consider when putting cybersecurity surveillance systems in place. When surveillance technology is introduced into an organization's digital ecosystem, employees may get concerned because it raises questions about their privacy, their sense of trust, and their sense of autonomy. To ensure the successful adoption and efficacy of surveillance systems, it is crucial to cultivate a culture of security awareness among personnel. The goals of monitoring must be openly shared by organizations, with a focus on how it protects digital assets and averts security breaches. Employee participation in the process, addressing their worries, and outlining the scope of the surveillance can all help to allay fears and promote a favorable response. Cultural acceptance depends on striking the correct balance between the necessity for security and the respect for personal privacy. Organizations can maximize the advantages of surveillance technologies while fostering employee trust and cooperation by fostering a culture of security consciousness. This improves the organization's overall cybersecurity posture.

FUTURE RESEARCH AND CONCLUSION

The study explores the use of surveillance systems as an important cybersecurity technique to protect online assets from numerous threats. It analyses their uses, difficulties, and future potential. Tracking systems are used to manage vulnerabilities, recognize external threats, respond to instances, and improve security frameworks. Information overload, privacy concerns, ignorance, and regulatory compliance are just a few of the problems that need to be fixed. The future of security surveillance involves integrating AI and ML for better threat detection, using behavioral analytics to identify hidden anomalies, adopting Zero Trust Architectures for enhanced safety, using cloud-based surveillance for effective data management, and implementing privacy-enhancing technologies. Improved monitoring may address user expectations and regulatory compliance, and predicted analytics will enable proactive actions. Current security measures and a thorough security strategy will likely complement one another and result in multiple-layered defenses against digital attacks. This route will develop security awareness and user confidence through breakthroughs in AI and ML, improved privacy, and a comprehensive protection approach.

REFERENCES

Antonakakis, M., April, T., Bailey, M., Bernhard, M., Bursztein, E., Cochran, J., . . . Zhou, Y. (2017). Understanding the mirai botnet. In *26th USENIX security symposium (USENIX Security 17)* (pp. 1093-1110). USENIX.

Asif, M., Abbas, S., Khan, M. A., Fatima, A., Khan, M. A., & Lee, S. W. (2021). MapReduce based intelligent model for intrusion detection using machine learning technique. *Journal of King Saud University. Computer and Information Sciences.*

Bin Sarhan, B., & Altwaijry, N. (2022). Insider Threat Detection Using Machine Learning Approach. *Applied Sciences (Basel, Switzerland)*, *13*(1), 259. doi:10.3390/app13010259

Chander, B., Pal, S., De, D., & Buyya, R. (2022). Artificial intelligence-based internet of things for industry 5.0. *Artificial intelligence-based internet of things systems*, 3-45.

Cybersecurity, C. I. (2018). *Framework for improving critical infrastructure cybersecurity*. https://nvl-pubs. nist. gov/nistpubs/CSWP/NIST

Drewek-Ossowicka, A., Pietrołaj, M., & Rumiński, J. (2021). A survey of neural networks usage for intrusion detection systems. *Journal of Ambient Intelligence and Humanized Computing*, *12*(1), 497–514. doi:10.100712652-020-02014-x

Golovko, V., & Kochurko, P. (2005, September). Intrusion recognition using neural networks. In *2005 IEEE Intelligent Data Acquisition and Advanced Computing Systems: Technology and Applications* (pp. 108-111). IEEE.

Goodfellow, I., Bengio, Y., Courville, A., & Bengio, Y. (2016). *Deep learning* (vol. 1). Academic Press.

Haghtalab, N., Roughgarden, T., & Shetty, A. (2022, February). Smoothed analysis with adaptive adversaries. In *2021 IEEE 62nd Annual Symposium on Foundations of Computer Science (FOCS)* (pp. 942-953). IEEE. 10.1109/FOCS52979.2021.00095

Jang-Jaccard, J., & Nepal, S. (2014). A survey of emerging threats in cybersecurity. *Journal of Computer and System Sciences*, *80*(5), 973–993. doi:10.1016/j.jcss.2014.02.005

Khaliq, S., Tariq, Z. U. A., & Masood, A. (2020, October). Role of user and entity behavior analytics in detecting insider attacks. In *2020 International Conference on Cyber Warfare and Security (ICCWS)* (pp. 1-6). IEEE. 10.1109/ICCWS48432.2020.9292394

Mekala, S., & Vennila, J. (2018). A Survey of Intrusion Detection and Prevention Systems in Cloud Computing. *Journal of King Saud University. Computer and Information Sciences*. Advance online publication. doi:10.1016/j.jksuci.2018.06.003

Narayanan, S. N., Ganesan, A., Joshi, K., Oates, T., Joshi, A., & Finin, T. (2018). Early Detection of Cybersecurity Threats Using Collaborative Cognition. *IEEE 4th International Conference on Collaboration and Internet Computing (CIC)*. 10.1109/CIC.2018.00054

Probst, C. W., Hunker, J., Bishop, M., & Gollmann, D. (Eds.). (2010). *Insider threats in cyber security* (Vol. 49). Springer Science & Business Media. doi:10.1007/978-1-4419-7133-3_1

Sarkar, Podder, & Roy. (2023). An Analysis of the Privacy and Security Related Problem with Social Networks. *ESP Journal of Engineering & Technology Advancements, 3*(2).

Scheibner, J., Ienca, M., Kechagia, S., Troncoso-Pastoriza, J. R., Raisaro, J. L., Hubaux, J. P., Fellay, J., & Vayena, E. (2020). Data protection and ethics requirements for multisite research with health data: A comparative examination of legislative governance frameworks and the role of data protection technologies. *Journal of Law and the Biosciences*, *7*(1), lsaa010. doi:10.1093/jlb/lsaa010 PMID:32733683

Schneier, B. (2015). *Secrets and lies: digital security in a networked world.* John Wiley & Sons. doi:10.1002/9781119183631

Thakur, K., Qiu, M., Gai, K., & Ali, M. L. (2015, November). An investigation on cyber security threats and security models. In *2015 IEEE 2nd international conference on cyber security and cloud computing* (pp. 307-311). IEEE. 10.1109/CSCloud.2015.71

Tipton, H. F., & Krause, M. (2006). *Information Security Management Handbook* (Vol. 3). Auerbach Publications.

Zawali, B., Ikuesan, R. A., Kebande, V. R., Furnell, S., & A-Dhaqm, A. (2021). Realising a push button modality for video-based forensics. *Infrastructures*, *6*(4), 54. doi:10.3390/infrastructures6040054

KEY TERMS AND DEFINITIONS

Adaptive Threats: Adaptive threats are cyber attackers who continuously adapt their tactics and methods to evade detection and compromise digital systems effectively.

Behavioral Analytics: Behavioral analytics is a method of identifying security threats by analyzing deviations from normal user, device, or network behavior, often using machine learning and statistical techniques.

Cloud-Based Surveillance: Cloud-based surveillance involves using cloud computing infrastructure and services for the storage and analysis of surveillance data, offering scalability and accessibility advantages.

Cultural Acceptance: Cultural acceptance refers to the development of a corporate culture within an organization that fosters security awareness and trust among employees regarding the use of surveillance systems for cybersecurity.

False Positives: False positives occur when surveillance systems generate alerts or warnings for behaviors or events that do not actually pose a security threat, potentially causing unnecessary concern or distraction.

Incident Response: Incident response is a structured approach used to manage and mitigate cybersecurity incidents, including security breaches and cyberattacks, to minimize their impact on an organization.

Privacy-Enhancing Technologies: Privacy-enhancing technologies are tools and methods designed to safeguard individual privacy while allowing for the collection and analysis of data for security purposes.

Surveillance Systems: Surveillance systems are integrated technologies and processes that continuously monitor digital environments to identify, analyze, and respond to cyber threats and security incidents effectively.

Vulnerability Management: Vulnerability management is the systematic process of identifying, assessing, and mitigating potential security vulnerabilities in an organization's digital infrastructure to reduce the risk of exploitation.

Zero Trust Architecture: Zero Trust Architecture is a security model that operates on the principle of verifying every user and device trying to access resources within an organization's network, even if they are already inside the network.

Chapter 16
Evolution of the Legal Status of Oceanographic Data Management in Europe

Enrique Wulff
https://orcid.org/0000-0001-8104-6147
Instituto de Ciencias Marinas de Andalucía (CSIC), Spain

ABSTRACT

This chapter provides an overview of ocean data legislation in the context of EU maritime policy. Its analyses give an insight into the implementation of the regulations, directives, decisions, and recommendations that address the European Union's approach to the management of its ocean resources. Methods adopted by European legislators to foster collaboration and innovation and harness ocean data to inform policymakers and other stakeholders are discussed. It provides an overview of how the EU has adapted its legal framework to the changing landscape of data management in ocean research and resource management. This insight is given within the specific geographical context of the European Atlantic and Mediterranean regions, allowing readers to understand how these legal responses to the data revolution impact their seas. This chapter could be a valuable resource for those interested in the particular interplay between regulations, data, and the changing landscape of fisheries management in the European Union.

INTRODUCTION

The content of this chapter is the evolution of the EU legislations (laws, directives and regulations) as they define clear objectives concerning the lifecycle of production-processing-consumption for publishing ocean data (Boyes et al., 2016). Yet Member States national laws are a matter of lack of coherence on data treatment rather than clear legal meaning, because while images, data products, and data files are copyrightable, data themselves are not (Reichman & Uhlir, 2003). Indeed, in spite of the fact that the availability of fisheries data has been improved from 2008, and marine data catalogues have been developed following successive EU research programs, EU searching to legally commit governments to

DOI: 10.4018/979-8-3693-0807-3.ch016

grant access to marine data and allow their re-use does not automatically apply to the large pools of data held by research institutions or other bodies with no formal role in government or public administration (European Commission, 2009).

In these times, government-related institutions are demonstrating a greater willingness to address problems concerning sea-related data, while scientific communities are lagging behind. This option may perhaps be due because the former reflect the national interest, whereas the latter join their efforts to the mainstream scientific activities This is already happening in nuclear fusion projects and satellite programs where datasets require more calculations than those provided by ocean management systems.

But the detailed analysis of the temporal evolution for the EU ocean legislation comprises three large types of data sets. Where large data sets get released allowing for analysis is in fishery (Osborne Clarke LLP, 2016). As a result, fishery data have been established as the de facto main structured ocean data over the Web, in the course of the development of the EU marine policy (including coasts, estuaries and wetlands). Marine data include all those designed to improve our understanding of how the seas behave (French et al., 2015), the research domains associated with them make that nearly all marine data could be considered environmental data. In accordance with EU legislation regarding maritime data, we have assembled all those with respect to maritime transport, particularly to such issues as safety, natural resource exploration and exploitation and protection of the marine environment and its biodiversity. Usually under the auspices of regional and international organizations relevant EU's maritime and fisheries policies are subjected to measures requiring scientific data in support of marine research.

In order to examine the many European legal resources concerned by oceanographic data, the fundamental types of data addressed here are (Figure 1 provides a numerical estimation showing data on other scientific data supporting the underlying marine research infrastructure facilities):

- Fishery data
- Marine and maritime data
- Other scientific data supporting the underlying marine research infrastructure facilities

Figure 1. Distribution of the typology of oceanographic data according to the number of legal texts of the European Union (EU)

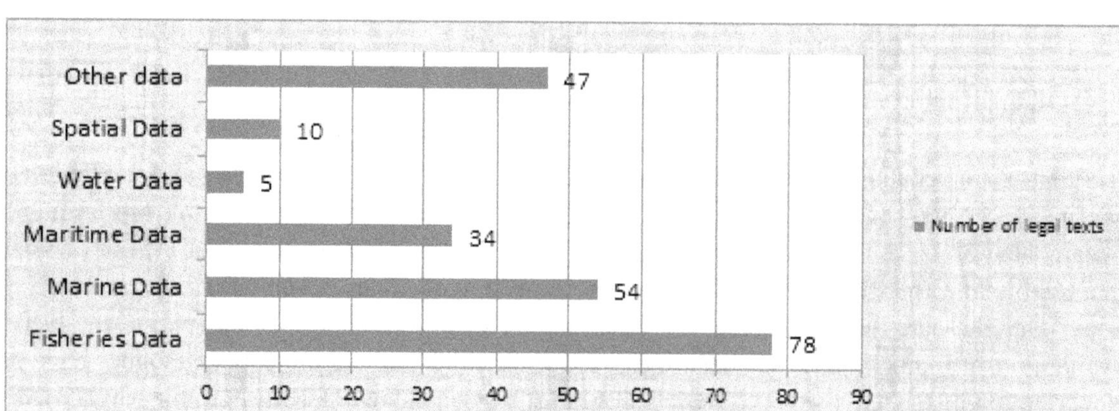

In Europe, the main normative element for the collection, management and use of data in the fisheries sector is the data collection framework (DCF) which establishes a Community framework for gathering these type of data, provides guides on their control and utilization and supports for scientific advice regarding the Common Fisheries Policy, also detailing the fishery data collection obligations with regard to indicators of the fishery sector knock-on effects on the marine ecosystem (It follows that those data, are a substantial part of impact assessments) (European Commission, 2008b). This Commission Regulation (EC) No 665/2008 lays down detailed rules for the application of Council Regulation No 199/2008, the current regulation on fishery data compilation, management and use (European Commission, 2008a).

Typically, the background of these records is the Common Fisheries Policy (CFP) which was initiated in 1983, reformed in 1992 and 2002, and that since 2005 (in compliance with the Action Plan submitted by the Commission) is in a new process of reforms oriented by the April 2009 Green Book. The current CFP entered into force on 1 January 2014 (Regulation (EC) No 1380/2013)[1], maintains among its prime objectives the collection of scientific data, and defines its end user as a science-based or management-based body concerned by the data sets for the scientific analysis in the fishery sector (European Commission, 2014a). At present, the point regarding data is the measures proposed to modify the 2008 Data Collection Framework (DCF)[2], to amend EU Regulation 199/2008[3]. It includes a proposal for a Regulation on the establishment of a framework of the European Union, for the collection of data, their use and management in the area of fishing focused on making scientifically informed decisions in connection with the needs of a common policy to manage fisheries. This proposal of regulation presented in June 2015, is particularly important for the Member States because their 23 national programs for the collection of fisheries data expired on 31 December 2016 (European Commission, 2013).

The discovery, visualization, access, process and evaluation of the marine and maritime data spans over four decades, since the 1976 Barcelona Convention on the Protection of the Mediterranean Sea Against Marine Pollution. Even though the shipping business deals with separate sectoral policies, with full integration of matters related to data since the Antarctic Treaty signed during the 1959 International Geophysical Year (IGY).

The evolution of European policy holds a high place on the international agenda of the oceanographic data, but it was only in 2006 that this heading was given an overarching element with the launching of the European marine observation and data network (EMODnet). It is a characteristic of the European legislation to consider a heterogenous set of outcome measures rather than a strategic approach, as a result of an excessive compartmentalization in tacking the impact of the human activities on the marine environment, and the lack of complete integration at Member State level over the maritime issues (commitments deriving from the obligations raised by a framework of governance that can integrate both the navigational interests of shipping and the protection of marine environment and biodiversity). Yet, it exists from 2010 onwards a common information sharing environment (CISE) for the EU maritime domain, with a step-by-step road map, the maritime CISE was implemented in 2016, on the basis of the objectives set out in 2014 by the European Parliament and Council (maritime security and safety, customs, border control, general law enforcement, fisheries control, marine environment protection/pollution response and defense). The maritime CISE data and service model is currently been tested and Member States have until 31 December 2017 to define their European interoperability solutions (final results will be delivered in 2018).

A patchwork of intergovernmental cooperation between the different legislations of the EU Member States determines the legal basis of the scientific data concerning the ocean in Europe (Suárez de Vivero & Rodríguez Mateos, 2012). To the UN's Institutional Strength in the European continent, thanks to the presence of FAO in Rome, is added the development of GIS (Geographic Information Systems) platforms as the technological basis for the marine spatial management (Stamoulis & Delevaux, 2015). This is a data technology that is based from 1996 on its own legal system, because of the approval of the INSPIRE (Infrastructure for Spatial Information in Europe) Directive (Bartha & Kocsis, 2011). Trends in spatial data infrastructures (SDI) are also borne out by the 2000 European Water Framework Directive (WFD) and by the 2008 Marine Strategic Framework Directive (MSFD) (Seip & Bill, 2016). A Shared Environmental Information System (SEIS) has been in place since 2008. SEIS ensures mutual support between INSPIRE and GMES, the Global Monitoring for Environment and Security system created in 2008 (Meiner, 2010). A list of provisions on scientific data at the service of the programs for marine research should include the Space Surveillance and Tracking (SST) support framework launched in 2014 and the Copernicus program introduced in 2013 with the same goals as those of the GMES program (Aschbacher & Milagro-Pérez, 2012).

Over and beyond the initial objective elements concerning ocean data policies, many more components of EU legislation for fisheries, marine, maritime, and other scientific data exist now than in 1976. The purpose of this study is, then, to describe (1) the fisheries data regulations along the evolution of the EU Common Fisheries Policy, (2) EU legislation supporting marine and maritime data, (3) other scientific data in ocean international settings under EU laws. Toward that goal the chapter explores these legal responses to the data revolution on sea inside the European Atlantic and Mediterranean framework (Figure 2).

Figure 2. European Union (EU) marine regions and subregions according to Article 4 of the Marine Strategy Framework Directive (MSFD)

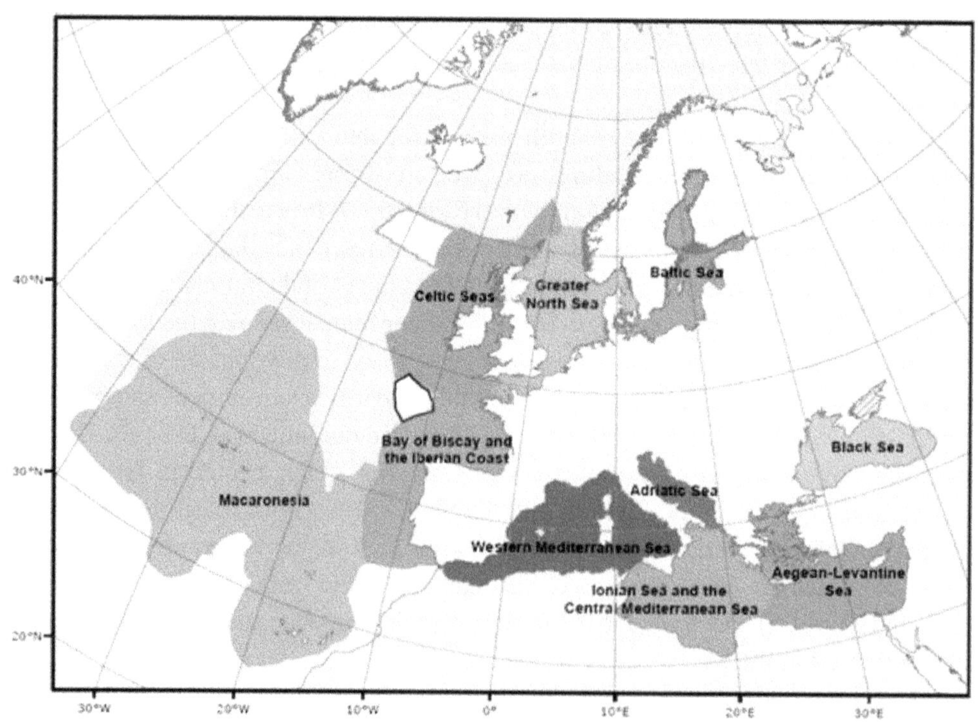

For studying the use of legal spaces in Europe concerning oceanographic data practices, information has been collected from: (1) the European Commission, Council and Parliament codes, regulations and handbooks and (2) published legal studies of data discovery, data access, and data management examining the European Union's policies.

BACKGROUND

The contributions of the literature for oceanographic data management are at the very heart of the standards for legislation, defining a community of interests of primary importance regarding research data. In the last twenty years, this effort has worked on the federation of databases in EU research infrastructures (Cesbron et al., 2021; Latapy et al., 2023; Tanhua et al., 2019; Beja et al. ., 2022), the harmonization of the regulation of private/open access to oceanographic research content (Sullivan, 2020), the alternatives for legal and technical regimes developed by scientists (Danobeitia et al., 2019), technical support for the preservation of research results through the standardization of open formats (ICCAT, 2007; JNCC, 2018) and content migration (Glaves, 2019), the dynamic distribution of metadata (Diviacco et al., 2023; Lamirault-Gall, 2011) and common property ontologies for data mining (Estrada et al., 2008).

The competitive development of indicators (Murillo et al., 2011), and the great development of data infrastructures (Tzitzikas et al., 2017; Delrosso et al., 2016; Martínez et al., 2021; Schaap et al., 2022; Jiang et al., 2023; Erkimbaev et al., 2017; Gómez-Pujol et al., 2021) make data legislation (Pehlivanoglou et al., 2006; Reed, 2013; Woker et al., 2023) and information systems (Cabrera Alvarado, 2020) in oceanography, a domain with extensive implementation of research data repositories. For open access policies, the common interests of this scientific community define the experiences of long-term conservation and publication (Teplitzky, 2017), data harmonization (Simoncelli et al., 2022), standards for metadata (IOC, 2017) and virtual environment for research (Leadbetter et al., 2016) are most abundantly documented. Its discussion in this chapter includes new work models in libraries.

THE EUROPEAN COMMUNITY'S COMMON FISHERIES DATA POLICY

The point of departure for this chapter is the EU legislation for fisheries data. Linking fisheries stock assessments with ocean data ensures that only the allowed quantities of fish are caught and so defines the Common Fisheries Policy (CFP) (Table 1). The CFP objectives and primary focus are on the collection and processing of fisheries data. These factors in both the supply and use of scientific data, determine the evolution of the CFP's legislation on which the design of the fisheries management is based. EU common policies undergo reforms in 10-year cycles, and as the generally accepted date of birth of the CFP is 1983 (Peñas Lado, 2012), the first reform of the CFP was undertaken in 1992, the second reform in 2002, and the more recent CFP reform was in 2013. Approaches required to improve fisheries data productivity, supported the development of successive CFPs establishing the importance of data collection for Member States. From the 1983 Community of 10 to the 2013 Union of 28 (of which 22 are coastal states), terms and conditions to implement the CFP were in line with a common vision and a sense of data discovery to ensure on a permanent and systematic basis, basic data for scientific advice. And this evolution has been done taking into account the different legal status in the various European Seas (the Baltic Sea, the North-east Atlantic Ocean, the Mediterranean Sea, and the Black Sea).

Table 1. Fisheries data regulations in the three CFP reforms

Data Regulation	Common Fisheries Policy (CFP) Regulation
COMMISSION REGULATION (EEC) No 2807 / 83 of 22 September 1983 laying down detailed rules for recording information on Member States' catches of fish	COUNCIL REGULATION (EEC) No 170/83 of 25 January 1983 establishing a Community system for the conservation and management of fishery resources
COUNCIL REGULATION (EC) No 1543/2000 of 29 June 2000 establishing a Community framework for the collection and management of the data needed to conduct the common fisheries policy	COUNCIL REGULATION (EEC) No 3760/92 of 20 December 1992 y establishing a Community system for fisheries and aquaculture
COUNCIL REGULATION (EC) No 199/2008 of 25 February 2008 concerning the establishment of a Community framework for the collection, management and use of data in the fisheries sector and support for scientific advice regarding the Common Fisheries Policy	COUNCIL REGULATION (EC) No 2371/2002 of 20 December 2002 on the conservation and sustainable exploitation of fisheries resources under the Common Fisheries Policy
Proposal for a REGULATION OF THE EUROPEAN PARLIAMENT AND OF THE COUNCIL concerning the establishment of a Union framework for the collection, management and use of data in the fisheries sector and support for scientific advice regarding the Common Fisheries Policy (recast)	REGULATION (EU) No 1380/2013 OF THE EUROPEAN PARLIAMENT AND OF THE COUNCIL of 11 December 2013 on the Common Fisheries Policy

Common Fisheries Policy (CFP): The First EU-Level Fishery Data Collection Instruments

Started as such in 1983, CFP Fisheries data collection procedures place a premium on reliability and replicable collection methods. To ensure the reliable provision of effort reports (which are communicated by masters of Community fishing vessels) detailed rules for recording information on Member States' catches of fish were defined by Commission Regulation (EEC) No. 2807/83; also data replication was mandated by this Regulation because information transmitted to radio stations was passed on in writing to the relevant authorities (and so executed on separate devices). This 1983 publication, first introduced the institutional dimension in the collection of fisheries data for scientific assessment as information was interpreted in terms of salience, credibility and legitimacy (Alcock, 2004). As such, it requires from log-books compliance with all relevant conservation provisions needed by the authorities. Credibility, indeed a major issue of importance in this Regulation, comes from the establishment of the TAC (Total Allowable Catch) format established by Article 3 of the Regulation (EEC) N°170/83, allowing 20% tolerance in estimates of the quantities of fish subject to a TAC that are retained on board. And legitimacy is associated to the relationship between environmental policy and fishing industry, as on several important aspects (estimates of discards, etc.) the authorities only report for scientific purposes.

The 1992 Reform: Data to Visualize the Fishing Effort

EU member states needed to be sure about the use of their exclusive economic zones (EEZ) data and information once the unity of the Community was challenged in 1985 with the withdrawal of the immense size of the Greenwald EEZ. The property of fish resources played a major role in this decision; and the new Spanish and Portuguese EEZs (included in 1986) were poor in stocks. Once the unity of the Community fishing industry was modified, the trend to improve the use of the State Members' data made the data processing chain conceptualize two new legal/institutional indicators designed to legislate for property rights in fisheries: fisheries effort and licensing regime.

What that means is that, although the content of the 1992 reform brought much continuity in respect to the CFP adopted in 1983 (Symes, 1997, 144), its associated data policy Regulation (EC) 1543/2000 established a knowledge framework for EU fisheries management. This Data Collection Regulation (DCR) introduced the concept of fishing effort, as criteria to inform the Commission on the use of the fishing availabilities allocated to Member States, so approaching the fact that their responsibilities include data gathering plans, while fisheries resources are shared. The following Commission Regulation (EC) 1639/2001 established the minimum and extended programs for the collection of data in the fishery sector (with different precision levels, parameters, and data requirements), and with its adoption, on 25 July 2001, the EC data collection framework (DCF) system became functional and effective.

While it is manifest that this fishing limitation measure engaged the possibility to formulate a right of innocent passage for EU ships with no regard to member states EEZs (Agyebeng, 2005), ownership rights generally come with certain associated rights (Cockburn, 2005). And doubts emerged on these "easement" rights, following the fact that the Council limits on the time vessels spent at sea conservation measures and recommendations from the Commission did not establish clearly the link between fish mortality and TACs. The consequence of this was that the quality of fisheries data improved, but concerns persisted as to how actually landing vs. catch data relationship was to be solved. So the new proposed data Regulation (EC) 1543/2000 did not drastically change through its input and output limitations the fisheries data management within the Community (Havstein, 2013).

The 2002 Reform: An Action Plan for the Improvement of Large Deficiencies in Nationally Collected Data

Since 2000, the adoption of the data collection regulation (DCR) (Regulation (EC) 1543/2000), was the base for the Common Fisheries Policy (CFP) receiving advice from basic data co-financed with Member States, as it meant that the same CFP has set aside funding to help national authorities collect both economic and biological data about all aspects of fisheries management and make them publicly available. These experiences were at the base when the new 2002 reform of the Common Fisheries Policy achieved its three main elements: the adoption of long-term strategies to manage European fish stocks and their recovery plans; the solution of subsidized capacity reduction associated to the suppression of funds for new vessel reduction; and to secure a channel through which stakeholders could engage with each other (the Regional Advisory Councils).

And the new data Regulation (EC) 199/2008 was able to take into account the complexities of the EU fishing fleets, to provide a regional approach and an approach by *métier* (i.e., it was based on the various fishing activities and not on stock-based sampling like before) to better describe multi-gear and multi-species fisheries. The new data collection framework (DCF) required Member States to collect data on fleets and their activities, biological data covering catches, including discards, survey information on fish stocks and the environmental impact that may be caused by fisheries on the marine ecosystem. It also included data on the economic situation of fishing enterprises, aquaculture and the processing industry, and of employment in these sectors (European Commission, 2011).

Although it can be said that the DCF is an improvement over DCR, however a problem remains which is that the data collection is not sufficiently driven by end-user needs, an example lies with the introduction of the *métier* based approach which disturbs DCR historical series, as far as eventual additional information is not able to reconstruct and readdress the previous data. Another area where improvements were in need concerned the availability of and access to data with confidentiality/ownership issues as for example, in the case of data collected under one instrument (control regulation) where synergies in requirements currently exists (European Commission, 2012).

2013 Reform: Data for Promoting Sustainable Fisheries

The basic texts of the CFP in the reform of 2013 (Regulation Nº 1380/2013) assembled the current EU legal drivers for fisheries data collection and monitoring, towards the quest for a sustainable fisheries management regime (as has been pursued ever since the 1983 regulation). It can be argued that the precautionary principle (an eminently political responsibility judging what is an "acceptable" risk for society) applied to fisheries management and introduced by the 2002 reform, constrained the issue of data limited stocks. And in particular that the data on *métiers* was seen as an important improvement in precision, and the usefulness and relevance of data collected under the DCF was relatively high. So the EC data collection framework system was becoming functional and effective, it was further stated that Regulation (EC) No 199/2008 is not time-limited and the Commission extended the Union program for data in the fisheries sector until 2016 (European Commission, 2015).

Searching to reform sustainable exploitation of fisheries, 2013 CFP (because the previous did not reduce sufficiently fish mortality) proposed conservation measures (costly and difficult to introduce), and a new legislative procedure after which the Council and the European Parliament together should have to agree on a common position. As such, the Council and European Parliament requested the Commission to integrate the principles and objectives for data collection laid down in 2013 CFP (and in particular Article 25 on data requirements for fisheries management) by amending Council Regulation (EC) Nº 199/2000 on the data collection for fisheries (Minutes, 2014). Questions like how much money would be saved with lower frequency of sampling, or if something could be considered no longer in need with regard to social and economic data go further in data political road.

EU MARINE AND MARITIME LEGISLATION SUPPORTING DATA

The EU's primary legal tools concerning marine and maritime data discovery, access and use understand the term "marine" as including all the data directly related to the sea, while 'maritime' retained a sense cross-sectoral: every data which relates to things associated with the sea. The EU has currently adopted over 200 directives, regulations and other kinds of policy developments related with the marine and maritime dimensions of the seas. Possibly the best known example of a technical directive bringing marine data progressively into line to enable free access without restriction of use is the Marine Strategy Framework Directive (2008/56/EC); and improving knowledge is one of the three main elements of the EU's Integrated Maritime Policy (IMP) (COM (2007) 575 final) with the ultimate intention of creating the European information and observation network on the sea (building inter alia on the GMES initiative) (DEFRA, 2010).

Table 2. European legislation that must be taken into account for marine and maritime data

Legislation	Date	Organization
Directive on the conservation of natural habitats and of wild fauna and flora (Natura 2000)	21/05/92	Council of the European Communities
An Integrated Maritime Policy for the European Union (IMP)	10/10/07	Commission of the European Communities
Directive establishing a framework for community action in the field of marine environmental policy (Marine Strategy Framework Directive) (MSFD)	17/06/08	European Parliament and the Council of the European Union
Building a European marine knowledge infrastructure: Roadmap for a European Marine Observation and Data Network (EMODNet)	07/04/09	Commission of the European Communities
Towards the integration of maritime surveillance: A common information sharing environment for the EU maritime domain (CISE maritime)	15/10/09	Commission of the European Communities
Directive establishing a framework for maritime spatial planning (MSP)	23/07/14	European Parliament and the Council of the European Union

At the EU level, a substantial body of marine and maritime legislation exists that must be taken into account because it could be relevant to data management (Table 2). The Marine Strategy Framework Directive (MSFD) (2008/56/EC) is to be highlighted, as it constitutes the marine pillar of the IMP (2009/C 279 E/06) and is of direct relevance for MSP in the EU (Juda, 2010). A critical need to make public authority more open in oceanography is access to marine and maritime data. And Europe's seas marine researchers access to DG Fisheries and Maritime Affairs funded data collections has been historically restrictive, compared to the fisheries related data accessible to anyone in the USA. Indeed, in the United States, the treatment of marine data as a public good is seen as contributing to overall economic development and value added. While in the EU, marine data is provided by a combination of public and private goods providers (as agencies seek to recover all or a proportion of the costs). To clarify these legal barriers to marine data access and re-use a first study was completed in 2008 (European Commission, 2008c), and to map out what Member States were spending on their current marine data infrastructures a second was launched in 2009 (European Commission, 2009b).

Natura 2000 Directives: Biodiversity Data a Way for MPA Networks

To satisfy EC Legislation, Natura 2000 (Habitats Directives 92/43/EEC) is the centerpiece of its nature and biodiversity policy, and it has identified 206 Natura sites comprising a marine area. It can be said that Natura 2000 data involved in policy advocacy for Marine Protected Areas (MPA) provide the legal means to protect essential fish habitats. The design of an MPA network inevitably depends on its overarching objectives, e.g. fisheries or habitat conservation. Documenting the use of tactical models in the planning of MPA networks, Natura 2000 data provide information on habitat, species distributions, larval, juvenile, and adult movements. But MPA networks are more easily applied in countries that have full control over their EEZs (e.g. the USA), and Europe Member States are just in the process of establishing its MPAs administered through the Natura 2000 sites because it poses a singular problem in terms of territorial use of their Exclusive Economic Zones (EEZs) in the context of the Common Fisheries Policy (CFP) (Fock, 2001).

However, in marine strategies the Natura Directives data are not prepared for prevention plans or projects. And the Technical assessment of the implementation of the Natura 2000 Directives nature conservation-oriented data (Natura 2000) needs to consider other Community legislation concerning multiple users of the marine environment. So when Natura 2000 data are taken as an initial baseline assessment, relevant elements emerge when they are compared with those collected under the MSFD and the Water Directive of October 2000 (WFD). As an element of ocean governance, the use of those data under Habitats and Bird Directives (Natura 2000) are meaningful for regional assessment of change, throw light upon regional consistency, and are included in standardized monitoring methodologies. The integration of all these data in a marine planning process is the principal challenge, by linking data on ecosystems with social and economic human impacts data (Caveen, 2013).

An Integrated Maritime Policy for the European Union (IMP): The European Atlas of the Seas

This European Strategy for Marine and Maritime Research searches to constitute a 'new form of governance' as a means of paving the way toward a more credible and legitimate use of scientific data. Due to data collection methods are not necessarily comparable from country to country, the European Union is in need of help in order to quantify the weight of the maritime economy (Fernández-Macho, 2016). And an European Atlas of the Seas was planned for the launch of the IMP from its Blue Book in 2007, as an educational tool and a means to underline a common maritime heritage, to take the full measure of the economic importance of oceans and the policies put in place for their sustainable exploitation (Dwyer & Wright, 2008). Marine and maritime data gathered, combined and interpreted are translated into indications on various maritime themes by coupling data into ecological and socio-economic indicators. These indicators are used in developing a scientific approach as a new form of governance where the focus is in paving the way for catering with the EU Maritime Spatial Planning community (Barale et al., 2015).

As a significant investment to develop a marine information system (IS) that seek to integrate fragmented data and cater to various users at different scales, also initiatives like broad-scale seabed habitat mapping and promotion of maritime spatial planning have prominent roles in light of the EU's IMP.

Marine Strategy Framework Directive (MSFD): Time Horizon to Achieve Good Environment Status

The Marine Strategy Framework Directive (MSFD) came into force on 15 June 2008, was required to conduct an initial assessment by 15 July 2012 and sets out to achieve in the European Seas a good environmental status (GES) by 2021. All Member States were required to achieve GES within a set of 11 key descriptors ranging from maintaining biological diversity to introducing energy in the marine environment (D3 is related to commercially exploited fish and shellfish) (Maier, 2014). This is a top-down prescriptive approach and a central concept in the Directive, and its utilization is similar to the stipulation of "good surface water status," "good groundwater status," and "good ecological status" as objectives in the EU's 2000 Water Framework Directive (Juda, 2010).

As a driving force the knowledge generated by MSFD reveals a significant number of information gaps, overcoming this lack of knowledge was one of the main aims of the Directive. Such efforts are urgently needed, because while some Member States (such as Portugal) although with extensive marine waters have to manage with the scarce available data, others like those on the coastal areas of the Baltic Sea have relatively broad databases on their marine waters (Maier, 2014).

As this action is needed at different jurisdiction levels, central to this Directive management is the principle of subsidiarity (de Vries et.al., 2016). It defines common objectives to be met, but gives Member States flexibility to implement it, because it is expected that the data can be retrieved in a suitable form for creating indicators of the state of the marine environment in a way that is coherent across national borders. As a legislative act the MSFD can be interpreted to foster and harmonize EU marine waters data with ecosystem approaches, to maintain or achieve GES inside territorial waters or EEZs with common goals.

European Marine Observation and Data Network (EMODNet): All Kinds of Marine Data for Free Download by Any User

As a result of the EU's Blue Book for Maritime Policy (European Commission, 2007), DG-MARE (the managing authority for maritime affairs and fisheries with the rank of directorate general) developed EMODnet to centralize European marine data according to one standard. In the past years, EMODNet portals have approached marine data themes: digital bathymetry, chemistry, physical habitats, geology, biology, physics and human activity. As one of the actions under EU Maritime Policy, the initiative search to improve availability of high quality data, and to encourage more data providers to come forward for data sharing and participating in the process of making complete overviews and homogeneous data products (Schaap, 2014).

The data management component of EMODNet is SeaDataNet. A set rule established by EMODNet is that marine data should be maintained by organizations that collect or own the data but accessed in a common way (European Commission, 2014a). These data stored in National Oceanographic Data Centers or other repositories, are linked through a Common Data Index (CDI), that indicates the type of data and that was developed through a 1st Innovation Cycle. The CDI Data Discovery and Access service is upgraded to ISO 19139 and it is fully INSPIRE compliant (Schaap, 2014). EMODnet gives access and discovery data services through a network of more than 100 interconnected data centers from 35 coastal states bordering the European seas. Although the focus of EMODNet is the distribution of data, attention is devoted to the ingestion of data by fostering a unique opportunity for new potential data providers, through an specific EMODNet Data Ingestion portal.

Best chances for a successful blue economy stems from the use of the EMODnet tool as the base for both DCF and the Integrated Maritime Policy, also the WISE-Marine tool as a part of SEIS, and the European Environment Agency (EEA) draw basic data from EMODNet to construct the indicators that meet their needs. Between Member States technical difficulties derived from marine data exchange policies and to obtain discovery and access of data from this Europe's marine data infrastructure database, tend to be improved by providing focus, continuity and sustainability.

CISE Maritime: Towards the Integration of Maritime Surveillance

Mechanisms for maritime surveillance activities, such as border control, general law enforcement and customs control are included within the framework of the Common Information Sharing Environment (CISE), because civil and military authorities (air patrols, coastguards and navies) are highly dependent on reliable marine data. The first regulation on CISE was put into force in October 2009, and the main pillar within this legal framework is its contribution to improved interoperability and connectivity between different EU actors in the civilian and military domains of the Member States. In this sense, special recommendations concern space generated data used in operations carried out by civilian and military authorities such as monitoring of maritime traffic, sea pollution and the fight against illegal activities at sea.

Searching to consider the enforcement of Community legislation to operate on the High Seas, the question arose of the diversity of legal frameworks and possible exchanges and the highly unlikely that one single technical solution will fit each and every exchange of information within the CISE. Moreover, data on illegal activities, catch information, and electronic data concerning all goods entering and leaving the EU customs territory can be highly sensitive and be transmitted between secured sectoral networks. CISE interoperability solutions fit for these purposes, and partners use the CISE Data Model ('common CISE language'). And that is why the CISE Architecture enables Member States to decide whether to nominate a single or multiple providers of CISE services at national level (European Commission, 2017).

Maritime Spatial Planning Directive (MSP): Freedom of Navigation and Data

Maritime spatial planning that can be defined as a process and as a means, has become a focal point of attention in EU institutions. Being "territorial cohesion" a common approach to MSP, the fact that EU legislation considers it as a shared competence intended to improve coordination made the Commission's Integrated Maritime Policy address this topic explicitly from November 2008. As it considers marine areas in terms of the best available data and information, this tool designates the location of different uses to assist in minimizing conflicts. A conception of ocean space that allows for varying uses in the different layers of the vertical spatial column of marine space (Juda, 2010).

MSP is a cross-sectoral thinking instrument, and this is why the term maritime is favored over marine, although there is an additional difference on the term and the US called it coastal and marine spatial planning (CSMP) (Cavalieri et al., 2016) in spite of the holistic cross-sectoral approach preferred in Europe of the process (European Commission, 2008d). Thankfully, like comprehensive marine knowledge and data systems, the challenge for the Commission entailed full development of a Framework Directive for MSP, what was achieved in 2014 (European Commission, 2014b). But MSP is also a mechanism which contributes data to protection and restoration of environmental sustainability and health through decisions on how to organize the sharing of information necessary for maritime spatial plans.

OTHER EU LEGAL TEXTS ON DATA SUPPORTING OCEANOGRAPHY

EU's primary legal tools offer coordinated access to space and in situ data which are involved in ocean activities (Table 3). Concerning this legislation on scientific data discovery, access and use, comprehensive documentation covers in-situ and satellite observing systems and provides data directly usable by forecasting systems.

Table 3. European regulatory framework for spatial data and other used in oceanography

Legislation	Date	Organization
Directive concerning urban waste water treatment (UWWTD)	21/05/91	Council of the European Communities
Water Framework Directive (WFD)	23/10/00	European Parliament and the Council of the European Union
Access to Environmental Information Directive (AEI)	28/01/03	European Parliament and the Council of the European Union
Bathing Water Quality Directive (BWD)	15/02/06	European Parliament and the Council of the European Union
Directive establishing an Infrastructure for Spatial Information in the European Community (INSPIRE)	14/03/07	European Parliament and the Council of the European Union
Towards a Shared Environmental Information System (SEIS)	01/02/08	Commission of the European Communities
Regulation on the European Earth monitoring program (GMES)	22/09/10	European Parliament and the Council of the European Union
Regulation establishing the Copernicus Program	03/04/14	European Parliament and the Council of the European Union
Decision establishing a Framework for Space Surveillance and Tracking (SST) Support	06/04/14	European Parliament and the Council of the European Union

Member States already collect much of these accurate and reliable spatial data which address the requirements of policy-makers and European regulations regarding the marine environment. These are mainly GIS (geo-referenced) data and, European choices concerning them search to improve their accessibility, that is usually restricted by financial or legal barriers. In this context the government of Europe deals with legal questions issued by the following codes:

1. UWWTD compels Member States to provide the Commission with all relevant information concerning studies on discharges not adversely affecting the environment (1991)
2. WFD determines Member States to provide sufficient data for a reliable assessment of the status of water relevant quality elements (2000)
3. the Environmental Information Directive which requires them to release the data when asked (2003)
4. the Bathing Water Quality Directive express that Member States shall ensure that sets of bathing water quality data are compiled (2006)
5. the Inspire Directive requiring Member States to adopt measures for the sharing data sets and services between public authorities (2007)
6. SEIS legal obligations concern Member States in that they must simplify data-gathering procedures at national and regional level (2008)
7. GMES data should maintain coherence with Member States' spatial reference data (2010)
8. Copernicus available contributing missions and in situ data) are provided mainly by the Member States (2014)
9. SST services operated sensors and processed data remain with the participating Member States (2014)

Under Maastricht Subsidiarity Principle: Urban Waste Water Treatment Directive Data

So activities related to marine knowledge are not confined to research but also include the use of best practices for the organization and availability (interoperability and open access) of marine and maritime data (Zervaki, 2015). Introduced in 1991, a first example was the Directive of Urban Waste Water (UWWTD) a relevant legislation given substantial deference to the role of member states concerning the methodology of data evaluation (principle of subsidiarity). At regular intervals EU Member states make their data submission, and the European Commission implements the Directive through reports on the situation of waste water treatment. Under Article 15(4), all the data reports follow the Water Information System for Europe (WISE) principles, and their current thematic and spatial scope is the Water framework policy directive (WFD).

So far, the EU's member states collectively have led to eight implementation reports from 1998 to 2015. With this division of authority between the European Union and its member states rules and sanctions are applied to encourage patterns of use in accordance with marine ecosystems. Based on data related to open coasts, these technical assessments involve the development of a governance system to improve the treatment of waste water and the improvement of water quality.

Water Framework Directive: Data Quality for Biological Elements in Transitional and Coastal Waters

The key piece of European legislation on water, the Water Framework Directive (WFD), identifies aquatic ecosystems (including estuaries and coastal waters) as an important focus for discussion on community policy to ensure protection of European waters status. Since the Directive was enacted in 2000, the EU called for filling the apparent policy and legislative gaps for the sea areas, what resulted in MSFD, UWWTD, and Natura 2000 Directives. Indeed, WFD integrates data to ensure its provision in conformity with international standards of scientific quality and comparability. Designed with an ecosystem approach (and not with a geographically defined approach), the strength of WFD (monitoring a range of biotic communities) is that potentially addresses complex mixtures of stressors in very different regions and water body types (Hering et al., 2010). What this means in terms of data management is that the objective of this directive is a ratio between defined parameters in a water body and relevant reference conditions. But when WFD focuses on this objective, it combines the assessment results, making use of the one-out-all-out rule, i.e., the lowest score of all assessment results determines the overall ecological quality class.

Access to Environmental Information Directive: The Context of Direct Effect of Data

The 2003 EU Directive on Access to Environmental Information (2003 AEI Directive) is the result of the revision of its 1990 predecessor. The Commission estimated in 1995 Data Protection Directive and 2003 Directive for the Re-Use of Public Sector Information that the driven forces of the market and technology tended to diminish the differences between Member States in terms of legislation on information. As such, the 2003 AEI Directive is the first pillar of the strategy to implement in Europe the 1998 Åarhus Convention, which guarantee the rights of access to information, public participation in decision-making, and access to justice in environmental matters.

These information provisions transposed into the EU level, makes the 2003 instrument stick very close to the environmental information definition inside the Aarhus Convention: it includes coastal and marine areas. Moreover, the revised 2003 AIE Directive represents a more explicit presence of scientific data than in the 1990 AIE (where only personal data were included). An innovative provision dealing with the quality of environmental data is contained in the 2003 Directive. Whereas number 20 of the Directive indicates that the method used in compiling the data should be disclosed as an important factor in assessing quality. Nevertheless, this duty does not apply to data not compiled by Member States and so the only competent authority to bring a legal action against an incorrect transposition of this requirement is the European Commission (Paradissis, 2005).

Bathing Water Quality Directive: A Common European Data Success Story

The regulatory standards of the bathing water directive are high, and data used to classify these European waters are based upon a 90- and 95-percentile evaluation for microbiological enumerations. This quality indicator is identified with beach awards, notably cleanliness of water and sand, revealed by a system of flags (blue flag, etc.). With a role in motivation to visit beaches, BWD Directive has in view article 175 TFUE to promote a high level of environmental protection on the basis of the availability of scientific and technical data. Member States must monitor the bathing waters annually, and Chapter III ('Exchange of information') regulates it in accordance with 2000 WFD. This environmental data management experience based on scientific knowledge, results in that bathing waters quality must be classified according to numerical criteria expressive of their level of quality: poor, sufficient, good or excellent.

Infrastructure for Spatial Information in the European Community: Increasing Attention to Marine and Coastal Spatial Data

In Europe, spatial data infrastructures (SDI) must support INSPIRE Directive requirements, eventually providing one central INSPIRE compliant entry point, whilst multiple community specific portals continue to be supported if necessary. This proven and fit for purpose set of technical standards is driven by geo-referenced data and based on standards established by Open Geospatial Consortium (OGC), with INSPIRE discovery metadata based on the ISO 19115/19119 Application Profile. The directive facilitates thematic data standardization with targeted data themes specifications needed for assessment of aquaculture facilities, oceanographic features (currents, salinity, wave heights, etc.) and sea regions (Meiner, 2013). By virtue of INSPIRE, European SDI discovery services are federated, the interoperability of spatial data sets is regulated and practices concerning spatial data sharing follow a uniform normative.

Shared Environmental Information System (SEIS) Principles and Its Marine Environmental Component WISE-Marine

SEIS, an European policy on environmental information, sets out a legal approach to simplify the collection, exchange and use of the data required for its design. In this way it is a vision that is based on the access to data held by Member States and the European Union, published on the 1st of February 2008. The first principle is simplification which means modernizations of the legal provisions associated with reporting on European environments. The second one is the improvement of collection and availability to supply high quality data for better regulation and policy. And the third principle searches to fit in with reporting requirements from thematic environmental legislation (INSPIRE, GMES, AEI, GEOSS). The SEIS initiative is also particularly intended to do away with paper environmental reporting data and move to an harmonized electronic reporting on electronic issues from the Member States to the European Commission (Janssen, 2009). A good example that follows the SEIS principles is the EMODnet, the European marine observation and data network.

Another marine domain component of SEIS is WISE-Marine, an extension of the Water Information System for Europe (WISE), the central water data web portal of EU that acts as platform for exchanging and sharing information and underlying data for the purposes of the 2008 Marine strategy framework directive (MSFD). Building on INSPIRE and SEIS principles, under the umbrella of EMODnet and, with data collected for other purposes, the stakeholders are trying to provide a coherent picture of the marine environment across multiple Member States. The European Environment Agency is leading this ingestion of environmental data from the WISE-marine system into EMODnet, and vice-versa, and the Commission intends to support the implementation of WISE-Marine in 2015-2018 (European Commission, 2014a).

Regulation on the European Earth Monitoring Programme: GMES Coordinates in Situ and Satellites Data From the Ocean

The European Earth monitoring program GMES (renamed Copernicus in 2014) is a flagship program of the European Union space activities (European Commission, 2016), and it aims to provide information services in the field of environment and security from satellite observation systems and from other sensors. The key objective of GMES is the integration of space monitoring data with corresponding in situ data of water quality, biological and physical-chemical parameters, what is an important and necessary step for improving the knowledge base for coasts and seas. GMES was launched in 2005 (although its origins date back to May 1998, 'Baveno Manifesto'), and its marine and atmosphere services were opened in 2008.

This Earth Observation (EO) program collects data from space with a satellite constellation as its primary infrastructure component. The data are provided by dedicated GMES missions (the Sentinels), as well as Contributing Missions from national and commercial providers. The in situ component is coordinated by the European Environment Agency (EEA) and includes ship- and buoy- based sensors and instruments. Six domains are involved in the production and delivery of GMES services; one of these domains is the marine which contributes to maritime navigation by creating and calibrating three-dimensional models used in prediction and forecasting, it also produces Essential Climate Variables (ECV) by ocean forecasting and monitoring. In this regard, it is noted that between the potential limitations to the full realization of GMES is the uncertainty around long term data policy (Booz & Co., 2011).

Regulation Establishing the Copernicus Program: Matching Data From Satellites and Ocean Buoys

In September 2008, the change of GMES's name to Copernicus was announced, however the European institutions still keep referring to GMES until 2013, and on the 3 April 2014 it was established as the Copernicus programme (repealing and replacing the former denomination). Moreover, the delivery of

GMES/Copernicus is a strategic objective of Europe 2020 (European Commission, 2013a). For the sake of Copernicus international dimension, its exchange of data system and access to observation infrastructure is more cost-efficient than data-buy schemes and enforces the global dimension of the programme. In this sense, the legal basis for this action at European level guarantees economies of scale from space based or in situ based sensors achieved from a more coherent and centralized management of input data than the one that can be offered by Member States. Moreover, if Member States lead Earth observations data duplication would render the implementation of EU environmental legislation difficult or even impossible.

At European level, a data policy that ensures full, open and free-of-charge access, combined with an strategy to preserve historic data, appears to be necessary factors for the private sector to invest in the use of Copernicus data to develop new businesses. The user community of Copernicus include the marine and atmosphere monitoring services of DG ENV, the DG MOVE for oil spill and ice monitoring, the DG MARE for ocean monitoring and forecasting and the DG CLIMA for climate change mitigation and adaptation.

Decision on a Framework for Space Surveillance and Tracking (SST) Support: European Ocean Tides and Maritime Surveillance

The European Commission use the concept of "space surveillance and tracking (SST)", for which they define the terms "SST sensor", "SST data" and "SST information". The main objective of this Decision is the development of a legally binding international instrument built around devices that measure size, location and speed of space objects. In many cases they are ground-based or space-based radars and telescopes, and these are called SST sensors. The distinction between the two last categories indicate an increasing level of refinement: SST data is the primary physical or orbital parameter of space object derived from SST sensors' observations and SST information is processed data enhanced by interpretation and inputs from sources (Kaiser, 2015) so that they can be readily meaningful to the recipient.

Critical data policy issues regarding SST data and SST information are enclosed by the decision rules oriented to ensure the security of SST data. Space weather data, are much more precise for ocean tides and maritime surveillance purposes than other environmental data, but they must follow recommendations on SST data security endorsed by the Security Committee of the Council (Council document 15715/11, 24.10.2011). These recommendations on security aspects for the Space Surveillance and Tracking Support data policy are the governance criteria for the exchange and sharing of information on national remote sensing activities. Indeed, space weather data are the subject of the widest distribution but they may have security significance regarding the governmental users, commercial significance and consequences regarding the international partners (Pasco, 2008).

RECOMMENDATIONS AND CONCLUSIONS

Tables 1, 2, and 3 highlight the main legislative orientations set out by the Commission, the Parliament and the Council in their efforts to secure a better environment for the EU depend on ocean data. Tackling today's data challenges, such as requesting access to the data source, discovering the data source and its documentation, viewing the datasets and displaying any relevant content of metadata, downloading datasets to be accessed directly, transforming data with a view to achieving interoperability and allowing data to be invoked - all this depend on the implementation of the different EU directives, regulations and laws. For that reason, where the Commission is concerned with the content, effectiveness and impact of the legislation the highest quality analysis are in need to be able to assess the impact of data policy proposals. And regulations could be improved by incorporating the recommendations set out from the points of view in the article.

Summary of the Commission's Approach to Common Fisheries Data Policy and Specific Proposals

The two key elements of the current framework for data collection (DCR) on the European fisheries are that Member States and fishermen oppose stricter conservation measures by arguing that there is not enough scientific evidence and data to justify such measures and the ability of the Commission on setting up a single authority for the collection and verification of fishing data. The implementation of the Common Fishing Policy respects the principles of data accessibility and sharing, but at various geographic scales and tailored to the needs of Member States authorities' problems involving citizens, enterprises and other stakeholders have repercussions on data flow elsewhere.

In support of this, improved research and data collection must be developed to identify the fishing industry with European data results on fishing activity and fishing grounds thus helping to improve fisheries management with regard to other uses.

Summary Scheme on the Actual European Legislation of Marine and Maritime Data and Recommendations

The very purpose of data access legislation is in conflict with an adequate protection of the interests concerned by the European ocean use management. EU action in the field of marine environmental data policy is biased by the problems coming from the exercise of jurisdiction that converts science to policy enabling the participation of the stakeholders in decision-making and keeping the stakeholders informed on the data activities of his government.

In so far as the EU objectives engaged in data policy, to develop a marine strategy to protect the marine environment and to encompass an integrated maritime policy, come in line with the interests of the Member States, the goal-oriented system of European data rules must be backed by a policy fully compliant with the subsidiarity principle.

Summary of Up-to-Date EU Scientific Data Legislation Concerning the Ocean and Recommendations Regarding Measures to Prevent Their Misuse

On the proposal of the European institutions, legal mechanisms for the exchange and sharing of wide-ranging online data for oceanographic research are subject of suitable governance and data policy models. Within and outside the space domain data assets are deeply embedded in developed blue economies and data legislations are critical for running large marine ecosystems and maritime surveillance.

The fight against undue implementation of the EU spatial data legislation appears as a result of Europe's ocean data policy being mainly part of a decision-making phase. The route towards a most subsequent adoption phase is through ensuring the Commission guidance on the key concepts of the directives and regulations, which aim to explain the way forward.

FUTURE RESEARCH

Helping to define the characteristics and governance structures of oceanographic data in Europe requires the examination of their legal contexts. To a first approximation, this means to take into account the large variance in the size of research infrastructures existing within the european region; notably recognising the risk of mixing together local knowledge spillovers with other sources of pecuniary externalities. This could require that legislation does not block the establishment of European public services within and between Member States and that there are clear agreements on how to manage legislative differences across borders, including the possibility of introducing new legislation.

In the most advanced sectors of oceanography carried out in Europe, the pursuit of a data policy is intensified by the fact that the resources it consumes are important enough to impress the public in terms of the digital economy (the general budget of SeaDataCloud is 10 million euros; SeaDataCloud was the 2016-2020 phase of the EU Project SeaDataNet). As this continues, analysis methodologies for oceanographic data and metadata will become available and technical obstacles can be resolved. The issue will consist of maintaining mandatory attention to the positioning data and conventions that refer to the formats; and a strong recommendation, regarding the levels of hierarchy and attributes of the parameters.

Going forward, the software perspective will focus on integrating AI into daily data management functions. Although it is critical, and this is perhaps its biggest problem, the imperative of having absolutely clean data, without which nothing is obtained from the Machine Learning (ML) models. This brings us to the concept of automated data management, so that humans do not move the data, which at some level eliminates the risk of errors in data manipulation. The current standardization of data management will lead to individual use of this automated instrumentation; just as the profession of automobile driver gave rise to the individual driving of these machines.

REFERENCES

Agyebeng, K. (2005). *Theory in Search of Practice*: The Right of Innocent Passage in the Territorial Sea. Cornell Law School Graduate Student Papers. Paper 9.

Alcock, F. (2004). The institutional dimensions of fisheries stock assessments. *International Environmental Agreement: Politics, Law and Economics*, *4*(2), 129–141. doi:10.1023/B:INEA.0000040416.45027.e4

Aschbacher, J., & Milagro-Pérez, M. P. (2012). The European Earth monitoring (GMES) programme: Status and perspectives. *Remote Sensing of Environment*, *120*, 3–8. doi:10.1016/j.rse.2011.08.028

Barale, V., Assouline, M., Dusart, J., & Gaffuri, J. (2015). The European Atlas of the Seas: Relating Natural and Socio-Economic Elements of Coastal and Marine Environments in the European Union. *Marine Geodesy*, *38*(1), 79–88. doi:10.1080/01490419.2014.909373

Bartha, G., & Kocsis, S. (2011). Standardization of geographic data: The European Inspire Directive. *European Journal of Geography*, *2*, 79–89.

Beja, J., Vandepitte, L., Benson, A., Van de Putte, A., Lear, D., & De Pooter, D. (2022). Data services in ocean science with a focus on the biology. In G. Manzella & A. Novellino (Eds.), *Ocean Science Data* (pp. 67–129). Collection, Management, Networking and Services. doi:10.1016/B978-0-12-823427-3.00006-2

Booz & Co. (2011). Cost-Benefit Analysis for GMES. European Commission: Directorate-General for Enterprise & Industry, London 19th September 2011.

Boyes, S. J., Elliott, M., Murillas-Maza, A., Papadopoulou, N., & Uñara, M. C. (2016). Is existing legislation fit-for-purpose to achieve Good Environmental Status in European seas? *Marine Pollution Bulletin*, *111*(1-2), 18–32. doi:10.1016/j.marpolbul.2016.06.079 PMID:27377000

Cabrera Alvarado, S. (2020). *In pursuit of openness. An analysis of the legal framework of the European Union's Copernicus' open data policy* [Doctoral dissertation]. University of Luxembourg, Luxembourg.

Cavalieri, S., McGlynn, E., Piotrowski, R., Reid, A., Cantral, L., Lee, E., & … . (2011). *Comparison: EU and US Ocean Policy. Report of the Cooperation Across the Atlantic for Marine Governance Integration (CALAMAR) Project*. Ecologic Institute.

Caveen, A. (2013). *A Critical Examination of the Scientific Credentials of Marine Protected Areas: Sound Science or a Leap of Faith?* [PhD thesis]. Newcastle University, Newscastle.

Cesbron, G., Melet, A., Almar, R., Lifermann, A., Tullot, D., & Crosnier, L. (2021). Pan-European Satellite-Derived Coastal Bathymetry—Review, User Needs and Future Services. *Frontiers in Marine Science*, *8*, 740830. doi:10.3389/fmars.2021.740830

Cockburn, S. (2005). *Developments in Marine Boundary Law to Construct a Legal Framework for Offshore and Coastal Spaces* [M.Sc.E. thesis]. University of New Brunswick.

Danobeitia, J., Beranzoli, L., Berry, A., Blandin, J., Cannat, M., & Chavrit, D. (2019, December). EMSO, a Large-scale European Research Infrastructure Delivering Harmonized Environmental Marine Data through a Distributed Ocean Observation System. In *AGU Fall Meeting Abstracts* (Vol. 2019, pp. OS53B-1525). Academic Press.

de Vries, P., Tamis, J., Thijsse, P., & Kater, B. (2016). Collecting literature for identifying data sets and data sources; Literature Review, Arctic Sea Basin Checkpoint. Wageningen, IMARES Wageningen UR (University & Research centre), IMARES report Final draft.

DEFRA. (2010). Marine data and observation. In *Great Britain. Parliament. House of Commons. European Scrutiny Committee. Fourth Report of Session 2010-11: Documents considered by the Committee on 20 October 2010*. The Stationery Office.

Delrosso, D., Clementi, E., Grandi, A., Tonani, M., Oddo, P., Girardi Feruzza, G., & Pinardi, N. (2016). *Towards the Mediterranean Forecasting System MyOcean V5: numerical experiments results and validation*. Rapporti Tecnici INGV.

Diviacco, P., Iurcev, M., Carbajales, R. J., Viola, A., & Potleca, N. (2023). Design and Implementation of a Crowdsensing-Based Air Quality Monitoring Open and FAIR Data Infrastructure. *Processes (Basel, Switzerland)*, *11*(7), 1881. doi:10.3390/pr11071881

Dwyer, N., & Wright, D. J. (2008). *Report of International Coastal Atlas Network Workshop 3 on Federated Coastal Atlases: Building on the Interoperable Approach*. European Environment Agency.

Erkimbaev, A. O., Zitserman, V. Y., & Kobzev, G. A. (2017). The intensive use of digital data in modern natural science. *Automatic Documentation and Mathematical Linguistics, 51*(5), 201–213. doi:10.3103/S0005105517050028

Estrada, M., Álvarez-Fanjul, E., Barragán, A., Bermúdez, Ó., García-Fernández, M. J., & Lavín, A. (2008). Reflexiones sobre la gestión y custodia de datos oceanográficos en España. *Recursos existentes y recomendaciones para el futuro.*

European Commission. (2007). An Integrated Maritime Policy for the European Union. Brussels, 10.10.2007 COM (2007) 575 final.

European Commission. (2008a). Council Regulation (EC) No 199/2008 of 25 February 2008 concerning the establishment of a Community framework for the collection, management and use of data in the fisheries sector and support for scientific advice regarding the Common Fisheries Policy. *Official Journal of the European Union, L, 60*, 1–12.

European Commission. (2008b). Commission Regulation (EC) No 665/2008 of 14 July 2008 laying down detailed rules for the application of Council Regulation (EC) No 199/2008 concerning the establishment of a Community framework for the collection, management and use of data in the fisheries sector and support for scientific advice regarding the Common Fisheries Policy. *Official Journal of the European Union, L, 186*, 3–5.

European Commission. (2008c). *Legal Aspects of Marine Environmental Data Framework Service Contract, No. FISH/2006/09 – LOT2*, final report. Brussels, October 2008.

European Commission. (2008d). *Roadmap for Maritime Spatial Planning*: Achieving Common Principles in the EU, 25.11.2008 COM(2008) 791 final. Brussels, 25.11.2008 COM(2008) 791 final.

European Commission. (2009). *Commission Staff Working Document. Building a European marine knowledge infrastructure: Roadmap for a European Marine Observation and Data Network*. Brussels, 7.4.2009 COM(2009) 499 final.

European Commission. (2009b). Marine Data Infrastructure Framework Service Contract, No. FISH/2006/09 – LOT 2 Executive Summary. Brussels, December 2009.

European Commission. (2011). *Commission Staff Working Document. Impact assessment - Accompanying Commission proposal for a Regulation of the European Parliament and of the Council on the Common Fisheries Policy* [repealing Regulation (EC) Nº 2371/2002]. Brussels, 13 July 2011 SEC(2011) 891.

European Commission, DG Mare. (2012). *The Evaluation of the Data Collection Framework (DCF) Lot 2*: Retrospective and Prospective Evaluation on the Common Fisheries Policy, Excluding its International Dimension.

European Commission. (2013). *Commission implementing decision of 30.8.2013 extending the national programmes for the collection of primary biological, technical, environmental and socio-economic data in the fisheries sector for the period 2011-2013 to the period 2014-2016*. Brussels, 30.8.2013. C(2013) 5568 final.

European Commission, (2014a). *Commission Staff Working Document. Marine Knowledge 2020: roadmap*. Brussels, 8.5.2014 SWD(2014) 149 final.

European Commission. (2014b). Directive 2014/89/EU of the European Parliament and of the Council of 23 July 2014 establishing a framework for maritime spatial planning. *Official Journal of the European Union, L, 257*, 135.

European Commission. (2015). *Proposal for a Regulation of the European Parliament and of the Council concerning the establishment of a Union framework for the collection, management and use of data in the fisheries sector and support for scientific advice regarding the Common Fisheries Policy (recast).* Brussels, 18.6.2015 SWD(2015) 118 final. COM(2015) 294 final.

European Commission. (2016). *Ex-post Evaluation on the European earth monitoring programme (GMES) and its Initial Operations (2011 to 2013).* Brussels, 2.8.2016 SWD(2016) 262 final.

European Commission. (2017). *Implementation of the Common Information Sharing Environment (CISE) for the EU maritime domain*: Ensuring interoperability of National IT Systems to allow for more efficient information exchange within and across borders. EMFF Work Programmes 2016/2017, Call for Proposals.

Fernandez-Macho, J. (2016). A statistical assessment of maritime socioeconomic indicators for the European Atlantic area. *Journal of Ocean and Coastal Economics*, *2*(2), 4. Advance online publication. doi:10.15351/2373-8456.1047

Fock, H. (2011). Natura 2000 and the European Common Fisheries Policy. *Marine Policy*, *35*(2), 181–188. doi:10.1016/j.marpol.2010.09.003

French, V., Chu, N.-C., Santoro, F., Sousa Pinto, I., Borges, D., & McDonough, N. (2015). *Review of Ocean Literacy in European Maritime Policy*. EU Sea Change Project.

Glaves, H. M. (2019). Developing a common global framework for marine data management. In Oceanography and Coastal Informatics: Breakthroughs in Research and Practice (pp. 179-199). IGI Global. doi:10.4018/978-1-5225-7308-1.ch008

Gómez-Pujol, L., Vallespir, J., March, D., & Tintoré, J. (2021). A Survey of Mediterranean Shoreline Change Data Infrastructure, Availability and Nature. *Monografies de la Societat d'Història Natural de les Balears*, (33).

Havstein, H. M. (2013). *Changes and continuity: 40 years of reforming the Common Fisheries Policy* [Master's thesis]. Institutt for historie og klassisdke fag, NTNU, Trondheim, Norway.

ICCAT (International Commission for the Conservation of Atlantic Tunas). (2007). *Basic texts.* https://www.iccat.int/Documents/Commission/BasicTexts.pdf

Intergovernmental Oceanographic Commission. (2017). *IOC Strategic Plan for Oceanographic Data and Information Management (2017-2021).* Author.

Jiang, F., Zhou, M., Zhou, F., & Hu, Z. (2023, May). Glider Network Observation Unraveling A Cyclonic Eddy in the Northwestern Pacific Subtropical Countercurrent. *Journal of Physics: Conference Series*, *2486*(1), 012009. doi:10.1088/1742-6596/2486/1/012009

JNCC (Joint Nature Conservation Committee). (2018). Open. *Data & Policy*, 1.

Juda, L. (2010). The European Union and the Marine Strategy Framework Directive: Continuing the Development of European Ocean Use Management. *Ocean Development and International Law*, *41*(1), 34–54. doi:10.1080/00908320903285463

Kaiser, S. A. (2015). Legal and policy aspects of space situational awareness. *Space Policy*, *31*, 5–12. doi:10.1016/j.spacepol.2014.11.002

Lamirault-Gall, M. O. (2011). *Metadata capture user guide for the Working Group on Marine Habitat Mapping (WGMHM) for ICES*. Academic Press.

Latapy, A., Ferret, Y., Testut, L., Talke, S., Aarup, T., Pons, F., Jan, G., Bradshaw, E., & Pouvreau, N. (2023). Data rescue process in the context of sea level reconstructions: An overview of the methodology, lessons learned, up-to-date best practices and recommendations. *Geoscience Data Journal*, *10*(3), 396–425. doi:10.1002/gdj3.179

Leadbetter, A. M., Shepherd, A., Arko, R., Chandler, C., Chen, Y., Dockery, N., Ferreira, R., Fu, L., Thomas, R., West, P., & Zednik, S. (2016). Experiences of a "semantics smackdown". *Earth Science Informatics*, *9*(3), 355–363. doi:10.100712145-016-0252-8

Maier, N. (2014). Coordination and cooperation in the European Marine Strategy Framework Directive and the US National Ocean Policy. *Ocean and Coastal Management*, *92*, 1–8. doi:10.1016/j.ocecoaman.2014.01.014

Martínez, E., García-Benadí, A., Toma, D. M., Delory, E., Gomáriz, S., & Del-Río, J. (2021). Metadata-driven universal real-time ocean sound measurement architecture. *IEEE Access : Practical Innovations, Open Solutions*, *9*, 28282–28301. doi:10.1109/ACCESS.2021.3058744

Meiner, A. (2010). Integrated maritime policy for the European Union — Consolidating coastal and marine information to support maritime spatial planning. *Journal of Coastal Conservation*, *14*(1), 1–11. doi:10.100711852-009-0077-4

Meiner, A. (2013). Spatial data management priorities for assessment of Europe's coasts and seas. *Journal of Coastal Conservation*, *17*(2), 271–277. doi:10.100711852-011-0173-0

Murillo, F. J., Kenchington, E., Sacau, M., Piper, D. J. W., Wareham, V., & Muñoz, A. (2011). New VME indicator species (excluding corals and sponges) and some potential VME elements of the NAFO Regulatory Area. NAFO SCR Document 11/73, Serial No. N6003pg. 20 pp.

Osborne Clarke, L. L. P. (2016). *Legal study on ownership and access to data: A study prepared for the European Commission DG Communications Networks*. Content & Technology.

Paradissis, J. J. (2005). *The right to access environmental information: An analysis of UK law in the context of international, European, and comparative law* [PhD thesis]. City University, London.

Pasco, X. (2008). Study on suitable governance and Data Policy models for a European Space Situational Awareness (SSA) System. Contract n° 21443/08/F/MOS, European Space Agency.

Pehlivanoglou, K. G., Rappou, M., & Martsoukou, M. (2006). Geological and oceanographic data determining the foreshore zone according to the Greek legislation. *Mediterranean Marine Science*, *7*(1), 15–26. doi:10.12681/mms.174

Peñas Lado, E. (2012). *The common fisheries policy: The quest for sustainability*. Wiley.

Reed, G. (2012). IODE Quality Management Framework for National Oceanographic Data Centres. Presented at *Twenty-second Session of the IOC Committee on International Oceanographic Data and Information Exchange (IODE-XXII)*, Ensenada, Mexico.

Reichman, J. H., & Uhlir, P. F. (2003). A contractually reconstructed research commons for scientific data in a highly protectionist intellectual property environment. *Law and Contemporary Problems*, *66*, 315–462.

Schaap, D. (2014). SeaDataNet II - EMODNet - building a pan-European infrastructure for marine and ocean data management. *Geophysical Research Abstracts*, *16*, EGU2014–EGU2735.

Schaap, D. M., Novellino, A., Fichaut, M., & Manzella, G. M. (2022). Data management infrastructures and their practices in Europe. In *Ocean Science Data* (pp. 131–193). Elsevier. doi:10.1016/B978-0-12-823427-3.00007-4

Seip, C., & Bill, R. (2016). A framework for the evaluation of marine spatial data infrastructures - accompanied by international case-studies. *GeoScience Engineering*, *62*(2), 27–43. doi:10.1515/gse-2016-0015

Simoncelli, S., Manzella, G. M. R., Storto, A., Pisano, A., Lipizer, M., & Barth, A. (2022). A collaborative framework among data producers, managers, and users. In *Ocean Science Data* (pp. 197–280). Elsevier. doi:10.1016/B978-0-12-823427-3.00001-3

Stamoulis, K. A., & Delevaux, J. M. S. (2015). Data requirements and tools to operationalize marine spatial planning in the United States. *Ocean and Coastal Management*, *116*, 214–223. doi:10.1016/j.ocecoaman.2015.07.011

Suárez de Vivero, J. L., & Rodríguez Mateos, J. C. (2012). The Spanish approach to marine spatial planning. Marine Strategy Framework Directive vs. EU Integrated Maritime Policy. *Marine Policy*, *36*(1), 18–27. doi:10.1016/j.marpol.2011.03.002

Sullivan, K. M. (2020). Documenting Sea Change: Ocean Data Technologies, Sciences, and Governance. *Environment and Society*, *11*(1), 82–99. doi:10.3167/ares.2020.110106

Symes, D. (1997). The European Community's Common Fisheries Policy. *Ocean and Coastal Management*, *35*(2-3), 137–155. doi:10.1016/S0964-5691(97)00030-6

Tanhua, T., Pouliquen, S., Hausman, J., O'Brien, K., Bricher, P., De Bruin, T., Buck, J. J. H., Burger, E. F., Carval, T., Casey, K. S., Diggs, S., Giorgetti, A., Glaves, H., Harscoat, V., Kinkade, D., Muelbert, J. H., Novellino, A., Pfeil, B., Pulsifer, P. L., ... Zhao, Z. (2019). Ocean FAIR data services. *Frontiers in Marine Science*, *6*, 440. doi:10.3389/fmars.2019.00440

Teplitzky, S. (2017). Open data, [open] access: Linking data sharing and article sharing in the Earth Sciences. *Journal of Librarianship and Scholarly Communication*, *5*(1). Advance online publication. doi:10.7710/2162-3309.2150

Tzitzikas, Y., Marketakis, Y., Minadakis, N., Mountantonakis, M., Candela, L., & Mangiacrapa, F. (2019). Methods and tools for supporting the integration of stocks and fisheries. In *Information and Communication Technologies in Modern Agricultural Development: 8th International Conference, HAICTA 2017, Chania, Crete, Greece, September 21–24, 2017, Revised Selected Papers 8* (pp. 20-34). Springer International Publishing. 10.1007/978-3-030-12998-9_2

Woker, H. J., Holst, R. J. R., & Harden-Davies, H. (2023). New technology and the protection of the marine environment. Research Handbook on International Marine Environmental Law: Second Edition, 409.

Zervaki, A. (2015). Introducing Maritime Spatial Planning Legislation in the EU: Fishing in Troubled Waters? *Maritime Safety and Security Law Journal, 1*, 95–114.

ADDITIONAL READING

Assante, M., Candela, L., Castelli, D., Cirillo, R., Coro, G., Dell'Amico, A., Frosini, L., Lelii, L., Lettere, M., Mangiacrapa, F., Pagano, P., Panichi, G., Piccioli, T., & Sinibaldi, F. (2023). Virtual research environments co-creation: The D4Science experience. *Concurrency and Computation, 35*(18), e6925. doi:10.1002/cpe.6925

Burgi, P. Y., Blumer, E., & Makhlouf-Shabou, B. (2017). Research data management in Switzerland: National efforts to guarantee the sustainability of research outputs. *IFLA Journal, 43*(1), 5–21. doi:10.1177/0340035216678238

Candela, L., Castelli, D., & Pagano, P. (2023). The D4Science experience on virtual research environments development. *Computing in Science & Engineering, 25*(2), 12–19. doi:10.1109/MCSE.2023.3290433

da Silva Marques, I., Santos, C., & Guerreiro, J. (2022). Comparative analysis of National Ocean Strategies of the Atlantic Basin countries. *Frontiers in Marine Science, 9*, 1001181. doi:10.3389/fmars.2022.1001181

Diviacco, P., Nadali, A., Nolich, M., Molinaro, A., Lurcev, M., Carbajales, R., & ... . (2021). Citizen science and crowdsourcing in the field of marine scientific research-the MaDCrow project. *JCOM, Journal of Science Communication, 20*(6).

Mikhaylov, A. S., Mikhaylova, A. A., & Kuznetsova, T. Y. (2018). Coastalization effect and spatial divergence: Segregation of European regions. *Ocean and Coastal Management, 161*, 57–65. doi:10.1016/j.ocecoaman.2018.04.024

Robinson, L. D., Cawthray, J. L., West, S. E., Bonn, A., & Ansine, J. (2018). Ten principles of citizen science. In S. Hecker, M. Haklay, A. Bowser, Z. Makuch, J. Vogel, & A. Bonn (Eds.) Citizen Science: Innovation in Open Science, Society and Policy (pp. 27-40). doi:10.2307/j.ctv550cf2.9

Van Wyk, J., Bothma, T., & Holmner, M. (2020). A conceptual virtual research environment model for the management of research data, a South African perspective. *Library Management, 41*(6/7), 417–446. doi:10.1108/LM-02-2020-0037

KEY TERMS AND DEFINITIONS

Data Management: Practices and projects to acquire, control, protect, disseminate, and increase the value of data.

Data Policy: Political tools available in the context of the European Union (EU), in defense of rights (intellectual property, etc.) that concern data, metadata and data products.

Data Services: Software services encapsulating operations with key data entities.

Fishery Data: Those with potential applications for fisheries management.

in-situ observations: Those direct measurements of seawater properties carried out using a combination of sensors on a wide range of platforms.

Interoperability: The ability to communicate and execute programs, or transfer data between multiple functional units, in a manner that is useful, transparent, and meaningful to the user.

Legal Compliance: Degree of compliance with EU regulations, communications, directives, and other types of legal documents regarding oceanographic data.

Marine Data: Those obtained regarding the marine environment, based on observations, studies or sampling.

Maritime Data: They are those of transportation, traffic, and maritime trade, bringing into play maritime safety and security, the prevention of maritime pollution, customs, border control and health.

Metadata: Data that defines and describes the characteristics of other data.

Métier: Work profiles in the context of the different fishing activities.

Open Access: The provision of immediate access, no registration, subscription, or payment requirements.

Spatial Data: It is the primary information necessary for geographic information systems (GIS), spatial data analysis software tools, and position-based mobile devices.

Water Data: These are data on the quality of bathing water and urban wastewater.

ENDNOTES

1 https://eur-lex.europa.eu/legal-content/EN/TXT/PDF/?uri=CELEX:32013R1380

2 https://eur-lex.europa.eu/legal-content/EN/TXT/PDF/?uri=CELEX:32017R1004&rid=3

3 https://eur-lex.europa.eu/legal-content/EN/TXT/PDF/?uri=CELEX:32008R0199

Compilation of References

Aboelmaged, M., Govindan, K., & Malik, M. (2023). Understanding the key determinants of IOT adoption for the digital transformation of the food and beverage industry. *Industrial Management &amp. Data Systems*, *123*(7), 1887–1910. doi:10.1108/imds-02-2022-0082

Acemoglu, D., & Restrepo, P. (2016). *The race between machine and man: Implications of technology for growth, factor shares and employment (No. w22252)*. National Bureau of Economic Research. doi:10.3386/w22252

Acemoglu, D., & Restrepo, P. (2019). *Artificial Intelligence, Automation, and Work*. University of Chicago Press. https://www.nber.org/chapters/c14027

Acemoglu, D., & Restrepo, P. (2020, March). The wrong kind of AI? Artificial intelligence and the future of labour demand. *Cambridge Journal of Regions, Economy and Society*, *13*(1), 25–35. doi:10.1093/cjres/rsz022

Achar, S., Patel, H., & Hussain, S. (2022). Data Security in Cloud: A Review. *Asian Journal of Advances in Research*, 1099-1106.

ACRL. (1998). *Task force on academic library outcomes assessment report*. https://www.ala.org/acrl/publications/whitepapers/taskforceacademic

Adamova, A. D., Zhukabayeva, T. K., & Ven-Tsen, K. (2021). Development of a digital educational platform using augmented reality and Gamification Technologies to intensify learning and cognitive activities of students in the course of studying the subject. *BULLETIN of L.N. Gumilyov Eurasian National University. Technical Science and Technology Series*, *137*(4), 39–47. doi:10.32523/2616-7263-2021-137-4-39-47

Adashi, E. Y. (2021). Cybersecurity in the internet of medical things. *Health Policy and Technology*, *10*(3), 100549. doi:10.1016/j.hlpt.2021.100549

Adil, M., Singh, Y., & Ansari, M. S. (2021). Asian. *Journal of Accounting Research*, *7*(1), 17–30. doi:10.1108/AJAR-09-2020-0086

Aghion, P., Jones, B. F., & Jones, C. I. (2019). *Artificial Intelligence and Economic Growth*. University of Chicago Press. https://www.nber.org/chapters/c14015

Agyebeng, K. (2005). *Theory in Search of Practice*: The Right of Innocent Passage in the Territorial Sea. Cornell Law School Graduate Student Papers. Paper 9.

Agyemang, F. G. (2019). From classroom to library: What are the transferable knowledge and skills teachers bring to library work. *Journal of Librarianship and Information Science*, *52*(3), 659–670. doi:10.1177/0961000619856401

Ahluwalia, M. S., & Chenery, H. (1974). Redistribution with Growth: The Economic Framework. In *Milestones and Turning Points in Development Thinking* (pp. 135–147). Palgrave Macmillan UK.

Ahmad, R., Alsmadi, I., Alhamdani, W., & Tawalbeh, L. (2021). Models versus datasets: Reducing bias through building a comprehensive ids benchmark. *Future Internet*, *13*(12), 318. doi:10.3390/fi13120318

Aicardi, C., Bitsch, L., Datta Burton, S., Evers, L., Farisco, M., & Mahfoud, T. (2020). *Trust and Transparency in Artificial Intelligence.* Technical report D12.5.4, Human Brain Project SGA2. Available at: https://www.humanbrainproject.eu/

Akça, D., Grün, A., Alkis, Z., Demir, N., Breuckmann, B., Erduyan, İ., & Nadir, E. (2006). 3D modeling of the Weary Herakles statue with a coded structured light system. *IAPRS*, (5), 46.

Alahi, M. E., Sukkuea, A., Tina, F. W., Nag, A., Kurdthongmee, W., Suwannarat, K., & Mukhopadhyay, S. C. (2023). Integration of IOT-enabled technologies and Artificial Intelligence (AI) for Smart City Scenario: Recent advancements and future trends. *Sensors (Basel)*, *23*(11), 5206. doi:10.339023115206

Alcock, F. (2004). The institutional dimensions of fisheries stock assessments. *International Environmental Agreement: Politics, Law and Economics*, *4*(2), 129–141. doi:10.1023/B:INEA.0000040416.45027.e4

Aldriweesh, E., Zakuan, N., Hafiz Bajuri, N., & Mufareh Alshammakh, A. (2022). The moderating role of organizational culture on the relationship between enterprise risk management dimensions and financial performance in manufacturing companies: A theoretical framework. *International Journal of Academic Research in Accounting. Finance and Management Sciences*, *12*(4). Advance online publication. doi:10.6007/ijarafms/v12-i4/15810

Alghofaili, Y., Albattah, A., Alrajeh, N., Rassam, M. A., & Al-Rimy, B. A. S. (2021). Secure cloud infrastructure: A survey on issues, current solutions, and open challenges. *Applied Sciences (Basel, Switzerland)*, *11*(19), 9005. doi:10.3390/app11199005

Alhashmi, S. F. S., Salloum, S. A., & Abdallah, S. (2020). Document details - Critical Success Factors for Implementing Artificial Intelligence (AI) Projects in Dubai Government United Arab Emirates (UAE) Health Sector: Applying the Extended Technology Acceptance Model (TAM). *Advances in Intelligent Systems and Computing*, *1058*, 393–405. doi:10.1007/978-3-030-31129-2_36

Ali, J., Madni, S. H., Jahangeer, M. S., & Danish, M. A. (2023). IOT adoption model for e-learning in higher education institutes: A case study in Saudi Arabia. *Sustainability*, *15*(12), 9748. doi:10.3390u15129748

Ali, M. Y., Naeem, S. B., & Bhatti, R. (2021). Artificial Intelligence (AI) in Pakistani University Library Services. *Library Hi Tech News*, *38*(8), 12–15. doi:10.1108/LHTN-10-2021-0065

Allioui, H., & Mourdi, Y. (2023). Exploring the full potentials of IOT for better financial growth and stability: A comprehensive survey. *Sensors (Basel)*, *23*(19), 8015. doi:10.339023198015

Allison, D. (2012). Chatbots in the library: Is it time? *Library Hi Tech*, *30*(1), 95–107. doi:10.1108/07378831211213238

Almugari, F., Bajaj, P., Tabash, M. I., Khan, A., & Ali, M. A. (2020). An examination of consumers' adoption of internet of things (IOT) in Indian Banks. *Cogent Business &amp. Management*, *7*(1), 1809071. doi:10.1080/23311975.2020.1809071

Almulla, S., Iraqi, Y., & Jones, A. (2013). A distributed snapshot framework for digital forensics evidence extraction and event reconstruction from cloud environment. *Proceedings of the International Conference on Cloud Computing Technology and Science, CloudCom*, 1, 699–704. 10.1109/CloudCom.2013.114

Alshohoumi, F., & Sarrab, M. (2020). Privacy concerns in IOT a deeper insight into privacy concerns in IOT based healthcare. *International Journal of Computing and Digital Systems*, *9*(3), 399–418. doi:10.12785/ijcds/090306

Altawalbeh, M. A. (2023). Adoption of academic staff to use the Learning Management System (LMS): Applying extended technology acceptance model (TAM2) for Jordanian universities. *International Journal on Studies in Education*, *5*(3), 288–300. doi:10.46328/ijonse.124

Ameyaw, S., & Frempong-Kore, A. (2021). Records management practices in Ghanaian tertiary institutions: A case study of ghana technology university college. *UDS International Journal of Development*, *7*(2), 461–472. doi:10.47740/503.udsijd6i

Anadolu Ajansı. (2023). *Hitit tabletleri yapay zeka ile analiz ediliyor.* https://www.aa.com.tr/tr/kultur/hitit-tabletleri-yapay-zeka-ile-analiz-ediliyor/2779718

Anandaram, Gupta, & Verma. (2023). IoT Wearable Breast Temperature Assessment System. *2023 7th International Conference on Computing Methodologies and Communication (ICCMC),* 1236-1241.

Anaya, E. A., Nakano-Miyatake, M., & Perez Meana, H. M. (2019). Network forensics with Neurofuzzy techniques. *52nd IEEE international Midwest Symposium on Circuits and Systems (MWSCAS '19)*, 848–852.

Anderson, E., & Jessen, S. (2003). Project maturity in organizations. *International Journal of Project Management, 21*(6), 457–461. doi:10.1016/S0263-7863(02)00088-1

Andrews, J. E., Ward, H., & Yoon, J. (2021). UTAUT as a model for understanding intention to adopt AI and related technologies among librarians. *Journal of Academic Librarianship*, *47*(6), 102437. doi:10.1016/j.acalib.2021.102437

Antonakakis, M., April, T., Bailey, M., Bernhard, M., Bursztein, E., Cochran, J., . . . Zhou, Y. (2017). Understanding the mirai botnet. In *26th USENIX security symposium (USENIX Security 17)* (pp. 1093-1110). USENIX.

Anurag. (2020, December 21). *Library Management System | Library Management Software in India.* https://www.skoolbeep.com/blog/library-management-system/

Araújo, C. A. A. (2014). *Arquivologia, biblioteconomia, museologia e ciência da informação: o diálogo possível.* Briquet de Lemos.

Archana Shreee, S., Maheshwari, B., & Jeevitha Sai, G. (2023). A Novel Method of Identification of Delirium in Patients from Electronic Health Records Using Machine Learning. *2023 World Conference on Communication & Computing (WCONF),* 1-6.

Aria, M., & Cuccurullo, C. (2017). Bibliometrix: An R-tool for comprehensive science mapping analysis. *Journal of Informetrics*, *11*(11), 959–975. doi:10.1016/j.joi.2017.08.007

Arias-Pérez, J., Tavera-Mesías, J., & Castaño-Serna, D. (2016). Construcción de un modelo de madurez de gestión del conocimiento para una multinacional de alimentos de una economía emergente. *El Profesional de la Información, 25*(1), 88-102. Disponível em: http://www.elprofesionaldelainformacion.com/contenidos/2016/ene/09.html

Arkeolojik Haber. (2023). *Çin Seddi yapay zeka ile restore edilecek.* https://www.arkeolojikhaber.com/haber-cin-seddi-yapay-zeka-ile-restore-edilecek-11684/

Aroba, O. J., & Abayomi, A. (2023). An implementation of SAP Enterprise Resource Planning – A Case Study of the south african revenue services and taxation sectors. *Cogent Social Sciences*, *9*(1). Advance online publication. doi:10.1080/23311886.2023.2228060

Artsın, M. (2020). A text mining application: Vosviewer. *Eskişehir Teknik Üniversitesi Bilim ve Teknoloji Dergisi B-Teorik Bilimler*, *8*(2), 344–354.

Aschbacher, J., & Milagro-Pérez, M. P. (2012). The European Earth monitoring (GMES) programme: Status and perspectives. *Remote Sensing of Environment*, *120*, 3–8. doi:10.1016/j.rse.2011.08.028

Asemi, A., & Asemi, A. (2018). Artificial Intelligence (AI) Application in Library Systems in Iran: A Taxonomy Study. *Library Philosophy and Practice (e-journal)*. Retrieved from digitalcommons.unl.edu/cgi/viewcontent.cgi?article=5134&context=libphilprac

Asemi, A., Ko, A., & Nowkarizi, M. (2020). Intelligent libraries: A review on expert systems, artificial intelligence, and robot. *Library Hi Tech*, *39*(2), 412–434. doi:10.1108/LHT-02-2020-0038

Asian Productivity Organization. (2010). *Knowledge management tools and techniques manual*. Tokyo: Asian Productivity Organization. Disponível em: https://www.apo-tokyo.org/publications/files/ind-43-km_tt-2010.pdf

Asif, M., Abbas, S., Khan, M. A., Fatima, A., Khan, M. A., & Lee, S. W. (2021). MapReduce based intelligent model for intrusion detection using machine learning technique. *Journal of King Saud University. Computer and Information Sciences*.

Attaran, M., & Attaran, S. (2020). Digital Transformation and economic contributions of 5G networks. *International Journal of Enterprise Information Systems*, *16*(4), 58–79. doi:10.4018/ijeis.2020100104

Lab. (2023). *MUES (Museum National Inventory System) Project*. https://b3lab.org/en/sayfa/mues_museum_national_inventory_system_project-32

Babiceanu, R. F., & Seker, R. (2019). Cyber Resilience Protection for Industrial Internet of Things: A Software-defined networking approach. *Computers in Industry*, *104*, 47–58. doi:10.1016/j.compind.2018.10.004

Bach, M., Zoroja, J., & Čeljo, A. (2017). An extension of the technology acceptance model for business intelligence system: Project management maturity perspective. *International Journal of Information Systems and Project Management*, *5*(2), 5–21. doi:10.12821/ijispm050201

Bais, P., & Bahadur, P. S. (2023). Agriculture in Indian Economy and Contribution of Science and Technology. *Asian Journal of Applied Science and Technology*, *7*(1), 167–176. doi:10.38177/ajast.2023.7116

Baker, H. K., Kumar, S., Goyal, N., & Gaur, V. (2019). How financial literacy and demographic variables relate to behavioral biases. *Managerial Finance*, *45*(1), 124–146. doi:10.1108/MF-01-2018-0003

Balcilar, M., Demirer, R., & Hammoudeh, S. (2013). Investor herds and regime-switching: Evidence from Gulf Arab stock markets. *Journal of International Financial Markets, Institutions and Money*, *23*, 295–321. doi:10.1016/j.intfin.2012.09.007

Balyan, A. K., Ahuja, S., Lilhore, U. K., Sharma, S. K., Manoharan, P., Algarni, A. D., Elmannai, H., & Raahemifar, K. (2022). A Hybrid Intrusion Detection Model Using EGA-PSO and Improved Random Forest Method. *Sensors (Basel)*, *22*(16), 5986. doi:10.339022165986 PMID:36015744

Bank, D., Koenigstein, N., & Giryes, R. (2023). Autoencoders. *Machine Learning for Data Science Handbook: Data Mining and Knowledge Discovery Handbook*, 353-374.

Barale, V., Assouline, M., Dusart, J., & Gaffuri, J. (2015). The European Atlas of the Seas: Relating Natural and Socio-Economic Elements of Coastal and Marine Environments in the European Union. *Marine Geodesy*, *38*(1), 79–88. doi:10.1080/01490419.2014.909373

Bareau, V., & Nettifee, E. (2023, April 10). *The Codex Metadata Model. - FOLIO Platform - FOLIO Wiki*. https://wiki.folio.org/pages/viewpage.action?pageId=1415393

Barré, P., Stöver, B. C., Müller, K. F., & Steinhage, V. (2017, July). LeafNet: A computer vision system for automatic plant species identification. *Ecological Informatics*, *40*, 50–56. doi:10.1016/j.ecoinf.2017.05.005

Bartha, G., & Kocsis, S. (2011). Standardization of geographic data: The European Inspire Directive. *European Journal of Geography*, *2*, 79–89.

Bashir, M. R., Gill, A. Q., & Beydoun, G. (2022). A reference architecture for IOT-enabled smart buildings. *SN Computer Science*, *3*(6). Advance online publication. doi:10.100742979-022-01401-9

Bates, M. E. (2019). *White paper: Insight as a service: Info pros and artificial intelligence*. Springer Nature. Available at: https://media.springernature.com/full/ springer-cms-preview/rest/v1/content/16773852/data/v1

Baxter, G., & Sommerville, I. (2011). Socio-technical systems: From design methods to systems engineering. *Interacting with Computers*, *23*(1), 4–17. doi:10.1016/j.intcom.2010.07.003

Bayanati, M. (2023). Business model of internet of things and blockchain technology in developing countries. *International Journal of Innovation in Engineering*, *3*(1), 13–22. doi:10.59615/ijie.3.1.13

Beal, A. (2004). *Gestão estratégica da informação: como transformar a informação e a tecnologia da informação em fatores de crescimento e de alto desempenho nas organizações*. Atlas.

Becker, J., Knackstedt, R., & Pöppelbuß, J. (2009). Developing maturity models for IT management: A procedure model and its application. *Business & Information Systems Engineering*, *1*(3), 213–222. doi:10.100712599-009-0044-5

Beja, J., Vandepitte, L., Benson, A., Van de Putte, A., Lear, D., & De Pooter, D. (2022). Data services in ocean science with a focus on the biology. In G. Manzella & A. Novellino (Eds.), *Ocean Science Data* (pp. 67–129). Collection, Management, Networking and Services. doi:10.1016/B978-0-12-823427-3.00006-2

Benos, L., Tagarakis, A. C., Dolias, G., Berruto, R., Kateris, D., & Bochtis, D. (2021). Machine learning in agriculture: A comprehensive updated review. *Sensors (Basel)*, *21*(11), 3758. doi:10.339021113758 PMID:34071553

Bentéjac, C., Csörgő, A., & Martínez-Muñoz, G. (2021). A comparative analysis of gradient boosting algorithms. *Artificial Intelligence Review*, *54*(3), 1937–1967. doi:10.100710462-020-09896-5

Bergkvist, L., & Zhou, K. Q. (2016). Zhou. *International Journal of Advertising*, *35*(4), 642–663. doi:10.1080/02650487.2015.1137537

Bertrand, S., Ben Ameur, R., Cerutti, G., Coquin, D., Valet, L., & Tougne, L. (2018, July). Bark and leaf fusion systems to improve automatic tree species recognition. *Ecological Informatics*, *46*, 57–73. doi:10.1016/j.ecoinf.2018.05.007

Bessadok, A., Abouzinadah, E., & Rabie, O. (2021). Exploring students digital activities and performances through their activities logged in learning management system using educational data mining approach. *Interactive Technology and Smart Education*, *20*(1), 58–72. doi:10.1108/itse-08-2021-0148

Bettin, A. (2023). Digital transformation for the water industry: How a data-driven business intelligence platform can improve operations. *Water Practice &amp. Technology*, *18*(7), 1599–1607. doi:10.2166/wpt.2023.091

Bhanumathi, S., Vineeth, M., & Rohit, N. (2019, April). Crop yield prediction and efficient use of fertilizers. In *2019 International Conference on Communication and Signal Processing (ICCSP)* (pp. 769-773). IEEE. 10.1109/ICCSP.2019.8698087

Bhargavi, P., & Jyothi, S. (2011). Soil classification using data mining techniques: A comparative study. *International Journal of Engineering Trends and Technology*, *2*(1), 55–59.

Bhosale, Thombare, Dhemey, & Chaudhari. (2018). Crop Yield Prediction Using Data Analytics and Hybrid Approach. In *Proceedings of the 4th International Conference on Computing, Communication Control and Automation*. IEEE.

Bin Sarhan, B., & Altwaijry, N. (2022). Insider Threat Detection Using Machine Learning Approach. *Applied Sciences (Basel, Switzerland)*, *13*(1), 259. doi:10.3390/app13010259

Bititci, U., Garengo, P., Ates, A., & Nudurupati, S. (2015). Value of maturity models in performance measurement. *International Journal of Production Research*, *53*(10), 3062–3085. doi:10.1080/00207543.2014.970709

Blockchain technology to enhance the public service capability of Digital Government. (2023). *Eurasian Law Journal*, *6*(181). https://doi.org/ doi:10.46320/2073-4506-2023-6-181-507-508

Booz & Co. (2011). Cost-Benefit Analysis for GMES. European Commission: Directorate-General for Enterprise & Industry, London 19th September 2011.

Borba, F. R., Knoll, E. C., & Todescat, M. (2013). Diagnóstico de níveis de maturidade em gestão do conhecimento: centro de empreendedorismo inovador da Fundação CERTI. Navus - Revista de Gestão e Tecnologia, 3(2), 163-176.

Bourguignon, F. (2004). *The poverty-growth-inequality triangle* (No. 125). Working Paper.

Bowen, G. A. (2009). Document analysis as a qualitative research method. *Qualitative Research Journal*, *9*(2), 27–40. doi:10.3316/qrj0902027

Boyes, S. J., Elliott, M., Murillas-Maza, A., Papadopoulou, N., & Uñara, M. C. (2016). Is existing legislation fit-for-purpose to achieve Good Environmental Status in European seas? *Marine Pollution Bulletin*, *111*(1-2), 18–32. doi:10.1016/j.marpolbul.2016.06.079 PMID:27377000

Bozdoğan, K. (2020). A bibliometric analysis of educational studies about museum education. *Participatory Educational Research*, *7*(3), 161–179. doi:10.17275/per.20.40.7.3

Bro, R., & Smilde, A. K. (2014). Principal component analysis. *Analytical Methods*, *6*(9), 2812–2831. doi:10.1039/C3AY41907J

Brougham, D., & Haar, J. (2020).Technological disruption and employment: The influence on job insecurity and turnover intentions: A multi-country study. *Technological Forecasting and Social Change*, *161*. doi:10.1016/j.techfore.2020.120276

Brucker, P., & Schlie, R. (1990). Job-shop scheduling with multi-purpose machines. *Computing*, *45*(4), 369–375. doi:10.1007/BF02238804

Budu, K. W., Yinping, M., & Mireku, K. K. (2018). Investigating the effect of behavioral intention on e-learning systems usage: Empirical study on Tertiary Education Institutions in Ghana. *Mediterranean Journal of Social Sciences*, *9*(3), 201–216. doi:10.2478/mjss-2018-0062

Butt, U. A., Amin, R., Mehmood, M., Aldabbas, H., Alharbi, M. T., & Albaqami, N. (2023). Cloud security threats and solutions: A survey. *Wireless Personal Communications*, *128*(1), 387–413. doi:10.100711277-022-09960-z

Cabrera Alvarado, S. (2020). *In pursuit of openness. An analysis of the legal framework of the European Union's Copernicus' open data policy* [Doctoral dissertation]. University of Luxembourg, Luxembourg.

Cardno, C. (2019). Policy Document Analysis: A practical educational leadership tool and a qualitative research method. *Educational Administration: Theory and Practice*, *24*(4). Advance online publication. doi:10.14527/kuey.2018.016

Carneiro, A. (2013). Maturity and metrics in health organizations information systems. In M. Cruz-Cunha, I. Miranda, & P. Gonçalves (Eds.), *Handbook of research on ICTs and management systems for improving efficiency in Healthcare and social care* (pp. 937–952). IGI Global. doi:10.4018/978-1-4666-3990-4.ch049

Cavalieri, S., McGlynn, E., Piotrowski, R., Reid, A., Cantral, L., Lee, E., & … . (2011). *Comparison: EU and US Ocean Policy. Report of the Cooperation Across the Atlantic for Marine Governance Integration (CALAMAR) Project.* Ecologic Institute.

Caveen, A. (2013). *A Critical Examination of the Scientific Credentials of Marine Protected Areas: Sound Science or a Leap of Faith?* [PhD thesis]. Newcastle University, Newscastle.

Cesbron, G., Melet, A., Almar, R., Lifermann, A., Tullot, D., & Crosnier, L. (2021). Pan-European Satellite-Derived Coastal Bathymetry—Review, User Needs and Future Services. *Frontiers in Marine Science, 8*, 740830. doi:10.3389/fmars.2021.740830

Chadwell, F. (2011). Assessing the value of academic library consortia. *Journal of Library Administration, 51*(7/8), 645–661. doi:10.1080/01930826.2011.601268

Chairunnisa, A., & Dalimunthe, Z. (2021). Indonesian stock's influencer phenomenon: Did financial literacy on millennial age reduce herding behavior? *Jurnal Akuntansi Dan Keuangan, 23*(2), 62–68. doi:10.9744/jak.23.2.62-68

Chaki, J., Parekh, R., & Bhattacharya, S. (2015). Plant leaf recognition using texture and shape features with neural classifiers. *Pattern Recognition Letters, 58*, 61–68. doi:10.1016/j.patrec.2015.02.010

Chakrasali, S. V., Kumar, C., Chaturvedi, A., & Jaisudhan Pazhani, A. A. (2023). Computer vision based healthcare system for identification of diabetes & its types using AI, Measurement. *Sensors (Basel), 27*, 10075.

Chander, B., Pal, S., De, D., & Buyya, R. (2022). Artificial intelligence-based internet of things for industry 5.0. *Artificial intelligence-based internet of things systems*, 3-45.

Chan, H. C., & Chan, L. (2018). Smart Library and smart campus. *Journal of Service Science and Management, 11*(06), 543–564. doi:10.4236/jssm.2018.116037

Chapple, C. (2017). *An Investigation into Viewers' Trust in and Response Towards Disclosed Paid-for-Endorsements by YouTube Lifestyle Vloggers.* https://www.semanticscholar.org/paper/An-Investigation-into-Viewers%E2%80%99-Trust-in-and-Towards-Chapple-Cownie/4ddff3ca932e45e225bdbcbe438546f85725cd14#citing-papers

Chatterjee, P., Bose, R., Banerjee, S., & Roy, S. (2023). Enhancing Data Security of Cloud Based LMS. *Wireless Personal Communications, 130*(2), 1123–1139. doi:10.100711277-023-10323-5 PMID:37168441

Chauhan, S., Kandhasamy, K., & Sakthivel, N. (2023). FOLIO: The Future of Library is Open. *SRELS Journal of Information Management, 60*(3), 150–156. doi:10.17821rels/2023/v60i3/171035

Chen, C.-L., Lin, Y.-C., Chen, W.-H., Chao, C.-F., & Pandia, H. (2021). Role of government to enhance digital transformation in small service business. *Sustainability, 13*(3), 1028. doi:10.3390u13031028

Chollet. (2017). Xception: Deep Learning with Depthwise Separable Convolutions. In *2017 IEEE Conference on Computer Vision and Pattern Recognition (CVPR)* (pp. 1800–1807). IEEE.

Chong, S. L., & Wan, R. (2018). Technological Infrastructure and Human Culture: Appropriating innovative teaching methods to 21st century classrooms. *SHS Web of Conferences, 53*, 05001. https://doi.org/10.1051hsconf/20185305001

Chong, C., Hean Low, M., Sivakumar, A., & Gay, K. (2006). A Bee Colony Optimization Algorithm to Job Shop Scheduling. *Proceedings of the 2006 Winter Simulation Conference.* 10.1109/WSC.2006.322980

Choo, C. W. (2006). *A organização do conhecimento: como as organizações usam a informação para criar significado, construir conhecimentos e tomar decisões. 2.* Editora SENAC.

Choudhary, H. (2023). Building Bridges to digital inclusion: Implications for curriculum development of digital literacy training programs. *International Journal of Technology Enhanced Learning*, *1*(1). Advance online publication. doi:10.1504/ijtel.2023.10059464

Chroni, A. (2018). Cultural Heritage Digitization and Copyright Issues. *Euro-Mediterranean Conference, Digital Heritage. Progress in Cultural Heritage: Documentation, Preservation and Protection*, 396-407. 10.1007/978-3-030-01762-0_34

Chubko, N., Morris, J. E., McKinnon, D. H., Slater, E. V., & Lummis, G. W. (2020). Digital Storytelling as a disciplinary literacy enhancement tool for EFL students. *Educational Technology Research and Development*, *68*(6), 3587–3604. doi:10.100711423-020-09833-x

Cimini, C., & Cavalieri, S. (2022). Industrial Smart Working: A Socio-technical model for enabling successful implementation. *IFAC-PapersOnLine*, *55*(2), 505–510. doi:10.1016/j.ifacol.2022.04.244

Citi Bank. (2016). *Technology At Work v2.0; The Future Is Not What It Used To Be*. Retrieved from https://www.oxfordmartin.ox.ac.uk/downloads/reports/Citi_GPS_Technology_Work_2.pdf

Cockburn, S. (2005). *Developments in Marine Boundary Law to Construct a Legal Framework for Offshore and Coastal Spaces* [M.Sc.E. thesis]. University of New Brunswick.

Collins, C., Dennehy, D., Conboy, K., & Mikalef, P. (2021). Artificial intelligence in information systems research: A systematic literature review and research agenda. *International Journal of Information Management*, *60*, 102383. doi:10.1016/j.ijinfomgt.2021.102383

Colt, J., & Howell, D. (2021). Cornell Library FOLIO Case Study. *International Journal of Librarianship*, *6*(2), 13–20. doi:10.23974/ijol.2021.vol6.2.205

Cooke-Davies, T., & Arzymanow, A. (2003). The maturity of project management in different industries: An investigation into variations between project management models. *International Journal of Project Management*, *21*(6), 471–478. doi:10.1016/S0263-7863(02)00084-4

Cornell University, INSTEAD, & WIPO. (2016). *The Global Innovation Index 2016: Winning with Global Innovation*. Geneva: WIPO. https://www.globalinnovationindex.org/gii

Cox, A. M., & Mazumdar, S. (2022). Defining artificial intelligence for librarians. *Journal of Librarianship and Information Science*.

Cox, A. M., Pinfield, S., & Rutter, S. (2019). The intelligent library: Thought leaders' views on the likely impact of artificial intelligence on academic libraries. *Library Hi Tech*, *37*(3), 418–435. doi:10.1108/LHT-08-2018-0105

Cox, A., Kennan, M., Lyon, L., & Pinfield, S. (2017). Developments in research data management in academic libraries: Towards an understanding of research data service maturity. *Journal of the Association for Information Science and Technology*, *68*(9), 2182–2200. doi:10.1002/asi.23781

Cox, A., Kennan, M., Lyon, L., Pinfield, S., & Sbaffi, L. (2019). Maturing research data services and the transformation of academic libraries. *The Journal of Documentation*, *75*(6), 1432–1462. doi:10.1108/JD-12-2018-0211

Cox, A., & Pinfield, S. (2014). Research data management and libraries: Current activities and future priorities. *Journal of Librarianship and Information Science*, *46*(4), 299–316. doi:10.1177/0961000613492542

Crosby, P. (1979). *Quality is free: the art of making quality certain*. McGraw-Hill.

Crowston, K., & Qin, J. (2011). A capability maturity model for scientific data management: Evidence from literature. *Proceedings of the American Society for Information Science and Technology*, *48*(1), 1–9. doi:10.1002/meet.2011.14504801036

Cumhuriyet (2023). *Blockchain teknolojisi, bin yıllık mağaraları daha erişilebilir kılıyor.* https://www.cumhuriyet.com.tr/bilim-teknoloji/blockchain-teknolojisi-bin-yillik-magaralari-daha-erisilebilir-kiliyor-2010544

Cybersecurity, C. I. (2018). *Framework for improving critical infrastructure cybersecurity.* https://nvlpubs. nist. gov/nistpubs/CSWP/NIST

da Silva, E. (2013). *Gestão do conhecimento e da informação como subsídios para a geração de inovação* [Master's Dissertação]. Universidade Estadual Paulista. Disponível em: https://www.marilia.unesp.br/Home/Pos-Graduacao/CienciadaInformacao/Dissertacoes/SILVA_E_da_Dissertacao.pdf

Dadzie, P. S., & Mensah, M. (2022). Change management in libraries: The case of the university of ghana library system (UGLS). *Library Leadership &amp. Management, 36*(1). Advance online publication. doi:10.5860/llm.v36i1.7496

Danobeitia, J., Beranzoli, L., Berry, A., Blandin, J., Cannat, M., & Chavrit, D. (2019, December). EMSO, a Large-scale European Research Infrastructure Delivering Harmonized Environmental Marine Data through a Distributed Ocean Observation System. In *AGU Fall Meeting Abstracts* (Vol. 2019, pp. OS53B-1525). Academic Press.

Dardzinska-Glebocka, A. (2007). Optimization Algorithm and Data Security Problem in Distributed Information Systems. *2007 Third International IEEE Conference on Signal-Image Technologies and Internet-Based System.* 10.1109/SITIS.2007.136

Das, P. (2015). Non-income Dimensions, Prevalence, Depth and Severity of Poverty: Spatial Estimation with Household-Level Data in India. In A. Heshmati, E. Maasoumi, & G. Wan (Eds.), *Economic Studies in Inequality, Social Exclusion, and Well-Being, Poverty Reduction Policies and Practices in Developing Asia* (pp. 187–203). Springer. doi:10.1007/978-981-287-420-7_10

Datt, G., & Ravallion, M. (1992). Growth and redistribution components of changes in poverty measures: A decomposition with applications to Brazil and India in the 1980s. *Journal of Development Economics, 38*(2), 275–295. doi:10.1016/0304-3878(92)90001-P

Davenport, T. H., & Prusak, L. (1998). *Ecologia da informação: porque só a tecnologia não basta para o sucesso na era da informação.* Futura.

Davis, F. D. (1989). Perceived usefulness, perceived ease of use, and user acceptance of information technology. *Management Information Systems Quarterly, 13*(3), 318–346. doi:10.2307/249008

Davis, M. C., Challenger, R., Jayewardene, D. N. W., & Clegg, C. W. (2014). Advancing Socio-Technical Systems thinking: A call for bravery. *Applied Ergonomics, 45*(2), 171–180. doi:10.1016/j.apergo.2013.02.009

Davis, M. C., Hughes, H. P., McKay, A., Robinson, M. A., & van der Wal, C. N. (2019). Ergonomists as designers: Computational Modelling and simulation of complex socio-technical systems. *Ergonomics, 63*(8), 938–951. doi:10.1080/00140139.2019.1682186

de Carvalho, R. B., Ferreira, M. A. T., & Silva, R. V. (2006). Análise da maturidade e do perfil de programas de gestão do conhecimento: pesquisa exploratória e comparativa em organizações brasileiras e portuguesas. *Revista Gestão Industrial, Ponta Grossa (PR), 2*(3), 15-28. Disponível em: https://periodicos.utfpr.edu.br/revistagi/issue/view/11

de Vries, P., Tamis, J., Thijsse, P., & Kater, B. (2016). Collecting literature for identifying data sets and data sources; Literature Review, Arctic Sea Basin Checkpoint. Wageningen, IMARES Wageningen UR (University & Research centre), IMARES report Final draft.

Deash, N., & Padhi, P. (2010). Quality assessment of libraries. *DESIDOC Journal of Library and Information Technology, 30*(6), 12–23. doi:10.14429/djlit.30.672

Defersha, F. M., & Chen, M. (2009). A parallel genetic algorithm for a flexible job-shop scheduling problem with sequence dependent setups. *International Journal of Advanced Manufacturing Technology*, *49*(1–4), 263–279. doi:10.100700170-009-2388-x

DEFRA. (2010). Marine data and observation. In *Great Britain. Parliament. House of Commons. European Scrutiny Committee. Fourth Report of Session 2010-11: Documents considered by the Committee on 20 October 2010*. The Stationery Office.

DeFranco, J. F., & Voas, J. (2023). Thoughts on automotive IOT. *Computer*, *56*(3), 13–18. doi:10.1109/mc.2022.3219637

Dekel, R. (2023). Despite How the Media Portrays It, AI Is Not Really Intelligent. Here's Why. *Entrepreneur – Science & Technology*. Available at: https://www.entrepreneur.com/science-technology/despite-how-the-media-portrays-it-ai-is-not-really/446894#:~:text=the%20training%20data.-,It%20is%20important%20to%20recognize%20that%20AI%20is%20not%20truly,decisions%20based%20on%20common%20sense

DeLone, W. H., & McLean, E. (2003). The Delone and McLean Model of Information Systems Success: A Ten-Year Update. *Journal of Management Information Systems*, *19*(4), 9–30. doi:10.1080/07421222.2003.11045748

Delrosso, D., Clementi, E., Grandi, A., Tonani, M., Oddo, P., Girardi Feruzza, G., & Pinardi, N. (2016). *Towards the Mediterranean Forecasting System MyOcean V5: numerical experiments results and validation*. Rapporti Tecnici INGV.

Demuyakor, J. (2020). Ghana Go Digital Agenda: The Impact of Zipline drone technology on Digital Emergency Health Delivery in Ghana. *Shanlax International Journal of Arts. Science and Humanities*, *8*(1), 242–253. doi:10.34293ijash.v8i1.3301

Deng, S., Tian, Y., & Zhang, H. (2009). Using the bibliometric analysis to evaluate global scientific production of data mining papers. *2009 First International Workshop on Database Technology and Applications*, 233-238. 10.1109/DBTA.2009.157

Diaz, R., & Montalvo, R. (2022). Digital Transformation as an enabler to become more efficient in sustainability: Evidence from five leading companies in the Mexican market. *Sustainability*, *14*(22), 15436. doi:10.3390u142215436

DibetleM.KalemaB. M. (2023). *Data security governance for Software-as-a-Service Cloud computing environment: A South African perspective*. doi:10.21203/rs.3.rs-3040096/v1

Dietterich, T. G. (2000, June). Ensemble methods in machine learning. In *International workshop on multiple classifier systems* (pp. 1-15). Springer Berlin Heidelberg.

Dillon, A., & Morris, M. (1998). From "can they?" to "will they?" Extending usability evaluation to address acceptance. In E. Hoadley, I. Benbasat (Eds.) *Proceedings Americas Conference on Information Systems (AMCIS)*. Univ. of Baltimore.

Diviacco, P., Iurcev, M., Carbajales, R. J., Viola, A., & Potleca, N. (2023). Design and Implementation of a Crowdsensing-Based Air Quality Monitoring Open and FAIR Data Infrastructure. *Processes (Basel, Switzerland)*, *11*(7), 1881. doi:10.3390/pr11071881

Djafarova, E., & Rushworth, C. (2017). Exploring the credibility of online celebrities' Instagram profiles in influencing the purchase decisions of young female users. *Computers in Human Behavior*, *68*, 1–7. doi:10.1016/j.chb.2016.11.009

Dobson, G. (2021). Lessons Learned about FOLIO's APIs. *International Journal of Librarianship*, *6*(2), 30–39. doi:10.23974/ijol.2021.vol6.2.206

Donthu, N., Kumar, S., Mukherjee, D., Pandey, N., & Lim, W. M. (2021). How to conduct a bibliometric analysis: An overview and guidelines. *Journal of Business Research*, *133*, 285–296. doi:10.1016/j.jbusres.2021.04.070

Dramani, I. E., Tang, Z., & Coffie, C. P. (2022). Usage intention of e-learning systems in Ghanaian tertiary institutions: A case study of the university for development studies. *Sustainability*, *14*(12), 7360. doi:10.3390u14127360

Drewek-Ossowicka, A., Pietrołaj, M., & Rumiński, J. (2021). A survey of neural networks usage for intrusion detection systems. *Journal of Ambient Intelligence and Humanized Computing*, *12*(1), 497–514. doi:10.100712652-020-02014-x

Drljevic, N., Aranda, D., & Stantchev, V. (2022). An integrated adoption model to manage blockchain-driven business innovation in a sustainable way. *Sustainability (Basel)*, *14*(4), 2873. doi:10.3390u14052873

Drucker. (1993). *Sociedade pós-capitalista. 2* (M. J. Tradução de Nivaldo, Ed.). Pioneira.

Duncan, A. S. P. (2022). The intelligent academic library: Review of AI projects & potential for Caribbean libraries. *Library Hi Tech News*, *39*(5), 12–15. doi:10.1108/LHTN-01-2022-0014

Dwivedi, Y. K., Hughes, L., Ismagilova, E., Aarts, G., Coombs, C., Crick, T., . . . Williams, M. D. (2021). Artificial Intelligence (AI): Multidisciplinary perspectives on emerging challenges, opportunities, and agenda for research, practice and policy. *International Journal of Information Management*, *57*, 101994.

Dwyer, N., & Wright, D. J. (2008). *Report of International Coastal Atlas Network Workshop 3 on Federated Coastal Atlases: Building on the Interoperable Approach*. European Environment Agency.

Ehms, K., & Langen, M. (2002). *Holistic development of knowledge management with KMMM*. Siemens. Disponível em: http://www.kmmm.org/objects/kmmm_article_siemens_2002.pdf

El-Abd, M. (2010). A cooperative approach to The Artificial Bee Colony algorithm. *IEEE Congress on Evolutionary Computation*. 10.1109/CEC.2010.5586007

Elsafty, A., & Yehia, A. (2023). Digital Transformation Challenges for Government Sector. *Business and Management Studies*, *9*(1), 11. doi:10.11114/bms.v9i1.6160

El-Zoghdy, S. F., & Ghoneim, A. (2016). A Multi-Class Task Scheduling Strategy for Heterogeneous Distributed Computing Systems. *KSII Transactions on Internet and Information Systems*, *10*(1), 117–135.

Emmert-Streib, F. (2021). From the Digital Data Revolution toward a digital society: Pervasiveness of Artificial Intelligence. *Machine Learning and Knowledge Extraction*, *3*(1), 284–298. doi:10.3390/make3010014

Erdogan, B. Z. (1999). Celebrity Endorsement: A Literature Review. *Journal of Marketing Management*, *15*(4), 291–314. doi:10.1362/026725799784870379

Erkan, I., & Evans, C. (2016). The influence of eWOM in social media on consumers' purchase intentions: An extended approach to information adoption. *Computers in Human Behavior*, *61*, 47–55. doi:10.1016/j.chb.2016.03.003

Erkimbaev, A. O., Zitserman, V. Y., & Kobzev, G. A. (2017). The intensive use of digital data in modern natural science. *Automatic Documentation and Mathematical Linguistics*, *51*(5), 201–213. doi:10.3103/S0005105517050028

Espina-Romero, L., & Guerrero-Alcedo, J. (2022). Fields touched by digitalization: Analysis of scientific activity in Scopus. *Sustainability (Basel)*, *2022*(14), 1–16. doi:10.3390u142114425

Estrada, M., Álvarez-Fanjul, E., Barragán, A., Bermúdez, Ó., García-Fernández, M. J., & Lavín, A. (2008). Reflexiones sobre la gestión y custodia de datos oceanográficos en España. *Recursos existentes y recomendaciones para el futuro.*

European Commission, (2014a). *Commission Staff Working Document. Marine Knowledge 2020: roadmap*. Brussels, 8.5.2014 SWD(2014) 149 final.

European Commission, DG Mare. (2012). *The Evaluation of the Data Collection Framework (DCF) Lot 2*: Retrospective and Prospective Evaluation on the Common Fisheries Policy, Excluding its International Dimension.

European Commission. (2007). An Integrated Maritime Policy for the European Union. Brussels, 10.10.2007 COM (2007) 575 final.

European Commission. (2008a). Council Regulation (EC) No 199/2008 of 25 February 2008 concerning the establishment of a Community framework for the collection, management and use of data in the fisheries sector and support for scientific advice regarding the Common Fisheries Policy. *Official Journal of the European Union, L, 60*, 1–12.

European Commission. (2008b). Commission Regulation (EC) No 665/2008 of 14 July 2008 laying down detailed rules for the application of Council Regulation (EC) No 199/2008 concerning the establishment of a Community framework for the collection, management and use of data in the fisheries sector and support for scientific advice regarding the Common Fisheries Policy. *Official Journal of the European Union, L, 186*, 3–5.

European Commission. (2008c). *Legal Aspects of Marine Environmental Data Framework Service Contract, No. FISH/2006/09 – LOT2*, final report. Brussels, October 2008.

European Commission. (2008d). *Roadmap for Maritime Spatial Planning*: Achieving Common Principles in the EU, 25.11.2008 COM(2008) 791 final. Brussels, 25.11.2008 COM(2008) 791 final.

European Commission. (2009). *Commission Staff Working Document. Building a European marine knowledge infrastructure: Roadmap for a European Marine Observation and Data Network*. Brussels, 7.4.2009 COM(2009) 499 final.

European Commission. (2009b). Marine Data Infrastructure Framework Service Contract, No. FISH/2006/09 – LOT 2 Executive Summary. Brussels, December 2009.

European Commission. (2011). *Commission Staff Working Document. Impact assessment - Accompanying Commission proposal for a Regulation of the European Parliament and of the Council on the Common Fisheries Policy* [repealing Regulation (EC) N° 2371/2002]. Brussels, 13 July 2011 SEC(2011) 891.

European Commission. (2013). *Commission implementing decision of 30.8.2013 extending the national programmes for the collection of primary biological, technical, environmental and socio-economic data in the fisheries sector for the period 2011-2013 to the period 2014-2016*. Brussels, 30.8.2013. C(2013) 5568 final.

European Commission. (2014b). Directive 2014/89/EU of the European Parliament and of the Council of 23 July 2014 establishing a framework for maritime spatial planning. *Official Journal of the European Union, L, 257*, 135.

European Commission. (2015). *Proposal for a Regulation of the European Parliament and of the Council concerning the establishment of a Union framework for the collection, management and use of data in the fisheries sector and support for scientific advice regarding the Common Fisheries Policy (recast)*. Brussels, 18.6.2015 SWD(2015) 118 final. COM(2015) 294 final.

European Commission. (2016). *Ex-post Evaluation on the European earth monitoring programme (GMES) and its Initial Operations (2011 to 2013)*. Brussels, 2.8.2016 SWD(2016) 262 final.

European Commission. (2017). *Implementation of the Common Information Sharing Environment (CISE) for the EU maritime domain*: Ensuring interoperability of National IT Systems to allow for more efficient information exchange within and across borders. EMFF Work Programmes 2016/2017, Call for Proposals.

Ex Libris. (n.d.). *Artificial Intelligence in the Library: Advantages, Challenges and Tradition*. An Ex Libris Whitepaper. Retrieved July 11, 2020 https://cdn2.hubspot.net/hubfs/2909474/Ex%20Libris%20Artificial%20Intelligence%20White%20Paper.pdf

Fadel, B. (2010). Gestão, mediação e uso da informação. In *Gestão, mediação e uso da informação.* São Paulo: Cultura Acadêmica. Disponível em: https://www.culturaacademica.com.br/catalogo-detalhe.asp?ctl_id=115

Falayi, A., Wang, Q., Liao, W., & Yu, W. (2023). Survey of distributed and decentralized IOT Securities: Approaches using Deep Learning and blockchain technology. *Future Internet*, *15*(5), 178. doi:10.3390/fi15050178

Fama, E. F. (1965). The behavior of stock-market prices. *The Journal of Business*, *38*(1), 34–105. doi:10.1086/294743

Fan, J., Bai, J., Li, Z., Ortiz-Bobea, A., & Gomes, C. P. (2022, June). A GNN-RNN approach for harnessing geospatial and temporal information: Application to crop yield prediction. *Proceedings of the AAAI Conference on Artificial Intelligence*, *36*(11), 11873–11881. doi:10.1609/aaai.v36i11.21444

Farias-Gaytan, S., Aguaded, I., & Ramirez-Montoya, M.-S. (2023). Digital Transformation and digital literacy in the context of complexity within Higher Education Institutions: A systematic literature review. *Humanities & Social Sciences Communications*, *10*(1). Advance online publication. doi:10.105741599-023-01875-9

Fekri-Ershad, S. (2020, November). Bark texture classification using improved local ternary patterns and multilayer neural network. *Expert Systems with Applications*, *158*, 113509. doi:10.1016/j.eswa.2020.113509

Ferguson, S., & Hebels, R. (2003). Library management systems. In Computers for Librarians: An Introduction to the Electronic Library (pp. 111–142). Woodhead Publishing Limited. doi:10.1016/B978-1-876938-60-4.50010-0

Fernandez-Macho, J. (2016). A statistical assessment of maritime socioeconomic indicators for the European Atlantic area. *Journal of Ocean and Coastal Economics*, *2*(2), 4. Advance online publication. doi:10.15351/2373-8456.1047

Fields, G. S. (2000). The dynamics of poverty, inequality and economic well-being: African economic growth in comparative perspective. *Journal of African Economies*, *9*(Supplement_1), 45–78. doi:10.1093/jafeco/9.Supplement_1.45

Finley, T. K. (2019). The democratization of artificial intelligence: One library's approach. *Information Technology and Libraries*, *38*(1), 8–13. doi:10.6017/ital.v38i1.10974

Fishbein, M., & Ajzen, I. (1975). *Belief, attitude, intention, and behavior: an introduction to theory and research.* Addison-Wesley.

Fitterer, R., & Rohner, P. (2010). Towards assessing the networkability of health care provides: A maturity model approach. *Information Systems and e-Business Management*, *8*(3), 309–333. doi:10.100710257-009-0121-9

Florio, M., Morretta, V., & Willak, W. (2018). Cost-benefit analysis and European Union Cohesion Policy: Economic Versus Financial returns in Investment Project Appraisal. *Journal of Benefit-Cost Analysis*, *9*(1), 147–180. doi:10.1017/bca.2018.4

Flynn, J., Dance, S., & Dirk Schaefer, D. (2017)1 Industry 4.0 and its Potential Impact on Employment Demographics in the UK. *5th International Conference on Manufacturing Research (ICMR).*

Fock, H. (2011). Natura 2000 and the European Common Fisheries Policy. *Marine Policy*, *35*(2), 181–188. doi:10.1016/j.marpol.2010.09.003

FOLIO Project. (n.d.). *Welcome to MOTIF: The FOLIO design system · FOLIO UX docs · UX prototypes, guidelines & assets.* FOLIO UX. Retrieved October 16, 2023, from https://ux.folio.org/docs/

FOLIO. (2022a, April 7). *Local KB Admin | FOLIO Documentation.* https://docs.folio.org/docs/erm/local-kb-admin/

FOLIO. (2022b, December 6). *Bulk Edit | FOLIO Documentation.* https://docs.folio.org/docs/bulk-edit/

FOLIO. (2023a, February 9). *Courses | FOLIO Documentation.* https://docs.folio.org/docs/access/courses/courses/

FOLIO. (2023b, February 9). *Organizations | FOLIO Documentation*. https://docs.folio.org/docs/acquisitions/organizations/

FOLIO. (2023c, February 9). *Requests | FOLIO Documentation*. https://docs.folio.org/docs/access/requests/requests/

FOLIO. (2023d, February 18). *Settings | FOLIO Documentation*. https://docs.folio.org/docs/settings/

FOLIO. (2023e, February 23). *Circulation log | FOLIO Documentation*. https://docs.folio.org/docs/access/circulation-log/circ_log/

FOLIO. (2023f, February 28). *Check out | FOLIO Documentation*. https://docs.folio.org/docs/access/check-out/checkout/

FOLIO. (2023g, March 31). *Invoices | FOLIO Documentation*. https://docs.folio.org/docs/acquisitions/invoices/

FOLIO. (2023h, April 18). *Receiving | FOLIO Documentation*. https://docs.folio.org/docs/acquisitions/receiving/

FOLIO. (2023i, May 2). *Users | FOLIO Documentation*. https://docs.folio.org/docs/users/

FOLIO. (2023j, May 2). *Welcome | FOLIO Documentation*. https://docs.folio.org/docs/

FOLIO. (2023k, July 27). *Licenses | FOLIO Documentation*. https://docs.folio.org/docs/erm/licenses/

FOLIO-Open Libraries. (2023, October 23). https://twitter.com/FOLIO_LSP/status/1187025363836297219?s=20

Fornell, C., & Larcker, D. F. (1981). Evaluating Structural Equation Models with Unobservable Variables and Measurement Error. *JMR, Journal of Marketing Research*, *18*(1), 39–50. doi:10.1177/002224378101800104

Forrester. (2017). *Artificial Intelligence with the Human Touch - Blend AI with Human Agents to Improve Both Customer and Agent Satisfaction*. Retrieved September 15, 2023 from https://www.genesys.com/resources/artificial-intelligence-with-the-human-touch

Foster, J., Greer, J., & Thorbecke, E. (1984). A class of decomposable poverty measures. *Econometrica*, *52*(3), 761–766. doi:10.2307/1913475

Fotouhi, A., Oudi, M., Gueni, B., & Mabrouk, M. B. (2021). User behavior analysis using IOT Data. *Nordic and Baltic Journal of Information &amp. Tongxin Jishu*. Advance online publication. doi:10.13052/nbjict1902-097x.2020.011

Fournie, J. (2020). Managing Electronic Resources Without Buying into the Library Vendor Singularity. *The Code4Lib Journal, 47*. https://journal.code4lib.org/articles/14955

French, V., Chu, N.-C., Santoro, F., Sousa Pinto, I., Borges, D., & McDonough, N. (2015). *Review of Ocean Literacy in European Maritime Policy*. EU Sea Change Project.

G. A., Naik, & HG. (2021). Covid-19 Prevention Kit Based on an Infrared Touchless Thermometer and Distance Detector. *2021 5th International Conference on Electronics, Communication and Aerospace Technology (ICECA)*, 358-362.

G20 Ministers of Culture. (2023). *Outcome Document and Chair's Summary*. G20 Development Ministerial Meeting Varanasi.

Ganesan, V.K., Sivakumar A.I., & Srinivasan, G. (n.d.). Heirarchical minimiation of completion time variance and makespan in job shops. *Computers and Operation Research*.

Gasso, G. (2019). Logistic regression. INSA Rouen-ASI Departement Laboratory: Saint-Etienne-du-Rouvray, France.

Geetharamani & Pandian. (2019). Identification of plant leaf diseases using a nine-layer deep convolutional neural network. *Computers & Electrical Engineering*, *76*, 323–338.

Geetha, V., Punitha, A., Abarna, M., Akshaya, M., Illakiya, S., & Janani, A. P. (2020, July). An effective crop prediction using random forest algorithm. In *2020 International Conference on System, Computation, Automation and Networking (ICSCAN)* (pp. 1-5). IEEE. 10.1109/ICSCAN49426.2020.9262311

Ghaffari, K., Lagzian, M., Kazemi, M., & Malekzadeh, G. (2019). A socio-technical analysis of internet of things development: An interplay of technologies, tasks, structures and actors. *Foresight*, *21*(6), 640–653. doi:10.1108/fs-05-2019-0037

Ghazi, M. M., Yanikoglu, B., & Aptoula, E. (2017). Plant identification using deep neural networks via optimization of transfer learning parameters. *Neurocomputing*, *235*, 228–235. doi:10.1016/j.neucom.2017.01.018

GhoshS.VermaS. K.GhoshU. (2023). *An Improved End-to-End Data Security Approach for Cloud Computing*. doi:10.36227/techrxiv.23553489.v1

Gkinni, Z. (2014). A preservation policy maturity model: A practical tool for Greek libraries and archives. *Journal of Insect Conservation*, *37*(1), 1–10.

Gkrimpizi, T., Peristeras, V., & Magnisalis, I. (2023). Classification of barriers to digital transformation in Higher Education Institutions: Systematic Literature Review. *Education Sciences*, *13*(7), 746. doi:10.3390/educsci13070746

Glaves, H. M. (2019). Developing a common global framework for marine data management. In Oceanography and Coastal Informatics: Breakthroughs in Research and Practice (pp. 179-199). IGI Global. doi:10.4018/978-1-5225-7308-1.ch008

Godin, B. (2009, July). National Innovation System: The system approach in historical perspective. *Science, Technology & Human Values*, *34*(4), 476–501. doi:10.1177/0162243908329187

Gohari, A., Ahmad, A. B., Rahim, R. B., Supa'at, A. S., Abd Razak, S., & Gismalla, M. S. (2022). Involvement of surveillance drones in Smart Cities: A systematic review. *IEEE Access : Practical Innovations, Open Solutions*, *10*, 56611–56628. doi:10.1109/access.2022.3177904

Goksen, Y., Cevik, E., & Avunduk, H. (2015). A case analysis on the focus on the maturity models and information technologies. *Procedia Economics and Finance*, *19*, 208–216. doi:10.1016/S2212-5671(15)00022-2

Golovko, V., & Kochurko, P. (2005, September). Intrusion recognition using neural networks. In *2005 IEEE Intelligent Data Acquisition and Advanced Computing Systems: Technology and Applications* (pp. 108-111). IEEE.

Gomes, J., & Romão, M. (2018). Information system maturity models in healthcare. *Journal of Medical Systems*, *42*(11), 235. doi:10.100710916-018-1097-0 PMID:30327955

Gómez-Pujol, L., Vallespir, J., March, D., & Tintoré, J. (2021). A Survey of Mediterranean Shoreline Change Data Infrastructure, Availability and Nature. *Monografies de la Societat d'Història Natural de les Balears*, (33).

Goodfellow, I., Bengio, Y., Courville, A., & Bengio, Y. (2016). *Deep learning* (vol. 1). Academic Press.

Gopal, A., Prudhveeswar Reddy, S., & Gayatri, V. (2012). Classification of selected medicinal plants leaf using image processing. *2012 International Conference on Machine Vision and Image Processing (MVIP)*, 5–8. 10.1109/MVIP.2012.6428747

Gorrell, M., & Colt, J. (2023, March 6). *FOLIO Governance Model - Community - FOLIO Wiki*. https://wiki.folio.org/display/COMMUNITY/FOLIO+Governance+Model

Government of India. (2009). *Report of the Expert Group to Review the Methodology for Estimation of Poverty, Press Information Bureau, Planning Commission Government of India (2012), Press Notes on Poverty Estimates 2009-10*. Press Information Bureau.

Grabis, J., Stankovski, V., & Zariņš, R. (2020, April). Blockchain enabled distributed storage and sharing of personal data assets. In *2020 IEEE 36th International Conference on Data Engineering Workshops (ICDEW)* (pp. 11-17). IEEE. 10.1109/ICDEW49219.2020.00-13

Graetz, G., Restrepo, P., & Skans, O. N. (2022). Technology and the labor market. *Labour Economics*, *76*. doi:10.1016/j.labeco.2022.102177

Grant, C. (2013). The Future of Library Systems: Library Services Platforms. *Information Standards Quarterly, 24*(4), 1–13. https://www.niso.org/sites/default/files/stories/2017-09/FE_Grant_Future_Library_Systems_%20isqv24no4.pdf

Graves, A., & Graves, A. (2012). Long short-term memory. *Supervised sequence labelling with recurrent neural networks*, 37-45.

Greenberg, E., & Sørensen, A. (1974). Towards a concept of psychological maturity. *Journal of Youth and Adolescence*, *3*(4), 329–358. doi:10.1007/BF02214746 PMID:24414373

Griffin, J. M., Ji, X., & Martin, J. S. (2003). Momentum investing and business cycle risk: Evidence from pole to pole. *The Journal of Finance*, *58*(6), 2515–2547. doi:10.1046/j.1540-6261.2003.00614.x

Grossberg, S. (2013). Recurrent neural networks. *Scholarpedia Journal*, *8*(2), 1888. doi:10.4249cholarpedia.1888

Guillermo, L. (2016). Deep learning for plant identification using vein morphological patterns. *Computers and Electronics in Agriculture*, *127*, 418–424. doi:10.1016/j.compag.2016.07.003

Gul, F., & Khan, K. (2019). An Empirical Study of Investor Attitudinal Factors Influencing Herd Behavior: Evidence from Pakistan Stock Exchange. *Abasyn Journal of Social Sciences*, *12*(1), 1–11. doi:10.34091/AJSS.12.1.01

Gul, S., & Bano, S. (2019). Smart libraries: An emerging and innovative technological habitat of 21st century. *The Electronic Library*, *37*(5), 764–783. doi:10.1108/EL-02-2019-0052

Guo, G., Wang, H., Bell, D., Bi, Y., & Greer, K. (2003). KNN model-based approach in classification. In *On The Move to Meaningful Internet Systems 2003: CoopIS, DOA, and ODBASE: OTM Confederated International Conferences, CoopIS, DOA, and ODBASE 2003, Catania, Sicily, Italy, November 3-7, 2003. Proceedings* (pp. 986-996). Springer Berlin Heidelberg. 10.1007/978-3-540-39964-3_62

Gupta, N. E., Kumar, K., & Sinha, K. (2023). The Nexus of War, Violence, and Rights: A History of War-Torn Afghanistan. In Handbook of Research on War Policies, Strategies, and Cyber Wars (pp. 334-351). IGI Global.

Gürsen, A. E., Öncel, A. G., Plaisent, M., Benslimane, Y., & Bernard, P. (2023). Artificial Intelligence Utilization in Libraries. *Athens Journal of Sciences, 10*(2), 83-94.

Gu, Y., Wang, Y., Yang, Z., & Gao, Y. (2017). A Distributed Privacy-Utility Trade-off Method Using Distributed Lossy Source Coding with Side Information. *KSII Transactions on Internet and Information Systems*, *11*(5), 2778–2791.

Haghtalab, N., Roughgarden, T., & Shetty, A. (2022, February). Smoothed analysis with adaptive adversaries. In *2021 IEEE 62nd Annual Symposium on Foundations of Computer Science (FOCS)* (pp. 942-953). IEEE. 10.1109/FOCS52979.2021.00095

Hair, J. F., Risher, J. J., Sarstedt, M., & Ringle, C. M. (2019). When to use and how to report the results of PLS-SEM. *European Business Review*, *31*(1), 2–24. doi:10.1108/EBR-11-2018-0203

Hair, J., Sarstedt, M., Hopkins, L., & Kuppelwieser, G. V. (2014). Article. *European Business Review*, *26*(2), 106–121. doi:10.1108/EBR-10-2013-0128

Halaç, H.H., & Öğülmüş, V. (2021). Kültürel miras verilerinin dijital olarak depolanması: OpenHeritage3D Örneği. *The Turkish Journal of Design, Art and Communication, 11*(2), 521–540.

Halder, D., Pradhan, D., & Chaudhuri, H. R. (2021). Forty-five years of celebrity credibility and endorsement literature: Review and learnings. *Journal of Business Research, 125*, 397415. doi:10.1016/j.jbusres.2020.12.031

Haralick, R. M., Shanmugam, K., & Dinstein, I. H. (1973). Textural features for image classification. *IEEE Transactions on Systems, Man, and Cybernetics, SMC-3*(6), 610–621. doi:10.1109/TSMC.1973.4309314

Harisanty, D., Anna, N. E. V., Putri, T. E., Firdaus, A. A., & Noor Azizi, N. A. (2022). Leaders, practitioners and scientists' awareness of artificial intelligence in libraries: A pilot study. *Library Hi Tech.* Advance online publication. doi:10.1108/LHT-10-2021-0356

Harmon, P. (2004). Evaluating an organization's business process maturity. *Business Process Trends, 2*(3), 1–11.

Harris, C. (n.d.). *Microservices vs. monolithic architecture.* https://www.atlassian.com/microservices/microservices-architecture/microservices-vs-monolith#:~:text=A%20monolithic%20application%20is%20built

Harvey, L., & Green, D. (1993). Defining quality. *Assessment & Evaluation in Higher Education, 18*(1), 9–35. doi:10.1080/0260293930180102

Hasan, M. Z., Hussain, M. Z., Mubarak, Z., Siddiqui, A. A., Qureshi, A. M., & Ismail, I. (2023, January). Data security and Integrity in Cloud Computing. In *2023 International Conference for Advancement in Technology (ICONAT)* (pp. 1-5). IEEE. 10.1109/ICONAT57137.2023.10080440

Havstein, H. M. (2013). *Changes and continuity: 40 years of reforming the Common Fisheries Policy* [Master's thesis]. Institutt for historie og klassisdke fag, NTNU, Trondheim, Norway.

He, Zhang, Ren, & Sun. (2016). Deep Residual Learning for Image Recognition. In *2016 IEEE Conference on Computer Vision and Pattern Recognition (CVPR)* (pp. 770–778). IEEE.

Heidari, A., & Jabraeil Jamali, M. A. (2022). Internet of things intrusion detection systems: A comprehensive review and Future Directions. *Cluster Computing, 26*(6), 3753–3780. doi:10.100710586-022-03776-z

Helgesson, Y., Höst, M., & Weyns, K. (2012). A review of methods for evaluation of maturity models for process improvement. *Journal of Software Maintenance and Evolution: Research and Practice, 24*(4), 436–454.

Hervieux, S., & Wheatley, A. (2021). Perceptions of artificial intelligence: A survey of academic librarians in Canada and the United States. *Journal of Academic Librarianship, 47*(1), 102270. doi:10.1016/j.acalib.2020.102270

Heydari, R., & Haj Seyed Javady, S. M. R. (2023). Application of Hybrid Data Mining Model (Genetic Algorithm-Wavelet-Deep Neural Network-Monte Carlo Method) for Forecasting the Price of Agricultural Products: A Case Study of Future Price of Saffron in Agricultural Commodity Exchange. Agricultural Economics and (Wagh, 2016). *Development, 30*(4).

Hira, S., & Deshpande, P. S. (2015). Data analysis using multidimensional modeling, statistical analysis and data mining on agriculture parameters. *Procedia Computer Science, 54*, 431–439. doi:10.1016/j.procs.2015.06.050

Hirschleifer, J. (1994). The dark side of the force. *Economic Inquiry, 32*(1), 1–10. doi:10.1111/j.1465-7295.1994.tb01309.x

Hogarth, J., & Wójcik, D. (2016). An evolutionary approach to adaptive capacity assessment: A case study of soufriere, Saint Lucia. *Sustainability, 8*(3), 228. doi:10.3390u8030228

Hollyhead, A., & Robson, A. (2012). A little bit of history repeating itself – Nolan's stages theory and modern IS auditor. *ISACA Journal, 5*, 46–49.

Hombalimath, Palanikkumar, & Patwari. (2023). Symmetrized Feature Selection with Stacked Generalization based Machine Learning Algorithm for the Early Diagnosis of Chronic Diseases. *2023 5th International Conference on Smart Systems and Inventive Technology (ICSSIT),* 838-844.

Howard, Zhu, Chen, Kalenichenko, Wang, Weyand, Andreetto, & Adam. (2017). *MobileNets: Efficient Convolutional Neural Networks for Mobile Vision Applications.* arXiv: 1704.04861.

Huang, Liu, Van Der Maaten, & Weinberger. (2017). Densely Connected Convolutional Networks. In *2017 IEEE Conference on Computer Vision and Pattern Recognition (CVPR)* (pp. 2261–2269). IEEE.

Huang, Y. (2020). Deep Q-networks. *Deep Reinforcement Learning: Fundamentals, Research and Applications*, 135-160.

Huang, Y. H. (2022). Exploring the implementation of artificial intelligence applications among academic libraries in Taiwan. *Library Hi Tech.* Advance online publication. doi:10.1108/LHT-03-2022-0159

Hu, L. T., & Bentler, P. M. (1999). P. M. *Structural Equation Modeling, 6*(1), 1–55. doi:10.1080/10705519909540118

Hunt, R., & Zeadally, S. (2012, December). Network Forensics: An Analysis of Techniques, Tools, and Trends. *Computer, 45*(12), 36–43. doi:10.1109/MC.2012.252

Hu, R., Jia, W., Ling, H., & Huang, D. (2012). Multiscale distance matrix for fast plant leaf recognition. *IEEE Transactions on Image Processing, 21*(11), 4667–4672. doi:10.1109/TIP.2012.2207391 PMID:22875247

Huston, S. J. (2010). Measuring Financial Literacy. *The Journal of Consumer Affairs, 44*(2), 296–316. doi:10.1111/j.1745-6606.2010.01170.x

Hwang, J., Nkenyereye, L., Sung, N., Kim, J., & Song, J. (2021). IoT service slicing and task offloading for edge computing. *IEEE Internet of Things Journal, 8*(14), 11526–11547. doi:10.1109/JIOT.2021.3052498

IAM. (2021). *Pathway to excellence – maturity scale and guidance.* Institute of Asset Management.

ICCAT (International Commission for the Conservation of Atlantic Tunas). (2007). *Basic texts.* https://www.iccat.int/Documents/Commission/BasicTexts.pdf

Intergovernmental Oceanographic Commission. (2017). *IOC Strategic Plan for Oceanographic Data and Information Management (2017-2021).* Author.

Islam, M. S. U., Kumar, A., & Hu, Y.-C. (2021). Context-aware scheduling in Fog computing: A survey, taxonomy, challenges and future directions. *Journal of Network and Computer Applications, 180*, 103008. doi:10.1016/j.jnca.2021.103008

Islam, N., Altamimi, M., Haseeb, K., & Siraj, M. (2021). Secure and sustainable predictive framework for IOT-based multimedia services using machine learning. *Sustainability, 13*(23), 13128. doi:10.3390u132313128

Jagatheesaperumal, S. K., Rajkumar, S., Suresh, J. V., Gumaei, A. H., Alhakbani, N., & Uddin, Md. Z., & Hassan, M. M. (2023). An IOT-based framework for Personalized Health Assessment and recommendations using Machine Learning. *Mathematics, 11*(12), 2758. doi:10.3390/math11122758

Jagtap, S. T., Phasinam, K., Kassanuk, T., Jha, S. S., Ghosh, T., & Thakar, C. M. (2022). Towards application of various machine learning techniques in agriculture. *Materials Today: Proceedings, 51*, 793–797. doi:10.1016/j.matpr.2021.06.236

Jaiswal, G., & Sinha, K. (2023). Yoga: An Ancient Healing Approach for Cyclical Mastalgia. In Perspectives on Coping Strategies for Menstrual and Premenstrual Distress (pp. 237-261). IGI Global.

Jaiswal, G., Karmakar, M., & Sinha, K. (2023). Yoga: A Stress Removal Toolkit During War From the Women's Perspective. In Acceleration of the Biopsychosocial Model in Public Health (pp. 137-167). IGI Global.

Jambekar, S., Nema, S., & Saquib, Z. (2018). Prediction of crop production in India using data mining techniques. *Fourth International Conference on Computing Communication Control and Automation (ICCUBEA).* 10.1109/ICCUBEA.2018.8697446

Janani, R., & Gopal, A. (2013). Identification of selected medicinal plant leaves using image features and ann. *2013 International Conference on Advanced Electronic Systems (ICAES),* 238–242. 10.1109/ICAES.2013.6659400

Jang-Jaccard, J., & Nepal, S. (2014). A survey of emerging threats in cybersecurity. *Journal of Computer and System Sciences, 80*(5), 973–993. doi:10.1016/j.jcss.2014.02.005

Jeevan, K., & Sathisha, B. M. (2020). Implementation of IoT Based Wireless Electronic Stethoscope. *2020 Third International Conference on Multimedia Processing, Communication & Information Technology (MPCIT),* 103-106.

Jeong, Y. (2023). Digitalization in production logistics: How ai, Digital Twins, and simulation are driving the shift from model-based to data-driven approaches. *International Journal of Precision Engineering and Manufacturing-Smart Technology, 1*(2), 187–200. doi:10.57062/ijpem-st.2023.0052

Jiang, F., Zhou, M., Zhou, F., & Hu, Z. (2023, May). Glider Network Observation Unraveling A Cyclonic Eddy in the Northwestern Pacific Subtropical Countercurrent. *Journal of Physics: Conference Series, 2486*(1), 012009. doi:10.1088/1742-6596/2486/1/012009

Jiankang, W. (2011). Knowledge management maturity models: A systemic comparison. International Conference on Information Management, Innovation Management and Industrial Engineering (ICIII), 606-609. doi:10.1109/ICIII.2011.420

Jing, Y. N., Tu, P., Wang, X. P., & Zhang, G. D. (2015). Distributed-log-based scheme for IP traceback. *The fifth international conference on Computer and Information Technology (CIT' 15),* 711–715.

JNCC (Joint Nature Conservation Committee). (2018). Open. *Data & Policy,* 1.

Joly, Goeau, Bonnet, Bakic, Barbe, Selmi, Yahiaoui, Carre, Mouysset, Molino, Boujemaa, & Barthelemy. (2014, September). Interactive ´ plant identification based on social image data. *Ecological Informatics, 23,* 22–34.

Juda, L. (2010). The European Union and the Marine Strategy Framework Directive: Continuing the Development of European Ocean Use Management. *Ocean Development and International Law, 41*(1), 34–54. doi:10.1080/00908320903285463

Kadir, A., Nugroho, L. E., Susanto, A., & Santosa, P. I. (2013). *Leaf classification using shape, color, and texture features.* arXiv preprint arXiv:1401.4447.

Kaiser, S. A. (2015). Legal and policy aspects of space situational awareness. *Space Policy, 31,* 5–12. doi:10.1016/j.spacepol.2014.11.002

Kakwani, N. (1993). Poverty and economic growth with application to Côte d'Ivoire. *Review of Income and Wealth, 39*(2), 121–139. doi:10.1111/j.1475-4991.1993.tb00443.x

Kamath, G., Mallya, J., Kamath, V., & Payini, V. (2022). LibQUAL+® based importance-performance matrix analysis for assessing library service quality: A case study. *Annals of Library and Information Studies, 69*(4), 269–276.

Kanagasabai, B., & Aggarwal, V. (2020). The Mediating Role of Risk Tolerance in the Relationship between Financial Literacy and Investment Performance. *Colombo Business Journal, 11*(1), 83–104. doi:10.4038/cbj.v11i1.58

Karaboga, D., & Basturk, B. (2008). On the performance of artificial bee colony (ABC) algorithm. *Applied Soft Computing, 8*(1), 687–697. doi:10.1016/j.asoc.2007.05.007

Karaboga, N. (2009). A new design method based on artificial bee colony algorithm for digital IIR filters. *Journal of the Franklin Institute, 346*(4), 328–348. doi:10.1016/j.jfranklin.2008.11.003

Karmakar, M., Priya, A., Sinha, K., & Verma, M. (2022, December). Shrinkable Cryptographic Technique Using Involutory Function for Image Encryption. In *International Conference on Advanced Network Technologies and Intelligent Computing* (pp. 275-289). Cham: Springer Nature Switzerland.

Kataria, C. D., & Choudhary, S. (2015). Herding behavior in financial market: Critical literature review. *International Research Journal of Commerce Arts and Science*, *6*(12), 16–26.

Kaur, K., & Attwal, K. S. (2017). Effect of temperature and rainfall on paddy yield using data mining. *7th International Conference on Cloud Computing, Data Science & Engineering*. 10.1109/CONFLUENCE.2017.7943204

Kavitha, R., Kumar, A., Kalpana, V., & Hariram, V. (2023). Artificial Intelligence based Health Monitoring System on IoTH platform. *2023 Second International Conference on Augmented Intelligence and Sustainable Systems (ICAISS)*, 1458-1463.

Kawale, S. R., & Diwan, S. P. (2022). Intelligent Breast Abnormality Framework for Detection and Evaluation of Breast Abnormal Parameters. *2022 International Conference on Edge Computing and Applications (ICECAA)*, 1503-1508.

Kayıkçı, D. (2019). Arkeoloji ve müzeolojide yapay zeka / derin öğrenme: 3B parça eşleştirme sistem modeli önerisi. *Proceedings of the 2nd International Conference on Technology and Science*.

Kayser-Bril, N. (2012). Become data literate in 3 simple steps. In J. Grey, L. Bounegru, & L. Chambers (Eds.), *The data journalism handbook*. O'Reilly Media.

Kebapci, H., Yanikoglu, B., & Unal, G. (2011). Plant image retrieval using color, shape and texture features. *The Computer Journal*, *54*(9), 1475–1490. doi:10.1093/comjnl/bxq037

Kelly, S., Kaye, S.-A., & Oviedo-Trespalacios, O. (2023). What Factors Contribute to the Acceptance of Artificial Intelligence? A Systemic Review. *Telematics and Informatics*, *77*, 101925. doi:10.1016/j.tele.2022.101925

Keynes, J. M. (1930). Economic Possibilities for our Grandchildren. Essays in Persuasion, 358-373.

Khaliq, S., Tariq, Z. U. A., & Masood, A. (2020, October). Role of user and entity behavior analytics in detecting insider attacks. In *2020 International Conference on Cyber Warfare and Security (ICCWS)* (pp. 1-6). IEEE. 10.1109/ICCWS48432.2020.9292394

Khan, B., Fatima, H., Qureshi, A., Kumar, S., Hanan, A., Hussain, J., & Abdullah, S. (2023). Drawbacks of Artificial Intelligence and Their Potential Solutions in the Healthcare Sector. *Biomedical Materials & Devices*, 1-8. doi:10.1007/s44174-023-00063-2

Khan, A. U., Zhang, Z., Chohan, S. R., & Rafique, W. (2021). Factors fostering the success of IOT services in academic libraries: A study built to enhance the library performance. *Library Hi Tech*, *40*(6), 1976–1995. doi:10.1108/lht-06-2021-0179

Khaydarova, G. (2023). Thermal characteristics of compositions of polyvinyl chloride with flame retardants. *Universum:Technical Sciences*, *107*(2). Advance online publication. doi:10.32743/unitech.2023.107.2.15077

Kim, J. (2021). Determining research data services maturity: The role of library leadership and stakeholder involvement. *Library & Information Science Research*, *43*(2), 101092. doi:10.1016/j.lisr.2021.101092

Kim, J. S., Kim, M., & Noh, B. N. (2014). A fuzzy expert system for network forensics. In *Computational science and its applications* (Vol. 3043, pp. 175–182). Springer.

Kingma & Ba. (2017). *Adam: A Method for Stochastic Optimization*. arXiv: 1412.6980.

Kirsch, C. (2000). MTO contingency model for the transferability of socio-technical methods - the Swiss KOMPASS method applied to the design and implementation of Advanced Manufacturing Systems in Australia. *Proceedings of the Human Factors and Ergonomics Society Annual Meeting*, *44*(36), 497–500. doi:10.1177/154193120004403612

Kishore Kumar, R., Pandidurai, M., & Senthil Kamalesh, M. S. C. (2023). Design of IoT based Rural Health Helper using Natural Language Processing. *2023 4th International Conference on Electronics and Sustainable Communication Systems (ICESC)*, 328-333.

Klasen, S., & Misselhorn, M. (2008). *Determinants of the growth semi-elasticity of poverty reduction* (No. 176). IAI Discussion Papers.

Koelmel, B., Borsch, M., Bulander, R., Waidelich, L., Brugger, T., Kuehn, A., Weyer, M., Schmerber, L., & Krutwig, M. (2023). Quantifying the economic and financial viability of Nb-IOT and Lorawan Technologies: A comprehensive life cycle cost analysis using Pragmatic Computational Tools. *FinTech*, *2*(3), 510–526. doi:10.3390/fintech2030029

Kohlegger, M., Maier, R., & Thalmann, S. (2009). Understanding maturity models. Results of a structured content analysis. In K. Tochtermann, A. Paschke (Eds.), *Proceedings of I-KNOW'09 and I-SEMANTICS'09* (pp. 51-61). Verl. Technische Universitat Graz.

Koo, B., Curtis, C., & Ryan, B. (2021). Examining the impact of artificial intelligence on hotel employees through job insecurity perspectives. *International Journal of Hospitality Management*, *95*. doi:10.1016/j.ijhm.2020.102763

Kotsiantis, S. B. (2013). Decision trees: A recent overview. *Artificial Intelligence Review*, *39*(4), 261–283. doi:10.100710462-011-9272-4

Kouper, I., Fear, K., Ishida, M., Kollen, Ch., & Williams, S. (2017). Research data services maturity in academic libraries. In L. Johnston (Ed.), Curating research data. Vol. 1: Practical strategies for your digital repository (pp. 153-170). ACRL.

Kranthi, M., & Tanguturi, R. C. (2023). Design of Intelligent Medical Integrity Authentication and Secure Information for Public Cloud in Hospital Administration. *2023 2nd International Conference on Edge Computing and Applications (ICECAA)*, 256-261.

Krasadakis, G. (2022). *60 Leaders on Artificial Intelligence*. https://krasadakis.medium.com/60-leaders-on-artificial-intelligence-d1be5b27431b

Krishnaji, N. (2012). Abolish the poverty line. *Economic and Political Weekly*, 10–11.

Krizhevsky, A., Sutskever, I., & Hinton, G. E. (2012). Imagenet classification with deep convolutional neural networks. In *Proceedings of the 25th International Conference on Neural Information Processing Systems* (vol. 1, pp. 1097–1105). Curran Associates Inc

Krizhevsky, A., Sutskever, I., & Hinton, G. E. (2017, May). ImageNet classification with deep convolutional neural networks. *Communications of the ACM*, *60*(6), 84–90. doi:10.1145/3065386

Kulkarni, A. M., Pandiyan, M., & Sonawane, C. S. (2023). An overview of FOLIO: An open-source library management system. *Library Hi Tech News*. Advance online publication. doi:10.1108/LHTN-08-2023-0138

Kultur Limited. (2023). *Kültürel miras için yapay zekâ tabanlı arşiv otomasyon sistemi: GAMOS*. https://kulturlimited.com/kulturel-miras-icin-yapay-zeka-tabanli-arsiv-otomasyon-sistemi-gamos/

Kumar, K., Singhania, D., Singh, K. P., Mishra, P., & Sinha, K. (2023). Navigating the Economic Challenges of the Russia-Ukraine Conflict on India. In Handbook of Research on War Policies, Strategies, and Cyber Wars (pp. 218-238). IGI Global. doi:10.4018/978-1-6684-6741-1.ch012

Kumar, N., Belhumeur, P. N., Biswas, A., & Jacobs, D. W. W. (2012). Computer Vision System for Automatic Plant Species Identification. In Computer Vision – ECCV 2012 (vol. 7573, pp. 502–516). Springer Berlin Heidelberg.

Kumar, S., Jaiswal, G., & Sinha, K. (2023). Skin Cancer Lesion Detection Using Improved CNN Techniques. In Handbook of Research on Technological Advances of Library and Information Science in Industry 5.0 (pp. 355-377). IGI Global.

Kumar, P. M., Surya, C. M., & Gopi, V. P. (2017, November). Identification of ayurvedic medicinal plants by image processing of leaf samples. In *2017 Third International Conference on Research in Computational Intelligence and Communication Networks (ICRCICN)* (pp. 231-238). IEEE. 10.1109/ICRCICN.2017.8234512

Kumar, S., Mishra, S., Khanna, P., & Pragya. (2017). Precision sugarcane monitoring using SVM classifier. *Procedia Computer Science*, *122*, 881–887. doi:10.1016/j.procs.2017.11.450

Kumar, S., Tiwari, P., & Zymbler, M. (2019). Internet of things is a revolutionary approach for future technology enhancement: A Review. *Journal of Big Data*, *6*(1). Advance online publication. doi:10.118640537-019-0268-2

Lamirault-Gall, M. O. (2011). *Metadata capture user guide for the Working Group on Marine Habitat Mapping (WGMHM) for ICES*. Academic Press.

Lappalainen, Y., & Narayanan, N. (2023). Aisha: A Custom AI Library Chatbot Using the ChatGPT API. *Journal of Web Librarianship*, *17*(3), 1–22. doi:10.1080/19322909.2023.2221477

Larsson, Maire, & Shakhnarovich. (2017). *FractalNet: Ultra-Deep Neural Networks without Residuals*. arXiv: 1605.07648.

Lartey, R. (2012). The banking regulatory and Market Framework in Ghana: Strengths, weaknesses, opportunities and threats. SSRN *Electronic Journal*. https://doi.org/ doi:10.2139/ssrn.2083237

Latapy, A., Ferret, Y., Testut, L., Talke, S., Aarup, T., Pons, F., Jan, G., Bradshaw, E., & Pouvreau, N. (2023). Data rescue process in the context of sea level reconstructions: An overview of the methodology, lessons learned, up-to-date best practices and recommendations. *Geoscience Data Journal*, *10*(3), 396–425. doi:10.1002/gdj3.179

Leadbetter, A. M., Shepherd, A., Arko, R., Chandler, C., Chen, Y., Dockery, N., Ferreira, R., Fu, L., Thomas, R., West, P., & Zednik, S. (2016). Experiences of a "semantics smackdown". *Earth Science Informatics*, *9*(3), 355–363. doi:10.100712145-016-0252-8

Lee, Chan, Mayo, & Remagnino. (2017). How deep learning extracts and learns leaf features for plant classification. *Pattern Recognition*, *71*, 1–13.

Lee, Chan, Wilkin, & Remagnino. (2015). Deep-plant: Plant identification with convolutional neural networks. *2015 IEEE International Conference on Image Processing (ICIP)*, 452–456.

Lee, I. (2020). Internet of things (IOT) cybersecurity: Literature review and IOT cyber risk management. *Future Internet*, *12*(9), 157. doi:10.3390/fi12090157

Lee, S., Choi, H., Kim, T., Park, H. S., & Choi, J. K. (2022). A Novel Energy-Conscious Access Point (eAP) System with Cross-Layer Design in Wi-Fi Networks for Reliable IoT Services. *IEEE Access : Practical Innovations, Open Solutions*, *10*, 61228–61248. doi:10.1109/ACCESS.2022.3181304

Lee, Y., Wu, W., & Lee, C. (2021). How COVID-19 triggers our herding behavior? risk perception, state anxiety, and trust. *Frontiers in Public Health*, *9*, 587439. Advance online publication. doi:10.3389/fpubh.2021.587439 PMID:33659231

Lemos, S.I.C., Ferreira, F.A.F., Zopounidis, C., Galariotis, E., & Ferreira, N.C.M.Q.F. (2022). Artificial Intelligence and Change Management in Small and Medium-Sized Enterprises: An Analysis of Dynamics Within Adaptation Initiatives. *Annals of Operations Research*, 1-27. . doi:10.1007/s10479-022-05159-4

Liang, X., & Chen, Y. (2018). Libraries in internet of things (IOT) era. *Library Hi Tech, 38*(1), 79–93. doi:10.1108/lht-11-2017-0233

Li, B., Chen, T., & Giannakis, G. B. (2019). Secure mobile edge computing in IoT via collaborative online learning. *IEEE Transactions on Signal Processing, 67*(23), 5922–5935. doi:10.1109/TSP.2019.2949504

Libris, E. (2019). *How AI Can Enhance the Value of Research Libraries.* Retrieved from https://www.libraryjournal.com/story/how-ai-can-enhance-the-value-of-research-libraries

Li, D., Nanseki, T., Chomei, Y., & Kuang, J. (2023). A review of smart agriculture and production practices in Japanese large-scale rice farming. *Journal of the Science of Food and Agriculture, 103*(4), 1609–1620. doi:10.1002/jsfa.12204 PMID:36069313

Likhadzed, V., & Klubnikin, A. (2023). *How Much does Artificial Intelligence Cost? Well, it Depends.* ItrexGroup.

Lima, B. F., Neto, J. V., Santos, R. S., & Caiado, R. G. (2023). A socio-technical framework for LEAN project management implementation towards sustainable value in the digital transformation context. *Sustainability, 15*(3), 1756. doi:10.3390u15031756

Lin, C., Zhitang, L., Cuixia, G., & Yingshu, L. (2019) Modeling and analyzing dynamic forensics system based on intrusion tolerance. *Ninth IEEE international conference on computer and information technology*, 230–235.

Lin, C., Wu, J. C., & Yen, D. C. (2012, January). Exploring barriers to knowledge flow at different knowledge management maturity stages. *Information & Management, 49*(1), 10–23. doi:10.1016/j.im.2011.11.001

Lin, H. (2007). Effects of extrinsic and intrinsic motivation on employee knowledge sharing intentions. *Journal of Information Science, 33*(2), 135–149. doi:10.1177/0165551506068174

Li-Pei Wong, Low, & Chong. (2008). Bee Colony Optimization with local search for traveling salesman problem. *2008 6th IEEE International Conference on Industrial Informatics.* 10.1109/INDIN.2008.4618252

Li, S., Hao, Z., Ding, L., & Xu, X. (2019). Research on the application of information technology of Big Data in Chinese digital library. *Library Management, 40*(8/9), 518–531. doi:10.1108/LM-04-2019-0021

Liu, T. (2021). How is FOLIO different from its predecessors? *International Journal of Librarianship, 6*(2), 40–48. doi:10.23974/ijol.2021.vol6.2.207

Liu, W. (2021). FOLIO and Smart Libraries: Meeting the future needs of Chinese Libraries. *International Journal of Librarianship, 6*(2), 73–83. doi:10.23974/ijol.2021.vol6.2.213

Liu, Y., Zhang, X., Gao, Y., Qu, T., & Shi, Y. (2022). Improved CNN method for crop pest identification based on transfer learning. *Computational Intelligence and Neuroscience, 2022*, 2022. doi:10.1155/2022/9709648 PMID:35341164

Liu, Z., & Feng, D. (2015). Incremental fuzzy decision tree-based network forensic system. In Y. Hao, J. Liu, Y. P. Wang, Y. M. Cheung, H. Yin, L. Jiao, J. Ma, & Y. C. Jiao (Eds.), *Computational intelligence and security* (Vol. 3802, pp. 995–1002). Springer. doi:10.1007/11596981_148

Li, Y., Zhuang, Y., Hu, X., Gao, Z., Hu, J., Chen, L., He, Z., Pei, L., Chen, K., Wang, M., Niu, X., Chen, R., Thompson, J., Ghannouchi, F. M., & El-Sheimy, N. (2021). Toward Location-Enabled IoT (LE-IoT): IoT Positioning Techniques, Error Sources, and Error Mitigation. *IEEE Internet of Things Journal, 8*(6), 4035–4062. doi:10.1109/JIOT.2020.3019199

Lohiya, R., & Thakkar, A. (2021). Application domains, evaluation data sets, and research challenges of IOT: A systematic review. *IEEE Internet of Things Journal, 8*(11), 8774–8798. doi:10.1109/jiot.2020.3048439

Looy, A., Backer, M., & Poels, G. (2011). Defining business process maturity. A journey towards excellence. *Total Quality Management & Business Excellence*, *22*(11), 1119–1137. doi:10.1080/14783363.2011.624779

Lundvall, B. A., & Johnson, B. (1994). The learning economy. *Journal of Industry Studies*, *1*(2), 23–42. doi:10.1080/13662719400000002

Lundvall, B. A., Johnson, B., Andersen, E. S., & Dalum, B. (2002, February). National systems of production, innovation and competence building. *Research Policy*, *31*(2), 213–231. doi:10.1016/S0048-7333(01)00137-8

M. R. G. & Anandaram. (2022). Extraction of Fetal ECG Using ANFIS and the Undecimated-Wavelet Transform. *2022 IEEE 3rd Global Conference for Advancement in Technology (GCAT),* 1-5.

Mackay, C. (2012). *Extraordinary popular delusions and the madness of crowds*. Simon and Schuster.

Macuácua, J. C., Centeno, J. A. S., & Amisse, C. (2023). Data mining approach for dry bean seeds classification. *Smart Agricultural Technology*, *5*, 100240. doi:10.1016/j.atech.2023.100240

Madhava Varma, K., Chowdary, N. D., Chandra, P. P., & Kumar, G. P. (2023). Cloud based ERP systems and Data Security for Cloud based ERP Applications - SAP S/4HANA. *International Journal Of Scientific Research In Engineering And Management*, *07*(02). Advance online publication. doi:10.55041/IJSREM17828

Maftei, A. A., Lavric, A., Petrariu, A. I., & Popa, V. (2023). Massive data storage solution for IOT devices using Blockchain Technologies. *Sensors (Basel)*, *23*(3), 1570. doi:10.339023031570

Maharaja, R., Iyer, P., & Ye, Z. (2019). A hybrid fog-cloud approach for securing the internet of things. *Cluster Computing*, *23*(2), 451–459. doi:10.100710586-019-02935-z

Maier, N. (2014). Coordination and cooperation in the European Marine Strategy Framework Directive and the US National Ocean Policy. *Ocean and Coastal Management*, *92*, 1–8. doi:10.1016/j.ocecoaman.2014.01.014

Mailapur & M. K. (2023). Implementation of GUI based Vital Track Ambulance for Patient Health Monitoring. *2023 8th International Conference on Communication and Electronics Systems (ICCES)*, 1417-1424.

Maimun, A., Siow, C. L., Khairuddin, J., & Hiekata, K. (2022). Digital transformation through data-driven and data-centric approaches with Artificial Intelligence. *ICCAS, 2022*. Advance online publication. doi:10.3940/rina.iccas.2022.19

Majumdar, Naraseeyappa, & Ankalaki. (2017). Analysis of agriculture data using data mining techniques: application of big data. *Journal of Big Data.*

Mallisetty, S. B., Tripuramallu, G. A., Kamada, K., Devineni, P., Kavitha, S., & Krishna, A. V. P. (2023, January). A Review on Cloud Security and Its Challenges. In *2023 International Conference on Intelligent Data Communication Technologies and Internet of Things (IDCIoT)* (pp. 798-804). IEEE. 10.1109/IDCIoT56793.2023.10053520

Mand, A. A., Janor, H., Rahim, R. A., & Sarmidi, T. (2021). Herding behavior and stock market conditions. *PSU Research Review*, *7*(2), 105–116. doi:10.1108/PRR-10-2020-0033

Mangalaraj, G., Nerur, S., & Dwivedi, R. (2022). Digital transformation for agility and resilience: An exploratory study. *Journal of Computer Information Systems*, *63*(1), 11–23. doi:10.1080/08874417.2021.2015726

Manyika, J., Silberg, J., & Presten, B. (2019). What do we do About the Biases in AI? *Harvard Business Review.* Available on: https://hbr.org/2019/10/what-do-we-do-about-the-biases-in-ai

K. Mao, & X. Jiang (Eds.). Local binary pattern based on image gradient for bark image classification. In *Tenth International Conference on Signal Processing Systems* (p. 39). SPIE.

Marcus, G., & Davis, E. (2019). *Rebooting AI: Building Artificial Intelligence We can Trust*. Pantheon Press.

Maresova, P., Krejcar, O., Barakovic, S., Barakovic Husic, J., Lameski, P., Zdravevski, E., Chorbev, I., & Trajkovik, V. (2020). Health–related ICT solutions of smart environments for elderly–systematic review. *IEEE Access : Practical Innovations, Open Solutions*, *8*, 54574–54600. doi:10.1109/access.2020.2981315

Marietza, F., Ridwan, N., Santi, F., & Saiful, S. (2023). The Impact of Cultural Shocks on Investor Sentiment and Herding Behavior: An Evidence during COVID-19 Pandemic. *Asian Journal of Economics, Business and Accounting*, 30–50. . doi:10.9734/ajeba/2023/v23i5933

Marin, L., Pawlowski, M., & Jara, A. (2015). Optimized ECC implementation for secure communication between heterogeneous IOT devices. *Sensors (Basel)*, *15*(9), 21478–21499. doi:10.3390150921478

Martínez, E., García-Benadí, A., Toma, D. M., Delory, E., Gomáriz, S., & Del-Río, J. (2021). Metadata-driven universal real-time ocean sound measurement architecture. *IEEE Access : Practical Innovations, Open Solutions*, *9*, 28282–28301. doi:10.1109/ACCESS.2021.3058744

Martínez-Peláez, R., Ochoa-Brust, A., Rivera, S., Félix, V. G., Ostos, R., Brito, H., Félix, R. A., & Mena, L. J. (2023). Role of digital transformation for achieving sustainability: Mediated role of stakeholders, key capabilities, and Technology. *Sustainability*, *15*(14), 11221. doi:10.3390u151411221

Masadeh, S. A., & El-Haggar, N. (2023). Analyzing factors influencing IOT adoption in higher educational institutions in Saudi Arabia using a modified TAM model. *Education and Information Technologies*. Advance online publication. doi:10.100710639-023-12039-2

Mate, M. H., & Kapse, S. R. (2015). Network Forensic Tool — Concept and Architecture. *2015 Fifth International Conference on Communication Systems and Network Technologies*, 711-713. 10.1109/CSNT.2015.204

Matousek, K. (2008). Security and reliability considerations for distributed healthcare systems. *2008 42nd Annual IEEE International Carnahan Conference on Security Technology*. 10.1109/CCST.2008.4751326

May, C. K. (2022). Complex adaptive governance systems: A framework to understand institutions, organizations, and people in socio-ecological systems. *Socio-Ecological Practice Research*, *4*(1), 39–54. doi:10.100742532-021-00101-7

Mazikana, A. T. (2023). How inflation, GDP growth, unemployment, interest rates and exchange rates affect an organisation. SSRN *Electronic Journal*. https://doi.org/ doi:10.2139/ssrn.4377852

McFeeley, B. (1996). *IDEAL^{SM}: a user's guide for software process improvement*. Carnegie Mellon University. doi:10.21236/ADA305472

Mcgee, J., & Prusak, L. (1994). *Gerenciamento estratégico da informação: aumente a competitividade e eficiência de sua empresa utilizando a informação como uma ferramenta estratégica*. Elsevier.

McNally, C., & Kuss, I. (2020, March 6). *Deployment Environments (general overview) - System Operations and Management SIG - FOLIO Wiki*. https://wiki.folio.org/pages/viewpage.action?pageId=7832871

McQueen, R. J., Garner, S. R., Nevill-Manning, C. G., & Witten, I. H. (1995). Applying machine learning to agricultural data. *Computers and Electronics in Agriculture*, *12*(4), 275–293. doi:10.1016/0168-1699(95)98601-9

Medar, R. A., & Rajpurohit, V. S. (2014). A survey on data mining techniques for crop yield prediction. *International Journal of Advance Research in Computer Science and Management Studies*, *2*(9), 59–64.

Meiner, A. (2010). Integrated maritime policy for the European Union — Consolidating coastal and marine information to support maritime spatial planning. *Journal of Coastal Conservation*, *14*(1), 1–11. doi:10.100711852-009-0077-4

Meiner, A. (2013). Spatial data management priorities for assessment of Europe's coasts and seas. *Journal of Coastal Conservation*, *17*(2), 271–277. doi:10.100711852-011-0173-0

Mekala, S., & Vennila, J. (2018). A Survey of Intrusion Detection and Prevention Systems in Cloud Computing. *Journal of King Saud University. Computer and Information Sciences*. Advance online publication. doi:10.1016/j.jksuci.2018.06.003

Merlette, D., & Pruthi, D. P. (2013). *Network security; NetDetector: Identifying real threats and securing your network*. Available: https://www.niksun.com/

Meskó, B. (2022). Covid-19's impact on digital health adoption: The growing gap between a technological and a cultural transformation. *JMIR Human Factors*, *9*(3). Advance online publication. doi:10.2196/38926

Mettler, T. (2009). *A design science research perspective on maturity models in information systems*. Report no. BE IWI/HNE/03. Universität St. Galen. https://www.alexandria.unisg.ch/publications/214531

Mettler, T. (2011). Maturity assessment models: A design science research approach. *International Journal of Society Systems Science*, *3*(1/2), 81–98. doi:10.1504/IJSSS.2011.038934

Migabo, E. M., Djouani, K. D., & Kurien, A. M. (2020). The narrowband internet of things (NB-IOT) resources management performance state of art, challenges, and opportunities. *IEEE Access : Practical Innovations, Open Solutions*, *8*, 97658–97675. doi:10.1109/access.2020.2995938

Momoh, E. O., & Folorunso, A. L. (2019). The Evolving Roles of Libraries and Librarians in the 21st Century. *Library Philosophy and Practice (E-Journal)*, 1–11. https://digitalcommons.unl.edu/libphilprac/2867

Monetary policy and herding behavior developed market and emerging market comparison. (2021). *Trikonomika Journal*. doi:10.23969/trikonomika.v20i1.1579

Montavon, G., Samek, W., & Müller, K. R. (2018). Methods for interpreting and understanding deep neural networks. *Digital Signal Processing*, *73*, 1–15. doi:10.1016/j.dsp.2017.10.011

Moore, D. (2003). *Technical Report. 03-39*. Social and Economic Sciences Research Center, Washington State University.

Moore, G. (1991). *Crossing the chasm: marketing and selling high-tech products to mainstream customers*. Harper Business.

Moore, S. (2019). Digital Government, public participation and service transformation: The impact of virtual courts. *Policy &amp. Politics*. Advance online publication. doi:10.1332/030557319x1558603936750

Moreira, P. (2008). Stealth Risks and Catastrophic Risks. *Journal of Travel & Tourism Marketing*, *23*(2–4), 15–27. doi:10.1300/J073v23n02_02

Morin, E. (1999). *O método 3: o conhecimento do conhecimento*. Sulina.

Morol, Md. K. (2022). Data Security and privacy in cloud computing platforms: A comprehensive review. *International Journal of Current Science Research and Review*, *05*(05). Advance online publication. doi:10.47191/ijcsrr/v5-i5-09

Moskal, B. (2000). Scoring rubrics: What, when and how? *Practical Assessment, Research & Evaluation*, *7*(3), 3.

Mostajer Kheirkhah, F., & Asghari, H. (2019, June). [Plant leaf classification using GIST texture features. *IET Computer Vision*, *13*(4), 369–375. doi:10.1049/iet-cvi.2018.5028

Moumtzidis, I., Kamariotou, M., & Kitsios, F. (2022). Digital transformation strategies enabled by internet of things and Big Data Analytics: The use-case of telecommunication companies in Greece. *Information (Basel)*, *13*(4), 196. doi:10.3390/info13040196

Msauki, G. (2021). Library 4.0 and sustainable development: Opportunities and challenges. *Examining the impact of industry 4.0 on academic libraries*, 31-44.

Munisami, T., Ramsurn, M., Kishnah, S., & Pudaruth, S. (2015). Plant leaf recognition using shape features and colour histogram with K-nearest neighbour classifiers. *Procedia Computer Science*, *58*, 740–747. doi:10.1016/j.procs.2015.08.095

Murillo, F. J., Kenchington, E., Sacau, M., Piper, D. J. W., Wareham, V., & Muñoz, A. (2011). New VME indicator species (excluding corals and sponges) and some potential VME elements of the NAFO Regulatory Area. NAFO SCR Document 11/73, Serial No. N6003pg. 20 pp.

Murray, P. (2023, August 17). *Information and User Guides for FOLIO Apps*. https://wiki.folio.org/display/FOLIOtips/Information+and+User+Guides+for+FOLIO+Apps

Murray, P., & Colt, J. (2023, August 14). *Welcome to the FOLIO Wiki - Community - FOLIO Wiki*. https://wiki.folio.org/

Murray, P., & Martin, K. (2022, March 3). *FOLIO Roadmap (2019-2020) - Product Council - FOLIO Wiki*. https://wiki.folio.org/pages/viewpage.action?pageId=1410538

Mutafelija, B., & Stromberg, H. (2003). *Systematic process improvement using ISO 9001:2000 and CMMI*. Artech House.

Na, S., Xumin, L., & Yong, G. (2010, April). Research on k-means clustering algorithm: An improved k-means clustering algorithm. In *2010 Third International Symposium on intelligent information technology and security informatics* (pp. 63-67). IEEE.

Naidoo, D. T. (2023). Integrating TAM and IS Success Model: Exploring the Role of Blockchain and AI in Predicting Learner Engagement and Performance in E-learning. *Frontiers of Computer Science*, *18*(Sept), 5. doi:10.3389/fcomp.2023.1227749

Namitha, Manu, Rashmi, & Chinamuttevi. (2022). IOT Based Smart Health Care System to Monitor Covid-19 Patients. *IJEER*, *10*(1), 36-40.

Narang, N. K. (2022). Mentor's musings on standardization imperatives for the connected vehicles for seamless integration in sustainable mobility. *IEEE Internet of Things Magazine*, *5*(2), 4–8. doi:10.1109/miot.2022.9889259

Narayanan, S. N., Ganesan, A., Joshi, K., Oates, T., Joshi, A., & Finin, T. (2018). Early Detection of Cybersecurity Threats Using Collaborative Cognition. *IEEE 4th International Conference on Collaboration and Internet Computing (CIC)*. 10.1109/CIC.2018.00054

Nareshkumar, A., & Gururaj, B. (2022). An Integrated IoT Technology for Health and Traffic Monitoring System with Smart Ambulance. *2022 IEEE North Karnataka Subsection Flagship International Conference (NKCon)*, 1-6.

Naveen, K. B., Ramesha, M., & Pai, G. N. (2020). Internet of things: Internet revolution, impact, technology road map and features. *Adv. Math. Sci. J.*, *9*(7), 4405–4414. doi:10.37418/amsj.9.7.11

Nduta, A. (2023, April 3). *A Brief History of Open Source*. https://www.freecodecamp.org/news/brief-history-of-open-source/

Nedelkoska, L., & Quintini, G. (2018). *Automation, skills use and training*. OECD Social, Employment and Migration Working Papers, No. 202. Paris: OECD Publishing. http://dx.doi.org/ doi:10.1787/1815199X

Nelson, R. R., & Phelps, E. S. (1966). Investment in humans, technological diffusion, and economic growth. *The American Economic Review*, *56*(1/2), 69–75.

Nguyen, L. D., Leyva-Mayorga, I., Lewis, A. N., & Popovski, P. (2021). Modeling and analysis of data trading on blockchain-based market in IoT networks. *IEEE Internet of Things Journal*, *8*(8), 6487–6497. doi:10.1109/JIOT.2021.3051923

Nguyen, L., Gallery, G., Newton, C., & Australasian Accounting, C. (2016). Article. *Business and Finance Journal, 10*(3), 3–22.

Nielsen, F., & Nielsen, F. (2016). Hierarchical clustering. *Introduction to HPC with MPI for Data Science*, 195-211.

Nielsen, J. (1993). *Usability engineering*. Morgan Kaufmann Publ. doi:10.1016/B978-0-08-052029-2.50007-3

Nischitha, K., Vishwakarma, D., Ashwini, M. N., & Manjuraju, M. R. (2020). Crop prediction using machine learning approaches. *International Journal of Engineering Research & Technology (Ahmedabad)*, *9*(8), 23–26.

Nolan, R. (1973). Managing the computer resource: A stage hypothesis. *Communications of the ACM*, *16*(7), 399–405. doi:10.1145/362280.362284

NTV. (2023). *Microsoft'tan tarihi ve yapay zekayı bir araya getiren proje*. https://www.ntv.com.tr/galeri/teknoloji/microsofttan-tarihi-ve-yapay-zekayi-bir-araya-getiren-proje-ilk-olimpiyatlara-katilmak-artik-mumkun,oAjB-S_jP-km86F_m8WF 7Lw

Nwaiwu, F., & Mbelu, S. (2020). Digital transformation in healthcare and surveillance capitalism: Comparative assessment of data and Privacy Protection Compliance across the European Union. SSRN *Electronic Journal*. https://doi.org/doi:10.2139/ssrn.3643838

O'Shea, K., & Nash, R. (2015). *An introduction to convolutional neural networks*. arXiv preprint arXiv:1511.08458.

Oakleaf, M. (2007). Using rubrics to collect evidence for decision-making: What do librarians need to learn? *Evidence Based Library and Information Practice*, *2*(3), 27–42. doi:10.18438/B8WS3W

Oikonomidis, A., Catal, C., & Kassahun, A. (2022). Hybrid deep learning-based models for crop yield prediction. *Applied Artificial Intelligence*, *36*(1), 2031822. doi:10.1080/08839514.2022.2031823

Ojha, A., Jindal, A., & Chanak, P. (2023). An intelligent indoor emergency evacuation system using IOT-enabled WSNS for smart buildings. *IEEE Internet of Things Journal*, •••, 1–1. doi:10.1109/jiot.2023.3321646

Okunlaya, R. O., Syed Abdullah, N., & Alias, R. A. (2022). Artificial intelligence (AI) library services innovative conceptual framework for the digital transformation of university education. *Library Hi Tech*, *40*(6), 1869–1892. doi:10.1108/LHT-07-2021-0242

Olsen, Konovalov, Philippa, Ridd, Wood, Johns, Banks, Girgenti, Kenny, Whinney, Calvert, Azghadi, & White. (2019, December). DeepWeeds: A Multiclass Weed Species Image Dataset for Deep Learning. *Scientific Reports*, *9*(1), 2058. PMID:30765729

Omame, I. M., & Alex-Nmecha, J. C. (2020). Artificial intelligence in libraries. In *Managing and adapting library information services for future users* (pp. 120–144). IGI Global. doi:10.4018/978-1-7998-1116-9.ch008

Ortigueira, R., Fraire, J. A., Becerra, A., Ferrer, T., & Cespedes, S. (2021). RESS-IoT: A scalable energy-efficient MAC protocol for direct-to-satellite IoT. *IEEE Access : Practical Innovations, Open Solutions*, *9*, 164440–164453. doi:10.1109/ACCESS.2021.3134246

Osborne Clarke, L. L. P. (2016). *Legal study on ownership and access to data: A study prepared for the European Commission DG Communications Networks*. Content & Technology.

Owens, H. (2022). AI Experts are in Short Supply. That's Making the Skills Crisis Worse. *ZD Net/Business*. Available on: https://www.zdnet.com/article/ai-experts-are-in-short-supply-thats-making-the-skills-crisis-worse/

Owens, N., & Thomas, C. (2019). The Future of Cataloging in a FOLIO Environment. *The Serials Librarian*, *76*(1), 66–71. doi:10.1080/0361526X.2019.1579692

Oyelude, A. A. (2021). AI and libraries: Trends and projections. *Library Hi Tech News*, *38*(10), 1–4. doi:10.1108/LHTN-10-2021-0079

Palanikkumar, D., Mary, P. A., & Begum, A. Y. (2023). A Novel IoT Framework and Device Architecture for Efficient Smart city Implementation. *2023 7th International Conference on Trends in Electronics and Informatics (ICOEI)*, 420-426.

Pallavi Asrodia & Sharma. (2013). Network Monitoring and Analysis by Packet Sniffing Method. *International Journal of Engineering Trends and Technology*.

Palmberg, K. (2009). Exploring process management: Are there any widespread models and definitions? *The TQM Journal*, *21*(2), 203–215. doi:10.1108/17542730910938182

Panigrahi, B., Kathala, K. C. R., & Sujatha, M. (2023). A machine learning-based comparative approach to predict the crop yield using supervised learning with regression models. *Procedia Computer Science*, *218*, 2684–2693. doi:10.1016/j.procs.2023.01.241

Paradissis, J. J. (2005). *The right to access environmental information: An analysis of UK law in the context of international, European, and comparative law* [PhD thesis]. City University, London.

Pasco, X. (2008). Study on suitable governance and Data Policy models for a European Space Situational Awareness (SSA) System. Contract n° 21443/08/F/MOS, European Space Agency.

paulderscheid. (2021, September 15). *Implications of the transition towards library services platforms*. https://medium.com/@paulderscheid/implications-of-the-transition-towards-library-services-platforms-7ad7f62034d6

Paulk, M., Curtis, B., Chrissis, M., & Weber, Ch. (1993). Capability maturity model, version 1.1. *IEEE Software*, *10*(4), 18–27. doi:10.1109/52.219617

Paul, M., Vishwakarma, S. K., & Verma, A. (2015, December). Analysis of soil behaviour and prediction of crop yield using data mining approach. In *2015 International Conference on Computational Intelligence and Communication Networks (CICN)* (pp. 766-771). IEEE. 10.1109/CICN.2015.156

Pavlidis, G., Koutsoudis, A., Arnaoutoglou, F., Tsioukas, V., & Chamzas, C. (2007). Methods for 3D Digitization of Cultural Heritage. *Journal of Cultural Heritage*, *8*(1), 93–98. doi:10.1016/j.culher.2006.10.007

Pawar, M. S., Perianayagam, L., & Rani, N. S. (2017, June). Region based image classification using watershed transform techniques. In *2017 International Conference on Intelligent Computing and Control (I2C2)* (pp. 1-5). IEEE. 10.1109/I2C2.2017.8321839

Pearline, S. A., Kumar, V. S., & Harini, S. (2019). A study on plant recognition using conventional image processing and deep learning approaches. *Journal of Intelligent & Fuzzy Systems*, (Preprint), 1-8.

Pedersoli, S., & Presbitero, A. F. (2023). Public Debt Management and private financial development. *Economic Systems*, *47*(1), 101010. doi:10.1016/j.ecosys.2022.101010

Pehlivanoglou, K. G., Rappou, M., & Martsoukou, M. (2006). Geological and oceanographic data determining the foreshore zone according to the Greek legislation. *Mediterranean Marine Science*, *7*(1), 15–26. doi:10.12681/mms.174

Peñas Lado, E. (2012). *The common fisheries policy: The quest for sustainability*. Wiley.

Peng, B., & Potipiroon, W. (2022). Fear of losing jobs during COVID-19: Can psychological capital alleviate job insecurity and job stress? *Behavioral Sciences (Basel, Switzerland)*, *12*(6), 168. doi:10.3390/bs12060168

Peng, G., Privette, J., Kearns, E., Ritchey, N., & Ansari, S. (2015). A unified framework for measuring stewardship practices applied to digital environmental datasets. *Data Science Journal*, *13*(0), 231–253. doi:10.2481/dsj.14-049

Petter, S., DeLone, W., & McLean, E. (2008). Measuring information systems success: Models, dimensions, measures, and interrelationships. *European Journal of Information Systems, 17*(3), 236–263. doi:10.1057/ejis.2008.15

Phung, K. A., Kirbas, C., Dereci, L., & Nguyen, T. V. (2022). Pervasive Healthcare internet of things: A survey. *Information (Basel), 13*(8), 360. doi:10.3390/info13080360

Planning Commission Government of India. (2013). *Press Notes on Poverty Estimates 2011-12*. Press Information Bureau, Planning Commission.

Popham, J. (2003). *Test better, teach better: the instructional role of assessment*. Assoc. for Supervision and Curriculum Development.

Pöppelbuß, J., & Röglinger, M. (2011). What makes a useful maturity model? A framework for general design principles for maturity models and its demonstration in business process management. In V. Tuunainen (Ed.), *Proceedings of the 19th European Conference on Information Systems*. https://fim-rc.de/Paperbibliothek/Verorffentlicht/327/wi-327.pdf

Pouliakas, K. (2018). *Determinants of automation risk in the EU labour market: A skills-needs approach*. IZA Discussion paper series, No. 11829. Bonn: Institute of Labor Economics (IZA). http://ftp.iza.org/dp11829.pdf

Pradhan, P. (2021). Library Services Platform (LSP): An Overview. *INFLIBNET, 26*(1), 12–22. https://www.researchgate.net/publication/333816851

Prasad, K., Dekka, S., Tanguturi, R. c., & Poornima, G. (2022). An Intelligent System for Remote Monitoring of Patients Health and the Early Detection of Coronary Artery Disease. *2022 International Conference on Smart Generation Computing, Communication and Networking (SMART GENCON)*, 1-6.

Prasad, S., & Singh, P. P. (2017). Medicinal plant leaf information extraction using deep features. TENCON 2017 - 2017 IEEE Region 10 Conference, 2722–2726. doi:10.1109/TENCON.2017.8228324

Prasad, S., Kumar, P., & Tripathi, R. C. (2011, September). Plant leaf species identification using curvelet transform. In *2011 2nd International Conference on Computer and Communication Technology (ICCCT-2011)* (pp. 646-652). IEEE. 10.1109/ICCCT.2011.6075212

Prasad, K., Anil Kumar, N., Reddy, N. S., & Ashreetha, B. (2023). Technologies for Comprehensive Information Security in the IoT. *2023 International Conference for Advancement in Technology (ICONAT)*, 1-5.

Prasad, S., Kiran, R., & Sharma, R. K. (2020). Influence of financial literacy on retail investors' decisions in relation to return, risk and market analysis. *International Journal of Finance & Economics, 26*(2), 2548–2559. doi:10.1002/ijfe.1920

Pratono, A. H., Nawangpalupi, C. B., & Sutanti, A. (2023). Achieving Sustainable Development Goals through digitalising creative works: Some evidence from social enterprises in Indonesia. *Digital Economy and Sustainable Development, 1*(1). Advance online publication. doi:10.100744265-023-00011-4

Prema, P., Veeramani, A., & Sivakumar, T. (n.d.). Machine Learning Applications in Agriculture. *Journal of Agriculture Research and Technology*, 126.

Priya, A., & Sahana, S. K. (2020). Multi-Processor Job Scheduling in High-Performance Computing (HPC) Systems. *FPGA Algorithms and Applications for the Internet of Things*, 168–203. . doi:10.4018/978-1-5225-9806-0.ch009

Priya, A., & Sahana, S. K. (2020). Processor Scheduling in High-Performance Computing (HPC) Environment. *Emerging Trends and Impacts of the Internet of Things in Libraries*, 151–179. . doi:10.4018/978-1-7998-4742-7.ch009

Priya, A., Sharma, S., Sinha, K., & Yogesh, Y. (2023, March). Community Detection in Networks: A Comparative study. In *2023 International Conference on Device Intelligence, Computing and Communication Technologies (DICCT)* (pp. 505-510). IEEE. 10.1109/DICCT56244.2023.10110206

Priya, C. A., Balasaravanan, T., & Thanamani, A. S. (2012, March). An efficient leaf recognition algorithm for plant classification using support vector machine. In *International conference on pattern recognition, informatics and medical engineering (PRIME-2012)* (pp. 428-432). IEEE. 10.1109/ICPRIME.2012.6208384

Priya, A., & Sahana, S. K. (2020). Multiprocessor Scheduling Based on Evolutionary Technique for Solving Permutation Flow Shop Problem. *IEEE Access : Practical Innovations, Open Solutions*, *8*, 53151–53161. doi:10.1109/ACCESS.2020.2973575

Probst, C. W., Hunker, J., Bishop, M., & Gollmann, D. (Eds.). (2010). *Insider threats in cyber security* (Vol. 49). Springer Science & Business Media. doi:10.1007/978-1-4419-7133-3_1

Probst, G., Raub, S., & Romhardt, K. (2002). *Gestão do conhecimento: os elementos construtivos do sucesso.* Bookman.

Proença, D., & Borbinha, J. (2016). Maturity models for information systems – a state of the art. *Procedia Computer Science*, *100*, 1042–1049. doi:10.1016/j.procs.2016.09.279

Pvloiu, Ancuceanu, Enache, & Vasileanu. (2017). Important shape features for romanian medicinal herb identification based on leaf image. *2017 E-Health and Bioengineering Conference (EHB)*, 599–602.

PwC Report. (2023). Retrieved from https://www.pwc.com/gx/en/issues/analytics/assets/pwc-ai-analysis-sizing-the-prize-report.pdf

Qazi, S., Khawaja, B. A., & Farooq, Q. U. (2022). Iot-equipped and AI-enabled Next Generation Smart Agriculture: A Critical Review, current challenges and future trends. *IEEE Access : Practical Innovations, Open Solutions*, *10*, 21219–21235. doi:10.1109/access.2022.3152544

Qian, C., Liu, X., Ripley, C., Qian, M., Liang, F., & Yu, W. (2022). Digital Twin—cyber replica of Physical Things: Architecture, applications and future research directions. *Future Internet*, *14*(2), 64. doi:10.3390/fi14020064

Qin, J., Crowston, K., & Kirkland, A. (2017). Pursuing best performance in research data management by using the capability maturity model and rubrics. *Journal of Escience Librarianship*, *6*(2), e1113. doi:10.7191/jeslib.2017.1113

Quazi, T. A.-M., & Patel, S. S. (2023). Socio-Technical Systems Engineering Perspectives towards a South African halaal blockchain system. *Advances in Logistics, Operations, and Management Science*, •••, 287–309. doi:10.4018/978-1-6684-7455-6.ch014

Quoc & Hoang. (2020). Vnplant-200–a public and large-scale of Vietnamese medicinal plant images dataset. In *International Conference on Integrated Science* (pp. 406–411). Springer.

Ram Vishal, Shankar, & K. A. M. (2023). Cardiovascular Disease Prediction Using LSTM Algorithm based On Cytokines. *2023 4th International Conference for Emerging Technology (INCET)*, 1-5.

Raman. (2020, March 24). *Monolithic vs Microservices architecture.* GeeksforGeeks. https://www.geeksforgeeks.org/monolithic-vs-microservices-architecture/

Ramesh Naidu, P., Guruprasad, N., & Dankan Gowda, V. (2020). Design and implementation of cryptcloud system for securing files in cloud. *Adv. Math. Sci. J.*, *9*(7), 4485–4493. doi:10.37418/amsj.9.7.17

Ramesh Naidu, P., Guruprasad, N., & Dankan Gowda, V. (2021). A High-Availability and Integrity Layer for Cloud Storage, Cloud Computing Security: From Single to Multi-Clouds. *Journal of Physics: Conference Series, 1921*(1), 012072. doi:10.1088/1742-6596/1921/1/012072

Rampersad, G. (2020). Robot will take your job: Innovation for an era of artificial intelligence. *Journal of Business Research, 116*, 68–74. doi:10.1016/j.jbusres.2020.05.019

Rao, B. K., Chaturvedi, A., & Hussain, N. (2022). Industrial quality healthcare services using Internet of Things and fog computing approach, Measurement. *Sensors (Basel), 24*, 100517.

Raorane, A., & Kulkarni, R. (2013). Role of data mining in Agriculture. *International Journal of Computer Science and Information Technologies*, *4*(2), 270–272.

Ravallion, M. (2000). What is needed for a more pro-poor growth process in India? *Economic and Political Weekly*, 1089–1093.

Ravallion, M., & Datt, G. (2002). Why has economic growth been more pro-poor in some states of India than others? *Journal of Development Economics*, *68*(2), 381–400. doi:10.1016/S0304-3878(02)00018-4

Rawat, G. S., & Singh, K. (2019). Beacon inter-reception time based adaptive beaconing (BIRA) for congestion-aware vehicular networks. *Journal of Discrete Mathematical Sciences and Cryptography, 22*(8), 1477-1487.

Rawat, G. S., & Singh, K. (2019). Detection and prevention of vulnerabilities in open source software: An experimental study. In *Communication and Computing Systems* (pp. 297–303). CRC Press. doi:10.1201/9780429444272-48

Rawat, G. S., & Singh, K. (2023). A bayesian-based distributed trust management scheme for connected vehicles' security. *Peer-to-Peer Networking and Applications*, *16*(5), 1–17. doi:10.100712083-023-01515-8

Rawat, G. S., & Singh, K. (2023). Evaluation and Optimization of a Congestion Control Scheme for Vanets. In *Advanced Computer Science Applications* (pp. 351–363). Apple Academic Press. doi:10.1201/9781003369066-29

Ray, R., & Sinha, K. (2014). Rangarajan committee report on poverty measurement: Another lost opportunity. *Economic and Political Weekly*, 43–48.

Reddy, S., & Patwal, P. P. S. (2022). Data Analytics and Cloud-Based Platform for Internet of Things Applications in Smart Cities. *2022 International Conference on Industry 4.0 Technology (I4Tech),* 1-6.

Reddy, S., & Patwal, P. P. S. (2022). Data Analytics and Cloud-Based Platform for Internet of Things Applications in Smart Cities. *2022 International Conference on Industry 4.0 Technology (I4Tech)*, 1-6.

Reed, G. (2012). IODE Quality Management Framework for National Oceanographic Data Centres. Presented at *Twenty-second Session of the IOC Committee on International Oceanographic Data and Information Exchange (IODE-XXII)*, Ensenada, Mexico.

Reichelt, J., Sievert, J., & Jacob, F. (2014). Jacob. *Journal of Marketing Communications*, *20*(1–2), 65–81. doi:10.1080/13527266.2013.797758

Reichman, J. H., & Uhlir, P. F. (2003). A contractually reconstructed research commons for scientific data in a highly protectionist intellectual property environment. *Law and Contemporary Problems*, *66*, 315–462.

Rekhis, S., Krichene, J., & Boudriga, N. (2018). DigForNet: digital forensic in networking. In *IFIP TC-11 23rd international information security conference* (vol. 278). Springer.

Ren, W. (2004) On a network forensics model for information security. *3rd international conference on Information Systems Technology and its Applications (ISTA 2004)*, 229–234.

ReportG. S. (2023). Retrieved from https://www.goldmansachs.com/intelligence/pages/generative-ai-could-raise-global-gdp-by-7-percent.html

Revanna, Kameswara Rao, & Sarma. (2022). Enhanced Diagnostic Methods for Identifying Anomalies in Imaging of Skin Lesions. *IJEER 10*(4), 1077-1085.

Rigatti, S. J. (2017). Random forest. *Journal of Insurance Medicine (New York, N.Y.)*, *47*(1), 31–39. doi:10.17849/insm-47-01-31-39.1 PMID:28836909

Robinson, R. R. R., & Thomas, C. (2015). *Ranking of machine learning algorithms based on the performance in classifying DDoS attacks. In 2015 IEEE Recent Advances in Intelligent Computational Systems*. RAICS.

Rogers, E. (2003). *Diffusion of innovations* (5th ed.). Free Press.

Ruminski, J. (2007). Security of Distributed Processing of Medical Image Data Using JINI Technology. *2007 29th Annual International Conference of the IEEE Engineering in Medicine and Biology Society*. 10.1109/IEMBS.2007.4353630

Russakovsky, Deng, Su, Krause, Satheesh, Ma, Huang, Karpathy, Khosla, Bernstein, Berg, & Fei-Fei. (2015, December). ImageNet Large Scale Visual Recognition Challenge. *International Journal of Computer Vision*, *115*(3), 211–252.

Sabir, S. A., Mohammad, H. B., & Shahar, H. B. (2019). The Role of Overconfidence and Past Investment Experience in Herding Behaviour with a Moderating Effect of Financial Literacy: Evidence from Pakistan Stock Exchange. *Asian Economic and Financial Review*, *9*(4), 480–490. doi:10.18488/journal.aefr.2019.94.480.490

Sabu, A., Sreekumar, K., & Nair, R. R. (2017). Recognition of ayurvedic medicinal plants from leaves: A computer vision approach. *2017 Fourth International Conference on Image Information Processing (ICIIP)*, 1–5. 10.1109/ICIIP.2017.8313782

Sahi, S. K., Arora, A. P., & Dhameja, N. (2013). An exploratory inquiry into the psychological biases in financial investment behavior. *Journal of Behavioral Finance*, *14*(2), 94–103. doi:10.1080/15427560.2013.790387

Said, O., Al-Makhadmeh, Z., & Tolba, A. M. R. (2020). EMS: An energy management scheme for green IoT environments. *IEEE Access : Practical Innovations, Open Solutions*, *8*, 44983–44998. doi:10.1109/ACCESS.2020.2976641

Salima, A., Herdiyeni, Y., & Douady, S. (2015). Leaf vein segmentation of medicinal plant using hessian matrix. *2015 International Conference on Advanced Computer Science and Information Systems (ICACSIS)*, 275–279. 10.1109/ICACSIS.2015.7415152

Salleh, S. Z., & Bushroa, A. R. (2022). Bibliometric analysis on the implementation digitization technologies in cultural heritage in Malaysia. *Geografia : Malaysian Journal of Society and Space*, *18*(2), 287–300. doi:10.17576/geo-2022-1802-22

Samaila, M. G., Sequeiros, J. B., Simoes, T., Freire, M. M., & Inacio, P. R. (2020). IoT-HarPSecA: A framework and roadmap for secure design and development of devices and applications in the IoT space. *IEEE Access : Practical Innovations, Open Solutions*, *8*, 16462–16494. doi:10.1109/ACCESS.2020.2965925

SambyalS.AroraB. (2023). Hybrid Security Model for Securing Healthcare Data on Cloud. https://doi.org/ doi:10.21203/rs.3.rs-2908979/v1

Samuel, K. C. (2022). Optimizing the internet despite threat to IP: How Fashion Designers in Nigeria are leveraging digital media platforms for market entry and growth. *Advanced Journal of Social Science*, *10*(1), 1–13. doi:10.21467/ajss.10.1.1-13

Santos, C. D., & Valentim, M. L. P. (2014). As interconexões entre a gestão da informação e a gestão do conhecimento para o gerenciamento dos fluxos informacionais. *Perspectivas em Gestão & Conhecimento, 4*(2), 19-33. Disponível em: http://hdl.handle.net/20.500.11959/brapci/49728

Santos, R., Borges, M., Canós, J., & Gomes, J. (2011). The assessment of information technology maturity in emergency response organization. *Group Decision and Negotiation*, *20*(5), 593–613. doi:10.100710726-011-9232-z

Sarkar, Podder, & Roy. (2023). An Analysis of the Privacy and Security Related Problem with Social Networks. *ESP Journal of Engineering & Technology Advancements, 3*(2).

Schaap, D. (2014). SeaDataNet II - EMODNet - building a pan-European infrastructure for marine and ocean data management. *Geophysical Research Abstracts*, *16*, EGU2014–EGU2735.

Schaap, D. M., Novellino, A., Fichaut, M., & Manzella, G. M. (2022). Data management infrastructures and their practices in Europe. In *Ocean Science Data* (pp. 131–193). Elsevier. doi:10.1016/B978-0-12-823427-3.00007-4

Scheibner, J., Ienca, M., Kechagia, S., Troncoso-Pastoriza, J. R., Raisaro, J. L., Hubaux, J. P., Fellay, J., & Vayena, E. (2020). Data protection and ethics requirements for multisite research with health data: A comparative examination of legislative governance frameworks and the role of data protection technologies. *Journal of Law and the Biosciences*, *7*(1), lsaa010. doi:10.1093/jlb/lsaa010 PMID:32733683

Schneier, B. (2015). *Secrets and lies: digital security in a networked world*. John Wiley & Sons. doi:10.1002/9781119183631

Schroeder, A., Naik, P., Ziaee Bigdeli, A., & Baines, T. (2020). Digitally enabled advanced services: A socio-technical perspective on the role of the internet of things (IOT). *International Journal of Operations &amp. Production Management*, *40*(7/8), 1243–1268. doi:10.1108/ijopm-03-2020-0131

Schubert, E., Sander, J., Ester, M., Kriegel, H. P., & Xu, X. (2017). DBSCAN revisited, revisited: Why and how you should (still) use DBSCAN. *ACM Transactions on Database Systems*, *42*(3), 1–21. doi:10.1145/3068335

Schucmacker, R. E., & Lomax, R. G. (2016). *A Beginner's Guide to Structural Equation Modeling* (4th ed.). Routledge.

Schuster, F., & Habibipour, A. (2022). Users' privacy and security concerns that affect IOT adoption in the home domain. *International Journal of Human-Computer Interaction*, •••, 1–12. doi:10.1080/10447318.2022.2147302

Scott, J. (2007). Mobility, business process management, software sourcing, and maturity model trends: Propositions for the IS organization of the future. *Information Systems Management*, *24*(2), 139–145. doi:10.1080/10580530701221031

Seip, C., & Bill, R. (2016). A framework for the evaluation of marine spatial data infrastructures - accompanied by international case-studies. *GeoScience Engineering*, *62*(2), 27–43. doi:10.1515/gse-2016-0015

Selam, M. N., & Ababu, A. (2021). Extemporaneous Compounding Practice for dermatologic preparations in Ethiopian Public Hospitals: Regulatory Requirements and quality concerns. *Risk Management and Healthcare Policy*, *14*, 1933–1938. doi:10.2147/rmhp.s300906

Sen, A. (1993). Capability and well-being. *The Quality of Life, 30*, 270-293.

Sen, A. (2005). Human rights and capabilities. *Journal of Human Development*, *6*(2), 151–166. doi:10.1080/14649880500120491

Sen, A., Ramammurthy, K., & Sinha, A. (2012). A model of data warehousing process maturity. *IEEE Transactions on Software Engineering*, *38*(2), 336–353. doi:10.1109/TSE.2011.2

Shanmugasundaram, K., Memon, N., Savant, A., & Bronnimann, H. (2003). ForNet: a distributed forensics network. In V. Gorodetsky, L. Popyack, & V. Skormin (Eds.), *Computer network security* (Vol. 2776, pp. 1–16). Springer. doi:10.1007/978-3-540-45215-7_1

Shareef, M., Kumar, V., Kumar, U., & Dwivedi, Y. (2011). E-Government adoption model (GAM): Differing service maturity levels. *Government Information Quarterly*, *28*(1), 17–35. doi:10.1016/j.giq.2010.05.006

Sharma & Sabitha. (2019). Identification of influential factors for productivity and sustainability of crops using data mining techniques. *6th International Conference on Signal Processing and Integrated Networks (SPIN).*

Sharma, A., Jain, A., Gupta, P., & Chowdary, V. (2020). Machine learning applications for precision agriculture: A comprehensive review. *IEEE Access : Practical Innovations, Open Solutions*, *9*, 4843–4873. doi:10.1109/ACCESS.2020.3048415

Sharma, V., & Hashmi, M. (2021). On the seamless integration and co-existence of chipless RFID in broad IOT framework. *IEEE Access : Practical Innovations, Open Solutions*, *9*, 69839–69849. doi:10.1109/access.2021.3078318

Sharpe, A. (2001). Estimates of relative and absolute poverty rates for the working population in developed countries. In Meeting of the Canadian Economics Association, Montreal, Canada.

Sheikhshoaei, F., Naghshineh, N., Alidousti, S., & Nakhoda, M. (2018). Design of a digital library maturity model (DLMM). *The Electronic Library*, *36*(4), 607–619. doi:10.1108/EL-05-2017-0114

Sheikhshoaei, F., Naghshineh, N., Alidousti, S., Nakhoda, M., & Dehdarirad, H. (2021). Development and validation of a measuring instrument for digital library maturity. *Library & Information Science Research*, *43*(3), 101101. doi:10.1016/j.lisr.2021.101101

Shettar & Angadi. (2016). Efficient data mining algorithms for agriculture data. *International Journal of Recent Trends in Engineering and Research, 2*(9).

Shin, D. (2014). A socio-technical framework for internet-of-things design: A human-centered design for the internet of things. *Telematics and Informatics*, *31*(4), 519–531. doi:10.1016/j.tele.2014.02.003

Shram, M. M. (2021). Data Processing by end devices in IOT Systems. *Connectivity*, *153*(5). Advance online publication. doi:10.31673/2412-9070.2021.052428

Shrivastava, G., & Gupta, B. B. (2014). An Encapsulated Approach of Forensic Model for digital investigation. *2014 IEEE 3rd Global Conference on Consumer Electronics (GCCE)*, 280–284. 10.1109/GCCE.2014.7031241

Siahaan, Y., & Gunawan, F. (2021). Measuring level of information and communication technology literacy of university students in Indonesia. *Advances in Economics. Business and Management Research*, *168*, 242–245.

Simoncelli, S., Manzella, G. M. R., Storto, A., Pisano, A., Lipizer, M., & Barth, A. (2022). A collaborative framework among data producers, managers, and users. In *Ocean Science Data* (pp. 197–280). Elsevier. doi:10.1016/B978-0-12-823427-3.00001-3

Simonyan & Zisserman. (2015). *Very Deep Convolutional Networks for Large-Scale Image Recognition.* arXiv: 1409.1556.

Singh, R., & Bhattacharjee, J. (2019). Measuring Equity Share Related Risk Perception of Investors in Economically Backward Regions. *Risks*, *7*(1), 12. doi:10.3390/risks7010012

Sinha, K. (2022). *Development of Enhanced Cryptography Based Model for Multimedia Security in Distributed Environment.* Academic Press.

Sinha, K. (2023). The Metaverse and Digital Libraries: Ensuring Safe and Secure Access to Information. In Handbook of Research on Advancements of Contactless Technology and Service Innovation in Library and Information Science (pp. 1-22). IGI Global.

Sinha, K., Choudhary, S., Paul, S., & Paul, P. (2018, September). Security of Multimedia in Cloud using Secret Shared Key. In *2018 International Conference on Computing, Power and Communication Technologies (GUCON)* (pp. 908-912). IEEE. 10.1109/GUCON.2018.8675031

Sinha, K., & Paul, P. (2021). Randomized Block Size (RBS) Model for Secure Data Storage in Distributed Server. *KSII Transactions on Internet and Information Systems*, *15*(12).

Sinha, K., & Paul, P. (2022). An Improved Pseudorandom Sequence Generator and its Application to Image Encryption. *KSII Transactions on Internet and Information Systems*, *16*(4).

Sinha, K., Priya, A., & Paul, P. (2020). K-RSA: Secure data storage technique for multimedia in cloud data server. *Journal of Intelligent & Fuzzy Systems*, *39*(3), 3297–3314. doi:10.3233/JIFS-191687

Sivaramakrishnan, S., Srivastava, M., & Rastogi, A. (2017). Attitudinal factors, financial literacy, and stock market participation. *International Journal of Bank Marketing*, *35*(5), 818–841. doi:10.1108/IJBM-01-2016-0012

Soderkvist. (2001). *Computer Vision Classification of Leaves from Swedish Trees* [Dissertation].

Sony, M., & Naik, S. (2020). Industry 4.0 integration with socio-technical systems theory: A systematic review and proposed theoretical model. *Technology in Society*, *61*, 101248. doi:10.1016/j.techsoc.2020.101248

Sousa, J. P., Cordeiro, P., & Cunha, C. R. (2022). The use of technologies in museums: A bibliometric analysis based on the Web of Science database. *Advanced Research in the Technologies, Information Innovation and Sustainability*, *1676*(PT II), 269–282.

Stamoulis, K. A., & Delevaux, J. M. S. (2015). Data requirements and tools to operationalize marine spatial planning in the United States. *Ocean and Coastal Management*, *116*, 214–223. doi:10.1016/j.ocecoaman.2015.07.011

Sternkopf, H., & Mueller, R. (2018). Doing good with data: development of a maturity model for data literacy in non-governmental organizations. In T. Bui (Ed.), *Proceedings of the 51st Hawaii Intern. Conference on System Sciences (HICSS-51)*, (pp. 5045-5054). Univ. of Hawaii at Manoa. 10.24251/HICSS.2018.630

Stevens, J. P. (1992). *Applied Multivariate Statistics for the Social Sciences* (2nd ed.). Erlbaum.

Stollenwerk, M. F. (2001). L. Gestão do conhecimento: conceitos e modelos. In *Inteligência organizacional e competitiva* (pp. 143–163). Editora UnB.

Suárez de Vivero, J. L., & Rodríguez Mateos, J. C. (2012). The Spanish approach to marine spatial planning. Marine Strategy Framework Directive vs. EU Integrated Maritime Policy. *Marine Policy*, *36*(1), 18–27. doi:10.1016/j.marpol.2011.03.002

Sullivan, K. M. (2020). Documenting Sea Change: Ocean Data Technologies, Sciences, and Governance. *Environment and Society*, *11*(1), 82–99. doi:10.3167/ares.2020.110106

Summers, L. H. (1986). Does the stock market rationally reflect fundamental values? *The Journal of Finance*, *41*(3), 591–601. doi:10.1111/j.1540-6261.1986.tb04519.x

Sun, R., & Meng, J. (2022). Looking at young millennials' risk perception and purchase intention toward GM foods: Exploring the role of source credibility and risk attitude. *Health Marketing Quarterly*, *39*(3), 263–279. doi:10.1080/07359683.2022.2053805 PMID:35343385

Suresh, A., Kumar, P. G., & Ramalatha, M. (2018, October). Prediction of major crop yields of Tamilnadu using K-means and Modified KNN. In *2018 3rd International conference on communication and electronics systems (ICCES)* (pp. 88-93). IEEE.

Suthaharan, S., & Suthaharan, S. (2016). Support vector machine. *Machine learning models and algorithms for big data classification: Thinking with examples for effective learning*, 207-235.

Su, X., Yan, X., & Tsai, C. L. (2012). Linear regression. *Wiley Interdisciplinary Reviews: Computational Statistics, 4*(3), 275–294. doi:10.1002/wics.1198

Swathi Pai, Shruthi, & Naveen. (2020). Internet of Things: A Survey on Devices, Ecosystem, Components and Communication Protocols. *2020 4th International Conference on Electronics, Communication and Aerospace Technology (ICECA)*, 611-616.

Symes, D. (1997). The European Community's Common Fisheries Policy. *Ocean and Coastal Management, 35*(2-3), 137–155. doi:10.1016/S0964-5691(97)00030-6

Szczepański, M. (2018). *Economic impacts of artificial intelligence (AI)*. EPRS | European Parliamentary Research Service.

Szegedy, Ioffe, Vanhoucke, & Alemi. (2017). Inception-v4, inception-resnet and the impact of residual connections on learning. In *Proceedings of the Thirty-First AAAI Conference on Artificial Intelligence, AAAI'17* (pp. 4278–4284). AAAI Press.

Szegedy, Liu, Jia, Sermanet, Reed, Anguelov, Erhan, Vanhoucke, & Rabinovich. (2015). Going deeper with convolutions. In *2015 IEEE Conference on Computer Vision and Pattern Recognition (CVPR)* (pp. 1–9). IEEE.

Taherdoost, H., Sahibuddin, S., & Jalaliyoon, N. (2014). Exploratory Factor Analysis; Concepts and Theory. Jerzy Balicki. *Advances in Applied and Pure Mathematics, 27*, 375-382. doi:10.1093/mind/LIX.236.433

Takeuchi, H., & Nonaka, I. (2008). *Gestão do conhecimento*. Bookman.

Tanguturi, S. R. C. K., & V. C. H. (2023). Implementation of Machine Learning Approach for Detecting Cardiovascular Diseases. *2023 3rd International Conference on Intelligent Technologies (CONIT)*, 1-6.

Tang, Y., & Daniels, T. E. (2015) A simple framework for distributed forensics. *25th IEEE International Conference on Distributed Computing Systems Workshops (ICDCS 15)*, 163–169.

Tanhua, T., Pouliquen, S., Hausman, J., O'Brien, K., Bricher, P., De Bruin, T., Buck, J. J. H., Burger, E. F., Carval, T., Casey, K. S., Diggs, S., Giorgetti, A., Glaves, H., Harscoat, V., Kinkade, D., Muelbert, J. H., Novellino, A., Pfeil, B., Pulsifer, P. L., ... Zhao, Z. (2019). Ocean FAIR data services. *Frontiers in Marine Science, 6*, 440. doi:10.3389/fmars.2019.00440

Taqi, F., Batool, S. H., & Arshad, A. (2023). Examining differences in perceived usability of Google Drive among Public Library Users. *Library Hi Tech*. Advance online publication. doi:10.1108/lht-05-2022-0275

Tariq, U., Ahmed, I., Bashir, A. K., & Shaukat, K. (2023). A critical cybersecurity analysis and future research directions for the internet of things: A comprehensive review. *Sensors (Basel), 23*(8), 4117. doi:10.339023084117

Taylor, M. P. (2021). Modularity in FOLIO: Principles, techniques and tools. *International Journal of Librarianship, 6*(2), 3–12. doi:10.23974/ijol.2021.vol6.2.208

Teplitzky, S. (2017). Open data, [open] access: Linking data sharing and article sharing in the Earth Sciences. *Journal of Librarianship and Scholarly Communication, 5*(1). Advance online publication. doi:10.7710/2162-3309.2150

Terra, J. C. C. (2001). *Gestão do conhecimento: o grande desafio empresarial. 3*. Negócio.

Thakur, K., Qiu, M., Gai, K., & Ali, M. L. (2015, November). An investigation on cyber security threats and security models. In *2015 IEEE 2nd international conference on cyber security and cloud computing* (pp. 307-311). IEEE. 10.1109/CSCloud.2015.71

Thelwall, M. (2008). Bibliometrics to webometrics. *Journal of Information Science, 34*(4), 605–621. doi:10.1177/0165551507087238

Thuraisingham, B., & Ford, W. (1995). Security constraint processing in a multilevel secure distributed database management system. *IEEE Transactions on Knowledge and Data Engineering, 7*(2), 274–293. doi:10.1109/69.382297

Tidd, J., Bessant, J., & Pavitt, K. (2008). *Gestão da Inovação. 3.* Bookman.

Tigre, P. B. (2006). *Gestão da inovação: a economia da tecnologia do Brasil.* Elsevier.

Tipton, H. F., & Krause, M. (2006). *Information Security Management Handbook* (Vol. 3). Auerbach Publications.

Tyagi, K., Yadav, S. K., & Singh, M. (2021). Cloud data security and various security algorithms. *Journal of Physics: Conference Series, 1998*(1), 012023. doi:10.1088/1742-6596/1998/1/012023

Tzitzikas, Y., Marketakis, Y., Minadakis, N., Mountantonakis, M., Candela, L., & Mangiacrapa, F. (2019). Methods and tools for supporting the integration of stocks and fisheries. In *Information and Communication Technologies in Modern Agricultural Development: 8th International Conference, HAICTA 2017, Chania, Crete, Greece, September 21–24, 2017, Revised Selected Papers 8* (pp. 20-34). Springer International Publishing. 10.1007/978-3-030-12998-9_2

U. K. N., & R. V. M. (2022). Arduino based COVID-19 Suspect Detection Device. *2022 6th International Conference on Electronics, Communication and Aerospace Technology,* 158-163.

Ugwuanyi, S., Paul, G., & Irvine, J. (2021). Survey of IOT for developing countries: Performance analysis of lorawan and cellular Nb-IOT Networks. *Electronics (Basel), 10*(18), 2224. doi:10.3390/electronics10182224

United Nations. (2022). *World Economic Situation and Prospects 2022.* https://www.un.org/development/desa/dpad/wp-content/uploads/sites/45/WESP2022_ANNEX.pdf

Uryadova, T., & Leshcheva, M. (2022). Analytical tools to justify investment decisions. *Research of Economic and Financial Problems,* (3), 1–10. doi:10.31279/2782-6414-2022-3-7-1-10

Uzun, M., & Abul, O. (2016). End-to-end internet speed analysis of mobile networks with mapReduce. *2016 International Symposium on Networks, Computers and Communications, ISNCC 2016.* 10.1109/ISNCC.2016.7746114

Valentim, M. L. P. (2013). *Gestão da informação e gestão do conhecimento: especificidades e convergências.* Infohome. Disponível em: https://www.ofaj.com.br/colunas_conteudo.php?cod=88

Valentim, M. L. P. (2008). Informação e conhecimento em organizações complexas. In *Gestão da informação e do conhecimento no âmbito da Ciência da Informação* (pp. 11–26). Polis/Cultura Acadêmica.

Van Eck, N. J., & Waltman, L. (2010). Software survey: Vosviewer, A computer program for bibliometric mapping. *Scientometrics, 84*(2), 523–538. doi:10.100711192-009-0146-3 PMID:20585380

Vanitha, C. N., Archana, N., & Sowmiya, R. (2019). Agriculture analysis using data mining and machine learning techniques. In *5th International Conference on Advanced Computing & Communication Systems (ICACCS).* IEEE.

Varinlioğlu, G., Alankuş, G., Aslankan, A., & Mura, G. (2019). Oyun Tabanlı Öğrenme ile Dijital Mirasın yaygınlaştırılması. *METU JFA, 36*(1), 23–40.

Velmurugan, C., & Kannan, M. (2012). Recent Growth and Developments in Open-Source Software on Digital Libraries in India. *Pearl. Journal of Library and Information Science, 6*(4), 173–178. doi:10.5958/j.0973-7081.6.4.019

Venkaiah & Sunitha. (2019). A new approach for predicting crop yield prediction using data mining techniques. *International Journal of Engineering, IT and Scientific Research, 3*(1).

Venkatakiran, S., Ashreetha, B., & Reddy, N. S. (2023). Implementation of a Machine Learning-based Model for Cardiovascular Disease Post Exposure prophylaxis. *2023 International Conference for Advancement in Technology (ICONAT)*, 1-5.

Venkataraman, D., & Mangayarkarasi, N. (2016). Computer vision based feature extraction of leaves for identification of medicinal values of plants. *2016 IEEE International Conference on Computational Intelligence and Computing Research (ICCIC)*, 1–5. 10.1109/ICCIC.2016.7919637

Venkatesh, R., & Singhal, T. K. (2022). Articulating Business Model Innovation, Digital Transformation and managed services: Case of Digital Transformation as a Service. *International Journal of Business and Globalisation*, *31*(4), 1. doi:10.1504/ijbg.2022.10040365

Venkatesh, V., Morris, M. G., Davis, G. B., & Davis, F. D. (2003). User Acceptance of Information Technology: Toward a Unified View. *Management Information Systems Quarterly*, *27*(3), 425–478. doi:10.2307/30036540

Verma, S., Kawamoto, Y., & Kato, N. (2021). A Network-Aware Internet-Wide Scan for Security Maximization of IPv6-Enabled WLAN IoT Devices. *IEEE Internet of Things Journal*, *8*(10), 8411–8422. doi:10.1109/JIOT.2020.3045733

VijayaLakshmi, B., & Mohan, V. (2016). Kernel- based PSO and FRVM: An automatic plant leaf type detection using texture, shape, and color features. *Computers and Electronics in Agriculture*, *125*, 99–112. doi:10.1016/j.compag.2016.04.033

Vinjosh Reddy, S., Sai Ramani, K., Rijutha, K., Mohammad Ali, S., & Pradeep Reddy, C. H. (2010). Wireless hacking-a WiFi hack by cracking WEP. *ICETC 2010 - 2010 2nd International Conference on Education Technology and Computer*, *1*. 10.1109/ICETC.2010.5529269

Vosviewer. (2023). *Visualizing scientific landscapes.* https://www.vosviewer.com/

Wagh, R., & Dongre, A. P. (2016). Agricultural sector: Status, challenges and it's role in Indian economy. *Journal of Commerce and Management Thought*, *7*(2), 209–218. doi:10.5958/0976-478X.2016.00014.8

Wang, C., Ahmad, S. F., Bani Ahmad Ayassrah, A. Y. A., Awwad, E. M., Irshad, M., Ali, Y. A., Al-Razgan, M., Khan, Y., & Han, H. (2023). An Empirical Evaluation of Technology Acceptance Model for Artificial Intelligence in E-commerce. *Heliyon*, *9*(8), e18349. doi:10.1016/j.heliyon.2023.e18349 PMID:37520947

Wang, C., Chi, C., Zhou, W., & Wong, R. (2015). Coupled Interdependent Attribute Analysis on Mixed Data. *Proc. Twenty-Ninth AAAI Conf. Artif. Intell. Coupled*, 1861–1867. 10.1609/aaai.v29i1.9480

Wang, D., Cao, W., Zhang, F., Li, Z., Xu, S., & Wu, X. (2022). A review of deep learning in multiscale agricultural sensing. *Remote Sensing (Basel)*, *14*(3), 559. doi:10.3390/rs14030559

Wang, D., Li, T., Liu, S., Zhang, J., & Liu, C. (2017). Dynamical network forensics based on immune agent. *Third International Conference on Natural Computation (ICNC 2017)*, 651–656.

Wang, Y., Liu, C., & Tu, Y. F. (2021). Factors Affecting the Adoption of AI-Based Applications in Higher Education: An Analysis of Teachers Perspectives Using Structural Equation Modeling. *Journal of Educational Technology & Society*, *24*(3), 116–129.

Wedajo, M., & Chekole, B. (2020). Attitude of employees towards change initiatives as influenced by commitment and job satisfaction: The case of selected higher education institutions in Ethiopia. *Journal of Process Management. Nuclear Technology*, *8*(3), 42–52. doi:10.5937/jouproman8-25868

Wedde, H. F., Farooq, M., & Zhang, Y. (2004). *BeeHive: An Efficient Fault-Tolerant Routing Algorithm Inspired by Honey Bee Behavior, Ant Colony, Optimization and Swarm Intelligence.* Lecture Notes in Computer Science. Springer Berlin.

Wei Tan, J., Chang, S. W., Abdul-Kareem, S., Yap, H. J., & Yong, K. T. (2018). Deep learning for plant species classification using leaf vein morphometric. *IEEE/ACM Transactions on Computational Biology and Bioinformatics*, *17*(1), 82–90. PMID:29994129

Weismueller, J., Harrigan, P., Wang, S., & Soutar, G. N. (2020). Influencer Endorsements: How Advertising Disclosure and Source Credibility Affect Consumer Purchase Intention on Social Media. *Australasian Marketing Journal*, *28*(4), 160–170. doi:10.1016/j.ausmj.2020.03.002

Wendler, R. (2012). The maturity of maturity model research: A systematic mapping study. *Information and Software Technology*, *54*(12), 1317–1339. doi:10.1016/j.infsof.2012.07.007

Wheatley, A., & Hervieux, S. (2019). Artificial Intelligence in Academic Libraries: An Environmental Scan. *Information Services & Use*, *39*(4), 347–356. doi:10.3233/ISU-190065

Wheeler, A. R., & Buckley, M. R. (2021). The current and future states of automation, artificial intelligence, and machine learning. In *HR without People?* (pp. 29–44). Emerald Publishing Limited. doi:10.1108/978-1-80117-037-620211003

Wicaksana, S. A., Purwoko, B., & Sihite, M. (2022). Role of organization culture on organizational agility for digital transformation in XYZ Government organization. *International Journal of Business Management and Economic Research*, *05*(03), 70–83. doi:10.35409/ijbmer.2022.3391

Wilson, F. (2015). The Quality Maturity Model: Your roadmap to a culture of quality. *Library Management*, *36*(3), 258–267. doi:10.1108/LM-09-2014-0102

Woker, H. J., Holst, R. J. R., & Harden-Davies, H. (2023). New technology and the protection of the marine environment. Research Handbook on International Marine Environmental Law: Second Edition, 409.

Wood, B. A., & Evans, D. (2018). Librarians' perceptions of artificial intelligence and its potential impact on the profession. *Computers in Libraries*, *38*(1).

Wu, Bao, Xu, Wang, Chang, & Xiang. (2007). A Leaf Recognition Algorithm for Plant Classification Using Probabilistic Neural Network. In *2007 IEEE International Symposium on Signal Processing and Information Technology* (pp. 11–16). IEEE.

Wu, S. G., Bao, F. S., Xu, E. Y., Wang, Y. X., Chang, Y. F., & Xiang, Q. L. (2007, December). A leaf recognition algorithm for plant classification using probabilistic neural network. In *2007 IEEE international symposium on signal processing and information technology* (pp. 11-16). IEEE.

Xiao, Q., Li, G., Xie, L., & Chen, Q. (2018, November). Real-world plant species identification based on deep convolutional neural networks and visual attention. *Ecological Informatics*, *48*, 117–124. doi:10.1016/j.ecoinf.2018.09.001

Xia, T., Wang, Z., & Li, K. (2014). Financial Literacy Overconfidence and Stock Market Participation. *Social Indicators Research*, *119*(3), 1233–1245. doi:10.100711205-013-0555-9

Xing, L.-N., Chen, Y.-W., Wang, P., Zhao, Q.-S., & Xiong, J. (2010). A Knowledge-Based Ant Colony Optimization for Flexible Job Shop Scheduling Problems. *Applied Soft Computing*, *10*(3), 888–896. doi:10.1016/j.asoc.2009.10.006

Xu, Y., Song, R., Korba, L., Wang, L., Shen, W., & Lang, S. (2005). Distributed device networks with security constraints. *IEEE Transactions on Industrial Informatics*, *1*(4), 217–225. doi:10.1109/TII.2005.843826

Xu, Z., Xu, L., Ling, X., & Zhang, B. (2022). Data-driven hierarchical learning and real-time decision-making of equipment scheduling and location assignment in automatic high-density storage systems. *International Journal of Production Research*, *61*(21), 7333–7352. doi:10.1080/00207543.2022.2148011

Yahata, S., Onishi, T., Yamaguchi, K., Ozawa, S., Kitazono, J., Ohkawa, T., ... Tsuji, H. (2017, May). A hybrid machine learning approach to automatic plant phenotyping for smart agriculture. In *2017 International Joint Conference on Neural Networks (IJCNN)* (pp. 1787-1793). IEEE. 10.1109/IJCNN.2017.7966067

Yang, M., Mamun, A. A., Mohiuddin, M., Al-Shami, S. S. A., & Zainol, N. R. (2021). Predicting Stock Market Investment Intention and Behavior among Malaysian Working Adults Using Partial Least Squares Structural Equation Modeling. *Mathematics*, *9*(8), 873. doi:10.3390/math9080873

Yang, Z., Zhu, R., & Zhang, L. (2016). Research on the Capability Maturity Model of Digital Library Knowledge Management. In B. Xu (Ed.), *Proceedings of the 2nd Information Technology and Mechatronics Engineering Conference* (pp. 333-337). Atlantis Press. 10.2991/itoec-16.2016.63

Yao, Q., Tang, H., Boadu, F., & Xie, Y. (2022). Digital transformation and firm sustainable growth: The moderating effects of cross-border search capability and managerial digital concern. *Journal of the Knowledge Economy*. Advance online publication. doi:10.100713132-022-01083-x

Yao, Y., Rosasco, L., & Caponnetto, A. (2007, August). On Early Stopping in Gradient Descent Learning. *Constructive Approximation*, *26*(2), 289–315. doi:10.100700365-006-0663-2

Yeh, S.-T., Arthaud-Day, M., & Turvey-Welch, M. (2021). Propagation of Lean Thinking in academic libraries. *Journal of Academic Librarianship*, *47*(3), 102357. doi:10.1016/j.acalib.2021.102357

Yigit, E., Sabanci, K., Toktas, A., & Kayabasi, A. (2019). A study on visual features of leaves in plant identification using artificial intelligence techniques. *Computers and Electronics in Agriculture*, *156*, 369–377. doi:10.1016/j.compag.2018.11.036

Yıldırım, A., & Şimşek, H. (2018). *Qualitative research methods in the social sciences* (11th ed.). Seçkin Publishing.

Yoon, J. (2020). Deep-learning approach to attack handling of IOT devices using IOT-enabled network services. *Internet of Things : Engineering Cyber Physical Human Systems*, *11*, 100241. doi:10.1016/j.iot.2020.100241

Yuan, J., & Yang, N. (2023). On factors affecting users' willingness to participate in the smart services of academic library. *Journal of Librarianship and Information Science*, *0*(0). Advance online publication. doi:10.1177/09610006221146298

Yu, K., & Huang, G. (2020). Exploring Consumers' Intent to Use Smart Libraries with Technology Acceptance Model. *The Electronic Library*, *38*(3), 447–461. doi:10.1108/EL-08-2019-0188

Zairi, M. (1997). Business process management: A boundaryless approach to modern competitiveness. *Business Process Management Journal*, *3*(1), 64–80. doi:10.1108/14637159710161585

Zakaria, N., & Mohd Yusof, S. A. (2016). Understanding Technology and people issues in Hospital Information System (his) adoption: Case study of a tertiary hospital in Malaysia. *Journal of Infection and Public Health*, *9*(6), 774–780. doi:10.1016/j.jiph.2016.08.017

Zan, B. U. (2012). *A comparative bibliometric analysis study in scientific disciplines at Türkiye* [Doctorate Dissertation]. Ankara University Social Sciences Institute.

Zawali, B., Ikuesan, R. A., Kebande, V. R., Furnell, S., & A-Dhaqm, A. (2021). Realising a push button modality for video-based forensics. *Infrastructures*, *6*(4), 54. doi:10.3390/infrastructures6040054

Zeng, R., Jiang, Y., Lin, C., Fan, Y., & Shen, X. (2012). A Distributed Fault/Intrusion-Tolerant Sensor Data Storage Scheme Based on Network Coding and Homomorphic Fingerprinting. *IEEE Transactions on Parallel and Distributed Systems*, *23*(10), 1819–1830. doi:10.1109/TPDS.2011.294

Zervaki, A. (2015). Introducing Maritime Spatial Planning Legislation in the EU: Fishing in Troubled Waters? *Maritime Safety and Security Law Journal*, *1*, 95–114.

ZhangB.DafoeA. (2019). Artificial intelligence: American attitudes and trends. *Available at* SSRN 3312874.

Zhang, C., & Lu, Y. (2021). Study on artificial intelligence: The state of the art and future prospects. *Journal of Industrial Information Integration*, *23*, 100224. doi:10.1016/j.jii.2021.100224

Zhang, J., Hu, X., Tan, X., Zhong, J. H., & Huang, Q. (2006). Implementation of an Ant Colony Optimization technique for job shop scheduling problem. *Transactions of the Institute of Measurement and Control*, *28*(1), 93–108. doi:10.1191/0142331206tm165oa

Zhang, P., Jiang, C., Pang, X., & Qian, Y. (2020). STEC-IoT: A security tactic by virtualizing edge computing on IoT. *IEEE Internet of Things Journal*, *8*(4), 2459–2467. doi:10.1109/JIOT.2020.3017742

Zhang, R., & Wu, C. (2011). An Artificial Bee Colony Algorithm for the Job Shop Scheduling Problem with Random Processing Times. *Entropy (Basel, Switzerland)*, *13*(9), 1708–1729. doi:10.3390/e13091708

Zhang, S., Zhang, C., & Huang, W. (2018, December). Integrating leaf and flower by local discriminant CCA for plant species recognition. *Computers and Electronics in Agriculture*, *155*, 150–156. doi:10.1016/j.compag.2018.10.018

Zhang, S., Zhang, C., Wang, Z., & Kong, W. (2018, June). Combining sparse representation and singular value decomposition for plant recognition. *Applied Soft Computing*, *67*, 164–171. doi:10.1016/j.asoc.2018.02.052

Zhang, W., Zhang, B., Zhou, Y., He, H., & Ding, Z. (2020). An IOT honeynet based on multiport honeypots for capturing IOT attacks. *IEEE Internet of Things Journal*, *7*(5), 3991–3999. doi:10.1109/jiot.2019.2956173

Zhou, G., Zhang, C., Ji, T., Zhou, J., & Zhang, Z. (2023). FOLIO Successfully Goes Alive in the Largest Public Library in China. *International Journal of Librarianship*, *8*(1), 3–10. doi:10.23974/ijol.2023.vol8.1.288

Zhou, Z. H. (2012). *Ensemble methods: Foundations and algorithms*. CRC Press. doi:10.1201/b12207

Zubi, Z. S. (2009). On distributed database security aspects. *2009 International Conference on Multimedia Computing and Systems*. 10.1109/MMCS.2009.5256696

About the Contributors

Barbara Holland is a Native New Yorker and a recent retiree from Brooklyn Public Library with over 21 Years of experience as a Sr Librarian. I received my Bachelor of Arts Degree in Psychology from the City College Of New York and a Masters degree in Library Science and Information Studies from Queens College of New York. My quest for knowledge and information continues to be ongoing. I have presented at the Georgia Conference On Information Literacy, and the Brooklyn Reading Council. I edited several books with IGI Global publishing: Emerging Trends and the Impact of Internet of Things and Libraries, Handbook of Research on Library Response to the COVID-19 Pandemic, and numerous papers over the years.

Keshav Sinha was born in Dhanbad, India, in 1991. He received the B.E. Degree in Computer Science and Engineering from Sri Chandrasekharendra Saraswathi Viswa Mahavidyalaya, Kanchipuram, India, in 2013 and an M.E. Degree in Software Engineering from the Birla Institute of Technology, Mesra, India, in 2016. Currently, as a research scholar, he is doing a Ph.D. from Birla Institute of Technology, Mesra, India, in Cryptography and Network security. In the future, this work will provide a secure environment for multimedia transmission. He published several papers in various conferences and journals as a research scholar. His current research interest includes Soft Computing, Cryptography, and Network Security, which provides flexibility in the computer science society.

* * *

Younes Benslimane is an Associate Professor at the School of Information Technology, York University in Toronto, Canada. He received his PhD in Information Systems (IS) from University of Quebec in Montreal, Canada. His research interests include IS analysis and design, business process management, methodologies and best practices for IS development and management, and skills requirements for IT professionals. His work has been published in refereed journals and conference proceedings.

Prosper Bernard has a solid multidisciplinary academic background, with a Ph.D. in Business Administration from the City University of New York and an MBA from St-John's University in New York. He also holds a B.A. from the University of Montreal, Summa Cum Laude, and a B.Sc. from McGill, a CDP in Data processing, a CMC in Management consulting, and an Adm. A. in Management. He has published several books and articles. He is an internationally respected lecturer and consultant with extensive experience in business strategy, project management, management of information systems, international Bbsiness/marketing, and international business education. He has served as vice-president at the University of Québec at Montreal, Dean of the School of Business, one of the largest in North America, as Director of the Executive MBA program, president of the graduate studies committee, and director of the PhD program in Business run in a Consortium of the four Montreal Universities. He has lectured and has acted as a visiting professor at many universities, including McGill University, the University of Alberta, St-John's University in New York, Ecole Polytechnique, Barry University in Miami, the University of Southern California, the Fundacão Getulio Vargas, São Paulo, Brazil, The University of Sarasota, INCAE in Costa Rica, the University Claude Bernard in Lyon, France, and many others. He has held managerial positions in Information Systems in the fields of banking, insurance, education, and transportation. Dr Bernard has received two medals from the China's government for its contribution to China- Canada friendship and his implication with education.

Frank Boateng is a lecturer and a researcher in a Higher Education Institution, he has experience in designing courses, mentoring students, and contributing to knowledge advancement through research. His leadership abilities, strategic planning, and technical expertise in Fiber Optic Technology and Information Systems Management have allowed him to work on initiatives requiring high technical expertise. He has received training from prestigious institutions like Coventry University, Ghana Institute of Management and Public Administration, and Admintelecom Academy. Currently, he is a faculty member of Ghana Communication Technology University Department of Information Systems, Ghana and pursuing a PhD studies in Library and Information Science at Durban University of Technology, he is endowed with transferable networking, leadership, strategic planning, and technical skills, making him an asset to any organization.

Fatma Sezin Doğruer, who was born in 1981, graduated from Department of Architecture in Middle East Technical University in 2003. She completed her Master's program in History of Architecture in Middle East Technical University in 2006. She attended British Museum's International Training Programme in U.K. in 2009. She took education for 6 months in 2016 with a state scholarship as a visiting scholar in graduate program of Museum Studies in Texas Tech University in U.S.A. during her doctorate programme in Conservation of Cultural Properties in Gazi University, to which she had started in 2014. She graduated from the doctorate programme in 2019. She gave lectures in Karabük University and Sakarya University, Department of Architecture as a guest instructor in 2020 and 2021. She gave lecture in English in Texas Tech University and Boğaziçi University as a guest in 2021. She deserved the title of Associate Professorhip in 2023. She presently works as a culture and tourism expert in General Directorate for Cultural Heritage and Museums in Ministry of Culture and Tourism. She works on the editorial board of the Turkish Journal of Archaeology and Ethnography. She has knowledge of advance English and intermediate German.

Hamid Farrokh Ghatte holds a Ph.D. degree in Structural and Earthquake Engineering from Istanbul Technical University (ITU). Currently, he is an assistant professor at the Civil Engineering Department of Antalya Bilim University (ABU), Turkey. Dr. F GHATTE has also worked as a research assistant at the Civil Engineering Department of Ljubljana University, Ljubljana, Slovenia. He has published several refereed publications and collaborated as a subject reviewer for different international scholarly journals. His current research focuses on the seismic performance and retrofitting of reinforced concrete structures, finite element analysis, rocking walls, and self-compacting concrete members to solve various issues during natural disasters like earthquakes. As a new area of investigation, he is working on machine learning in civil engineering, optimization, and artificial intelligence in civil and structural engineering.

Vasanthakumar G. U. obtained B.E., M.E., and Ph.D. from University Visvesvaraya College of Engineering (UVCE), Bangalore University, Bengaluru, India. Blended with rich experience of around 17-years in Industry, Teaching, Administration and Research, he has accomplished the responsibilities in various capacities and currently working as Associate Professor in the Department of Computer Science and Engineering at Nitte Meenakshi Institute of Technology (NMIT), Bengaluru, India. He is recognized Research Supervisor affiliated to Visvesvaraya Technological University (VTU), Belgaum, India. He has evaluated the research progress of 1-Ph.D and 1-M.Sc. (Engg) by Research Scholars so far and is currently supervising 2-Ph.D scholars. His research interests focus on Data Mining, Social Network Analysis, Pattern Recognition, Information Security, Internet of Things, Artificial Intelligence and Robotics. He has been granted with 1-UK Design Patent and has published 2-Patents in Indian Patent Journal, Authored and Edited 1-Book, 5-Book Chapters, and published 25-Research papers in refereed International Journals and Conferences. He is an Innovation Ambassador of Ministry of Education's Innovation Cell and College SPOC for Smart India Hackathon. He is awarded as Certified Microsoft Innovative Educator. He is also certified Peer Reviewer of Elsevier Researcher Academy, Program Committee and Editorial Review Board Member of reputed International Journals and Conferences and Jury member for various Project Competitions. Being an active member of various Professional and Academic bodies including IEEE, he has volunteered in organizing various Conferences, Hackathons, Workshops, Seminars and Technical Talks.

Shivnath Ghosh is a Professor & Head in the Computer Science & Engineering department at Brainware University.

Dankan Gowda V. is currently working as an Assistant Professor in the Department of Electronics and Communication Engineering at BMS Institute of Technology and Management in Bangalore. Previously, he worked as a Research Fellow at ADA DRDO and as a Software Engineer at Robert Bosch. With a total experience of 14 years, including teaching and industry, Dr. Gowda has made significant contributions to both academia and research. He has published over 60 research papers in renowned international journals and conferences. In recognition of his innovative work, Dr. Gowda has been granted six patents, including four from Indian authorities and two international patents. His research interests primarily lie in the fields of IoT and Signal Processing, where he has conducted workshops and handled industry projects. Dr. Gowda is passionate about teaching and strives to create an engaging and effective learning environment for his students. He consistently seeks opportunities to enhance his knowledge and stay updated with the latest advancements in his field.

Aslı Gül Öncel is a faculty member of the Department of Management and the Director of the Business Research Center at Galatasaray University in İstanbul, Turkey. She is also a member of the academic council of ATINER institute in Athens, Greece. She earned her bachelor's degree in Electrical Engineering from Yıldız Technical University and master's degree in Industrial Engineering from Galatasaray University. She received her Ph.D. in Information and Communication Sciences from Picardie Jules Verne University in Amiens, France and completed a one-year of post-doctorate at University of Québec at Trois Rivières (UQTR) in Canada. Dr. Aslı Gül Öncel served as the organizing committee member of the 2013 European Academy of Management (EURAM) conference in İstanbul. Since 2009, she has been teaching statistics, mathematics, and courses on energy and environment politics at Galatasaray University. Her primary research interests are focused on climate change, the environment, and quantitative techniques.

Venkatesan H. has completed his BHMS, MD (Hom) (Practice of Medicine) and PhD (Hom) at Vinayaka Mission's Homoeopathic Medical College and Hospital, Salem, Tamilnadu, India. He was the 1st Rank Holder in both BHMS (2007) & MD (Hom) (2010) and was awarded with Gold medals for the same. He has additionally acquired Post Graduate Diploma in Bio-statistics at Madurai Kamaraj University on 2015. He has joined as Assistant Professor on 2010 and currently working as Professor and Head, Department of Practice of Medicine at the same College. He is also serving as PG Guide, PhD Supervisor and Research Coordinator of the Institute. He has been the Principle Investigator of 05 Research Projects. He has more than 20 Peer Reviewed and Indexed Publications. He has also Presented Various Research Papers at National and International Conferences and Seminars. His areas of interest are Artificial Intelligence in Health Care Sector, In Vitro Analysis and Standardization of Herbal Medicines, Medical Research Methodology, Design of Experiments & Research Writing.

Navkiran Kaur is an Assistant Professor in the Department of Library and Information Science at Punjabi University, Patiala (Punjab, India). She holds a Ph.D. in Library and Information Science on the topic 'Role of Medical College Libraries in Health Information Literacy in Punjab and Chandigarh: An Analytical Study' and has a strong research background with contribution of more than 30 research papers in journals, conference proceedings, and edited books. She has jointly edited two books. Dr. Kaur has traveled to different parts of the country for academic and professional assignments. She has been actively participating in national and international conferences, seminars, workshops, webinars, and training programs. She is a life member of the Indian Library Association (ILA), the Indian Association of Teachers of Library and Information Science (IATLIS), and the Punjab Library Association (PLA). Her areas of interest are Health Information Literacy; Information Literacy; Information Sources and Services; Knowledge Organization and Information Processing; Information Storage and Retrieval; and Information Analysis, Consolidation and Repackaging.

Kishlay Kumar was born in Ranchi, India, in 1992. He has completed his BBA and MBA with Human Resource and Marketing as a specialization from Birla Institute of Technology, Mesra, Ranchi in 2013 and 2016 respectively. Currently, as a research scholar, he is pursuing Ph.D. from Sarala Birla University. He has a 6 years of experience in the field of Sales and Marketing in various organizations such as DTDC Express Limited, Byjus, Vodafone. In future, this work provides an idea on digital marketing.

Jayanti Kumari is a research scholar, she is working in field of Data mining Techniques. In future, this work provides a secure environment for increasing income using data mining techniques. As a research scholar, she published several papers in various conferences and journals. Her current research interest includes "Analysis of agricultural data for increasing income using data mining techniques" at Jharkhand Rai University. As a research scholar, she published few papers in journals & attends few conferences. Currently she is working as an Assistant Professor and also HOD of CA & IT department in Yogoda Satsanga Mahavivdyalaya, Ranchi-4, Jharkhand.

Khushbu Kumari is a motivated Assistant Professor in Computer Science & Application with 6+ years of progressive experience. Currently, she is working as an Assistant Professor in department of Computer Application & Information Technology at Yogoda Satsanga Mahavidyalaya, Dhurwa, Ranchi. She has submitted her research on the topic of "An Empirical Study of Fusion Framework for Content Based Image Classification" in Department of Computer application at Vinoba Bhave University, Hazaribag. She has 4+ year of research experience in the domain of Content Based Image Classification and published 7 research articles. She has published 6 Scopus indexed papers to contribute her research in the field of content-based image classification. She has a huge interest in the research areas like Image Processing, Feature Extraction, Fusion Technique Representation, Machine Learning, Artificial intelligence & Optimization etc. and also working progressively to contribute in the concerned field.

Priyanka Kumari is presently associated with Yogoda Satsanga Mahavidyalaya in the Department of CA/IT. She is having 6+ years of experience in computer science. As a research scholar, she published several papers in various conferences and journals. Currently she is working in the field of image classification. In future, this work provides a secure environment for high accuracy for the images. As a research scholar, she published several papers in various conferences and journals. Her current research interest includes Soft Computing, Computer Vision.

Akshita Maliyal pursuing a BTech degree in Computer Science and Engineering with a specialization in Cyber Security and Forensics from the University of Petroleum and Energy Studies Dehradun, India. Her research interests include data security, cloud data security, and Distributed data security.

Prabhakar S. Manage received his B.E. degree in Electronics and Communication Engineering from VTU Belagavi, Karnataka, India in 2009 and M.Tech. Degree in Electronics from VJTI Mumbai in 2011. Prabhakar S Manage is currently pursuing the Ph.D. degree in Electronics and Communication Engineering with the Visvesvaraya Technological University (VTU) Belagavi, Karnataka State, India. With a broader scope of Wireless Communication, AI his areas of interest are Biomedical engineering., Antennas, MIMO Antennas, Meta Heuristic algorithms. He has published papers in various National and International conferences and journals.

Shrabanti Mandal obtained her Ph.D. in the field of Artificial Intelligence from National Institute of Technology, Durgapur, India in the year 2020. Currently she is working as Associate Professor in Computer Science & Information Technology department at Guru Ghasidas Vishwavidyalaya, Bilaspur, Chhattisgarh. Before joined as Associate Professor, She worked as Assistant Professor in Computer Science and Applications department at Dr. Harisingh Gour Central University, Sagar, Madhya Pradesh, and National Institute of Technology, Srinagar J&K, India. Her areas of specialization include Fuzzy Logic, Data Mining and Soft Computing. She has published around ten research articles in International and National Journals and Conferences

Marek Nahotko is employed at the Institute of Information Studies of the Jagiellonian University, Kraków, Poland. He is the head of the IIS Department of Information Research Methodology. He obtained his doctorate at the University of Wrocław (2002) and habilitation at the University of Warsaw (2012). He specializes in the organization of information and knowledge, metadata of electronic documents and in the use of the Internet, electronic documents and research data in scientific communication and information processes. He is the author of 180 publications, including 19 books.

Subhajit Panda is currently pursuing his Ph.D. at Punjabi University, Patiala, and concurrently holds the position of Assistant Librarian at the Central Library, Chandigarh University. He earned his B.Sc. (Non-Med.) in 2017 and was honored with the University Gold Medal for his BLIS & MLIS Degrees from Panjab University, Chandigarh, in 2018 and 2019, respectively. Mr. Panda boasts an impressive publication record, including 31 National & International Journal Articles (6 Scopus Indexed), 10 Book Chapters (2 Scopus Indexed), 1 Book, and 5 Conference Proceedings (1 International). He is a life member of esteemed organizations such as the Indian Library Association (ILA), Madras Library Association (MALA), and Bengal Library Association (BLA). Mr. Panda has also served as an associate editor for The International Journal of Information Studies & Libraries (IJISL). His expertise lies in Digital Literacy, Information Retrieval, Library Management, and Subject Analysis. His research interests encompass e-Learning, Change Management, Cloud Computing, Open Access, Web Accessibility, Virtual & Augmented Reality, and Metrics Studies.

Sulaiman S. Patel is a lecturer in the Department of Information Systems at Durban University of Technology in South Africa. He also co-ordinates postgraduate and research within the Department. Dr Patel completed his PhD in Electronic Engineering in 2018 from the University of Kwa-Zulu Natal, at which point he was heralded as the youngest ever PhD graduate from the university in his field. He had previously completed his Bachelor of Science in Engineering (Electronics) at the same institution Summa Cum Laude in 2015. His research interests span wireless communication systems, socio-technical systems, carbon literacy, the Internet of Things and applications of artificial intelligence.

Michel Plaisent is a full professor in the University of Quèbec in Montréal (Canada). After a bachelor in Information technology, a M.Sc. in project management and a Ph.D. in Information Technology Management, he joined the Business school in 1980 where he held different position while developing his research career, namely IT program director for 6 years. His doctoral research was pioneer as he studied the use of computer mediated communication systems by CEO. Since then, Dr. Plaisent's researches continue to focus human factors of IT, namely cognitive ergonomics, learning problems and personal productivity tools for managers. Among his new researches let's mention: Education 4.0 concepts and tools, AI and e-learning and more broadly the impact of internet on life and society. He has published more than 25 books and more than one hundred of articles in international conferences and academic indexed journals. He is engaged with several universities in Asia.

Amitava Podder is as an Assistant Professor in the Computer Science & Engineering department at Brainware University.

K. D. V. Prasad is a Research Professor at the Symbiosis Institute of Business Management. His research interests are AI, Machine learning and Business management in particular and Psychology and Behavioral Science in general. Dr Prasad published over 150 research articles in reputed journals.

Annu Priya received her B.E. degree in Computer Science Engineering from Bangalore Institute of Technology, India in 20014, and her M.E. (Software Engineering) and Ph.D. (Computer science &

Engineering) from the BIT, Mesra, India in 2016 and 2021, respectively. She is currently working as an Assistant Professor in the Department of CSE, Chitkara University Punjab, India. She has published many research articles in various international conferences as well as journals. Her major field of study is in Computer Science. Her research and teaching interests include High Performance Computing, Image Processing and Swarm, and Evolutionary Computing.

Piyush Ranjan is working as a Professor & Registrar with Jharkhand Rai University, Ranchi. Dr. Ranjan holds double post-graduate degree in Management and Computer Application and also double graduate degree in Physics and Computer Application. He has over 17+ years of experience in corporate sector and academics. Apart from being an IT Consultant, he has also taught in various educational institutions in Delhi and other places. His area of expertise includes MIS, Operating System, Database Management System and Network Administration. His area of research includes Environmental Impact of Microprocessor Technology, Threat of dumping Obsolete Computers, Sustainable Development of Computer Technology etc. Prof. Ranjan has contributed and edited chapters in various books both for National & International publishers and also published few books like 'Challenges to Higher Education', 'Online Learning', 'Changing Role of Teachers in Education' and many more. He is also on the Board of 'Advisory Editorial Member' of various National & International Journals and has conducted many workshops and FDP in institutes across India. He has also presented various papers in National & International Conferences organized by FMS Delhi, IIT Roorkee, ISB Hyderabad, BITS Pilani, IMT Ghaziabad, NIRMA University etc. He is also a recipient of various awards and achievements including "special acknowledgement Certificates" for the contribution in different Management Development Programs from All India Management Association (AIMA) for four consecutive years (2007- 2010). He has also been awarded as an "Innovative Academic Leader" in year 2017 for his outstanding and exemplary contribution to education and skill by Global Education and Skill Summit.

Piyal Roy is an Assistant Professor in the Computer Science & Engineering department at Brainware University.

Saptarshi Kumar Sarkar is an Assistant Professor in the Computer Science & Engineering department at Brainware University.

Harshita Sharma currently pursuing a B.tech in computer science with a specialization in cyber security and forensics from the University of Petroleum and Energy Dehradun, India. With a strong passion for cyber security, they are constantly exploring the intricate realm of digital systems and online safety. And also have a keen interest in IoT(Interest of things) and distributed systems.

Elaine Silva earned her post Doctorate in Information Science in the area of concentration Information, Technology and Knowledge by Universidade Estadual Paulista Júlio de Mesquita Filho (Unesp). Invited professor in the Postgraduate Program in Information Science (PPGCI) of Unesp and in the specialization courses in Information, Technology and Innovation and Innovation in Information Units of the Teaching, Research and Extension Program in Information, Technology and Innovation (ITI UFSCar). Assistant Coordinator of the Working Group Information and Knowledge Management in Organizations (GT-4), of the National Association of Research and Graduate Studies in Information Science (ANCIB), management 2021-2023. PhD in Information Science from Unesp with Sandwich Doctorate developed at the Doctoral Program Formación en la Sociedad del Conocimiento of the Universidad de Salamanca (USAL) in Spain. It works mainly in the following themes: Knowledge production; Information management; Knowledge management; Innovation generation and management, Public innovation policies and National innovation systems.

L. G. Honey Singh was born in Ranchi, India, in 1994. She received her B.Com Degree from St. Xavier's college, Ranchi, Jharkhand, India, in 2016 and M.Com Degree in the field of Finance from St. Xavier's College, Jharkhand, India, in 2018. She also completed her MBA Degree in the field of Global Financial Market in 2021. As a Research Scholar, she is currently pursuing Ph.D. from Ranchi University in the field of Finance. In future, this work provides an idea on the investor behaviour in the market.

Naman Srivastava is an undergraduate student, he is currently pursuing a Bachelor's degree in Cybersecurity from the esteemed University of Petroleum and Energy Studies (UPES). With a profound interest in the dynamic realm of cybersecurity, their goal is to contribute to the enhancement of digital security and privacy in our increasingly interconnected society.

Priyanka Srivastava is presently associated with Sarala Birla University in the Department of CSE. Being a coding expert, she organizes various events as Convenor of Coding Club at Sarala Birla University, Ranchi. She is having 13+ years of experience in reputed educational organizations. She completed her Ph.D. from BIT, Mesra in the area of Digital Image Processing. The topic of her doctoral dissertation is "Investigation of NEAR System in terms of Image Resemblance". She did her Master in Information Technology from Birla Institute of Technology, Mesra. Apart from teaching she was also associated with Examination Department as 'Assistant Registrar (Examinations)' and also handled the work of SWAYAM as 'University SWAYAM Coordinator at Jharkhand Rai University. She is also associated with "Spoken Tutorial Project" by IIT Bombay. She is having teaching experience in reputed organizations like Jharkhand Rai University, Birla Institute of Technology (Lalpur), Metas Adventist College, Usha Martin Academy, Dr. Zakir Husain Institute. She has great interest in Research and Publications with few publications in reputed Journals indexed with SCI, SCOPUS, International Conference Proceedings and many more. She has been awarded with "BEST PAPER AWARD" twice while presenting her research article. She guided an M.Tech candidate and currently five research scholars are under her guidance. Recently, she has been nominated by UGC for Master Trainers Training Program.

Mohammad Taj received the M.Tech. degree in VLSI system design from NCET. He is pursuing the Ph.D. degree in nanotechnology with the Vignan's Foundation for Science, Technology and Research. Four inertial sensors fabricated from MEMSCAP Foundry with collaboration of ISSS community chip, IISc Bengaluru. His research interests include MEMS/NEMS and VLSI System Design.

Daniel Tomiuk is a Professor of Analytics, Operations and Technologies, Dr. Tomiuk is also an expert in marketing. His research focuses on educational applications of technologies, such as e-learning. He has directed several theses and dissertations on social networks.

Marta Valentim is a full Professor at São Paulo State University (Unesp). https://orcid.org/0000-0003-4248-5934.07687f82-a466-492b-b10b-fd7cab8f154d

Madhav Verma is a passionate Computer Science student, I've dedicated myself to research in cryptography for 4 dynamic years. My journey in research field has equipped me with a profound understanding of data security and data privacy. Guided by a strong belief that data privacy is an important human right. I'm continually inspired to contribute to the research field. Beyond working, I find joy in solving puzzles and playing chess. I'm thrilled to forge ahead, leaving an impact in data security and cryptography, all while fostering meaningful connections with fellow professionals.

Yogesh is working as an Assistant Professor-III in the Department of CSE, Chitkara University Punjab, India with over 10 years of experience in teaching. He has filed 27 patents and published around 60 research papers in various international conferences and journals of repute (indexed in SCI/Scopus). Received " Best Researcher Award "in the International Scientist Awards on Engineering, Science, and Medicine 2021. Winning Best Paper Award during IEEE conference ICRITO 2017. Also received Digital Badge from IBM. The current research interest includes computer vision, machine learning, and deep learning. He is an active member of many professional societies like The IEEE Technical Committee on Scalable Computing (TCSC), The IEEE Computer Society Big Data Special Technical Community (STC), IEEE Environmental Engineering Community, Parallel Model, and System: DataFlow and Beyond, IEEE Computer Society Technical Community, Internet of Everything, IEEE Computer Society Technical Community Enterprise Architecture, IEEE Computer Society Technical Community, Cyber Security, IEEE Computer Society Technical Community & IEEE SIGHT.

Cataldo Zuccaro obtained a Ph.D. in marketing and statistical modeling at the University of Quebec in Montreal in 1989. He is a professor of marketing at the University of Quebec in Montreal. He has been the director of the MBA Research and the chair of the department of business strategies at the University of Quebec in Montreal. Dr. Cataldo Zuccaro is a specialist in Data Analysis, Business Analytics, Data Modelling and Market Strategies. His areas of research are marketing research methods, business modeling, customer scoring and segmentation, business analytics and research methods. He has taught and continues to teach in the university's Executive MBA program in such countries as Romania, Poland, France, Morocco, Algeria, Tunisia, Lebanon, Mexico and Peru. He has also consulted for large multinational corporations and government agencies. Dr. Zuccaro has published his research in such journals as Journal of the Market Research Society, Journal of Social Psychology, Journal of Modelling in Management, International Journal of Bank Marketing, Social Research Indicators and the Journal of Economics and Economic Education Research. He is the winner of the silver medal for the best paper published in the International Journal of Market Research awarded yearly by the Market Research Society.

Index

A

B

C

D

E

F

G

H

I

J

K

U

V

W

Z